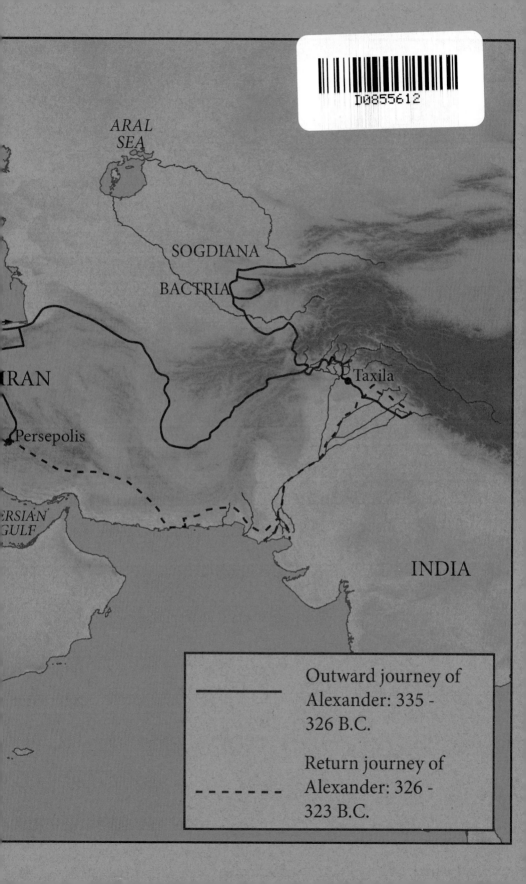

Soldier, Priest, and God

Soldier, Priest, and God

A Life of Alexander the Great

F. S. NAIDEN

OXFORD
UNIVERSITY PRESS

OXFORD
UNIVERSITY PRESS

Oxford University Press is a department of the University of Oxford.
It furthers the University's objective of excellence in research, scholarship,
and education by publishing worldwide. Oxford is a registered trade mark of
Oxford University Press in the UK and certain other countries.

Published in the United States of America by Oxford University Press
198 Madison Avenue, New York, NY 10016, United States of America.

© Oxford University Press 2019

Library of Congress Cataloging-in-Publication Data
Names: Naiden, F. S., author.
Title: Soldier, priest, and god : a life of Alexander the Great / F.S. Naiden.
Description: New York, NY : Oxford University Press, [2019] |
Includes bibliographical references and index. Identifiers: LCCN 2018011264 (print) |
LCCN 2018036455 (ebook) | ISBN 9780190875350 (updf) |
ISBN 9780190875367 (epub) | ISBN 9780190875343 (hardback : alk. paper)
Subjects: LCSH: Alexander, the Great, 356 B.C.–323 B.C.—Religion. |
Greece—Kings and rulers—Biography. | Generals—Greece—Biography. |
Middle East—Religion. | LCGFT: Biographies. Classification:
LCC DF234.2 (ebook) | LCC DF234.2 .N35 2019 (print) |
DDC 938/.04092 [B]—dc23 LC record available at
https://lccn.loc.gov/2018011264

Endpapers: A Topographical View of the Asian Expedition, 334–323 BC.
Ancient World Mapping Center.

1 3 5 7 9 8 6 4 2

Printed by Sheridan Books, Inc., United States of America

Ζει ο βασιλιάς Αλέξανδρος;
Ζει και βασιλεύει
   —*From a Greek Folktale*

Contents

Acknowledgments

THIS BOOK OWES much to audiences at New York University's Institute for the Ancient World, the University of California at Berkeley, the University of North Carolina at Chapel Hill, the University of Reading, Tulane University, Washington and Lee University, and Camp Schwab, United States Marines, Okinawa, who all heard lectures of mine on Alexander. I also thank audiences at the conventions of the Association of Ancient Historians, the Society for Classical Studies, and the Society for Military History, and I gratefully thank Stefan Vranka and Oxford University Press for shepherding this book to publication. For work on the maps thanks go to the Ancient World Mapping Center, especially director Richard Talbert, and to the Loeb Classical Library Foundation, which defrayed the cost.

Special thanks for comments, corrections, or suggestions go to Eugene Borza, Andrew George, Peter Green, Waldemar Heckel, Julith Jedamus, Joseph Manning, Francesca Rochberg, Robartus Van der Spek, Andrew Stewart, Richard Stoneman, Dorothy Thompson, Christopher Tuplin, and Everett Wheeler. I cannot adequately thank Ann Loftin, who copyedited most of the manuscript, except to say to her, as I would to each reader I have named, that the errors are mine and the felicities yours, insofar as they are not treasures deposited by centuries of tradition.

Soldier, Priest, and God

Introduction

IN 336 BC, the twenty-year-old Alexander succeeded his father, Philip, as king of the Macedonians, a rural Balkan people. Within a decade or so, a tale spread that Zeus and not Philip was his father. This tale was no more improbable than what happened in the meantime. Alexander and his army had overthrown the Persian Empire, which stretched from Asia Minor to India by way of Egypt. Bigger things have happened, such as the spread of Christianity and Islam, but more slowly. It took several centuries for Jesus's followers to spread his message across the Roman Empire, and followers of the Prophet Muhammad fought for nearly 200 years to spread Islam from Arabia to Spain and Central Asia.[1]

Whatever we may think of Alexander—whether great or only lucky, a civilizer or a sociopath—we do not regard him as a religious leader. We do not expect that much religion from a military commander. Before deciding when to cross the English Channel in 1944, General Eisenhower consulted meteorologists, not diviners. He encouraged his men with prayerful words, but he accepted enemy surrenders without ceremony and assigned the burial of the dead to chaplains. Alexander depended on diviners scrutinizing sheep livers to learn when to cross the Hellespont and the Indus. Along with prayerful words, Alexander made a display of hacking sacrificial animals to death. When enemies surrendered to him, he often obliged them to perform a ritual of supplication. Rather than assign the dead to chaplains, Alexander conducted funerals himself. Every dead comrade could turn into a friendly or unfriendly ghost, a being to be pleased or placated.[2]

Religion was much more than these rituals. Temples were also treasuries, so religion affected war finance. Many rituals were very public events, so religion affected diplomacy and the administration of conquered territory. Religion provided legitimacy, and so it affected the solidarity felt among soldiers and the loyalty of subjects.

Religion dominated warfare because gods dominated everything. The Indus River was a god, and Zeus controlled the weather. Zeus also watched over suppliants, and he blessed a special religious fraternity, called the cult of the companions, to which Alexander and his subordinates belonged. Alexander claimed

Heracles and Zeus as ancestors. In this sort of world, atheism was virtually impossible, and religious freedom was a risk no community would take. If the gods abandoned a community, an eclipse might pluck the sun or moon out of the sky, a hostile river might leap out of its bed, or an earthquake pitch a city into the sea.

All ancient commanders played religious parts, but Alexander played the most. He uttered or inspired the most prayers and made the most sacrifices, and he did so in the most places, languages, and rituals. We may think of him as the Pope, the Holy Roman Emperor, and the head of the Church of England, all in one.

Piety did not make Alexander overly scrupulous. As a priest, he mostly observed festival days on which fighting was forbidden, but he sometimes found religious reasons to ignore festival days and fight anyway. Told by a seer to defeat the enemy by the end of the month, he lengthened the month. Told not to sacrifice in a temple, he besieged the city where the temple stood, and persevered until he captured the temple and made the sacrifice, even though—or just because—the city was Tyre, the Manhattan of the ancient world.

When Alexander used religion astutely, he and his army prospered. At the start of his reign in Macedon he rallied his late father's companions, and in neighboring Greece he gained kudos by refurbishing temples and sponsoring festivals. In Egypt he performed the ceremonies needed to be pharaoh and thus became a god as well as a priest. Babylon surrendered to him partly because he agreed to become a sacred king of another kind. All over the Levant, he demoralized enemies and pacified subjects by worshipping as the locals did.[3]

When Alexander neglected or mismanaged religion, he and his army suffered. The farther he got from the Mediterranean, where he knew some of the gods and had a feel for others, the less skill he displayed, and the more men he killed or lost. In Iran, where he refused to be crowned and even destroyed a shrine, resistance against him mounted. In India, the Buddhists, Jains, and Hindus baffled him, and he killed them by the hundreds of thousands. Then his officers, men he regarded as companions of a religious kind, rebelled against him and forced him to abandon his campaign of conquest.[4]

Although he never fully recovered from this disappointment, he continued to perform his priestly duties. As far as we know, the last time he rose from his bed was to sacrifice.[5]

———— ◦ ————

AMONG THE HUNDREDS of Alexander biographies, none has focused on the topic of religion. Well-known lives of Alexander in English mention the subject incidentally. Peter Green's biography notes episodes such as Alexander's sacrifice at Tyre but does not ask why any act of sacrifice should be important. Robin Lane Fox's longer biography mentions some Greek and Macedonian religious practices but is largely silent about the religions of the Near East. Mary Renault's novel delves least into religion, apart from its psychological treatment of Alexander's becoming a kind of god in Egypt.

These writers assume religion meant little to Alexander. Many British writers have thought of Alexander as a proto-Anglican, punctilious in matters of ceremony but otherwise indifferent.[6] In riposte, German writers seized on Alexander's becoming an Egyptian god and interpreted this event as a psychotic break.[7] For late twentieth-century German writers, Alexander was a pagan Führer and his men were virtual Nazis. For some Americans, Alexander was a religious cynic, like a gangster dropping occasional contributions into the collection plate.[8]

Some modern soldiers have written about Alexander, notably the British general J. F. C. Fuller, but they say nothing about religion. Fuller preferred military operations, and others have concentrated on logistics and equipment. Writers on Alexander's strategy omitted religion despite the importance of the gods for war aims and propaganda. Recent writers on the role of religion in ancient warfare omitted Alexander and his campaign.[9]

It is easy to understand why writers have not attempted a religious portrait of Alexander. Ancient sources take religion for granted. They record Alexander's daily morning sacrifices during his last days, but not at other times. Although they record a few rituals that went wrong, they skip many that went right, and they seldom pay attention to any religion other than that of the ancient writer and his original readers. For that matter, only a few sources from Alexander's own time exist. He kept no record of his religious activity, and indeed wrote nothing except letters, only a few of which survive. What we do know comes from memoirs by the companions who worshipped alongside Alexander. Of these books only fragments remain—scattered glimpses of sacrifices, coronations, and omens.[10]

The best-known companion, Ptolemy, a boyhood chum of Alexander's who succeeded him as pharaoh, glorified Alexander and himself at others' expense. His Alexander was a flawless priest, impeccably Greco-Macedonian among his own men but suavely adaptable among foreigners. What Ptolemy thought of Alexander's deification is impossible to say, except that Ptolemy thought it was good policy in Egypt. The writings of less servile generals, such as Alexander's viceroy Antipater, are lost.[11]

The Greek admiral Nearchus and Alexander's helmsman Onesicritus mentioned religious matters mainly with respect to India, and Onesicritus indulged in fanciful propaganda. Alexander was realistic about him. After listening to Onesicritus read from his manuscript Alexander said, "How I should like to return from the dead some time, and see how your stuff strikes people. . . . For now, they have good enough reason to praise and welcome it. That is their way of angling for a share of my favor."[12] More propaganda came from companions who became governors and minted coins that likened Alexander to Heracles and other heroes or gods.

Alexander's chief engineer, Aristobulus, cared more about Alexander's interest in hydraulic engineering than about religious practices. Aristotle's nephew Callisthenes, who signed on as court historian, pointedly refused to acknowledge Alexander as a god and supplied only a few religious details, mostly about the Levant. More valuable are the surviving fragments of the "Stories of Alexander" written by Chares, the royal chamberlain. While Ptolemy typically noticed brief, standard offerings, such as those made for crossing rivers, Chares described a unique nine-day festival for Zeus that provided sacrificial meat to every man under arms. Chares takes the reader aside to explain that the same trumpet brought worshippers to a sacrifice, companions to a meeting, and soldiers to a muster. Another royal servant, Ephippus, described the funeral of Hephaestion, the companion who was closest to Alexander. A hostile source, Ephippus reported that Alexander performed acts of sacrilege as well as sacrifice.

All these memoirs by Alexander's companions survive thanks to three writers of the Roman era: Curtius Rufus, Arrian of Nicomedia, and Plutarch. The first two wrote histories of Alexander's invasion of the Persian Empire, while Plutarch wrote a biography of Alexander to match his life of Caesar. All three take religion for granted, and for the same reason: good relations with the gods remained indispensable for military success. They nonetheless miss important religious distinctions. Curtius, writing in Latin, does not know Alexander's subordinates were companions. Arrian, writing in artificially classical Greek, knows better, but he often describes the companions as "the king's friends," a turn of phrase that lacks any religious accent. Arrian reports no ceremonies performed by companions, as though sacrifice and other rituals were royal prerogatives. Only Plutarch calls the companions just that, and mostly avoids using other terms. He knows about ceremonies performed by several companions. Plutarch, as it happens, was a priest.[13]

Roman influence shows itself in all three of these writers. Plutarch, characteristically, is the only one who endows Alexander with any personal religious life, and that is decidedly Greek or Macedonian. Arrian, who was a Roman general, is the only one who gives detailed information about meetings between Alexander and the companions. Curtius Rufus reports the most rituals, and also makes a show of knowing Macedonian customs, but does not know one kind of sacrifice from another.

These writers knew little about Near Eastern religions, no doubt partly because it was difficult to travel into the interior of Egypt, to visit Babylon, and especially to visit India. When Curtius Rufus describes relations between

Alexander's army and the worshippers of Yahweh in Samaria, he misunderstands Hebrew henotheism, and when he and the others describe relations between Alexander's army and the people of India, they fail to distinguish among Hindus, Buddhists, and Jains.

Yet the rest of Greek literature, including Greek public documents, reveals the norms that these writers mostly omit. Whereas Curtius Rufus and others report a few dozen acts of sacrifice, this literature reports thousands. The same holds true for omens, acts of supplication, and the practices that bound Alexander to his companions. And the same holds true for the practices of the various African and Asian religions that he and his men encountered—Semitic, Egyptian, Mesopotamian, and Persian as well as Indian. This cornucopia of evidence reveals part of what Alexander, who was a newcomer as well as an invader, had to understand and accomplish.[14]

In the last thirty years, Egyptologists and Assyriologists have written the first thorough accounts of Alexander's religious doings in Egypt and Mesopotamia. A 2008 republication of an inscription proves that Alexander was crowned pharaoh in a religious ceremony. That makes it all the more certain he was crowned king in Babylon. We already knew he made himself priest-king in Tyre.[15] Since 2000, a number of scholars led by Pierre Briant responded to this new evidence by putting Greek and Near Eastern material on a par. Scholars also began writing articles in which "Alexander" and "religion" were keywords, if not words that often found their way into article or book titles.[16]

Drawing on all these sources, old and new, this book tells a religious version of a familiar but evolving story. It is for lay readers, not specialists, but it includes endnotes for those interested in the sources being used. The sources for religious rites such as acts of sacrifice also appear in several appendices. The endnotes refer to these appendices as well as to the bibliography, which is wide-ranging but not exhaustive.[17]

This book also draws on eighteenth- and nineteenth-century European travel writers' descriptions of the flora and fauna that were a mainstay of ancient paganism. These adventurers rambled all over Alexander's empire, especially Iran and Central Asia, places that had changed little since antiquity (but have changed greatly during the last hundred years).

Finally, some Near Eastern legends about Alexander appear in these pages. Most come from the *Alexander Romance*, an Egyptian story of his life written in Greek in Alexandria in the first few centuries after his death and revised by writers throughout the Near East. Fanciful though the *Romance* is, it reveals how the people of the region remembered the Macedonian invasion. A religious biography should include the afterlife of the subject, wherever and whatever this afterlife may be.[18]

Sometimes these legends find humor in Alexander's improbably successful enterprise. Sometimes they find the enterprise repellent, and transmute it into fantasy, and sometimes they turn it into a kind of miracle and then ask what such a miracle could be for. In this way, Christians, Jews, and Muslims strove to understand how a king and his corps of officers could conquer the known world in about the time it took the Soviet Union and the United States to go from putting dogs into orbit to putting men on the moon.

I

The Mediterranean Comes of Age

ALEXANDER'S EUROPE EMERGED from a cataclysm. For many millions of years, North Africa's Atlas Mountains had reached north across what later became the strait of Gibraltar and merged with the Spanish Cordillera. The Atlantic Ocean lay to the west of the mountains, and to the east a large lake stretched as far as the undivided lands of Italy and Sicily. A second lake lay farther east, beyond Italy, alongside Asia and Egypt. Then, about 5 million years ago, the bed of the ocean shuddered, the mountains linking Spain and Africa cracked open, and a torrent moving more than sixty miles an hour flowed through. The lake to the east rose by as much as ten yards a day for two years. The Greeks thought it took a Titan, Atlas, to steady the land beside the waterway.[1]

Italy became a peninsula; Macedon acquired a coastline. The entire seacoast filled with bays and channels, the short hops for sailing that made sea voyages the best way to travel the Mediterranean. The one great river, the Nile, acquired a new destination. The Arabian and Anatolian peninsulas bumped against the water as if halting an invader. Only Macedon and the neighboring lower Balkans could compare with these two land masses. Greece was an appendage. Greek rivers were creeks, and the biggest Greek lake was little more than a marsh. The Greek version of a big island was Crete. Everything Greek was small, including the communities that spread along the Mediterranean coast like frogs, Socrates said, on the shore of a pond.[2]

Farther east, the Taurus and Antitaurus mountain ranges watched over Anatolia. More mountains, the Caucasus and the Zagros, watched over Mesopotamia. The biggest range of all, the Himalayas and the Hindu Kush, faced the other direction, eastward, and separated the Indian subcontinent from the rest of Asia. The tops of these ranges were little better than snow-capped deserts, and the plateaus beyond them were dry and hard to cultivate. The biggest plateau, in central Iran, lay farther from the Nile and Mediterranean than any other large part of this region.

Which gods should worshippers bless or blame for this apportionment of soil and water? Egyptian priests said eight or nine creator gods had suspended the world amidst waters, like a disk. Mesopotamians and Indians also conceived of the world as a disk in water; at first, so did Greeks. The Egyptians called the waters surrounding the disk "the great circle." The Mesopotamians thought that the Mediterranean and the Persian Gulf were both part of the encircling ocean, and that another large body of water might be, too—Lake Van in Armenia, or the Caspian. The Greeks thought the encircling ocean was the Atlantic, but perhaps the Caspian flowed into it.[3]

Then, most priests thought, the gods flooded the earth. Mesopotamian priests explained that the gods had built the world's first irrigation system but had grown tired of the work of maintaining the canals. They had created mankind to do the work instead, and then the insolent human laborers had raised a ruckus of complaint. The subsequent flood had punished mankind and taught them a lesson: more worship, less complaint.

The Hebrews knew the story but changed the meaning of the events. The great flood had not been an irruption that pitted Europe and Asia against each other. It had been a punishment that pitted Yahweh against mankind. The Greeks knew the story, too, but localized it. God punished mankind by starting the Trojan War, not by sending a flood. The reason for the punishment remained the same: humans complained too much and made too much noise. Egypt did not tell some version of this story. The gods there had never needed irrigation, so they had never punished a workforce.[4]

History, the ancients thought, began sometime after the flood. One of the two main centers, Egypt, was not unified until around 3000 BC and did not reach its greatest extent, including Palestine and part of Syria, until 1,500 years later. Even then, the Egyptians knew little about places farther east. They knew almost nothing about Iran. The Mesopotamians knew more about Iran than the Egyptians did, and more about Asia Minor, but they were not mostly unified until around 2300 BC, and not fully unified until around 750.

The pharaoh, who was one of the two chief kings in the region, would march from his center, Egypt, south past the first cataract to the confluence of the Blue and White Nile. Then the kingdom of Punt came into view. The other chief king, who ruled Assyria or Babylonia, would march from his capital in every direction. He became King of the Four Corners of the World, all linked to neighboring peoples, such as Elam to the east. Instead of the Blue and White Nile, the Mesopotamian ruler referred to the upper and lower seas, the Mediterranean and the Persian Gulf, as well as to the Tigris and Euphrates. The Greeks had to sail, not march, but Jason and the Argonauts sailed as far as Egypt and the Caucasus. They were perhaps the first tourists, visiting the same outer chaos that great kings wished to subdue.

If the king failed to protect his frontiers, chaos encroached. In Egypt chaos roamed the deserts that lay outside the Nile valley. In Mesopotamia it lurked outside the city gates, bringing disease and ruin. By the time of Herodotus, chaos lay beyond the Black Sea, or in the farthest reaches of the Sahara, home to invincible monsters. Macedonians located chaos to the north, in the Balkans, or a ways to the east, whence hordes of Persians one day came marching down the coastal road.

All these stories—Egyptian, Babylonian, Greek, and also Macedonian— originated in leading shrines. Egypt had two, at Memphis and Thebes, or perhaps three, if the priests at Heliopolis were to be believed. Mesopotamia had one preeminent shrine, in Babylon, and others, such as the temple of Eanna at Uruk. All were hives of priests, kings, citizens, subjects, and slaves. They were the tallest buildings on earth—far taller than any royal palace, dozens of times as large as any palace in Macedon or house in Greece. Only the dead were better housed, and only a very few of those, in Egypt's pyramids. Sacrifices in these shrines were the biggest events a worshipper could conceive, the axis of human communion with god—Amon-Re in Egypt, Marduk in Babylon, Zeus in Greece and Macedon. The celebrant was a cross between a priest and a king.

Offerings kept the priest-king victorious, and they kept the Nile or the canals flowing. If they did not, he had failed, and a new priest-king replaced him. If the king prospered, the lowly begged him for help. Just as sacrifice suited him, supplication suited them. In both rites, the weak beseeched the strong. The shrine and the city around it lived under a double hierarchy, one for sacrifice in the shrine and one for supplication in the city or palace. Only the priest-king fully understood. He ranked below the god and above everybody else, a son to one and a father to all others, an indispensable self-contradiction. He was always partly divine, but tradition and personal success determined how much. Tradition also determined the importance of other priests. They might serve as substitutes for the king, as guardians, or as acolytes.[5]

The priests assisting the king were more diverse than the word "priesthood" implies. In Greece and Macedon, amateurs did much of a priest's work. Every chieftain, magistrate, and householder performed rituals, including animal sacrifices to learn the future. A favorite method, reading sheep's livers, came from Babylonia. The most sought-after Greek priests, the diviners, specialized in reading livers for the petty kings and magistrates of Greek cities. If the king or magistrate killed a sheep with a shapely liver, he could prosper. Or, if the king did not have an expert, or did not want to consult one, he could watch the tail of a sacrificial animal and see whether it curled in the right way once he threw it on the fire.

In Greece or Egypt, gods also gave oracles, and demanded sacrifice as a payment (always made in advance). Then the priest or sometimes the priestess delivered the oracle to the worshipper. In Egypt a pharaoh could receive oracles privately, but in Greece oracles were public knowledge.[6]

For starting a war, a favorable oracle was almost indispensable. After that, the king needed sacrifices to get a divine blessing. Sacrifices also fed his priests, and in Greece they provided feasts for his men. Then came an offering to get divine permission to march. Another came at every river. The king or his priest must know the river's name, its taste in sacrificial animals, its biography. Which river would do what for whom, and at what price? The same went for every lake, marsh, strait, or sea.

Just before battle, the king would sacrifice again. The Greeks, among the poorest nations, often used the cheapest animal, a goat. They seldom splurged on a cow, let alone a bull. (And they did not use wild animals. Worshippers seldom did, and kings never did. A domesticated animal made a much better impression. The worshipper was giving up something of his own—something tasty, perhaps something hefty.) After a battle, victorious troops gave thanks and feasted again. If an army lost, the priests might declare the king's sacrifices unacceptable. The god had rejected them, and the proof was not just defeat but a bad liver or a tail that curled the wrong way.[7]

After combat came supplication. The defeated supplicated on the battlefield, prostrating themselves or waving palm fronds. In Greece and Syria, but not Egypt or Babylonia, they might retreat to a shrine, where the conqueror would find it hard to refuse to listen to them. Others in distress took refuge in shrines, too.

Zeus had laid down the rules for this practice. Spoils belonged to the victor, and that included human spoils. The duty to hear and evaluate a suppliant also belonged to the victor. While begging for mercy or just for help, the suppliant, like a worshipper, would besiege the superior being with gestures and pleas. Babylonians kissed the king's feet. Greeks clasped knees. Kissing the royal hand was the height of temerity, but sometimes it helped. If the king decided to aid the suppliant, he would offer him a right hand and raise him up. In the Near East the king acquired new subjects this way, and in Greece a city could acquire new residents, allies, or trading partners. Or the king might decide not to help. That suited Zeus. The lord of Olympus was a god of due process but not of mercy.

For the ancients, these ceremonies were not a fraud or a formality. If they were a kind of theater, the gods wrote the script. Worshippers might read this script by studying the stars. Belief in a heavenly script led kings and their armies to regard the most violent events in the heavens, eclipses, as signs of whether a king should risk war. Eclipses did not cause victories or defeats: the script was far more subtle than that. Celestial events sent messages. The king who got them wrong came to the end of his own story.[8]

The gods remained aloof, like cops in a crime-ridden neighborhood. They were too few, came too late, and were too unpredictable to be relied on. Sometimes they brought order, sometimes disorder. Could they be bribed or begged? What would it take to become a being like that?

BY THE STANDARDS of the Near East, or even Greece, Macedon was a small and modest kingdom. The original cantons were Lyncestis, meaning "land of lynxes"; Orestis, "mountain men"; Elimaea, "tribe of millet"; and Emathia, "beachcombers." When the kingdom grew, it added Pieria, "grassland," Eordaea, "land toward the dawn," and Bottiaea, "clods of earth," also to the east. Towns were few, and none of them governed themselves like Greek *poleis*. As late as the time of Philip, Alexander's father, the one good road swung around Mount Olympus, which divided the country from Greece.[9]

The Macedonians, in a word, were "barbarians," Greek for "babblers." Although the Greek and Macedonian languages were similar, no Macedonian name sounded right to a Greek ear. The Greeks pronounced "Philip" as "Philippos," whereas Macedonians said "Bilippo." The Macedonians ate too much meat, drank too much milk, and did not dilute their wine. They were a Balkan people, foresters and cowboys, not cultivators.[10]

The Macedonians believed in the same gods that the Greeks did, especially Zeus, whom they worshipped under several epithets, including one for suppliants, another for guests, and yet another for kings. Perhaps the Macedonians worshipped Zeus more vigorously than the Greeks did. At the shrine of Dium, they sacrificed as many as one hundred victims at a time, each one tied to an iron ring. From this place the peak of Mount Olympus, the gods' home, was visible in the distance on any clear day. This sight conveyed what any mountaintop will—icy indifference, unbridgeable distance, and latent power.[11]

In some places, the Macedonians worshipped Zeus in combination with the supreme god of Egypt, Amon. The oracle of Zeus at Dodona, in the mountains of Epirus west of Greece, instructed them to. All things Egyptian were prestigious, and so the Macedonians obeyed the oracle and worshipped Zeus and Amon together. Later, when Alexander came to the throne, this local idiosyncrasy would provide him an introduction to Egyptian religion.[12]

The Zeus of the Macedonians let the king keep any land he conquered, provided that he plunged his spear into land to be invaded and then captured it. The Macedonians who helped him also got some part of it. This custom differed from the military practices of the Greeks and the Macedonians' other neighbors. Conquering another community was deemed risky, for the local gods might resent it. The worshippers of Zeus should be warlike but not rapacious.[13]

The Macedonians worshipped other leading Greek gods, but with a military bent. In the palace at Aegae, the royal family worshipped the warlike Heracles as an ancestor. Outside the palace, commoners worshipped Heracles, too, along with Zeus and the primeval Mother of the Gods. Athena ranked as a war goddess more than as a goddess of crafts and knowledge. Dionysus presided over many cults promising a good afterlife, yet the Macedonians also worshipped this god as

the "phony man" of a military incident: One day some young women worshipping Dionysus by running around outdoors with sticks encountered some enemy
soldiers. These men thought the Bacchants were fighting for the Macedonians,
and fled.[14]

The Macedonians followed the oldest Greek methods of sacrificing. They paraded a domesticated animal to an outdoor altar and slaughtered it, burning
enough of the carcass to send smoke up to the god. The fat of the animal made the
fire flare, and so did libations of wine. Then the king, or whoever else was in
charge, said a prayer of his own choosing. He nibbled the liver and other innards,
assuring himself that the victim was good enough for the god and also good
enough to eat, and then he distributed the rest of the meat to the royal entourage,
or just to a family gathering.

If no animal could be spared, or if no man was at hand to slaughter it (a task
not given to women and children), Macedonians sacrificed cereals or tiny bits of
costly incense imported from the Near East. Anyone might do it, and many
people did it every day. At dawn the sun received a burnt offering. At every ford a
river received one. Macedon hosted hundreds of gods, some local, some familiar
Olympians under local names. What a Greek would have found odd about these
customs was not the plentitude of gods but the paucity of written rules. The
Macedonians mostly practiced a folk religion, different both from the regulated
religion of a Greek city-state and the hieratic religion of a Near Eastern kingdom.

The poverty of Macedon made incense rarer than in Greece or the Near East,
and it also made offerings rarer. A Macedonian was more likely than other people
to be reduced to making a prayer without an offering, or a prayer with a vow
promising an offering in the future. This poverty made the king all the more important. His sacrifices on behalf of his people far surpassed anything they could
do for themselves. This contrast would not have surprised a Greek or an Egyptian,
but in Macedon the king had fewer religious rivals. In Macedon, the king was the
only famous priest.

Sacrifices, offerings, and prayers let Macedonians not just talk to gods but also
celebrate them. As in Greece, song and dance accompanied sacrifices and offerings, but comparison between Greece and Macedon was always more or less misleading, because the Greeks did their fanciest celebrating in shrines, and the
Macedonians and their kings did theirs at home or in the open. The biggest
Macedonian rite we know of, the annual purification of the army, took place in
some open field big enough for thousands of men to assemble and then walk, one
by one, between the severed limbs of a slaughtered sheep. The sheep's blood
washed away the army's sins without multiple animals having to be killed. Then
the troops fought a mock battle that showed the gods blessed them, and that also
let them practice maneuvers.[15]

Any god might send an omen, and the kings of Macedon were especially alert in detecting them. If the king had a dream, he would summon a priest to interpret it. Then he would doubt whether this priest was right, and summon another. Birds worried rulers most. Gods were aerial creatures, and so birds were ominous. They might swoop down and spoil a sacrificial ceremony. An eagle, representing Zeus, might fly away from the king rather than toward him. If no omens came the king's way, he could manufacture some. He would kill a sheep and use the Babylonian technique of reading livers, or let an expert try it. Sacrifice of this kind kept omens flowing, and so they kept the king in touch with the gods.

To interpret this barrage of omens, the Macedonian king imported diviners from abroad. He and his diviners dominated official Macedonian religion. Temples and temple priests mattered less than in urban societies such as Greece, Babylon, and Egypt. Household religion mattered more. Every head of every household was also a priest and had sons or nephews to assist him. The fickleness of the gods was every man's worry, not just the king's.[16]

Zeus expected the king of the Macedonians to be a descendant of Heracles through Temenus, a Macedonian hero supposedly of Greek origin. Any Temenid might claim the crown, and leading Macedonians would choose among contenders. They tended to choose the best commander, who would be the man with the most or best companions. All princes had companions, some acquired, some inherited, all tested in battle. They did not need to have any larger following among Macedon's shepherds and vagabonds or the farmers and fishermen of the coast.[17]

Save for the king, the Macedonians had little in the way of government. A government has a constitution, a law code, magistrates, and a constabulary to safeguard the people and the territory. Macedon had a batch of traditions for conducting royal business and a circle of companions who rode with the king and helped him enforce his will. When Alexander's father, Philip, became regent in 360, he addressed his companions, whether chieftains or local landlords, by name, and not according to any office. They addressed him the same way. It would take Philip some years to establish that his own people, and foreigners, should address him as king and not as first among equals.[18] Philip never was crowned. The Macedonians did not crown their rulers. Had they done it, they would not have been sure who was "Macedonian." The king's chums were Macedonians. Other people were not, unless under arms. Some of the towns had mainly priests for magistrates. Other officials were simply called "the gray ones."[19]

The king's companions, although loyal in battle, intrigued against him. They resented many a king for being a sexual omnivore. The king could keep concubines as well as a wife, and often seduced young men at court. Sometimes a discarded youth would kill him. The century before Philip came to power repeatedly illustrated this pattern of courtly homosexuality, murder, and revenge.[20]

The leading powers in the region, Persia and the Greek states, had sometimes trifled with wretched Macedon. The Persians had passed through when they invaded Greece in 480. They asked the Macedonian king to submit, and he agreed. He and his chums could neither resist nor rebel. They failed to join the Persians because the invaders did not want them. During the Peloponnesian War, Athens punished Macedon for sometimes supporting Sparta, and Sparta punished Macedon for sometimes supporting Athens.[21]

Early in the fourth century, the brigands of nearby Illyria attacked Macedon. The first Illyrian king, Bardylis, had taught his bravos to fight like Greeks. They used standard equipment, mainly spears, and they drilled, lined up, and obeyed rudimentary orders. Macedonians were still fighting like Homeric individualists. When Philip was thirteen, Bardylis killed the Macedonian king in battle and annexed territory. The surviving members of the royal family and the companions bribed Bardylis to make peace, partly by offering Philip and thirty others as hostages. Philip ended up in Thebes, where he saw good troops drill and met their officers.[22]

He was far better off than he would have been in Macedon. A brother of his had got the throne, only to be assassinated within a year or so at a war dance held at court. A second brother of Philip's became king, but he died in battle against Bardylis. The companions then decided to give the throne to a child, perhaps to suit themselves, but perhaps at the behest of princes who were raising troops abroad. Needing a guardian for the child, they sent for Philip.[23]

The Thebans gladly let Philip go home to this disastrous situation. Not long after returning to Macedon, he became regent. Neither the Thebans nor Bardylis realized this twenty-two-year-old novice ruler carried an entire army in his head.[24]

———

TO SURVIVE, THE new regent of Macedon needed to turn the companions into military leaders. Philip had no school for them to attend, and so he could not assign them a curriculum. He did have religion, and so he gave them a cult.

The Macedonian word "companion" had a rustic, Homeric flavor. The Macedonian companions worshipped together, hunted together, and fought together. Common worship taught them that they shared the same god; the hunt taught them that they shared spoils; war taught them that they shared command. Their leader, the king, was priest, master of the hunt, and commander. There was no procedure for admission to this circle, save that the candidate had to be acceptable to the king and had to kill a boar without a net. Until then, he wore a halter instead of a belt. Afterward, he could join the sword dances performed at court.[25]

Even more than war, hunting revealed the ethos of the companions. This ethos was to preserve one's fellows at all costs. The best description of it appears in the

Iliad. In this poem, men are companions to one another because they are in imminent danger, as they would be when hunting big game. Social ties do not matter. In the heat of combat, even strangers can be companions. Just as hunters would rally around a wounded member of their party, Homeric warriors fight harder because their companions are wounded. Just as hunters may feel vengeful toward an animal that has killed one of them, Homeric warriors take vengeance because a companion has been killed. A great warrior would be indomitable in revenge, just as Achilles is indomitable once his companion Patroclus has been killed.[26]

In a hunt, neither the king nor anybody else gave many orders. They made suggestions or acted spontaneously. Homeric companions did not give orders to one another, either. That made fighting in formation impossible. Warriors did not maneuver or even line up.[27]

Philip needed to instill a different ethos in his men. Loyalty must be irrevocable. Companions must obey orders, yet be free to modify them. They must belong to an institution, and belong for life. On his authority as king, Philip brought his men into a cult in which they pledged themselves to Zeus, the patron of companions. Since the king was the cult leader, they also pledged themselves to him as well. This pledge was the most sacred possible oath. If the companions were in his company, they would join him in daily offerings to the gods.[28]

Before, companions had been courtiers, just as they had been comrades in arms in Homer. Philip made companionship both formal and portable. It was not revocable. A companion in a military post might be sacked, but he could not lose his status. He would remain senior or junior according to his service and reputation.[29]

Companions were no longer mostly landlords or chieftains of the original Macedonian cantons. More and more of them were outsiders and even Greek immigrants. One companion was a dancer; another had been a serf in Thessaly.[30] Philip's Greek biographer, Theopompus (not a companion himself), complained, "His companions had been scarfed up from everywhere....Any sexpot, wretch, or arriviste from Greece or abroad would do. Practically everybody like that gathered in Macedon so that they could be addressed as companions of Philip." To the Greeks, a "companion" was not typically a military officer. He was a member of an oligarchic political club or a prostitute. So Philip had to teach the new arrivals companionship, or, as Theopompus saw it, teach them to be immoral: "If a man wasn't like that when he came, Macedonian life and manners made him the same as everybody else."

In the course of Philip's reign, the number of companions increased from several dozen to 800. An entourage became an organization. A tradition of worship and fellowship turned into something more adaptable but better controlled, a sort of religious guild for military officers.[31]

Where did Philip get this idea? Perhaps from the Spartans and Cretans. All Spartan infantrymen banded together with those in the same platoon and swore an oath. The commander of the platoon conducted the ceremony. The words of the oath have not survived, but the recruits likely pledged to obey their superiors and especially the king of Sparta. Members of the platoon may have dined together in civilian life. Like Philip's companions, they did not all come from the same family or neighborhood. These social aspects would have appealed to Philip, as would the pledge to the king.[32]

Some Cretan cities enrolled future soldiers into a cult. A magistrate rather than a king performed the rite, and the troops pledged to be loyal to the city instead of an individual. Zeus was the patron god, and all citizens of military age belonged. The religious ceremony gave companionship a touch of mystery lacking in Sparta. Although Philip could not have known exactly what happened in this ceremony, he had joined a cult on the island of Samothrace. The gods there promised to protect voyagers. In Philip's rite, Zeus would protect soldiers who followed Philip's orders.

Greek cult ceremonies sometimes culminated in an epiphany, but no one would expect Zeus to appear in person amid the participants in Philip's cult. The king thus would not find himself upstaged. Greek ceremonies also conferred the blessing of a happy afterlife, another irrelevant feature. The afterlife was not Zeus's business, and it was not Philip's, either, once he buried the dead.[33]

The formalization of companionship did not deprive the king of any traditional privileges. At the annual purification of the army, the king still cut a sheep in half, put the remains on both sides of a road, and marched his men between them. To found a city, he would circumambulate the site, making offerings to welcome the gods and ward off demons. He celebrated victories by sacrificing animals, and he received suppliants. He still had the duty of burying his dead comrades—burning the body on a pyre, pouring offerings, and building a tomb.[34]

After formalizing and enlarging the cult, Philip assigned military tasks to the companions. Many became officers in the heavy infantry. The most important of them commanded regiments of about 1,500. Philip named each regiment after its commander, like Rogers' Rangers in the French and Indian Wars, or Merrill's Marauders in World War II. He (or perhaps it was Alexander) gave them purple cloaks, the same color as the king's. The color that marked social rank in the Near East marked military rank in Macedon.[35]

Philip turned the royal pages, so tempting or dangerous for earlier kings, into companions-in-training. Many would become infantry or cavalry officers or hold other high posts. Some of Alexander's childhood friends may have been pages. Because they served the king at table and in his bedchamber, they may have seen Philip more than Alexander did.[36]

When companions did wrong, who would punish them? Sometimes the king did. At other times he asked the senior companions to. Deferring to these veterans was not mere politesse on the king's part. To wield power, he sometimes had to share it. In the same spirit, he rarely killed political opponents except when he took power. He apparently never killed any of the companions. So, although Philip made the use of force his main business, he did not make slaughter his business. Philip behaved professionally (not that he used that word), and he expected his officers to do the same.[37]

How would Philip bind his companions to the mass of Macedonian shepherds, vagabonds, and peasants serving in the infantry regiments? He acknowledged them as "foot companions." He inducted them into the cult of the companions, ordered them to attend some offerings to this god, and to make a pledge. He also gave them eighteen-foot cherrywood pikes to keep men and horses at bay and drilled them ceaselessly. Alexander would later promote some "foot companions" to the rank of officer.[38]

By establishing "foot companions," Philip spread a new military ethos throughout his Macedonian forces, and to spread it farther, to allied troops, he sometimes put Macedonians in command. The entire force counted as a kind of elite, like the special forces of the twenty-first century. Philip, though, was not creating helicopter-borne squads of experts. He was assembling the largest as well as the best army in Greek history. Yet he was not megalomaniacal. He shared operational control with his companions.

Through companionship, Philip offered his men a career open to talents, but not on a democratic, secular basis. For new companions who were immigrants, he was the best available employer. For old companions, raised in Macedon, he was a mixed blessing. Before Philip, the Macedonian elite had dominated royal councils. Some princes and their relatives cosigned treaties with foreign powers. Now that they had more money, higher commands, and bigger reputations, but Philip alone signed the treaties. Philip had done to the companions what Louis XIV did to the French nobility: they left their estates and came to Versailles, where they lived better but less freely. Philip had replaced the quasi-Homeric world of family and friendship with a bigger world of institutions.[39]

For the females surrounding him, Philip had a simpler but no less radical idea. Before, Macedonian rulers had had one wife at a time. Eager to form diplomatic ties with his neighbors, especially those with good armies, Philip turned polygamous. He married seven times, and most of his wives may have been alive at the time of his death. Against the odds, he had only two sons, one of whom was militarily incompetent and thus ineligible for the throne. Alexander, who served in the army from the time he was a teenager, was the other.[40]

PHILIP COMMENCED HIS reforms as soon as he became regent. The Illyrian brigand Bardylis refused to return all the territory he had taken from Philip's predecessors, and Philip picked a fight with him. As soon as Philip reorganized and reequipped his army, he led it against Bardylis, now ninety years old but still vigorous after half a century of success against the Macedonians and other neighbors. In 358 Philip prevailed in a clash in a remote valley between the two kingdoms. His new army had won its first victory against an opponent fighting in the modern, Greek manner. Rather than humiliate Bardylis, he made him an ally and married his daughter—the first of his seven wives.[41]

Philip fought in all directions, including eastward, at the port town of Olynthus. His siege engines and slingers rained terror on the city. Some of the troops inscribed messages on the lead shot they were firing—Philip's sort of message, imperious but good-humored: "Here's one, swallow it," "It rained," and "Ouch." And, in case of a prospective female captive: "Conceive." Olynthus retaliated with artillery fire of its own. As Philip was inspecting his catapults, a bolt shot from the city walls put out one of his eyes. The city fell after a siege of only two months—something of a military record. Thanks to immigrant companions, Philip had built the best siege train in the Greek world.[42]

To the south, Philip struck a bargain with the neighboring Thessalians, and married two of them. This important Greek region made him their chief military magistrate and gave him use of their cavalry. Unlike the Macedonians, who rode in a wedge-shaped formation, the Thessalians rode in a diamond, and they were even better trained. Although not companions, they let Philip conduct religious ceremonies on their behalf. Even as his army grew, Philip maintained his religious primacy.[43]

Next, Philip married the daughter of the king of Epirus, to the southwest. This princess, Polyxena, became his fifth wife—a more prestigious consort than the other four, for the Epirote royal family claimed descent from Achilles. She may have met Philip at a cult ceremony. In their different ways, both of them were keen about cult membership. She also had the recommendation of being able to read and write (Philip's mother had not learned to read until late in life). Polyxena bore Philip's first healthy son, Alexander, in 356.[44]

Alexander became Philip's next project, albeit one that he and Polyxena both neglected at first. Female slaves largely raised the infant Alexander, and they told him his first religious stories, about monsters as well as gods or heroes. Alexander's chief nurse, Lanica, was the Macedonian daughter of a herdsman rich enough to own horses. Her brother, a cavalry officer, later saved Alexander's life. A horse was the one gift Alexander's parents are said to have given him. They did not give him a saddle or stirrups, two conveniences that did not yet exist. Good riders guided their horses with their knees, leaving both hands free to hold a spear. Alexander soon mastered these equestrian skills.[45]

By the time Alexander was eight or ten, Philip assigned to him some male slaves who taught him Greek. One tutor flattered the boy by calling him Achilles, the hero of the *Iliad*. Alexander memorized the whole poem. Unlike the monsters evoked by the slaves, some of Homer's characters were ancestors—Achilles, Heracles, and collaterally the god Dionysus. Like Heracles, Alexander descended from Zeus.[46]

By age thirteen he needed a better tutor, and Philip gave this post to the son of a physician to the royal family. It may seem that Philip was now taking his son much more seriously, for the tutor was Aristotle. Yet the Aristotle of Alexander's youth was not the fountainhead of knowledge that posterity would admire. Athens, where Aristotle had studied under Plato, had become unfriendly toward him, and his income was flagging, so he came home to Macedon to tutor a pupil whose father would pay on time. He taught other pupils, too, including a son of Antipater, Philip's senior subordinate.

Alexander may have learned some geography from Aristotle, but not much warfare or religion. Aristotle contributed most by stimulating his pupil's curiosity. Much of Aristotle's work depended on gathering and classifying specimens, some of which were political, not natural, such as his collection of hundreds of constitutions from the Greek world and elsewhere. Alexander would eventually collect political specimens, too, but as subjects to rule and not texts to study. Whereas Aristotle studied large bodies of water to learn what was in them, Alexander would want to know how to appease them, cross them, and if necessary move them.[47]

Alexander learned ritual from his parents. Since his mother was a priestess of Dionysus, he could watch her as well as Philip make offerings, and he made some himself amidst his friends. (A tutor told him to sacrifice modestly, and he resented it.) Soon he knew some of the tricks of the trade: when the tail of a sacrificial animal was cut off and thrown on the altar, it would curl the wrong way, downward, before it straightened up and curled upward as the fire got hotter. Watching it was like dialing a familiar phone number. One surely would get through, but would the god answer, and if he did, what would he say? That was an advanced religious subject.[48]

Alexander learned to be exacting. One day as he was sacrificing and an assistant—a Macedonian noble's son—was swinging a thurible full of hot coals, the youth dropped a coal on his arm. The boy did not dare cry out. That would irritate the god, and Alexander, too. Alexander did not know what had happened until he smelled the boy's burning flesh. Rather than stop, he continued the ceremony. He wanted to test the boy.[49]

Alexander was always one to raise standards. Tradition required dozens of cattle be given to Zeus annually at Dium, but Alexander set one hundred dining couches for a banquet in honor of Zeus's daughters, the Muses. That would show Zeus, and show his future Macedonian subjects, too.[50]

Alexander learned more about Zeus from his mother. Her family were the patrons of the important shrine to Zeus at Dodona in her native Epirus. Rather than a temple, it was a grove, where the priestesses of the god received oracles by listening to the breeze in the oak trees. Sometimes the priestesses, called doves, received messages from the god without having to listen. Sometimes a clinking sound made by bronze tripods, a common Greek religious object, replaced the breeze. However the god spoke, the priestesses delivered his message to those who had come to obtain an oracle. This method of communicating with Zeus had supposedly come to Dodona from an African shrine sacred to Amon, the Zeus of the Egyptians. Thus did the Zeus at Dodona become the Zeus-Amon known to Macedonians.[51]

Alexander matured into an unprepossessing specimen. Cowlick and all, he was very short, his voice grated, his neck was twisted to one side, and his eyes were out of kilter. He did not wrestle as his father did. His will and his concentration were preternatural. To avoid falling asleep as he was being read to, he held a silver ball at the end of an arm he extended over a basin. When he dropped the ball it clanged, and he would wake up. Physically and temperamentally unlike his father, he was intellectually like him, and Philip trained him to be a cavalryman and commander from an early age, no doubt long before Alexander fought his first important battle, at age eighteen. In this contest, at Chaeronea near Thebes, he would learn both military and religious lessons.[52]

CHAERONEA MARKED ALEXANDER'S emergence as a military leader and Philip's emergence as the leader of Greece. By now Philip had advanced far enough to the south to arouse the opposition of both Thebes and Athens. In 338 these two joined forces and sent an army against him. Other Greeks held back— Sparta out of pride, some out of fear, more thanks to Philip's bribes. The two armies, Macedonian and Thessalian on one side, and Athenian and Theban on the other, clashed at Chaeronea. Philip marched south on the same road the Persians once took, and the Thebans and Athenians marched north to meet him. They knew the city's walls would not protect them against his artillery, and they also knew they had more soldiers.[53]

Philip put his light infantry, known as the shield bearers, on his right by some hills opposite the Athenians. On the left he put the heavy infantry and cavalry under Antipater, who faced the Thebans. The eighteen-year-old Alexander, who had already been fighting for several years, commanded the mounted companions. A stream bordered one side of the battlefield and hills bordered the other, so the cavalry could not outflank the enemy, the tactic used against Bardylis. Philip would need to create an opening through which Alexander could lead his several thousand troops.[54]

Ancient World Mapping Center 2017

ILLYRIA

LYNCESTIS

Aegae • • Pella

EORDAIA   BOTTIAIA/
           EMATHIA

ORESTIS   Olynthus •

ELIMEIA   PIERIA ←Dium

Mt. Olympus

EPIRUS
       • Dodona

THESSALY

Delphi •   Chaeronea
              X   Lake Copais
        Thespiae • • Thebes
                    Athens •
        • Corinth

ARCADIA

        Sparta •

— — — — — Boundaries of
           Macedon in 359 BC

———————   Boundaries of
           Macedon in 336 BC

/ / / /   Controlled
           by Macedon

        • Taenarum

0   50   100 mi

Philip's Macedon and Philip's Greece, 360–336 BC.
Ancient World Mapping Center.

Just before battle, the two sides made animal offerings, worshipping in the same way for the same thing. For the Macedonians, Philip presided, perhaps with the help of diviners. Among the Greeks, Athenian and Theban leaders acted separately. The Greeks may also have puzzled over oracles from shrines such as Delphi. Not the Macedonians, who never consulted shrines in military matters. The companions thought of their duty to aid and obey, the Athenians of their oath to stand fast by their comrades. The Macedonians were mostly veterans. The Athenians were mostly youths, under commanders who had never fought a big land battle. The Greeks were superior athletically, thanks to their gymnasiums; the Macedonians were superior technically, thanks to their officers. The Greeks, all prosperous citizen-soldiers, had larger, better-made shields. The foot companions took shelter behind a forest of pikes. The Greeks were proud to fight. The companions were glad to, as fighting was better than digging ditches.[55]

When combat began, the difference between the two sides increased. More of the Macedonians were on horseback, and so they could see more. More of them were commanders, and the rank and file heard more orders, even if they did not hear or see more of any gods or heroes thought to be patrolling the battlefield. Philip played a different role than the Athenian and Theban generals. They led from the front. He may have been in combat, but not in the thick of it. Rather than make a visible display of courage, he controlled the passage of time and the use of terrain. Perhaps that appealed to Zeus as Philip conceived him—a god of force, but one who preferred an economy of force.

Philip made a mock retreat and the Athenians fell for the trick, breaking ranks as they advanced. Philip gave an order to halt and stand fast, and the spears carried aloft during the retreat swung down by the hundreds, row upon row. The Athenians fell where they stood.[56]

The Athenians' advance created the gap Philip had hoped for. Alexander spotted it and led his cavalry through it and then around the Thebans. Alexander could pick his target, and he headed for the most important Theban unit, the Sacred Band. Relentless as well as aggressive, Alexander virtually exterminated this elite of 300 men. The remaining Greeks broke and ran. Macedonian solidarity, hierarchy, and expertise had defeated Greek solidarity, equality, and amateurism. As Philip put it, deer led by lions defeated lions led by deer.[57]

Philip's corps of doctors, another of his military innovations, tended to the wounded. Military doctors dated back to the time of Homer, but Philip organized his physicians better than the Greek states, even Sparta. Perhaps on this occasion Philip invited doctors from the other side to join his own, and also admitted enemy wounded into the makeshift hospital erected after the fighting ceased. He did not wish to humiliate the Greeks after defeating them.

The Macedonians cremated their companions and put the ashes in a mound that reached seven yards high and seventy yards wide. This Macedonian site dominated the battlefield, but it lacked any statuary or enclosure. Philip did not wish to be profligate. He spent some money on a small circular building at Olympia, where he put statues of himself, Alexander, and other members of his family. By this gesture he thanked Zeus and advertised himself.[58]

Capping these ceremonies were acts of thanksgiving by both sides. The Macedonians thanked the gods for victory and drank the unmixed wine that gave them a reputation for drunkenness. The Greek troops, back in their cities, thanked the gods because they were still alive. Religion encased the trauma of the battlefield as a frame completes a painting or a window, making it tolerable to contemplate. Sometimes the religious perspective on combat included additional ceremonies. At Athens, it included plays performed at festivals. Although the Macedonians did not write plays, they did read plays such as those of Euripides. Alexander and other companions quoted Euripides as readily as a Victorian gentleman would quote Shakespeare. Homer was their Bible, quotable for every purpose.[59]

Chaeronea showed Alexander how to use subordinates, play tricks, manage gods, and secure peace. Above all, it taught him the paradoxical lesson of unified purpose before a battle, shared responsibility during it, and mercy afterward. Zeus symbolized unity, the companions shared responsibility, and the king himself, acting in Zeus's name, showed mercy.

Out of respect for Euripides, and regard for his own reputation, Philip treated the Athenians mildly. He nonetheless garrisoned several cities. He controlled nearly all of modern Greece, all of European Turkey, and most of the Balkans. As Theopompus admitted, Philip was now the greatest man in Europe—the greatest man who had ever been in Europe. He began to sit on a raised dais, something previous Macedonian kings had never presumed to do. Alexander, who had proved himself worthy to succeed Philip, would have a true throne to inherit.[60]

Philip now took aim at a new target, the Persian Empire, heir to the empires of Egypt and Babylon, and much else besides. The Greeks, who wished to be rid of him, encouraged him to invade, saying that he should punish the Persians for destroying Greek shrines when they invaded in 480 BC. The oracle at Delphi agreed. The Greeks had destroyed Asian shrines, and also destroyed each other's shrines, but this embarrassing fact did not prevent them from turning to Philip, a third party, and asking him to avenge Greek losses.[61]

Whatever Philip thought of these religious appeals, Persia was the greatest state in the world, and Philip was nothing if not ambitious. He had made himself the most important member of the federation that ran the oracle at Delphi (explaining why the oracle endorsed his plan), and he had backed the winning team in a horse race at Olympia, perhaps the most prestigious Greek sporting event.

When some Greeks in Asia Minor rebelled against the Persians, he sympathized, and they encouraged him to intervene by putting a statue of him in the biggest temple in the region's biggest city, Ephesus.[62]

Philip was not the only ambitious member of his family. Alexander's vexatious mother, Polyxena, now called herself Olympias, "the Olympian woman," after Philip's victory. She wanted to be Philip's chief wife. Alas, Philip had never given her this position. She resented it, and passed on her resentment to her son, Alexander. Meanwhile, Philip married yet another wife, a Scythian princess. He had dealings with the Scyths on his northern, Danube frontier.[63]

Imitating his father, Alexander tried to contract an advantageous marriage. The year after Chaeronea, he sent some of his companions to Western Anatolia to arrange a marriage with a daughter of a Persian vassal, Pixodarus. Pixodarus received the young men but refused their suit. Philip had already arranged for this girl to marry Alexander's feeble half-brother. Philip punished Alexander for interfering. The punishment was characteristically Macedonian: Philip exiled some of Alexander's friends, but did not act against Alexander himself. (The girl did not wind up marrying the half-brother. Perhaps Pixodarus feared his daughter would be one wife among many.)

Philip had now taught his son another religious lesson: marriage and the goddess of marriage, Zeus's wife Hera, were subordinate to the needs and gods of war. Alexander learned this lesson, but his mother, Olympias, refused to.

———◆———

NO SOONER HAD Philip laid plans for the invasion of Persia—sending Attalus and Parmenio, two top commanders, to Asia Minor with an advance force—than a jealous bodyguard assassinated him. Philip had more land, money, and soldiers than all his royal predecessors, but he was still a Macedonian—a sexual omnivore. His lovers and his in-laws combined to bring about his sudden death in the early fall of 336.

The most important of Philip's in-laws was Attalus, who happened to be the uncle of one of his wives. Not coincidentally, Philip's latest male lover was Attalus's protégé. The lover Philip had just discarded, Pausanias, hated this new favorite, and mocked him by calling him a hermaphrodite. Attalus retaliated: a gang of his stable boys got Pausanias drunk and raped him. Greek gossip said that the gang used him as though he were an *hetaera*, a "female companion" or prostitute.[64] Pausanias complained to Philip, but when Philip did nothing, Pausanias decided to kill him.

Like some other ancient assassins, Pausanias acted during a religious festival. Philip planned a parade at Aegae, and Pausanias wished to kill him in a way that showed the gods hated Philip. The only account of the assassination, adapted from an unknown companion's memoir, criticizes Philip:

Everyone paraded at dawn. Statues of the twelve gods, elegantly sculpted and richly adorned, dazzled the public. There was also a thirteenth statue, suitable for a god, which was of Philip himself. The parade reached the open-air, unfinished theater. Every seat was taken when Philip appeared wearing a white cloak. At his insistence, his bodyguards stood back, and followed at a distance. He wanted to show publicly that the goodwill of all the Greeks protected him. He had no need of an armed guard.

After posting horses at the gates of the city, Pausanias came to the theater entrance carrying a dagger under his cloak. As Philip bade his friends precede him into the theater at Aegae, Pausanias saw the king was alone. He rushed him, pierced him through his ribs, and struck him dead.

A group of bodyguards hurried to the corpse of the king and the rest pursued the assassin. Pausanias would have mounted his horse before they could catch him, but he caught his boot in a vine and fell. As he sprang to his feet, the rest approached and killed him with their javelins.[65]

The assassination precipitated a succession crisis. Without delay, Alexander gathered the companions present at the scene of the crime. Other companions were a day away, in Pella, the capital, or far away on assignment, as were Parmenio and Attalus. Some asked whether Olympias had hired Pausanias to kill Philip. The rumor was absurd: however resentfully, Olympias depended on Philip. Alexander spread a counter-rumor that the Persians might have wanted Philip dead. He could not so easily scotch a rumor that an oracle had predicted Philip's death. The oracle had vaguely said some "sacrifice" would soon take place.[66]

Besides battling rumors, Alexander plotted against enemies and cultivated allies. He began by acting against Attalus, whom he hated for a remark Attalus had made about Olympias. Attalus told Philip he hoped Macedon would start having legitimate and not illegitimate kings. This allusion to Olympias's foreign birth, and Philip's failure to object to it, had prompted Alexander and his mother to retreat to her home in Epirus for several months. To dispatch Attalus, Alexander offered to give Parmenio sole command in Asia Minor in return for killing his fellow general. Couriers took the offer to Parmenio, and he accepted it.[67]

To gain the support of Antipater, Alexander offered to give a high command to Antipater's son-in-law, a prince who could have made a claim to the throne. Alexander did not need to worry about his half-brother, the incompetent Arrhidaeus.[68]

Alexander made just one decision that evinced immaturity: he ordered his supporters to kill the young man who had been king of Macedon very briefly before being deposed by Philip. Philip had never felt threatened by this onetime child king and had spared him, but Alexander saw a threat where none existed. Olympias envisioned another such threat, and she ordered the death of Attalus's niece. For Olympias, this young wife of Philip's had been one wife too many.[69]

Meeting and drinking in the many banquet rooms of the palace at Aegae, the companions coalesced around Alexander. He had fought well at Chaeronea, and he was taking the throne in a traditionally irregular manner.[70]

Alexander now conducted his first funeral, held beside the Aegae palace. This ceremony would be traditional and irregular, too, because of Alexander's need to act quickly. He burned his father's body on a pyre and prayed for his father's ghost, but he did not pause to hold funeral games in Philip's honor, as was the Macedonian as well as Greek custom. Instead he immediately had a small mausoleum built in a cemetery on a slope below the palace. The two-room, one-story tomb was a trifling affair, no larger than many of the private houses in the village nearby. The workmanship showed haste. The plaster on the interior walls was never finished and thus could not be painted. After putting the sarcophagus inside, Alexander added a few weapons and other military gear, but no throne. Remains of the pyre lay about the tomb. Alexander shut up the high marble doors and rode to the capital at Pella for more alliance-building and killing.[71]

A quorum of companions gathered at Pella and acknowledged Alexander as king. No one crowned him, as the archbishop of Canterbury crowns the king of England. The companions worshipped alongside him, he acted as their priest, and he became, Zeus willing, king of the Macedonians. Among his first duties, he made a purificatory offering in which the blood of a pig, poured over himself and his coadjutors, would wash away the gore of so many killings. Would Zeus approve this legerdemain? The god disapproved of murder, but Zeus approved of vengeance upon the guilty, and he preferred that thrones be occupied.

The larger body of companions—the Macedonian army—acknowledged Alexander, too. He prayed for them, and they listened. He sacrificed, and they ate. He drilled them, and they obeyed.

In now quiet Aegae, the builders painted a commemorative picture on the façade over the marble doors. It depicted Philip and ten companions hunting in a Macedonian grove. Two men had speared a buck and a doe, and two more were dispatching a boar with the help of four dogs. A third pair, one with a spear and another with a double-headed axe, attacked bigger game, a lion, as did some more dogs. A man on a rearing horse led the attack, aiming his spear at the back of the lion's shoulders. That would be the fatal blow, but he had not yet struck it. To the side, a wounded bear had got the better of another hunter and was chewing his spear. A spearman and a man with a net made ready to deal with another bear. Although the trees are leafless and the weather must be cold, one of the hunters is naked. He looked young enough to be a royal page. Only the man with the net was well clothed, and he wore skins, like a mountaineer.[72]

The Frieze atop Tomb II, Vergina, 336 BC.

Museum of the Royal Tombs at Aegae. Artistic rendering by Daniel Lamp. Courtesy of the Trustees of the American School of Classical Studies at Athens.

None of the hunters had distinguishing features except for the man on the rearing horse, whose face was partly obscured but was plainly the late king. Only the left profile was visible, for Philip had been blinded in the right eye. And there was one other distinctive figure, a young man with dark, darting eyes, astride a horse in the center of the whole picture, not striking any animal, but spear aloft, as though he would finish off the lion himself. That was Alexander, wearing a laurel wreath that set him apart. Alexander was the one companion who was not interchangeable with the rest—the princely one fit to replace the dead king.[73]

There was one distinctive animal in the picture, the lion—a species at home on Olympus and other Macedonian mountains. He looked at the hunters with not just ferocity but royal contempt. His death would be regrettable, for killing a brave opponent was always regrettable, and it would not go unremembered.[74]

Three small statues atop a column identified the grove as sacred. Everything here happened according to the gods' will. If the gods wished, they could change the setting, and replace the hunters with soldiers and the animals with enemies. The killing would go on.

For all the violence of this scene, it was soundless and motionless, like a frame in a movie. Alexander and his comrades could step out of the frame, forswearing the moment of action, and then step back into the frame to reclaim it.

The builders left the tomb unfinished. Perhaps Alexander never returned to see it. Once he departed for Asia, he would never have the chance to visit Aegae again.

———————

ANOTHER ACCOUNT OF Alexander's birth appeared in the anonymous *Hebrew Book of Alexander of Macedon,* written somewhere in the Near East centuries later. Some features of this account are Jewish, and so Alexander resembles Moses, for he was to be put to death as an infant and then was spared. Other features are Egyptian, and so Alexander is the son of the ruler of Egypt. That ruler is Philip, an ordinary king of an important country, not an upstart regent of an unimportant one.[75]

Long ago a man named Philip ruled over the land of Egypt. He was generous and kindly, he ruled righteously, and no ruler equaled him. All his people loved him. His wife was named Cleopatra.

A certain Bildad, the son of Anson, lived in Egypt, an astrologer and a wizard unequalled in cleverness. Whatever he wished, he accomplished by means of witchcraft. He laid eyes upon Cleopatra and desired her, and pined away because of his lust for her. When he saw that the king had left Egypt, he went to a field where he had buried a certain herb, dug it up, and worked some witchcraft with it, and went to the Queen. He said, "Listen, my lady. I have brought a message from Digonia, our god. He wishes to

De la natiuite alixandre le grat et de la fume Neptanabus en ma cedome. Le premier chapitre.

En lan de ochus roy des perses v.ᵉ et de phe lippe roy de macedome vi.ᵉ et de Neptanabus roy deegip te vi.ᵉ qui fu du quint eage Lan iii. vbb. et du monde vraie ment iii.ᵐ vi.ᶜ et lxxx. selon euse be fut Alixandre fils de phelippe et de Olimpiade ne. Laquelle chose certes nest pas veue du tout accorder a celle mesmes comune histoire de alixandre. Laquelle raconte icellui auoir este engendre de neptanabus la mesme hore du royaume lan du re gne de ochus viii. et de phelippe v. et de Neptanabus vb. septime eusebe lescript. Cestui ochus und egipte Neptanabus toute hore ethiope. ouquel le regne degypte est destruit. Or ensiuuons donge de cestui neptanabus. et du nau sement alixandre histoire vraie. Lystoire dalixandre / Entre les saiges degypte est neptanabue vementembre auoir este le plus excellent ne pour pauie de ba taille ne auoit icellui, ne doit ne machinemeus du dieu de batailles ne se mettoit. mais lui entrez es lieux secrez de sa mai son royal vng bachin portoit auec lui tout seul. et sans compaignie emploit le bachin de fontaine tresclere. et faisoit samblance de nefs de cire. et mettoit illec samblances de gens. Lesquiek toit estoient venz mouuoir et viure. Et adiousoit auec vne vertue du fust de besemus. et di soient paroles par lesquelles

Anonymous Flemish illustration of Bildad, aka Nectanebo, and Olympias in the *Alexander Romance*, ca. 1475.

Ghent Museum, ms. Ludwig XIII 5, v. 2, fol. 1V.

visit you in order to lie with you and beget a son, who will also become a god." When the Queen heard this, she said, "Give me a sign by which I may know that you tell the truth." He answered, "Let this be the sign. When the god comes to you, the room will be full of light, and he will have a burning light on his forehead." When the Queen heard this, she rejoiced, and bowed and prostrated herself.

That night Bildad came into the court of the Queen after he had put all the members of the Queen's household asleep. He entered one chamber after another until he came before the Queen's bed. He performed the sign that he had told her of, and she welcomed him, and so he went in to her, and she conceived. Then she asked him, "What shall be the name of the boy who is going to be born?" He replied, "Alexandron," for "Alexandron" in the Egyptian language means "Lord over all."

When Philip returned from abroad, rejoicing because of his victories in battle, the Queen ran to meet him, embraced him and kissed him, and told him everything that had happened to her. When the king heard it, he became enraged, for he knew that Bildad the wizard had gone to her. He sent a messenger for Bildad, and Bildad was very much afraid, and fled Egypt, and lived in a cave all the rest of his life. The King sought him at all the frontiers of his kingdom, to slay him, but he had hidden himself, and could not be found. The King then said to the Queen, "You shall not be punished by being put to death, but stifle the report, so that no man shall know of this, lest we come to shame."

It came to pass that the Queen bore a son, and she said to the midwife, "Strangle this son of mine, and I will give you a shekel of gold." But the midwife answered, "Far be it from me to stretch forth my hand against a prince in whom I see all the signs of royalty, and who will reign over the whole world, although he shall die in his youth in a strange land." The Queen heard this, but refrained from replying, and so the child escaped.

This was the form of him. From the soles of his feet up to his navel he was covered with hair. Between his shoulders he had the image of a lion, and upon his chest that of an eagle. One eye resembled that of a lion, and he looked with it toward the sky, and the other resembled that of a cat, and he looked with it toward the earth.

This story does not explain how Philip went about creating a new army, but the image of Alexander as a monster does suggest the effect this army would have on a large part of the civilized world. The newborn monster also foreshadows Alexander's career as an aberrant celestial being. ("Alexandron" means nothing in Egyptian.)

2

A *Macedonian Priest-King*

IN LATE 336 BC Alexander asserted himself as Philip's successor in the roles of Thessalian general and leader of the Greeks. Then he turned north, asserting himself along the Danube. In this campaign, he handled the companions differently than Philip had. Philip took some risks, but Alexander took more, leading by example. Rumors spread that Danube tribesmen had wounded or even killed him.[1]

Encouraged by these rumors, some Greeks revolted in the summer of 335. Patriots attacked the Macedonian garrison Philip had posted in Thebes and drove hundreds of men into the city's acropolis. There, amidst the temples of the Theban gods, the beleaguered Macedonians waited for Alexander to come to the rescue.

He and the army marched to Thebes at the rate that Philip had trained them to attain, and Greek allies joined them. They could have invested the city and deployed artillery. Unwilling to destroy it, they merely camped in front. The Thebans did not sally forth to fight, and a lull ensued. The Macedonians may have thought that the gods wanted the city and the shrines spared. Dionysus was especially fond of the city, where he had paid a tumultuous visit and established Bacchic ceremonies. Yet the gods did not send any signs that the Macedonians should withdraw.

The lull ended when the guards atop the city walls began insulting the Macedonians. Infuriated, Alexander let one of his regimental commanders, Perdiccas, attack some of the Theban fortifications. The Thebans counterattacked, and Alexander committed more troops to the developing battle. Then the Thebans staged a mock retreat, as Philip had at Chaeronea. Turning around, they surprised the pursuing Macedonians and drove them back. Now it was the Thebans' turn to be surprised. Advancing too fast, they fell into disarray, and Alexander pounced. The enemy panicked and fled through the city's main gate. They forgot to close it, and the Macedonians pursued them into Thebes.[2]

Chaos engulfed the city. The Greek allies of the Macedonians perhaps did the worst of the slaughter, but the Macedonians did most of it. Some Thebans supplicated in shrines, and the Macedonians killed them. Alexander spared a few who managed to reach him and appeal in person. At his most politic, the king spared a woman who killed an officer after he attacked her.[3] This *beau geste* did not compensate for the offense done to the gods of the violated shrines.

Alexander decided to sell the population into slavery. Zeus would not object: spoils belonged to the victor. Alexander spared Theban priests, a traditional religious exception to this rule. He also spared those who had shown hospitality to his father or to him. Doing that was a traditional social exception to the rule. To show respect toward Greek culture, Alexander spared descendants of the Theban poet Pindar. The exceptions added up to a fraction of the population. Some 30,000 were enslaved, the highest reported total for a single Greek city.[4]

A trip to the tents of a field hospital revealed casualties rivaling those at the battle of Chaeronea. Perhaps Alexander paid more attention than he had after Chaeronea, or after any other previous battle. The casualties were now of his own making.

The doctors plied their iron knives and rasps and their copper probes, and inserted tin and lead tubes for draining fluids. The occasional drill perforated a wounded skull to create drainage in cases where there was no fracture. For all the equipment—far more elaborate than anything other armies had—the doctors could do little but cut and thrust in ghastly imitation of the soldiers they were treating. Since there was no known soporific or anesthetic except mandrake root, slave nurses often restrained patients. Doctors ignored shock, including common symptoms such as pallor in the extremities, and they treated inflammation by opening veins and letting patients bleed. They passed over blows to the viscera, limiting themselves to superficial wounds. But they followed manuals, including Hippocratic writings they consulted as men screamed. Given the chance, they worked skillfully. Although Alexander's father lost the sight in one eye to an arrow, a doctor prevented him from being disfigured.[5]

Although he was the chaplain of every one of these wounded men, Alexander did not presume to offer them any pious hope or consolation. The lives of these men lay in the gift of Asclepius, the god of health, and not in the gift of Alexander, or even another god. The doctors were serving or abetting Asclepius. It was they who were the wonder-working priests, so to speak, on this occasion. King Alexander had the same duty as other men who had escaped unscathed, which was to give thanks.

Some 500 Macedonians had died. For these men Alexander now conducted his first mass funeral. In a pious but shrewd touch, he let the Thebans do the same for their own dead.[6]

The ceremonies conducted by the two sides were alike—prayers, libations of wine poured on the fire, and mementos such as coins, weapons, and strigils (for scraping away body oil) added to the flames. Yet the expectations for the dead were altogether different. The Macedonians had died in battle and would go to the Elysian Fields. Some of the Thebans were children who had died in shrines, along with unmarried young men and women. Tradition said they would become unhappy ghosts, haunting the place of burial.

Perhaps to make amends for the blunder of killing the suppliants, Alexander offered to drain nearby Lake Copais. The lake had flooded fields and pastures in the region after an earthquake. The local cities refused to let Alexander's engineer do the work. Alexander may not have realized the mistake he had made earlier, in Thrace. A commander who was also a king and a chief priest needed to stay alive, and his enemies had to know he was alive. Otherwise they would be more likely to resist.[7]

The destruction of Thebes had two momentous results: Greek opposition to the Macedonians collapsed, and Greek resentment of the Macedonians increased. Alexander now had every reason to leave Greece behind him and take up his father's plan to invade the Persian Empire. Invading Persia was a huge project, suitable for Alexander's ambitions. It was also a complex religious project, attractive to a devout king who believed his god, Zeus, ruled Asia and Africa, even if Alexander did not grasp how.

WHO WERE THE Persians and who were their gods? Every educated Greek knew, and Alexander knew, that the Persian Empire included Egypt and Mesopotamia. In Egypt, Zeus was Amon, as he was in some places in Macedon, and in Babylon Zeus was Marduk, familiar to Alexander thanks to Herodotus and other Greek writers. The Persian Empire also included Phoenicia and Persia proper. The Phoenician god Alexander knew best was Heracles, his ancestor, who, he thought, was the chief god of Tyre, the biggest eastern Mediterranean city. Persia's ruling dynasty came from the southwestern corner of modern Iran, called Persis, as did many of the best soldiers. The Greek writer and mercenary Xenophon had fought against these troops some sixty years before. Farther east, in Central Asia, the empire reached into the former Soviet Union, Afghanistan, and western Pakistan as far as the Indus. Alexander knew good soldiers came from here, too, but he knew much less about the gods and people of these regions than he did about Egypt, Mesopotamia, and Phoenicia.

The remaining lands—Palestine, the region south of the Caspian Sea, and the Anatolian peninsula—were mostly poor and lacking in soldiers. The Macedonians knew only Anatolia, which lay across the Hellespont. This province might serve as a stepping-stone for the invaders. From there they could reach Egypt and Mesopotamia, plus Phoenicia and Persia proper. Central Asia and Pakistan, "India" to the Greeks, would come last.

Had the king of Persia ruled this empire as Philip or Alexander ruled Macedon, he would have been the chief priest of all these places. The Persian king did not play this multinational role. Instead he acted only as a Persian ruler. He took the throne in a Persian ceremony and did not become a king anywhere else but Egypt, where he acted as pharaoh in absentia. He left religion to local priests and delegated the administration of the empire to notables from leading families, especially the royal clan of the Achaemenids. These notables were the king's bondmen, or servants, a position that the Greeks and Macedonians misunderstood as rendering them slaves and making the king a despot. They formed an ethnoclass drawn from a smaller ambit than Philip's companions. The title given them, "satrap," meant a defender of royal perquisites, not a subordinate. The king could remove them more easily than he could control them. Rather than be removed, some rebelled.[8] Whether rebellious or loyal, satraps depended on local troops, plus a few Persians or other Iranians. The royal army served the king alone. The garrisons in leading cities throughout the empire also served the king. Persia had several military forces because it had two authorities, the king and the isolated satraps.[9]

Below the level of the satrap, the empire formed congeries of dependencies. Local kings and tribal chieftains survived, each with their own gods, priests, and shrines, and the Persians relied on them to provide levies and collect tribute. Caria, the home of Pixodarus, Alexander's would-be father-in-law, was one of these autonomous areas. The Great King lacked any administrative or religious instruments with which to replace men such as Pixodarus. Even where the empire was strong, in and around garrisons, it was not mainly Persian, any more than the British Raj in India was mainly British.

The unity of the empire—one ruler, always an Achaemenid, and some two dozen satraps, all from the ethnoclass—was misleading. Babylon, Egypt, and other western provinces, such as Phoenicia, had been restive for generations. The typical rebellion featured a descendant (or a supposed descendant) of a native ruler such as an Egyptian pharaoh or a king of Babylon. The chief native god would back this descendant against the Persians, and then the god would fall silent once the Persians defeated the rebellion. Time would pass, and the cycle would recur.[10]

The present Persian king, Daryamush, was a prince from a cadet line who got the throne after the murder of his predecessor in a palace intrigue. He began as a royal courier known as Artashata. (Greeks also knew him under a nickname, Codomannus, but they did not know what it meant. They did know Darius had some Mesopotamian ancestors.) Then Darius volunteered to defend Persian honor by challenging a rebel chieftain in the mountains south of the Caspian Sea. He killed the rebel and received the post of satrap of Armenia, an embattled frontier. At the beckoning of the vizier who murdered the previous king, he took the throne in 336, the same year as Alexander. Since then, he had suppressed a rebellion in Egypt and asserted himself elsewhere.[11]

To legitimize himself, he adopted the name Darius, borne by several Achaemenid kings.[12] For the same reason, he bore several titles—Great King, King of Kings, King of the Great Earth Far and Wide. These titles legitimized him by being grand and also by being Babylonian. In Asia, Babylonia was as ancient, successful, and prestigious as Egypt was in the Mediterranean.[13]

Philip, who knew Darius's record, respected the Persians. His lieutenants Parmenio and Attalus led only a small force, and they confined themselves to the northwestern corner of Anatolia, closest to Macedon. Philip and his generals realized the Macedonians had a far smaller army than the Persian king's and a far, far smaller navy than Phoenicia could provide Darius. Philip had briefly been allied with Persia. After Philip's death, everything about the military, naval, and diplomatic situation recommended caution—the successes of Darius, the cynical, unpredictable behavior of the Greeks encouraging the invasion, and Alexander's own inexperience.[14]

Yet Alexander saw no need for caution. He regarded Darius as illegitimate—a cadet who got the throne by murder. Although Darius had visited Egypt, he did not serve the Egyptian gods as a pharaoh would. Although he ruled Babylon and Tyre, he did not serve as a king or a priest there. Macedonians expected a ruler to do both, and so in Alexander's eyes several great thrones in the Near East were effectively vacant. This ex-courier from Persia, a mediocre part of Asia, was an interloper, and he was not even a priest.[15]

To replace Darius, Alexander would have to remove him. He must either kill him or capture him and compel him to supplicate, and he must do it in person at the head of a strike force of his best cavalry and infantry. He had to seize the Persian Empire the Macedonian way, by the spear, and rule it under the tutelage of Zeus and Zeus's foreign counterparts, including Amon in Egypt and Marduk in Babylon.[16]

Alexander's plan was less preposterous than it seemed. Another conqueror, Cyrus the Great, had done much the same thing. Cyrus had created the empire in a way that resembled Alexander's plan to seize it.

Like Alexander, Cyrus was an outsider. Kurash, as Cyrus called himself, started as the king of Anshan, a small mountain state that lay to the northeast of Mesopotamia. The people of Anshan were an amalgam of Elamites, who lived in a plain next to lower Mesopotamia, and illiterate Iranian herdsmen, who lived in the mountains and valleys to the north. The Elamites worshipped gods like Mesopotamia's, and the Iranians made some of these gods their own, but they added Ahura Mazda and Anahita, a water goddess. At some time or another the prophet Zoroaster had put his stamp on Iranian religion, giving it a dualistic character missing from the polytheism of the Mesopotamians or other peoples. The chief city of Anshan was Susa; some of the kings were called rulers of Anshan or of Susa and Anshan, titles that went back 1,500 years before Alexander. The ethnic term "Persian" came into use only at the end of this period.[17]

Cyrus began his conquests in Iran and Asia Minor around 559. He had a knack for recruiting talented generals from among his enemies, and he employed some local notables as administrators. All this must have appealed to Alexander, who recruited companions in much the same way. Cyrus was Philip on a grand scale—an opportunist, a genius, and an arriviste.[18]

To conquer Babylonia, Cyrus posed as the restorer of neglected cults. That helped him defeat the native ruler, who appeared impious. Taking the hoary title of King of Babylon, Cyrus was crowned accordingly, and made sure to sacrifice geese, ducks, and turtledoves in addition to the usual sacrificial pigeons. By quoting the inscriptions of earlier kings, he posed as something of an antiquarian. A long-established elite continued to manage the city's religious life, but Cyrus arranged for temple revenues and other imposts to flow to his coffers. And he did small things to remind the Babylonians who was in command, such as wearing Elamite dress on the day he proclaimed his son his successor.[19]

Cyrus wore several crowns. When dealing with Iranians, he wore the crown of Anshan. When dealing with Babylonians, he wore the Babylonian crown. When dealing with the Jews, he wore no local crown at all. He knew they were sensitive on this point. Whereas the Babylonian king Nebuchadnezzar had destroyed the temple in Jerusalem and driven the Hebrews into exile, Cyrus let them return and rebuild the temple.[20]

Cyrus died in 530, fighting in Central Asia, and so the task of conquering Egypt fell to his son, Cambyses. Cambyses was the first man to rule all of Egypt as well as the Fertile Crescent. He governed Egypt as pharaoh, Mesopotamia as king of Babylon, and the rest under the Mesopotamian title King of the Lands. From Cambyses, the Persian Empire went downhill to the present usurper, the so-called Darius, who had titles, yes, but was not king of Babylon, and who had recovered Egypt only two years earlier.[21]

Alexander was not the first European to admire Cyrus but disparage subsequent Persian rulers. For centuries, Greek intellectuals had maintained a sort of fan club for Cyrus. Xenophon wrote that Cyrus was pious, abstemious, and attentive to the needs of his soldiers rather than to his own—all good qualities for a leader of companions. Xenophon's Cyrus was a diviner, like Alexander and all Macedonian kings. The Cyrus of Herodotus was another kind of Greek fantasy, a mountaineer who lived simply and warned the Persians against the temptations of life in Babylon and other low-lying metropoles. This image must have appealed to the Macedonian soldiery. In any war against Persia, the Macedonians would be the rustics—the mountaineers with stronger limbs and simpler and healthier diets than an army of lowlanders.[22]

Alexander proposed not so much to conquer and absorb the Persian Empire as to take it apart and reassemble it. At the level of operations and tactics, Alexander had the advantage of an army of companions. At the level of strategy, he had the advantage of audacity.

———————

DURING THE WINTER of 335–34, Alexander held council meetings to form a plan to attack the Persians. At these meetings the king and his companions transacted both military and political business in an atmosphere established by offerings to Zeus, who was the god of public business as well as of companionship. Participants were on their best behavior. Violence was unthinkable; the companions, writing their memoirs years later, attributed violence at meetings only to gatherings of the followers of Darius.[23]

The council met often. Before big battles, a large group might gather several times. On campaign, a small group gathered every morning to discuss the line of march. Years later, when some of the companions were writing, they recorded only the most exciting meetings, such as those before battles, or courts-martial, or special sacrifices. Yet meetings covered all sorts of business, from the line of march and the king's health to diplomacy and strategy.[24]

As always, the king's heralds issued a summons to those invited. All stood until Alexander bade them sit. He spoke first and presented the day's business. Then he asked the formulaic question "What does it please you to do?" As custom provided, the first ones to reply were the senior councilors. On one occasion, Antipater and Parmenio removed their headgear (another custom) and asked why the king should make plans to go to Asia before securing his position in Europe. He needed to marry and get an heir, in case the next rumor of his death in battle proved true.[25]

Alexander refused. After a debate, Parmenio, Antipater, and their supporters gave way. Because of the solemn atmosphere imparted by Zeus and tradition, disagreements like this did not lead to a break. Councilors never even voted. They reached consensus, even if they had to pretend to.[26]

Alexander's secretary, a Greek companion named Eumenes, told the council about the cost of the Persian invasion in talents, the biblical weight of silver widely used as a standard of value. Alexander would have to meet a payroll of about 45,000 soldiers costing about 225 talents a month.[27]

Now add the cost of the necessary ships and crews. Crossing the Hellespont would take sixty ships, plus some merchant vessels. Alexander would also have to pay for a battle fleet of comparable size. Cost per ship, including maintenance of each vessel as well as maintenance and wages for the crew: a little over a talent per month. Although the Greek allies might pay some of these costs, Alexander had to pay the entire cost of building vessels. Few if any shipwrights would be slaves. Alexander must pay them, too.[28]

Now the arithmetic: a base of 225 talents a month for the 45,000 soldiers, and up to 300 for ships, plus the cost of fodder and everything from horse hair to spear points. The grand total might be 7,000 to 10,000 talents a year. This sum was eighty or a hundred times what Athens spent to build the fleet that defeated the Persians in 480. It far exceeded Philip's annual revenue. On top of that, Alexander had inherited Philip's considerable debts and reduced his own revenue by exempting Macedonians from taxation. That gesture had won him the support of his soldiers, but now it made paying them harder. To make matters even worse, Alexander had already borrowed money from the companions, and so he would have to repay these loans as well as pay their salaries.[29]

Paying the religious costs of the invasion would be a solemn matter of honor. Besides providing sacrifices on behalf of his army, Alexander would have to provide accompanying rewards for his companions. He would have to provide sacrifices on behalf of conquered populations, too. Whatever the local god, Alexander would have to build or rebuild shrines and dedicate costly statues, altars, and the like. He would have to make some costly promises to suppliants. Then he would have to keep his word.

These practical and religious requirements dictated the invaders' itinerary. In the words of the bank robber Willie Sutton, they must go where the money was: the great shrines and the cities around them. Once they got there, Alexander must make sacrifices and dispense largesse as well as seize assets, and so the cycle of high costs, temple visits, and more high costs would begin anew. Worship and finance were intertwined.

Once the council made plans, Alexander sacrificed to Zeus at Dium, the chief Macedonian shrine, and gave his men a feast. He wanted a portent or two, and his father's diviner, Aristander, found one for him. Out in the countryside, a wooden statue of Orpheus, a poet but also an epic adventurer, had begun to ooze sap as though it were a living tree. That, Aristander said, showed that Alexander's deeds would inspire another Orpheus.[30]

After the feast, Alexander led his men from Dium to the frontier, at Abdera, on the coastal road to Asia. Parmenio came from Anatolia to join Alexander and together they marshaled the army.

Parmenio knew the army better than Alexander did. In the course of a long career, he had led a campaign in Illyria, gone to Athens as a diplomat, and suppressed a pro-Athenian rebellion against Macedon on Euboea. Besides being experienced, he was ruthless. Although Attalus had married his daughter, Parmenio ordered Attalus's death. Wherever Alexander looked, he would see Parmenio or Parmenio's sons and in-laws, a number of whom were high commanders.

And everywhere Alexander looked, he would see officers trained by Philip. In the Macedonian infantry, there was an officer for every seven men. (Only the Spartan army had as many officers, and it was far smaller. The Persian army had fewer officers.)[31] Macedonians would command most allied troops.

Alexander mustered the officers and men of his strike force, which would serve as the right wing of the army in big battles and sometimes operate independently. Parmenio's oldest son, Philotas, headed the most important unit, the 1,800 lancers of the companion cavalry. Another son, Nicanor, commanded the second-most-important unit, the 3,000 shield bearers, a post he had held since before Chaeronea. Third came hundreds of javelin throwers from the mountains in the upper valley of Macedon's chief river, the Strymon. In battle, they formed a screen for the Macedonians. They served under a commander appointed by their own king, a longtime friend to Philip.[32]

Alexander also selected hundreds of archers from the Greek islands. The best-equipped, the Cretan archers, served under their own commanders. Fewest in number, but first in the line of march, were hundreds of scouts, from Thrace in the Balkans.

Parmenio's larger but somewhat less select force centered on the 9,000 foot companions of the heavy infantry known as the phalanx. Half came from the Macedonian highlands. Coenus, one of the best regimental commanders, was Parmenio's son-in-law. Parmenio also received the 1,800 Thessalian cavalry lent to Alexander because he was general of the Thessalians. Parmenio had fewer javelin men and archers than Alexander, but he did have the services of hundreds of Greek cavalry and 7,000 Greek infantry useful as reserves or garrisons. These men employed more slaves than Macedonian or Balkan troops, and consumed that much more food and water.[33]

Thousands of noncombatants such as boatmen, artillerists, and surgeons marched mostly with Parmenio. The army would need boatmen as soon as it reached the Hellespont, and artillery for fortified cities. It would need surgeons from start to finish. Each life counted, especially each Macedonian life. A medical corps was cheaper than replacing companions.

Parmenio also marshaled hundreds of wagons and many hundreds of teamsters, not to mention thousands of mules. To keep the baggage train from being miles longer than it was already, the quartermasters struck a balance between making animals carry food and fodder and relying on comestibles kept in storehouses en route. For now, the army would carry several days' worth of comestibles, amounting to more than a ton. Storehouses would supply the rest. Once the army left friendly territory, storehouses would be harder to come by. The mules would have to work harder, and the army would have to work harder, too, sending foragers far and wide.[34]

One day a week, the mules would insist on resting. The behavior of the men was harder to predict. If the omens and offerings proved unsatisfactory, they would not advance, just as they would not fight at forbidden times. These human factors were Alexander's responsibility. As priest, he would decide which omens were propitious. As king, he could adjust the forbidden times in the calendar. One was the month of Daisios, the Macedonian harvest time, only weeks away. They must cross soon. If they did not reach Asia in spring, while the grain was milk-ripe, they would face shortages that no miracle of logistics could cover.[35] Finally, Alexander needed to leave behind a prestigious commander with enough troops to control Macedon, Greece, and the Balkans. He allotted half of the Macedonian cavalry and heavy infantry, plus other personnel ranging from artillerists to surgeons, to Antipater. Alexander had no choice but to assign this task to the oldest of all Philip's associates, just as an American vice president who succeeds an assassinated president must stick with senior members of his predecessor's cabinet.[36]

Like Parmenio, Antipater had won battles before Alexander was born, and Alexander grew up watching Antipater serve as Philip's replacement on occasions such as the Pythian Games at Delphi. Now Antipater as well as Parmenio would command more troops than those assigned to Alexander's strike force. Antipater would also serve as regent in Macedon, in charge of Alexander's relatives. In spite of—or because of—the responsibilities he gave Antipater, Alexander did not quite trust him. Antipater, he said, was white on the outside, but royal purple on the inside. Alexander's mother, Olympias, regarded Antipater as a covert usurper. For his part, Antipater regarded Olympias as a nuisance.[37]

On the eve of the army's departure, Parmenio built a shrine to Zeus, the patron of companions. He gave the customary offerings to Zeus and added offerings to Jason, the leader of the Argonauts, asking for good luck on the forthcoming expedition. Macedonians and Greeks regarded the voyage of Jason and his men as the supreme example of a long, successful journey. Jason, a mere youth, led Heracles, Orpheus, and other heroes on a search for the Golden Fleece, a treasure kept under guard by the family of the sun god at the far end of the Black Sea. With Medea's help they stole it, and Jason and most of the others returned safely.[38]

Jason's were the first companions to worship Zeus, preceding the companions of the Trojan War by a generation. Like Macedonian companions, the Argonauts made a sacrificial pledge to serve their leader and cooperate with one another. Like Alexander, Jason promised pelf and glory, or, failing that, honorable burial.[39]

We do not know whether Alexander attended this ceremony. He could not have welcomed the tacit comparison between himself and Jason, a novice soldier who led by consensus yet was honored as a hero. Nor could he have liked seeing Parmenio take the religious lead.

Parmenio and his fellow worshippers made an elaborate inaugural sacrifice at the shrine. Perhaps they swore a vow, promising some gift to Zeus and Jason if the expedition prospered. Many of them did not keep it. Like Alexander, they would never return home.

———————

THE ARMY NOW began a two-week march to the Hellespont. When they arrived they camped at Sestos, the usual place of embarkation for Asia. Behind them rose the cliffs of Europe, where crops grew on the heights. Before them stretched the Dardanelles and Anatolia, all beaches and marshy flats. Although Anatolia lay close to Macedon, it was in some respects less well known than some faraway lands such as Phoenicia or Egypt. Europe seemed solid, small, and easy to view at a glance, Anatolia vast but tenuous.

To get supplies, and also bullion, the army should head for the nearest Persian provincial capital, Dascylium, about seventy-five miles southeast. From there they could take a local road eastward and merge with a main road lined with wells and storehouses. It was broad and well maintained until it reached the Cilician Gates, a pass leading to the rest of Asia through the Antitaurus Mountains.[40]

If they wanted more gold than Dascylium offered, they should sail south and head inland, via Ephesus, a rich town, and then Sardis, a provincial capital that was the richest in Anatolia. Xenophon and 10,000 fellow mercenaries had followed this route. After passing Sardis, they had gone up the valley to Celaenae, another store of wealth, and then due east, toward the Cilician Gates.

Meeting with his generals, Alexander opposed targeting Dascylium, and he also opposed heading south, into the valley. Rather than take a town or valley, he wished to defeat the enemy in battle as soon as possible. He could offer an obvious military reason. The previous year Parmenio had fought unsuccessfully against the Persians. Cyzicus, a Greek port city in this region, had rebelled, and Parmenio tried to capitalize on the rebellion. Parmenio and 10,000 troops set out from Abydos, near Troy, and moved south, only to be attacked by Memnon of Rhodes, a mercenary serving as the local Persian commander. Memnon captured Cyzicus and then drove Parmenio back to Abydos. If the Macedonians did not defeat Memnon, their reputation for prowess would suffer. They must inaugurate their campaign with a victory over Memnon and the Anatolian satraps fighting alongside him.[41]

The generals agreed, only to hear Alexander announce a plan that seemed to contradict the first one. Rather than cross the strait, land at Abydos, and then march against the Persians, Alexander wished to loiter while he performed religious duties. First he would perform water-crossing rites at the Hellespont, and then he and an escort would leave the army at Abydos and go to Troy, which lay well to the south. He wanted to worship at the shrine of his ancestor Achilles, a gesture that would increase his own prestige. The rest of the army must stay at Abydos and wait for him. Once he returned, the reunited army would march out and draw the enemy into a fight.

On military grounds, the council might object to this diversion, but because it was religious, Alexander could insist on it. The councilors could not tell him that rites before crossing a body of water were normal but rites in honor of an ancestor such as Achilles were not.

Parmenio and the main body left from the port at Sestos, but Alexander left from a nearby spot, the tomb of Protesilaus, one of many heroes buried along the waterway. Protesilaus had been the first Greek killed at Troy, falling when he stepped ashore from his boat. Honoring him would please the Greeks in the army, and stepping ashore without mishap would show them that Alexander did not mean to be defeated. After honoring Protesilaus, Alexander sailed out into the strait, pausing to sacrifice a bull to Poseidon and to pour libations to the sea nymphs. Then he joined the rest of the fleet and crossed to Asia.

Their destination, near Abydos, lay several miles downstream. The dozens of boats all had to travel some way against the current, then swerve into it and float into the middle of the channel. When they reached the shore, Alexander leapt out first and threw his spear into the sand, claiming all the lands of the Persian Empire. Zeus and the heroes would give it to him—provided that he took it. Then he erected altars and prayed to Zeus, Athena, and Heracles, his favorite trio of gods, to convince enemies everywhere to accept him as king.[42]

With this piece of showmanship, Alexander turned the invasion into a world war. Zeus, the king, and the companions would take on all of civilization (or as much as the Macedonians were aware of). Civilization would resist, but how well and how long would depend on the attitude of more gods—Amon, Marduk, and many others. If these gods turned out to be allies or alter egos of Zeus, the companions would prevail in the struggle. Civilization would be theirs to rule.[43]

Alexander proceeded to Troy with some cavalry. Described by Homer as a city, Troy was merely a village, with supposedly ancient shrines and bric-a-brac. The visitors put a garland on Achilles's tomb and borrowed some heroic weapons from the shrine of Athena for use in battle against the Persians (offered the lyre of Paris, Alexander rejected it). In spite of his debts, Alexander promised to build Athena a better shrine, and found a new city besides.

Alexander also went to a household altar of Zeus and spoke to the ghost of Priam, king of Troy during the Achaean attack. Achilles's son, Alexander's ancestor, had killed Priam while the old man was supplicating at what was supposedly the same altar. Alexander begged Priam for forgiveness.[44]

Even more than the rituals performed at the Hellespont, the pilgrimage to Troy set the terms for the peculiar war Alexander had envisioned. To him and to all Greeks and Macedonians—one might almost say, to all literate Europeans—Troy symbolized Asia. They thought of Troy as one of Asia's greatest cities, like Babylon or Susa. When Alexander's ancestor Achilles and the other Achaean heroes attacked Troy, the Trojans supposedly appealed to Babylon and Susa for help. In defeating Troy, the Achaeans had defeated the rest of Asia, too. Under Alexander, Greek-speaking invaders would do it again.[45]

By associating himself with Achilles, who had fought so famously to protect and avenge his own companions, Alexander assured his Macedonians that he would protect them, even placing their lives ahead of his own. By taking arms from Athena, he assured them that he and they would prevail and that Athena would be of help in this region in particular. So far so good, but emulating Achilles also implied that, like Achilles, Alexander would die young, and that the Asian territory he captured would eventually belong to the companions, not to him. Since Greeks worshipped Achilles as a hero, Alexander was implying that his own men and others would worship him, too, but after his death.

By promising to build a new city and shrine at Troy, Alexander defined for the companions his notion of ruling Asia. If a city had declined, Alexander and the companions should restore it. Above all, they should restore shrines and worship in them, honoring the gods' altars and the rights of suppliants. They should never think that the ghosts of the dead were unobservant or powerless. Ancient kings such as Priam were still alive, if only as wraiths, and conquerors needed not only to respect them but also to regard them as models.

When Parmenio worshipped Zeus and Jason at Abdera, a few weeks before, the old general sent altogether different messages. Parmenio said nothing at all to the people of Asia. He addressed himself only to the god, the hero, and the companions—three parties that the companions knew from their own cult of Zeus. Rather than offer them victory, as Alexander did by invoking Athena, Parmenio offered them solidarity. Rather than the prospect of empire, he held out hope of a successful adventure. In Parmenio's mental map, Troy, Babylon, and Susa were not especially important. In Alexander's map, these places and Egypt were all-important.

Parmenio and Alexander might have objected to each other's religious choices. If Alexander imagined Zeus with Achilles, and Parmenio imagined the same god with Jason, both men could not be perfectly right, even if they had the best of intentions toward Zeus, the heroes, and each other.

The Macedonian expedition into Asia had begun twice. First Parmenio and the army set out from Abdera, at the frontier of Philip's kingdom, and they assembled as though they were embarking on an argosy. Next, Alexander and his entourage set out from Troy, on the frontier of Asia, as though he and they were men of a different stamp, Iliadic warriors. A united army carried within it a seed of conflict and division.

———————

WHY DID ALEXANDER separate himself from Parmenio at this juncture? One ancient story about Alexander's youth suggests that the young king regarded fathers and father figures as burdens rather than parents or companions. In this fanciful tale from ancient Armenia, Olympias is Alexander's mother, but his father is Nectanebo, an Egyptian exile known to the Macedonians as a priest. As in the Hebrew story at the end of Chapter 1, Alexander does not know the truth about his parentage.[46]

Alexander asked Nectanebo, "May all the signs of the Zodiac be recognized, as you have said?" When the Egyptian nodded, Alexander said, "I wish to see them."

"Come with me out into the plain tonight, and you shall see them, if the sky is clear," Nectanebo answered. Alexander agreed, but said, "Let me ask you another question. Tell me how you will die."

Nectanebo answered, "I shall perish at the hands of my own son," as an Egyptian oracle had foretold.

Once night fell and the moon had risen, and the signs of the Zodiac were visible, they went outside the city. Nectanebo lifted up his eyes and said to the boy, "Observe how gloomy Saturn is, and how Ares looks like blood, and Venus is joyful, and Nabu, Marduk's scribe, is favorable, and how bright Marduk is." While the eyes of Nectanebo were fixed on the signs, and both of them were walking along together, Alexander pushed Nectanebo and cast him into a pit. After he had fallen, Nectanebo said, "What were you thinking, my son Alexander, when you stretched out your hand against me and cast me into this pit?"

Alexander answered, "Sir, you are a fool who does not know what is on earth, yet investigates the sky. I also blame you for being ignorant, for you said that you would die at the hands of your son. You did not know that you would die by my hands."

"I did say that," Nectanebo replied, "and I have not lied."

"Am I your son?" Alexander asked.

Nectanebo told Alexander how he had impersonated the god Amon, gone into Olympias, and begotten him. When he had finished, his soul departed from him and he died.

Alexander was afraid to leave the body in the pit for animals to devour, so he put it over his shoulders and took it back with him, and buried it in the Egyptian way, but in secret.

The Egyptian burial Alexander gives his father points to the origin of this story, which was Egyptian. From Egypt the story traveled to other Near Eastern lands, thanks to its being part of the *Alexander Romance*. The *Romance* was popular everywhere, but each version of it, and each story derived from it, catered to local or regional taste. The Hebrew story at the end of Chapter 1 compared Alexander to Moses, and this story mentioned two Mesopotamian gods, Nabu and Marduk, both identified as stars.

Yet both stories told a symbolic truth about the Macedonian invasion. Just as the Hebrew story captured the fabulous or monstrous aspect of the enterprise, this one captured the vulnerability of the invaders. Egypt had the power to define Alexander, and Mesopotamia, with its gods among the stars, had the power to help or hurt him. The invaders were mighty, but the invaded were not helpless.

3

The S-Curve

ALEXANDER'S TRIP TO Troy cost the Macedonians about a week they might have spent advancing on the Persians. Instead the Persians had time to prepare, and after Alexander returned they had more, for the army's long columns made slow progress on the coastal road. The Macedonians would have been glad to take the first big town on the way, Lampsacus, but had to veer away from it to avoid crossing a swift-flowing river. Alexander sent messengers there for food and help, but the Lampsacenes replied with an act of supplication. They begged to refuse, and Alexander was in no position to object to this perverse request. As the army approached the next town, Parium, mountains blocked the way, and they had to turn inland. The third town, Priapus, gave food and aid.[1]

Then the army entered a valley that stretched from the coast into the mountains. This, Callisthenes told the companions, was the plain of Adrastus, named after a supplicating Trojan prince killed by Agamemnon. The first shrine to Nemesis, a goddess of revenge, had been built here. A few miles ahead lay another Trojan landmark, the tomb of another Memnon, a general who died at the hands of Achilles in the Trojan War. This Memnon arrived from Susa, one of the capitals of the Persian Empire, even if he was not a Persian. Farther up the coast, Parmenio's hero, Jason, awaited the Macedonians. Jason had built the temple of Apollo at Cyzicus.[2]

The rear of the column had just entered the plain when the scouts approached the Granicus, the first of several rivers on the way to Dascylium. There were few fords and no nearby bridge, and the riverbanks were mostly too steep for horses, especially the small animals the Macedonians rode. For an army on the other side, the river offered a stout defensive position. Persian cavalry lined the opposite bank.

COMMANDING THE CAVALRY, and all the Persian forces in the region, was the Memnon who had defeated Parmenio. After serving Darius in Egypt, Memnon had received command of all Persian forces in Anatolia, and the defeat of Parmenio had justified the king's confidence in him. The Persian satraps—one

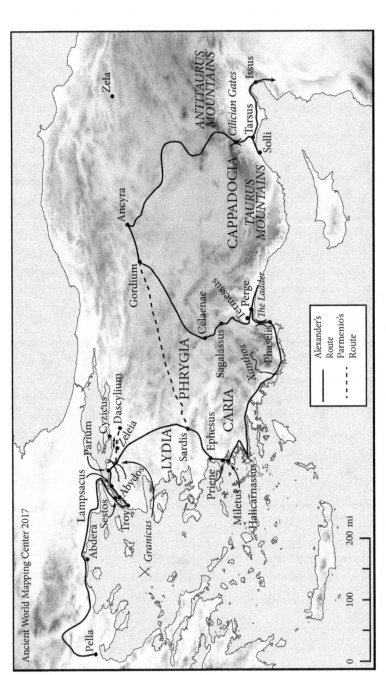

The Route of the Expedition Through Anatolia, 334–333 BC.
Ancient World Mapping Center.

in Dascylium and three more in adjoining territories—reluctantly cooperated with this Greek mercenary.

Several days before the Macedonians arrived at the Granicus, Memnon marshaled his troops at Zeleia, on another of the rivers between the Macedonians and Dascylium. At first he had planned to wait there and let the Macedonians come to him. Zeleia stood beside the only local bridge big enough for an army to cross. Alexander would find it hard to get around or over the bridge, and Memnon would find it easy to receive reinforcements. If the Macedonians somehow got past Zeleia, the Persians could burn the ripening fields and orchards, and empty the granaries. The invaders would eventually starve.[3] They could not extricate themselves. The mountains and the coastal marshes prevented that.

Memnon had taken a Macedonian or two captive in the fighting against Parmenio, and so he knew that the month of Daisios would soon begin and then the Macedonians would not fight. Zeus expected them to worship him instead (and bring in spring crops). This delay would keep them from battling their way to Dascylium and getting supplies there.[4]

Memnon called a council of war that all four of the Persian Anatolian satraps attended. When they heard his plan to avoid battle and burn the fields, they objected. The satrap Arshita, who ruled the town of Dascylium and the country to the east, regarded Alexander as a dangerous regional rival. Spitadatha, the satrap of the lands to the south, including some Greek cities, was a member of the Persian royal family and fielded a personal guard of forty of King Darius's cavalry. He regarded Alexander as both a rival and a parvenu. The other two satraps had traveled from eastern Anatolia. They objected because they were unfamiliar with Greek and especially Macedonian military prowess. Memnon remonstrated, but they replied that his kind of war would be dishonorable. The Persians must advance and fight. Ahura Mazda, their chief god, expected it.[5]

Memnon, the Rhodian mercenary, lost the debate with the cowboys from the high plains of Asia, and not without cause. Unlike the Europeans, the Persians put armor on some of their horses, an innovation, and some riders wore chain mail superior to any Greek or Macedonian armor. The Persians also fielded horse archers using a compound bow better than what the Greeks had. Persian cavalry did not fight in formation, as the Macedonians and Thessalians did, but they surpassed them in skill and athleticism. They could swarm around European armies consisting mainly of infantry and decimate them. (The satraps conceded their own infantry were inferior, and so they employed thousands of Greek mercenary foot soldiers as well as infantry officers such as Memnon. The Persians had no "foot companions," just cavalry somewhat like the mounted companions.)[6]

Memnon and his forces now took up positions on the side of the Granicus opposite the Macedonians. Marshes made the lower part of the river impassible,

and the upper part, beyond the confluence of the Granicus and the main tributary, the Koca Çay, was too rugged for most troops, so they stayed in between.
Throughout this mile-long stretch, banks up to five yards high would impede the
enemy. Perhaps the banks were partly wooded. Today many scrub oaks grow
there. The water was deeper than the two to four feet now typical in the springtime. There must have been a ford or two, for there is a very shallow one now,
about two miles from the modern shoreline. If the Macedonians crossed, the
Persians would attack the advancing column. Memnon knew his enemies fought
in formation. He would catch them before they had a chance to assemble.[7]

The Macedonians had not reached the river until late afternoon, but they
were ready to fight, and Alexander proposed to cross, no matter how steep the
banks. He wanted his battle, and he wanted to maintain momentum. The councilors demurred. Every foot companion would need to disassemble his pike and
carry the two pieces over his shoulder as he crossed the river. Even if the horses
could all swim, the men could not. Supposing the troops did cross, they would
fall out of line, and the Persians would be waiting.[8]

No, Alexander replied. He had obtained the blessing of Achilles and they
must fight. To wait would be dishonorable.

Parmenio and others disagreed. Alexander suggested that they cross as early as
possible the next day, and all agreed.

Some councilors reported that Macedonians were objecting to fighting during
Daisios, which would begin the next day. Speaking as king, Alexander declared
that he had postponed the start of Daisios. The calendar needed adjusting, he
explained, for it was out of sync with the sun and moon. To this tergiversation the
council did not object. The heavenly bodies were his province, not theirs.[9]

That night Alexander said his prayers. He would do it before crossing any
river, but especially a river guarded by enemies. Zeus was a likely god to invoke on
this occasion, and so was Athena, who for Alexander was a goddess of victory.
Callisthenes may have suggested a prayer to the spirit of the captured Trojan
Adrastus, or to Nemesis, the spirit of revenge, or to the Homeric Memnon, slain
by Achilles.[10]

A prayer of this sort resembled a legal brief. Zeus, Alexander would explain,
must favor the Macedonians over the satraps, just as he had favored Agamemnon
and Achilles over the Trojans. The local ghosts of the dead should submit to
Macedonian force majeure. The river Granicus should also cooperate. Other
local rivers had submitted to the king's ancestor Achilles.

The choice of god dictated the offering that should accompany the prayer. An
Olympian received a slaughtered animal and some grain tossed on the altar, if
there was one. A spirit drank blood from a slaughtered animal poured into the
ground. The river received an animal slaughtered beside the water. The king

decided who got what. The Macedonians did not have a liturgy. They had only a tradition that the king must adapt day by day.

These religious customs informed the coming battle. They imparted respect for the terrain, a sense of mission, and an awareness of the vagaries of combat. European and North American soldiers fighting in this region today bring along anthropologists and psychologists. Alexander sought out the gods who were already there.

***

THE NEXT MORNING Alexander led his strike force—scouts, companion cavalry, quick-marching shield bearers, and some light troops—across the river at a ford the Persians neglected to defend. Parmenio and the main body crossed after them. As the sun rose over the field beside the river, the parts of Philip's war machine moved at a speed that may not have surprised Memnon but surely surprised many of the Persians. The Persians now confronted a battle line of about 40,000 extending east of the riverbank.[11]

Both armies were trapped. To the north lay the marsh; to the south, broken ground only scouts and other light troops could cross. To the west ran the mostly unfordable Granicus. To the east lay the only bridge, at Zeleia.

Parmenio, with heavy troops on the left, would hold the enemy fast, and Alexander, with the strike force on the right, would probe for weaknesses. The Greek troops lined up behind the phalanx. The troops stationed in the middle could switch from one commander to the other, depending on circumstances. The Macedonian artillery and the myriad mules would wait in the rear.

The Persians fought in two lines. Iranian cavalry stood in front, with Arshama and Spitadatha against Alexander, and other Iranians against Parmenio. The Greek mercenary infantry waited in back. The Persian commanders, like many other Near Eastern generals, assumed that the cavalry would attack and disperse any enemy riders, and then do the same to the enemy infantry. The Persians' own infantry—their best-organized soldiers, the Greek mercenaries—would do nothing more than mop up. The Persian baggage train waited miles away, at Zeleia.

The gods naturally attended, as they did all battles. Soldiers thought the gods would appear out of nowhere, terrifying enemies. More often the gods were spectators, like the herdsmen who roamed the hills as they would on any other day, or leaned on their crooks to watch. They knew the Persians as the owners of a few local estates and as avid hunters. They knew Troy as a market town, and they associated the Macedonians with Parmenio.[12]

Almost all of Alexander's battles began with Alexander, and so did this one. After ordering the companion cavalry forward, he rode at the front, conspicuous for the two plumes on his helmet. Beside him rode Clitus, his nurse's brother, who commanded a company of the companions known as the king's own, and Philotas. Like their men, who were fanning out behind them, they carried no shields and no body armor besides helmets and cuirasses. They depended on cohesiveness, a quality that came partly from the horses. The best horse, the leader of the herd, led the way. That was Bucephalas, Alexander's mount. Other bold horses ran just behind him. Those belonged to Clitus, Philotas, and the other top officers. Then came the less intrepid animals, following along. The enlisted men rode those. At the back corners of the formation, outstanding mounts kept the herd together. Lower-ranking officers rode those. The horses were companions, too, guided by instinct. The Thessalian cavalry controlled by Parmenio operated the same way.[13]

Although the horses trotted and did not gallop, the shield bearers could not keep up. The heavy infantry, beginning with Perdiccas, could not keep up with the shield bearers, and so the army advanced in echelon. Once the antagonists drew near, two engagements began.

Alexander and the companions brushed aside the inferior cavalry of the satrap Arshita, and this force fled toward Dascylium. Alexander now re-formed his men and turned toward the next satrap, Spitadatha of Ionia. These Persians fought harder. Their leaders led from the front, no less than Alexander did. Again and again they strove to kill him. One struck Alexander in the head with a scimitar, cutting off one of the two plumes, but Alexander's helmet deflected the blow. Spitadatha himself raised his scimitar to hit Alexander from behind, but Clitus, still beside his king, swung his own sword, shaped like a curved meat cleaver, and cut off Spitadatha's arm at the shoulder. In this sector of the battle, Spitadatha's death proved decisive. His very best men dispersed, and so did the rest of his troops.[14]

A second engagement pitted the Thessalians, stationed at the far end of the line, against the Bactrians, who attacked, circling and shooting arrows. Since the Macedonian phalanx stood nearby, in the middle of the battlefield, the Bactrians lacked room to maneuver. The Thessalians carried shields, unlike Macedonian cavalry, and withstood the barrage. Eventually they made contact and began the work of stabbing the Bactrians and their mounts. Once the Bactrians fell to the ground, the Thessalians dispatched them, for the Bactrians lacked helmets. The satrap Mithrobouzanes was killed, and the Bactrians retreated, following their standards.[15]

Now both Alexander and the Thessalians advanced farther and encountered the Greek mercenaries that the Persians had left in reserve. For a second time, the Macedonians re-formed. They followed a version of the battle plan Philip had used twenty years before, against Bardylis and the Illyrians. The phalanx and shield bearers advanced to engage the enemy. Alexander and the cavalry moved to the side and rear, closing off retreat. The enemy formed a square but broke under pressure. Unlike Philip, who had let the Illyrians escape, Alexander ordered more attacks. The Macedonians killed all but 2,000 mercenaries. These were the best enemy troops in Anatolia, and he did not wish to encounter them again. He also wished to warn other Greeks against serving on the Persian side.

Macedonian casualties amounted to a few hundred, Persian casualties to some thousands. Memnon survived, but two satraps were dead, and one who had fled committed suicide. The Macedonians had destroyed the Persian field army in Anatolia and decapitated the Persian administration, but they had not eliminated the Persians. The cavalry escaped, and many Persian garrisons remained. Nor had they destroyed all potential local resistance. The invaders would now have to deal with dozens of cities, valleys, and regions.[16]

After the battle, Alexander dispatched Parmenio, the previous year's loser, to Dascylium for the money and supplies there. Alexander's personal physician checked to see whether he had suffered a dent to his skull as well as his helmet. If Alexander was badly wounded, who would give the orders to care for the enemy, a courtesy that armies did not always extend? Who would make sure that the troops immediately received all their pay but the creditors were put off? Who would bury the dead?

The next day, Alexander did this duty, and also buried the dead enemy mercenaries. Flames sanctified by libations consumed the hundreds of bodies, and then the victors shoveled all manner of bones into the funeral mound—shinbones with cut marks, skulls rent front to back or temple to temple by sword blows, or punctured by butt-spikes of spears. Bone buttons survived from the men's shoes. The Greeks lay beside their sword handles and straight and curved sword blades. The Macedonian army could not afford to waste usable weapons, and buried their dead without them.[17] Alexander saved his largesse for the families of the dead, giving them cash and tax exemptions.[18]

Next Alexander returned to Troy, to give thanks. Like Achilles, he had defeated an opponent named Memnon, and he had done it near Troy. He commissioned equestrian statues of the twenty-five Macedonian dead who were companion cavalry, plus an accompanying statue of one companion who had survived—himself.[19]

This gesture was tantalizing. Was he truly just one more companion, or was he the most powerful man in Europe and Asia Minor? The same question arose from a commemoration that he made with Greeks in mind. To Athens he sent some gold and silver valuables taken from the abandoned Persian baggage train. On the biggest piece, he wrote this inscription:

Alexander, the son of Philip,
And the Greeks save for the Spartans dedicate
These spoils taken from the Barbarians dwelling in Asia.

He did not call himself a king. He did imply that his accomplishments surpassed those of the Spartans who had refused to help him. Absurdly, he shared these accomplishments with "the Greeks." More Greeks fought against him than for him, and he sold the 2,000 survivors into slavery.[20]

Last, he set his engineers to digging wells and making other preparations for building the city that he had vowed to found, to be called Alexandria, among the Trojans. He now possessed a mere smidgen of Anatolia. If the Persians had concentrated even more on killing him and had succeeded, they would have driven the Macedonians back into Europe. No one could immediately replace Alexander as chief priest and as king, and without a priest-king the army could not function.

———※———

AFTER THE GRANICUS battle, Alexander experienced what for him, as for other ancient conquerors, was the best part of victory—accepting the supplications of local people who were fearful, if not defeated, and came to him to surrender. That introduced him to the worst part of a victory over the Persian Empire. How would he rule these people? He was not king of Persia. He did not wish to take the throne of each and every local king; it would take too long.

To get money, he laid down a rule that all income paid to the Persians would now go to him or his representatives. To make sure the money was collected, he preserved the Persian post of satrap, and appointed one of his companions. He also replaced any Persian garrisons with new ones, under companions who would report to him. Besides being his subordinates, the satraps and the garrison commanders would need to remember they were companions, and act independently yet cooperatively.

Alexander and his generals discussed Memnon, who was now organizing a fleet of Phoenician ships. Memnon might counterattack and hit Alexander in the rear in Greece, using his fleet and his remaining mercenaries. If Memnon could manage that, the Persians in Anatolia would fight harder, and the Greeks there would be less welcoming to the Macedonians. Rich now, thanks to Dascylium, Alexander might eventually be unable to pay his men. To quash Memnon before that happened, the army would move south, targeting the enemy fleet.[21]

The Macedonians marched down the coast, going from one market town to the next, and Alexander's ships accompanied them. The grain was now high, and Parmenio and the others in charge of logistics, such as the king's close friend Hephaestion, seized supplies in some places and bought them in other places, especially towns and islands with which Alexander made alliances. In return for being given tax breaks, these places would refuse to supply Memnon's navy. In the biggest town, Miletus, the Persian garrison resisted, but the people stayed in Alexander's good graces by supplicating. To announce themselves, they waved palm leaves. Although this supplicatory gesture was common in Asia, the Macedonians might not have seen it before.[22]

In a week or two the Macedonians reached Sardis, the capital of the wealthy satrapy of Lydia. They seized the treasury, which was far bigger than Dascylium's, and Alexander paid more of his debts. He also spent some of the money and built a shrine to Zeus (who thundered in approval). Since the Persian in charge of the place surrendered without a fight, Alexander made him part of his entourage. Alexander also left behind many of his Greek allied troops, giving them the task of occupying this region, one Greeks had known for centuries. This was the first of many exchanges in which Europeans left Alexander and Asians joined him.[23]

To satisfy his curiosity, he and some of the companions visited Sardis's well-known garden and game park next to the Persian palace. Here they discovered the Persian version of an old religious idea. To keep chaos at bay, the Persian kings built a high wall and put a garden behind it. That was their tidy and attractive response to the Greek tradition of building walls around shrines. No doubt the visitors were charmed. They had seen many Greek gardens, small places devoted to education and romance. Now they saw a grand one, devoted to kings and lions.

Alexander's first religious problem arose at Ephesus, a few more days down the road. This port city surrendered but took advantage of Alexander's arrival to expel the tyrant who had governed the city under Persian rule. A crowd dragged the tyrant from an altar he had run to for refuge and put him to death. As a suppliant, he deserved a hearing; as a tyrant, he might not. Perhaps his death was sacrilegious, but Alexander was not sure he had the authority to interfere.[24]

The altar stood before the newly finished temple of Artemis, the largest building in the Greek world. The city assembly invited Alexander to celebrate his Granicus victory there, and he did, bringing his troops. The Persians had taken down the temple's statue of Philip, and the assembly let Alexander put it back up. He wanted to do more than that, and asked them to let him dedicate the temple to the goddess. The assembly refused. Dedicating the temple was their prerogative, and giving this prerogative to a king would deprive them of their autonomy. The king of Persia had never tried to impose himself on the Ephesians in this way, and they would not let the king of the Macedonians do it. He might enter the shrine and honor their customs, sacrificing goats rather than fancier species and using altars made entirely of pairs of goat horns. They might even let him worship, but they would not let him be the chief worshipper.[25]

This attitude should not have surprised either Alexander or companions who had dealt with Athens and other Greek cities. These cities were hypersensitive and legalistic—and Ephesus was nearly as large and as rich as Athens, with a marketplace and public buildings to match, and more sumptuous marble than in all the cities of Macedon together. He marched out of town, dissatisfied. He had got no dedication and he had set a precedent for letting Greek cities in Asia Minor replace unpopular governments with democracies. Even a commission Alexander gave to the painter Apelles went badly. The famous artist happened to be in Ephesus, and Alexander asked him to paint Bucephalas carrying him into battle. Apelles could not get the horse right, even after Alexander had the animal brought into the studio.[26]

On the Macedonians marched. If a port lay out of the way, Alexander would dispatch Parmenio or other companions to extract a surrender. At Priene another, less imposing temple was going up. By letting the townspeople establish a democracy and giving them tax breaks, Alexander got to dedicate the temple. That put him ahead of the Persian kings and their policy of benign neglect of Greek religion. It also raised Alexander's position among the Greeks. He was now doing what the city itself would otherwise do.[27]

Memnon fled again, farther south, to the southwestern tip of Anatolia. He was running out of strongholds, and also out of ports. The Macedonians overtook him at Halicarnassus, on a desolate peninsula where the rocky fringe of Anatolia spills down into the water. Memnon and his forces withstood a siege of weeks. When Alexander called a halt to the Macedonian attacks, Memnon and his Persians set fire to the city and abandoned it, but kept two fortified strongholds. The exhausted Macedonians largely withdrew, leaving Memnon his strongholds. A few troops stayed on to prevent the enemy from moving by land. The Persians could still move by sea.[28] Memnon had fought Alexander to a draw.

Unable to vanquish Memnon, Alexander gained a victory of a sort over Pixodarus, who had refused to become his father-in-law. Passing through Pixodarus's kingdom of Caria, Alexander gave it to his sister, Ada, who had ruled the country before but lost it to her brother. Using an odd turn of phrase, he said that Ada was like a mother to him. Ada, in turn, adopted him as her son. That way he could inherit the throne of Caria once she died. Alexander was giving the first example of how he would disassemble the Persian Empire kingdom by kingdom, and then reassemble it as so many appanages of his own. The religious implication of this policy was that he would have as many gods as he had thrones.[29]

The invaders had been fighting in Anatolia for six months and they were no closer to Babylon or Susa, Persia's capitals, than when they started. Yet Alexander would now lead the army on a colossal detour.

AFTER THE WITHDRAWAL from Halicarnassus, Alexander and the council faced another choice of route. If they wanted to be quick and safe, they ought to go back to Sardis and pick up the main road used by the Persian kings' couriers. This road ran northeast to Gordium, an old Anatolian town, then east, past ancient and modern Ancyra, then south, toward the best exit from Anatolia, the narrow road at the Cilician Gates. If they chose this route, they would have to winter in Gordium. They could get out of Anatolia sometime early the next year, 333. If they wanted to be quick but not safe, they could go east and follow the dry and barren route used by Xenophon and the mercenaries. That led toward the Gates, too.

A third route went south, toward the southwest coast of Anatolia, a more rugged country than any the Macedonians had encountered. The mountains broke apart in gray cliffs piled thousands of feet high. At this time of year, early winter, snow capped the heights. Torrents of water rushed down into ravines, leaving room for a highway but allowing no bridges and no navigation. The Persians had once sent an army down the road, and when it reached the main town, the citizens, amazed that any enemy had come so far, took their families and slaves to the acropolis and burnt them alive before making a suicide attack. The Persian grasp on the region was tenuous.

Alexander proposed to take this route and seize coastal towns that might be used by the Persian navy. The baggage train and most of the infantry would follow Parmenio in the opposite direction, north, on the safe, swift route to Sardis and the Persian road. The council agreed. Many of them, after all, would go with Parmenio. Besides, they had no navy to attack the ports with.

Alexander and his force turned into the mountains and debouched into a valley some twenty miles wide, where friends of Homer's Trojans had held estates. When Alexander reached the Xanthos River, he seized on an omen that would justify these new, avoidable risks. In the riverbed someone had found a bronze tablet with incomprehensible markings. That did not keep Alexander and his priests from reading it after a fashion. The markings, which were letters of some long-lost Near Eastern alphabet, happily predicted the overthrow of the Persian Empire. That interpretation kept the Macedonians from feeling lost. When they passed the tomb of Sarpedon, a son of Zeus who died in battle, Alexander avoided acknowledging this reminder of heroic mortality. They pressed on, to the first coastal port. The diviner Aristander, who was serving Alexander as he had Philip, happened to be from this town. That made the town's surrender all the easier to arrange.[30]

Like the mountain road, the coastal road was rough. For the first time, the army built itself a highway. Near the town of Phaselis, below a mountain called the Ladder, there was no room for a road, and the army marched along the beach, another first. Only favorable winds kept them from drowning, and Callisthenes was surely not the only one who called it a miracle that the troops survived. Supplications were few, and the army had to settle for conditional surrenders instead. At Phaselis, the people crowned Alexander with a golden wreath, a Greek way of putting a crown on his head. A crown of this kind implied that he was their ruler but that they were free. Accepting the compliment, he led revelers through the street in order to pay honors to a statue of a local man who had been a pupil of Aristotle.[31] This community sacrificed goats, like the Ephesians, and turned the hides into a favorite item of apparel, goat-hair shirts, which they gave to the Macedonians.

Some fifty miles farther, the beach disappeared—permanently. That had not happened before, either. Alexander had come far enough along the coast to reach the western end of the Taurus, the massif dividing Anatolia from the rest of Asia. For some one hundred miles, there was no practicable way of traveling farther eastward. With the Taurus in front of him and the sea beside him, Alexander was trapped, as he had been at the banks of the Granicus, and his predicament was now more serious, even though it did not involve the Persian army. If the Macedonians stayed put, they would alienate the towns they were living off. If they went into mountains, they might starve. If they picked the wrong way out, they would be stranded. If they split up, they would be picked off.[32]

They struck north, through the mountains beyond Perge, the last of the ports. First they tried a passage via the small and isolated city of Termessus. Termessus refused to let them pass, not because the city sided with the Persians but because they objected to a foreign army. Alexander laid siege to the place, but it took too long, and the army started to run out of food. To get more, they retreated the way they had come.[33]

Once resupplied, they went north again, the wind in their faces. Soldiers from Termessus shadowed them. Once the Macedonians reached the next town, Sagalassus, 2,000 feet high, the troops from Termessus joined the local people in defending a ridge in front of the city. Although defeated, this force escaped into the mountains. That always infuriated Alexander, just as surrender always disarmed him. He killed all he could, took Sagalassus, and reached the plateau of Anatolia for the first time.[34]

As the army approached their next destination, the Persian provincial capital of Celaenae, the mountains gave way to plains of olive trees and to vineyards that produced a wine potable if mixed with honey. The mercenaries holding Celaenae proposed to surrender in sixty days if no Persian rescuers arrived. These were the most unfavorable surrender terms offered so far. Alexander's engineers surveyed the mercenaries' stronghold, a tower of stone glowering over a palace built by the Persian king Xerxes. They described the difficulties of a siege, and Alexander, wishing to avoid another Halicarnassus, agreed to the mercenaries' terms. He gave the task of waiting (and drinking wine) to a detachment under one of his best officers, Antigonus. The treasure obtained at Celaenae let Alexander pay his remaining debts, with money to spare for the defense of shipping lanes in the Hellespont.[35]

Farther north, the road improved. Here, about halfway between Sardis and Gordium, the army hit the central route across Anatolia. It was broad enough for ten men abreast. Parmenio had already passed this way. He had spent the winter in Gordium and was waiting there when Alexander reached the city in early spring.[36]

Gordium proved tiny, with no notable temples and a small citadel built by the Persians. The army was loitering in a country without any large towns—and, of course, without ports. That complicated logistics. The barrenness of the country also affected morale. Before Gordium, the soldiers had named several places after their leader—"Alexander's palisade," "Alexander's inn," and "Alexander's well." Once they reached Gordium, they stopped.[37]

Parmenio gave Alexander bad news about Memnon. After the siege of Halicarnassus, Memnon had led his fleet on a counteroffensive to win back the port towns taken by the Macedonians. To convince the Greeks to change sides, he paid bribes, and to acknowledge Greek liberty, he signed treaties. He was now besieging the big port of Mytilene. The expedition might have to turn around and go back to the western coast of Asia Minor to fight Memnon.[38]

Morale also suffered for another reason. The soldiers knew, just as the officers knew, that there was one good road out of Anatolia, and that it passed through the Cilician Gates, where the Persians ought to be waiting. The alternative to passing through the Gates lay through the Antitaurus, a route of 215 miles at heights of up to 5,000 feet. Xenophon's mercenaries had traveled through the Antitaurus at the end of their service in Asia. To avoid starvation, they had given up their slaves and animals. They could not avoid frostbite, and some died of exposure. The Macedonians numbered six times this group of 10,000. That would spell greater confusion, and much greater losses.[39]

Then a religious problem arose, and solving it raised morale. The shrine of Zeus at Gordium had a Macedonian touch, or so the locals said. A Macedonian exile, Midas, had come to Gordium, become king, and built a shrine to Zeus. Yes, this was the Midas best known for turning objects into gold. Here in the local shrine was the wagon he had traveled in. He had dedicated it to the god, and tied it in place with a knot. Zeus would part with this piece of memorabilia only if the knot was untied. Would Alexander care to try? Perhaps the priests would discreetly assist him. Perhaps he would endow their shrine, which was only a house and a lot.[40]

Undoing the knot, the priests went on, would be significant. After the era of Midas and his descendants, Cyrus the Great seized the country. To undo the knot was to undo Cyrus's empire. The priests even said that the man who untied the knot would rule Asia. Of course, they had made the knot difficult to untie.

What truth was there in this palaver? Rather than the name of a king, Midas was a dynastic title of the Phrygians, who made an early attempt to unify Anatolia.

Far from being rich in gold, they used cloth for money. One ambitious ruler married a Greek. To resist this particular Midas, the Assyrians entered Anatolia. Midas responded by preventing them from passing through the Cilician Gates. He had divided Anatolia from the East—in effect, had linked Anatolia to Greece. Now the priests had invited Alexander to do the opposite and unite Macedon to Asia.

Although ignorant of this history, Alexander accepted the offer to untie the knot. Then he panicked, or became infuriated. (Perhaps the first of these feelings inspired the second.) Rather than untie the knot, he drew his sword and cut it open. No priest could claim to have helped him. That night, Alexander's soothsayers greeted thunder and lightning as good omens. Zeus (who had got power by rude strokes of his own) approved of Alexander. The king reciprocated with offerings by which he gave thanks to the god and shared his apparent good fortune with his men. He told the engineers (or let them believe) that he loosed the knot by pulling a pin, not by cutting.[41]

Then true good fortune came. Memnon, Alexander learned, had fallen ill and died. The siege of Mytilene ended, and the danger passed. For lack of an adequate replacement for the dead commander, the Persian fleet dispersed.

Had Alexander ever prayed for this stroke of luck? Not in public. Greek and Macedonian leaders did not pray for such a thing publicly, any more than Achilles prayed for Hector to die in bed of an illness. Perhaps, after hearing of Memnon's death, Alexander prayed on behalf of Memnon's widow, Barsine. She had lived in Macedon as a child, for her family were Persian exiles who took refuge with Philip, and so Alexander knew her. Born around 360, she was only a few years older than he. Now she was a widow with three children. If Alexander did pray, his prayers came true, for she reached Damascus, where he would eventually encounter her again.[42]

Once the army left Gordium and went east, on the Persian road, the plain became barren. To avoid hunger and drought at that time of year, the late summer and early fall, the expedition hoped to draw on royal storehouses along the road. The storehouses were available, but to feed an army the size of Alexander's, all must be filled, and so the king sought logistical help from a new source. After reaching Ancyra, he appointed a native, Sabictas, as satrap of the next region, Cappadocia. Alexander feared there would be too little grain otherwise. Towns would not provide them a market, and there was little to plunder.[43]

He had never appointed a native before. He had let Ada take the throne but not appointed her. In Celaenae he picked a top officer, Antigonus. For the port towns on the coast he picked one of his sea captains, in Sardis a brother of Parmenio. These men would stand guard against Memnon's forts on the peninsula, the Persian navy, and restive locals. Sabictas might not. He lacked any religious or cultural ties to the Macedonians. He was not a companion—not a Homeric henchman and not an Argonaut.[44]

Of the several wells named after Midas, the one in Ankara was the last from which the army would drink.[45] They marched on through country so empty that later writers could not tell what road they used. Homer told them nothing about the country around them, and neither did Xenophon or Herodotus. Local informants may have told them that Cyrus the Great had founded the local town of Zela after defeating nomadic invaders from Central Asia, a region the Macedonians knew almost nothing about. Cyrus had built a shrine there to the Persian goddess Anahita—an odd shrine in the eyes of a Greek, for it consisted only of an ashen mound surrounded by a circular earthen wall. The ashes were the remains of fires tended by Magi who killed their sacrificial victims not by slitting their throats, as Greeks did, but by bashing them with a log. If the generals heard of Zela, they did not bother to turn aside and stop. The Macedonians cared much less about Persian religion than about Persian troops, roads, and gold.[46]

As the Macedonians continued east and then south, heading for the Cilician Gates, the Antitaurus range rose on their left. The local people said one peak was so high that in good weather both the Black Sea and the Mediterranean were visible. If the Persians stopped the Macedonians, they would either have to find a way through these mountains or go back the way they had come.[47]

The men knew that even if some favored going back, Alexander would not, and Alexander would likely prevail. He would declare the omens for a retreat unfavorable, and those who disagreed would need to produce more persuasive omens. Earlier, when Parmenio produced an omen in favor of fighting the Persians at sea, Alexander reinterpreted the omen.[48] The omen came from Zeus, the king said, and so it was the king's business to read it. He did not let Aristander or any other diviner interfere.

How many Persians were guarding the Gates? They would not know until they arrived. They did know that the narrow road through the Gates stretched for some miles. At the tightest spot, the road was two yards wide and cliffs rose more than a hundred yards overhead. A rockslide could stop them. Several hundred Greek mercenaries could, just as several hundred Spartans stopped the Persians at the pass at Thermopylae. Barriers could block the way, and archers and perhaps catapults could decimate them as they removed the barriers. Flash floods could stop them. Skirmishers could slow them down, mile after mile.[49]

At the Granicus they had been trapped on three sides. The river ran beside them; marshes blocked them on one side and the rough ground on another. At the Ladder, in the coastal mountains, they had been trapped. The beach disappeared behind them, the mountains rose on one side, and the tide came in on the other. Now they had gates in front of them—battlements of well-guarded rock. The fairy-tale march had stopped at the door of the ogre's castle.

A force of Persians—small, but more than enough to hold the pass for days—knew the Macedonians were approaching. They did not expect them to arrive as soon as they did, and the defenses remained minimal. Their commander had withdrawn to Cilicia. He thought he could defeat or delay the Macedonians in a pitched battle there.

When the Persians saw Alexander's Thracians clambering up the pass, they panicked. In the distance, they saw the long Macedonian line. Behind them they saw open road. They took to the road.[50]

Hour by hour, for nearly a day, Alexander's army passed through the Gates. Not a weapon or a rock swooped down on them.

Once the army passed the Gates and descended into the lowlands of Cilicia, Alexander collapsed with a fever. As he lay sick, it occurred to him that his doctor might have been paid to kill him. Darius was trying to bribe Alexander's courtiers to assassinate him, and Parmenio suspected the doctor, a Greek named Philip. Ignoring Parmenio and the other councilors, Alexander decided to trust his father's namesake. He recovered from the illness and would not be seriously ill for another eight years. Two common camp diseases, typhus and typhoid, would bypass him. In spite of his many wounds, gangrene, tetanus, and blood poisoning would spare him, too. His mother had good reason to dedicate a statue to the goddess Health in that most prominent of places, the Athenian Acropolis.[51]

The army's path through Anatolia described an enormous, sideways S. The first part made some sense: the religious stop at Troy, then the battle, then the sweep of the treasure houses and the attempt to neutralize the Persian fleet. That, though, was only the first turn in the S. The army split and drove north, in the opposite direction, and circled back south toward the Gates. That second turn followed the Persian royal road, but the first had not. The S-curves kept the Persians guessing.[52]

Religion accounted for some of the risks the expedition had taken, and for some of the success. The side trip to Troy, taken for the sake of the hero Achilles, was a religiously motivated risk, and the failure to get greater control of places such as Ephesus was a religious compromise. The morale-saving bravado displayed by Alexander at Gordium was a piece of good religious luck, and passing through the Gates, even more than escaping trouble at the Ladder, was a piece of luck that a Macedonian or a Greek might think due to a god.

Religion was also an occasional liability. Alexander wanted pitched battles, no matter the odds, because he wanted proof Zeus favored him. He trusted his companions, men he worshipped with, but when they could not help him, as happened in Cappadocia, he had to turn to strangers. Yet religion also supplied an invincible motive to carry on. Every favorable sacrifice and every supplication said that the gods had chosen Alexander's side. That seemed to explain the invaders' spectacular success. Big and forbidding as it was, Anatolia had given way to them, river by river and peak by peak.

The Anatolian campaign had closed the gap between the military experience of Alexander and that of his senior companions. Now a new gap opened between them. When Alexander led the companions in a rite of thanksgiving at Solli, the first important Cilician city, they thought of him as priest of the Macedonians, but this twenty-two-year-old had begun to think of himself as more than a priest. After he left western Anatolia, several cities had changed their calendars, so that his arrival there marked the start of a new era.[53] More such honors would follow. Alexander was becoming a man apart. In the apprehensive minds of some Greeks, he was becoming godlike.

THE JEWS AND Armenians told stories of Alexander that made him an Egyptian. The Persians told another story, put in writing in the Middle Ages by the poet Firdausi.[54] Alexander was the son of Darab, the king of Persia. He was called Sikander because the first syllable of his name, "Al," was the definite article in Arabic, the most widely spoken language. He became "the Sikander," or simply "Sikander." His father was Failakus, who ruled Rum, or Rome. In this story, the march through Anatolia is merely part of a journey Alexander makes to Persia.

> The king of Persia, Darab, had ruled well, defeating his Arab enemies, and then attacked Failakus, king of Rum, whom he defeated with great loss. Failakus begged for peace, and Darab agreed, if Failakus would send one of his daughters to marry Darab. Failakus sent his daughter Nahid with many presents to the king of Persia, who married her.
>
> Nahid had bad breath, and so, although she became pregnant, she was so disagreeable to the king that he let her return for a time to her father in Rum, where she gave birth to a son. Failakus had no sons, and decided to keep the baby, spreading the word that it was a son of his own. He called the child Sikander.
>
> Darab married another wife, by whom he had another son, named Dara, who succeeded his father. Dara governed as his father had, claiming tribute from inferior rulers like Failakus. Sikander, who became king of Rum after Failakus's death, refused to pay tribute. Through an ambassador, he told Dara, "The time is past when Rum acknowledged the superiority of Persia. It is now your turn to pay tribute to Rum. If you refuse my demand, I will invade your dominions. Do not think not that I shall be satisfied with the conquest of Persia alone. The whole world shall be mine."

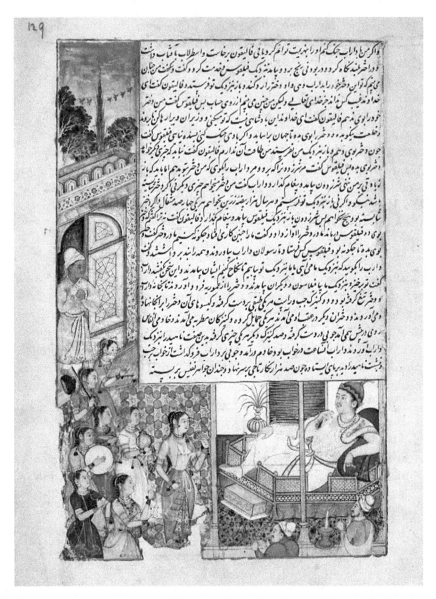

Anonymous Persian illustration of Nahid and Darab in the *Dārābnāmah* of Abu Tahir
Tarsusi, late sixteenth century.

British Library, London, or. 4615, fol. 129r.

Dara had no choice but to assemble his army, for Sikander was already marching against him. As Sikander drew near to the border of Persia, he disguised himself as an envoy, traveled to the camp of his half-brother, Dara, and told the king, "Your majesty, Sikander has not invaded your empire for the sake of fighting, but to know its history, its laws, and customs. He wishes to travel through the whole world. Why should he make war on you? Give him free passage through your kingdom, and nothing more is required."

Dara was astonished at the airs put on by this envoy, and asked, "What is your name, and who are your parents? Are you Sikander?"

"Nothing of the sort," answered the envoy.

Dara entertained the envoy, and ordered his cup-bearer to bring him wine. After Sikander drank, he refused to return the cup, and instead put it in his sack, explaining that it was the custom in Rum for an ambassador to keep any cup from which he drank. Amused, Dara gave him more wine, and let him keep four cups, with which the ambassador returned to his own camp.

"They have been generous," Sikander said, displaying the jeweled cups. "I have eaten at their table, and learned everything about them, including their numbers. Prepare to attack."

The Alexander of this story, a deceitful player of parts, was not one that the companions would have recognized in late 333, when the army passed through the Gates and reached Cilicia. Yet the events in Syria, Egypt, and Mesopotamia during the next few years would lead some of them to change their minds and have the same opinion as Firdausi. They would watch Alexander play the part of a priest-king in several foreign cultures, and each time they would object, as Dara did in the story, but Alexander would prevail against them. Like Barrymore or Olivier, he could play all royal roles.

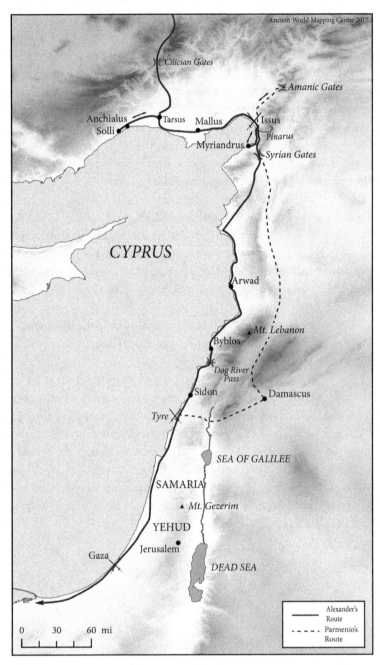

The Route of the Expedition Through Syria and Palestine, 333–332 BC.
Ancient World Mapping Center.

4

The Throne of Tyre

ONCE ALEXANDER SURVIVED the worst of his illness, he and the companions thanked both Asclepius and his doctor, Philip, for saving his life. They did not expect either the hero or the doctor to do away with the need for a period of rest and recovery for the patient and his companions. They lingered in Cilicia, enjoying a return to the shore of the Mediterranean. As a defensive measure, Parmenio went west with ample forces to guard the chief pass between Cilicia and Mesopotamia. The rest of the army remained with the king.

The generals were glad for the pause. Parmenio needed time to secure the pass, and the council of war needed time to learn Persian intentions. When would they attack, and where? The pass offered one route, but the generals also feared an attack from another direction, the south. If the enemy chose the south, another important provincial capital, Damascus, could serve as the Persian headquarters. They could attack the Macedonians and shield Phoenicia and Egypt. The generals were not sure that the Persians wanted to defeat them more than they wanted to protect these territories.

Alexander wanted to pause in the hope that Darius would seek out the Macedonians and lead his Persians into battle against them, just as the satraps had done. The Macedonians should wait for the enemy in the narrow country along the coast, which resembled the terrain in Greece and Macedon. Alexander hoped not so much to defeat the Persians as to kill or capture Darius. At best, he would make Darius beg for mercy.[1]

There was another reason Alexander wished to wait. He had never before been in a mostly Semitic country, and he wanted to learn about the gods, people, and landscape. At the first town he visited, Anchialus, he saw ruins far larger than at Troy. The colossal alabaster stele of the Assyrian king Sennacherib, found in the center of the city, confounded Callisthenes and the others, who could not read the inscription. They relied on a mistranslation that turned a boast about the king's sybaritic opulence into a cynical rejection of pleasure and riches. No one realized that Sennacherib had erected the stele around 698 BC as part of the Assyrian struggle against Midas and the Phrygians. No one knew that Sennacherib's god, Ashur, was another version of Zeus.[2]

After the sojourn in Anchialus, Alexander and the army marched on to Solli, a Greek city, which surrendered and let Alexander make a thank offering. Seeing the city had a mint, Alexander exacted a levy of 200 talents in order to produce coins to pay troops and debts. He then compensated the city by letting it establish a democracy. Mallus, the next stop on his tour of Cilicia, worshipped the hero Amphilochus, and that made for an agreeable pause: Amphilochus was a supposed ancestor of Alexander as well as the citizens. Instead of a levy, Mallus got a tax break, and Alexander brokered a settlement between competing political factions in the city. Mallus also had a mint that had produced coins for the Persians, and would keep producing them.[3]

Alexander did not object to other kinds of money, even coins bearing the name of Mazdai, the former Persian satrap. Mazdai's money would remain legal tender, and so would Persian darics, gold coins bearing a stereotypical image of the king kneeling and shooting an arrow. So would local money from a dozen mints, including coins issued in his name with Semitic legends. Alexander was all for money, the more the better. He needed streams of it, and whenever he got bullion, he minted new issues. Eventually he started twenty-four mints in Egypt and Asia. From Philip he had inherited just two, both Macedonian.[4]

At Mallus the generals met. Since Parmenio and 14,000 men now held the pass, they decided to advance at a saunter from town to town and spring to spring. Some food was seized, some bought from Aramaic-speaking merchants. The granaries were full, the orchards ripe. Then the coast narrowed, and the road began zigzagging through mountains and cliffs. To the east rose the mountain that the people called Haman, after the local god. To the west valleys opened on the Mediterranean. The scouts rode ahead, with Syrian or Phoenician interpreters. Next came Philotas and the lead troops of companions. Alexander and the rest of the troops followed, with Parmenio still watching the rear. The young and fleet in the lead, the old and slow at the rear: the army of 40,000 moved with the feral logic of a pack of wolves.[5]

Inscriptions stared down from some outcroppings. One, a ways ahead of them, at the Dog River pass, commemorated the king who had built the road—Nebuchadnezzar, who had besieged Tyre and overthrown Jerusalem 250 years before. The inscription, which is still there, says:

> I did what no former king had done: I cut through the high mountains, I crushed the rocks. . . . I prepared a passage for the cedars for Marduk—tall and thick, splendid . . . and supreme. . . . I bundled them like reeds and planted them in Babylon like so many Euphrates poplars. I let the people of Lebanon lie in safe pastures . . . and I wrote an inscription in the mountain passes and on it established my royal image forever.[6]

Marduk was Nebuchadnezzar's Zeus. This god had assigned the people of Lebanon to Nebuchadnezzar as a farmer assigns sheep to a shepherd. The Macedonians would not have understood this image of a human flock. Sheep were offerings, not human beings.

Some days later the army came to the town of Issus, and there they paused to build a hospital. They also left behind a few men who had taken ill in Cilicia. Parmenio recently had quit the pass and joined the march south. Now the Macedonians would be blind to enemy movements, as they sometimes had been in Anatolia.

The next day they crossed the Pinarus, one of many small rivers, and the day after that they reached a narrow 600-yard stretch of shoreline lined with high rocks and empty towers and walls. They did not know the Hebrew story that the great whale had disgorged Jonah at this spot, but they might have guessed it, for the unmanned defenses seemed to swallow them, as they spent nearly an entire day marching through.

The following day, the Macedonians headed toward the next defile, twenty miles south. Xenophon and his mercenaries, who had used the same road, had turned east there. The Macedonians turned south and reached the coastal town of Myriandrus. Their scouts had no word of Darius and the Persians. Was the enemy to the south of them, as the generals feared? Then one of the medical personnel left behind at Issus rode into camp and reported that the Persian army had entered Issus the same day the Macedonians left and had mutilated the patients recuperating there.[7]

The two armies had dropped into a funnel. First came the Macedonians, then the Persians. Neither could escape. The Mediterranean blocked them in one direction, and the Arabian plate, throwing up mountains to oppose the sea, blocked them in the other direction. The funnel had narrowed, and they were both stuck. More than 100,000 men would now collide.

LIKE THE MACEDONIAN generals, Darius thought in military terms. When word reached him of the defeat at the Granicus, he responded calmly and confidently. Although he began to gather an army at Babylon, he declined to send more men to Anatolia or go there himself. He did not see the need. The northern third of Anatolia remained in friendly hands, Cappadocia had acknowledged Alexander under duress, and the Greeks might change sides. Alexander's campaign to control seaports had only partly succeeded.

Then came word that Alexander had slipped through the Gates. This piece of luck alarmed Darius, as though a burglar had found the one unlocked door in the house. In the early fall of 333 he summoned his advisers, especially Mazdai, who knew the region because he was satrap of Syria as well as former satrap of Cilicia. He had governed Greeks and fought against them.[8]

Darius's Greek mercenary commanders warned the king of the superiority of the enemy infantry. A pitched battle against these forces would be a mistake, no matter how big an army the king raised. Forces like Alexander's had beaten the Persians at the Granicus, had beaten them decades before, when Xenophon's mercenaries invaded, and had beaten them in Greece during the Greco-Persian wars 150 years earlier. The king must fight battles of another kind, harassing the Macedonians with mounted archers or surrounding them in open country in either Cilicia or Syria. This advice resembled Memnon's to the satraps a year earlier.[9]

Mazdai, who knew the Macedonians from scouting reports, surprised the king with his news about Alexander's army. The invaders had not continued to advance, as Xenophon's men had, and they had not secured their supply line through the Gates to the rest of Anatolia, or rebuilt their navy. Alexander was an armed tourist, going where he liked—a young man, slight and ungainly, and not long arisen from his sickbed.[10]

Weighing this portrait of Alexander against the mercenaries' warnings, Darius decided to lead his troops out of Babylon and head west, seeking a battle. He may not have consulted Babylonian astrologers or priests about obtaining Marduk's blessing. He was not king of Babylon, a long-abolished title. He did consult his own Persian priests, the Magi, who served Ahura Mazda, Anahita, and other Persian gods.[11]

After several weeks, the Persian army arrived at the main ford on the upper Euphrates and crossed the half-mile-wide river, an exertion that took several days. Then they headed west over flat, sandy country toward the Mediterranean. The Iranian cavalry led the way, followed by the king and his sacred fire, to be kept burning until the hour of his death, and select water from Susa in Elam. Boiled and then cooled, it was stored in silver vessels.[12]

To make better time, Darius left behind the women, the baggage, and the heavy troops, sending some to the rear and others to Damascus. The lead elements reached the pass Parmenio had been guarding a few hours after he left. They might have caught the Macedonians just south of Issus, but they stopped there to capture the patients in the hospital. After that the Persians proceeded south, reaching the Pinarus River.[13]

The Macedonians were just a dozen miles away, at Myriandrus. The story of the mutilated prisoners stiffened their resolve to fight. The war council debated whether the Pinarus should be the place. They could go farther and choose another spot. Fight at the Pinarus, Parmenio urged, and all agreed.[14]

That night Alexander and a few of his priests climbed the mountain beside the coastal road to make offerings. This rite would be harder to perform than it had been the night before the Granicus battle. The gods here were Phoenician, and so Zeus and others Alexander might want to worship would have new names. Zeus turned out to be Baal Haman, the master of the mountains, shown on Persian coins minted in Cilicia. The Phoenician Athena was Baal's virgin sister, Anat—an odd thing, since Athena was not Zeus's sister. Anat appeared on Cilician coins, too. Alexander wanted to worship his ancestor, Heracles, and could find something like this hero in the person of Nergal, a warrior whose familiar was a lion.[15]

To identify these gods, Alexander did not need to be a religious expert. He did not need to know, for example, whether the local people thought of the mountain Haman as a god in its own right, or whether they sometimes called the mountain by the name El, another god. He needed Zeus's authority, Athena's skill, and Heracles's strength. By the same token, he did not need to give up his own gods in favor of Phoenician ones. If Zeus could be Amon, as was true at home, he could be Baal.[16]

The particulars of worship differed somewhat from a Greek or Macedonian ceremony. The Semites sacrificed cattle, sheep, and goats, but unlike the Europeans, they did not use pigs. Some goddesses had a taste for birds; the chief god had a taste for beef. That was the same, and so were offerings of grain in addition to animals. Incense was more popular among the Semites than among the Europeans, who regarded it as a luxury import. For Alexander, and for the Greeks, the acme of the offering was not the ceremony but the request. Worship, like supplication, centered on benefactions.[17]

The next morning Alexander performed the usual offerings at the start of the day. The ceremony went well, and so he could regard the mountaintop encounter with the local gods as propitious. He ordered the army to turn north, back through the narrows and toward the Pinarus. They reached the southern side of the river late in the afternoon. The Persians were waiting on the opposite side, several hundred yards away.[18]

The land alongside the Pinarus ran about a mile and a half from the sea to a hillock that marked the beginning of the mountains. Unlike the Granicus, the river was fordable throughout, but in some places the far bank was steep enough to slow down infantry. For the Macedonians, the terrain posed two dangers. To attack the Persians, they must cross the river. That would expose the infantry to attack from above. Troops along the seashore, where the river broadened and became shallow, could be outflanked.

The Macedonian order of battle alleviated the coastal danger. Parmenio, stationed by the sea, assigned the Greek cavalry to cover the beach. Next to them came the six regiments of the phalanx. Alexander's strike force included the shield bearers, lining up next to the phalanx, and then the companion cavalry plus the

Thessalians. Archers and Balkan mountaineers faced the heights. Alexander rode with the cavalry, beside Clitus and Parmenio's son Philotas. He was somewhat to the right of center, as he had been at the Granicus, and as Philip had been against Bardylis. The Greeks guarded the baggage train, and also a pass that the Macedonians feared that the Persians might use if they attacked from the south.[19]

Darius drew up his order of battle after consulting veterans of the Granicus defeat. Opposite each of the main Macedonian forces, he stationed a force well suited to fight it. All the Persian cavalry faced Parmenio's cavalry. Darius put his brother, Huxshathra, in command of them. Opposite Parmenio's infantry he put his Greek mercenaries, including a Macedonian exile, Amyntas. To one side, he stationed an ethnically mixed force of infantry with shields. Some of these faced Parmenio, some the shield bearers. Since the Persians reached the battlefield first, Darius got the chance to post infantry on the hills on the Macedonian side of the river. They looked down on Alexander's flank. Less valuable troops waited along the coastal road, to the rear. In the very center of the line stood the best infantry, 10,000 "Immortals," so called because the unit was always at full strength, and his personal guard. A mere forty guardsmen had fought at the Granicus. Now the full complement of 2,000 protected Darius.[20]

Darius reckoned that his cavalry could outride their opponents in any melee, and that the archers among his infantry could make any Macedonian assault costly. Sooner or later the Persian cavalry would break through and surround the Macedonians. If, in spite of everything, the Macedonian phalanx advanced, the Greek mercenaries would meet them as they climbed up the banks of the Pinarus. To impede the phalanx, Darius built a palisade along part of the river. If Alexander advanced, the Immortals and the guards would give up their lives to stop him. If put in danger, Darius would leave his chariot and mount a gray mare held by a servant. Until then he would control his officers by issuing written orders.[21]

A mile or so away, Alexander took alarm at some of the Persian dispositions. To ward off the Persians in the hills, he put his archers and javelin men opposite them. They would do best at firing or charging uphill. To ward off the Persian cavalry facing Parmenio, he sent the Thessalians to that side of the field.

By now the sun hung low over the Mediterranean. In the nearest towns, Issus and Myriandrus, a few Persian or Greek soldiers stood guard. The people prayed to Baal in their homes and shrines. Alexander's men spread the password, the name of a god or hero. Darius's men did not all speak the same language, nor worship alike, and could not share a password.

On one end of the field, by the mountains, the javelin men and the archers drove the Persians from the hillock. The enemy retreated to the heights stretching away from the battlefield to the east. On the other end of the battlefield, by the sea, the Persian cavalry began to advance against the Thessalians and the other cavalry under Parmenio. In between, Alexander readied the troops nearest him, the companion cavalry under Philotas and Clitus, and then trotted toward the enemy. He led the first wedge, and this wedge led the others. The shield bearers and phalanx advanced, too, but could not keep pace, and so they and Alexander's men moved in echelon, as at the Granicus.

Alexander and the companion cavalry crossed the stream and flung back the Persian infantry and archers. Alexander could now see a way to Darius's chariot, and he directed the troops toward it. Alexander hoped to reach the king and kill, capture, or humiliate him. If Darius fled on his gray mare, the enemy might still retreat or surrender. Alexander did not need to fight a duel with Darius. He needed to turn the contest between them into a ritualistic encounter that would make one of them legitimate and the other illegitimate.[22]

As the enemy drew near, the king and his entourage must have recognized Alexander by the two plumes atop his burnished iron helmet. The swift advance surprised those who had never fought Macedonians, but no one withdrew. Darius continued to give orders, and his Immortals continued to fight. For Alexander and his cavalry, the battle slowed down. Each yard gained took longer. Yet they drew nearer to Darius. First they were hundreds of yards away, then dozens. Although wounded in the thigh, Alexander drove on. Darius stood firm. The number of Persians between the two kings diminished. Bucephalas and the mare could almost see each other.[23]

SEVERAL HUNDRED YARDS to the left and rear of Alexander, the shield bearers strove to keep up with him. Then came the phalanx, toting their fifteen-foot spears across the stream and up the steep bank full of brambles. The lead regiments moved so fast that a gap opened up between them and the back three. Darius's palisade made the gap hard to close.

Some of the Greek mercenaries stationed near Darius spied the gap and marched into it. Once they reached this point, which lay just to the Persian side of the riverbank, they wheeled and attacked the three trailing regiments in the side. The nearest regiment was Ptolemy's. He was not the same man as Alexander's childhood friend, who eventually became pharaoh. This Ptolemy would not travel so far as Egypt.[24]

A young man, he had started the war as one of the royal bodyguards, and then took part in the siege of Halicarnassus. Just afterward he and Coenus led newly-wed Macedonian soldiers home for the winter. The next spring, Ptolemy and Coenus led these men back to Asia to rendezvous with the army at Gordium.

Ptolemy now stood some dozens of yards away from the Greeks. He marched to the right of his men, hurrying them along, conspicuous in his purple cloak.

The Greeks smashed into them. Their short spears caught the Macedonians in the side. As the Macedonian officers stepped forward to rally their companies, they made themselves targets, and were stabbed. Ptolemy fell dead. So did one officer after another. When junior officers stepped forward to reform the companies, the Greeks speared them, too. Square by square, the companies disintegrated. Most of Ptolemy's hundred or so officers were now slain, fatally wounded, or trampled to death.[25]

Surviving officers sounded trumpets calling men to regroup and other units to help. Alexander's nearby strike force heard the call better than Parmenio's wing. Alexander halted his advance on Darius and turned to observe the fighting some hundreds of yards behind him. Coenus, commander of the front half of the phalanx, turned and watched also. He was closer to the beleaguered regiment. In the Persian army, a man in Coenus's position would have waited for orders from the king. Not in this army. As Alexander watched, Coenus gave the order for his regiment, and those beside it, to turn around and head toward the fighting. Once Coenus arrived on the scene, he positioned his men so that they could hit the Greeks on the side. What the Greeks had done to Ptolemy, Coenus now did to them.[26]

The Greek mercenaries needed help, but that would have to come from Darius. The Persian king could see the fighting, or some of it, and so he saw the need. If he ordered reinforcements for the mercenaries, the order did not get through. None of Darius's officers took it upon themselves to march to the aid of the mercenaries.[27]

Left to their own devices, the mercenaries looked for some escape from their predicament. Coenus was attacking from one side, and Ptolemy's remnants were attacking from the other. The gap in the Macedonian line remained. They realized the Macedonian baggage train might be that way. Seeking plunder as well as escape, they headed toward it, and marched themselves out of the battle.

Parmenio, farther away, did not respond to the regiment's call for help. The Iranian cavalry, far outnumbering his own riders, were attacking in swarms. The Iranians dodged Parmenio's infantry; their horses typically avoided lowered spears. Instead the Iranians charged up the beach and attacked the Thessalian cavalry. Most rode past the diamonds and attacked from behind, but the Thessalians could change front and counterattack. Horse-to-horse fighting was ill suited to the bows and arrows of the Iranians but well suited to the javelins of the Thessalians. The Iranians rallied to their standards and attacked repeatedly, but suffered more casualties than they inflicted. Eventually they withdrew to the other side of the river.[28]

Only now, after Parmenio had prevailed and Coenus had saved Ptolemy's remnants, did Alexander resume his attack. He was too late. Darius knew that the cavalry had withdrawn and that some of the mercenaries had disappeared.

The time had come for the indispensable man to leave the field on his gray mare, like a modern leader forced from his limousine. He left his robe and his shield behind him in the chariot.[29]

Alexander did not pursue him into the gathering dusk. Instead he and the other Macedonians turned on some of the troops Darius had kept in reserve. These troops had no horses and no officers of any account. The battle ended with the cries of fallen men in the dark. Friendly torches moved toward the voices that called out in Macedonian or Greek, only to find that some of the wounded were not friends.

Alexander's officers reported some 1,200 Macedonian deaths, mostly in the infantry. Persian deaths numbered many thousands. Darius retreated toward the Euphrates, 300 miles east, and from there to Babylon. Some troops escaped to the north and sailed to Egypt, and others marched to Anatolia, where they plagued the Macedonian commander Antigonus.[30]

After the battle, Alexander's doctors treated his wound, and the king in turn visited the other wounded, and ordered the dead be cremated and given a shrine. With plunder from Darius's baggage, which he captured after the fighting, he paid donatives to the relatives of the dead and conducted funeral games in the traditional Greek and Macedonian manner. Naked sprinters competed in one race, and men in armor in another. Horses and chariots competed, the most prestigious event; wagons and mules competed, too, a concession to the realities of army life. Most events were military, like the javelin. That gave honor to the dead soldiers.[31]

Yet funeral games were not merely for the dead. Greeks and Macedonians liked to compete, no matter what the occasion. The Macedonians in particular could think of war itself as a game played by companions according to rules partly invented by Philip II. As for Philip or any other king, he would regard staging games partly as a way of manipulating his men. In this case, Alexander wished to distract attention from how the Macedonians had nearly lost the battle. The reason for the near defeat was Alexander's headlong pursuit of Darius, undertaken to delegitimize rather than defeat the enemy. A political and religious goal had come into conflict with military requirements.

To gain more plunder, Parmenio went to Damascus to seize the baggage that Darius had sent there. Lacking a map, he forced peasants to guide him. The governor of the city surrendered and gave the Macedonians 2,600 talents in coin, the largest haul so far. He also helped Parmenio capture a fleeing caravan of Persian servants and concubines who had quit Damascus so hastily they left clothes, furniture, and royal treasures strewn along the road. Parmenio wrote Alexander a letter enumerating "concubines who play music, to the number of 329, and 277 caterers and 70 wine-clarifiers," but only "14 perfume-makers." The letter showed how far the Macedonians had come since seizing Dascylium and Sardis. If Alexander did not sell this multitude of servants into slavery, they would slow down his army.[32]

Alexander eventually returned to the place where he had worshipped before the battle and erected altars to the gods he knew as Zeus, Athena, and Heracles. These altars would survive for centuries. When Cicero arrived in the vicinity, almost 200 years later, he chose this spot to be acclaimed by Roman troops and give them a donative. He knew the place under the local name Hieron, Greek for "sacrosanct." Alexander's three altars had become a place of pilgrimage. It was Alexander's Midas touch—every place he consecrated turned into an occasion for largesse. In contrast, he never finished the shrine that he planned to build in honor of the sacrifice made by the dead.[33]

Alexander handled battle captives assiduously. He acknowledged the accomplishments of the Persian cavalry commander Huxshathra, and admitted the Persian into the entourage. He interviewed the queen mother, Sisygambis, who waited for him in the captured royal chamber. She decided to take the initiative and supplicate him. She probably knew enough about Greek customs to take the person she approached by the knees, and perhaps the hand; perhaps she had rehearsed the scene. She may also have kept a translator handy, since the ranking companions who knew Persian were not nearby.

When Alexander entered the chamber accompanied by the bodyguard Leonnatus, she took Leonnatus for the king, and supplicated the wrong man. Alexander smiled and said she had made no mistake: the other man was Alexander, too. He called her "mother," as he had Ada. He could pay no higher compliment to a female (or offer any plainer criticism of Olympias). Sisygambis was not deceived. She replied that she was a slave, as were the other captured women, including her daughters and her daughter-in-law, Darius's wife. What, she asked, was Alexander going to do with them?[34]

This was no motherly question, he must have thought, but the first words in an exchange among Sisygambis, himself, and Darius, who would want the captives returned to him. If Alexander did return them, even at a price, that would legitimize Darius. Rather than answer Sisygambis, he embraced Darius's little son, another captive, and left Sisygambis to his subordinates. (They had been dealing with female Persian suppliants of their own. No doubt some of these suppliants became concubines.)[35]

When Parmenio returned from Damascus, he brought two noteworthy captives. He gave the less prepossessing one, a young Macedonian woman named Antigone, to his son Philotas, who was already acquiring a string of concubines. A Macedonian captured at sea by the Persians in 333, she had somehow made her way to the court of the Great King, where she may have been the most prominent

Macedonian. She was both a survivor and a social climber. Philotas soon made the mistake of remarking to her that Alexander was one companion among many. Philotas's mistake lay not in what he said but in telling Antigone, who began to search for someone to whom she could profitably confide more damaging indiscretions.[36]

Parmenio's other noteworthy captive was Barsine, the widow of Memnon of Rhodes. Her elderly father ranked high in the Persian court, even though he had once been an exile in Macedon. His ancestors had been satraps in western Anatolia—Macedon's neighbors—for nearly a century. He had named one of his sons Ilioneus, after the city of Troy.[37]

You might have died on the battlefield without an heir, Parmenio told Alexander; take up with Barsine. Alexander agreed. Within several years she gave him a son, Heracles. This boy could become Alexander's heir. If Alexander preferred, he would not. Barsine was no more important to Alexander than most of Philip's seven wives had been to Philip.[38]

Why had Alexander changed his mind about children? Perhaps because he had now accomplished something his father had not done, which was to defeat a Persian king, and so he felt ready to take this step. Or perhaps his reason may have had to do with Barsine, not his father. Barsine was a Greco-Persian. Marrying her—or, if that is too strong a word, using her as a concubine who might have legitimate children—showed that Alexander was flexible. He would welcome enemies into his entourage. They would not become companions, and Barsine would not become a queen, but they could prosper as subordinates, and she could prosper as a mate. And perhaps he chose her for a reason that had to do with himself. He and Barsine had known each other as children. In that sense, if not in any other, she was a companion.[39]

Alexander did not like much of the rest of the booty he had received. Shown some of Darius's furniture, he was embarrassed, and said, "Knowledgeable people seem to think that this means being a king." He melted down much of it, keeping the regalia he found in the Persian baggage train, yet found he could not dispense with all of Darius's tents. He needed several of them to house Darius's women.[40]

Soon after the battle, he rejected wealth of another kind, conveyed by an offer from Darius. From east of the Euphrates the king wrote and asked Alexander to return the captured women. Alexander could keep one of them, Darius's daughter, and marry her. And in return for evacuating Syria and most of Anatolia, Alexander would receive ample silver.

Alexander suppressed news of this letter. He may not have feared that the companions would accept this bargain, but the offer of money might tempt them, and they might pressure him to negotiate with Darius. He replied as follows:

I made war after you began the quarrel. I have already prevailed over your generals and satraps in battle, and now, since the gods have given everything to me, I control you and your country. As for those who served under you and did not die in battle, I have taken care of them and they do not stay with me unwillingly, but instead willingly fight alongside me.

No longer write to me as an equal. If you ask for anything, think of me as the master of everything you have. You will have whatever you can persuade me of.[41]

Alexander had invited Darius to supplicate. To provoke him further, Alexander avoided mentioning the women.

Darius did not deign to answer. By angering him, Alexander had induced him to raise another army, a matter of months or even years. Meanwhile, Alexander could pursue his next two goals, seizing Phoenicia and then Egypt. After that, Darius would have another chance to beg for his life.

IN THE MILD weather of early winter, the army entered Phoenicia, a coastal strip of cities that abounded in resources of every kind. These cities resembled Greece, but also Asian kingdoms. In Arwad, Sidon, and Tyre, priest-kings ruled, but they differed from Greek or Macedonian kings with religious duties. They served as admirals, not generals, and so they were often overseas. Although of royal birth, they sometimes did not take office until acclaimed by a citizen assembly. As Alexander had learned, they worshipped in a familiar way, but did not always worship familiar gods. Inland, in neighboring Syria, some Semites were henotheistic, worshipping one god in preference to all others. Identifying this god with Zeus or Baal Haman would be an error.[42]

Since Phoenicia consisted of independent cities, Alexander could not rule it as a whole. Nor could he appoint satraps and garrison commanders and leave administration to them. He would have to make use of the position of priest-king. Would he appoint himself to this post, or leave it to the incumbents?

For a third time, the army marched through the 600-yard coastal narrows where the Hebrews said Jonah had come ashore. As they walked south for a week, to Arwad, a few warships accompanied them. Alexander's scouts confirmed the surveyors' warning: Arwad was an island. Part of the city was there, two miles offshore, and part on the mainland. The city's fleet was absent, serving under the Persians, and so was the king.

Alexander's engineers advised that besieging the mainland settlement would be easy, but besieging the island would be difficult without more ships. To knock down the thirty-five-foot-high walls, they would have to put catapults on the ships, turning them into artillery platforms. So far as they knew, no navy had ever done this.[43]

The citizen assembly in Arwad preempted any siege. At their behest, the crown prince sailed to the mainland and offered the throne of Arwad to Alexander. Alexander accepted, and the new king received a gold crown surpassing anything kings of the Macedonians wore. In return, Arwad received two considerations more valuable than the crown: Alexander would leave the prince in charge, and Arwad's citizens would pay no more tribute than they had to the Persians.[44]

Alexander wanted no more crowns on these terms. At the next city, Sidon, a week down the road, he declined to become king. He delegated negotiations to a trusted companion, Hephaestion, but Hephaestion, a novice, made a kind of religious mistake.[45]

In Sidon, the king and the citizen assembly were at odds with each other. When the king, a Persian loyalist, refused to negotiate, the assembly sent delegates who surrendered to Hephaestion. They proposed that he name a new king. Hephaestion suggested one of the delegates, but they proposed a puppet—a royal relative who was a gardener. The gardener, they said, would know the royal family's ceremonies. For the sake of the ceremonies, it seems, Hephaestion agreed.[46]

Instead of being king, Alexander ended up with a vassal controlled by an assembly. That would make it harder to raise taxes, get ships, and unify Phoenicia. The winner in the negotiations, the assembly, got a priest-king who would not be a king. Rather than object, Alexander gave the new government most of the Persian wealth kept in the city. He took the rest and moved on to Tyre, a few days down the road. Here, in the biggest of the cities, Alexander got neither a crown nor a puppet. Instead he got a fight.

At Tyre, stone and mortar walls 150 feet high encircled a community of about 100,000 crammed into a square mile. Tyre was the ancient world's Manhattan, with outer boroughs of the city lining the shore half a mile away. The Macedonians arrived and overwhelmed these settlements with money, demands, and news that all the other Phoenician ports had fallen, and had also lent their navies to the invaders.

The great powers of the past had seized the mainland towns, but no one had ever captured the island. Nebuchadnezzar, who had cut through the mountains and cut down the forests, besieged Tyre for thirteen years and then gave up. The Persian authorities, who maintained a garrison in Sidon to prevent revolts, never set foot in Tyre. In that era before catapults, the walls were impregnable. To be captured, a strongly walled city would have to be betrayed from within. That often happened in Greece, but not in Tyre.[47]

The balanced, stable government of Tyre made betrayal less likely. An assembly of the people joined a council of elders and a priest-king in running the city.

Over centuries, power had shifted from one to another, or to judges who umpired conflicts, but in Alexander's time the people were strongest, and they were chauvinist. At most, the priest-king might sway the sailors in the fleet, which he commanded as admiral.

The chief god, Melkart, was the priest-king's partner. The god's name meant "king of the city," and the priest-king alone could lead worship at Melkart's shrine, the most opulent in Tyre, built with gold and sapphire columns. Each spring this god, who also ruled the underworld, rose from the dead at the king's request and came to Tyre. An image of Melkart was set afire, put aboard a boat, and sent out to sea, blazing, to warn the world that Tyre, like Venice, had renewed its marriage to the waters. When the Macedonians arrived, this festival was some weeks away. Ambassadors from Carthage, Tyre's most important colony, would shortly arrive for the celebrations. Between them, Tyre and Carthage had enough first-class warships to challenge all Greeks together. Melkart was an avatar of naval, royal, and intercontinental power—a Titan, the columns of whose shrine, the highest spot in the city, shone in the distance at night.[48]

Alexander thought Melkart was Heracles. (Heracles, after all, had come back from the underworld, even if he was not king there.) As a descendant of Heracles and Melkart, too, Alexander could claim the position of Tyrian king. For this purpose, he did not need a vote of the assembly or the elders. He needed access to the temple of Melkart. If he could make an offering there at festival time, he would be king as a result. The present king, he knew, was absent with the Persian fleet. When this king returned, he would protest, but Alexander, Melkart's descendant, would outrank him. Heracles-Melkart had appeared to him in a dream and laid out the plan for Alexander. The binational god conveniently spoke to him in Greek.[49]

The assembly of Tyre did not endorse Alexander's scheme. They invited him to sacrifice in a lesser temple, on the mainland. Alexander declined. The assembly persisted. Only a Phoenician, they reasoned, could be a scion of Melkart. To gain access to Melkart, Alexander concluded, he would have to capture the city, doing what the Persians, Nebuchadnezzar, Cyrus, and the pharaohs never had.[50]

Summoning his councilors, Alexander proposed a siege. They thought it unnecessary. The Macedonians needed to keep watch over Tyre, not capture it. The Persians now had few ships, and Alexander would soon receive ships contributed by Arwad, Sidon, and Phoenician ports on Cyprus. This fleet could isolate Tyre, and a small force of Macedonians could do the same on land. The rest of the army should leave Tyre behind, just as they had left Halicarnassus behind.[51]

Polyidus and the engineers offered another objection to a siege. Deep, treacherous waters protected the city. How could the Macedonians build a mole a half mile long across the strait and reach the walls? Even if they could, it would take months, and they would run out of food. Alexander answered that somehow or other they would turn the island into a peninsula and bring their siege engines close enough to knock down the walls. Food would come from the hinterland, as it had for the Tyrians.[52]

Alexander also placated the councilors with a last attempt to negotiate. He officiously sent a herald to Tyre under Hermes' protection. When the man did not return, Alexander claimed that the Tyrians had put him to death. That was sacrilege. The story was surely untrue: heralds enjoyed divine protection in Phoenicia as well as in Greece and Macedon. Yet the army believed the story. Alexander now had a moral advantage in the council debate, and he prevailed.[53]

Perhaps Alexander also had to convince himself. For that he turned to the soothsayer Aristander. Alexander told Aristander he had dreamed that Heracles was leading him into Tyre, and Aristander replied that Tyre would fall, but only after labors to compare with those of Heracles. Alexander's troops had reservations, too. When red specks appeared in some of the army's bread, they panicked because of the bad omen. Aristander calmed this constituency by saying that the blood the soldiers saw was that of the Tyrians. When the men saw a whale in the harbor, that was bad news for the Tyrians. Then Aristander killed a sheep and inspected the liver: it looked propitious.[54]

From the commander in chief to the common soldiers, the Macedonians had been in disarray. This double dose of religion provided a tonic. It did not provide a guarantee. Aristander's predictions would flow back and forth with the tides of war.

Operations began in midwinter with Macedonian work on the mole. The engineers battered down buildings in the seaside towns and hauled the earth and rubble to the shoreline. As boats carried the debris out to sea and dropped it, the Tyrians ridiculed Alexander for warring upon the god of the sea, then attacked the Macedonians with catapults from their own vessels. The Macedonians protected themselves with dozens of skins and sails; the Tyrians landed marines and butchered the longshoremen loading rubble onto Macedonian boats. Still, the mole rose to sea level, and the engineers commenced building towers and battering rams to roll up to the city walls. Modular towers devised by the engineer Diades would let catapults and archers fire down on the citadel.[55]

Then the Tyrians called upon their allies living on Mount Lebanon, east of the city. Alexander's foresters, who were stripping the mountain of timber for towers and rams, found themselves ambushed. Angered, Alexander left the siege of Tyre to Perdiccas and others and took a strike force into Mount Lebanon and beyond, killing any who resisted. One night when he and a companion had no fire, he ventured alone among some enemy sentries, killed them, and brought back a firebrand.[56] When food ran low, he demanded help from peoples to the south,

including the worshippers of Yahweh around Samaria and Jerusalem. Some refused, but some gave, impressed by the slaughter on Mount Lebanon.

A victorious Alexander returned to Tyre to find the siege faltering. Tyrian fire
ships had destroyed some of the siege towers, and many Macedonians had to leap
into the water. Rather than kill them, the Tyrians crushed their hands with sticks
and stones. Wind and storm waters had dislodged the material on the top of the
mole. Now it was out of sight.

Alexander ordered it rebuilt, broader and bigger than before, using tree
branches as a skeleton for the earth and rubble. Teams of Tyrian divers swam underwater and pulled away the branches. The mole submerged again. Diades's
towers would never reach their destination.

The siege had now lasted weeks. The king of Tyre had returned, with some
ships but no food or money. Becoming desperate, Tyrians hunted down birds and
turned wine into vinegar. Some sold their own children into slavery, then sold
themselves. After a citizen said he dreamed that the healing god Eshmun had left
the city, the people chained the god's statue to the altar beside it. They would have
killed the hapless citizen, but he fled to the temple of Melkart and supplicated.
The city magistrates shamed the populace into leaving him be.[57]

Then the ships from Arwad, Sidon, and Cyprus appeared. These reinforcements served as cruisers to repel enemy vessels and battleships bringing artillery
to bear against targets on the island. With Alexander serving as one of the admirals, the fleet drove the Tyrians from the waters around the island and surrounded
the city's damaged ramparts. The attackers also improved their tactics, partly by
imitating the Tyrians. They put catapults aboard ships, and to increase the fire-
power of these vessels they lashed the prows together and built decks linking one
ship to another. The fleet put catapults to a half dozen uses—blind fire against
civilians in the city, sniping against enemies on the battlements, interdictory
fire against Tyrian catapults, barrages to knock down the walls, covering fire if
Alexander's troops disembarked, supporting fire once they entered combat. The
Tyrians responded with hot sand that scalded the attackers, and they flung scythes
and hooks at the invaders.[58]

The engineers also reconfigured ships to carry more marines, especially
Coenus's regiment. To make it easier for men to land, they added drawbridges,
another invention by Diades. When Coenus and his men disembarked to attack
the city, they would not have to step into deep, turbulent water. A bridge would
lower them to some spot where projectiles had demolished the wall.[59]

Aristander had assured the king that the city would fall on the last day in the
month. When it did not, Alexander made the month a day longer. The next day
the wind changed, letting ships draw closer. The bridges swung down, and the
shield bearers disembarked and broke into the city. An axe blow to the head killed

the lead officer almost immediately, but Alexander led the troops onward. He took the royal palace, then led his men to the shrine of Agenor, the reputed ancestor of the Thebans of Greece. He cut down all who resisted him. Coenus's men broke into the rest of the city, and so did Phoenicians and Cypriots. Some Phoenicians showed mercy to the enemy, but the Macedonians did not. They slew some 8,000 Tyrians, and then calmed down enough to spare 30,000 to sell into slavery. Some of these had fled to shrines. Fifteen thousand later fled to Sidon with the help of the Phoenicians.[60]

The king and the Carthaginian ambassadors had fled to the shrine of Melkart. There they supplicated, and Alexander spared them. Then he directed Diades and the engineers to wheel a catapult into the shrine. At the altar of Melkart, he prayed to the being he knew as Heracles, and asked this club-wielding hero to accept a more efficient weapon presented by a descendant. An accompanying offering went well, showing that Heracles welcomed the novel gift. After this cross-cultural flourish, Alexander buried his 400 dead in the Macedonian way. He held athletic games in their honor and gave an ample donative to his men.[61]

The siege had lasted six months. Alexander assigned administrative duties to a garrison commander, then left the city to march south, toward Egypt.

Disastrous for Tyre—which never fully recovered—the siege raised Alexander's confidence. Never had he made such good use of allies or learned so much from enemies. He got the local god wrong, but got tactics and equipment right, and so he concluded that he had the god right, too. Centuries later, thanks to sand deposits, the abandoned mole became the peninsula that Alexander had envisioned.

The people of Tyre, and those of the other Phoenician cities, soon accommodated themselves to the Macedonian invaders. For merchants, Alexander and his Macedonians were ideal customers—hungry, thirsty, rich, and eager to sell their numerous captives into slavery—and the Phoenicians were willing to go anywhere. From Tyre onward, they dominated the business of serving Alexander and his men. They became the expedition's sutlers—its profitable, private commissariat. Parmenio and Hephaestion would now have the help of the world's most energetic traders.

DARIUS HAD GONE on to Babylon. During the siege he wrote Alexander again, asking for the return of the captive queen and princesses. As before, he offered a marriage alliance, but this time he added more silver. He also promised to yield all Anatolia and Syria. Darius left the status of Egypt unclear. The Persians maintained a garrison in Gaza, on the only road into Egypt. If Darius evacuated Syria, he could no longer help the Gaza garrison, and so he could scarcely defend Egypt. Without mentioning this province, he seemed to be conceding it.[62]

This time Alexander did not, or could not, keep news of the offer from the companions, and the council gathered to debate it. No one favored the marriage proposal. It legitimized Alexander, but it also turned him into a subordinate. Thanks to Parmenio's capture of Damascus, the Macedonians did not need the money. (Nor did they need Syria and Anatolia, which they had already conquered).[63]

The questionable feature was Egypt. Alexander thought of it as the greatest of godly prizes. Some Greeks who fought the Macedonians at Issus were heading there in hopes of finding employment and plunder. Other Greek mercenaries might join them. If they sided with native Egyptian rebels, a new Egyptian monarchy might emerge. Then Sparta and Athens, always eager to oppose Macedon, would send men and ships to Egypt.[64]

As council custom dictated, Parmenio, the senior general, spoke first, and said they should accept Darius's offer. This offer would let them grab Egypt and erect a Mediterranean empire. Alexander disagreed: he wanted more than what Darius offered. Some of the generals wished to reject the offer, too, but they were less ambitious. They said going to Egypt would not accomplish the goal of conquering the Persians. It would be another detour, like Alexander's visit to Troy. Other generals favored rejecting the offer for a related reason. Couriers had brought news of increasing Greek resistance to Antipater, Alexander's viceroy in Macedon. Persians in Anatolia were helping the Greeks, as they had been for several years, and were resisting Antigonus, Alexander's other lieutenant. The Macedonians should move to obliterate these Persian forces, the generals argued, not make peace with Darius.

In effect, some companions wanted to go home. Alexander wanted to satisfy his curiosity and ambition. They thought of the expedition as just that, an expedition. He thought of it as a personal holy war. He again prevailed: the army would make Egypt its next target.[65]

This had not been the first difference of opinion between Alexander and Parmenio, and between the king's closest supporters, many of them his friends, and the old general's supporters, many of them veteran commanders. Some differences were tactical. Alexander wished to fight at the Granicus immediately, and Parmenio preferred to wait; Parmenio, not Alexander, picked the Pinarus River as the spot to fight Darius. The latest difference of opinion was strategic. Alexander wanted to expand quickly, Parmenio perhaps eventually.

Every one of these disputes involved religion. Parmenio was all for Zeus, and for the companions. He wanted to limit casualties and fight close to home. Alexander was all for Zeus, Athena, Heracles, and now Baal, Nergal, and Melkart, and next Amon and Marduk. He wanted to sanctify casualties and fight beyond the Mediterranean basin.

Aside from these military disputes, Alexander and the companions drifted apart for another reason: the challenges of administering the empire. Alexander thought Anatolia, Egypt, and eventually Babylon could form a whole under his rule. Perhaps he could add Iran and places farther east. Parmenio and the others had no ecumenical ambition. For them, the lands along the Mediterranean would suffice. They obeyed the topographical dictates of the great flood that shaped the Near East thousands of years before. Alexander disobeyed.

FOR PARMENIO AND for the other companions, new conquests meant not new gods but new satrapies and other posts. So far, seven companions were serving as satraps. Antigonus, the most important of them, was fighting the Persians in central Anatolia. Three served elsewhere in Anatolia. Two more held Cilicia and Syria, the old posts of the Persian Mazdai. The remaining companion, who was serving in Thrace, on the western side of the Bosporus, had lost control of much of this satrapy to Thracian chieftains.[66]

If enough of these men failed, the empire would fall apart, almost in the foot-steps of Alexander's army. Yet Alexander could do little to help them. Army life provided no time or place to train satraps. The school for pages taught only some warfare, and perhaps a little diplomacy, but not the administration of Persian sa-trapies. Competent in warfare, whether on land or sea, a satrap might prove in-competent in dealing with his subjects. He might not know their gods, languages, or customs.

Unlike the companions, Alexander knew how to handle the religious and cul-tural aspect of power. He had been a priest-king for years, and had watched his father serve as one. He even had his older, simpleminded half-brother, Arrhidaeus, accompany him on the expedition to help him perform ceremonies. He always had help. What help would a companion have, especially among Semites?

As the army marched south on the coastal road, two Semitic communities, Samaria and Yehud, surrendered to the invaders, and Alexander presented the chal-lenge of dealing with them to a middling companion, Andromachus. Alexander might have reserved this task for himself, or for Parmenio. Instead Alexander and Parmenio went on, without pausing, toward Egypt, and Andromachus turned inland in order to serve as companion in chief for what is now the land of Israel.

Samaria and Yehud worshipped Yahweh, not a polytheistic set of gods such as Baal and Melkart. The bigger community, Samaria, centered on a temple at Mount Gerizim, and smaller Yehud centered on an unfinished temple in Jerusalem. Both communities spoke Aramaic and read a scripture written in an early form of Hebrew. It consisted of the five books of Moses. Other religious writings had not yet become canonical. Both communities were poor. They minted few coins.

Accompanied by a small number of troops, Andromachus came first to Samaria. He summoned the local ruler, called a *pihatum*, who had served the Persian satrap in Damascus. Defying the Persians, this official had brought troops to Tyre to fight alongside Alexander.[67] Andromachus told him to keep his post and be attentive to the wishes of Damascus now that a Macedonian ruled there.

Andromachus visited the shrine at Mount Gerizim, which for the Samaritans was the navel of the world, like Delphi among the Greeks. The small temple was ashlar masonry, not smooth stone, with Phoenician serpent motifs on the columns. A small cairn in the middle contained the remains of the usual animal offerings, cattle, sheep, and goats, but no pigs and many pigeons and doves. The nearby town had never fully recovered from an Assyrian attack centuries before. It served as the depository for the taxes Andromachus had come to take charge of—some due to the *pihatum*, some to the satrap, some to the king, and some to the shrine. The high priest of the shrine was the most important Samaritan. The *pihatum* was a foreigner, such as a Babylonian.[68]

Andromachus now traveled south some fifty miles to his other responsibility, Yehud. In Jerusalem, the only town, some thousands lived within the ruins of the walls of the city of David. The city's temple, which was rising atop the older temple destroyed by Nebuchadnezzar, was far from finished. Cyrus the Great, who had authorized the Jews to build it, had left the costs to them, and they were even poorer than the Samaritans. Yehud was more arid than Samaria. The 600-yard water tunnel built by King Hezekiah snaked back and forth amid geological faults in the rocky earth below Jerusalem. Had Alexander's geometrically minded engineers come to inspect this well-known piece of engineering, they would have left disappointed.[69]

The hands claiming a share of the meager local revenue were many. As in Samaria, the high priest took his share, and the *pihatum* took his. The Persians had spent some of their share on a common official perquisite, specially enriched black soil for the garden next to their palace. This originally Elamite refinement let the Persians cultivate exotic fruits and flowers.[70]

And this local money, what was it? The legends bore the names of long-vanished kings of Israel and Judah, as well as those of local Aramaic administrators. Sometimes the Persian king appeared in a traditional pose, kneeling and shooting an arrow. Even Zeus appeared, but not for any religious purpose. The coins were as confused as the taxes. Yet the local god, Yahweh, let his people worship no other beings.[71]

To the Macedonian mind, that explained the backwardness of Samaria and Yehud. Since there was only one god, there were fewer shrines; the divine received less attention and so gave fewer blessings. Since Yahweh was not like Hermes, god of commerce, the people were poor, and since Yahweh was not like Athena, goddess of crafts, the imagery on the coins was unsystematic and there was little art. Although Yahweh did not go so far as to deny that Hermes and Athena existed, he insisted on his monopoly over Samaria and Yehud. He was not the only heno-theistic god in the region. In the desert, the tribes of Moabites worshipped only Chemosh. Perhaps Yahweh was more demanding. Everything that belonged to him was consecrated and made irrevocably his. The whole people of Yehud be-longed to him.

Yahweh's enemies also belonged to him. On his say-so, they might be irrevo-cably destroyed. Yahweh might even command that they be burned alive. Foreign armies might be punished in this way, as would violators of Yahweh's shrine, and committers of incest and fornication with women in the high priest's family. Samaria and Yehud, which quarreled about other religious matters, thought alike about the consecration of goods and men to Yahweh.[72]

Greeks and Macedonians did not have any such ideas. They could melt down sacred objects in an emergency and replace them later. A slave might be dedicated to a god, to serve in a shrine, but a whole community could not be. Gods did not con-secrate human beings to destruction. The wrath of the Olympians was unceremoni-ous—a lightning bolt, a plague, or a flood. Worshippers did not burn criminals alive.[73]

Although the Samaritans had aided Alexander, Andromachus squeezed them harder than he did the people of Yehud, who were to be spared taxation one year in every seven. While the army was in Egypt, the Samaritans rebelled. The troops who had aided Alexander turned on Andromachus and his garrison. They killed the Macedonian soldiers, drove them off, or sold them into slavery. They pre-sented Andromachus to Yahweh, who consecrated him to destruction. The Samaritans burned him alive. Perhaps Andromachus had moved some valuable (or even trivial) items from the shrine at Mount Gerizim and melted them down, as no doubt happened at Solli, when the inhabitants had to give Alexander 200 talents. Perhaps he had seized temple livestock for the Macedonian offerings. Perhaps he had fornicated with the priest's wife or daughters.[74]

Only later, on his way back from Egypt, did Alexander send Perdiccas to sup-press the rebellion. Perdiccas's regiment assaulted Mount Gerizim and the settle-ment around the Persian fort. The Samaritans fought back, but Macedonian pro-ficiency was too much for them. Although the settlement had resisted the Assyrians for three years, it fell to the Macedonians in a matter of weeks. Some of the defenders withdrew and escaped to caves in the desert. They had supplies and records with them, even registries of slaves. They may have expected to live in hiding. Perdiccas discovered, attacked, and slaughtered them. He then estab-lished a Macedonian colony in Samaria, peopling it with ex-soldiers and fugitives from Tyre. He and his regiment rejoined the army, and another minor compan-ion replaced Andromachus.[75]

The Macedonians adjusted to the Semitic brand of polytheism that they en-countered in Syria and Palestine. They expected the Semites to adjust in return.

Some, like the people of Sidon, adjusted readily. Others, like the people of Tyre, adjusted reluctantly. When the Macedonians encountered henotheism, they did not realize that they needed to adjust in another way. For their part, the Samaritans refused to adjust to the invaders. A slaughter ensued. Alexander and his men had made their first religious mistake, but it was a small one, and they did not suffer from it. Only the Samaritans did. The community never recovered, and so Yahweh worship became largely and permanently Jewish.

———◆———

PERDICCAS DID NOT attack the people of Yehud. They peaceably paid their taxes, and the Macedonians took some land from Samaria and gave it to them. A few of them enlisted as mercenaries in the invading army.[76]

As for Alexander, he never visited Yehud. According to the Hebrew *Romance*, however, the conqueror not only visited this small country but invaded it:

> Alexander turned toward Jerusalem, for he had heard of the might of the Jews, and thought that if he did not conquer them, his glory would amount to little. He and his men arrived at Dan, in the north of Israel, and he sent messengers to Jerusalem, saying, "Send me your taxes and send me all the treasures of the house of Yahweh as tribute." When the people heard this, they were afraid, and clothed themselves with sackcloth, fasted, and prayed. The high priest wrote to Alexander and offered to send him a dinar of gold for every house in the city, but asked him to spare the treasures their ancestors had dedicated to God. When Alexander read the letter, he became angry, and swore by his idol that he would not leave the land of the Jews until he had made Jerusalem and the temple a heap of ruins.
>
> One night, as the king was lying in his bed and could not sleep, he rose and opened his window, and saw before him an angel dressed in linen holding a sword. He trembled and bowed down, and said, "Why will my Lord smite his servant?"
>
> The angel answered, "Am I not he who subdues kings for thy sake? Why, then, wilt thou do evil in the eyes of the Lord?"
>
> Alexander said, "I shall do whatever you tell me."
>
> The angel ordered him to go to Jerusalem and give up his treasure and dedicate it to God. "If thou dost rebel against my word, know that thou shalt surely die, thou and all thy companions."
>
> The king and his host journeyed to Jerusalem. When he arrived at the gate, the high priest and eighty-eight Levites clad in holy garments came forth to meet him. When Alexander saw the high priest, he alighted from his horse and prostrated himself on the ground, kissing

"Alexander the Great in the Temple at Jerusalem," by Sebastian Conca, 1737. Oil on canvas. Prado Museum, P00101, Art Resource.

the priest's feet. The soldiers of Alexander became angry and said to the king, "Why do you humble yourself before this old man? What will the world say?"

"Do not be surprised," answered the king. "This old man is like the angel who goes before me in battle, and tramples the nations that are my enemies, and so I honor him." To the high priest the king said, "Show me the temple of the god who subdues nations before me."

The king brought forth vessels of gold and silver and precious stones and went into the temple and placed them in the treasury. He told the high priest and the others who took the gold and silver to make a statue of him and place it in the temple as a remembrance.

The high priest replied, "We cannot do this thing and make a graven image in the temple. Listen to our advice. Take this gold that you want turned into a statue and give it to the priests so that the poor and the crippled of the city will be maintained. As for thy good name, all the males born this year will be named Alexander."

This thing pleased the king, who weighed forty talents of gold and put it in the hands of the high priest and the other priests, and said, "Pray for me always." After leaving the temple, Alexander and his host stayed in the city for three days, and he lavishly gave away his gold and silver, so that learned men said such riches had never been seen in Jerusalem since the days of Solomon. All the country people brought food and drink to Alexander's host.

The king then journeyed from Jerusalem, passed over to Galilee, and left the land of Israel.[77]

Stories like this one, which surely went back to a time not very long after Alexander's death, marked the beginning of a new phase of his career. Besides dealing with religions that he sought out himself, he would deal with religions that sought him out. Judaism, Christianity, and Islam would all do so in the hope of turning the king into one of their own. This hope was not original with these three religions. In turning Alexander into a half-brother of King Dara, the Persian poet Firdausi was trying to do the same thing. The religions of the book added a new dimension to this project: they would try to convert Alexander as well as nativize him.

5

The Throne of Egypt

AFTER THE FALL of Tyre, Alexander and the army marched straightaway to Gaza, arriving in late 332. They feared any delay would encourage the Persians in Egypt to resist the invaders, or would even encourage the Egyptians to overthrow the Persians and become independent. Only six years before, the Persians had struggled to reclaim Egypt from the last native pharaoh, Nakhtnebef, who had been betrayed by some of his Greek mercenaries. Barsine's father had fought as a mercenary in Egypt.[1]

As the army drew near to Gaza, it began to run out of water, and the Phoenician-ruled towns where the army was stopping did not have enough. No amount of gold could buy it. Hephaestion, the quartermaster, had to transport water by boat. All along the 300 miles from Lebanon to Gaza, his little saltwater navy carried fresh water for the army. Like the troops, the boats hopped from town to town. Otherwise they would run out of water, too.

When the army reached the hilltop fort of Gaza, the garrison of Persians and Arab mercenaries refused to surrender. The engineers threw up their siege towers, only to jump for their lives as the structures sank into the sand and toppled over. As Alexander offered a sheep to the gods in the hopes of reading its liver and finding a good omen, a crow passed overhead, dropped a clod of dirt on him, and alighted on one of the towers. It got stuck in an oily spot and could not flap its wings. Aristander said the clod of dirt spelled risks for Alexander, but the stuck bird showed the city would fall. The soothsayer was again administering a religious sedative laced with a warning.[2]

This time Alexander ignored Aristander. Rather than avoid taking risks, the king led the defense of an artillery emplacement. A bolt from a Persian catapult struck him in the breastplate and lodged in his shoulder. When Alexander's doctor and his assistants cut away the breastplate and pulled out the bolt, Alexander fainted from loss of blood and for a moment appeared to be dead. Before the bleeding stopped, he was back in command, taking more risks.[3]

The ceremony of supplication also turned against the king. An Arab pretending to be a deserter threw himself at the king's feet, and when the king bade him rise, hoping for some intelligence about the enemy's dispositions, the suppliant

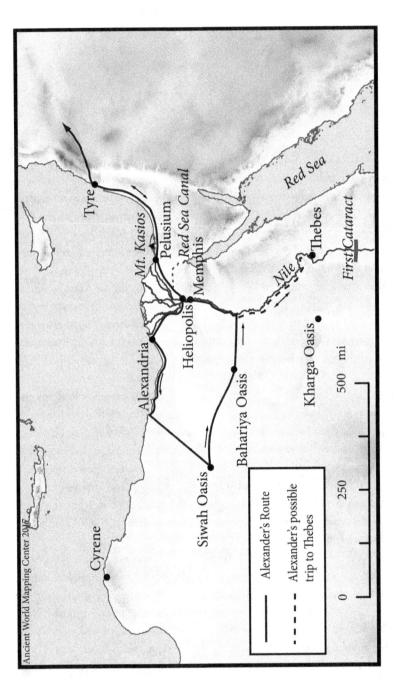

The Route of the Expedition Through Egypt, 332–331 BC.

Ancient World Mapping Center.

drew a sword and tried to stab him in the ribs. Alexander had been unkind to suppliants in Thebes but kind at Miletus and Tyre, even if his men had not. Now he found himself traduced. He ordered the engineers to throw up higher towers, and the Macedonians finally built platforms so tall that their catapults could bombard the city from above. In spite of having to work in the sand, sappers brought down a rampart. Using ladders put against the damaged walls, regiment after regiment entered the city. None of the males in the city asked for mercy, or got it. Alexander ordered the women and children sold into slavery. They surely supplicated, but that did not keep them from being enslaved.[4]

The garrison chief, Betis, died in combat, depriving Alexander of any chance to capture him and watch him fruitlessly beg for mercy. Alexander's anger inspired some companion or other—we do not know which one—to tell a false tale that the king not only captured Betis but killed him when he failed to submit, then dragged the corpse around the city, just as Achilles had dragged the corpse of Hector around Troy. (To do that, Alexander would have had to tie Betis to a wagon or a chariot, and Alexander never drove wagons or chariots. He was a Macedonian, and rode a horse.) Alexander merely killed the men and enslaved everyone else. The Gazans had wounded him, and also wounded his pride.[5]

The Macedonians commandeered the most valuable spots in the city, the wells, and began drawing the water they would need for the march across the Sinai Peninsula to Egypt. Gaza had little else to offer besides incense imported from Yemen. (Poor Greeks and Macedonians used pinches of it as a substitute for sacrificial animals.) Alexander now seized fourteen tons of the stuff and sent it to his tutor Leonidas, who had once told him to be parsimonious when making offerings. Now Leonidas would have more incense than even a profligate could use. Selling it would make the prim old tutor a fortune. With this sardonic grand gesture, Alexander bade farewell to Syria and to the Greek world, too, and made ready to enter Egypt.[6]

Loaded with water, Hephaestion set sail again, periodically stopping to set heaps of water jugs and bags of fodder on dunes close to shore. The army marched along the beach, on the damp strip of sand that would not be too wet or too dry for men and horses. Just inland ran a long, marshy lake that protected them from attacks by hostile Arabs. In any event, the Arabs were nowhere to be seen. They had expected the Macedonians on the roads.

The troops marched for a briny, searing week before reaching Mount Kasios, the Zeus of all sand dunes, on the edge of the Nile delta. In several more days they came to the Persian fort at Pelusium. Surprised by the arrival of the Macedonians, the Persians surrendered. While the army drank the local beer, the officers learned the news from Egypt. The local satrap had died defending Darius at Issus, and the Macedonian exile Amyntas had escaped and invaded Egypt with his 4,000 mercenaries. Hoping to become satrap of Egypt, Amyntas seized Memphis, but he made the mistake of plundering the country. The Egyptians turned against him and exterminated him and his troops.[7]

After several days in Pelusium, the army headed for the easternmost tributary of the Nile. The generals put as much of the army as possible aboard boats and headed to Memphis, some eighty miles upriver. They waited there for Alexander, who marched behind them, accompanied by a few mounted companions and other troops. Nobody challenged him, not even the son of the native pharaoh Nakhtnebef, who lived some thirty miles away.[8]

Alexander rode on to his destination, the City of the Sun, or, as the Egyptians sometimes called it, the Place of Pillars. Several large temples and a village stood atop a mound beside the river, like a college on a hill.

At the temple of Re priests came out to greet Alexander, and so did those of another great temple, that of Atum, the god of sundown. The temple of Re was the chief depository of Egyptian royal records. Herodotus visited it about a century before, and now Alexander came, hoping to be acknowledged as pharaoh. The priests welcomed him, but how did they address him? The companions, left outside, could not be sure. Perhaps the priests coached him in his first offerings to Re, a falcon-headed god with a sun disk hovering over him. The companions did know that the gold and silver vessels on display in the shrine surpassed anything Macedonian or Phoenician. The statuary was huge, even by the standard of Zeus at Olympia, the biggest statue any of them had ever seen.[9]

The Persians had taken the biggest piece of all, a statue of a Persian king, back to Susa. This ruler was the first Darius, who had invaded Greece. The inscription on this statue read: "The king commanded that this stone statue be made in Egypt. Let all who see it know that the Persian holds this land." Yet "the Persian" was no longer in Egypt. Like the statue, he had vanished.[10]

Before bidding Alexander goodbye, the priests took him to the shrine's tree of life, called the *ished*. The gods Seshat and Thoth would write the king's name on the leaves.[11]

LIKE AMYNTAS, ALEXANDER wished to seize Egypt. Unlike him, he wished to become pharaoh. The twenty-five-year-old king of the Macedonians had much to learn, and limited time to learn it.[12]

The pharaoh made offerings, but far more than any Greek king or priest, he received honors. He was the son of the chief god, Amon-Re, who bequeathed Egypt to him as his personal property. Unlike any Greek god, Amon-Re was a double or a composite. As Re, he was the sun god, at home in the City of the Sun. As Amon, he was the god of the heavens, the earth, the underworld, the air, and the water, at home in Thebes, far upriver. The priests at the City of the Sun called him

The one who made millions of himself,
The one who forms his name with his own hands, in any shape he likes.
He lights up the sky's circle with his diadem
While he travels the sky like the sun
And wanders nightly through the Underworld.
He makes the Nile overflow and rise in the fields,
The earth submits to his plans, the gods are under his hands,
Men under his feet.[13]

Amon-Re gave life without procreation. To bring some creature into being, the god spoke its name. Then the god vivified the creature by imparting a liquid ray of sunlight. So much for mothers—for Ada, Olympias, or even Hera.[14]

As son of Amon-Re, the pharaoh was obliged to imitate, or merge with, Horus, Amon-Re's chief offspring. When the pharaoh made offerings to Amon-Re, received oracles from him, or built shrines for him, he must do so as Horus.

Horus bestowed a life force, or *ka,* on each pharaoh. Only the pharaoh possessed a life force of this particular kind, and so the pharaoh's *ka,* unlike the life force bestowed on other people, had a personal name. So long as his *ka* was with him, the pharaoh could play all his roles—son of the god and successor and heir to the god. If the *ka* departed, the pharaoh lost his powers. Egypt's leading priests would know whether the *ka* had come or gone, much as Tibetan monks know how to locate the soul of the Dalai Lama once it has been reincarnated in his successor.[15]

Since the pharaoh had to perform rites in many places, he could not carry out all his duties, and priests acted as substitutes. In some rites, priests impersonated gods. When the pharaoh was crowned, a priest impersonating Horus brought the candidate before a priest impersonating Amon-Re, and the threesome repaired to the "king's house," which was Amon-Re's, where the disguised priests purified the candidate, and Amon-Re's "daughter," a priestess, imparted divine fluid to him. To the acclaim of the nine chief gods, the Amon-Re of the ceremony crowned the candidate and gave him his royal insignia. Later in the ceremony, the priestly impersonators proclaimed the new king. No Greek tragedy presented so many impersonated gods, or ever presented them in a temple rather than on a stage. Missing was the audience for the performance. Only priests and royalty attended.

In other rites, the priests used a statue to impersonate a god. This kind of impersonation happened in Greece and many other places, but in Egypt the priests did not merely carry the statue or escort others who were carrying it. They tilted the statue to show favor or disfavor to worshippers.

The priests also staged festivals and mythic reenactments meant to reinvigorate the pharaoh's authority. Every year the pharaoh celebrated the victory of Amon over the dragon Aphet, as well as that of Horus over the monster Typhon. The pharaoh played the part of Horus, and the priests played other parts. Or, if the pharaoh was absent, the priests played all the parts.

The pharaoh, the priests, and the pharaoh's architects and builders collaborated in the pharaoh's building programs. Next to conducting rituals in shrines, building and repairing them was the pharaoh's chief religious duty. Sometimes he performed this task in person, and sometimes he delegated it. It took him up and down the country and into the desert, where shrines stood at the important oases.

For Alexander, all this was novel. A king of Macedon was a descendant of Zeus but not the god's son. He did not treat his kingdom as personal property and could not be impersonated. Antipater was a viceroy, not a double, and Alexander's brother, Arrhidaeus, was an occasional substitute, not a double. A Macedonian king had to fight in person and lead councils, and no double could do it for him. Instead of a double, the Macedonian king had companions. He shared some powers with them. Alexander let Leonnatus receive suppliants under false pretenses, and he let Parmenio command the main body. He left Antigonus and others to their own devices. The only important priest was the king himself. No one, not even a king, impersonated a god. At his most theatrical, Philip merely led a parade of divine statues that included one of himself. His statue was built for the occasion. The divine statues came from shrines.[16]

Alexander wished not only to become the pharaoh but also to become a more popular ruler than his Persian predecessors. After Cambyses, Cyrus's son, only two of the Persians had spent time in Egypt. (One was the Darius who was Alexander's opponent. He had fought there.) The priests had impersonated these Persians from start to finish, and the many decades in which the Persian pharaohs had been absent encouraged the priests and the population to regard them as illegitimate. Only Darius I made a strong, positive impression, revising Egypt's laws and repairing a Red Sea–Nile canal. Alexander would try to outperform Darius. He also wished to outperform Cambyses.[17]

These two goals did not match those of the priests he would encounter at Memphis and Thebes. They would tell him what he wished to hear about Darius and Cambyses, but they intended to direct him, not help him. They did not expect him to settle in Egypt. They did not require that, and did not want it. Let Alexander's ambitions take him elsewhere. They would remain in control.

Alexander's goals would eventually displease the companions. They regarded Egypt as a piece of pelf for Alexander to divide among them. They regarded the *ka,* the divine fluid, and the mummery as nonsense, and they did not wish for the Macedonians to be popular as well as powerful. They did not want the duties of being priest-king to delude Alexander. That had already happened at Tyre.

They may have noticed that not a single Egyptian had supplicated Alexander. This defeated people acknowledged him, but they did not beg. Rather than exalt him that way, something the Macedonians welcomed, they exalted him in another, which the Macedonians did not.

———◦———

FROM NOW ON, Alexander would travel mostly by boat, the preferred mode for pharaohs and divine statues as well as generals. On the Nile, boats could make twenty miles a day, triple that with wind in their sails. On the best roads anywhere—the royal roads of the Persians—a soldier could make fifteen to twenty miles a day at most, about the same as a mule. A man riding a horse all day would not do much better. For the first time, Alexander and his entourage would be able to outpace the army.[18]

Sailing for Memphis, he and they passed the pyramids and the island fort known as Babylon, which the Athenians had once besieged. At Memphis, Alexander's generals and the remaining Persians received him at the royal pier, beside the official Nilometer for measuring the level of the river. The priests now took him in hand, and his companions surrendered themselves to the local Greeks, who would tell them which god was which as they passed countless Egyptian temples and headed for the main Greek shrine in the city, amidst the coops of pigeons bred for manure and geese bred for sacrifice.[19]

Memphis resembled a gigantic royal barge that had run aground. Flood walls protected the Nile side, dominated by the walnut trees of the royal garden, the palace, and the biggest building, the temple of Ptah. On the inland side, a mile or so away, a canal that often overflowed passed through the middle of a plain protected by dikes. Most foreigners lived outside the dikes—Persians, Syrians who worshipped Baal, and Greeks and Carians worshipping Zeus. Many native Egyptians lived beside a necropolis farther to the west. For the first time, the Macedonians saw tombs for animals. Egyptian shrines baffled them. They were not allowed to see most divine statues there, and so they found it hard to know which god was which. Amon-Re was Zeus, but Re was also the sun. Ptah, the god of Memphis, was Hephaestus, the Greek smith god—or was he? Ptah was a potter, not a smith. He had created the world at a potter's wheel, modeling it on an egg.[20]

As in the City of the Sun, priests brought Alexander to holy ground and acknowledged him. Then they took him inside and presented him to Ptah, who was subordinate to Amon-Re but led his own set of gods. Perhaps the coronation occurred here. After being acknowledged in one place, a new pharaoh could be crowned in another. Later, he would be virtually recrowned through the ceremonies that reinvigorated him.

The coronation centered on Alexander's receiving some version of each of the five names bestowed on every pharaoh. These names, and not the word "pharaoh" (which meant "great house"), designated the ruler of Egypt. The names mostly involved the gods Horus and Amon-Re. The Horus name, which showed that the pharaoh was the son of Amon-Re, described him as an embodiment of youth and strength, often a bull. The Two Ladies name referred to the goddesses who represented the Nile delta, depicted as a cobra in a basket, and the Nile Valley, depicted as a vulture. This name showed that the pharaoh owned Egypt, and sometimes described him as conquering new lands. The golden Horus name showed that the pharaoh was pure and incorruptible, with mature qualities to balance those of youth. The solar name indicated that the pharaoh succeeded Amon-Re as ruler of Egypt. The personal name came very much last. The priests left this name up to the pharaoh.[21]

One script for a pharaonic coronation survives. It describes the enthronement of a much earlier pharaoh, Haremhab, who like Alexander was not of royal stock. To make him ready to receive his names, a priest impersonating Amon purified him with water, and a priestess imparted the divine fluid. Then Amon crowned him and announced his names, and the gods who had assembled for the ceremony (and who were impersonated by more priests) exclaimed to Amon, "Thou hast brought us our savior." The ceremony concluded as Amon embraced the pharaoh and presented him to priests impersonating another set of characters, the Nine Bows, a traditional group of foreign powers, only one of which was Greek. The Nine Bows humbled themselves, the pharaonic *ka* arrived, and Haremhab became the last pharaoh of the Eighteenth Dynasty. He had overthrown Tutankhamen. In much the same way, Alexander, who overthrew the Persians, became the 467th king of Egypt.[22]

Then Alexander emerged from the temple and the priests coached him through a public, not secret, offering to a bull incarnating Ptah. The bull made his appearance at a window in the temple court, displaying his characteristic white markings on a black coat. After the bull watched the king pray and make the offering, he returned to his stall and private water supply. The priests told Alexander that he had performed well in his first public act as pharaoh; the bad pharaoh Cambyses had supposedly killed Ptah's sacred bull.[23]

Soon after, Alexander made reassuring offerings in the Greek and Macedonian manner. He killed some oxen, and as his holy men and butchers gutted and flayed them, he put the best pieces, thighs wrapped in fat, on a temporary altar. The flame jolted upward for a few minutes, like fireworks, and libations of wine kept the fire burning for another ten minutes, until only the charred bones remained. The king raised his hands, palms outward, and prayed to Zeus as everyone kept still, lest any sound or movement spoil this moment of communion with the patron of the companions.

Bas-relief of Alexander and Amon-Re, temple sacred to Amon, Mut, and Chonsu, Luxor, 330–323 BC.

Photograph: Heritage Image Partnership, Art Resource.

Then the little drama gave way to a traditionally raucous barbeque. Alexander staged games that attracted the best talent in the army's entourage and in Egypt. A panel of generals judged a competition among tragic poets.[24]

In spite of these touches of home, the companions found Alexander's position ambiguous. First he stood beside Ptah, in secret, and then he stood before them, in the open. First he was a demigod, and then a master of ceremonies. He worshipped a bull, and then he killed oxen. Was he a butcher and a hunter or a stable boy?

Alexander left the troops at Memphis and sailed upriver with his senior companions. None of the surviving accounts says how far they went, but a likely destination was the shrine of Amon at Thebes. The royal party had seen other shrines of this god in Memphis, and they knew about Amon because Macedonians and Greeks worshipped him under the double name Zeus-Amon. Alexander had heard about him from his mother, whose family controlled the oracle of Zeus-Amon at Dodona. Above all, Amon had just made Alexander pharaoh, and Thebes was Amon's home. The Greeks called this city "the City of Zeus," as though it were Zeus's home. Alexander would not want to miss this, the shrine of shrines.[25]

The voyage to Thebes must have disconcerted the companions. They had left the Mediterranean, with its rocks, woods, and clear streams, for a landscape of sand, palms, and the brown waters of the Nile. At the City of the Sun the companions had stayed in the visitors' compound used by Plato, and they knew Greeks had lived in Memphis for centuries, but now the Macedonians docked at temple after temple with little sign of Greeks or foreigners. Instead of the pyramids they had seen earlier, they spotted enormous tombs cut into the cliffs on the western side of the river.

Alexander traveled in a different spirit from the rest. A calendar of rituals obliged him to be here, there, and everywhere. He could land at a shrine like the one at Luxor, near Thebes, and envision priests impersonating him there at a festival months earlier or later. He could also foresee that he would be present in shrines through pictures. He was already making plans to build and refurbish shrines, and so he could imagine new temple friezes that would show the pharaoh Alexander making offerings to the gods—those family-style offerings that only a pharaoh could make, since only the pharaoh could approach gods as though they were relatives.

A frieze built at Luxor during Alexander's reign describes these rites in a series of forty-two panels. Each panel contains the name of the king, some of his titles, some instructions, and a statement by Amon-Re. The first panel says,

The perfect god, the lord of both lands, Alexander

and turns to the rite:

Lead the king into the temple.

This instruction is for Amon, who turns to Alexander and says,

> I have put the nine peoples with bows in your power. I have given you all life, happiness, and health.

Alexander carries out his instructions:

> Mount the steps. Approach the throne.... For the sake of your father, kiss the ground. Do homage with the holy pitcher. Burn incense for your father. Gaze on him. Bring lotus blossoms.... Give milk. Bring the god to his meal. Purify the shrine with natron balls.... Put makeup on Amon's eyes. Apply ointment.

More instructions appear on other panels.[26]

A Macedonian worshipper would not know about natron, a compound of salt and soda ash, or about makeup for men. He might give milk to Zeus, but he would not see the god drink it. A god was a horrific being, manifest in lightning, like Zeus, or in a pillar of fire, like Yahweh. Amon should be that way, too, for the sun in Egypt could be destructive. Yet Alexander, a man like any other, bashed in the head at the Granicus, stabbed in the thigh at Issus, and stuck in the ribs at Gaza, would touch the sun and dress it. He had the blessing of a pharaonic *ka*. The Luxor shrine where he dressed Amon was dedicated not just to the god but to this special *ka*. When Alexander was shown worshipping there, he was in some sense worshipping himself.[27]

So far, the companions were only beginning to grasp this relationship. They could not enter temples, just the courtyards outside, and so they did not see Alexander officiate, or see pictures of other pharaohs whom Alexander would imitate. They could not fully understand the claims the priestly impersonators made on Alexander's time, his self-image, and his purse.[28]

"THE CITY OF Zeus," or, as the Greeks sometimes said, "the greatest city of Zeus," proved to be a mere string of neighborhoods on the western bank of the Nile. A few residences clustered around temples, but Thebes lacked a marketplace or a stronghold like an acropolis. The deserts beyond the Nile Valley walls provided the only defense, and the river the only highway.

The king disembarked at the riverside neighborhood of Karnak. The street leading from the dock led immediately to the largest shrine the Macedonians had ever seen or heard of. As priests led him through the gate, Alexander discovered the first of the temple's secrets. A 1,000-year-old composite, the shrine was deteriorating at different rates in different spots.[29]

Alexander and the priests walked past the outside walls, twelve yards thick and about fifty yards high, built by Nakhtnebef, and then past the inside walls built a thousand or so years earlier by the conqueror Djehutymes, the Thutmosis of the Greeks. A colossal stone entryway ushered them into a forecourt as long as a football field. Next, a colonnaded court built before the supposed date of the Trojan War. Only now did they reach the temple. The grandfather of Thutmosis erected it around 1520 BC, generations before the supposed lifetime of Heracles. Thutmosis built the inner sanctum, the Akhmenou. Pharaohs communed here with Amon during one of the festivals that restored their powers.

Alexander had now walked about 600 yards, a longer distance than most running events at the ancient Olympics. Temple walls blocked any view of the outside and any sound other than that of the royal party. Hundreds of wall paintings of pharaohs and gods bombarded him, as did far more epigraphical text than in any Greek shrine or precinct. Many of these pictures and inscriptions identified pharaohs performing the same duties as Alexander's. "He, too, is Alexander," said these images—but "he" was Egyptian.

Some of the priests could not go farther. Only a select few guided Alexander into a ceremonial hall forty yards long. On one side stood nine chambers for ritual foods, unguents, perfumes, and vestments, and three chapels occupied the other side. At the far end stood a chapel for the obscure god Sokar, a room housing the boat used by Amon to sail the Nile, and another for Amon's image. Alexander had reached Thutmosis's Akhmenou.

He cannot have had time to examine it. Perhaps the priests led him to one unremarkable, typical spot in an antechamber past the storage rooms and the god's boat. In a frieze on the lower part of a wall, the first scene showed the pharaoh purifying Amon-Re with water from a vase. In another scene, the pharaoh gave the god four pieces of incense, and in a third scene he opened the mouth of the ithyphallic form of the god with an adze. On the upper part of the wall, the pharaoh, accompanied by the personified Nile River, announced offerings listed on a tablet.[30]

After more than a month in Egypt, Alexander would find this frieze familiar. The priests, though, could point out an odd feature. The pictures were out of kilter. The water in the vase flowed erratically from one piece of the frieze to the next, and the Nile River split in two. Would the new king repair these damaged pieces? If Alexander agreed to make the repair, his cartouche would go into a prominent spot over a nearby door.

Alexander agreed, and the priests made the repair sometime during his reign. Perhaps he agreed without having entered the shrine. Then a priest made the decision on the king's behalf. Or perhaps the king did enter but made no decision, and the priest did later. No matter which of these things happened, the effect was the same. One course of events merged with another, the nominal with the actual, the way tributaries merged with the Nile.

Alexander or his ministers went up and down the country, building mostly for Amon and especially near Thebes. Outside the temple of Amon-Re, Alexander consecrated a chapel to the Egyptian Heracles, Chonsu. He also restored the pictures and inscriptions on a gate in a Chonsu temple erected around 1050 BC. New pictures depicted him in a leopard skin, the garb of Chonsu's priests.[31]

In recompense, the priests of Amon gave Alexander a set of titles that may have differed slightly from those bestowed elsewhere. These titles were:

Ruler of Rulers of the Entire Land
The Lion, Great in Might, Who Takes Hold of Mountains, Lands,
  and Deserts
The Bull, Who Protects Egypt, the Ruler of the Great Green
And of What the Sun Encircles
The King of Upper and Lower Egypt, Beloved by Amon and Chosen by Re,
Alksandros.[32]

The priests had called the Persian Darius "Ruler of Rulers." They had called Thutmosis a bull, and many rulers lions. They had never called any pharaoh world ruler and lord of the sea and sky. Only gods like Horus had ever received these titles. Since the titles would be part of the pharaoh's cartouche, the evidence of deification would appear throughout Egypt. It would, of course, be written in hieroglyphics that only priests could read.[33]

The priests knew their man: regal, ambitious, and increasingly megalomaniacal. They did not want anyone else to know him. The companions no longer knew their man. He had become not just a new kind of priest but a new kind of king.

———

TO SPREAD WORD of his apotheosis, Alexander needed an oracle from the highest authority. Zeus gave oracles only at Dodona, near Macedon, at the rural shrine familiar to his mother. For Alexander to return there and make an inquiry would be inconvenient, and for Olympias to ask on his behalf might not lead to the desired result. By contrast, Amon gave oracles throughout Egypt. Sometime during his trip to Thebes, or afterward, when Alexander sailed downriver, he learned about these oracles.

As pharaoh, Alexander could speak to Amon directly. Many shrines provided a station reserved for exchanges between the god and the pharaoh. In this intimate setting, the king would not even need to ask a question. Instead, the god would anticipate his request and render judgment in an epiphany.[34]

Or the king might do as other Egyptians did, and wait outside a temple for the moment when Amon's statue, or some other image of the god, left one shrine on the way to visit another. Then the worshippers could ask a question and the statue would answer by moving side to side. This sort of oracle resembled the oracle at Dodona, where Zeus caused leaves to rustle and the priestesses listened for a message. Elsewhere in Greece, divine statues did not budge or tilt, but they did express themselves by dropping tears or bursting into flame.[35]

Both methods appealed to Alexander. He would speak privately to Amon, and the god would acknowledge him as a son. Priests would announce this conversation. His companions would wait outside the shrine and approach a tilting statue or other divine image. They would ask whether they should worship Alexander, and the priests would say yes. Alexander would obtain a twofold oracle, partly Egyptian, partly quasi-Greek. He would disseminate the quasi-Greek oracle and eventually adapt it for subjects who were not Greek-speakers.[36]

Alexander and his advisers knew which Amon shrine would serve this purpose. In the Libyan Desert, in the oasis at Siwah, a ten-day march from central Egypt or the Mediterranean coast, an oracle of Amon served Egyptian and Greek clientele. The Egyptians came from the Nile valley and traveled west to Siwah via other oases. The Greeks came from coastal cities in Cyrene, on the Libyan coast, and traveled south into the desert. They knew about Amon thanks to a temple of Zeus-Amon in Cyrene that ranked as the largest Greek building in Africa. Jason and the Argonauts had made the trip from Cyrene to Siwah. Alexander believed that Cambyses had tried to attack the Siwah shrine. As always with Cambyses, Alexander would do the opposite, and go there as a pilgrim.[37]

Small though Siwah was, it did have a shrine where Alexander could speak to Amon in private, and it also had a satellite shrine a quarter mile away. Since Amon liked to travel, he regularly went from the main shrine to the satellite and back again, and since he preferred to travel by boat, the priests put him in the form of a solar disk on a small sailing vessel that they carried on their shoulders. Alexander's followers could wait for the boat and disk to make this journey and then ask the priests their question. The bobbing of the boat on the priests' shoulders would give them their answer.[38]

In return for the help he received at Siwah, Alexander would build a shrine to Amon at another oasis, Bahariya. Siwah would have been a better spot, but Thutmosis and others had already built everything that Siwah required. At neglected Bahariya, Alexander could make more of an impression. He could outbuild Darius I, who had decorated the fifty-by-twenty-yard temple of Amon at a third oasis, Kharga. Alexander would also top Darius II, who had put an inscription on the wall of the Kharga temple in the late 400s. Alexander's Darius, who was the third, had done nothing comparable.[39]

Alexander struck a bargain. With the help of the Egyptians, Alexander would speak to god, and an oracle would recommend that he be worshipped. With Alexander's help, the pious would get a new shrine. He did not make this bargain cynically. For him, Amon was a very real being.[40]

FOR THE TRIP to Siwah, Alexander selected a force of top companions and some infantry and cavalry—no extras. His group headed west from the edge of the Nile delta via the coastal road. The next big city, Cyrene, lay hundreds of miles away. In spite of the distance, the Greeks there feared an impending attack, and sent emissaries to Alexander. After receiving Cyrene's submission, the expedition replenished its supply of fresh water, and in early 331 it headed southwest into the Sahara.

For comfort and safety, the new pharaoh and his companions dressed like the Berbers who were guiding them. At some oases, the Macedonians saw camels grazing and learned that nomads brought them over from the delta in the winter. If it was hot enough, the travelers got bread by starting fires with twigs and camel dung that made the sand hot enough to bake on. It might still be cold enough at night to sleep beside the camels, much as they stank. The officers and cavalry rode, and the infantry walked.

The first stages of the journey kept them to the north of the rocks and wastelands of the Qattara basin. The oases were few, but they were adequate for a caravan of hundreds. The last big stage, four days mostly beyond the basin, was arduous. An unexpected, refreshing rain fell, but the water at the next oasis, Gara, was brackish. The nine springs up and down the valley were all bitter. In one more day, they reached the outskirts of Siwah, where salt marshes framed the road. They stepped down into a gorge where hostile Berbers could have slaughtered them. Then the twenty-mile-long strip of the oasis opened before them. Two miles before they reached the shrine a pair of hills rose like stone pillars, the last remains of a plateau that the desert winds had blown away. Mile after mile of date-bearing palms stretched into the distance.[41]

Alexander came at the time of the date harvest, or just after, and many caravans of camels were heading back from the oasis with baskets of fruit. They left not by Alexander's route but by another, going east toward Bahariya. Pilgrims on this easterly route had the pick of the fruit—the best about four inches long and sugar-sweet, the worst bright yellow and fit only for camels.

The temple of Amon stood half a mile south of the settlement. Compared to the temple at Karnak, it was minuscule, a mere chapel attached to a sandstone redoubt built for local princes. Before this small compound stretched a grove of palms. The satellite shrine built by Nakhtnebef stood on the far side of the trees. Alexander passed into the temple alone. An image of Amon appeared on one side of the entryway and an image of a local dynast on the other. The god was ram-headed, a feature never seen in the Nile valley. A legend read, "Amon-Re, the lord of oracles, proclaims life, health and happiness for the chief of the two deserts, Soutekhirdisou, son of the chief of the two deserts, Leloutek."[42] Alexander was not a descendant of Leloutek, yet here he was, hoping for his own proclamation from Amon, as though he were one more sheik.

Alexander now communed with Amon. As the king stood in a small room, a priest impersonating the god spoke to him from behind a wall pierced by a series of small holes. The companions had no way of knowing what was said. The king returned outside, accompanied by more priests, who served as translators, and addressed his men.[43]

He was, Alexander said, the son of Amon. Amon had said so.

He also told the companions that he asked the oracle a question about Philip, whom they knew to be his true father. Were those responsible for Philip's murder all dead? Amon had said yes, and the companions accepted this answer, even though Alexander had told them Darius was one of those responsible.

Alexander did not tell the companions everything that passed between him and the god. That, he knew, would be impious. In a way, Amon had initiated him, and as an initiate, Alexander must keep secret what transpired.

At the customary time, the sacred boat carrying the sun disk proceeded from the main temple. Pilgrims approached and conveyed their questions to the priests. At least one companion from Alexander's entourage joined them and asked a question that Alexander or his advisors had planted: Should the army give Alexander the offerings due to a god?

With one exception, no Macedonian king had ever received sacrifices as though he were a god. That was Philip, and the occasion was an attempt to mollify him by a city about to be attacked. The companion asking the question knew this history, but the Egyptian priests answering the question did not. They knew that Alexander, like any pharaoh, should be regarded as an incarnation of Horus. For that reason, they answered yes.[44]

The expedition could not stay long in Siwah without depleting the resources of the oasis, and so the royal party departed for the Nile Valley. Rather than go back the way they came, they headed east on the pilgrims' way to Bahariya. En route, they got their share of the dates. Unlike the wastelands to the north, the terrain was picturesque: first a black desert formed by small black volcanic stones atop the sand, then, around the oasis, a white desert of chalk and limestone outcroppings sculpted by the wind. They clambered up and down deep gulches until they reached a plain sloping down to the oasis.

Here, in a tiny settlement, the pharaoh did his customary work of turning the first spade for the building of a new shrine. So small a place did not take long to build. It comprised a temple with a forecourt of pale yellow sandstone and attached mud-brick buildings, and a surrounding wall with a single stone door. A temple wall showed Pharaoh Alexander making an offering, contained in round vases, to Horus and Isis. On another wall the recipient of the royal offering was Amon-Re. At the rear of the temple a painting showed Alexander offering the grounds for the temple to Amon-Re and Mout, the mother goddess of Thebes.[45]

Alexander and a local notable, Horhetep, commissioned inscriptions on a piece of sandstone at the entrance to the shrine. On one side Horhetep would make a dedication in hieroglyphics as "first prophet of Amon-Re." Alexander would use two sides. A hieroglyphic inscription on one side would list Alexander's five pharaonic titles and call him "beloved of Amon, the lord who gives oracles." The adjacent five-word Greek text would say only "King Alexander for Amon his father." Alexander could have used a good Greek stonemason, but he had not brought one. Instead he had to use a local Egyptian, who misspelled his name and botched the word "his." Readers would not be able to tell whether Amon was Alexander's father or not. The errors showed that Alexander left before the letters were cut, for he surely would have corrected the flaws.[46]

The royal party marched east two and a half days to the Nile Valley, and then Alexander boarded a royal barge and sailed downriver to inspect troops. Sometime during the trip, an accident occurred. The royal barge was so crowded that one companion, a young son of Parmenio named Hector, could not find a spot. He boarded another overcrowded boat, it sank, and he died of exhaustion after swimming to shore. Alexander gave him a funeral surpassing anything done for the dead at Issus, Tyre, or Gaza. A son of Parmenio was a virtual prince.[47]

Soon Alexander was again in Memphis, where he sacrificed to "Zeus the King," in other words, the Zeus of the Macedonians. At this time, if not before, his importunate mother sent him a slave skilled in Macedonian sacrifice. He also told the army about the oracle at Siwah, and about the new idea that he should be worshipped as a god.[48]

Alexander's indirect role in the young man's death more or less influenced the army's response to the oracle. Hector's brother Philotas ridiculed the idea that Alexander was the son of Amon. Parmenio told his son to be discreet, but Philotas told any who cared to hear that Philip was Alexander's father, and that Olympias knew it. Perhaps the Arabs would worship Alexander. They had only two gods and might want a third.[49]

Alexander could not have readily explained to Philotas, or any of his men, that he now had a heavenly father as well as an earthly one. Macedonians and Greeks put human beings on one plane and gods on another. Heracles, an exception, proved the rule. They allowed for a kind of intermediary, a hero, but a Greek or Macedonian hero (or heroine) was a peculiar being, honored much like a god, but only after his or her death. Alexander was no hero to his men. He was alive, and they wanted to keep him that way. After his death, the companions expected Callisthenes to have him. The official historian had promised to immortalize Alexander, an orthodox literary aim different from divinizing him.

For the time being, Philotas went unrebuked. He did not go unwatched. Antigone, his concubine, had found someone to confide in—Craterus, a senior regimental commander. When Antigone began telling Craterus about Philotas's religious opinions, and Craterus began passing the news to Alexander, the king did not discourage him. Alexander respected Craterus, an imposing man with social standing to match, for he was the oldest son of a leading companion from the mountain district of Orestis. At Sidon he stalked lions with Alexander in the Persian paradise, and he took accidental spear wounds without complaining. Alexander liked him for that. The king also realized that Craterus and Philotas were jealous of each other. Each wanted fame and would be glad to have it at the expense of his rival. Philotas went further, wanting fame for himself and his father at the expense of Alexander. In Philotas's opinion, the king got more fame than he deserved. Alexander's claim to be son of Amon would not only divide him from men such as Philotas, who rejected it, but also divide his men from each other.[50]

Whatever the companions thought, Alexander continued to serve the Macedonians as a priest. No talk of divinity would spoil the winning formula of what was still Philip's army.[51]

ALEXANDER, WHO LIKED war better than administration, struggled to find some way to govern his new province. He recognized that Egypt had reoriented him, and he feared it might have the same effect on the administrators he would leave behind once he departed in pursuit of Darius.

He did not want to appoint a satrap, as the Persians had. A satrap of Egypt would be an acting king with more money and subjects than any other subordinate. A satrap would also have to deal with Egypt's priests, who would try to avoid being taxed through flattery, bribes, and intrigue. To resist this onslaught, he would need to appear emphatically regal. A Macedonian might not understand the dangers of this position, or, if he did, might fancy himself independent. He would watch the priests impersonating Alexander and resent this charade performed for an absentee ruler. The first Persian appointed satrap of Egypt had proved disloyal.[52]

Alexander found nothing to emulate in the rest of the Persian administrative hierarchy, either. The Persians appointed two lieutenant governors for Thebes and the south but ruled the delta directly, without lieutenants. The Persians made this lopsided arrangement because they distrusted the priests of Amon-Re at Thebes, and hoped to intimidate them, and because brigands and rebels might ambush lieutenants sent into the delta. Brigands infested this region, and a great rebellion had begun there seventy years before.[53]

To replace the Persian machinery, Alexander divided Egypt into two parts of equal size, one centered on Thebes, and one including both Memphis and the delta. He gave Upper Egypt to a Persian with long experience in Egypt, and the delta to an Egyptian. Whereas the Persians put Egypt, Libya, and Sinai under one satrap, he separated them and gave Libya and Sinai to Greek administrators. No other place in the empire was as complicated, costly, or lucrative as Egypt.[54]

This new arrangement suited the Egyptians, and at the same time it confined them to the Nile valley. It did not assure Alexander of the revenue he hoped to extract, and so he appointed a Greek companion, Cleomenes, chief of finance for the entire region. Except for Alexander's own treasurers, Cleomenes would be the highest-ranking financial official in the empire.[55]

Since the Egyptians had no effective army of their own—and since Alexander wished to rule Egypt firmly—he stationed more troops there than the Persians had. Along with garrisons at Pelusium and Memphis, he established two small armies, one for Upper Egypt and one for Memphis and the delta. He chose Peucestas, the best linguist among the companions, for Upper Egypt. Balacrus, who had commanded allied infantry at Issus, got Lower Egypt, where he would suppress brigands or rebels.[56]

In all, Alexander put eight men in charge of Egypt and environs—an Egyptian, a Persian, two Greeks, and four Macedonians. Three were governors, four generals, and one, Cleomenes, was a financier and also governor of Sinai. Even that was not the whole story, for Alexander reserved to himself one important duty, that of appointing new priests. Priests must be Egyptians, of course, and probably would come from leading priestly families, and he alone knew this elite. One such family was that of the last native pharaoh, Nakhtnebef, whose son held a high place in Egyptian society during Alexander's reign and just afterward.

Besides reorganizing Egypt, Alexander established a new capital. During the last two periods of native rule the capital had been in the delta, and before that the capital had been Thebes. Alexander's dynasty would be Greco-Macedonian, and so he decided to build a capital in the place on the coast closest to Greece. Here he could establish a cult for himself as founder of the city. Priests there would depend on royal patronage, and most revenues would flow to him. As with his colony near Troy, he named the city Alexandria. Alexander conducted the inaugural ceremony in April, shortly before he left Egypt.[57]

The Egyptians for a long time called the city Raqote, which means "under construction." The chief builder, the financier Cleomenes, set to work even before Alexander and the army left. Since the city did not have any fresh water,

Cleomenes and the engineer Diades devised an expensive solution for this water shortage. Conduits would flow from the Nile to each house and building. At the end of the conduit, the water would settle and become clear enough to drink. Greeks benefited from these water mains, but poor Egyptians, obliged to live beside the river, would not. Like their countrymen elsewhere in Egypt, they continued to hoist their water from the Nile.[58]

Next came public buildings, none completed before Alexander's death. Even so, Alexandria became an emporium within a few years, and surpassed Memphis as the largest city in Egypt.

Alexandria developed a mix of religious practices. The cult of Alexander flourished, as did other cults willing to pray for the ruler of Egypt. In exchange for priestly support, the Macedonians protected Egyptian clergy. Peucestas, for example, posted a No Trespassing sign at the entrance to a priest's chamber.[59]

As Alexandria grew, the use of currency also grew. Earlier, coins had been scanty. Athenian "owls" had circulated in Greek emporia and the authorities had struck some imitations of Athenian coins with hieroglyphic legends. Most Egyptians relied on barter, or used silver and copper as monies of account. Only the pharaoh, the priests, and a few others paid in silver or gold bullion. Money was not an important form of wealth. Now Cleomenes started Egypt's first big mint, and Alexander continued to open mints as the empire expanded. Only a dozen years after Alexander left, an Egyptian hoarding money in the upriver town of Demanhur accumulated more than 8,000 coins minted by Alexander in Phoenicia, Babylon, Macedon, and Egypt, along with others minted by satraps and cities. This trove, discovered by British archaeologists in 1908, remains the largest numismatic find ever made in the Middle East. Alexander taught the Egyptians to think financially.[60]

Egypt taught Alexander to think theologically. Once only a priest, he now conceived of himself as a priest and a god, a recipient as well as a performer of rituals. The old idea that Greek gods were foreign gods coexisted with the new idea that Alexander was one of the cross-cultural gods. He had become a religious innovator, and after he left Egypt for other places he might innovate again.

This new disposition deepened the split between him and his companions. To them, Alexander remained a young leader like Jason of the Argonauts. If Jason could enlist the aid of the sorceress Medea, Alexander could enlist support from the Egyptian priests, but he should not do their bidding, and he should not expect his soldiers to do it. In that spirit, the army left Egypt behind, about six months after arriving, and went in pursuit of Darius. For them, this crucial event in Alexander's life had been an overlong vacation.

THE COMPANIONS REPORTED that the king founded Alexandria after receiving an omen any Greek would understand: when he marked the perimeter of the new city by throwing barley grains, birds came and devoured them. The birds showed that many foreigners would come and settle there. Near Eastern stories about Alexandria mention omens, too, but add that the ram-headed god Amon blessed the city.[61]

In an Armenian tale, Alexander asked Amon how to become immortal, and Amon spoke to him about Alexandria instead. Amon and Alexander conversed in a dream. The early Christian writer of this tale mistook Parmenio for an architect.

"I, the ram, say to you that if you wish to remain ageless, build a noteworthy city on the island of Proteus, the Old Man of the Sea, on the coast of Egypt, and name it for yourself."

Looking at the god, Alexander said, "Give me a sign that you are the god of this land."

The god answered, "Alexander, have you forgotten what happened while you stood at prayer, making offerings at a Greek altar? A great eagle swooped down, seized the entrails of your sacrifice, and flew off into the air. It circled around and dropped them on an Egyptian altar. Was it not plain to you that I am the guardian and protecting god of all?"

Alexander entreated the god and asked: "Will this city remain true to the name Alexandria, for which it will be built? Or will my name be changed to that of another king?" The god took him by the hand and led him to a high mountain and said: "Alexander, can you move this mountain to another place?" Alexander thought and answered, "How could I, Lord?" The god said to him: "So too, your name can never be changed. Instead, Alexandria shall flourish and overflow with bounty."

To this, Alexander replied, "Lord, disclose this to me, too: how am I destined to die?"

The god said: "It is better and more honorable for a man not to know when his life will end. Life seems boundless and infinitely varied only when men are ignorant of its evils. But if you wish to learn your fate, I shall tell you forthwith: with my help, you, a callow young man, shall subdue all foreign nations; and then, by dying and yet not dying, you shall come to me.

"The city of Alexandria that you build will be coveted by all the world, and be a home in which gods shall dwell for a long time to come. It will abound in beauty, size, and crowds of men. All who settle there shall stay on and forget their place of birth.

"Kings shall forever revere you as one who has become a god according to the customs of this land. Many kings shall come to Alexandria, not to make war, but to revere you as one who has been apotheosized. Once you have died, you shall receive gifts from kings forever. For you shall dwell here both when you are dead and when you are still alive. This city you are building is to be your grave."

When Alexander awoke and recalled the oracle which had been delivered to him, he recognized the Lord of all. He built a great altar and ordered that fit offerings be brought for the gods, and he had the architect Parmenio build the city's holy places.[62]

The prophecy given by the "Lord of all" would prove true. Alexandria would venerate its founder for centuries, but not in a way Alexander would have understood, or even the Christian author of this passage would have. Alexander's religious future lay with neither Christians nor pagans nor Jews.

In the spring of 331, when he left Egypt, this future was very distant. Meanwhile, the Macedonians, who knew him as a priest-king of one sort, did not accept him as a king of any other sort. The Tyrians had accepted him, but under duress. The Egyptians had accepted him, too, but on their own terms. That would also prove true of the next people Alexander would encounter, in Babylonia.

6

The Throne of Babylon

IN THE SPRING of 331 BC, the Macedonians left Egypt the way they had come in. The army gathered at Pelusium, at the eastern end of the delta, and marched up the coastal road. Uncooperative before, the Arabs were now officious. Once the army reached Palestine, Perdiccas took a detachment, headed inland, and made short work of the Samaritans. When the army reached Tyre, Alexander made sumptuous offerings to Melkart, the Semitic patron god, and added Greek games and a donative. In an expansive mood, he received ambassadors from Athens and granted a request of theirs that he had previously rejected. They wished to ransom Athenians who served the Persians as mercenaries and had then been captured. Alexander chose to regard the prisoners as suppliants, and he let them go for nothing. In the same mood, he let Harpalus, who had deserted him before Issus, return and resume his post as treasurer. Harpalus, one of his original companions, had sat next to him in classes taught by Aristotle.[1]

He also took on a new diviner, a Syrian woman who suffered prophetic fits and who was right often enough that Alexander came to trust her. She, not Barsine, slept beside him every night. She would tacitly compete with Aristander. So would others, including a specialist in the Babylonian art of reading sheep's livers.[2]

From Babylon, Darius wrote Alexander a third time, asking for the return of the women captured at Issus. If Alexander would give up Darius's mother, other members of the royal family, and their servants, Darius would allow him to keep one of the women, his own daughter, and marry her. Alexander would also receive 10,000 talents, or twenty times the previous offer, and obtain all land west of the Euphrates. Alexander probably could not keep this big an offer secret, and thanks to his recent successes did not think he had to. He summoned a council meeting, disclosed the offer to the generals, and asked for their advice.[3]

The older companions, Philip's men, wanted to take the offer. Parmenio spoke politely on behalf of these veterans. He did not like the odds in a battle against Darius on the plains of Syria or Mesopotamia. The Persian cavalry would run rings around them. Perhaps Parmenio and the other generals did not like what little they knew of Babylon. It might be another Egypt, seducing their king into promoting natives as well as companions.

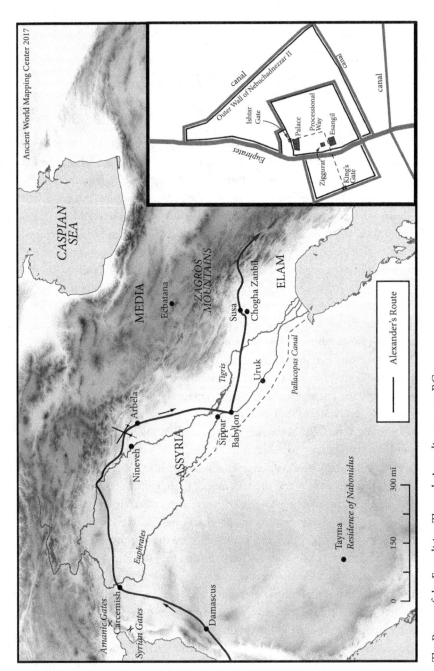

The Route of the Expedition Through Anatolia, 334–333 BC.
Ancient World Mapping Center.

Alexander replied impolitely to Parmenio. If he were Parmenio, he said, he would take the offer, but since he was Alexander, he would refuse it. Or so some companions remembered years later in their memoirs. Alexander never said anything so witty. He said many things that were this pointed, and made a pointed reply now. His marriages were his business, and he would not take a Persian for a wife. His Persian captives were his property, and he would not return them for a mere 10,000 talents. Alexander would return the captives only if Darius surrendered the Persian Empire. He dismissed the council, who returned to their tents more aware than ever of their commander's indomitable zeal.

Insulted yet again, Darius made no reply.

For the first time, the Macedonians could foresee the course of the war. Alexander had demanded that Darius capitulate, and Darius had refused, and so Alexander must again try to capture or kill him. If that failed—as it had at Issus— the Macedonians must seize Mesopotamia, especially Babylon and Susa, both of which were capitals of the empire. Then Darius would become marginal. Alexander could carry the war into Persia and Central Asia, or, if the generals could persuade him, he could satisfy himself with Babylon and the Near East and leave Persia to the Persians. Perhaps Persian men would learn to do what the women had done and beg for mercy.

After just three years of fighting, Alexander may have thought he could unify the Near East as easily as his father unified Greece in the course of a lifetime. So far he had achieved seductive economies of scale. He had seized half the Near East at the cost of a few thousand of his own men. He had killed tens of thousands of the enemy once, at Issus, and he had killed thousands of civilians twice, at Tyre and Gaza. Some foes were now in his service. In Syria and Egypt he had got rich, and so had his companions. One of them, Antipater, ruled Greece; another, Antigonus, ruled much of Asia Minor, and piece by piece would acquire much of the rest. Only Zeus's favor (and Amon's) could explain such victories. Babylonian Marduk would welcome him. Alexander knew this god had welcomed the victorious Cyrus, if not other conquerors.[4]

THE MACEDONIANS LEFT Syria in July 331. Between them and the Persian army, now at Babylon, flowed the Euphrates River, easiest to cross at the Carcemish ford used by Xenophon and later Darius. If the Persians wished, they could block the ford, or catch the Macedonians in midstream. Alexander and the generals nonetheless took the risk of advancing straight to Carcemish. When they reached the Euphrates, they threw two pontoon bridges across the river, no matter the risk. A few Persian scouts under Mazdai were watching, but soon they withdrew over the horizon.[5]

For the next five days Alexander's army marched over the bridge. Next they might go down the Euphrates, or travel a little farther and go down a tributary. Xenophon had. The generals rejected this route for lack of forage and fear of the heat. Instead they went east, heading toward the higher ground and lower temperatures in the valley of the Tigris. None of the Egyptians now in the entourage knew it, but by crossing the Euphrates Alexander had marched farther into Asia than any pharaoh.[6]

Alexander drove the army hard, marching the 300 miles to the Tigris in several weeks. The only road to Babylon lay on the far side, and to reach it the Macedonians again had to use a ford. They found one that was unguarded. Mazdai and his scouts had merely burned the granaries nearby. Around September 1 the army reached the road to Babylon, 360 miles to the south. This was Assyria, once the home of an empire, now a string of ex-capitals reduced to small towns or desert mounds, like Nineveh.[7]

Before the Macedonians lay a more complex objective than Egypt had been. Far to the south, the land between the Tigris and Euphrates was marshy, like the Nile Delta. Near Babylon, the land became firmer. Irrigation canals made any route other than the highway impracticable. Aside from patches of irrigated land, all was desert, and so the invaders must hop from one settlement to the next. That way they could feed on dates, and on beer and bread made from recently harvested grain. Village livestock would be in reach. Other flocks and herds belonged to camel-riding nomads and would not be worth the trouble to capture. Above Babylon, at the narrow point between the two rivers, stood the longest wall in the Near East. It ran from the Tigris to Sippar, on the Euphrates. Nebuchadnezzar had built it to block invaders.

The most important part of the environment lay overhead. The sky seemed larger than elsewhere, and brighter day and night. During their march south, on the thirteenth day of the Babylonian month of Elulu, a lunar eclipse occurred. The army had just pitched camp that evening. The eclipse lasted sixty-four minutes. A sandy west wind blew.[8]

The troops had seen eclipses before. One occurred in Egypt that spring, but they were not on campaign at the time, and so they ignored it. Three more occurred during the fighting in Anatolia but did not frighten them. Alexander and his seers, who could not predict eclipses, followed a formula for responding to them. The seers would declare the eclipse a good omen for the Macedonians and a bad one for the enemy. If the troops thought that the gods were favorable to them, this explanation would suffice. If the troops doubted the gods, they would need reassurance, and Alexander would resort to other devices.[9]

They needed reassurance now. They had been skirting a desert, and their route lacked shade trees and clear water. The gods of the locality were incomprehensible, and the troops had not seen any shrine betokening a Greek god for many weeks. They did not believe Alexander's claim to be the son of Amon or

Zeus-Amon, and so they got no reassurance that way. Beleaguered, they decided they would not march farther, and refused to stir from camp.

Alexander consulted the priests of Amon in his entourage. The Egyptians knew there had been several lunar eclipses since the expedition began, and that after each eclipse the Macedonians had continued to advance. They declared that the disappearance of the moon always boded ill for the Persians.[10]

Calling a meeting of seers and generals, Alexander announced this interpretation. Aristander agreed with it, and the generals welcomed it. The troops required something ceremonial, so the king ordered offerings to the sun, the moon, and the earth. These went well: the victims were slain, their entrails examined, their tails watched to see whether they would curl when put above the flames. Smoke trailed upward to divine nostrils. No eagle spoilt the affair, as happened at Gaza. Aristander predicted a battle by the end of the month. He knew—the officers told him—that the army would reach the enemy by then.[11]

After the sacrifice, the men ate, drank, and sang hymns. They did not object to beer instead of wine. Priest Alexander had calmed his troops.

The next morning Alexander rose early, as he commonly did, and made the daily offerings that assured him that the men should march on. When the offerings proved favorable, the army fell in and marched toward Arbela, the favorite residence of the goddess Ishtar. Like Athena, to whom he sacrificed before Issus, Ishtar was a warrior. If he prayed to a local goddess again, she would be his choice.

IN THE YEAR and a half since the battle of Issus, Darius had replenished his forces and built up a new army in Babylon. His troops were mostly Central Asian cavalry, suited to a fight on the plains of Mesopotamia. A few had ridden ahead under Mazdai. Babylonians and their Iranian neighbors contributed infantry, and so did India. Mountain peoples—Armenians, Medes, and troops from the southern Caspian—formed another detachment. The western part of the empire contributed little, the Greeks even less. The Persians contributed mainly the Immortals and the king's guard.

Some of Darius's men were inexperienced, most far from home. All had heard of Alexander, now ruler of half the empire, but only the Immortals, the guard, and the cavalry had fought him. Mazdai and another general, Bessus, the satrap of Bactria, had fought at Issus, but not in Anatolia.

Once the Macedonians crossed the Tigris, Darius led the main body north from Babylon and occupied Arbela. A road to Iran passed through this Assyrian town, and he wished to control the junction. He had pitched camp north of the city and was preparing a battlefield when the eclipse occurred.[12]

Like Alexander's men, Darius's panicked. The Great King looked to priests to calm them. His Persian Magi used some formula that satisfied the king, his satraps, and his Persian troops. The army, though, was not mostly Persians, and these other subjects of Darius's would look elsewhere for an explanation of the eclipse. The most likely place was an omen text. Babylon's priests had produced a large literature of astronomical omens. Astronomy—which they did not separate from astrology—was their specialty. They predicted events such as eclipses, and they also interpreted them as divine signs.[13]

Babylonian astronomy had been developing for several hundred years. Continuous records of celestial observations dated from the eighth century BC, approximately the time of Homer. By the time of Nebuchadnezzar, astronomers had identified the twelve signs of the zodiac. By the time of the Persian wars with Greece, they had cast the first horoscopes.[14]

When this eclipse occurred, the priests had an omen text to explain it. The text said, "The enemy will inflict a defeat on the land. The enemy"—that was Alexander—"will take all royal possessions." Darius probably did not hear of this prediction. If his Mesopotamian soldiers heard of it, it made their panic worse.[15]

This text also revealed a gap between Darius and the astronomers, who were the leading priests in Babylon. Rather than serve Darius, these priests were disinterested. If the eclipse was ominous for Darius, they would regard this piece of information as something for them to know and Darius to find out. They would not try to reverse the omen by means of a sacrifice. Since the omen came from the gods, it was irreversible except by special rituals that Darius did not ask them to perform.

Aristander and the other diviners on whom Alexander relied were traveling practitioners who had to please and persuade their royal client. The same went for Darius's Magi. The Babylonian astronomers were experts attached to shrines, especially the shrine of Marduk in Babylon, rather than to kings and armies. Rather than guess, they calculated. Rather than disagree with a ruler, as Aristander sometimes did with Alexander, they kept their own counsel. Military morale was not their concern.[16]

⸺◦⸺

WORRIED ABOUT FOOD and water, the Macedonians had kept moving, and eight days after the eclipse scouts riding at night sighted the constellation of Persian campfires lit mile after mile across the plain. They were stunned. They did not know the enemy was dispirited.[17]

Meeting the next morning, the leading companions fell into sharper disagreement than ever before. Many favored attacking later that same day, for they feared the enemy might encircle them if they waited. Parmenio preferred to pitch camp. He told his fellow councilors that the Macedonians should survey the terrain. It was, he noted, a battlefield chosen by Darius. Although Alexander presided over this meeting of the generals as he always did, he took no position. Parmenio prevailed.[18]

Taking the companion cavalry with him, Alexander rode the four miles of ground between the two sides. He discovered that the Persians had cleared one area for scythed chariots, cavalry, and creatures called elephants. A Greek mercenary deserter revealed that the Persians had booby-trapped another area. Returning to camp, Alexander called a meeting later the same day. He proposed to attack the next morning, but Parmenio proposed a surprise attack during the night, now that Macedonians knew the ground. A night attack might cause the enemy to panic, and negate the Persian advantage in numbers.[19]

Some agreed with Parmenio, but Alexander did not. In rebuking them, the king avoided challenging Parmenio and instead singled out a new regimental commander, Polyperchon, a veteran of Philip's wars. Alexander told him the army should not strike at night, like a burglar, but attack in the light of day after the customary ceremonies. Other generals agreed with Alexander for a practical reason: they feared losing control of their men in the dark. This time Alexander prevailed. The meeting went on to discuss sidestepping the chariots and posting a reserve. Once the battle began, it would be too late to give orders for maneuvers like these. The council must give the orders now.[20]

After the meeting, the officers told their men to wait until morning. That night, the sight of the countless Persian fires demoralized them.

Alexander wanted help from the gods, but Callisthenes could not give him suggestions. The Greek intellectual did not know this country, and neither did Alexander's Egyptian advisors. At a late hour, Alexander prayed alone to the local Athena, surely Ishtar, and to the local Zeus.[21] Ishtar was an especially good choice, for she had been the dry nurse to the Assyrian conqueror Assurbanipal and a goddess much revered by Cyrus the Great. Instead of praying to Heracles, another god he typically invoked, Alexander addressed the Greek god Panic. Aristander attended as the king asked Panic to visit the other side, not his own, and cause a Persian rout. After returning to his tent exhausted, Alexander overslept.[22]

At dawn, Parmenio and the top commanders met by the tent, and found they must wait. They ordered that the army take breakfast, but did not disturb Alexander. Then, after more time passed—too much time—Parmenio went in and awakened him. The old general asked him how he could relax before a battle, and the king replied that by marching unchallenged through the deserts of Mesopotamia the Macedonians had already won. Just before the Macedonians broke camp, the king summoned a larger circle of commanders to remind them of the battle plan, take questions, and boost morale. As the battle drew near, he became calmer.[23]

When the Macedonians marched out, the day was fair, but the wind was already brisk, a sign of a coming sandstorm. The officers led long columns of men to the fore, ordered them to wheel, and extended them left and right until the front stretched about two and a half miles across the sandy plain. Amid the rising dust, the 50,000 men moved almost silently, at the nod of their officers and the blare of trumpets. From half a mile away, the Persians watched the choral parade.[24]

The Thessalian and allied cavalry patrolled the left flank, under Parmenio, and that was standard, as was the phalanx in the center. Four of the six regimental commanders had served since the start of the expedition. Craterus led the regiment at one end, Coenus the regiment at the other. The right side of the line, Alexander's, began with the shield bearers and the companion cavalry, both under sons of Parmenio. That was standard, too. Yet the battle of Issus had inspired some changes. On the far right, Alexander put archers and light Balkan troops, refusing to prevent encirclement by the Persians. The same change appeared on the left, where other cavalry and light troops from Thrace stood at an angle. In the rear, a reserve protected the baggage train with its prisoners and wounded.[25]

Alexander rode with the companion cavalry, next to Philotas and Clitus, and Parmenio commanded his flank from a post between Craterus and the Thessalians. The two men were more than a mile apart, farther than in past battles, and so they planned to communicate by messenger.

A tired Persian army awaited them. Darius had expected a night attack, just as Parmenio proposed, and so he had kept his men up all night. Like Alexander, he had prayed, but not to Panic. Instead he invoked one or more Persian gods, notably Mithra, the god of duty and fidelity. He now deployed his troops in traditional fashion. His chariots and elephants occupied the cleared ground at the foot of a hill resembling a camel's hump. To the left of them he put Bessus, the Bactrian and Central Asian cavalry, and the cavalry from Elam; in the center, behind the chariots, he put Indian cavalry ahead of the Babylonians and their neighbors; on the right, he put Mazdai and the troops from the Caucasus and nearby Parthia and Media. He stationed his men ethnically, whereas the Macedonians stationed theirs functionally. To Darius, troops were subjects. To Alexander and Parmenio, they were instruments. A continent was fighting an army.[26]

Darius stood in a chariot in the center, protected by his remaining Greek mercenaries as well as the Immortals and the guard. The gray mare he rode in emergencies waited beside him.[27]

Darius started the battle, sending Bessus's men to the flank. He wished to confine Alexander's troops to the area the Persians had cleared for chariots. Alexander ordered his light troops to counter the move. Then came the chariots. The Macedonians stepped aside, and the horse-drawn machines raced through the lines and off the field. Alexander now spied a chance to slip into the gap Bessus had left behind him. Avoiding the booby traps, Alexander and the companion cavalry trotted forward, and the shield bearers followed. An eagle soared over Alexander's head, and Aristander, marching nearby, encouraged the men to regard this as a good omen. Alexander led the advancing wedge in search of Darius. He was pursuing his objective of capturing or killing one man, not defeating an army.[28]

Alexander's pursuit of his goal led to the same mishap as at Issus. The Macedonian army split, the lead element under Alexander, the rest under Parmenio. Ordered by Darius to rescue the Persian prisoners, Mazdai saw a chance to accomplish this mission by passing between the two parts of the Macedonian army. He plunged through, leading his cavalry toward the baggage train.[29]

The generals had warned the Macedonian reserve about such an attack. As Mazdai reached the baggage train, the reserve struck back, spears lowered, and drove away Mazdai and his cavalry. Darius had squandered some of his best men on a futile attempt to free some of his noblest women.[30]

Other Persian cavalry swung wide and outflanked Parmenio and his Thessalians. Parmenio was again in trouble, but Alexander had no occasion to stop and see how Parmenio was faring. The swirling dust blinded him. Parmenio sent a messenger saying that Mazdai had broken through but that the reserve had blunted this attack. Enemy cavalry were harassing him, and the phalanx had split in two. Two regiments were with him, and the other four were trying to follow Alexander. The time had come for Alexander to face about and attack Mazdai.[31]

Afterward, the companions did not agree whether Alexander got the message. In any event, he trotted onward and his four regiments followed. They advanced in squares of several hundred men apiece, each led by a mounted officer conspicuous because of his breastplate and his horse. In the van rode the commander, even more conspicuous because of a purple cape. Coenus led the first regiment, Perdiccas the second. They could not make themselves less vulnerable by charging, stopping, or turning aside. They must go at the pace of infantry toting fifteen-foot spears.[32]

The Persian archers spotted them, and concentrated their fire on the purple capes visible above the rising dust. They wounded Coenus and Perdiccas, who fell out of line. The mass of Alexander's cavalry offered them another easy target, and they brought down a hundred of them. Hephaestion, leading some of the shield bearers, took a spear in the shoulder. All for naught: they missed Alexander and Bucephalas, too. Subordinates replaced the wounded commanders, and the decimated companions regrouped and trotted on. Where Alexander led, the shield bearers followed, and so did Coenus's and Perdiccas's regiments. They struck the Persian line, and under the impact the enemy wavered and began to break. The Indian troops were among the last to go. After a time, only the Immortals were defending Darius.[33]

As at Issus, the Persian king faced the choice of fighting or retreating. He had little news to go on. Dust from the battle prevented him from seeing whether

Mazdai had liberated his relatives or whether other cavalry had defeated Parmenio. Perhaps Mazdai or other commanders sent reports that did not get through. After waiting until the last possible moment, Darius left his chariot, got on his gray mare, and rode off the battlefield, heading for Arbela. The Immortals blocked any close pursuit. The rest of the Persians had already quit the field. Parmenio had defeated some of them and the reserves had defeated the rest.[34]

When Darius reached Arbela, he called a meeting of his advisers. He wished to know whether to turn east, to Iran, or continue south, to Babylon. If he went east and Alexander followed him, he would draw the Macedonians away from Babylon. That would spare the city, and it would not endanger Darius, who could outrun his pursuers. Darius could reach Ecbatana, a Persian capital in northwest Iran, and regroup. If he went south, to Babylon, Alexander would follow him and besiege the city. Darius knew of the Macedonians' success at Tyre, and he may have assumed Babylon would eventually fall. Then Alexander would capture him and the city both.[35]

To deny Alexander this victory, he and the advisers decided that he should head east, into the mountains. Darius quit Mesopotamia, but purposefully, the way he had quit the battlefield.

After Darius decided to withdraw to Iran, his top subordinates split. Mazdai went south to Babylon, and Bessus followed Darius. The remains of the Persian army, including troops that had not yet done any fighting, clogged the road to Arbela. The one bridge Darius had built over a river just down the road helped a few to safety, but blocked more. Many turned away from the road to find something to drink. The water in the irrigation canals made them sick, and easier for the pursuing Macedonians to dispatch. For the first time in two years, Alexander's army killed many thousands. Their own casualties numbered less than 1,000. The Phoenician sutlers prospered. They bought many tens of thousands of Persian captives from Alexander, and sent them up the Tigris, to be sold into slavery.[36]

Because of the stench of the Persian corpses on the battlefield, Alexander could not bury his hundreds of dead there. He brought the bodies to the vicinity of Arbela and buried them at a victory memorial on a hill. Then he paraded to the citadel of the city, the location of Egasankalamma, the gold-and-silver-plated temple of Ishtar. He gave a victor's customary thanks for success in battle and also for the discovery of a trove of gold and silver abandoned by Darius. He knew that Ishtar could not crown him king of Mesopotamia. The priests of Babylonian Marduk kept that privilege for themselves. He must go on to Babylon, and never mind pursuing Darius. Although Darius was a prize, Babylon and Marduk were bigger ones.[37]

Alexander perhaps took note of the municipal water supply piped from three rivers. He did not know it, but Sennacherib, whose monument had bewildered the companions in Cilicia, two years before, had built the tunnels. Besides being the world's best astronomers, the Mesopotamians were the world's best engineers, as shown by ziggurats and walls as well as irrigation canals and water mains. They had learned to use naphtha to make asphalt, and just south of Arbela Alexander and his courtiers encountered naphtha for the first time, as it bubbled up from the ground. Curious about the substance, Alexander cast about for some way to learn more about it, and had one of his slaves doused with it. The man accidentally caught fire and nearly died of his burns.[38]

Like naphtha, Mesopotamia would need careful handling. Egypt had its mysteries, but Mesopotamia packed more surprises and disappointments. No one here would suppose Alexander had a special life force, a *ka*.

WHILE AT ARBELA, Alexander changed his policy toward his subjects. To win friends, he announced the overthrow of tyrants throughout the empire. That had helped him at Ephesus, and it might help again. He also wanted to find some new, more plausible title for himself. He might call himself king of Asia, a term the Greeks would understand, but there was no kingdom of Asia. The people of Asia did not think of themselves as Asians, and would not recognize him as their king. He hit upon another phrase, "master of Asia," as though Asia were his household or his estate. Soon after the battle he tried out this phrase in a personal rather than official way. He sent some spoils to an important shrine of Athena located in Lindos on the island of Rhodes. The Lindians received a donation inscribed: "King Alexander, having bested Darius in battle and become Master of Asia, Made offerings to Athena of Lindos." Not far away in this shrine stood a statue dedicated to Athena by a pharaoh of two hundred years before.[39]

The Lindians thanked Alexander. He was welcome to be master of Asia, but not master of any Greeks. They assumed that he would not tax their property, occupy their city, or usurp their ceremonies. Other Greeks adopted this attitude. Alexander now wielded more power than before, but not over them.

Despite the victory, Alexander and the army found themselves somewhat at odds with each other. During the battle at Arbela, the army fought in three parts that did not communicate effectively. The officers felt isolated, if not slighted. The companions had won without acting like companions.

Philotas voiced this feeling when he remarked that he felt sorry for the defeated Persians, since they were fighting a demigod, and sorry for the cavalry, since they had to ride hard to keep up with one. This witticism and others came to Alexander's ears from Craterus, who had heard it from Philotas's concubine. For the first time, he had passed along some of her gossip to Alexander.

Soldiers who shared Philotas's skepticism expressed themselves to Philotas and not to Alexander. A cavalry officer named Hegelochus came to Philotas and said that the troops felt insulted to serve under a so-called Egyptian god.

He offered to kill Alexander. Alexander, after all, had done away with Philip, his true father, and so he was a virtual parricide. He deserved to die at the hands of a regicide.

Philotas rebuffed Hegelochus, but told Alexander nothing. Hegelochus and his mounted scouts had been the first men to reach the Granicus River the day before the big battle. After Philotas told Antigone about Hegelochus, this tale reached Alexander, too. It did not matter that Hegelochus would soon die in battle. The tale told by Antigone would outlive him.[40]

Craterus and many others realized that the main danger to morale came from another quarter. Many men who had no thoughts of murder—and no political thoughts at all—wanted to serve in less trying circumstances closer to home. News of military successes in Anatolia and Greece heightened this feeling.

Antigonus, Alexander's top commander in Anatolia, had cleaned up the spots missed during the Macedonians' S-curve march through the peninsula. Antigonus had defeated several Persian armies, and he and Parmenio's younger brother had eliminated the main Persian garrisons. The Macedonians serving under Antigonus mostly commanded native troops. They ran fewer risks than Alexander's forces, and administered the territories they conquered. Antigonus not only made himself look good but made service under Alexander look worse.[41]

The news from Macedon and Greece made the same impression on the troops. Antipater, Alexander's viceroy, suppressed a rebellion led by Sparta. The Spartan leaders knew that Alexander had left the Mediterranean region, but they did not know of the victory at Arbela, and so the moment to overthrow the Macedonians seemed to have arrived. The Spartan king Agis assembled 20,000 infantry and 2,000 cavalry, an army comparable to Philip's, and more than equal to what Alexander had left to Antipater. Agis threw back the Macedonian forces in southern Greece.

Antipater responded by raising troops and attacking Agis in Arcadia, in central Peloponnesus. In many hours of hard fighting, Antipater's men inflicted 5,000 casualties on the Spartan core of the enemy force, and killed Agis. The Spartan defeat, the worst they ever suffered, finished them as a Greek military power.

To companions of Philip's generation, this, and not the battle of Arbela, was the best achievement of Alexander's reign. Although Alexander had sent Antipater 3,000 talents, the money may have arrived too late to do any good, and so Antipater may have won by himself. Alexander belittled his viceroy's victory, calling it a "battle of mice." He told the companions that his own military reputation, now greater than ever, would overawe future enemies. Babylon would put any such claim to the test. The city and its leaders expected to negotiate with Alexander before surrendering.[42]

GREEKS REGARDED BABYLON as the largest, richest city in the world.[43] Many workmen were paid in silver, and quit if not paid on time. Thousands worked in just one industry, baking bricks. In the Persian period, wages rose, and private houses got bigger. Great trading houses sued each other, and the courts stayed busy.[44] To judge from the surviving records, Babylon led Tyre, Athens, and everywhere else in kinds and numbers of commercial documents—contracts, leases, bills of sale, mortgages, loans, promissory notes. Whereas Athens and Phoenicia fought incessant wars and Athens prosecuted intellectuals, Babylon did neither.

Astronomers and other clergy ran Babylon, giving the Persian satrap and garrison their cut. The palace of Nebuchadnezzar, where the satrap lived, might be the city's biggest residence, but the temple of Marduk was the biggest building, and the attached ziggurat, where the astronomers worked, was the tallest building on earth, save for the pyramids. The astronomers formed a college like All Souls or the Princeton Institute for Advanced Study. They and other leading priests belonged to a local assembly that was the most important center of power other than the Persian garrison.[45] The assemblymen wished to keep their posts, income, and perquisites. Mazdai, who had taken charge of the Persian garrison, wished to be spared, and to have his men spared. Neither group could be sure of Alexander's aims. Did the invader want plunder, power, or a general massacre?

As Alexander marched south, Mazdai's troops kept watch along the wall of Nebuchadnezzar some twenty-five miles north of the city. Then Mazdai sent emissaries to his foe. Would Alexander spare him and his troops? Perhaps, Alexander replied. Would Alexander spare the city? Perhaps. Did Alexander wish to become king? When Alexander answered yes, Mazdai put him in touch with the administrator of the shrine of Marduk, called the *shatammu*. He was not a royal impersonator, like an Egyptian priest, or a civil servant, like a Greek one. He served as a chief executive.

The *shatammu* gave Alexander a Babylonian history lesson translated into Greek by Mazdai's staff and Alexander's Phoenicians. The Babylonians had been without a king since the Persians abolished the position a century and a half ago. Before that, Cyrus the Great and Cyrus's son Cambyses had served as king and respected temple privileges. At Cambyses's death, the usurper Darius I became the ruler of Persia, and Babylon rebelled against him, making a descendant of Nabonidus, the last native prince, the new king of the city. Darius suppressed the rebellion, and to punish Babylon he abolished the position of king.[46]

That was an error. The Babylonians waited until Xerxes succeeded Darius, and rebelled again. Xerxes suppressed this brief outbreak, removed temple officials, and seized some temple and business archives. That provoked the Babylonians to rebel a third time. This affray lasted the better part of a year, and culminated in a siege. Now that Alexander had arrived, the Babylonians hoped for a king who, unlike the Persians, would perform the two complementary tasks of keeping chaos at bay and protecting the temple.[47]

Alexander, alas, was a foreigner, but the *shatammu* would instruct him. Then Alexander would swear an oath to Marduk. Other gods, like Ishtar, would witness the oath. The *shatammu* did not explain how the gods would manifest themselves—a professional secret.

If Alexander did not swear the oath, neither the assembly nor Marduk would cooperate with him.

However little Alexander knew about Marduk and chaos, he did not need a lesson in the history of sieges of Babylon. Aside from Xerxes's troubles, the Assyrians had once needed two years to capture the city, and even Cyrus needed months. Cyrus had to divert the waters of the Euphrates River. This feat reminded Alexander and the engineers of their labors at Tyre.[48]

At the last moment, when the Macedonians reached the wall, at Sippar, the three sides struck a bargain. Mazdai and his men would be unharmed. So would Babylon. Mazdai would administer the city, but not in the manner of a satrap. Alexander would swear an oath to Marduk and become king of Babylon—king of the four corners and king of the world. Then he could do in Babylon what he had done in Tyre and Egypt: make prestigious sacrifices. Once he did, he would rule legitimately.[49]

The *shatammu* brought word of the agreement to the assembly, which met in the usual place, the juniper garden beside the temple of Marduk. They agreed to offer the throne to Alexander as of 336, six years earlier. That way Darius would never have ruled Babylon. Back among the Macedonians, Alexander announced his newest crown to the companions, along with the news there would be no more fighting around Babylon or elsewhere in Mesopotamia. Mazdai and some of his men escorted the army toward the city. Mazdai, who knew his Greeks, arranged for town notables to approach the army and supplicate. The suppliants called the invaders "Ionians," or "Hanaeans," the name of a long-vanished tribe from northwestern Mesopotamia. They used a gesture Greeks avoided, prostrating themselves. By supplicating this way they did obeisance to the invaders.[50]

As the army trudged toward the city, led by Persians and accompanied by Babylonians, they passed one irrigation canal after another. The invaders noticed the large, regular, and impressively carved milestones, but they saw few people and fewer settlements. Then they spied a ridge—but no, the ridge was a seventy-five-foot wall of burnt brick hundreds of yards long. Scouts who swung away and approached the city sideways saw the next section of the wall, also interminably long.[51]

Coming to a cedar and copper gate, they passed an embankment and then not one wall, as they expected, but two walls twelve feet apart. For an overly long time they marched alongside a stretch of uncultivated ground. Every walled settlement had room for gardens, pastures, and muster grounds, but this space was bigger than small Greek cities. For the first time, they were walking on asphalt. Then they passed block after square block of unpainted mud-brick buildings, unrelieved by the sight of an alley, a courtyard, or even a window. Every house shared walls with its neighbors. And every house—every wall—was crumbling. The mud bricks eventually fell apart because of impurities in the sand used to make them. Or did the sun burn everything to bits? It bore down on the marchers, block after block.

Once the army reached downtown, crowds of people appeared on the rooftops and threw bunches of green twigs. Then the army wheeled onto a broad street of white limestone bordered by red and white crushed breccia—a sacred way. High along the buildings on either side, a band of enameled blue brick flowed past the mounted Macedonians at the head of the column. Sixty bas-relief white lions with yellow manes leapt from the blue brick. So did sixty yellow lions with red hair.[52]

After some more blocks, all crowded with admirers, a pair of towers built of more blue enameled bricks dwarfed the parading soldiers. They noticed a few slits for archers, for these towers dated to a time when the outer walls did not exist and the city extended no farther than this spot. Near the top of the towers, 150 bulls and snakes glared down from the blue enamel. Another gate, and the troops glimpsed the palace of Nebuchadnezzar, a towering building with a rooftop garden watered by water screws. Mazdai's men were still on duty at the doors. In another direction, a citadel loomed beyond a pavement of limestone and black basalt. Guarding the citadel gate were basalt lions, one shown treading on a prostrate man.[53]

They have come to their destination: Esangil, the temple of Marduk. Copper dragons protect the gates, and the high wall around the temple keeps them from seeing most of this four-story building. Yet even here, the edges are crumbling. Soon they stop in a street that has widened to eighty yards, far broader than any in Egypt or Tyre. Alexander dismounts, and the priests, all depilated and in white robes, usher him inside. The troops disperse, fleeing the lethal sunlight.

Entering Esangil, Alexander cannot tell whether it is a temple or not. First comes an outer court or hall, as in Egypt or Greece, but which the Babylonians call the "gateway." Tradesmen bringing food and drink for the gods crowd the place, a vulgarity the Egyptians would never allow. There is no altar, as there would be in Greece, and so there is nowhere for the tradesmen to deposit their goods. Then the new king comes to the next court, which the translators call the "house." Where, though, is the temple? To the right, the translators answer. With its forest of pillars and lofty steps, this building looks like a temple, and so Alexander, remembering Egypt and Greece, expects to go inside. There the priests will crown him, or, if he can find some way to improvise, he will crown himself. He did that in Tyre.

No, the translators inform him. Like everyone but the depilated priests, called "insiders," he will not be allowed to enter. He would desecrate the place, except, of course, on New Year's Day, when his presence in the temple is obligatory. Asking when New Year's Day is, Alexander and a few companions learn that it is twice a year, but not at the present time.[54]

The same day, or soon afterward, the priests crown Alexander according to a ritual script that is no longer preserved but may have resembled the script used for the last native ruler. That would be the man for Alexander to imitate.

First the priests explain that Alexander must once again avoid the sacred precincts. A throne and a footstool of solid gold, 800 talents' worth, are there, but they are for Marduk. Alexander must follow the *shatammu* to another place, where the chief priest seats him on a less impressive throne. The assemblymen raise their fists in approbation, and the *shatammu* crowns him with headgear that looked like a battle standard. A priest of Nabû, Marduk's scribe, bestows a scepter on him. The gods now proclaim Aleksandari king of the four corners, king of Babylon, and king of the world.[55]

In words he does not understand, Alexander swears to do something he certainly does understand—guarantee temple privileges. With that, the priests squire him to an altar where he makes his first offerings, a bloodless affair, since a priest has already done the work of killing the animal. Alexander need only prostrate himself while a priest presents meat, bread, and beer to Marduk, courtesy of the god's servant, the new king. Babylonian sacrifice, Alexander now sees, is less a way of making a gift to a god, or of paying courtesies, than of feeding him. As a grace note, Alexander has to sprinkle cypress dust on the offerings. Mainly he will offer beer. (The priests commonly drink the leftovers, but this time the king will.)[56]

Out they march into the courtyard of the temple. Beyond them rises the seven-story ziggurat that looms over the city. The summit of the ziggurat is the artificial Olympus of the Babylonians, where gods mingle with astronomers. The king of the world can never go there.[57]

After the ceremony, Alexander repaired to the water-cooled palace of Nebuchadnezzar to quaff his beer and consider his fate. In Macedon, Greece, and Egypt, he had not received leftovers and priests had not taken him by the hand. They guessed the future through omens, but they did not predict it through observations. In Babylon, even the calendar belonged to the priests, who had just altered it in order to change his accession date. They would not let Alexander himself alter the calendar, as he had done several times. Eventually they would explain why: by making the lunar and solar years correspond, the Babylonians made the calendar perfect.[58]

This innovation threatened Alexander, other kings, and Greek magistrates. These rulers all governed men partly by controlling time. Now the proto-scientists would control time. Worse, they would control it mathematically. No bribes, no offerings, no pleas. No religion as Alexander knew it. He sent copies of the calendar to Aristotle, and news of it spread throughout the Greek world. Some cities reformed their calendars the next year.[59]

AFTER THE PARADE halted and the companions dispersed, some toured the city. If they were lucky, they had guides who knew schoolboy texts listing waterways, streets, and as many as forty-three shrines identified by neighborhood. Shrine names ran to the grandiose—the House That Gathers All Decrees, Ishtar's House of Lapis Lazuli, the Foremost Mound of Cream, the Foremost House in the Universe (not an especially famous place), the House That Bestows the Scepter. Along with these Babylonian shrines, the companions saw unlisted Persian ones. Marduk presided over one shrine, the Persian Ahura Mazda over the next. Ishtar presided over one, and her Persian counterpart Anahita over another. Hebrews worshipped Yahweh. The companions found no Greek shrines, and they did not know which gods to compare to which.

They did not even find the famous hanging gardens. Greek reports of these gardens were wrong, said the guides. The gardens were one more achievement of

Sun god tablet of Nabu-aplu-iddina, ninth century BC.
Photograph: Trustees of the British Museum, BM 910000+.

Sennacherib, who had built the pillar at Anchialus in Syria. The Assyrian king had built the gardens at Nineveh, a city long since destroyed.[60]

To make offerings—and get the beef that went with it—the companions worshipped outdoors in their own way. One of the astronomers recorded a Macedonian offering in a marginal note for the fourteenth of Tishrutu, the month following the battle: "These Ionians [slew] a bull [—] / [some number of] short [ribs?] and [some number of] fatty tissues." Although some words are missing, since the tablet, too, has crumbled, some Macedonian officer slew a bull and removed some of the "tissues," in other words, the innards. To the surprise of the Babylonian observer, he did so on the spot. He was going to feed his men, not the god. That oddity struck the writer as noteworthy.[61]

Rather than offer a religious or cultural welcome to the Macedonians, Babylon treated them as tourists. The city that had taken the measure of Alexander took the measure of his men and furnished them beer and temple prostitutes.

Alexander's work would differ from the pharaoh's in Egypt. There he built new shrines and repaired old ones. Here he would need to concentrate on maintenance, especially for Esangil. Recent Persian rulers had not maintained the temple as well as Cyrus had. The ziggurat was in some disrepair, and the astronomers wanted it restored. The *shatammu* and Mazdai did not succeed in simplifying the finances of this perpetual project. Alexander wanted to know whether he should pay or whether the priests should, but the Babylonians did not answer unanimously.[62]

If the priests refused to cooperate, Alexander could replace them, but he could not dismiss them in a body. Priests could challenge any act of his by declaring it ominous and asking the astronomers for the last word on the subject. If the astronomers had no word to give, a struggle would ensue between priests who challenged the king and those who supported him. The king could win these battles, but at a cost in time and trouble.[63]

When Alexander tired of these planning sessions, he took boat trips. He soon discovered that in spite of the canals the Euphrates and the Tigris were not navigable all the way to the Persian Gulf. One day Alexander discovered what he took to be a royal tomb, and summoned translators. Another day he started a food fight between boats, throwing apples. No one fell into the water and died afterward, as Hector had in Egypt.[64]

In Egypt, Alexander had supposedly owned all the land, and in Macedon he could make gifts of all the land he owned or conquered, but in Babylon he was neither a monopolist nor a benefactor. Instead he was a leading landowner competing with Babylon's temples and merchant banks. Beyond Babylon, the king must maintain the canals on which agriculture and prosperity depended. He also must collect taxes from the nomads who owned some of Mesopotamia's livestock. He would not need to swear an oath to respect their rights, but he would need camel-riding police to catch them should they flee his tax collectors.

Mesopotamia had resources all its own, like naphtha, yet was short of currency. Like the Egyptians, the Mesopotamians used silver as a money of account, and they also used silver bullion and Persian coins, but they lacked a coinage of their own. That made it harder for Alexander to collect taxes, pay troops, refurbish temples, and rebuild waterways. The currency shortage also impeded small transactions. To buy beer or hire prostitutes, Macedonian soldiers had to pay with silver bits snapped off ingots like pieces of a chocolate bar. When Babylonians were paid in foreign coins, they treated them like raw silver and assayed them. Alexander and Mazdai had to erect a mint, then compel Babylon's merchants and bankers to switch from silver to coins.[65]

These challenges would consume months or years of Alexander's time, and he preferred to chase Darius. His men expected as much, and so did observers throughout the Persian Empire. Darius aside, Alexander wished to capture Susa, the next important Mesopotamian city. He must bequeath crumbling, opulent Babylon to legates.

As in Egypt and Phoenicia, he divided power. Although he appointed Mazdai governor, he gave him no troops. He assigned several thousand infantry to two companions who would remain in Mesopotamia, and tapped a third man to command a Macedonian garrison that would occupy a big fort on the other side of the river. He assigned the treasury to a fourth man. Mazdai observed, "There was one Darius, but Alexander has made many Alexanders."[66]

This compliment did not please the companions who overheard or later got word of it. Mazdai, who was not a companion, had received the best post in the empire outside of Macedon. Would this Persian be another Antipater, brown on the outside and purple on the inside?

To mollify the companions, Alexander distributed massive donatives during offerings in the palace and elsewhere. He kept relatively little for himself. The officers lived like generals, and the generals like kings. The only person to complain was Olympias, who learned of these donatives and reproached the king for living like a general.[67]

Alexander also offered the companions a new kind of power—central administration. Babylon, he decided, would be capital of the empire, and it would need a cadre that understood the empire as a whole, not men like Mazdai who knew only some part of it. A top financier would need to work in Babylon, which would engross Alexander's massive revenues. To this post Alexander appointed Harpalus, who had been the army paymaster. Others, including Eumenes, his secretary, and Chares, his chamberlain, would work in Babylon eventually, but for the time being they would accompany Alexander on the march to the east. Alexander needed to see these men daily and could not afford to leave them behind.[68]

The companions could not object to these arrangements. No place in Macedon could be the capital of an expanding Asian empire, and the companions disliked Egypt. Because Babylon surrendered without a fight, it was better than Tyre or Damascus. Someone had to police Babylon's traffic in men, whores, and money, and since Harpalus had a limp he could not serve in combat.

Alexander and the army spent thirty-four days in Babylon. They would not experience so long a break from fighting, marching, or cold weather for another seven years.[69]

———·———

THE ARMY NOW moved south along the eastern bank of the Tigris, with Alexander accompanying them by boat. The tribesmen of lower Mesopotamia must have gawked at this column of 50,000 men in tunics and skirts. Where were the long pants and kepis of the Persians, their chariots, covered wagons, and bottled water? And what was the rush? Like Philip, Alexander marched his men double time.

To avoid the marshes on the lowest part of the Tigris, the army turned east and followed freshwater tributaries. Much of the year, this flat country was flooded, but now, in late fall, it was passable, and the wheat and barley grew luxuriant. They entered the province of Elam, Cyrus's homeland, and passed a large abandoned city capped by a four-story ziggurat. Then they approached Susa.[70]

Like Babylon, Susa announced itself from afar. The army was now marching on a paved road, and mountains framed the city on its shelf of land. The blue glaze of the temple and palace walls shone like jewelry atop a colossal table. Memnon had built all this—the original Memnon, buried near Troy—and also the drainage and irrigation system that brought water to sacred groves around the city. Cyrus, Alexander knew, had marched down out of the mountains and conquered Susa, and his successors had made it a Persian capital. Although smaller than Babylon, Susa had distinct quarters: the Apadana palace and grounds, a citadel, a residential neighborhood, and date groves in the open ground within the walls. Temples were everywhere, identified by cattle horns attached to the walls.[71]

The Persian satrap, Attalitta, came out of the Apadana and surrendered. A few of his soldiers may have resisted, angering the Macedonians. What is certain is that when Alexander and his party entered the palace and found the statue of Darius I the Persians brought back from Egypt, they vandalized it. Someone who knew Egyptian zeroed in on the cartouche containing Darius's Egyptian titles and defaced it.[72]

They also found some Greek statuary taken from Athens in 480. The most famous of the Greek pieces was a pair of statues to Harmodius and Aristogeiton, Athenian youths who attempted to kill the last of Athens's tyrants. Alexander, with his penchant for political gestures, made sure these statues would be returned to their spot in the Athenian marketplace. The Athenians worshipped these youths as heroes.[73]

The famous chandelier in the main reception room of the Apadana went undisturbed. Alexander might someday use this room, and until then his satrap might. Alexander also spared the life-size bas-relief images of Darius's guard throughout the palace. There was much for these guardian spirits to protect—the chandelier and the cotton curtains and hangings tied with linen cords, the silver rings and marble pillars, and the gold and silver couches placed on a mosaic of porphyry, marble, and mother of pearl. Here the resources of the Persian kings merged with the finery of the Mesopotamians.[74]

The king and his men left the Apadana and passed through the House of Lapis Lazuli, dedicated to Ishtar. Straight ahead they saw the shrine of the "Lord of Susa," Inshushinak, surrounded by a deep moat lined with stone. The water was luminous, the shrine as small and tidy as a Greek temple. Alexander crossed the bridge, opened the temple door, and beheld Inshushinak, who was not much more than life-size. Several nearby statues had been dedicated to Inshushinak, but the king and his party learned to their surprise that these were statues of Babylonian kings. One was a life-size diorite image of King Manishtushu; another was a statue of the most famous Babylonian king, Hammurabi, seated atop a copy of his laws. The statue of Manishtushu had stood in Babylon for about 1,000 years before being removed to Elam around 1158 BC. Hammurabi's statue had stood in Sippar for 600 years before being removed at the same time. The Elamites had captured the statues and brought them to Susa. They had also defaced them. After scratching out part of the Akkadian inscriptions on these statues, they had written Elamite inscriptions dedicating them to Inshushinak.[75]

By questioning translators, Alexander and his entourage learned some of the history of these artworks. Long before Cyrus led his Elamites to power, Elam had conquered Babylon. Babylon had also conquered Elam. Each time, the statues of kings were captured and carried away, like slaves. So were statues of gods, even the Babylonian god Marduk and Inshushinak himself. Then they were defaced. Alexander knew that many peoples carried the statues of their own gods from place to place—even the Greeks did. Now he learned that the Elamites and Babylonians pilfered the statues of their enemies' gods and kings. Inshushinak captured Marduk, and Marduk captured Inshushinak.

This perpetual rivalry compromised Alexander. He was the son of Amon, the ward of Marduk, and the intimate of Inshushinak, roles that should be complementary. Apparently, they were not. Rather than form some international consortium, the chief gods warred upon one another. They acted the way Alexander and his men had acted toward the statue of Darius.[76]

Alexander did not become king of Susa thanks to a ceremony of Inshushinak's. The ceremony in Babylon sufficed. Although the Greeks thought of Susa as a great Persian capital, he did not attempt to make himself king of the Persians. He regarded Susa as a way station.

The army spent several pleasant weeks there. They celebrated a munificent sacrifice of thanksgiving in the Greek fashion, and they collected the Persian royal silver kept in the city—a haul ten times as great as the booty after Issus and Arbela. Babylon had just as much silver, but the army had not taken it. Instead Alexander had left it to Mazdai and the *shatammu*.[77]

Alexander's administrative appointments offended the companions. Parmenio got a house, but Alexander retained the Persian satrap, Attalitta, despite his having fought the Macedonians at Arbela. Only command of a garrison went to a Macedonian. Troops too old for more campaigning would man the garrison.[78]

Alexander did not reject the companions because Susa was far from Greece. He would soon appoint Macedonians as satraps in more remote places. Rather, he thought them incompetent to run cities centered on great shrines. That was a religious, not military, duty, and it belonged to him. Yet if he was in the field, who would do this duty? Would Alexander appoint a Sidonian in Sidon, a man with a Babylonian family in Babylon, and a Persian in Elam? Then Alexander was putting himself in the position of appearing Phoenician in Phoenicia, Babylonian in Mesopotamia, and Persian in Central Asia. Besides being the son of Amon in Egypt, he was the son of circumstances everywhere else.

While in Susa, Alexander mismanaged a gift that he gave to his most important Persian royal captive, Sisygambis. He presented her with some purple wool, telling her that his own sister weaved, but she knew that servants did most weaving in Macedon, the same as Persia, and she said she did not wish to work with her hands. Taken aback, Alexander withdrew and gave the wool to a slave of his own. He had had enough of Sisygambis, and decided to leave her and the other captives in the palace at Susa. That would show unflappable magnanimity. Perhaps it would make her less hostile.[79]

That mattered to him. Sisygambis was the queen mother, often a powerful position in the Persian court. He called her "mother," confirming her position. Difficult as she was, he might want to cooperate with her.

By now, the army had received all of the 15,000 reinforcements who had been arriving since Babylon. Always reliable in regard to reinforcements, Antipater had outdone himself—and depleted Macedon's manpower. He sent 6,000 Macedonian infantry plus 500 Macedonian cavalry, 3,000 Thracian infantry plus 600 of their cavalry, and 4,000 Greek mercenary infantry with 380 cavalry—far exceeding all previous reinforcements, and including the last Macedonians who

The four-story ziggurat at Choga Zanbil, Khuzestan, Iran.
Photograph: Toos Foundation.

would join the expedition.[80] In this way as in others, Susa marked the beginning of the end.

⸺⟐⸺

ACCORDING TO THE Babylonian Talmud, Alexander held a conclave of sages after capturing Babylon.[81] The Talmud does not say who these sages were, and other stories about the conclave identify them as Greeks or Indians. The Talmud calls the sages "elders of the South":

> Alexander of Macedon put ten questions to the elders of the South. He asked, "Were the heavens created first, or the earth?"
> They answered, "The heavens were created first, as it says, 'In the beginning, God created the heaven and the earth.'"
> He asked, "Was light created first, or darkness?"
> They replied, "This question cannot be answered," for if they said "darkness," since it is written, "The earth was without form, and void, and darkness was upon the face of the deep," they would also have to explain the verse "And God said, 'Let there be light, and there was light,'" and if they answered "light," they would have to explain "darkness was upon the face of the deep." They thought to themselves, "Perhaps he will go on, and ask what the face of the deep was, and what was above the firmament, and

Anonymous illustration of Alexander and the sages in Firdausi, Isfahan, ca. 1330.
Photograph: Artokoloro Quint Lox, Alamy Stock Photographs.

what below." Then they thought they should not have answered either this question or the one before it.

Next, he asked, "Who is wise?"

They answered, "He who discerns what shall come to pass."

"Who," he asked, "is powerful?"

They answered, "He who controls his passions."

"Who is rich?"

They answered, "He who rejoices in his portion."

"What shall a man do to live?"

"Mortify himself," they said, "through the study of God's works."

"And what," he asked, "shall a man do to kill himself?"

"Let him," they said, "stay alive."

"What," he asked next, "shall a man do to make himself acceptable to others?"

They said, "Let him shun his king."

He answered, "I have a better answer. Let him befriend his king and do good for mankind."

"Which of you is wisest?" he asked.

They replied, "One is as wise as another, for we answer in unison."

Before asking his last question, he paused, and then he asked, "Why do you refuse to accept my religion, and cherish your own? You are my subjects."

They answered, "We are, but every day Satan is victorious, and leads men astray."

"Behold," he concluded, "I will slay you by royal decree."

"Power is in the king's hands," they answered, "but it does not behoove a king to be false."

Pleased by their replies, Alexander gave them purple garments and chains of gold to put round their necks, and said, "Go back to your God and study His works in the sky above and the earth below."

To judge from these questions, Alexander and the sages both puzzled over the creation story in the book of Genesis. The sages allude to the Psalms and the commentaries known as the Mishnah, and Alexander to the Mishnah. The king is still something of a Jew, as he supposedly was in Jerusalem, but he is also a very Babylonian ruler, interested in astronomy, and a very Greek one, favoring friendship and philanthropy. To be the king of the world is to be all things to all sources, East and West. The chief difficulty between the king and his subjects is that he wants them to adopt his religion, and they want him to adopt theirs.

7

A Vacant Throne

JUST AS A flood created the Mediterranean Sea, a collision produced the Zagros Mountains. Fifty million years ago, when the land that would become the Indian subcontinent collided with the rest of Asia, the Iranian plateau moved upward and westward, and pressed against the Tigris and Euphrates. This uplift, the Zagros Range, marked the boundary between low country and high, desert and steppe, and, by Alexander's time, between the Semites of the plains and the Iranians of the mountains and the plateau.

Darius had withdrawn to the Zagros stronghold of Ecbatana, where he gathered a new army of some 40,000 troops, almost all Iranians and Central Asians. This army was smaller than the army he brought to Issus, and much smaller than the one he brought to Arbela, but more coherent. The most important commander, Bessus, had led a wing at Arbela.[1]

Darius knew that the Macedonians would need time to reach him. All roads to Ecbatana were narrow and rough, and the direct road from Susa into the Zagros was worse, for it went through a very narrow pass, the Persian Gates. Near the Persian Gates, at Persepolis, Darius maintained a garrison. Like Ecbatana, Persepolis served as a royal residence in the time of year when the roads were open.

Alexander and his surveyors knew little about this region. They thought of the Zagros not as a barrier between Mesopotamia and Iran but as part of a range they called the Caucasus, which supposedly ran from Anatolia to the Himalayas. They did grasp that they could not march up into the mountains at this time of year, the late fall, and reach Darius before the snow stopped them. They must try to reach him in two steps. The first step would take them through the mountains to winter quarters at Persepolis, the first place big enough to feed them and their animals. Alexander wished to visit nearby Pasargadae, site of a palace built by his rival Cyrus the Great and of Cyrus's tomb. Step two would take them from these places to Ecbatana, in the north. They could make this long march once the snow melted.[2]

Once Alexander caught Darius, he must consider what to do next. He could not become a priest-king in Persia as he had in Egypt. This position did not exist in Persia. Would he simply become king, as he had in tiny Phaselis in Asia Minor?

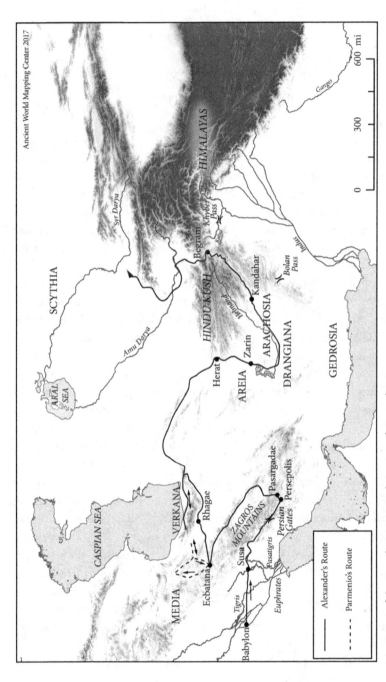

The Route of the Expedition Through Persia and Central Asia, 330–327 BC.
Ancient World Mapping Center.

An anonymous nineteenth-century drawing of the tomb of Cyrus at Pasargadae.
William Smith, *A Smaller History of Greece* (New York: Harper Brothers, 1882), 45.

Would his men be willing to accept him as the king of their enemies? Meanwhile, what of the Persian gods? Alexander had never ignored the gods of any locality, especially before battle. Would he now?

Alexander and the army left Susa in December 331, moving expeditiously before the snow season. Alexander and the strike force would take whatever route they could to seize the Persian Gates and reach Persepolis. Parmenio would take the main body on a long route suitable for carts. These movements resembled the campaign in southeastern Anatolia, where Parmenio and Alexander divided forces the same way.

The campaign began with a surprise. In the mountains north of Susa, on the fringes of Elam, the invaders encountered tribes that had never submitted to the Persians. They had once acknowledged Cyrus, but not later rulers like Darius. They would not acknowledge Alexander, either. When they tried to block the way, Alexander's force had to march day and night to circumvent them. Finding themselves surrounded, they begged Alexander for mercy, but he refused. Then they sent emissaries back to Sisygambis, in Susa. They asked her to intercede with Alexander. She wrote him, he gave way, and the mountaineers became Alexander's subjects.[3]

As the Macedonians trudged upward, the palms gave way to tamarisk and pistachio trees. Boars and gazelles crisscrossed meadows of wild alfalfa and oat grass. The hunting was excellent, the water clear, but this idyll would not last long: ahead, the peaks were covered with snow. Within a few days they reached ridges through which streams hurtled down toward Susa and Mesopotamia. As they climbed, the streams turned into ribands, thousands of feet below at the bottom of one gorge after another. At one spot, a horse or even a man could leap across the gorge.

When Alexander's men reached the Gates, a pass ten yards wide, lichen and snow covered much of the rocky heights. Catching sight of some Persian troops, the Macedonian vanguard rushed forward, and the Persians fled. Then the Persian commander, the satrap Ariyabrzana, gave the signal from an outpost overhead, and a cascade of rocks and arrows struck the attackers. Some officers fell, and their companies scattered. The army tried to turn back, but the rear was still advancing and blocked the way. Once they could turn back, they had to abandon their dead. Ariyabrzana had done what Darius and the satraps of Anatolia could not, and stopped the Macedonians.[4]

Then the Persian commander made the mistake of doing nothing in the hope that a superior position would protect him. Alexander asked Aristander to consult the gods, and when that did not help, he called a war council and dispatched Macedonian reconnaissance teams who used Persian prisoners of war to lead them around the Gates. Picked troops followed. In thirty-six hours they marched twelve rugged miles and caught the enemy by surprise. In the melee, the unarmed Persians grabbed the attackers' weapons or dragged them from their horses. The more numerous companions showed no mercy. Most of the Persians fell to their deaths while fighting or retreating.[5]

Like the mountaineers, the Persians gave way, and the army could now march from the Gates to Persepolis. The few men Ariyabrzana had left at Persepolis surrendered. Only twenty-four days had passed since the Macedonians left Susa. Soon Parmenio arrived, and the reunited army occupied this, the third capital they had seized.

———————

THE SETTLEMENT AT Persepolis was a brown monotone, like the fields below. A two-story sandstone platform supported a dozen buildings mostly amounting to outsized storehouses. The biggest building, another Apadana, resembled the one in Susa but lacked the brilliant blue enamel. Alexander found no place worth worshipping in, and he visited only a few of the famous halls of government. The population was surprisingly small: a few men who had not fled, and more women, luxuriously dressed.

After rounding up the inhabitants, the captors inspected and catalogued tons of royal possessions: food, drink, clothes, crockery, linens, furniture, and mineral samples sent as tokens of obedience (including electrum from Lydia, choice but malodorous Nile water from Egypt, naphtha from Mesopotamia, lapis lazuli from Bactria, and turquoise from Sogdiana). And more and more gold and silver, dwarfing what Susa provided. The inspection teams tallied sums that would be as absurd as billions today. And for what? The Persians minted only a fraction of it. A king like Darius would say that Persepolis showed he was rich in the most important currency, gifts, but the Macedonians thought the most important currency was coin.[6]

Alexander killed the male captives. Perhaps he did not know or care that some of them were Persian priests. He sold the women into slavery, then turned to the bigger problem of disposing of all the loot. Shown a jeweled box of cream scented with palm wine, he emptied the box and put his scrolls of the *Iliad* in it. He ordered Darius's bullion shipped to Babylon to be minted, and other valuables, like furniture, shipped to Susa. The satrap there could store it, or give some to Darius's mother and her children, now sequestered in the Apadana. Twenty thousand mules and 5,000 camels carried it all away.[7]

The council of war met and debated how to dispose of the rest of the property. They decided to burn the timbers, stores, and incidentals, but not try to destroy or remove walls or foundations. The engineers said that would take months, and besides, Alexander wished to use Persepolis as a provincial center. Alexander gave orders to leave the Persian royal tombs untouched. He would not dishonor the dead.[8]

Before departing, he staged a sacrifice to his own gods, and feasted the army. During his stay in Persepolis he had paid no honor to the Persian gods. Persepolis records that survived the fire show that these gods were many.[9]

The army's next stop, Pasargadae, twenty-six miles up the road, gave the Macedonians their first prolonged encounter with the religion of their enemies. To the surprise of the Macedonians, Cyrus's ceremonial center covered only two and one-third square miles and lacked fortifications and defensive walls. It even lacked a garrison. There was no other capital like it, not even Sparta, which lacked walls but not soldiers. Cyrus supposed no one could or would attack Pasargadae. Extensive gardens stretched from end to end. Two palaces nestled among them, and the tomb of Cyrus stood in a grove in one corner.[10]

The Persian governor greeted Alexander and his entourage at the gatehouse, Pasargadae's tallest building. The thirty-foot-high doors swung open, and a four-winged figure wearing an Egyptian crown peered down from a door jamb. What would Pharaoh Alexander make of it? Was it a god or a winged man? From the gatehouse, they walked through a hall flanked by fluted Ionic columns in a checkerboard pattern of black and white stone. They emerged into a series of gardens fed by canals of mountain water and dotted with carved wooden pavilions. The guide informed Alexander that this was the original Persian garden attached to a palace—the model for the gardens in Sardis, Samaria, and elsewhere, the first *paradeisos*, or "paradise."[11]

Where, the Macedonians demanded, was the treasury? Although the guide said there was none, Alexander and the soldiers set about finding it. From the water gardens they approached the columned hall of another palace—Cyrus's model for the Apadana palace at Persepolis and Susa. On one of the doorposts, the Babylonian god of fresh water, rendered as a man wearing the skin of a fish, peered down as if to answer the question of what the other odd figure, the winged Egyptian, was doing in the gatehouse. Cyrus collected gods.

The Macedonians found some silver and gold, but trifling sums compared to what they had already seized elsewhere, and so they decided to try the temples. Yet there were none. The Persians did not conceive of their gods as dwelling in houses, and so Pasargadae and other places had open-air altars where priests maintained perpetual fires and occasionally made offerings. Animals were disemboweled and burnt whole, a kind of sacrifice familiar to the Macedonians.

The invaders found altars of this kind outside the palaces. Nearby stood a low stone tower. As the visitors drew near, the guide confirmed what Alexander's advisers had already told him: all Persian kings were crowned at this spot. The goddess Anahita presided over the brief and simple ceremonies. The new king must take off his purple cloak and tunic and don nomadic clothes supposedly worn by Cyrus. After eating a meal of nomadic fare, and chewing red terebinth leaves that smacked of turpentine, he must climb the stone tower, appear on the parapet, and take the scepter in his right hand and a lotus blossom in his left. His followers would acclaim him and priests would burn animal offerings at the altars.[12]

Alexander and his men visited Cyrus's tomb nearby. A raised platform kept the burial vault out of profane contact with the earth. The entryway was so small that the taller companions had to bend over, although Alexander did not. They passed a cuneiform inscription they could not read but which Onesicritus claimed said, "Here lies Cyrus, king of kings," as though Cyrus were a Mesopotamian ruler.[13]

Cyrus had commissioned a mostly Babylonian burial chamber, evident in the workmanship of the golden sarcophagus and the thick purple robes atop it. He ordered a display of Babylonian tunics to complement his Iranian jackets and trousers, and a table to hold his scimitars. The Great King wished to make a small museum out of his death, but not a shrine. An adjacent building housed Persian priests who made monthly sacrifices of sheep and horses to the Sun.[14]

This eclectic display invited Alexander, already king of Babylon, to imitate the quasi-Babylonian Cyrus and become king of the Persians. Since Alexander considered Darius illegitimate, he had good reason to be crowned king. After taking a crown from the Phaselitans, he had accepted a kingdom a year, at Arwad, in Egypt, and at Babylon. At Arwad he replaced a local king, and in Egypt he replaced Darius. Sometimes he underwent a ceremony, and sometimes he took the throne without one.

Rather than become king of the Persians, Alexander ordered the priests there to maintain it and fulfill their duties, and then he quit Pasargadae, with only a little silver and gold to show for his visit.[15]

Why did he make these decisions? Perhaps because he had conquered only part of Cyrus's empire. Besides, no Persians other than the guide and a few priests would see the ceremony. In Phaselis the people had been watching, and in Egypt the clergy had been watching in the City of the Sun, Memphis, and Thebes. A religious reason may have occurred to him also. If he became king of Persia while Darius was still alive, the Persians might think him impious. For them, Darius was legitimate. Pasargadae helped Alexander understand this point of view. Perhaps he thought that Darius, who was illegitimate elsewhere, remained a true king in Persia. Until Darius abdicated or died, Alexander must continue to pursue him.[16]

With this prospect before him, Alexander prepared the army to march north, via Persepolis, toward Ecbatana. Alexander had begun to grasp the size and complexity of Iran, and he marched with renewed urgency. Antipater sent more reinforcements, but only Greek mercenaries. Alexander's companions would continue to age and their zeal would flag, yet his zeal would increase. It was now early spring 330, four eventful years since they landed at Abydos.[17]

ALTHOUGH ALEXANDER MAY have decided that Darius was a true king, Darius's commanders came to the opposite decision. The Great King had lost half the empire and all the Persian capitals other than Ecbatana.

These commanders, led by Bessus, did not act against their king forthwith. Instead they lent themselves to a new strategy of Darius's. After meeting with his advisers, Darius decided to withdraw from Ecbatana, which he could not hold against the Macedonian siege train. He planned to lay waste to the country as he fled to the east. His own people would suffer, but the Macedonians would run out of food and water. If they tried to make long marches between wells and springs, the Persian cavalry could surround and shoot them. The king still had 3,000 good horsemen, plus Greek mercenaries. Memnon had proposed this strategy four years before, in the Anatolian campaign against the Macedonians. Darius would now follow it in Iran.[18]

The Persian king divided his forces, sending some troops and the baggage train eastward. Eventually he and a light force led by Bessus would join them. Until then, he would harass the invaders.

Bessus and his co-conspirators planned to take Darius prisoner and try to negotiate with Alexander. If Alexander ceased his pursuit, they would surrender

Darius to the Macedonians. Otherwise, they would kill Darius. Either way, Bessus would replace him. Since Alexander held Pasargadae, Bessus could not be crowned, but his present position as satrap of Bactria made him heir apparent according to Persian custom, so he could rally support. Bessus would claim the crown that Alexander had refused.[19]

While Darius planned and Bessus conspired, Alexander and the Macedonians waited for the snow and ice to melt. In spite of harsh weather, Alexander and his light force moved ahead to procure food and fodder for the 500-mile trip to Ecbatana. At one point the horses could not carry the men through the snow and the storms, and Alexander dismounted and walked. Then the officers around him did, without being told. After them all the other officers in the column did. Finally everyone did. They got through. By late spring, Alexander had prepared the needed storehouses of supplies. The grain was milk-ripe and the army could move.[20]

Alexander hurried his men along but kept them and the horses well fed, and turned what should have been a march of several months into one of weeks. Only seven days after Darius left Ecbatana, Alexander and the companion cavalry reached the city. The tiny Persian garrison surrendered. As at Pasargadae, the Macedonians spared the Persian shrines, including a temple containing a famous statue of Apollo that had once stood in a shrine near Miletus. They also spared the rest of Ecbatana, except for seizing the ample gold and silver in the royal palace. Perhaps the landscape and the weather softened their attitude. Ecbatana lay in a valley of gardens, orchards, and forests reminiscent of northern Greece. Alexander could have some apples. Those he had eaten in Babylon had come from this and similar regions in Persia. The men got a donative. None of the companions made a record of what the gods got. Surely the gods' emolument was ample.[21]

Alexander would have liked nothing better than to revictual and press on after Darius. To his dismay, he found he could not. Many of his soldiers were unwilling. None wished to kill him, as Bessus wished to kill Darius, but many had tired of fighting. Under the impact of years of war, both Alexander and Darius were losing control of their men.

Although casualties had been few, the difficult terrain in Persia had discouraged the army, and the mountains of western Iran promised more of the same. If the army went east, as Alexander wished, they would be entering territory of which they had no conception. Persian gods were mere names to them. Indeed, some of these gods were not even that. Some, like Anahita, were known by epithets. This one meant "pure"; no Greek or Macedonian knew the goddess's name.

Alexander's Greeks, including the valuable Thessalian cavalry, wanted to go home. In their view, he had nothing left for them to do. He had already fulfilled the Greeks' goals of punishing Persia for invading Greece and of liberating Greek

Asia Minor. Now he should release his Greek troops. He had always offered high wages and ample plunder, but beyond Ecbatana there would be few cities worth plundering. Where would he get gold and silver to pay his men?

Alexander's Macedonians found him erratic. He prayed and sacrificed well, but recently he had distributed less largesse. He had not appointed a Macedonian as provincial governor since leaving Syria, three years before. East of Ecbatana, there would be few provinces worth governing. These troops wished to halt at Ecbatana and declare victory.

For his part, Alexander may have felt some of his troops were becoming useless. Heavy infantry were too slow to battle mountaineers, and cavalry were more useful in pursuit than in attack. He needed mounted light infantry, plus more light cavalry, and fewer foot soldiers. He also needed more engineers. Sooner or later the Macedonians would have to besiege mountain strongholds like those they had seen in the Zagros.

Only days after arriving in Ecbatana, Alexander summoned his generals to the Persian palace and adjacent paradise. There he announced several decisions that the war council would not presume to debate.[22]

To accommodate his homesick Greeks, Alexander dismissed them all with full pay, plus a substantial donative. When these well-paid veterans returned to their hometowns, Alexander earned a better reputation than he had ever had before. Some commonplace religious gestures showed how opinions changed. Some Boeotian veterans—from a town that had sided with Macedon against Thebes—returned to their home in Thespiae and dedicated some of their earnings to Zeus, in the form of a tripod. On it they wrote their names, and also these words:

> *The people of wide-wayed Thespiae sent these hoplites*
> *To barbarous Asia to avenge their ancestors. With Alexander,*
> *They captured the towns of the Persians.*
> *They have erected this handsome tripod to Zeus.*

To these Boeotians, Alexander was not the son of Zeus-Amon or even King Alexander. He was simply "Alexander," just as his father had often been simply "Philip."[23]

To convince Greeks and Thessalians to stay, Alexander announced that any individuals who wished to continue to fight could remain with him at higher pay than before. Many thousands accepted this offer. They became mercenaries, as opposed to the allies they had been before. Some of the Phoenician sutlers stayed with the army, too, but fewer than those who had accompanied the Macedonians through the Near East.

To placate the Macedonians, Alexander assigned 6,000 of them to guard the treasures at Ecbatana. This detachment included a large part of the heavy infantry and some of his best Balkan troops. In all, he gave up one-third of his best men. Most had served under Parmenio in the three big battles, or marched under him in the main body whenever Alexander rode ahead.

Parmenio was Alexander's next target. Rather than have him help pursue Darius, Alexander assigned him command of the troops in Ecbatana. Alexander was putting the old man behind him, as he had put Antipater behind him in Europe. He also was separating Parmenio from two of his sons, Philotas, in command of the cavalry, and Nicanor, in command of the shield bearers. Both would accompany Alexander. Alexander was creating a new, young circle of companions to replace the old circle created by Philip. By centering on Alexander as an individual, not on Alexander as priest of the cult, this new circle departed from one of Philip's ideals.

The army broke in two: the field force and the growing force of garrison troops, now many thousands, if not as large as the number he had brought to Asia. Alexander would need fewer meetings of his war council and more task forces, less solidarity and more loyalty.

Did Alexander anticipate the costs? He had divided the old from the young, the infantry from the cavalry, Parmenio from his two sons—companion from companion. His remaining men were entering a country where sacrificial animals would be hard to find. If the men got celebratory bonuses, they would have little chance to spend them. Few merchants other than the traveling Phoenicians would accept any coined money. Greek-speakers would be few, and Greek shrines would be nil.

With the approval of the council, Alexander left Ecbatana in pursuit of Darius, who was riding somewhere to the east, between Ecbatana and the Caspian Gates, a distance of some 250 miles. Alexander split his task force. He left most of the men behind, with orders to follow up, and rode ahead with some companion cavalry, a part of the phalanx, and light troops. He drove the foot soldiers until they dropped out and the horses died in the heat. In a dozen days he reached Rhagae, a caravan station of Jews and Zoroastrians (and now a suburb of Teheran) fifty miles from the Gates. Darius had already reached the Gates. He could now be heading in one of two directions, north to the Caucasus or east into Iran. To the south lay a sparsely inhabited desert.[24] Whatever route Darius chose, he did not dare slow down and lay waste to the country.

Alexander rested his men, and reached the Gates a week later. Here two Persian defectors appeared with news that Bessus and other satraps had arrested Darius. Unless Alexander overtook them, the satraps and not Alexander would decide Darius's fate.[25]

Alexander quickened the chase, leading picked cavalry carrying two days' rations. He drove them for twenty-four hours, let them water their mounts, and drove them again, through the night, until they reached the place where the defectors had last seen Darius. Bessus had fled, taking Darius with him.[26]

One of the men Bessus had left behind, Darius's ailing Greek interpreter, informed Alexander that Bessus would surrender Darius in exchange for silver and free passage to Bactria, his own province. Alexander spurned this offer and pressed on, riding through a desert all night and into the next day. His men drew water from wells fed by runoff from distant mountains via underground pipes. Then Alexander learned of a shortcut without any wells, and he took that. To combine speed and power, he dismounted the cavalry and put 500 of the best infantry on horseback. He left the other men to Nicanor, who took a road with water. During an all-night ride of some forty-five miles, most of the men dropped out.[27]

Only about sixty overtook Darius and Bessus. Amazed that Alexander had caught up with them, the more numerous enemy fled. Bessus and the other satraps, who did not want Darius left alive to make a deal with Alexander, had just enough time to stab him. Alexander arrived a few minutes later. He found Darius dead in a driverless wagon. The oxen pulling the wagon had led it down into a dale in search of water. Alexander took off his purple cloak and covered the body. He had not been willing to remove his cloak in order to become king at Pasargadae. That would have meant dressing like a nomad. He would remove it to honor a fallen enemy.

Some companions later claimed that Alexander wept beside the corpse. He might well have wept from a sense of frustration and loss. For three years he had stalked Darius across Asia at the price of several thousand Macedonian lives. Now he had finally caught him at the price of several hundred more, but it was too late. Alexander buried his dead soldiers somewhere in the wastelands east of Ecbatana.[28]

In spite of these losses, the companions shared some of Alexander's sympathy for Darius. They later spread stories that Darius had uncovered the conspiracy against him, yet had forgiven the conspirators after they begged him for mercy. Then these suppliants betrayed him, a hideous offense.[29]

Alexander cursed Bessus's treachery and swore to bring him to justice. Then he gave orders to bury Darius in the Persian manner, in the royal tombs at Persepolis. He did not attend himself, or order any acts of mourning. He enrolled Darius's Greek mercenaries in his own army and gave his soldiers most of the gold and silver taken from the Persian baggage train. Corrupt officers got the rest. They would have money enough to pay the Phoenician sutlers, who provided some of what the deserts and mountains would not supply. One companion used camels to bring Egyptian sand for his gymnastic exercises. Actors, ballplayers, clowns, and concubines remained with the entourage, as well as intellectuals such as Callisthenes and the painter Philoxenus, who sketched during battles. Slaves read to their masters, concubines submitted: court life went on.[30]

———————

THE MACEDONIANS COULD expect their new quarry, Bessus, to retreat to his own province, Bactria, well to the east. Bessus could recruit more troops there, including Scythians, and as heir apparent could claim the throne.[31] Alexander wished to eliminate him.

Alexander surely found Bessus a less attractive foe than Darius. Darius had more men, more territory, and much more right to be king of Persia. Alexander had protected Darius's family and called Sisygambis his mother. He despised Bessus.

In spite of long distances and rugged terrain, he might have accomplished his task in some months. Instead it would take a year and involve a 1,000-mile detour through the deserts of the Iranian plateau and the heights of the Hindu Kush. The delays began with a decision to head north, toward the wooded valleys of Verkana, beside the Caspian Sea. Because the Persians still controlled this region, Alexander and the generals wished to seize it in order to protect lines of communication. They also wished to give the men some less arduous duty. The abundant water and Mediterranean climate of Verkana would persuade unwilling soldiers to keep fighting by letting them campaign in a place like home.[32]

The Macedonians invaded Verkana from several directions. Alexander directed the main body, while Craterus led a second force that marched in parallel and attacked mountaineers. Erigyius, a Greek companion with long experience, led the baggage train by a nearby lower road. Although Parmenio had stayed at Ecbatana, a hundred miles to the east, he would lead 10,000 from there into Verkana.[33]

The invaders met little resistance, but Alexander treated the enemy more harshly than he had earlier. While Craterus accepted surrenders, Alexander killed many men of one tribe while they fled. In a valley known for a long underground river, Alexander decided to measure the river's length by throwing in two local men at the spot where it disappeared. He sent scouts downstream to watch the place where it reemerged. When the two men bobbed up, drowned, Alexander's surveyors concluded that this was indeed the longest known underwater river.[34]

Within a month or so of summer campaigning, the Macedonians had captured the chief towns, including the capital. There they encountered Barsine's father, Ashavazdan. This former exile in Macedon had long served Darius as an adviser. Now he wished to serve Alexander, who welcomed him for several reasons. The simplest was that, like Mazdai, he knew the Greeks and Macedonians well. He spoke some Greek and used the Hellenized name Artabazus. Connections like this gave Alexander hope that he could find Persians of broad experience to help him rule Central Asia. Rather than enslave some tribesmen, Alexander released them. He did punish one tribe that was clever enough to steal Bucephalas in a raid. These raiders promptly returned the horse, with many propitiatory gifts, but Alexander took their leaders hostage.[35]

To celebrate the new successes, Alexander performed a sacrifice of the customary Macedonian kind. That pleased the army, but he did not please the companions when he split Caspian administration among a Persian who fought at Arbela, another Persian who had joined the entourage in Egypt, and a companion. Alexander further angered the companions by giving a neighboring region to the satrap who surrendered it.[36]

Parmenio, who had done much of the work for this campaign, returned to Ecbatana. In spite of the summer heat, Alexander marched the other way, into the desert, pursuing Bessus. The fugitive had reached Bactria, where his supporters proclaimed him king under the royal name of Artaxshasa. Persian priests gave the new king their blessing. Rumors surely reached them about Alexander's killing priests at Persepolis.

To reach the next big settlement, at Herat, Alexander had to lead the army 500 barren miles. The heat banged down on them. Afraid of moving slowly and running out of water, Alexander burned the baggage train. When Nicanor fell sick and died during the march, Alexander did not dare stop to bury him. Instead Alexander left behind Nicanor's brother Philotas and gave him the thousands of men needed for a parade, a sacrifice, and funeral games. Parmenio had now lost two sons, and Alexander had lost his first top commander. Philotas received the ambiguous honor of conducting a great funeral in the middle of the desert.[37]

As the army pressed on, one of the satraps in the region, Shatibrzana, rode up from Herat and surrendered. Shatibrzana offered to furnish supplies, and Alexander confirmed him as satrap. He sent him back to Herat escorted by forty mounted infantry under the command of the companion Anaxippus. The king thought these forty would suffice to remind the satrap of Macedonian power.

Within weeks, however, came news that Shatibrzana had killed Anaxippus along with his men and was mounting a rebellion. For the first time, a satrap had betrayed Alexander's trust, and Persians had annihilated a Macedonian unit.

Alexander moved fast, with his usual mix of cavalry and a few infantry, and reached Herat after a forced march of seventy-five miles in two days. Shatibrzana had already escaped eastward into the foothills of Hindu Kush, so Alexander had to content himself with enslaving some would-be suppliants.[38]

At the rear, Craterus, leading the main body, encountered a mass of rebels who had taken refuge on a butte. The western side, where Craterus camped, rose 2,000 feet above the plain, far beyond the reach of any tower or drawbridge. Atop the massif, a spring and a grassy meadow four miles in circumference provided the defenders the essentials for a long siege. Some 13,000 men defended the perimeter.[39]

Craterus's troops attempted to scale the 2,000-foot cliffs, but high winds blew men off the precipices. Next the engineers built a ramp of felled trees, but it did not reach the tableland and collapsed when they tried to extend it.

Alexander had to turn around and help Craterus. After he arrived at the butte, he and his men accomplished nothing against the rocks, the foe, and the vertiginous winds.

Only an accident rescued the Macedonians. The ramp caught fire, and the wind carried the flames onto the tableland. Nearly all the rebels burned to death. The first siege east of the Zagros Range ended not with a victorious assault but with a natural disaster. Zeus the sky god was as fickle as ever.

The army regrouped and marched to their original destination, Herat. At the sight of the Macedonian siege engines, especially a drill invented by Diades, the defenders supplicated.[40] Once in possession of the city, Alexander convened the most important strategy meeting since the discussion of Darius's peace offers. Alexander presented two choices to the council.

First, they might resume their march on the man Alexander still called Bessus, but who was now King Artaxshasa. If they used the main road eastward, they would be well supplied, but Artaxshasa would know they were coming. He might attack their flanks, using the cavalry of Scythian allies.

Second, they might turn away from Artaxshasa and campaign in the swath of Persian territory to the south. They would find what water and food they could, and kill or run off all who would not surrender. The landscape was traversable, the people vulnerable. A large part of this region, the watershed of the Helmand River, was broad and fertile, thanks to irrigation; the crops were in. After living off the Helmand, they would turn around, go northeast, and approach Artaxshasa that way, rather than use the main road. That would surprise him. If he fought, he would likely lose. If he did not fight, they could force him into the wastelands to the north. They would control most of the Persian Empire, and he would control only the men who followed him.[41]

Alexander and the council preferred the second choice, which meant a detour of many months. They did not realize that the route from the Helmand country to Bactria lay through the Hindu Kush, some of the highest mountains in the world. For an ancient army, which thought of mountains as the abodes of gods or titans, this line of march would be a religious as well as topographic challenge.

———

IN THE FALL of 330, the Macedonians entered the Helmand valley. The Helmand did not turn out to be a river as they understood it. Partly dry, the riverbed was not firm enough to march in, and it was too wide for engineers to bridge. Wells along the unpaved road were far apart, and the water in the irrigation canals proved undrinkable. Even now, in October, the hot sun could fry an egg on a rock. On three sides, a wavy surface of brushwood spread across a sea of reddish sand. On the fourth side, foothills faded into the northeast.

The army reached the Persian citadel of Zarin just as food was running low. The satrap there had sided with Artaxshasa and fled to India. The mud-brick buildings suggested a very provincial Babylon, and some of the bricks even bore cuneiform stamps. Yet if a Babylonian king ever came this way, it was hard to see why. The shrine of the Persian gods Ahura Mazda, Anahita, and the sun god Mithra was a trifling affair, three stone altars seven feet high in a small roofless court without a sanctuary, and Alexander ignored it. Bored, he ordered books from Harpalus.[42]

South of Zarin, the river gave way to a network of lakes that watered orchards and fields. The harvest was in, but one lake gave the men fever, and the army had to rely on water skins carried on donkey or camelback. Only the hunting was good: fish, wild fowl, and wild asses by the hundreds galloping into the undrinkable water to cool off. The natives, besides not knowing how to read, write, or build houses, did not know how to eat and drink: no bread or wine, or even Near Eastern beer. Though the days were sometimes still warm, the nights turned gelid. The soldiers called the one friendly tribe the Euergetae, or "Doers of Good Deeds." They had reportedly helped Cyrus the Great, too. Alexander granted them autonomy at a price in food and animals.[43]

The surveyors could not tell Macedonians much about where they were. To the south, reddish cliffs made of sand and silt guarded a thousand miles of desert. Out of it rode raiders on dromedaries from the neighboring province of Gedrosia. Gedrosia, the surveyors said, faced the ocean that encircled the world. India, where the satrap went, faced the ocean, too, and lay at the world's edge. Rumors about the size of the mountains to the north, the Hindu Kush, now reached the troops. Artaxshasa—the man they called Bessus—was on the far side. How would they reach him?

The Persians who were now part of Alexander's entourage also worried the troops. The Macedonians especially disliked Alexander's new favorite, the eunuch Bagoas. The king even took Persian advice about clothes. He did not put on trousers or give up his Macedonian hat, but he wore a Persian tunic, belt, and diadem. The companions thought the belt effeminate and wondered why Alexander would not let them wear diadems, the headbands favored by Persian notables. The final insult was Alexander's decision to put Darius's brother, the cavalry commander Huxshathra, in charge of a new force of 1,000 Persian cavalry. Alexander also made Huxshathra a companion. That was worse than an insult.[44]

When Macedonians voiced these complaints, Alexander answered that he was not the Persians' king. Although he had captured Darius's regalia at Issus, and again at Arbela, he did not use it. He never wore the upright tiara, or Persian crown, and did not ask to be called a Persian king. He did not speak Persian or worship their gods, and so he needed Persian intermediaries. He judged Persians according to their merits. Mazdai received good treatment, and the commander at Gaza received the worst treatment Alexander could inflict. Darius was hunted down, but he was duly buried, the minimum due to an honorable enemy. As for Persian cavalry, he needed them to replace the much-missed Thessalians.[45]

Soon afterward discontent among the soldiers intersected with court gossip and with Alexander's resentment of Parmenio and Philotas. The army was camping at Farah, another scraggly Helmand valley stronghold. Philotas had long since rejoined them. Now that Parmenio had gone, Philotas was the leading companion, seeing Alexander twice a day. Men such as Craterus had more seniority but less access. Philotas did not know that Alexander was spying on him through the concubine Antigone.

As one of his lesser duties, Philotas kept watch over the dozens of royal pages. In previous reigns, pages were privy to most plots against Macedonian kings. When talk of a plot began in late 330, Philotas inevitably learned of it. After a meeting of the council, Philotas was the last to leave, and a page who was waiting at the entrance to the council chamber spoke to him. He repeated a rumor of a plot against Alexander. He had heard the rumor, he said, from his brother, another page. The ringleaders were rumored to be a bodyguard plus a few commanders, none highly placed.[46]

The rumors were especially doubtful because no one knew who was supposed to replace Alexander. There were only two possibilities. One was Alexander's incompetent half-brother, but no officer would participate in a plot to replace Alexander with this nonentity. The other was Antipater's son-in-law, the prince of Lyncestes, who was also named Alexander.

The Lyncestian had lost his command back in Asia Minor. The councilors thought he was in touch with Darius at the time, put him on trial, and wanted to execute him. The voluble Aristander agreed., for not long after the council meeting a swallow had landed on Alexander's head while he was napping, and that was a sign that they should kill the Lyncestian.[47] Alexander had preferred to put Antipater's son-in-law under house arrest, and he had remained under arrest for the next four years. He had no recent military record, and his years under arrest had made him timid and simpleminded.[48] A plot against Alexander was unfeasible, and Philotas, for one, knew it. He chose not to report the page's accusations.

Frustrated, the page went to the king through other parties. Alexander investigated, and learned that Philotas had kept the information from him.

Alexander now confronted three possibly guilty parties: the conspirators, the pages who knew about them, and Philotas. Had he feared the conspirators, he would have dealt with them first. He ignored them, and he did not punish the pages, who begged for mercy. Instead he concentrated on Philotas. The man who ridiculed his investiture as pharaoh had failed to protect him. It did not matter to Alexander that Philotas was innocent of any involvement in the conspiracy. Philotas was guilty of lèse-majesté, a very contagious offense.

In an army with any kind of military law, Alexander would have had to make some charge against Philotas and bring it before a tribunal. In a court like that of Darius, the monarch would decide. Alexander could not do either. Instead he had to engineer a consensus against Philotas among the council of officers. To convince them, Alexander would employ Craterus, who hated Philotas and perhaps envied Parmenio. If Philotas was sentenced to death, an assembly of soldiers must agree to carry out the sentence. To influence the assembly, Alexander would employ trusted officers.

Alexander interviewed Philotas privately, and Philotas confirmed the details: two royal pages, braggadocio, no feasible plans. Philotas begged for mercy, and the king gave a pledge of future favor. Next, Alexander convened a council of just six, including Craterus but not Philotas. The king suppressed the supplication and the pledge, and Craterus warned that a pardon for Philotas would not assuage Parmenio. Although Parmenio was 500 miles away, many soldiers remained loyal to him. The unity of the army, Craterus implied, required that Philotas and Parmenio both die. That same day, the king invited Philotas to dinner and told him nothing.[49]

Next he convened an assembly of the Macedonian soldiers. Six thousand attended, mostly from regiments Alexander thought reliable. Keeping Philotas out of sight, he recounted the plot, accused Philotas of leading it, and added that Parmenio had masterminded it. Next he paraded witnesses before the assembly. Several admitted their own guilt, but no one accused Philotas, let alone Parmenio. Alexander produced a letter from Parmenio to Philotas, but it was not incriminating. In his peroration, he added an accusation of impiety. Philotas, he said, ridiculed his claim to be the son of Zeus-Amon.

Alexander now presented Philotas, hands tied behind his back and head covered. Generals rose at the front of the assembly to denounce him, especially Craterus and Coenus, who had married Philotas's sister. The king ordered Philotas's head uncovered, and asked him to speak in Macedonian, even though he and the generals had spoken in Greek. After this appeal to the prejudices of the troops, Alexander left the rostrum. He wanted the officers to carry on the attack without him. They did, but Craterus, Coenus, and the others were less effective than another, lower-ranking infantry officer, Bolon. This senior veteran of Philip's wars spoke against Philotas and Parmenio, too. Either Alexander or Craterus had coached him.[50]

At last allowed to speak, Philotas rebutted the attacks, conceding only that he had failed to report some idle talk. The troops pitied him and refused to execute him. After begging Alexander for mercy and being betrayed, Philotas was successfully begging the troops for help. The Zeus of suppliants seemed to support Philotas.

Switching tactics, Alexander remanded Philotas to the council of generals and left the initiative to them. Craterus persuaded them to torture Philotas, yet Philotas failed to confess to any crime worse than indiscretion. Now the king had failed twice. Yet he was gaining. Each time the army drew nearer to a consensus against the accused.[51]

Alexander brought Philotas before a second assembly and asked them to stone Philotas. This manner of punishment would show that the Macedonians regarded Philotas as hateful to the gods rather than merely guilty of a crime. At last, the cascade of lying and bullying succeeded. As the leading officers watched, a few angry soldiers began to stone Philotas. Others joined them, and stoned him to death.[52]

Alexander knew that news of the execution of Philotas would reach Parmenio in several weeks. Within six weeks or so, it would reach Harpalus, Antigonus, Cleomenes, and Antipater. At the very least, these men could stop the flow of money and troops to Alexander. More likely they would make war on Alexander. Whatever they did, Parmenio would have to organize and lead them. He would know first, he commanded the most men, and he had the strongest motive.

Grasping this, Alexander summoned Polydamas, a senior officer Parmenio would trust since he had carried the message from Parmenio to Alexander at Arbela. The king gave him a letter to hand-deliver to Parmenio and another letter to read to Parmenio's men, and put him and two nomads on camels, with orders to ride day and night to Ecbatana. Not quite two weeks later, Polydamas reached the city and brought the letter to Parmenio. It brought good news about the army's progress and the exploits of Philotas. As Parmenio read parts of the letter aloud, so that his subordinates could hear the news, too, Polydamas and the nomads stabbed Parmenio to death. Polydamas unrolled the other letter Alexander had given him and read it aloud. It proclaimed that Parmenio and Philotas had conspired against the king, and that the council of war approved their deaths.[53]

After some hubbub, Parmenio's subordinates accepted this explanation. The letters were evidently genuine. They did not know that the letters were untruthful.

To prevent a coup that had never been planned, Alexander had carried out a countercoup. Then he was perspicacious enough to stop. He made no attempt to purge Parmenio's associates such as Coenus and Polyperchon. Some leaders have purged their corps of officers—Stalin did—but Alexander avoided handicapping an army in the middle of a hostile continent. Alexander allowed some of Philotas's alleged co-conspirators to be acquitted. He did arrange for the soldiers to put Prince Alexander of Lyncestis to death.[54]

Although sparing his fellow officers, Alexander damaged another of his assets, the cult of companionship. Parmenio symbolized this cult, which Philip had formalized about thirty years before. Philotas led the second generation of companions. Philip would not have killed these men. Alexander killed them partly because Philotas had denigrated the new, unwelcome cult of Alexander as the son of Zeus-Amon.[55]

Until this point, Alexander's religious policy in the Near East had never conflicted with his role as priest of the cult that helped make the Macedonian army strong. Now a conflict had arisen, and Alexander had chosen the cult proclaimed at Siwah over the cult organized by his own father. Cyrus the Great may have astutely combined cults, but Alexander could not.

The last word belonged to Antipater. When he learned of Parmenio's death, he asked, "If Parmenio plotted against Alexander, who can be trusted? If he did not, what should we do?" The answers to these questions would not come immediately. Instead they would emerge years later, in even more remote parts of Asia.[56]

———◦———

ALEXANDER DISPERSED THE powers wielded by Philotas and Parmenio. He gave half the companion cavalry to the administrator Hephaestion and the other half to Clitus, the cavalry veteran who had saved him at the Granicus. He promoted those in Ecbatana who had assented to the assassination, he immediately segregated Macedonians of doubtful loyalty in a brigade assigned to hazardous or humiliating duty, and he gradually dispersed the Balkan troops who served under Parmenio in all the great battles.[57]

No sooner did the army leave the Helmand country to turn north, toward the Hindu Kush, than the Iranians struck again. Shatibrzana rebelled a second time, threatening the line of communication to Ecbatana and the rest of the empire. Alexander dispatched companion cavalry under Erigyius, the column commander in the Caucasus. Erigyius acted much as Alexander might have. Instead of using the army's route along the Helmand, which was a half circle, he cut across the middle, along the granite outcroppings of the Hindu Kush. Winter storms descending from the mountains tore up trees by the roots and brought blocks of rock down the hillsides. The temperature dropped forty degrees in minutes. Sometimes the men could take shelter in a cave, but seldom in a tent and never a house. Fresh water was rare, and foodstuffs rarer. Erigyius should have lost many of his men. He had Alexander's good luck, and so he lost only a few.[58]

After weeks in the saddle, Erigyius and his detachment fell upon the larger force of Shatibrzana. In the ensuing melee, Erigyius speared Shatibrzana in the face, killing him, and the enemy fled. The Macedonians had beaten the Iranians at their own kind of fighting, but the credit went to Erigyius and his bravos, not Alexander or the main body. In another, smaller battle against the rebels, Parthians fought on the Macedonian side. For the first time, Alexander employed Asiatics in land warfare.

As these troops fought, the army had marched upriver toward the next Persian satrapal capital, at modern Kandahar. The Helmand stretched 250 yards across, with snow wreaths melting on the banks. Cliffs guarded the southern side. The satrap fled toward the Bolan Pass and India, and Alexander did not bother to appoint another. The army ate well, for it was now late spring, and the wheat and barley in the upper Helmand valley were milk-ripe, but as they went farther upriver, the air became colder and the snow did not melt. The riverbanks turned into massive rocks, and the stream ran so fast it was hard to scoop up, or even put a foot in. Then the stream gave out, and so did all the trees, save for solitary junipers, and the road ended. Pinnacles of rock guarded the steeply rising path. The army marched for weeks, yet they were too late. The mountain passes visible in the distance had filled with snow.

The army now camped in tiny villages of brick huts, where the people burned dung to keep warm. The soldiers suffered from frostbite and food stocks dwindled. There were no birds, no beasts of prey, no temples, and thus no gods. Move, Alexander ordered them, or starve. And they did move, over the snowy mountains down into the Kabul River valley, a long drop that led them into settled country with wells, and barns full of fodder and food. The army did not so much stop as collapse for several months.

They did not know where they were. Alexander called the chief town in the valley, now Begram, "Alexandria in the Caucasus." Even after a year in Iran, the surveyors clung to the notion that the Caucasus Mountains ran west to east for thousands of miles.

Partly because the army had more camp followers than before, supplies eventually diminished. First olive oil ran out, and the men used sesame sap. The price of the sap skyrocketed, as did the price for any remaining wine. The grain gave out, and they began killing and eating their horses (but not the more valuable mules). And then, in May 329, after months of waiting, the snow diminished enough for the army to march. Alexander learned of several passes, but Artaxshasa had blocked the better ones. Alexander chose a pass more than a mile higher than Begram. Infantry and mules could travel two abreast, but not porters carrying goods on long poles. Horses could not walk abreast, either, for there was no room for a man to stand beside them and hold the reins. For men and animals alike, the snow was sometimes shoulder deep. Resting against the rocks was dangerous, for the men might be stuck to them by their own frozen sweat. As food and fuel ran out, they butchered and ate more of the animals, and drove away some of the slaves. The cavalrymen dismounted and tugged at their horses, and the infantrymen toted all their own gear. They ignored the plight of the camp followers bringing up the rear. As the climb became steeper, the soldiers slung the walking wounded over the backs of mules. In two weeks, they covered only forty-five miles.[59]

From his position in front, Alexander could not see what became of those at the rear. He saw the snow, rocks, and sky ahead of him. When the blue air claimed the whole prospect, he could look down and descry the flatlands and hills of Bactria, and a tangle of rivers flowing northward, away from him, into the unknown.

At the rear of the column, four days behind, the last Macedonian slogged in the mud and dung left by tens of thousands of men and animals. The vanguard sheltered him from the cold, but he saw only the trail in front of him. When he began to descend, he glimpsed the prospect of food, wine, and sacrificial meals stretching out across miles of towns, fields, and valleys. Days later, he and his comrades discovered that Artaxshasa had destroyed everything, especially the wells and vineyards. The men hauled the wounded off the backs of the mules and ate the animals. They had entered the homeland of the Iranians, where Cyrus died and Zoroaster was born.

Alexander had brought an army through the Hindu Kush, the "Killer of Hindus." He knew the legend that his ancestor Heracles led an army into India, so perhaps Heracles came this way. In Euripides, Dionysus led an army, or at least a band of revelers, to India. These were gods and heroes. No human had accomplished this feat, not even Cyrus the Great. The son of Philip was the first.

Apparently, no local gods helped him. He had failed to make contact with them, just as he had failed to make contact with the Iranian gods at Persepolis, Pasargadae, and Ecbatana, or with the dying Darius. If he thought the Titan Prometheus was chained to a mountain somewhere in the Hindu Kush (and he might have, since Prometheus was chained to the Caucasus), he overlooked this Titan as well. Although he must have prayed to Zeus on high, he had run the risk of displeasing the chief god by the mistreatment of Philotas, a suppliant and a companion. Murder also offended Zeus, even or especially if the victim was an old man, like Parmenio.

The Macedonians had now traveled as far from home as if they had gone to Newfoundland, in Canada, in a new world.

FIRDAUSI CONTINUED HIS story of Alexander and Dara (his name for Darius) down to the Persian king's death. In this version of events, the

Macedonians, or Rumis, made peace with the Persians, Alexander and the dying Dara were reconciled, and Alexander became king of Persia:

The armies engaged, and they fought seven days without striking a decisive blow. On the eighth day, Sikander compelled Dara to flee, and the Rumis pursued the Persians to the banks of the Euphrates. Afterward, Dara collected his scattered forces, and tried his fortune again, but Sikander defeated him a second time. Following this success, the Sikander devoted himself to winning the affections of the Persian people, telling them: "Persia is my inheritance: I am no stranger to you, for I am myself descended from Darab. I wish only to pass through your country and go on to other conquests."

Disaffection now spread in Dara's army. A few troops, still faithful to their unfortunate king, offered to fight once more, and Dara was too grateful and too brave to discourage them. A sliver of an army went into action, and afterward Dara was again a fugitive, escaping with 300 men into the desert. Sikander captured his wife and family, but restored them to Dara. The Persian king now asked Sikander for a place of refuge somewhere in his own dominions. In return, Dara promised Sikander all the buried treasure of his ancestors. Sikander declined the offer, and said Dara should come and visit him. Although advised by his nobles to accept the invitation, Dara refused.

Two of Dara's ministers, named Jamusipar and Mahiyar, learned from astrologers that their king would soon fall into the hands of Sikander. In order to gain Sikander's favor, they decided to put Dara to death themselves. One night as the king was traveling in his wagon, and his guards were dispersed, Jamusipar rode up and plunged his dagger into Dara's side, and Mahiyar struck another blow, which felled the king. The two immediately sent word to Sikander, who hastened to the spot. Dismounting, he sorrowfully placed the head of Dara on his lap.

Dara was still breathing. When he lifted up his eyes and saw Sikander, he groaned, and Sikander said, "We shall take you to safety, and tend to your wounds."

"It is too late for remedies," Dara answered. "I leave thee to Heaven. May thy reign be peaceful."

"Never did I wish to see this sight," Sikander said. "If God will spare your life, you shall be king again." He added, "On my mother's word, you and I are sons of the same father." The tears rolled down his face and fell on the face of Dara. "I shall punish your murderers to the utmost," a promise Sikander soon kept.

Dara blessed him, and said, "I die with my mind at rest. Do not weep. Preserve the honor of my family. Marry my daughter, Roshung. If God gives you a son, call him Isfendiyar" [which means "teacher of truth"] "and let him propagate the Avesta of Zoroaster. Let him hold the festivals I love, and tend the holy fire at the altars, and never cease his labors until the worship of Ahura Mazda is accepted everywhere, and all believe the true religion."

Sikander promised that he would fulfill Dara's wishes. Then Dara placed the palm of his brother's hand on his mouth and died. Sikander wept, and then put the body on a golden couch and attended it to the grave.[60]

Illustration of the death of Darab in Nizami by Dharm Das, 1595. Walters Museum, ms. W.613.26b.

In fact, Alexander would soon marry an Iranian, and then marry another, and he would have a half-Iranian heir. Yet neither the heir nor Alexander would propagate the religion of the Avesta. Like the Jews who told the story of Alexander visiting the temple in Jerusalem, Firdausi used religion to conquer the conqueror. In truth, Alexander remained wedded to his eclectic band of gods and epithets— Zeus as Amon, and the Zeus of the companions, Zeus as Marduk and Heracles as Melkart, and a Macedonian favorite who would reemerge in Central Asia and later India, Dionysus.

8

Sogdian In-laws

THE ARMY HAD reached the edge of Bactria and Sogdiana, two Texas-size provinces that would strike a Greek or a Macedonian as crazily diverse. Outlying ridges of the Hindu Kush rose near many broad, fordable rivers, but the Vaxshu River, today's Amu Darya, and the Yaxsha, now the Syr Darya, were too broad to ford. Deserts lay between the rivers, and steppes between the mountains. Sandstorms, floods, and brigands often blocked the roads. Artaxshasa was king, but he was not fully or perfectly crowned. Militarily speaking, he was the same leader he had been when he was only a general. He shared control of Bactria and Sogdiana with warlords leading tribal, local followers. The death of Darius had created many Dariuses.

In language and culture, the people of Bactria and Sogdiana were Iranian. They differed from the Persians as much as Welshmen differ from Englishmen, or New Englanders from Southerners. Like the Persians, they believed that a legitimate king served Ahura Mazda through Anahita. Artaxshasa claimed to be legitimate, but the Iranians could reject him and still oppose Alexander, who was utterly illegitimate. The Persians in Alexander's entourage could do little to help Alexander. They knew mainly the cities they had governed or visited. Warlords generally controlled the country people.[1]

The Persians had pioneered civilization in Bactria and Sogdiana. They improved irrigation, and collected more tribute than in many provinces. More remained to be done: Persian roads ran only between a few cities, and signal fires on mountaintops provided better communication than the Persian king's famed postal riders. Whereas Persia was partly Mesopotamian in culture and social norms, Central Asia was overwhelmingly Iranian and nomadic. The most important Persian was the Elamite ruler Cyrus, but the most important Central Asian was reportedly the Iranian prophet Zoroaster.[2]

In a meeting with his generals—all Macedonian and Greek—Alexander said the army should ignore the warlords and stick to the mission of pursuing Artaxshasa. Alexander thought that once he captured or killed him, resistance would collapse. He did not consider the danger that eliminating Artaxshasa would leave the warlords on their own, and that they might fight rather than

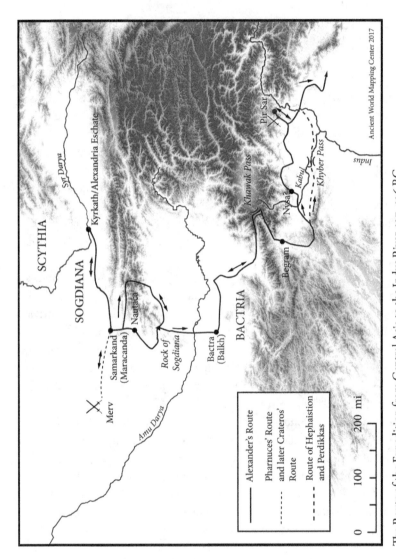

The Route of the Expedition from Central Asia to the Indus River, 327–326 BC.
Ancient World Mapping Center.

surrender. The councilors did not consider this danger, either. Like Alexander, they worried that if Artaxshasa escaped he would go north to Scythia, an Iranian land outside the Persian Empire, and recruit more cavalry there.

Still short of food, the Macedonians hastened north, pursuing Artaxshasa. They found ample supplies at Bactra, or modern Balkh, which surrendered straightaway. The army got mail from home and restored the baggage train, and local Phoenicians joined the expedition. Then came rumors that Artaxshasa and his cavalry had run ahead and swum across the wide, unbridged Amu Darya. When the tens of thousands of Macedonians reached the river, they could not cross so nimbly. For lack of timber to build pontoons or boats, most crossed the water on thousands of floats made of chaff wrapped in hides. It took six days. Rather than force unfit men to cross, Alexander pensioned them off. As the young swam the river and headed north toward Siberia, the old turned back into the welcoming arms of the sutlers, who provisioned them for the return to Europe.[3]

Farther north, in Sogdiana, the invaders encountered one of the deserts dividing one river valley from the next. The early summer heat made moving the main body impossible, so Alexander rode ahead with his strike force. Travel by day would cause sun-blindness, so the troops marched by night, peering at wagon tracks to stay on the road.

One of Artaxshasa's supporters, the warlord Spitamanah, soon approached some Macedonian scouts and told them he and his men could kidnap the king and bring him to Alexander in exchange for being left in peace. They were offering the invaders a bargain: Artaxshasa would cease to be king, a gain for Alexander, but Alexander would not become their master. Alexander did not wish to accept these terms, but in order to get Artaxshasa, he pretended to agree.[4]

Alexander dispatched his childhood friend Ptolemy with crack troops who covered ten days' march in four days. They found Artaxshasa alone in a village where Spitamanah had left him. Once Ptolemy brought Artaxshasa to Alexander, Alexander set about humiliating him as well as putting him to death, all in as public a manner as possible. He put him, naked and chained, on a wagon and had him driven south, out of Sogdiana, to Bactra, where many Iranians could see him. From there, Alexander had him sent on the main road westward, to Ecbatana, one of the Persian capitals. Darius's brother, Huxshathra, led the way. After Huxshathra arrived in the city, an assembly of leading Persians gathered to watch the execution of Artaxshasa, torn apart after being tied to two bent saplings.[5]

This sudden success surprised Alexander, and he had to devise some new military objective. He decided to ride on and gain control of the rest of Sogdiana. He advanced by night to Maracanda, today's Samarkand. This caravansary, which was the capital of the Persian province, surrendered. Soon afterward, the inhabitants of a nearby mountain stronghold snuck down and attacked a detachment of foraging soldiers. Alexander pursued them and they withdrew to their strong-hold. He advanced and besieged the place, but they replied with stones, spears, and arrows. One arrow broke Alexander's shin and he had to quit the field. He had not suffered any wound since Gaza, two and a half years before. No less disconcerting, some of the defenders hurled themselves from the battlements rather than supplicate.[6]

In about four months, the Macedonians had overcome the Hindu Kush, seized two satrapies, and disposed of Darius's heir. The Persian throne was now vacant. Since Alexander was not king of the Persians himself and would not become their king, the throne would be vacant permanently. The Macedonians thought this meant peace. They did not grasp that the throne belonged to Ahura Mazda, Mithra, and Anahita. This trio bestowed it and preserved it. No one could rule without it. Many Iranians were very sure of this—sure enough to fight for years against the invaders.[7]

————— ❧ —————

ALEXANDER AND THE council reacted to this new kind of war as though it were the old kind, between armies. Since the biggest hostile force belonged to the Scyths, they marched north to attack them near the second big river, the Syr Darya. They ran out of water and more men died of thirst than in most battles, yet in spite of the councilors' appeals to Alexander he pressed on to Kurkath, the "City of Cyrus" that guarded the Persian frontier. After it surrendered, the troops pulled out their ox hides and floated across the Syr Darya. To their surprise, they met with no opposition. The Scyths invited Alexander to send emissaries farther north, and he dispatched Craterus and others.[8]

Then came more guerrilla war. Kurkath rose in revolt, and so did lesser towns. Craterus returned and laid siege to the city, while Alexander attacked other Iranian centers. Each time he burned a place, the inhabitants of the next town saw the smoke and fled, and his cavalry would pursue and annihilate them. Then back to Kurkath, where Alexander deployed the siege train the Macedonians had hauled piece by piece over the Hindu Kush. Alexander led the assault under covering fire from the artillery and drove the defenders to an inner citadel. He took a blow on the head and neck from a stone, collapsed, and was struck dumb. He had suf-fered his first severe concussion. Recovering overnight, he accepted the enemy's surrender the next day. The Iranians had run out of water. The Macedonians sold many of the survivors to sutlers, who shipped them westward, to the Near East. The Macedonians had not sold them so many slaves for two years.[9]

To replace Kurkath, Alexander founded a stronghold nearby, and named it Alexandria *Eschate,* "The Ultimate (or Last) Alexandria." The engineers threw up seven miles of circuit walls in twenty days. To celebrate, and to raise morale, he made offerings of cattle and sheep, hosted a feast, and presided over games: tag-team wrestling, chariots drawn by horses and mules, poetry recitals. While gathering fruit for the feast, his men came upon dwarf apples, a kind they had never seen, and Alexander sent some of the trees back to Aristotle.[10]

Scythians assembled on the far side of the river and soon spoiled the occasion by firing arrows at the athletes. Alexander responded with an offering of another kind, to learn the omens for a counterattack. The entrails of the slaughtered sheep showed that the counterattack would fail, but Alexander pressed Aristander to alter the result. The companions objected, and after Alexander insisted on new results, they begged him, something they had never done before and would never do again. They could not overrule him. He made more offerings, and when the omens remained poor he ignored them, halted the festivities, and ordered his best troops to counterattack.[11]

After Macedonian catapults drove the Scythians from the bank, Alexander and the companion cavalry crossed on rafts and pursued them into the desert. Overcome by the heat and perhaps sickened by contaminated water, the king gave up the chase. Rather than go on, the companions accompanied him back to camp. This display of impiety and horsemanship had cost 160 Macedonian lives.[12]

Spitamanah now joined the resistance. He and his cavalry rode through Sogdiana, behind Macedonian lines, and besieged Samarkand. Alexander sent some 2,000 reinforcements and for the first time assigned Macedonians to a foreigner, the Lycian Pharnuces, chosen because he spoke Iranian languages. The Macedonian officers disliked Pharnuces, and they especially disliked his order to pursue Spitamanah, who had withdrawn into the deserts to the north.[13]

Spitamanah soon reached Scythia, recruited 600 Scyths, and turned around and traveled south. He found Pharnuces at the oasis of Merv and sent his men in circles around the Macedonians. To escape the Scythian arrows, the Macedonians withdrew to a glen where the Scyths could not maneuver. Then Pharnuces lost control of his officers. One Macedonian commander tried to lead his men across a river to safety, and the Scyths annihilated them. Most of the Macedonians died in the fighting, and the Scyths captured the rest and put them to death. Alexander's rescue column arrived too late to do much more than bury the dead. The Scyths had vanished into the desert.[14]

Two thousand Macedonians died in this engagement, more than in any other since Alexander left Europe. Stunned, the companions could not agree about whom to blame. Some blamed Pharnuces, the foreigner. Others blamed Caranus, the officer who led his men across the river. Others had heard a rumor that Pharnuces tried to resign his command before the troops left Samarkand but that his subordinates shirked the responsibility of replacing him. Many blamed Alexander, who had appointed Pharnuces, put Macedonians under him, and arrived too late.[15]

In another month, the weather turned cold, and the army returned to the comparative comfort of Bactra, where Alexander installed himself in the satrapal palace. That winter he made one of his best decisions. He had already refounded Persian settlements as Alexandrias, but these were few and far between. In Bactria and Sogdiana, he set out to establish more cities, closer together. Some would be refoundations, some new settlements. Both Phoenicians and Greeks would be welcome, and so would Macedonians too old for service with the army but suitable for garrisons or militias. Greek and Macedonian immigrants would run local governments, Greeks and Phoenicians would dominate local markets, Macedonians would provide military officers and infantry, and Iranians would provide cavalry. Captured Iranians would provide a source of slaves for the settlements. The first generation of women would almost all be captive natives.[16]

The new cities, Alexander must have hoped, would regard him as a divine founder. Iranians would join others in this worship. A new society, partly Greek, partly Iranian, would emerge in Bactria and Sogdiana.

The religious aspect of this plan fared badly. Alexander mistakenly assumed that Iranian and Greek gods and rituals were mutually compatible. He did not reckon with Anahita and the funeral rites at her shrine in Bactra.

Like other Iranians, the Bactrians worshipped Anahita as a protector of irrigation. The ancient Iranian hymnal, the *Avesta*, described her as a wellspring that flowed from a mountain in the center of the world. Her original, esoteric name, Harahvati, meant "possessing all water." The shrine in Bactra, luxurious by local standards, featured a statue of Anahita with a golden crown of eight rays and a hundred stars, gold shoes and jewelry, and a dress of thirty beaver skins. Participants in one of her festivals wore Scythian dress, giving her local appeal.[17]

The worship of Anahita accounted for burial customs very different from those of the Macedonians and Greeks. Since Iranians regarded groundwater as sacred to the goddess, they kept corpses out of contact with watercourses and the soil. Sometimes they embalmed corpses in wax. More often, stone or ceramic caskets kept out water. Cyrus lay in such a casket at Pasargadae. If the Iranians did not insulate a corpse, they exposed it on a platform, to be devoured by dogs or birds kept in the shrine. Once the bones were picked clean, relatives put them in ossuaries. They never burned remains. Like water, fire was sacred.[18]

The Macedonians and Greeks did the opposite: they buried or burned human remains. What they saw in Bactra offended them. When they objected, the worshippers and priests of Anahita explained that burial would contaminate the groundwater and harm the goddess, and that cremation would contaminate the fire and harm other gods. The companions disagreed: groundwater and fire were both profane, and important bodies of water were divine males, like Ocean Stream and Poseidon. No mountain stood in the center of the Greek world, and no goddess issued from it. They reported the exposed bodies to Alexander, and he ordered soldiers to kill the dogs and birds and bury or burn the corpses on the platforms.[19]

After ignoring Anahita at Pasargadae, Alexander had now insulted her. This misstep evoked others: the harm he had done at Persepolis two years before, the enslavement of town after town, and the mutilation and execution of Artaxshasa. In the spring of 328, the guerilla war resumed, fiercer than ever.

The campaign began with a misunderstood omen. After Alexander left winter quarters and pitched camp near the Amu Darya, the army ran short of water, and the engineers began digging wells. Instead of striking water, the engineers discovered petroleum burbling up out of the ground. They thought it was olive oil. Alexander ordered Aristander to interpret this oddity, and the diviner said that the Greek gods were on Alexander's side. Yet some companion or other (was it Aristobulus?) remembered otherwise. The engineers eventually struck water, not olive oil. The Macedonians did not thank Anahita for giving them the water.[20]

Another omen at this time showed how worried Alexander and his troops had become. One of the army's herdsmen brought Alexander a lamb with a misshapen forehead that looked like a royal tiara. The lamb also had double testicles. Horrified, Alexander summoned his most learned experts, the Babylonian diviners. They purified him using their own chants and incense. Unsure at first whether the ritual had worked, he told his companions that he feared not only for his own life but for theirs as well.[21]

Alexander's main foe, Spitamanah, went among the Scythians, village to village and yurt to yurt, recruiting horsemen. Encouraged by his defeat of Pharnuces, he and his cavalry probed behind Macedonian lines. They rode as far as Bactra, where only a small garrison remained, plus a military hospital and some royal servants. The garrison chief, Peithon, commanded only a small mercenary force, so he summoned convalescents from the hospital and armed Alexander's pages. He defeated the more numerous attacking force but lost control of his congeries of hirelings, walking wounded, and boys. Spitamanah counterattacked, killed most of the Macedonians, and captured Peithon, the first ranking Macedon to fall into the hands of the enemy.[22]

Craterus, commanding a nearby detachment, marched on Bactra and attacked Spitamanah, who retreated to the north. Spitamanah recruited still more Scythians with promises of plunder and returned to Bactria. There he ran into Coenus, who defeated him. Most of the Sogdians and Bactrians fighting alongside Spitamanah lost hope and deserted him. Spitamanah's Scyths stripped these deserters of their weapons and food.

Now the Scyths heard a false report that Alexander was heading toward them. Tired of fighting, and wishing to appear hospitable yet formidable, they cut off Spitamanah's head and sent it to Alexander.[23]

Alexander now had the head of a warlord, but the Scythians had Peithon, and Alexander did not control Bactria and Sogdiana. In the fall of 328, after he returned to winter camp, he began to plan for a third year of war in Central Asia.

———————

WHEN THE MACEDONIANS camped that winter, Alexander chose rude quarters in Samarkand. Some officers and men had to stay in Bactra, about 300 miles to the south, or in Nautaca, a post on the snowy road in between.

Because of the weather as well as the long distances, Alexander met less with the companions than before, and mostly communicated with them by letter. He dropped the familiar Greek salutation *xairein,* reserving it for Antipater and a few intimates. He also began censoring the soldiers' letters home. He didn't want Antipater, or the soldiers' families, to learn that casualties had risen and that the men were getting less loot and fewer captives than before. Inevitably, he stopped worshipping with the companions as a group.[24]

Against the troops' wishes, Alexander planned to station a garrison of 13,500 in Bactria, including 3,500 cavalry. He also contemplated a total of 23,000 troops for Bactria and Sogdiana. He could find this large number of men more easily than he could find someone eager to command them. He had to turn to the man who had always been closest to him in battle, Clitus the Black, who had saved his life at the Granicus, and whose sister had been his nurse. Since the death of Philotas, Clitus had held the prestigious position of top cavalry commander.[25]

Clitus, Alexander announced, would give up his cavalry command and govern the provinces of Bactria and Sogdiana. He would command not only Macedonians and mercenaries but thousands of Persians and other Iranians—a first. Alexander did not predict when Clitus would get Macedonian or mercenary reinforcements, or when he might rejoin the army and have his share of any new conquests. A reluctant Clitus could not refuse the appointment.[26]

Had Macedonians done less drinking, Clitus might have served in the post for years, but the Macedonians drank hard, especially that winter in Samarkand. On the night that Clitus and Alexander both drank too much, the witnesses were not sober enough to remember quite what happened.

They did remember that Alexander and others had gone hunting during a warm spell. When the party returned, Alexander went to the palace and made an offering to Castor and Pollux, two brothers, one mortal and one immortal. These two were gods of safe homecoming, and also symbols of how Alexander saw himself, part man and part god. Clitus went to his quarters and was about to make an offering of three sheep when the invitation came to dine with Alexander. The sheep followed him as he went to the king's, and Aristander, surprised, called this a bad omen. The king ordered Aristander and another diviner, the Spartan

Cleomantis, to sacrifice for Clitus's safety, and Clitus joined other leading companions at the party. Ptolemy and Perdiccas took couches on a large dais beside the king. Clitus and others found couches on a lower level. As bodyguards watched the entrances to the dining room, cupbearers poured wine, starting with the king.[27]

After dinner the boasting turned from hunting to war. Unhappy with the situation in Bactria, some of the companions went so far as to disparage the expedition into Asia. They also knew the sharpest way to express themselves—to contrast Alexander with his genuine, human father, Philip. Clitus, the unhappiest of all, and one of the most senior, spoke most. Did he taunt Alexander? Or did he rise from his couch and challenge him? No one who remembered the party agreed about what he did, only about Alexander's being to blame for what happened next. One companion wrote:

> Alexander began to belittle the deeds of Philip, and boasted that the well-known victory at Chaeronea had been his doing. A wicked and jealous father had deprived him of the glory of this deed. These things and others like them pleased the young, but displeased the older men. The older men had lived longer under Philip than under Alexander.
>
> Clitus turned to the people reclining below him and quoted a lyric of Euripides, so that the king could overhear the sound rather than the words. When the king suspected that the conversation was tending in a hostile direction, he began to ask those on the dais whether they had understood what Clitus said. They kept silent. His voice slowly rising, Clitus recalled Macedonian deeds in Greece. Then he said that the names of kings should not be inscribed on war trophies. The names of soldiers should. They did the killing and the dying. That was the truth, and if Alexander's father Zeus would not tell him, an old soldier would. Parmenio and Attalus were not alive to tell him. The king had put them to death.
>
> Drunk, the king jumped up from his couch. In order to restrain him, his neighbors threw away their cups and rose. Alexander took a spear from a bodyguard and was going to strike Clitus, but Ptolemy and Perdiccas took him by the arms and stopped him. Leonnatus took away the spear. Alexander cried out and said that his close friends had seized him, something that never happened to Darius. He ordered that the trumpet be sounded to bring troops to the royal quarters.
>
> Ptolemy and Perdiccas released him and threw themselves at his knees, begging him to give up his headlong anger. The king ran into the vestibule, took a spear from a guard, and waited by the exit. One by one, the companions left, and the lights were put out. Clitus, who had stayed, stepped

forward in the dark, and the king asked who he was. He said he was Clitus, and that he was leaving. Alexander struck him in the side, and as Clitus died, Alexander said, "Go and join Philip, Parmenio, and Attalus."[28]

This story implied that Alexander had caused the death of all four men, even his own father.

Other companions remembered differently. The chamberlain, Chares, said Clitus quoted Euripides's play *Andromache,* about a Trojan captive enslaved by Achilles's son. Clitus did not have to remind the Achilles-obsessed Alexander that Andromache was an ancestor of the king's. Impersonating her, Clitus said, "What bad government the Greeks have!" Alexander, Clitus implied, was a tyrant. According to Chares, Alexander immediately killed him with a spear. This version of events condemned Alexander by proving Clitus right.[29]

In his memoirs, Ptolemy tried to exonerate Alexander. He wrote that after Clitus provoked Alexander, Ptolemy hauled Clitus away, but Clitus broke free, returned to the party, and challenged Alexander. Enraged by Clitus's insults, Alexander killed him.[30]

About the aftermath, the memoirists agreed. The grieving Alexander took to his bed and refused to eat, calling himself the murderer of his own friends. Cool after causing the death of Philotas, and indifferent to Parmenio's death, he now became deranged. The ministrations of the doctors did no good, and neither did those of Callisthenes. The companions urged him to take food, and to make an offering to Dionysus. They knew that Alexander had skipped an offering to Dionysus and suspected that the god had let Alexander drink too much, or had driven him mad. They felt sure that Dionysus was accompanying the expedition. Callisthenes and the other intellectuals in the entourage pointed out that Dionysus had visited this region and subdued it, establishing his cult there. When the army discovered some Scythian burial stones, the intellectuals identified them as boundary markers erected by Dionysus.[31]

When Alexander arose and went to look at the corpse of Clitus, he called out to Clitus's absent sister, who had been his nurse. In the course of the war, she had lost two sons and now her brother. Three times Alexander had failed this woman, who was like a second mother.[32] He wished to kill himself.

Whatever the companions thought of Clitus's death, they were not prepared to lose their military and religious leader. They convened a meeting of the army, and the soldiers, following the senior officers' lead, declared the king could legitimately kill a subject who defied him. No one asked whether a king could legitimately kill a companion. Aristander reminded them that Clitus had ominously failed to complete a sacrifice just before his death. If that did not satisfy them, they could blame Dionysus.[33]

This verdict let Alexander put an end to his grief. It could not supply him a grand strategy for the intractable war in Central Asia. He needed help, but who would give it? He had warred on the Scythians, caused the death of Spitamanah, and expelled Artaxshasa, so he could not expect help from the associates of these men. The Parthians who had helped him before, in suppressing Shatibrzana, were too far away. His sundry diviners had done little for him. The local gods were among his enemies.[34]

THE CAMPAIGN OF 327 began with a near disaster due to ignorance of local conditions. Alexander marched out too soon, and a hailstorm struck the army as they were heading up a forest road. The column scattered to take shelter in the woods. After the hail stopped, the temperature dropped suddenly. The king and the companions went from man to man, trying to keeping them from lying down and freezing to death, but some nevertheless died of cold. Later, the troops managed to set fires to warm themselves. Alexander saved one soldier by putting him on his throne in front of a fire. Then the flames from the fires spread. Although most men escaped to nearby meadows and a village, some burned to death. Altogether the storm cost Alexander's army 2,000 lives. Rather than attempt to bury the dead, Alexander left them frozen in the woods.[35]

Although he did not promise to bury them later, he did say he would replace all missing animals and equipment. He kept his word thanks to a friendly warlord whose scouts caught sight of the army. The troops received 2,000 camels among other new beasts of burden. On the Macedonians marched, and attacked the Scythian nomads Alexander had made his next target. Alexander captured 30,000 sheep and cattle from the nomads, and repaid the warlord.[36]

Next the king directed his forces against an uncooperative warlord, Huxshiartas, who had served under Artaxshasa. Huxshiartas had gathered his family and troops atop a tableland the Macedonians called the "Rock of Sogdiana." The wells and fields could support 1,000 households, and nine miles of mountains reaching as high as 9,000 feet ringed the place. Most of the year, heavy snow made the ascent arduous. Alexander and his officers debated whether to undertake a siege or withdraw and wait for the enemy to climb down. A taunt from one of the defenders settled the matter. He asked whether the Macedonians had wings to climb the highest mountain protecting the tableland. If they did not, they should give up.

Alexander offered a reward of twelve talents to the first man to scale this mountain—twelve times the bonus he had paid to those who reenlisted at Ecbatana. He also offered prizes for runners-up, no matter how many. Three hundred men, most from the Balkans, volunteered. The engineers wove linen cords and adapted iron tent pegs for use in the frozen snow and rocks, and the volunteers dispensed with their weapons and armor.

They waited until nightfall to climb the steepest, least guarded approach. Using the pegs and cords, they fashioned a rope ladder reaching many hundreds of feet to the top. Thirty men fell and died. Like the victims of the hailstorm, they lay unburied in the cold. By sunrise, 270 reached the peak, and sent Alexander a flag signal.[37]

Alexander sent a herald to shout up to the defenders that they should surrender. The Macedonians had wings, he said, and had flown to the top of the mountain, above the defenders' position. The king did not say that this unarmed force amounted to a company. Thinking the climbers armed and numerous, Huxshiartas and his troops surrendered.

Huxshiartas expected to march down with his men and beg for mercy. Presumably Alexander would take them captive. The Macedonians would enslave some, especially the women, and sell the rest to the Phoenicians, who would send them in coffles to the slave markets of Persia and Mesopotamia. Instead Alexander asked to enter the citadel under a flag of truce. Huxshiartas sent guides to lead Alexander and a detachment up the mountain, and when they met, Alexander told Huxshiartas that the Macedonians would take no captives. He gave Huxshiartas to understand that the defenders should act as hosts. Alexander would be his guest.

As the two sides ate at Huxshiartas's table, Alexander and Huxshiartas turned from mutual compliments to negotiations. Alexander offered autonomy to Huxshiartas and any warlords he might recruit. Macedonians would control the cities in Bactria and Sogdiana, but the warlords would control much of the countryside. Alexander promised high pay to any Iranians who joined his cavalry. Alexander summoned Eumenes, who led Huxshiartas's lieutenants to the baggage train to marvel at the Macedonians' store of bullion and coin. After some give-and-take, Huxshiartas accepted Alexander's proposition. Alexander probably did not explain his plan to colonize Bactria and Sogdiana. Alexander was buying time, and Huxshiartas was buying peace.[38]

To seal the agreement, Huxshiartas offered to Alexander his daughter Rauxshna (the name means "Bright Star") as a wife. Like Clitus before him, Alexander could not afford to refuse. Rauxshna, whom the Greeks called Roxana, became his second mate.[39]

As the father of the bride, Huxshiartas set marriage terms that were probably typical of the ancient Iranian countryside. The groom must be of sound mind, innocent of the crime of murder, and able to provide for his wife. He must allow the bride to remain an Iranian, which meant, among other things, that Roxana could keep her religion. The groom need not pledge to be faithful, which meant that Alexander would not have to repudiate Barsine, and could take additional wives or keep concubines.

On the day of the ceremony, Alexander repaired to a room in Huxshiartas's citadel. Roxana entered separately, in a veil. Macedonian and Iranian witnesses to the nuptials gathered around. The room smelled of smoke from a sacred plant, perhaps soma, used in rituals for Anahita and the Iranian sacred fire. At Huxshiartas's bidding, bride and groom came forward and took their seats at a table. Then Roxana unveiled herself, but custom required that Alexander look at her through a mirror standing on the table. The mirror symbolized light from the sacred fire of Iranian cult, and a candelabra symbolized the fire. Perhaps Alexander did not understand that aspect of the ceremony, but he liked the apples on the table, and the pomegranates. No book was read, and no priest was necessary.⁴⁰

At the end of the ceremony, the couple received a round, flat loaf of bread. Iranians believed that whoever took bread first would be more loyal.⁴¹ Confronted with this domestic version of the Gordian knot, Alexander halved the loaf with his sword. Then the two of them took bread simultaneously.⁴²

After the ceremony, victors and vanquished celebrated. Food and drink flowed down to the Macedonian army encamped below the citadel. The mountain climbers spent their reward money on luxuries provided by the Phoenician sutlers.

Philip would have approved. Just as he had married the Scythian Meda, Alexander had now married an Iranian. Whether Roxana and Barsine were better-looking than Philip's wives, as some companions thought, they were more fecund. In 327, Barsine had given birth to a son, Heracles, and a few years later Roxana gave birth to Alexander IV. Of the thousands of women in the baggage train, these two were the best treated and the safest, but not among those closest to their partners. Alexander often left his baggage, and his wives, far behind him.⁴³

Alexander now had an Iranian wife and an Iranian ally. He was already using some Iranian cavalry, and even a few Iranian bodyguards, and he now recruited thousands more Iranians from warlords who chose to cooperate rather than resist or flee. The Macedonians could leave Central Asia in peace, rather than in discord. Alexander had accomplished all this not as king of Persia, ruler of the four corners, or pharaoh, but as the son-in-law of a warlord.⁴⁴

IN THE SPRING of 327 Alexander decided to change social formalities in his court. He wanted to unify his followers, many of whom were now Iranians. He did not tell his companions to act or dress like Iranians, still less speak Persian, but he did want the Macedonians to acknowledge him in the same way Persians did. That was the Persian custom Greeks called *proskynesis*.⁴⁵

Proskynesis let Persians acknowledge their betters. When ordinary Persians greeted notables, they bowed. When notables greeted the king, they bowed low.

Commoners and foreigners went farther, or lower, and prostrated themselves. Macedonians and Greeks thought of prostration as a gesture of worship, but Persians regarded it simply as a form of address. It had no religious meaning. When foreigners came to the court of the Persian kings, they used this form of address, too. The Greek exile Themistocles had prostrated himself before the Great King—an ironic gesture, considering that he had destroyed the king's navy a few years before.[46]

At one of Alexander's nightly dinner parties, some Iranian guests prostrated themselves while approaching him, as usual, and then some Greeks did, too. He rewarded each one with a kiss. Then he slyly suggested his Macedonians do the same. Craterus, who had helped Alexander kill Philotas, ignored the request, as did Coenus, and Alexander did not presume to rebuke these two leading companions. When Parmenio's sometime ally Polyperchon mocked those doing it, Alexander rose, strode across the room, and rolled the reclining Polyperchon from his couch and onto the ground. That, he said, was doing as the king wished. Alexander returned to his dais, and Polyperchon rose and returned to his couch. The other generals merely watched. Alexander received more prostrating Persians and Greeks that evening, and some less prominent Macedonians prostrated themselves, too, but none of the generals did. They thought the incident closed. Alexander had insulted them and they had politely but successfully rebuffed him. Polyperchon went on to high commands.[47]

The generals, however, had set an unwitting example to two other groups at court, the pages and the Greek intellectuals. Both were indispensable to Alexander and his army, and both were becoming disaffected.[48]

Over many generations, Macedonian pages had conspired against unsuccessful or unpopular kings, including Alexander himself two years before. They bore arms and learned to use them in preparation for future careers as army officers. Unlike most companions, they could approach the king at any time. In their eyes, the king was no god, any more than any master is a hero to his valet.

The pages had no important leader within their own ranks. They needed guidance from some mature man of consequence, such as Callisthenes, the chief intellectual at court. Besides being the historian of the expedition, he was their instructor.

In the role of instructor, Callisthenes succeeded his great-uncle Aristotle, who had instructed Alexander, Ptolemy, Nearchus, and other leading companions. Callisthenes had a far less congenial task. The number of pages had grown to about a hundred, and the Greek ambience of the court in Macedon had evaporated as the army moved east and Alexander dealt with more Iranian leaders, Phoenician sutlers, and sundry foreign priests. Callisthenes had publicly declaimed portions of his official (but Homeric) "History of the Deeds of Alexander," only to meet with ridicule from men such as Philotas and Clitus. They denied that any miracle had saved the army as it was marching along the beach near the Ladder in southern Anatolia. They also rejected the Greek oracles that Callisthenes said recognized Alexander as son of Zeus, not just Amon.[49]

The night when Alexander introduced *proskynesis,* Callisthenes, of all people, objected more boldly than any of the generals. As other Greeks prostrated themselves and went away with a kiss, Callisthenes came forward to receive his kiss without prostrating himself. Alexander averted his face, like an offended deity, and Callisthenes said aloud, "I go away the poorer for a kiss." Callisthenes's reaction was somewhat hypocritical. In describing how favorable winds saved the army at the Ladder, he said the waves fell and did obeisance to Alexander. The elements could worship Alexander, but Callisthenes would not.[50]

The pages added the insult to Callisthenes to their growing list of complaints: the death of Philotas, the assassination of Parmenio, the murder of Clitus, Alexander's failure to bury the dead, and his marriage to the barbarian. Must their teacher prostrate himself, treating Alexander as though he was a Persian god?

And one more thing: where were they going? Alexander had not said. Rumors circulated of an invasion of India. The pages had no reason to believe the campaign in India would be any easier than the one in Central Asia.

On a royal hunt some weeks later, a page named Hermolaus killed a boar that the king wished to take. The king whipped him and took away his horse. Alexander had insulted the wrong page: Hermolaus's father had been an officer in the companion cavalry for as long as Alexander had been king. Hermolaus did not speak to his father, but he plotted with his lover, another page, to kill Alexander. Soon more pages joined the conspiracy. They planned to replace the king with the only available royal prince, Alexander's half-brother. They settled on a night when they would all be on duty in the king's quarters and could easily kill him in in his sleep. Alexander stayed up all night drinking, something they did not expect, and foiled their plan. The next morning an informant told a sleepy Alexander about the conspiracy.[51]

Since the Syrian prophetess who slept in his quarters had told him to spend that night drinking, Alexander thanked her for saving his life. Now he had to deal with those who had tried to kill him. That would require a meeting of the companions.[52]

Alexander summoned a select group that avowed their loyalty to him. Reassured, he summoned another, larger group, which put the pages on trial. Hermolaus spoke frankly, even without being tortured, and his father was so surprised that he tried to put his hand over his young son's mouth. Explaining his motives, Hermolaus cited the deaths of Parmenio, Philotas, and Clitus, and said that the Macedonians were no longer companions but slaves. He absurdly accused Alexander of being king of the Iranians instead of the Macedonians.

He plausibly accused Alexander of insulting Zeus by calling himself a god. Other defendants testified in the same vein.[53]

Although the companions agreed with some of what the defendants said, they did not wish to encourage plots against Alexander. As for the rumored campaign in India, they believed it could make them richer than ever. They decided to execute Hermolaus and the other defendants. Like Philotas, Hermolaus and the others were stoned to death.[54]

The generals thought the conspiracy laid to rest, but Alexander wished to prosecute one more conspirator. He called another meeting and accused Callisthenes of provoking the conspiracy of the pages.[55]

Alexander had no evidence against Callisthenes, whom the pages had not implicated, but when Callisthenes spoke in his own defense, he inadvertently strengthened the case against him. He said that Alexander should rule not by compulsion but according to the custom of the Macedonians. In the mouth of a soldier or even a general, this remark would be unobjectionable, but coming from Callisthenes it was provocative. The word for "custom," *nomos,* could also mean "law." Callisthenes insinuated that Alexander ruled unlawfully, like a tyrant. Callisthenes added that neither the Macedonians nor the Greeks should worship Alexander as a god. Many had thought as much, but no one had dared to say so in public.[56]

The council could not reach a verdict in the case of Callisthenes. At least two members, Ptolemy and Aristobulus, blamed him for encouraging the pages' plot, and Ptolemy thought Callisthenes should be executed. The majority agreed that Callisthenes was guilty but did not think the council should punish a Greek civilian, as opposed to a companion or a soldier. They recommended that Alexander jail Callisthenes and dispatch him to Greece for trial before a panel of Greek delegates. That would show that the companions respected the law.

Alexander complied and jailed Callisthenes, but delayed sending him back, and treated him poorly enough that some months later he died in captivity. So perished the only man on the expedition who knew Homer better than Alexander did.[57]

That same spring someone more important than Callisthenes died. The companion Erigyius had fought under Parmenio at Issus and beside Craterus at Arbela. He killed the rebel Shatibrzana face-to-face and wisely warned Alexander to accept the omens against crossing the Syr Darya into Scythia. But the campaign in Central Asia weakened Erigyius, as it had so many others, and he died of illness. Year by year, Alexander was losing far more good men to the rigors of campaigning than he could ever put on trial, assassinate, or betray. Erigyius received an honorable burial, but no honor given to the dead could banish this thought from the minds of the living.[58]

Alexander left the lands of the Iranians without ever having become their king and without worshipping the gods of the region. These two departures from his practice in Egypt and Babylon inspired Iranian resistance. At the same time, his neglect of Macedonian rites had lowered his own troops' morale. Alexander's new enterprise, India, would show whether he learned from the mistakes he made in Central Asia.[59]

——⊸⊶——

IN LATE SPRING 327, the main body of the army retraced its route through Bactria and Sogdiana and reached the former camp at Alexandria in the Caucasus. After suppressing resistance in nearby mountains, Craterus and Polyperchon soon joined them. After months of rumors, the council of war was preparing an Indian invasion plan.

The first order of business, as always, was securing supplies. The army was now larger and harder to feed than ever. Although no Macedonian reinforcements arrived after Susa, some 45,000 new troops had arrived since the expedition started, along with a comparable number of Iranians. Even after sending some 10,000 troops home to Greece and Macedon and leaving many thousands in garrisons, especially in Central Asia, Alexander led at least 100,000. Only the Macedonians, barely a fifth of the total, could be counted on to tolerate short rations. With so many to feed, the generals could not afford to travel through India's ample mountains and deserts. They must head for the Indus River.[60]

The best Greek authority on India, Scylax, had led a small force of Persian explorers down the Indus around 500 BC.[61] He reached the Indus by way of the Kabul River, a tributary flowing through the Khyber Pass. After sailing downstream, he returned to the Near East by hugging the coast of Pakistan and Iran. Scylax showed that the Khyber Pass was a suitable invasion route, and also reported that another pass into India, the Bolan, lay too far south. Scylax and the other authorities agreed that little land lay east of the Indus. The only important area was the Punjab, Persian for "the land of five rivers," all of them Indus tributaries in the northwest.

Who ruled India? Scylax reported a number of kingdoms, and so did Sasigupta, an Indian who had joined Alexander after fighting for the Persians at Arbela. Scylax said nothing about India's Brahmins, Buddhists, and Jains. Unless he mistook India's caste of warriors, the Kshatriyas, for kings, he said nothing about the caste system. Sasigupta—and lessons learned from experience—would have to explain these complications.[62]

The soldiers of India were no question mark. At the battle of Arbela, Indian troops had been among the last to leave the field. Indian mahouts rode the elephants deployed by Darius. After these formidable soldiers returned home,

India became effectively independent. The Macedonians would find no Persian officials willing to surrender, no settlements like Kurkath, and no merchants speaking Aramaic or anything like it.[63]

Several Greek writers said that Cyrus the Great wanted to invade India but never did, and that Semiramis, an Assyrian queen, tried to invade but only temporarily succeeded. To learn more about Semiramis, the Macedonians consulted the Babylonians in the entourage, but the Babylonians reported there was no ruler named Semiramis. They knew of a few important Assyrian queens, even one with a similar name, but none of them had invaded India.[64]

Only Heracles and Dionysus had ever invaded India successfully. Why should merely mortal Macedonians try to match this feat? To reach the end of the world? The end of the world was the one thing the Macedonians felt sure they would find beyond the Indus. This notion derived not only from Scylax but also from better-known writers, such as Herodotus. A similar notion appeared in Homer, who supposed that an ocean stream encircled the world. China did not exist for Homer, any more than the Western Hemisphere did, and so the stream ran just east of India and then swept round it to the south.

Alexander had more than predatory reasons for invading India. He was curious, just as he had been about underwater rivers south of Caucasus or about

Lithograph of the Khyber Pass by James Rattray, 1848.
Photograph: Paul Fearn, Alamy Stock Photographs.

the temple of Melkart in Tyre. He had already collected many oddities and sent them to Aristotle—cotton and rice as well as naphtha from Mesopotamia, and enough animals, dead or alive, to help fill fifty volumes on Asian fauna compiled by Aristotle's assistants. He had just sent home information about elephants.[65]

Alexander wanted Indian subjects, not just specimens, yet he was partial to subjects who were specimens. These Indians promised to be remarkable specimens. One Greek writer, Ctesias, who had heard tales of India while at the Persian royal court, said that Indian tigers had three rows of teeth and goads in their tails.[66]

Alexander and the generals decided to funnel their forces into the Khyber Pass. Hephaestion and Perdiccas would lead the main body from town to town, gathering supplies, leaving garrisons and colonists behind them. Alexander would lead a smaller, partly Iranian strike force to clear the highlands of hostile tribes. Craterus would follow with the siege train and infantry regiments recruited from rugged parts of Macedon.[67]

Not long after Hephaestion descended toward the Khyber Pass and began the 200-mile march to the Indus, Alexander turned toward gorges and heights that offered a diet of mulberries and cold water sometimes flavored by junipers carried down torrents of runoff. The first people he encountered retreated into the mountains.

During these opening weeks of the campaign, Alexander sought in vain for some religious justification for the invasion. He talked to his men about Dionysus, and also Heracles, but encountered no traces of either god. Then he and his light force arrived in Nysa, a town ensconced in a forest in the Kabul River valley, and camped outside. When the night turned cold, the soldiers cut timber and made fires so big that the flames sprang out of control, leapt into a cemetery full of wooden monuments, and destroyed them. This omen frightened the inhabitants, but they did not know whether to surrender or flee. Their priests suggested a third response. Ambassadors from Nysa supplicated Alexander and informed him that the town was the birthplace of Dionysus. To the north, toward the Himalayas, rose the mountain where the god was born, called Meru. Would Alexander take possession of the town and join them in worshipping this god?[68]

Alexander believed they said the name of the mountain was Meros, which was the Greek word for "thigh." "Meros" commemorated Dionysus's birth from the thigh of Zeus. These people even worshipped the god by wearing fawn skins, as Greeks did, and like Dionysus they played cymbals—the same cymbals the Macedonian heard Indian soldiers playing before the battle at Arbela. The soldiers remembered the Central Asian boundary stones erected by the god. The intellectuals remembered Midas, who had invited Alexander to invade Asia. Midas had sent the Greek satyr Silenus to India, to join Dionysus's expedition.[69]

Were the Nysaeans Greeks? Alexander had come upon Greeks in the Near East, but here, in the heights above the Kabul River, the people spoke Pakrit, a language much like Sanskrit, and worshipped the gods of north India. Interpreters turning Pakrit into Aramaic, and then Greek, told the following story: Dionysus left the place of his birth, headed to the Indus, and conquered all India, bringing the cultivation of vines. Starting from Meru, the god invaded India by going from one high place to the next and avoiding the heat and flooding—a tactic Alexander could imitate. The Macedonians assumed that once they reached a bigger city with better informants, a genealogy of the god's Indian descendants would be forthcoming.[70]

At the invitation of the local priests, Alexander climbed Mount Meru, retracing the god's steps. A wooden shrine satisfied his notion of Dionysus among the Indians. After descending, he granted autonomy to the people of Nysa, who responded by giving him supplies and a few volunteers.

No one informed Alexander that Lord Shiva sat on the mountain, not Dionysus, or that Shiva's son, Scanda (the name means "Seed"), was born on the froth of the Ganges, not of his father's thigh. Scanda was a war god, not a god of the vine or the arts, a god of theft and not drink, with no kingdom and no dynasty. Nor would Alexander have listened. For the first time since Babylon, he had got himself a god. For the first time since Syria, he could share his god with his men.[71]

He had not, however, found any way to share his god with the other settlements in the Kabul valley, which resisted him without even attempting to communicate. At the first fort the Macedonians reached, an arrow shot without warning hit him in the shoulder. Two more hit Leonnatus and Ptolemy. The defenders would regret their accuracy. After the Macedonians scaled both rings of walls, the defenders burst from the gate in flight. The Macedonians slew every prisoner they took. The rest of the enemy scrambled up to the heights. Alexander razed the site and ordered Craterus to stay behind and destroy all settlements that did not surrender.[72]

This, the first big battle in India, gave the invaders a false impression of enemy fecklessness. In the next valley, the enemy remained behind the mud walls of the biggest fort in northern Swat. Some were mercenaries, not tribesmen. Alexander's officers staged a mock retreat to lure some troops out of the fort, and the Macedonians routed them, but Alexander took an arrow in the leg while leading the way. For four days catapults battered the walls and decimated the defenders, yet assaults with ladders failed to penetrate the fort. The engineers lowered a bridge from a siege tower onto the fort's outer wall, but it collapsed. Alexander found it prudent to negotiate. He would spare the enemy, provided that their mercenaries join his army. The mercenaries agreed, but then withdrew to a nearby hill rather than join him. The other defenders escaped at night. Infuriated,

Alexander attacked the mercenaries, exterminated them, and captured a now empty town.[73]

Alexander sent Coenus to attack a second settlement. Unable to take this fortified position, Coenus made a mock retreat. Out came the defenders, as unschooled as before, and the Macedonians turned and pounced, killing 500 of them. Meanwhile, Alexander besieged a third settlement. Panic spread among the defenders, and their commander, Abisaras, led a general withdrawal to Pir Sar, a redoubt more formidable than those the Macedonians had faced so far. The defenders knew it simply as Avarna, "the fortress." This mountain stood 5,000 feet above the Little Una River, or 8,000 feet above sea level. A tableland twenty-five miles in circumference, it provided ample springs, timber, and arable land. Like the warlords in Sogdiana, Abisaras wished to compel Alexander to grant him autonomy. Failing that, he would cut Alexander's supply lines.[74]

Hearing that Pir Sar was sacred to Krishna, the Indian counterpart to Heracles, the officers told their men Heracles had once attacked it, and that they would do likewise. Ptolemy built a camp and a palisade partway up the ravine below the enemy position, but Macedonian assaults from this spot failed twice. The engineers now did their best work since Tyre. They poured earth and rocks into the ravine, and in the face of enemy volleys they built a mound 200 yards high in one day. Stationing catapults atop the mound, they maintained artillery fire as they continued to build it higher. In two more days they filled the ravine. Amazed, the enemy opened negotiations, but Alexander, mistrustful after the recent episode with the mercenaries, set a trap. While the negotiations were under way, he withdrew some of the troops surrounding the redoubt, and gave the enemy a chance to escape. Forgetting negotiations, they left the redoubt and ran down the mountainside. As soon as they were gone, Alexander stormed the redoubt. Then he directed his men to march downhill and attack the fleeing enemy from behind. Those the Macedonians did not kill hurled themselves from rocky outcroppings and perished. Only Abisaras and a few others escaped. Alexander had once again prevailed, but without the benefit of obtaining a surrender. His foes yielded up their lives and their land, but they did not cooperate, let alone supplicate.[75]

Alexander made offerings to Heracles amidst the rocks and the funeral pyres of many dead Macedonians. To the north stretched barren country rising up to the Himalayas. More ravines and mountains blocked the western view, and to the south the Little Una, a rivulet beside a dirt road, dribbled down to the Kabul River between a few settlements. Eastward, in the direction of the subcontinent, Alexander and his acolytes glimpsed the Indus watershed in Punjab. They had never seen anything so green or so utterly boundless.[76]

Anonymous illustration of Alexander's flight in the *Histoire du bon roi Alexandre* of Jean Wauquelin, ca. 1440.

National Library of France.

SEVERAL VERSIONS OF the *Alexander Romance* tell how somewhere in Asia he came to a dead end but wished to go on. This version, written in Byzantine Greek, apparently derives from a story in the Talmud. The story may have originated in the Babylonian legend, Etana, about a king and an eagle.[77] Alexander is writing about his travels to his mother:

I began to ask myself if this place was really the end of the world—the place where the sky touched the earth. How could I discover the truth?

I ordered my men to capture two of the large, white birds that lived there. Since these birds fed on carrion, the dead horses around our camp attracted them, and a great many of them drew near us. Powerful but tame, they did not fly away when we approached them. Some of the soldiers climbed on their backs, hung on, and flew off. I captured two of the birds and ordered them to be given no food for three days. On the third day I had a wooden yoke built, and tied it to their necks. Then I had an ox-skin made into a large bag and tied it to the yoke. Holding two spears about 10 feet long, I climbed into the bag. After fixing a horse's liver to the point of each spear, I held them out. When the birds soared up to seize the livers, I rose up with them into the air. I thought I must be close to the sky. As the birds' wings beat, and pushed the cold air against me, I shivered all over.

Soon a flying creature that looked like a man approached me and said, "Alexander, you have not yet secured the whole earth. Why are you exploring the sky? Return to earth as soon as you can, or you will become food for these birds." He went on, "Look down on the earth, Alexander!" Fearfully, I looked down and saw a dragon curled up in a circle, and in the middle of the circle a tiny threshing-floor. Then my companion said to me, "Point a spear at the threshing-floor. That is the world. The dragon is the Ocean that encircles the world."

After this warning, I lowered both spears, leading the birds downward, and returned to earth. Frozen and half-dead with exhaustion, I landed about seven days' journey from my army. I soon encountered one of the generals under my command. Levying 300 horsemen from him, I returned to camp. Now I have decided to make no more attempts at the impossible. Farewell.

In India's high country, Alexander flew into the heavens. Once he arrived in the low country, he would end up traveling in the other direction.

9

Self-Defeat

THE BABYLONIANS THOUGHT Asia was 40,000 years old, and the Hebrews thought it was younger, but Asia came into being 10 million years ago. After the Indian plate moved across the Gulf of Arabia, a journey of millions of years, it reached the rest of the continent and forced it northward. The Zagros arose, and so did the Himalayas and the Hindu Kush. East of the mountains two troughs opened. The western trough became the Indus, which reached the Gulf of Arabia. The eastern trough became the Ganges, which reached the Bay of Bengal.[1]

About 7000 BC, after the last ice age, melting glaciers in the mountains filled the troughs. The Himalayas and the Hindu Kush hemmed in the rain clouds coming from the Gulf of Arabia during the monsoon and sent down more water. The flow of water in both the Indus and the Ganges became far greater than that of the Nile before the building of the Aswan Dam—so much greater that no one has ever even attempted to build such a dam in India. Every flood season, the rivers move and divide. Once there were two rivers to the west, the Indus and the Sarasvati. The Sarasvati flowed just east of the Indus, and perhaps reached the Rann of Kutch. The first Indian writings, the Rig Veda, called the Sarasvati the holy river. Some of the authors of the Veda lived beside it.[2]

The Indian plate kept moving, and around 2000 BC it shoved a tributary of the Sarasvati into the Indus. The Sarasvati diminished until it could no longer reach the Rann of Kutch. It expired in the desert that bordered the Indus. Or it would have expired had it not been a goddess as well as a river. The Hindus say that Sarasvati dove underground and took her waters the other way, toward the Ganges, into which she flows at a spot in the upper Ganges valley. This démarche occurred about 1000 BC.[3]

The plate kept moving, and the mountains kept rising. Even now, the Himalayas are rising inches every year. Each peak yields to another, bigger mountain, leading to some supernal or world mountain described in Sanskrit writings later than the Veda. It should be tall, of course—so tall that stars circle it as if in a whirlpool. Great rivers, including the Indus and the Ganges, should flow from it. The water at the foot of the world mountain should be sweet, calm, and stable—an object lesson to the rivers of the subcontinent. Gods should live on the mountain,

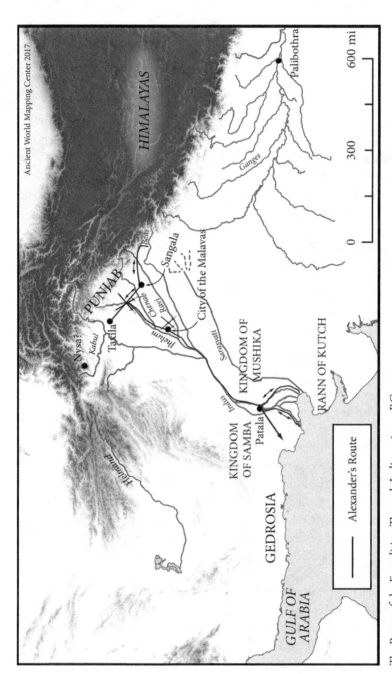

The Route of the Expedition Through India, 326–325 BC.
Ancient World Mapping Center.

and people should worship it—as they still worship Mount Kalaish in southern Tibet, where Buddhist pilgrims circle the mountain in a thirteen-mile circuit. Of course, these worshippers will never scale the world mountain. Rivers and mountains lie between it and us, seven concentric rings, the Hindus think, running outward from the mountain to the edge of the world.[4]

In Alexander's time, only the people of northern India knew this story. The Iranians possessed shards of it, and other foreigners knew even less. Foreigners knew little about India. The Veda does not report that any foreigner ever invaded it. The isolation of India explains why foreigners, even as late as the empire of the Achaemenids, did not know it was a subcontinent.[5]

When Alexander's men encountered Anahita in Bactria, they did not realize that Harahvati, Anahita's original name, was the Persian for Sarasvati, the fugitive water goddess of the subcontinent.[6]

AFTER DESCENDING FROM Pir Sar and going back to the Kabul River Valley, Alexander and the light force reached the lowlands he had glimpsed from atop the mountain. The winter had now begun, but they scarcely knew it, for they were entering tropical jungles for the first time. As the engineers labored to clear a path, Alexander and his companions came upon some war elephants that fleeing Indian troops had abandoned. The king now learned to hunt them. The royal party captured some and dressed them for military service. Two others escaped capture by flinging themselves from a cliff.[7]

In spring 326, half a year after the Indian campaign began, Alexander reached the banks of the Indus. His chief engineer, Aristobulus, had a pontoon bridge ready and waiting. They had chosen the right season for crossing. Had they tried later, they would have faced a six-mile-an-hour current flowing several hundred yards wide, and the bridge would have been impossible to build. However confident he was in the bridge, Alexander gave the river two offerings, one before he crossed and one after. He had done this only twice before, at the Danube and at the Hellespont. In histories of the subcontinent, this crossing is the first event securely dated to a particular year. Along with his pontoons and his prayers, Alexander brought linear time to India.[8]

The army traveled a local road for several days to the first important city, Taxila, where Alexander hoped to extract a surrender, supplies, and information. The ruler of Taxila, Ambhi, had already contacted Alexander through ambassadors and sent a gift of elephants. He now marshaled some of his troops as an honor guard and marched out of town to receive the invaders. Mazdai had done the same to good effect, but Alexander doubted whether Ambhi was surrendering, and so he prepared the Macedonians for battle. The prince reassured the invaders, but he communicated with them very imperfectly, and so Alexander's entourage mistook Ambhi's hereditary title for a personal name.[9]

Ambhi presented his city to Alexander, along with thirty elephants. In return, Alexander appointed Ambhi as satrap over his own kingdom, which ran from the Indus to the Jhelum, the next river in the Punjab. Never before had Alexander turned a king into a satrap. In Ambhi's eyes, Alexander made him autonomous. In Macedonian eyes, Ambhi was surrendering unconditionally.

In Taxila, the leading city in the Punjab, Alexander and the companions could form realistic ideas about India. The society of the Aryas, as many Indians called themselves, extended east into Punjab and the Ganges valley, and also south, along the banks of the Indus, much as Egypt extended along the banks of the Nile. To the north rose the Himalayas, visible in good weather. Contrary to what the people of Nysa had told the Macedonians, Mount Meru was in the Himalayas, far to the north.[10]

To learn more about the gods, Alexander and his interpreters could use Ambhi's library of religious literature—the tales of the Puranas and the hymns and formulas of the Vedas, plus sacred commentaries and ritual manuals. The priests called Brahmins were both librarians and the practitioners of the polytheism described in the Vedas. This long-predominant religion differed from the polytheism of the Iranians and Greeks. Animal offerings were important, but the victim might be strangled, not clubbed or stabbed. The innards, crucial in a Greek sacrifice, might be cast aside, along with the excrement. The worshippers never ate even the smallest part of the animal. Instead they burned it whole, a very odd thing in Greek eyes.[11]

More important than any animal offering was pouring milk into a fire. Like the Babylonians, the Indians tended to pour offerings, not burn them, the Greek preference. Instead of wine, worshippers drank the hallucinatory juice of the soma plant and offered the rest of the plant to the god. Persians used soma, too, but Alexander probably had not noticed. So far as later writers knew, he had not taken part in any Persian religious rituals.[12]

When not hallucinating, the Indians followed rules as complex as any in Egypt or Babylon. One kind of priest chanted mantras from the Veda; others made libations or killed animals; others prepared soma. The most important priest watched the proceedings in silence, detecting any errors, and mending them in his mind without interfering. Indian kings did not act as priests, but the priests, eager for royal patronage, made kings the chief beneficiaries of some prayers and offerings. These rites let a king ascend to the realm of the gods and return safely to earth. Heracles had never done that. He had gone to Hades and back, not to heaven and back.

In Taxila, the invaders also encountered ascetics whom the Greeks called sophists, or, since they were half naked, gymnosophists, or "sophists with no clothes on." These were the Jain and Buddhist monks whom the Indians called Shramanes, and whom the companions took to be Cynics. These two sects rejected animal sacrifice—a perverse idea to the Macedonians—but some aspects of the Jain religion might have appealed to them, and especially to Alexander. *Jina*, or Jain, meant "victor." One of the titles of the Jain holy men, *tirthankara*, meant someone who gains a victory by finding a ford in a river and leading others safely across. Victors, water, fords—here was military intelligence, but what sort? It came from half-naked beggars sweeping the dust from their paths lest they crush a beetle or a seed.[13]

One of the ascetics, whom the companions called Calanus, joined Alexander's entourage. He and others explained Indian basics to the Macedonians. According to the Brahmins, he said, Alexander did not need to be Zeus's son. He only needed to underwrite royal rituals. According to the Jains, Alexander needed only to be a pilgrim, leading others to god. Other kings had embraced these sects. One Indian king on the Ganges turned to Buddhism in order to console himself after the death of his wife. For military purposes, Calanus or others recommended the cult of the warrior and sage Vasudeva. An image of this legendary champion appeared at the head of Indian armies, including the next army Alexander would fight. This god would make a suitable Heracles.[14]

How did Alexander respond to this opportunity? The historical record is blank. None of the companions seems to have written about this subject, and neither did any later writers. After embracing the religion of the Egyptians and accepting the instructions of the Babylonians, Alexander apparently did nothing to respond to the Indians. At Mount Meru he had found a Greek way to rule India, and it seems he never looked for another. Perhaps he disliked the soma. He cannot have admired the temples. Rough-hewn stone affairs, they clung to the ground and often culminated in a stupa containing relics of a holy man. For the Indians, a stupa was a miniature version of Mount Meru. For the Greeks and Macedonians, these buildings suited the worship of a hero, not a god.[15]

When Alexander offered gifts to Indian priests, he was vexed to see the gifts rejected. (He was unaware that, as a foreigner, he did not belong to the caste entitled to give them gifts.) The prestige of the Buddha and the *tirthankara* surprised the Macedonians. They knew little about religious reformers. Only the king, being the chief priest, could alter the religion of the Macedonians.[16]

Although Alexander collected gifts and tribute in Taxila, he disbursed far more in spoils. To Ambhi he promised 1,000 talents of future booty, prompting one Macedonian to congratulate Alexander for finding a foreigner who deserved so great a reward. Ordinary soldiers did not begrudge Alexander this gesture. Besides getting their pay, they got sacrificial largesse. Alexander gave the wounded lodgings in Taxila, where they would eventually serve as a garrison. These men would not need to wonder how far into India Alexander would go.[17]

ANOTHER INDIAN KING, Puru, waited beyond the Jhelum. This torrent of a river swept downward in a muddy spate over a rugged bed of boulders, shooting forth green waves and swirling into eddies and backwaters beside crumbling banks. When Alexander arrived, in flood season, the river was unfordable. Confident in this natural barrier, and also in his archers, Puru refused to submit to the Macedonians. Even if the Macedonians somehow crossed, Puru would meet them with elephants. The men and horses would never get out of the water and up the bank.

Alexander convened the council and made a plan to divide the army in three parts. Craterus would take charge of heavy infantry and cavalry stationed in a riverside camp. Other commanders would take charge of the mercenaries and disperse them elsewhere along the river. These two parts would immobilize the Indians and make it possible for the third part, under Alexander, to find and attack the enemy's corps of elephants. Alexander's experience with elephants, limited though it was, had led him to target this element in Puru's army. If he could destroy it, or even neutralize it, his Macedonians would defeat the rest. As for Puru, he would either die with his elephants, supplicate, or retreat. All three outcomes would serve Alexander's wish—as strong now as ever—to maintain his own prestige through victories in battle. He assumed that Ambhi would betray him if he failed to defeat Puru.[18]

Puru wished to meet Alexander in battle and survive, or at least see to it that his army survived, and demonstrate to India's soldiers that the outlandish invader was not invincible. He patrolled his side of the river looking for Alexander, and ignored Craterus and the mercenaries.

To deceive his foe, Alexander spread word that he would wait some months for the water to go down. Then he made mock attempts to cross. That exasperated the Indians, who eventually reduced their patrols. Next he moved his men to a bend where the river was only several hundred yards wide. The weather was right: a torrential rain at midnight. The engineers had already hidden boat parts in nearby woods and now assembled them. Ambhi's officers showed the Macedonians how to use inflatable sheepskins. These were more buoyant than the Macedonian floats full of straw, and less soggy in the rain.[19]

Five thousand cavalrymen crossed on the floats, the horses swam, and some 6,000 infantry crossed in reassembled boats, or two apiece on the inflated skins. The storm made them inaudible and invisible. When the men and horses got across, they saw their mistake: they had reached an island. They would have to make another crossing. At last they managed to reach the other bank. To their relief, Puru and his elephants were nowhere in sight. Alexander's charades had distracted him.[20]

Once across, Alexander did not delay. He lined up his force of 11,000, cavalry in the van, and made for Puru's position, several miles away. When 120 enemy chariots appeared, the Macedonians dealt with the attackers the same way as at Arbela: they let the enemy pass through, and then struck them from the side and rear. The chariots got stuck in the mud or were overturned. Alexander pressed on. Soon he and the cavalry caught sight of Puru's army, centered on a force of elephants that made the enemy position look like a castle.[21]

Open country lay all around. Alexander could dispatch his ample cavalry to either his left or his right, and Puru, who had fewer cavalry, could not stop them. In the center, Alexander's phalanx, which had not yet reached the battlefield, would face Puru's infantry and elephants. Although Alexander had the advantages of speed and maneuverability, Puru, riding atop the neck of an elephant in the middle of the line, could see more of the field. He had also brought a bigger proportion of his men to the battle. Most of Alexander's men were still across the river.

Alexander and the cavalry resumed their advance and drew somewhat closer to the elephants, but did not attack them. The horses would have taken fright. Instead Alexander swerved right, around the Indian flank. The rest of the cavalry broke left, under Coenus.[22]

Puru saw that Alexander was trying to encircle him, and he ordered his own cavalry to thwart the Macedonians by riding parallel to them. In response, Alexander rode farther to the right. Meanwhile, Coenus and the rest of the Macedonian cavalry rode around the other end of Puru's line and began attacking the Indians from the rear. Puru ordered some of his cavalry to face about and resist Coenus. The Macedonians had met their match in formation-fighting.[23]

Then Alexander attacked, and Puru responded by sending some of his elephants against the Macedonian cavalry. That blunted Alexander's assault, but exposed the elephants to attack by the Macedonian phalanx. So far they had held back, for fear of the animals' trunks and tusks. Now they struck the animals from the side and gradually drove them into a mass. The elephants inadvertently trampled Indian foot soldiers and caused some Indian cavalry to be trapped between the two sides. The mahouts tried to redeploy their animals, but the Balkan javelin men targeted them, and one elephant after another lost its guide. The Macedonians struck down hundreds of Indians, penetrating the damaged formation. Craterus and the other troops on the far side of the river crossed over and joined the attack. Puru eventually found himself surrounded, but refused to surrender, and the Macedonians, tired and overawed, did not attempt to take him captive. Their own casualties numbered at least 1,000, the largest for any pitched battle.[24]

As soon as Alexander heard that Puru was surrounded, he rode to the scene, spotted him, and sent Ambhi as a messenger. Regarding Ambhi as a traitor, Puru

raised his javelin in order to kill him. Ambhi withdrew, and Alexander sent another Indian messenger, known to the Greeks as Sandracottus. A political exile,
Sandracottus had presented Alexander a plan for invading India. He might have
the skills and connections to reach Puru.[25]

After speaking to Puru, Sandracottus reported the Indian king was wounded
but still atop his elephant. It would not do to have him meet Alexander that way,
since the Macedonian rode only a horse, so Sandracottus returned to Puru and
asked him to dismount. The Indian king balked, but then Alexander rode up with
only a few companions, and dismounted himself. Puru did the same. The two
commanders, one wounded and one unharmed, stood face-to-face. Sandracottus
and some of Puru's men acted as translators, but the Macedonians did not quite
understand whom they were dealing with. The man they called "Porus" did not
have this personal name. Puru was a dynastic name. Had Alexander borne such a
name, it would have been Temenid, the Macedonian royal family name. The dynasty of the Puru or Paurava had once lived by the Sarasvati River, and then
moved to western Punjab.[26]

The companions strove to overhear the ensuing conversation. Alexander asked
what he should do for Puru, and Puru answered, "Treat me like a king," or, as one
companion heard it, "Treat me as this day shows you should." Puru would not supplicate, and so Alexander would have to establish some other tie with him.[27]

Alexander responded complaisantly. Besides allowing Puru to continue ruling
his kingdom, Alexander promised to give him additional territory. That was more
than Ambhi got. Alexander also made Puru satrap, the same as Ambhi. And one
more thing: Alexander would make Puru a companion. Neither Ambhi nor
Mazdai got that. Alexander had changed his method of dealing with the defeated.
Rather than turn Indian rulers into subjects, Alexander planned to convert them,
king by stubborn king, to the Macedonian royal cult. Every defeated enemy could
be an ally gained—a firm ally, bound to Alexander by the Zeus of companions.[28]

In the past, Alexander had participated in the cults of foreign nations, especially Egypt. Now he expected the ruler of a foreign nation to participate in a
Macedonian cult. As in Persia, Alexander's religious policy toward foreigners was
coming into conflict with his role as leader of the cult of the companions.

Puru accepted Alexander's offer and agreed to become an ally. He did not put
his army at Alexander's disposal, and Alexander did not ask him to. Instead Puru
and a smaller force would march with the Macedonians.

After the two kings finished their impromptu negotiations, the two sides
withdrew to separate camps. Alexander buried the dead and then celebrated the
victory and the new alliance with offerings and games. Mindful of rainy weather,
he worshipped the sun and prayed for a dry way eastward.[29]

Silver tetradrachm minted in Babylon, 323–322 BC.
American Numismatic Society 1959.284.86.

The officers did not like the prospect of going east. Several Indian rulers had bigger armies than Puru, especially the Magadha rulers on the Ganges. These foes could deploy enough elephants to trample the Macedonians. The companions also objected to Puru being one of their number. As a king, Puru was too powerful to be a companion.

Alexander might have reasoned with them: When he was only king of Macedon, he needed companions who were commoners, but now, as son of Zeus, or king of the world, he needed companions who were kings. Instead, Alexander gave the companions games and sacrificial meals. He could not give them bonuses. India was not yielding up treasures as had Persepolis and Susa. The Indians minted some coins, but they were punched and not struck.

The most impressive images of the conquest of India came from faraway Babylon. Alexander ordered the Babylonian mint to commemorate the battle with medallions featuring an elephant and coins featuring Alexander on Bucephalas, armed with a long spear and attacking an elephant with two mahouts.[30]

Some of these medallions showed a mounted Alexander attacking an elephant not just with a spear in one hand but with a thunderbolt in the other. The thunderbolt was Zeus's weapon of choice. By carrying it, Alexander became godlike. Yet he was not threatening a god, a titan, or some human sinner, as Zeus would. He was fighting a battle, and he might even seem to be hunting the elephant. The religious purpose of the medallion, which was to associate Alexander with Zeus or Zeus-Amon, was at odds with the commemorative purpose, which was to portray one king's victory over another.[31]

AFTER THE CELEBRATION, the army campaigned farther east. As the rain increased, it drove the main body of the army from the roads and valleys toward higher ground. When the army reached the next tributary of the Indus, the Chenab, in late June, the water had risen some fifty feet, leaving its bed and inundating the plains. Even after Alexander went as far as dry land would take him, he faced a stream of 3,000 rocky yards. Out came the stuffed skins and the reassembled boats. The skins still worked. Some boats broke up on the rocks, causing hundreds if not thousands to drown.[32]

The sight of some lotuses led Alexander to believe that he had discovered the source of the Nile. He had seen these plants in Egypt, where they had been a tourist favorite since Herodotus. Perhaps he could sail down the river and end up in the Nile valley. But no, the local informants told Alexander, the Chenab ran down to the Gulf of Arabia, not to Africa. Forget the Nile, and head for the hills: it was flood season. Sleeping on roofs helped, but not for long. Snakes fleeing the rising waters infested the trees and the roofs, too. Alexander and his men fled northward, following the locals. Eventually, he reasoned, the waters would recede, and then he would need more boats. Once in the hills, he had his foresters cut teakwood.[33]

Still fleeing the rain, the army traveled up toward the Himalayas. They had left any enemies far below, but did not know it. Potential informants shunned them, and the remaining population were specimens of a new kind. One companion wrote:

> In the forest were fabulously big monkeys with tails, and a fabulous number of them. The Macedonians once saw them standing on some open hilltops, staring. The monkeys have a human attitude, no less than elephants do, and so the Macedonians fancied that this was an army, and they attacked them as though they were enemies. The Indians there with Alexander had to tell the Macedonians to stop.

Other writers said that the apes (or monkeys, as the Greek writers called them) replied by throwing stones.[34]

In August Alexander reached the next river, the Ravi. The floodwater had receded, clearing the way to the city of Sangala, three days farther east. To induce a surrender, Alexander assaulted a nearby town, sparing no one, and then burned it to the ground. Then he advanced on Sangala, which begged for mercy. He granted it. At the end of the campaign the Macedonians buried their own dead, who totaled about ninety, with pomp and circumstance.[35]

Leaving Sangala in the hands of some of Puru's troops, the army headed toward the river Beas. By this point they had crossed most of Punjab. In a few days more they would reach the edge of the Indus watershed. Beyond lay some 120 miles of low, open land between the Indus watershed and that of the Ganges. This country, which now straddles the border between Pakistan and the Republic of India, became the site of the British imperial capital, New Delhi.

Alexander knew little about the Ganges. After his experience at the Chenab, he could believe the reports that the Ganges was more than three miles wide, and that it was a very considerable god. Sandracottus and others gave him conflicting reports about the Ganges kingdom of Magadha, with its capital in the riverside stockade of Palibothra. Sandracottus minimized the difficulty of attacking Magadha, but other informants did not. Alexander's generals remained pessimistic.[36]

The army reached the Beas amidst ceaseless rain. Up and down the broad stream massive boulders confronted them. On the far side barren country stretched as far as the Ganges, twelve days distant. Alexander, leading the van, ordered preparations for a crossing, and in a few days Hephaestion and the rest of the troops caught up with him, after campaigning elsewhere in Punjab. As the army hewed rafts and stuffed skins, the rain poured and knots of soldiers gathered to complain. The Macedonian infantry and cavalry wanted to go home, and they told their officers as much.[37]

Complaints of this kind had begun as soon as the army left Ecbatana, four years before. At that time the officers either shouted down the malcontents or relayed promises from Alexander. The men received sacrificial meat plus money and a place to spend it, and got more food when Alexander let them go foraging. They took captives, and sometimes they were supplicated. In India, they got little or none of this.[38]

Rather than reprove the men, the officers sympathized with them. Since Taxila, the officers had gotten no appointments, and they were hearing more and more rumors about Ganges armies and elephants. Suppose they won a new war in the Ganges valley and reached the edge of India. Was that the end of the world? What would they accomplish there? A thanksgiving enabling them to return? Why not turn back now?

Coenus, Perdiccas, and other veteran officers were aging, and soldiers without mounts were aging faster as they slogged through the Punjab. If Alexander wished to make more conquests, he ought to produce a favorable omen. Instead, Zeus had sent seventy consecutive days of rain.[39]

What would the officers do? They could not appeal to faraway Antipater or Antigonus. They did not trust Puru or Ambhi, who were using the Macedonian army to advance their own interests. Without a summons from Alexander, they could not even meet.

Then Alexander made the worst mistake of the expedition. He called a council of war.

AFTER HEARING FROM Hephaestion, Ptolemy, and Leonnatus about the new attitude among the officers, Alexander convened a meeting of all the commanders of phalanx regiments, plus other leaders. The bodyguards attended, too, making about twenty in all. Perdiccas and several of those present had commanded infantry regiments throughout the expedition. Craterus being absent, the most senior officer was Coenus, who had commanded not only an infantry regiment but also half the companion cavalry. All told, Coenus had led more independent commands than anyone but Craterus.[40]

In Ptolemy's account of the meeting, Alexander began by saying, "When you follow me into danger you are not of the same mind as before. I see it, and that's why I have summoned you. Persuade me to go back, or let me persuade you to go on." This gambit acknowledged the perspective of his listeners: he was Jason, and they were the Argonauts.[41]

Alexander claimed that the enemies awaiting them in the Ganges Valley would flee, and that the mouth of the Ganges, the most remote part of Asia, lay close by. If they did not go the distance, unconquered nations would attack them and deprive them of what they already ruled. After they did go the distance, they might go home via an interesting new route, sailing around Africa. Perhaps Alexander had heard that the Phoenicians circumnavigated Africa. Now his companions would.

Go to the end of the world, he summed up: no cowardice, no delay. Plunder and satrapies for the taking, and pensions for all who wish them, once the army had gone as far as possible. Remember the examples set by Heracles and Dionysus. The members of the expedition will become famous, if not divine.

For a time, no one replied. Then Coenus removed his helmet, as custom required, and addressed the council. "In the light of the reputation that I have, thanks to you, and that I have in the eyes of the troops," he began, and went on to say, "My age gives me the right not to hide what seems best."

Coenus was raising the dead against Alexander. Everyone in the meeting knew that Parmenio and Clitus, the two officers Alexander had murdered, would have favored calling a halt. Parmenio had wanted to call a halt before they invaded Mesopotamia. Clitus was killed after he challenged Alexander's decision to leave him in Central Asia.

Coenus now made Alexander a somewhat insulting offer. If Alexander would go home to visit his mother, and dismiss his troops, Coenus and the other officers would help him raise a new force and attack peoples closer than the Indians, such as the Carthaginians. Coenus concluded with a commonplace that Alexander may have taken as another insult, or even a threat: "Divine power can do unpredictable things. Human beings cannot be protected against them."

Infuriated, Alexander dismissed the councilors.

A day later, Alexander reconvened the council. If they wished, he said, they could go home with donatives. He would persevere, helped by whoever would stay. With this new gambit, he hoped to split the opposition. Friends such as Hephaestion would speak up, he thought, and refuse to abandon their king. Once Coenus and the rest saw that the officers were split, they would yield to Alexander for unity's sake. Then the officers would help Alexander convince the men.[42]

The king waited for some response but got none, not even from Hephaestion. Ptolemy was among those who said nothing.

Alexander dismissed them a second time.

After these two days of deadlock, some companions approached him privately and tried to talk him into going back to Macedon. No doubt Hephaestion was among them. Perhaps Ptolemy was. They all chose to keep their fruitless conversation with Alexander secret. They did not suggest he call another meeting. That would show the army that Alexander had lost the confidence of his war council, and perhaps lead to disorder.

A third day went by, and then another, and then another. Alexander refused to speak to any of the commanders, or even to come out of his tent. A mutiny had broken out, a royal mutiny of one: the son of the god of companions versus the companions, the priest versus his congregation.

One hundred miles away, the Ganges princes were surely mobilizing. In Macedon, Antipater perhaps was editing his own correspondence. The people there were suffering from famine, and so were many Greeks. To appease the gods who had sent the famine, thousands of acts of sacrifice were occurring every day. Yet no one sacrificed on behalf of this army, a community the size of Athens or Memphis. Only Alexander could perform these rites, and he refused.[43]

Then one morning the king stepped out of his tent. For what may have been the 10,000th time, he slew a sheep and inspected the entrails. They proved unfavorable. Perhaps he performed this ritual three times, the maximum custom allowed. The bad omens persisted. Although he had ignored or manipulated omens before, Alexander did not challenge them this time.

He convened a third meeting, summoning the closest and oldest of his companions. He announced bad omens for crossing the river. The army would turn back. Where they would go, he did not say.[44]

When the news spread, the troops rejoiced. Rushing to his tent, they called down the gods' blessings on him, thinking he had at last let himself be defeated, by his companions.[45]

In reply, Alexander announced that before withdrawing, the army must erect twelve brick altars as tall as siege towers. Ten thousand men would work on each one. For weeks men and animals labored in the rain to build the complex. Then the sky cleared, and Alexander sacrificed to a different Olympian god atop each altar, and decreed games for the men. After days of celebration, they turned back the way they had come, toward the Jhelum River.[46]

The twelve altars counted as prominent oddities on Alexander's Indian itinerary, along with crocodiles, pearls, and monsoons. One later writer, Plutarch, believed that Indian kings worshipped at them, but eventually these piles of brick faded into the landscape and vanished.[47]

One person in the expedition might have preserved them: Sandracottus. He left at about this time, for he no longer had any prospect of enlisting Alexander's help once the army turned back. His future seemed unpromising. In the next twenty years he nonetheless raised an army and conquered most of northern India. Besides overthrowing the Magadha kingdom, he conquered all of Alexander's territories in the subcontinent. He would have found it easy to preserve the riverside altars, the building of which may have been the last act of Alexander's that he witnessed. Perhaps they did not suit his religious taste. He was a syncretist, combining traditional Indian cult with Buddhist ideas. Alexander's altars looked like ziggurats, not stupas.[48]

Anonymous color drawing of the western bank of the Beas River, 1848.
Illustrated London News.

IN EARLY FALL, the army marched back to the place on the Jhelum where they had fought Puru some months before. Two thousand teakwood boats were waiting there. So were new leather corselets and cherrywood pikes brought from Europe via the Khyber Pass. The men burned their old corselets and prepared the flotilla while Alexander made travel plans with his councilors and gave Puru charge of the Indian frontier. He had founded a city at the site earlier, but now he named it after Bucephalas, who had lately died, a victim of one wound too many. Coenus died of illness, and received the most elaborate funeral since Erigyius. Even Alexander's favorite dog had recently died—and got a city named after him, too. The sick and wounded were numerous enough to form garrisons for these cities.[49]

The king and council were embarking on a risky plan—descending the Indus to the Gulf of Arabia. They knew this downriver voyage would take months, but they could not know how many. Bad weather might delay them indefinitely. The trickle of mail and supplies through the Khyber Pass would no longer reach them, and Alexander's orders to his subordinates would no longer get through. Men such as Antipater, Antigonus, and Harpalus, used to hearing from him after several weeks or months, might not hear from him again for up to a year. The descent of the Indus would test not only the army but the strained ties of companionship.

To save time and lives, they might have gone back the way they came. The council knew that Alexander would reject this plan with all his native vehemence, exacerbated by resentment at having to turn back. No one even proposed it. Instead the councilors let Alexander approach them individually and borrow money to build the ships.[50]

That October, amidst further rains, Alexander propitiated the river in the name of Amon and Heracles and the army set sail. Craterus took infantry and cavalry down the western bank, and Hephaestion took more troops plus baggage and 200 elephants down the eastern bank. The fleet of 1,800 vessels, led by Alexander, traveled just behind. Crowds of curious villagers gathered along the banks or poured down from neighboring hills, and Craterus and Hephaestion had to police them. Alexander waved from on deck, and river dolphins bobbed beside the royal barge.[51]

The voyage soon turned rough. At the confluence of the Jhelum and the Chenab, in central Punjab, a whirlpool destroyed two ships. Lookouts called warnings to helmsmen, drums beat the pace for the rowers, sawyers broke up against the hulls of the ships, and rescue teams on shore hollered back and forth as boats went aground. Tributaries flowed into the river and threw up waves and spume.[52]

Every day they put in for rest, food, and forage. Whenever they failed to secure cooperation from the locals, Alexander ordered his troops to seize villages and supplies.

The troops complained. They had thought fighting would come to an end once they turned back at the Beas River. Alexander and the officers had to convince them to keep at it.[53]

When the Malava federation of southern Punjab refused to cooperate, Alexander regarded this as resistance by a mere tribe. Rather than negotiate, Alexander marched his strike force day and night through a fifty-mile stretch of desert and launched a surprise attack on a Malava city. For lack of a palisade, he stationed a ring of thousands of cavalry around the place. When civilians tried to flee, he killed them before they could supplicate. He had treated Central Asian rebels in much the same way, but the Malavas were not rebels, and their cities surpassed anything in Central Asia. Their warriors had fought in the chief battle described in the Indian epic, the *Mahabharata*.[54]

Perdiccas, sent against another city, found it deserted. Pressing onward, the two commanders killed fugitives on the roads or fleeing into marshes. Advancing on a third city, the Macedonians encountered a garrison of crack troops who were Brahmin priests under arms. More impulsive than ever, Alexander led the way in mounting the wall, and the Macedonians followed him to victory, but this time the Indians burned the city rather than desert it, and died fighting amidst the flames.

To the south, the Indians marshaled another, bigger army of 50,000. When Alexander outmaneuvered them, they took refuge in a fourth Malava city, and the biggest siege since Tyre ensued. Alexander and Perdiccas attacked, driving the Indians from the outer wall to a citadel. Rather than wait for the siege train, Alexander ordered an assault with scaling ladders. Not even a diviner who wished to warn him to wait could delay him. He told the diviner he had already found good omens by killing an ox himself, and ordered his men to mount the walls with ladders.

When he thought they were shirking their duty, he went up a ladder himself, mounting the wall and cutting down the enemies in his way. Arrows rained down from the citadel towers, and Indians standing near him on the parapet flung javelins. Alexander had only his sword and his shield. Aghast that their king was in danger, the shield bearers scrambled up the ladders to join him. Then the ladders broke. Only the bodyguard Leonnatus and two others had reached Alexander.[55]

Rather than retreat, or offer an easy target atop the parapet, Alexander jumped down into the city, landing beside a fig tree. He continued fighting with his back against the wall of the citadel. The Indians hemmed him in, flinging spears and rocks. They would have overwhelmed him had not Leonnatus and the other two Macedonians leapt down after him. An arrow in the face killed one Macedonian. Another arrow pierced Alexander's armor and struck him in the lung. As blood flooded his breastplate, he fainted and dropped to the ground. The two Macedonians left standing were wounded, too. The king was minutes away from death.

Frantic because they had lost sight of Alexander, the shield bearers climbed the wall of the citadel by standing on one another's shoulders. Leaping down into the city, they repelled the Indians and carried Alexander out through the gate to his tent. Seeing that the arrow was barbed, the surgeons made a large incision, so they could extract all of it, and more blood gushed. The king opened his eyes, only to faint a second time. The anxious surgeons dressed his wound, and the body of a very fit thirty-year-old began, breath by breath, to recover. The surgeons had saved him. The enraged Macedonians took the life of every Indian in the city. Stunned by this onslaught, the Malava federation surrendered unconditionally, as did the cities of the neighboring Ksudrakas.[56]

Meanwhile, some troops heard a rumor that the king was dead. They panicked, and pandemonium broke out. To calm them, Alexander ordered that he be brought from his tent and put on a barge. After he came alongside the place where the men were camped, he showed himself by removing a screen that sheltered him from the sun. The men shouted in amazement and held up their hands as though praying. When slaves brought his litter, he ordered them to bring his horse instead. He mounted and came ashore to resounding cheers. Weeping men came forward and touched him or threw flowers. He had never come so close to receiving the divine honors Amon proclaimed were his due.

Later, the companions gathered unsummoned at his bedside and criticized him for recklessness. Craterus, the leader of the delegation, reminded him he was a king, not a soldier. If he continued to suffer grave injuries, more rumors of his death would spread and encourage rebellion. Philip took risks, too, Craterus reminded Alexander, and they cost him an eye, but he did not repeatedly put himself in the lead. Craterus and the other officers thought that Alexander no longer needed to take grave risks. Earlier he did it to capture Darius. Now he did it only to capture a small city.[57]

Alexander neither protested nor changed his conduct. He preferred the individualism of Homer's Achilles to the collective thinking of Craterus, Parmenio, and Philip. Yet sometimes he knew better than to imitate this selfish hero. His favorite verse in Homer praised Agamemnon, the beleaguered Achaean leader, not Achilles.[58]

Alexander was torn. As leader of his companions, he had to take risks. As commander in chief and king, he had to order his companions to take the risks. If he tried to strike a balance between these duties, a companion such as Craterus would complain Alexander was too much a soldier, and a companion such as Clitus would complain that Alexander was merely a general. This problem of balance is a perennial one, affecting leaders today when they decide whether to command from the front line or from the rear. Alexander's religious bent compounded the problem. He took risks because he wanted his men to revere him.

He also understood their religious needs as opposed to his own. An army in its right mind will not stand and fight; it will run away. Alexander strove to give his men the outlook—the supernal, self-sacrificing zeal—they would need to persevere. He tried to motivate them by invoking omens, propitiating gods, and sending dead comrades on a safe trip to the underworld.

Over the next few weeks Alexander recovered from his wound, and the men from their distress. The king gave thanks to the gods, called another meeting, and appointed a Macedonian satrap to govern the Malavas. (Only one new province had gone to a Macedonian since Clitus received Bactria.) From the Malavas, Alexander demanded 1,000 hostages. Once he received them, he felt the Indians had proved their loyalty, and he returned the hostages. Kindness toward captives, not suppliants, was his new token of mercy.[59]

The army now reached the Indus and built more ships before resuming the voyage downstream. As they left Punjab for the flats of the lower Indus valley, the river became smooth, falling only half a foot per mile. The flotilla meandered around sandbanks and sawyers, passing rafts made of stuffed skins and bundles of reeds. From a distance, the men could see the peaks of Hindu Kush. Yet marshes and oxbow lakes obscured the configuration of the land along the Indus, and often they could not tell where to put in for the night. Thankfully, resistance ceased. The Macedonians' reputation preceded them, and when they reached the Ambashthas, the people hailed them as an army of gods—the Macedonians did not know which ones—and surrendered.[60]

For the first time, a community would do what Amon said, and worship Alexander. Alas, this community had never heard of Amon, or Zeus-Amon, and so whatever they did was incomprehensible to the god whom they worshipped. If they gave Alexander a ticket to the heavens, as the Brahmins could have done, apparently no companion recorded it.

After several more weeks' voyage, the Macedonians encountered the ruler of a large kingdom in the central Indus Valley. They called him Mushika, confusing his name with that of his people. The outcome of the encounter was also confused. He refused to cooperate, then changed his mind, and then changed it again and rebelled, the first Indian leader to do so. The next king they encountered, in the desert and mountains to the west of Mushika, was another royal question mark. The companions called him Samba, confusing him with a legendary son of Krishna. Samba refused to cooperate, like the Mushika and the Malavas, but some cities in his kingdom submitted and then rebelled.[61]

Brahmin priests and soldiers led the rebellion. Rather than take any prisoners, Alexander executed them. He apparently did not know that this policy violated the norms of Indian warfare. Later some of them begged for mercy, waving palm fronds, and a surprised Alexander spared them. At a city farther south, Hamartelia,

Brahmins defied the Macedonians, and Alexander besieged them, but in time they begged for mercy, too, waving fronds, and Alexander spared them also. They had gotten the knack of this Greek ritual: resist, then beg. Yet these supplications did Alexander little good. For the most part, Indians did not submit to him. The king could no longer manage the business of surrender with aplomb. Farther south, deep in the lower Indus valley, Alexander's troops massacred a tribe that identified itself with Dionysus.[62]

Casualties in the southern Indus Valley were high—as many as 80,000 in the kingdom of Samba, and tens of thousands in other places. One-third of all casualties reported during the entire expedition were Indian. About half of those enslaved were Indian. This policy of mass enslavement may have angered the Indians more than the casualties, for the Vedic religion did not allow for the enslavement of worshippers of the gods of India. In contrast, the religion of the Macedonians and Greeks allowed for the enslavement of anyone, except priests in important shrines. Even more than vegetarianism, this Indian norm divided the locals from the invaders.[63]

At some point, Alexander asked the Indians in the entourage about the tenacious resistance to an obviously superior invader. Calanus, the ascetic who had joined the expedition in Taxila, answered without words. He spread a dried cowhide and stepped on the edge of it. Another part of the hide rose. He stepped on that part, and somewhere else rose. Then he stood in the center and the hide stayed flat. What did Calanus mean? Was he suggesting that Alexander could control India only by reaching the center? Where was that?[64]

The army reached the delta in springtime, as the Indus began to flood. The entire region became a motile sea of mud, turning the Gulf of Arabia brown for several miles below the river's mouth. The banks of the Indus changed without warning. A second glance and a stretch of bank disappeared, taking a hastily abandoned village with it. Alexander found even the town of Patala, located well above the flood plain, abandoned by its people. He needed help to feed and move his army, so he chased them, and when that failed, he negotiated to lure them back.[65]

Then came another, bigger surprise—the ocean. Twice a day, waters from the Gulf pushed sixty miles upriver, creating a tidal bore. At high tide, even the mangrove swamps slipped from view. As Alexander's admiral, Nearchus, later wrote:

> When the tide carrying the whole mass of the sea reaches the river channels, the rivers reverse course for miles. Nothing can withstand them. Suddenly the river bottom appears, and just as suddenly the land is under water. Ships end up sailing on dry land.
>
> These tides appear at the new and full moon for three days. . . . At the new moon, the tide comes on so strong that people living near the river's

mouth can hear it as though hearing the roar of battle. Soon the waves come charging over the shoals with a great hiss.[66]

When Alexander and an advance party arrived on the shore of the delta, they knew nothing of this dangerous tide. They assumed they could safely draw up their boats and leave a few men to guard them while they explored. When the tide came in, those men almost drowned. The party regrouped and made for higher ground many miles upriver, where most of the army had pitched camp.[67]

Alexander now began to make preparations to leave India and return to Mesopotamia. He dispatched generals to gather food and forage, cut wood for a new fleet, and seek out native shipwrights and sailors. Curious about the number and location of the Indus River's mouths, he dispatched Nearchus on voyages to chart the coast of the delta while rounding up vessels and checking for pirates.

On one such trip, Nearchus and his crew saw the greatest of all Indian specimens. As he wrote:

> The crew saw water blowing out of the sea at daybreak. A hurricane might have stirred it. When men familiar with the region explained, the crew was amazed. Animals swimming in the sea blew the water into the air.[68]

Whenever the sperm whales drew near, the men panicked and dropped their oars, and Nearchus went forward and ordered the crews to row as if going into combat—raise the battle cry with a shout, pull hard, and make a racket.

> That way the crew had the nerve to go on together. So, when the ships drew near these beasts, the men would raise the battle cry . . . the trumpets would sound, and they would row as noisily as they could. When the beasts neared the front of the ships, they would be taken aback, and would dive. Not much later, they would surface astern and blow water again.

Nearchus sympathized with his underwater foes:

> Some of the beasts went aground. A low tide caught them and left them in the shallows, or storms thrust them ashore. That way they sickened and died, and the flesh dribbled off them. People built houses with the bones. Some of the ribs were big enough for bearing beams.

Here, in the waters south of modern Karachi, the Indian venture came to an end. Alexander erected a commemorative altar along the coast and thanked the Greek and Egyptian gods for his success. Amon, he explained, had given him an oracle about this ceremony. This, his only oracle about India, had come from Egypt. Aristander did not contribute to the Indian campaign, and neither did any other diviner.[69]

Before leaving India, Alexander brought some bulls aboard a ship and sailed out to sea for the last time. Once out of sight of land, he sacrificed to Poseidon, just as he had at the start of the expedition. As his men flung the carcasses into the water, he prayed to the god for a safe return to Mesopotamia, and he also prayed that no one should ever sail farther into the Indian Ocean. When he turned and sailed back toward shore, his lookouts could not see any land for some time. The reason was that the shoreline was low and treeless. Then the subcontinent materialized, like a crease between the sea and sky.[70]

MANY VERSIONS OF the *Alexander Romance* include a story of how the king ventured not only out to sea, but also underwater. In this Byzantine version, Alexander describes his adventure in a letter written to his mother and Aristotle:

> We traveled through a desolate region toward the sea, seeing the sky and the earth but no birds or other animals. For ten days we no longer even saw the sun, just mist. Once we got to a place on the seaside and pitched camp, we stayed for some weeks.
>
> In the middle of the water lay an island, and I wanted to explore what was there. I ordered a fleet of boats built, and about a thousand of my men and I sailed in these boats to the island, which was not far from shore. As we approached, we heard the voices of men laughing, but we could not see them. They spoke Greek, but we could not understand what they said. Some of the troops swam ashore to explore, but straightaway crabs came out, dragged the men into the water, and killed them. Frightened, we returned to the mainland. As some of us were disembarking and walking along the beach, we saw a crab coming out of the water onto dry land. It was as big as a breastplate, with legs a foot long. We attacked it, but metal could not break through the shell and the creature's legs fended off wooden spears. After we picked it up and crushed it, we found seven valuable pearls inside. No one had ever seen pearls like these.
>
> I wondered what else the boundless sea had to offer, and ordered an iron cage be built, and inside the cage a glass jar three feet wide. Then I ordered that a sleeve be put in the bottom of the jar for a man to put his hand through. I wanted to submerge with the sleeve shut and learn what was at the bottom of the sea. When I got down, I would stick my hand out, catch fish, and then pull it back and shut up the sleeve. Once I built

this device, I ordered a 308-foot chain, and gave orders that no one pull me up unless I tugged on the chain by jostling the jar. "Once I get to the bottom," I said, "I'll tug, and you raise me."

Once I had got ready, I entered the glass jar for my foray into the deep. After entering by a lead hatch, I closed it, and descended 120 feet. A fish banged the cage with his tail and they brought me up when I tugged the chain. I tried again and the same thing happened. I tried a third time, descending 308 feet, and saw many kinds of fish circling me. Then a huge fish came and swallowed me and the cage and brought me to shore a mile away. After tearing up the cage with its teeth, the fish belched me up on the dry land. Three hundred sixty men sailed to the rescue, but the fish dragged them all away along with their four boats. Half senseless and dumb with fear, I fell down and did homage to divine providence for saving me from the frightful beast. I said to myself, "Stop striving for the impossible,

Anonymous illustration of Alexander and the diving bell in the *Roman d'Alexandre*, fifteenth-century French vellum.

Belgian National Library, ms. 9342 fol. 182, CHT169065.

Alexander, lest you lose your life fishing in the deep." I found my way back to my troops and ordered them to quit this country by retracing their previous line of march.[71]

Like the story of flying on birds' wings, this story of submarining described limits. Mortality set one limit. Alexander's time in India showed that religion set another. An invader with no local god to help him had made unwinnable wars on priests, monkeys, and rivers. The companions refused to go on. Now they would have to retreat.

After playing many parts well, Alexander had played the part of Indian rajah according to his own script, and this script had failed him. Why? Which god should he blame? Amon, who gave bad advice in a very foreign country? Dionysus, who got Alexander drunk with power? Zeus and his seventy days of rain? Sarasvati? Who was she?

Alexander had more gods to blame than ever, but also more reason to blame himself and not them.

10

Persian In-Laws

ENTERING INDIA RESEMBLED walking the length of a swimming pool with weights on. After the shallow end, the bottom sloped down toward the jungle, the Indus, and the floods. Leaving resembled walking back, but with no water in the pool. One trudged out of India only to enter the bumpy plateau of the Makran Desert, in southeastern Iran. For fear of dying of thirst, few ventured into the Makran. Alexander was prudent enough to send in only some of his men, but imprudent, or brave, enough to lead them himself. He would make this march his personal failure, but let his soldiers and camp followers suffer for it. Unlike Napoleon in Russia, he would never admit he was retreating.[1]

That summer of 325 Alexander and the generals met and divided the army in three parts. The king would take a fast-moving force of infantry and cavalry, and some baggage, on the 1,200-mile desert route from India to Susa, the nearest center of communication and transportation. The king would stay within a few days of the shoreline, so that he could send or receive supplies by way of a second force, traveling by sea under Nearchus. The sea route might well be faster and easier, but the Macedonians lacked the ships to put the entire force on board.[2]

Nearchus would carry enough marines to meet any threat from pirates, and he would perform the hydrographic tasks Alexander always insisted on—find rivers and seas, map and traverse them, pinpoint potable and navigable waters, worship local gods, establish an emporium or two. Alexander knew some companions would turn down the command, and told Nearchus so. That got the modest Nearchus to volunteer. The two men had been childhood friends. Among leading companions, only Hephaestion and Ptolemy had known Alexander as long.[3]

Alexander and Nearchus would both lead light, fast, vulnerable forces. Craterus, Parmenio's successor, would lead the heavy force by the only known road, which went from the Indus valley through the Bolan Pass to Kandahar and the province of Arachosia. Since the army had taken the Khyber Pass into India, the generals wanted someone to take the other pass, the Bolan, out. Then they would know the topographical fundamentals of the easternmost part of the empire. Unlike Alexander, Craterus could begin administrative work very soon,

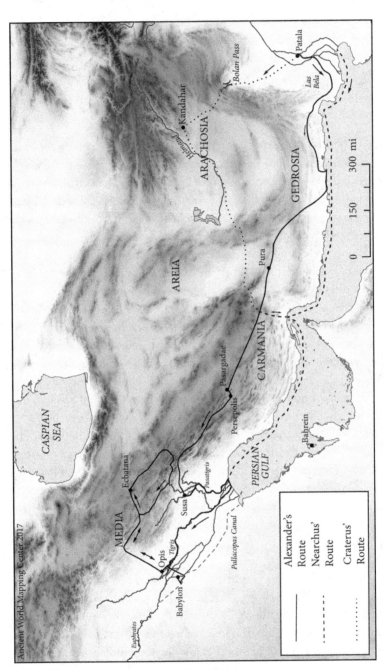

The Route of the Expedition from India to Babylon, 325–324 BC.
Ancient World Mapping Center.

Engraving showing the Bolan Pass, by Louis and Charles Haghe, 1842.
Photograph: Paul Fearn, Alamy Stock Photographs.

in Kandahar. From there he could travel passable roads to fertile country just east of Persepolis and Pasargadae. He would arrive from the north, and Alexander, coming west, would meet him. Nearchus could send a detachment inland, and meet, too. Then Craterus and Alexander would both head for Susa, and Nearchus would go back to the coast and continue sailing. After reaching the head of the Persian Gulf, Nearchus would sail upriver and reach Susa from the south. In Susa they would meet a second time.

Why not move the whole army by the safe route assigned to Craterus? That would have saved time, lives, and money. Rather than think of these advantages, Alexander thought of his personal competition with Cyrus the Great. Cyrus, he heard, had tried to cross southeastern Iran and reach India, but had to give up for lack of supplies. Alexander would do better. His fleet, sailing along the coast, would resupply him, and the prevailing winds would let the ships keep up. Thanks to Herodotus, Alexander knew that the few inhabitants along the way were so poor they ate little but fish, and had no horses or mules. They were no threat.[4]

The generals thought of this plan as another, grand version of the formula Philip had devised for the Macedonians decades before: Divide the army. Put the young men on horseback, under a young leader, and send them on a raid. Put the old men in the infantry, under an old leader, and send them into battle. Philip had used this method on the battlefield. Alexander and Parmenio used it in Anatolia, Syria, and Persia. Alexander, Craterus, and others did the same in Central Asia. In India, they added boats and elephants to the formula.

All in all, some 120,000 combatants would participate, plus many thousands of camp followers. Alexander had brought somewhat fewer people into India, and far fewer people into Asia at the start of the expedition. The return would be an epic in its own right—far bigger than the returns of Homer's heroes, not to mention Jason and his crew of fifty-five Argonauts.[5]

———————

WHILE NEARCHUS BUILT ships and recruited rowers and pilots, and Craterus marched his part of the army up the Indus valley, Alexander waited in the Indus delta for the summer heat to pass. He had decided to bring some of Puru's elephants with him, along with the indispensable Phoenician sutlers and the portable bureaucracy led by Eumenes. In all, he led some 60,000 to 70,000.[6]

He did not expect to encounter much opposition, or much in the way of Persian administration over the vast region known as Gedrosia. He and his staff remembered the Gedrosian nomads they had chased away from the baggage train five years before, as they traversed the Helmand Valley. The main enemies would be thirst and hunger. Each man needed up to a gallon of fluids a day, and thousands of animals needed a dozen times as much. Temperatures would top 100 degrees Fahrenheit.[7]

The army crossed the first stretch of the Makran Desert in a single night, a feat of marching comparable to what they achieved on the coast of Sinai, and then descended to the small, fertile plain of Las Bela, in modern Baluchistan, at the opportune time just before the harvest. Some of the people surrendered, but more ran and hid until the main body had passed on. Alexander left Leonnatus behind with some of the best of the light troops. The natives turned on him and defeated him in skirmishes where they took advantage of the terrain. Then they made the mistake of gathering their forces and fighting a battle in the open. The Macedonian troops slaughtered them.[8]

Alexander now learned that he had erred in regard to the prevailing winds. In the fall, when Nearchus would be sailing, the monsoon would cause headwinds. The admiral would not be able to travel alongside and furnish supplies. The local sailors who knew the seasonal winds had failed to inform the Macedonians.[9]

Alexander had no choice but to march on, food and fodder piled high in the wagons, and cross the Makran west of Las Bela. Unlike Arachosia and Sogdiana, the Makran had no oases, no big rivers like the Helmand, no inland seas like the Caspian. The mountains of this southern edge of the Iranian tableland drew close to the water, as in Anatolia, so the expedition headed inland, only to find just a few small, dry valleys leading into the interior. No native force guarded these valley entryways, for little worth guarding lay beyond. Even villages were rare. Rather than report strange buildings or customs, Aristobulus catalogued odd plants: the myrrh trees, plus tall, thorny mangroves growing in shallow salt water, and cutch trees with thorns so big and strong they ensnared hares and brought down passing horsemen. The garish rocks crumbled in a man's hand, and the occasional volcano spouted mud.[10]

In early fall, the Iranian coast was no longer too hot for a lizard or a snake to cross the road without being burned to death. It was still too hot for horses to be ridden and not walked, or for men to march by day rather than by night. Monsoon runoff from the mountains provided water and greenery, but not enough edibles. One night a flash flood hit the camp and carried away some of the wagons, slaves, and concubines.[11]

Stocks dwindled, but no supplies came from the fleet that should have been sailing along the coast, a few days' march away. The men went hungry, and the camp followers starved. The profits of the Phoenician sutlers went up as prices rose, and then fell as the men began to steal supplies. When Alexander heard the fleet was low on food, he ordered a convoy to take grain to the coast, but the troops stole the grain. Always enterprising, the Phoenicians gathered the gum from the myrrh trees that grew in this region, and packed the stuff on to their mules, but the men stole some of the mules. The Phoenicians also tried to gather nard roots, but failed, since the soldiers trampled the roots and used them, along with myrrh plants, as bedding.[12]

One of Alexander's top mercenaries, a Thracian, led plundering raids on native villages, but these scattered places yielded no wine or even beer, and so it seemed that the natives did not make offerings to the gods. They venerated wild animals. A snake could stop a local caravan, and so could wild asses approaching in two groups. The Macedonians found other customs peculiar, too. The natives attacked on foot, one man's tunic tied to the next man's, so no wounded would be abandoned. They bedded down a hundred yards from each other, each with his dromedary. And they were incorrigible. All these customs survived for 2,000 years, to be reported by wayward travelers in the nineteenth century.[13]

After a few weeks, the runoff from the monsoon dribbled away, and the army grew thirsty. Even a saltwater creek would be welcome, and the odd deposit of rainwater beside the road would be miraculous. When anyone found a water hole, many soldiers would rush toward it and plunge in, armor and all, only to drown underneath those piled on top of them. Alexander could not successfully order them to stop. He had to set an example of self-control, and he did it one day when scouts returned with a small supply of water from a hidden spring. They poured some water into Alexander's helmet. The king took the helmet and poured the water into the sand. That showed men they must wait their turn.[14]

Farther on, they ate their animals, as they had in the Hindu Kush. Some of the men became delirious.[15]

After a sandstorm, the guides told them they were lost. Alexander led a mounted detachment toward the coast, relying on the stars to guide him. The sea was still there. Digging in the shale, his men found a watering hole. He sent word to the army to come and join them. The army would not die of thirst—not yet.[16]

After two months they reached the Persian outpost at Pura, some 500 miles from the Indus. From here rivers and roads led to the Helmand valley, Pasargadae, and Persepolis. The generals who commanded Parmenio's old troops in Ecbatana had marched down with food and fodder. They had heard of the desert march and ignored rumors of Alexander's death. Two neighboring satraps to the north also sent supplies.[17]

No supplies came from the Persian appointed satrap in Susa, to the west. He, too, had heard the rumors, but believed them to be true.[18]

Many or most of Alexander's soldiers had survived, even if no animals remained to eat the fodder. The leading companions had all survived, and some Phoenicians, too. Many or most camp followers died. The survivors marched a joyfully banal 400 miles to another outpost, where they waited for Craterus. They had nothing to fear from any enemy. Save for Cyrus, no large army had ever entered this region, and none would try for many centuries.[19]

Hundreds of miles to the north, Craterus faced the obstacle of too many men rather than too little food. He was leading three of the six phalanx regiments, about 500 archers, some 10,000 superannuated companion cavalry, and other Macedonians destined for home, plus some 200 elephants needing up to 500 pounds of grain and 60 gallons of water a day. Camp followers raised the total to some 50,000 people and several thousand animals of all kinds. Alexander's two wives, Barsine and Roxana, went with him. Parmenio had led that many people only once, when he followed Alexander into the Zagros, and he had no royal wives to escort. After marching up the Indus and crossing at a ford, Craterus would have to wedge this mass through the Bolan Pass.[20]

The Bolan was much like the Cilician Gates—a gorge between perpendicular walls 200 or 300 feet high, crisscrossed by a brisk stream almost too cold to drink and just deep enough to ruin men's boots. The worst danger was the occasional flood when there was no sign of rain. The army learned to camp strung out over many miles of conglomerate rocks jutting into the gorge. That would protect them against floods, yet tempt no enemies, for the Macedonians' reputation preceded them. Beyond the pass lay the Iranian tableland they had seen five years before. There was no timber there or even brush for fuel, but the pasture was rich, and the flocks of sheep and goats were large and numerous: a good country for mealtime sacrifices. They reached Kandahar about the same time of year as in 330, and this time, unlike that one, the army stopped and stayed for the winter. The little colony of Macedonians still held the place. These men were among those Alexander had suspected of being loyal to Parmenio and had punished by assigning to remote outposts.

Alexander and the council assumed they had subjugated this region, but Craterus discovered that the commander, Menon, had died fighting rebels the year before. Craterus himself now defeated the rebels and compelled their chiefs to surrender. When he headed west, to meet Alexander, he left a strengthened guard at Kandahar and took the captive chiefs with him. He had cleaned up part of the mess left by an army too small to occupy what it conquered. His own casualties were negligible, and he found leading an army from atop an elephant agreeable. On his march westward, no one presumed to molest him. He soon caught up with Alexander, and learned to his surprise that his own forces now outnumbered those of the king. The reconstituted army was now smaller than it had been since before the invasion of India.[21]

Marching east, the Macedonians acquainted themselves with yet another Persian province, Carmania, famed for its wines and its system of water pipes. The population was Persian, the climate Greek, the mines and smithies efficient enough for a Greek to envy. The satrap, one of the Persians Alexander had kept in office five years before, had more or less encouraged rebels operating in the mountains, and so Alexander executed him and replaced him with a Macedonian.[22]

The king then announced a celebratory vacation. With no concession to things Egyptian or Babylonian (let alone Persian or Indian), Alexander's chamberlain, Chares, organized the largest Greco-Macedonian sacrifice since the expedition left the shores of the Mediterranean seven years before. Unlike all its predecessors, this festival celebrated survival, not victory, and it did not involve a large civilian population.

With no big city to parade in, Alexander and his companions dawdled in the wine country for a week, riding about on wagons. Eight horses drew the royal car, which held a dais where the king and his companions drank from golden bowls and goblets. Slaves waved boughs to shelter the carousers. Wagons with more companions, but covered merely by purple canopies, strove to keep up. The enlisted men had to walk, but thanks to the casks of wine and the mixing bowls rolling beside them, they gratefully fell out of line to be rescued by flute girls and camp followers. From time to time the revel stopped and the king ordered contests in singing and dancing. When his favorite, the Persian eunuch Bagoas, won the prize, he sat Bagoas beside him and gave him a kiss, to the cheers of the Macedonians.[23]

This revel beat Babylon, and so did Alexander's next marvel, imitating Dionysus. He got off the dais and rode in a chariot drawn by asses, the same as the god.[24] Wearing a wreath in his hair and a leopard skin over his shoulders, he christened the camp followers Bacchants, and put bowls of wine before the doors of houses on the route. Then he poured libations, as gods often did (gods never sacrificed animals). Dionysus was a son of Zeus, as Alexander wanted to be, but he was more military than Horus, the son of Amon, and more convivial than Heracles, who was not a god of wine country. Once the performance ended, Alexander resumed his usual duties and presided over sacrifices and games.[25]

The soldiers relished this spectacle. They had recovered their king. Their refusal to worship him had given way to a horror of parting with him. Estranged from many of his officers, Alexander was now closer to his men than ever.

———

NEARCHUS MADE THE slowest progress of the three commanders. By the time he learned about the winds, it was too late to give up. Alexander had left for the desert, so he would have to try to catch him. He knew he ought to rendezvous with Alexander at certain valleys and other points, but he did not know exactly where these places were, any more than Alexander did. He must ward off any attackers, but not pursue them and fall farther behind. He must return with interesting specimens and useful information about the naval and commercial potential of the route he was traveling, but he did not know how hard he would have to look, or how far out of his way he would need to go. To satisfy the curiosity of Alexander's surveyors, he operated what may have been the first nautical odometer. He would have been better off if he had the first compass, a device that had not yet been invented.[26]

In the first place, of course, he would have to sacrifice on behalf of the expedition. That meant replacing Alexander. Nearchus celebrated games, and so he replaced Alexander as organizer and chief judge. Everything that followed would require replacing Alexander, too.[27]

It took the fleet a week to reach the mouth of the Indus, where the crews had to stop and dig a channel through a reef blocking the way. Adverse winds kept them in camp for a month. Food ran low; the men fished to survive and drank brackish water. Finally the wind changed, and they reached the edge of the Indus delta at a harbor called the Ladies' Place, now Karachi. Nearchus did not find a trace of any Persian occupation—no men, weapons, Persian coins, or imperial documents.[28]

Day after day they passed sandstone cliffs with no sign of animals, plants, or human beings. Then good luck arrived. Halfway between Karachi and the Strait of Hormuz, they reached a rendezvous and met Leonnatus and a detachment sent by Alexander. Assuming that Leonnatus's march was less arduous than a sea voyage, Nearchus gave his sick or injured sailors to Leonnatus in exchange for fresh men.[29]

Bad luck soon proved his assumption right. At one anchorage, Nearchus could not land because 600 locals ran out of their seaside huts and lined the shallow waters along the beach, brandishing lances. The lances lacked metal tips and the warriors wore no metal gear of any kind. Nearchus ordered the ships to advance close enough so that his men could safely jump overboard but stay far enough away to be out of range. Once they got off, they had to stand or tread water as the rest joined them. Then they had to swim or trudge to shore while under fire. Nearchus had apparently sent them to their deaths. Then good luck again: the enemy could not believe that the Greek marines, in their heavy armor, were advancing through the surf. They shouted and gesticulated but did not attack. Nearchus, who had already primed his catapults, ordered them to fire, and a shower of iron bolts fell on the natives. Some fell, some ran, and some mounted camels and fled. The men they took prisoner had fingernails long and tough enough to gut fish, but no knives.[30]

After winning the battle, the Macedonians put their own tools to work repairing their ships. They could not afford to keep the prisoners as slaves. Nearchus ordered the men set free as though they were suppliants. The Macedonians never laid eyes on any women and children.

Later, coasting along a fertile country, Nearchus caught sight of a town. He told the fleet to wait a little ways offshore, as though they would not land, and then swam to the beach with a handful of men and asked the people to let him visit. Nearchus gladly accepted their tuna, cakes, and dates, but as soon as he got inside the main gate, he ordered two of his archers to climb to the top and stand guard. Once they had secured the spot, Nearchus joined them and sent a prearranged signal to the ships. The sailors came ashore on the run and the townspeople, amazed, flew to arms. Still atop the gate, Nearchus told his interpreter to make an offer: no attack on the town in return for one particular kind of food, fish meal. This was the only food that would keep and let them avoid frequently coming ashore. The people denied they had any, and tried to ascend the town walls and take up positions in order to ward off the sailors. Nearchus's archers shot them down. The sailors were now drawing near the town. Fearing that they might be enslaved as well as defeated, the people begged the Macedonians to take what meal they had and spare the place.

Nearchus agreed. After the fleet sailed away and came upon a nearby shrine, they landed and ate their fill. The gods no doubt received their share of the fish meal, a very un-Macedonian offering.[31]

The fleet was now approaching the mouth of the Persian Gulf. They heard about an island local mariners called enchanted: every ship that anchored there disappeared. Nearchus himself had just lost a vessel, and when the island came into view his crews panicked. He insisted on landing in order to prove the legend false. It was characteristic of him, and of his contemporaries, that when he wrote about this island he added an appendix about a local nymph who turned everyone who shared her company into fishes. The sun god rebuked her, and in response she turned the people of the coast into eaters of fish meal. In a second appendix, Nearchus discredited this story. He believed in the gods implicitly, but interrogated the beliefs of others.[32]

He had not made a rendezvous with Alexander's force for hundreds of miles. Then, after more weeks of voyaging, a scouting party came upon a man wearing Greek clothes. When he spoke Greek in reply to their questions, they burst into tears. With whoops and hollers they brought him to Nearchus. Nearchus reluctantly ordered all his men to stay behind and guard the ships as he set out with a small party. On the way inland a detachment of Alexander's men found them but did not recognize them. When they arrived in Alexander's camp, the king first thought only these few men had survived and the fleet was lost. After learning the truth, he played the same game with Nearchus as he had at the start of the expedition. He told his admiral he did not have to sail onward, to Mesopotamia, and Nearchus insisted on doing so.[33]

Nearchus returned to the fleet with supplies. Once again he replaced Alexander and led a collective sacrifice for good luck during the rest of the voyage.[34]

Next Nearchus reached islands in Persian Gulf, some of them prosperous because of the cultivation of dates and a pearl fishery. Phoenician crewmembers told him this region was their ancestral home. The Persian Gulf was then known as the Red Sea, and hospitable locals led him to the tomb of the Phoenician ancestor who had given his name to the gulf, a King Rufus or Red. The temples looked Phoenician but were built of wood, not the stone that Greeks and Phoenicians both preferred. At the head of the gulf, near the mouth of the Euphrates, Nearchus discovered an island emporium that brought incense and myrrh from Arabia to Babylon, whence the Phoenicians carried them to Greece. Nearly every lump of incense, the most common sacrificial offering—far more common than animals, which were troublesome and costly—reached the Greeks from this source. Nearchus discovered that the gods had the tastes of Arabs.[35]

After traveling up the Persian Gulf, he entered the river Pasatigris, east of the Tigris and Euphrates. It led to Susa, but Alexander did not meet him in the city. Instead Alexander intercepted him downstream, by a pontoon bridge on the Susa highway. The king staged games and sacrifices without any of the excesses of Carmania, but with perfect generosity. It all could have been much worse. Craterus returned with almost no losses, and Nearchus with only a few. Unlike Alexander's hero Achilles, no leading companion had died in combat.[36]

Alexander and the surveyors debriefed Nearchus. The Greeks and Macedonians, Nearchus told them, misunderstood the Euphrates and Tigris rivers. Although the Euphrates flowed into the Gulf, the Tigris flowed into a lake, and so did the Pasatigris. The two rivers became one. Several channels connected the lake to the Persian Gulf. Other waterways led into interminable marshes. The fleet had been lucky to reach the lake. On the way, marshes and rocky shallows forced the ships to advance single file.[37]

From this conversation, among others, emerged Alexander's biggest building project, a canal that would give Babylon easy access to the sea. Earlier rulers had built a canal of this kind, but the shifting of the rivers and Persian neglect made it impassable. Alexander would build another. He was not like an American soldier who regards the Corps of Engineers as an inferior branch of service.

Nearchus had traveled in a way that differed from the one Parmenio imagined when he sacrificed to Jason at Abdera, and also from the one that Alexander took when he sacrificed to Achilles at Troy. Parmenio followed the guideposts of religious conservatism and solidarity among cult members. Alexander, who in some ways might have imitated Agamemnon, leader of the Trojan expedition, preferred to imitate Achilles, who had a divine parent and cherished companions who were close friends, like Patroclus. Nearchus took a path of religious exploration, as Odysseus had done.

Each path had its dangers. That of Nearchus was the most adventurous yet the least aggressive.

———•———

WHILE THE ARMY marched on to Susa, Alexander detoured to Pasargadae. He wanted to revisit the sepulcher of Cyrus and also the rest of this ceremonial center, which resembled the palace at Aegae in Macedon. Compared to the great palaces of the Near East, both were small and intimate. The similarity between them may have suggested to Alexander how much Cyrus was like Philip. Both men were founders of armies and builders of empires and both were indispensable to Alexander's achievement. Cyrus gave him something to conquer, and Philip gave him something to conquer it with.

At Pasargadae, Alexander and his companions learned, the Persian whom he left as satrap had died while the army was in India. No Macedonian had stepped forward to replace him, and so a Persian officer who had fought at Arbela took charge. Amid the disorder in the province, robbers had come and ransacked Cyrus's tomb, carrying away everything but the sarcophagus and the couch. Cyrus's body lay on the floor, mutilated after being wrenched from the sarcophagus. The sarcophagus had fallen victim to the robbers, too. To make it easy to carry, they had hacked off corners and crushed the lid. Then they had given up trying to remove it, and abandoned it. Alexander covered the remains with his cloak, doing for Cyrus what he once had done for Darius.[38]

Enraged, he ordered his men to torture the priests and learn who had robbed the tomb, but the priests refused to say. One companion remembered later that Alexander blamed a Macedonian official for neglecting his duty and put him to death. Other companions blamed the disorder that the invading army inevitably left behind it. Aristobulus got orders to restore everything, down to the last detail, save for the door, which should be walled up. Alexander put the shrine under a stronger guard, so that no harm would come to the compound, and departed without the satisfaction of encountering Cyrus on what Alexander, after seizing the empire, would regard as equal terms.[39]

He had never become king of the Persians—never succeeded Cyrus. Now it was too late. The desecration of the tomb made Alexander's coronation unthinkable.[40]

At Pasargadae, Calanus, the one Indian who had gained Alexander's trust, killed himself. He had become sick during the trip through the desert, and when his condition worsened, he committed suicide Heracles-style, as a Greek would say, by burning himself to death atop a pyre. Since he was a Brahmin, his choice of a fiery death implied that he felt he had committed some kind of impiety. He did not say what it may have been. His last words were only that he would soon see Alexander in Babylon. What did he mean? Since he believed in reincarnation, as other Indian ascetics did, was he predicting that he would somehow rejoin Alexander once the king reached Babylon? Or did he imply that Alexander would die there, as Calanus died at Pasargadae? The companions apparently did not record any answers to these questions.[41]

The events at Pasargadae betokened larger troubles for Alexander's rule. Since Alexander had not let himself be crowned, many Persians thought him illegitimate, and some of them rebelled. Shatibrzana had come first. After Parmenio's death, a pretender to the Persian throne raised a rebellion in Media. In the eastern Caucasus, Alexander's satrap had defied him.[42]

In India, Roxana's father held the approach to the Khyber Pass, but the Macedonian satrap put in charge of the west bank of the Indus had died fighting rebels. Indian mercenaries murdered the Macedonian satrap in charge of the east bank. Without Macedonian officials nearby, Alexander's two allies, Ambhi and Puru, would likely renounce their allegiance. Calanus had predicted these difficulties, using the cowhide as an object lesson.[43]

After Alexander traveled on to Susa, he learned the tomb of Cyrus was not the only important site recently desecrated. Both Macedonian and Persian officials had plundered tombs, shrines, and palaces throughout Iran. The generals put in charge of Media after the death of Parmenio plundered the palace and shrines in Ecbatana. Alexander learned from Bagoas that the Persian satrap who failed to protect the tomb of Cyrus despoiled other royal tombs. These acts of sacrilege would alienate worshippers and gods alike.[44]

The western provinces were faring only a little better. Building continued at the site of Alexandria in Egypt. Antigonus controlled most of Anatolia, but Persian relicts controlled the rest. One companion had marched north, beyond Macedonian territory, and crossed the Danube, into the steppes of the Ukraine. Bad weather and the Scyths annihilated his small army.[45]

While in Susa, Alexander took countermeasures. He executed the pretender in Media, and he executed the disloyal Susa satrap and gave the region to a Macedonian companion. At Bagoas's suggestion, he executed the satrap of Persia and gave the post to Peucestas, the one linguist among the companions. He executed the sacrilegious generals in Media, even though they had brought him food after the march through the Makran. He blamed some of their troops as well, and executed them, too.[46]

To deter future rebellions, Alexander decided to militarize the administration of the marcher territories of the empire. For that he needed veteran commanders, but he had fewer than before. Among the top commanders traceable down to the year 324, a half dozen had died of illness or wounds; two more, serving in Media, had been put to death for sacrilege; just one had been sent home; and four had died at the hands of Alexander and fellow councilors. In all, Alexander had lost a third of his top talent.[47]

Among less important commanders, he had suffered more losses. He could not look to Persian commanders to make up the difference. He had put five of them to death, including two who fought at Gaugamela. One who fought for him had retired.[48]

He chose to combine the most demanding assignments. He gave two rebellious satrapies, Areia and Drangiana, to a Cypriot who had performed well in the fighting there. He combined part of the Caucasus with central Iran, putting both under one of the few trustworthy Persians. He combined sparsely populated Kandahar and the Makran into a single, mammoth satrapy given to a Macedonian. In India, Alexander combined territories running from Begram to the eastern Punjab, and gave this vast region to the Macedonian lieutenant of the satrap murdered by the Indian mercenaries. Recognizing that this assignment was too much for one man, Alexander named Ambhi as co-satrap. Throughout the easternmost part of the empire, satrapal boundaries dating back centuries gave way to zones of occupation. In India, these zones amounted to buffers.[49]

These administrative difficulties sprang from Alexander himself. He ruled India in the name of Dionysus but did not explain Dionysus to the Indians. Although he ignored the leading Persian gods, he expected his subordinates to respect them. The companions were his mainstay, except when Asiatics were. A veteran officer sent to some remote purlieu did not know which Alexander he represented—the agent of Dionysus, the son of Amon, or the self-appointed sheriff of Asia.

————

SEVERAL YEARS BEFORE, in Central Asia, Alexander had recruited Iranian cavalry by promising plunder and marrying a warlord's daughter. This policy had served him well in both Central Asia and India. Now, in Susa, he decided to recruit more Iranians. Besides adding Iranian units to his army, he would establish mixed units. In the infantry the Iranians would serve in the middle of each file, with Macedonian officers at the front and the back. The higher-ranking officers and garrison commanders would, of course, remain Macedonian. Satrapies would remain mixed, but more Macedonian than in the years just before the invasion of India.[50]

Alexander also decided to create more Persian companions. So far, he had created only one, Darius's brother, who switched sides after Issus. (The only other foreign companion was Puru.)[51]

Reprising his marriage to Roxana, he decided to wed Darius's daughter, one of the captives he left in Susa in 330. That ought to pacify the girl's obstreperous mother, Sisygambis, who had rejected his gifts, called him a slave master, and yet somehow induced him to call her "mother." To involve the companions, he decided to give them Persian wives, too. No one would need to divorce his present wife, any more than Alexander would divorce Roxana. Like Philip and Alexander, the companions would turn polygamous. The new wives would breed reinforcements to the Macedonian elite.

Alexander was no egalitarian. He did not intend to let Iranian men marry Greeks or Macedonians. Like other Macedonians (and like the Persians), he was patriarchal: the son of a Macedonian was a Macedonian, and never mind the mother. Otherwise, Alexander would be an Epirote, like Olympias. As for the complication of his being the son of Amon, he kept it to himself. The Persians would not understand this subject any better than the Macedonians and Greeks did.

The king now staged the most costly of his celebrations. The quartermasters rounded up the cattle and Alexander sacrificed at an altar in plain view of Inshushinak, the local Zeus, and the other Elamite gods. Ambassadors from the Greek world and elsewhere attended the ceremonies, contributing 15,000 talents to defray the costs. Thirty thousand young Iranians recruited into Alexander's service stood guard. Some thousands of Macedonians commanded (or stood guard over) the Iranians. Persians as well as Macedonians guarded Alexander. Nearchus and the column leader Leonnatus received the usual Greek honors— money, golden crowns, accolades. Some of Nearchus's captains and sailors got honors, too, but Craterus and his men, who had not discovered any new lands or fought any fish-eaters, got nothing more than the ample sacrificial meal given to all of Alexander's tens of thousands of troops.[52]

Next came the group wedding. The wedding tent held a hundred couches, and each couch came with paraphernalia worth a fifth of a talent. That was a Persian touch. So were the silver and the purple clothes and cloths, and the gold and silver plating for the tent pillars, inlaid with jewels, and the curtains embroidered with figures of wild animals. Alexander ordered a bridal chamber built for every couple. He might have used the Susa palace, but he preferred a tent, the kind of place he had lived in for most of the last ten years.[53]

Alexander took not one but two Persian wives, Darius's daughter and also a daughter of Darius's predecessor, Artaxerxes. (This second thought occurred to him when he recalled that Darius's family were usurpers.) Alexander assigned a daughter of Darius to Hephaestion. That would make Alexander and Hephaestion in-laws. Craterus got a niece of Darius. Two top companions, Ptolemy and Eumenes, got daughters of Artabazus, Alexander's father-in-law as well as the first important Persian to take Alexander's side. The regimental commander Perdiccas, a veteran of all the big battles, got a daughter of the Persian satrap of Media, and another commander got a daughter of Spitamanah, the Bactrian insurgent. That match showed the Central Asians that Alexander remained friendly toward them. Eighty more companions got wives from leading Persian families.

Every one of these ninety-odd couples got a dowry from the king and a bedchamber in the tent. In addition, all men with concubines got a gratuity. Through these acts of largesse, Alexander provided for any and every Asian son of a ranking Macedonian, even those born out of wedlock. His own Barsine had just presented him a son he named Heracles.

Where did Alexander get the idea for these marriages? Not from the brides. He got it from Philip, who had married a Scyth as well as an Epirote and several Greeks. Alexander now had an informal harem of his own.

After the ceremony, Chares presented conjurors from Sicily and Iona, harpists and flautists from Athens and elsewhere, and actors in scenes from Euripides and other tragedians. A Macedonian touch was a drinking contest—unmixed wine, which might discourage Greek competitors who customarily diluted wine with water. The winner received a talent for his feat of drinking three gallons of wine, but died of the aftereffects. Chares, who was a Greek, claimed that forty-one contestants died. Most were Macedonian soldiers, the same as the winner, the Homerically named Promachos, "fighter in the front rank."[54]

To give his Macedonian soldiers something to celebrate, Alexander offered to discharge their debts, but they did not wish to tell him how much they owed. He promised to pay in full, no matter what, and then they informed him. Alexander disbursed 10,000 talents, or 5,000 less than the contributions by the ambassadors. He was still the richest man in the world—the richest who had ever been. The coins he minted for his troops and government contained more gold and silver than the U.S. currency of the sound-money decades after the Civil War. That made him richer than all Gilded Age American millionaires put together.[55]

ONLY ONE LEADING companion in the eastern part of the empire failed to attend the weddings. Harpalus had managed imperial finances for seven years from his post in Babylon. When Alexander emerged from the desert and began to punish wayward administrators, Harpalus decided to flee to the west.

Harpalus was a lifelong companion of Alexander's. When Alexander and Philip quarreled about the prince's getting married, Harpalus had gone into exile with Ptolemy, Nearchus, and Alexander's other intimates. In 333, before the battle at Issus, he fled, thinking Darius would defeat the Macedonians, but Alexander coaxed him to return two years later. After that, he performed well as a financier. He took the money seized at Ecbatana—the last great haul of gold and silver—to Babylon and centralized finances there. He paid for Alexander's expedition to India, sending the king fancy gear for 25,000 men and 7,000 mercenaries. And he kept some monies for himself. All companions did. Cleomenes kept more, and Harpalus kept the most.[56]

Much went to the upkeep of Pythonice, the Athenian courtesan who lived with him in the palace of Nebuchadnezzar. He erected statues of her and himself, as would be normal if he were king of Babylon and she were queen.[57] Although she was a slave and the daughter of a slave, Harpalus eventually married her, and she bore him a daughter. When she died, he erected cenotaphs to her in both

Babylon and Athens. He paid the nephew of an important Athenian politician a hefty thirty talents to build the Athenian memorial. For centuries it remained the biggest private funerary monument in Greece.[58]

Unlike the administrators Alexander punished after arriving in Iran, Harpalus had not rebelled or neglected his duties, and so he did not fear Alexander for these reasons. He fled for the same reason that the army wished to stop going eastward. He was quitting, and he feared that once Alexander returned to Babylon, he would never be allowed to quit, or would have to give up the money he had amassed. Although his limp made him unfit for fighting, he thought like an Argonaut. He had captured his snatch of the Golden Fleece, and he wished to go back to Greece.

In early 324 he headed for Athens with 5,000 talents and about as many troops. Once there, he would face a choice. He could present himself in proper, diplomatic fashion and ask to become a permanent resident of Athens. For that, he would have to supplicate. Or he could barge into the city. If he preferred supplicating, he must leave his troops behind, enter Athens without fanfare, and take refuge in a shrine. (The Acropolis would be rather showy; better a shrine in the port of Piraeus.) While the Athenian assembly considered his case, he would be safe from arrest by the Macedonian garrison stationed in town.

Harpalus should have supplicated, but he was Harpalus, and so in May 324 he paraded into the harbor with thirty warships. The chief of the Macedonian garrison warned the city not to admit him. Realizing his mistake, Harpalus withdrew to Taenarum, a Peloponnesian port of call for mercenaries, and paid off his men. He returned to Athens with just three ships but most of his money. He supplicated and began to distribute bribes to further his cause.[59]

Athenian politics now enmeshed Harpalus. Leading Athenians feared that Alexander and his viceroy Antipater would make war on the city unless Athens surrendered Harpalus to the Macedonians. Antipater soon requested that the city extradite Harpalus, and so did Alexander's mother, Olympias. The orator Demosthenes maintained that Antipater and Olympias did not matter. Only Alexander did, and he was months away. Let the king send a message demanding the extradition of Harpalus. Until then, Harpalus should remain in the city. The Athenians agreed. Some had already pocketed bribes from Harpalus, including Demosthenes.[60]

When news of Harpalus's flight to Athens reached Alexander, the king was furious. A rumor circulated that he killed the messenger who brought the news. Alexander threatened to besiege the city. The flight of Harpalus obsessed him so much that his armorer, hoping to win favor, offered to donate the siege equipment.[61]

The Athenians temporized. First they posted guards around the shrine where Harpalus was staying (or sometimes staying, allowing for trips to drinking parties), and then they let him escape. He sailed back to Taenarum, where he picked up a few mercenaries and embarked for Crete, where he turned freebooter. Soon after, Athenians heard that his slaves had murdered him but could not find his money. Some said that Harpalus's steward absconded with the money and sailed to Rhodes, where a Macedonian official caught him. But what became of Harpalus? Perhaps he fell in with a Spartan soldier of fortune who killed him after robbing him but getting no money.

Unable to bag Harpalus, Alexander asked Antipater to pursue Demosthenes. When Antipater told the Athenians to surrender him, they hesitated, giving Demosthenes a chance to escape. The orator fled the city and supplicated in a rural shrine of Poseidon on the far side of the Saronic Gulf, some forty miles away. Antipater, white on the outside, would never arrest a suppliant in a shrine. Instead he blockaded the shrine, cutting off Demosthenes's supply of food. Demosthenes faced the choice of starving or surrendering to Antipater, who would surely execute him. He decided to poison himself. The priests at the shrine hastened to remove him before his death on holy ground offended the god. They hauled the dying man, convulsed by poison, out of the little temple with its serene view of the sea, and heaved him in front of the Macedonian troops who had surrounded the place.[62]

Demosthenes expected to die, but Harpalus expected to survive through supplication. Then Alexander rendered supplication ineffectual. Harpalus's large fortune did not rescue him. Although Alexander made large fortunes possible, he also made these fortunes insignificant in the face of overwhelming military power. He caused the suppliant Harpalus to die in obscurity.

Distorting the rite of supplication was a new kind of religious misstep. In the past, Alexander had offended or ignored foreign gods such as Anahita. Now he put himself at odds with Zeus, who expected suppliants to be treated with respect, if not kindness. Alexander himself apparently did not grasp this change. He had come to see Zeus as Zeus-Amon, or simply Amon, a god with other attributes.

———

THE PERSIAN-LANGUAGE POET Nizami, writing in the Middle Ages, said that Alexander invented the mirror and along with it the custom of using mirrors at wedding ceremonies. This episode occurs in "Alexander the Great as a Prophet," part of Nizami's *Sikander Nama*, or *Book of Alexander*.

When Sikander became the key to the world, the first mirror image appeared. He saw it when he had a sword made and looked at the reflection on the blade. He had never seen the like, and so he decided to create a true and perfect mirror. First, his men cast gold and silver into a mold and polished it to a high sheen, but no recognizable image appeared. They tried several metals from Alexander's mines, but the metals showed weird images.

Finally, they tried iron. Rassam, the blacksmith, polished it until it shone. The character of the metal emerged, and Rassam saw identifiable shapes. Yet no matter what Rassam did, he did not see an accurate likeness. If he broadened the mirror, it made the face look too broad; if he lengthened it, it made the forehead long. Then, when he made it round, he saw accurate likenesses. No matter how he took it up and held it, he saw himself as he was. He had perfected the mirror. Through knowledge of geometry—and out of the pith of the iron—Sikander's servant wrought a display of true forms.

Pleased at seeing his own image, Sikander gave a kiss to the back of the mirror. Ever since, brides do the same thing on their wedding day. They give a kiss as a present to the mirror that displays their faces.[63]

Other Persian and Arabic tales explain how Alexander used the mirror. In one, the mirror caused everyone who looked at it to die, so Alexander put it atop a tower in hopes that a dragon would see it. The dragon did, and perished, but so did curious passers-by. In several tales, the whole world appeared in Alexander's mirror, and so Alexander kept the mirror secret until his death. Afterward, the companions discovered the mirror and looked into it, but its magical power vanished and they saw only themselves.[64]

II

The Waters of Life

IN THE SPRING of 324 Alexander confronted the first enemy he could not vanquish—his responsibility to rule an empire. In the two years since the generals compelled him to turn back at the river Beas in India, he had avoided this invisible opponent. He sailed down the Indus rather than leave India the way he came. Once at the mouth of the Indus, he slogged through the desert rather than take the whole army on the short, safe route assigned to Craterus. He delayed again by cavorting in the Persian wine country. In Susa, he diverted himself with mass marriages. Now he must go and sit on the throne once held by Cyrus and Nebuchadnezzar, and become a ruler rather than a commander and an adventurer. Rather than risk his life, he must risk being bored.[1]

The generals welcomed the return to Babylon, the city chosen as the capital of the empire. It was rich, central, and cosmopolitan. Harpalus, one of the top administrators, had lived like a king there, and they expected to do likewise. Babylon had treated the generals better than any other captured city, and they knew that if they and the army went home, Antipater and his forces would make them superfluous, if not unwelcome.

The infantry and cavalry wanted to bypass Babylon and go home to Macedon and Greece. They wanted Alexander to go home with them, and play Jason to their Argonauts. In spite of everything, they thought of him as the epic chieftain of the Macedonians, not as king of Babylon or Egypt.

What did Alexander want? To resume exploring, and probe the obstacles to navigation discovered by Nearchus in lower Mesopotamia. He headed south by boat and left Hephaestion the task of marching the main body of the army into the marshes of lower Mesopotamia. The current wafted Alexander and a light force all the way to the Persian Gulf while Hephaestion battled mosquitoes, snakes, and crocodiles. Next Alexander sailed along the coast and up the Tigris, removing barriers to navigation as he went. Hephaestion strove to keep up.[2]

Alexander sailed as far as Opis, at the head of navigation, and pitched camp. From Opis one road went to Iran and another went north to Europe and south to Babylon. Once the troops of Mazdai had guarded this spot. Now Alexander and Hephaestion's waterlogged men rested there under the dry Mesopotamian summer sun.

The king now sprang another surprise on his army. Summoning his officers, he ordered them to send the older Macedonians and Greeks home with bonuses. Young soldiers would remain with Alexander in Mesopotamia. So would most of the officers, and all the Iranians, who would replace the departing veterans.

Dividing the army by age insulted the older men, and preferring Iranians insulted everyone. The soldiers replied that they wished to go home together, and threatened to quit. Let Alexander manage without them and ask his "father," Amon, for help. Agitators emerged among the troops, and some lower-ranking officers expressed sympathy with their men.[3]

Alexander responded by calling a meeting of officers and soldiers. The generals, led by Craterus and the regimental commanders Perdiccas and Polyperchon, stood beside him on the dais. Around the dais stood the lead company of the shield bearers. The ex-bodyguard Seleucus commanded this elite light infantry, which Parmenio's son Nicanor had led until he died in the Iranian desert.

Alexander turned to the generals beside him and ordered them to arrest the leading agitators, including some lower-ranking officers. The generals said and did nothing. Rather than repeat his order, Alexander peered into the crowd, picked out thirteen agitators, and ordered the shield bearers to arrest them. Seleucus and his lieutenants marched into the crowd. Raising his voice, Alexander ordered Seleucus to lead the thirteen away and execute them. Seleucus complied. Everyone else was struck dumb.[4]

The king now made the army a speech showing what he had learned from the fiasco in India.[5] He began by acknowledging Philip was his father. He eulogized Philip for enriching the Macedonians, for rescuing them from their neighbors, and for enlarging the kingdom, defeating one enemy after another. Then Alexander turned to the subject of his own reign. When he took the throne he owed some 1,200 talents, but since then had acquired the wealth of Anatolia, Egypt, the Levant, and Persia. He had paid his debts and his men, and given them offices, concubines, and lands. He had nothing more to show for his labors than a priest would—a place of honor, a purple cloak, and a diadem—and, like a priest or the head of a modest household, he ate and drank what his companions did.[6]

He then turned to the subject of his military service. He fought as hard as the men had, he said, and was wounded as often. He buried the dead with honor. Although he sometimes quarreled with his companions, he always provided for them.

Nothing about Egypt, Babylon, the crown of Persia, or the follies of India; no Amon, Marduk, Heracles, or Dionysus. There was no empire of Alexander, only the expedition of Alexander and the Macedonians.

He had them now, and he knew it. He told them all to go home, with bonuses. If that was the sort of companions they were—deserters and traitors—he would not complain. He would stay behind, stuck with soldiers who were Persians and barbarians.

With that he sprang down from the platform and went to his quarters. Lest the men think he would change his mind, as he had in India, he ordered leading Persians to come to the tent and accept commands replacing Macedonians. Using Persian terms, he called these officers kinsmen. When the Macedonians learned of this, they became distraught. How could their king treat the Persians as kinsmen and deny them this honor?[7]

A veteran officer, the cavalry commander Callines, now went among the men, and encouraged them to go to Alexander's quarters and beg to be reconciled with him. They came en masse and threw their weapons on the ground, supplicating. Until Alexander took pity on them, they said, they would not budge.[8]

Alexander opened the door, and when he saw some of them weeping he wept himself. All of you are my kinsmen, he told the Macedonians. Callines approached him and kissed him. Then Alexander let any Macedonian who wished approach and kiss him. Although he comforted them, he did not accede to their wishes. Only the old soldiers would go home. The rest would remain, alongside Persians, and so would he.

They had succumbed to Alexander as though he were a god. Yet they never would have succumbed had he insisted on being treated as a god. On that score, they had always resisted him. They adored him only when he sank down on the brink of death, on the battlefield, or now, when he threatened to withhold his affection and they begged for his blessing.[9]

An arduous day had only begun. Alexander sacrificed to Zeus, Heracles, and Dionysus but invited Persian priests to participate. He had never done that before. Then he prayed aloud for the Persians, Greeks, and Macedonians to be like-minded. He was not making an egalitarian gesture. He was praying to his own gods, not those of the Persians. He was, however, trying to undo the harm done to Iranian religion at Persepolis, Pasargadae, and Bactra.[10]

At the feast afterward, he put Macedonians in the best places, but Persians in the second-best. Next came donatives—the promised bonuses for those who would go home, and help for soldiers worrying about how they would support illegitimate children born in Asia. The king would provide for these children by paying for their upbringing and keeping them in Babylon.

Alexander promised all departing soldiers a safe return. If these men were exiles from their own cities, he ordered the cities to welcome them. He also made sure that civilians displaced by war could return home. Going farther still, he ordered cities to allow exiles of all kinds to return. The number of returning soldiers, refugees, and exiles under Alexander's protection would reach tens of thousands. The governments of these cities would object to welcoming home so many, especially the hardened soldiers, but Alexander allowed exceptions only for murderers and traitors. Those who were hateful to Zeus because of these two crimes should remain in exile. All others deserved help, and they would get it from Alexander and Zeus both. Alexander had these orders announced soon afterward at the Olympic Games, the largest gathering in the Greek world. Stunned, the Greeks delayed complying.[11]

Alexander, of course, had created the problem he was trying to solve. Some of the returning soldiers were men he was pensioning off. Others were mercenaries who had been serving his satraps but found themselves dismissed the previous year, in 325. Alexander did not want his satraps to have so much manpower. Still others were mercenaries who had served under Darius. Harpalus probably recruited all three types.[12]

Alexander sprang more surprises at Opis. He ordered Craterus and Polyperchon, two of his leading subordinates, to leave court. He gave them the honorable exit of taking the returning veterans home. When they arrived in Macedon, Craterus would take charge there. Alexander also ordered Antipater out of Macedon, which the old man had governed for ten years, and summoned him to Babylon to assume unnamed responsibilities. Antipater must bring all his troops with him and turn them over to Alexander. Along with breaking up the army, Alexander was breaking up the companions.[13]

His last surprise reflected the same suspicious attitude toward subordinates. Alexander ordered several satraps to stay with him rather than go to their posts. He was filling his court with men he had promoted but would not put to work.[14]

The king triumphed: a mass supplication, an opulent sacrifice, a horizon without enemies. Next he should go to Babylon to establish a central administration with Antipater as lord president of the council. Yet he did not. He was already inviting sixty or seventy to meals. Why go to Babylon, where he would have to invite more?[15]

Alexander preferred to go sightseeing. As soon as Craterus and the retirees marched away, he and his light force headed up the road from Opis to Iran. The weather was better than in 330, when they first traveled this way, and they had no one like Darius to chase. The stony road—better stones than dust—wound up the hills past skirts of wildflowers and fields of hollyhock. Bees teemed by day, stars by night. Days later they reached Ecbatana, in a valley of country estates, all greensward and vineyards, occupied by Parmenio's old officers. The exuberant army celebrated a seven-day festival to the Olympian gods, and also an annual feast in honor of Dionysus.[16]

During the holiday, Alexander's lifelong friend Hephaestion fell ill. Alarmed, Alexander prayed to a local god he took to be Asclepius, but Hephaestion died some days later. Alexander's grief was Homeric, down to cutting the manes of his horses. He had always modeled himself on Achilles, and now he had lost Hephaestion, just as Achilles lost Patroclus. And, like Achilles, he was to blame: Achilles had let Patroclus die in his place, and Alexander had let Hephaestion take part in this ill-fated trip.

Boredom gave way to frenzy. Alexander killed Hephaestion's physician and destroyed the shrine of the mistaken god. Turning on the Persians, he ordered them to put out the sacred fires of their religion. They found this request ominous. If the fires went out, that would harm Alexander, the king. Alexander even pressured the oracle of Amon in distant Siwah. He asked the oracle to raise Hephaestion to the godhead. The oracle surely said no, but the messenger Alexander had sent told him Amon had said yes.[17]

For the funeral, he ordered an altar brought up from Babylon at a cost of 10,000 talents. He had the body embalmed, not cremated, as though Hephaestion were Egyptian royalty. He more or less bullied the companions into dedicating their weapons to Hephaestion, an honor Greeks gave heroes. After the funeral, Alexander staged games with 3,000 competitors from throughout the empire. The prizes far exceeded any offered in Greece.[18] Next Alexander started two memorials, a shrine in Alexandria and a mausoleum in Babylon shaped like a mini-ziggurat to resemble the tomb of Cyrus in Pasargadae. That would show Harpalus. He also sent an ironic offering to the chief shrine of the uncooperative Asclepius, in Epidaurus. The god did not deserve it, Alexander said, but would get it anyway.[19]

Alexander rued losing his friend, just as he resented having to turn back in India. He expressed his chagrin through an insult. According to Macedonian custom, Alexander should have given Hephaestion's cavalry unit the name of its new leader, Perdiccas, but he refused. Having lost Hephaestion, he did not value other companions as highly as before.[20]

The funeral and the shrines consumed the summer of 324. To get Alexander out of Ecbatana, the companions proposed a military campaign against a tribe of highwaymen living near the Babylon-Ecbatana road. He annihilated them in just a month that fall. Alexander did not know it, but he had fought his last battle. Now he must go to Babylon and be king.[21]

———◦———

AS LONG AS Alexander was away, the Babylonian priests paid little attention to him. They busied themselves with perpetual repairs to Babylon's crumbling mud-brick shrines. Alexander helped fund the work, but they supervised—after an exorcist dressed in white laid the first brick while toting his ceremonial leaden axe. Provided the priests knew where Alexander was, they routinely mailed him cuts of sacrificial meat. They prospered during price rises caused by Alexander's new currency. Even during a shortage of barley, the staple of the Babylonian diet, they amassed enough gold to make Marduk a new crown.[22]

As Alexander drew near the city, ending his seven-year absence, priests began issuing warnings and reporting omens. After checking the stars, top astronomers advised the king that entering the city would be inauspicious. A Babylonian liver-reader told the companion in charge of the city garrison that Alexander's very life was in danger. A prestigious deputation said Alexander should not enter from the east, with his face toward the setting sun. Instead he should enter from the west and face the rising sun. Otherwise the sun would set on his reign, as had happened to Darius. Alexander tried to comply, but marshes blocked the western approaches, forcing him to enter from the east.[23]

Alexander moved into the palace of Nebuchadnezzar with his wives, bodyguards, and a handful of close companions. He lived more modestly and less gaily than Harpalus, the previous occupant. During the heat of the day he held court outdoors, reclining on a silver-footed couch beside the artificial streams in the palace gardens. Mesopotamian dignitaries arrived from many cities, asking for tax exemptions and other privileges given to Babylon. Alexander dispatched Aramaic-speaking companions to the palace library, where they consulted the scribes in charge of vast stores of clay tablets on every subject from royal land holdings to the size and shape of the world (including maps). He needed to form a mental picture of his empire and especially of his new capital.[24]

Alexander and his companions had never lived in a large city. They had merely visited Susa, Memphis, and Tyre, all smaller and less diverse. Now Babylonian priests, officials, and merchants crowded into the palace. How many Babylonians should he add to the imperial elite? He had replaced the now dead Mazdai with a Macedonian, but he assigned Mazdai's half-Babylonian son to the companion cavalry. He decided that no one, either Macedonian or Babylonian, should replace Harpalus as financier for the entire empire.[25]

Foreign emissaries pressured him, too. Greek ambassadors arrived, bringing gifts and making requests for help in dealing with returning soldiers and exiles. They thanked him for the temples he had built or expanded in Greece, but they failed to honor him as a god. When Carthaginian ambassadors came hoping to establish peaceful relations, he chastised them for aiding the enemy during his siege of Tyre. Then he threatened to make war on them, adding he would pardon them for the time being. When Arab sheiks came out of the desert bringing impressive gifts such as frankincense, he demanded that they submit to him. To his amazement, they refused.[26]

News from Macedon and Greece also disappointed him. Besides refusing to adore him in person, the Macedonians and Greeks did not build altars to him and worship that way. The Macedonians worshipped Hephaestion as a hero, but not Alexander. Spartans gave a laconic reply to a suggestion about divine honors. Alexander, one of them said, could be "called" a god. Some Athenian citizens or other residents worshipped at an altar for Alexander and Hephaestion, but the community did not. Instead it watched the proceedings with dismay. One orator said the worshippers should purify themselves after each sacrifice. Another brought a lawsuit against an Athenian who had proposed that the community join in. A third joked that he did not care whose son Alexander was—Amon's, Zeus's, or Poseidon's.[27]

Alexander did not expect good religious news from Asia. A Greek oracle from western Asia Minor declared him to be a god, but a Persian oracle circulating there said that the Persians would overthrow the Macedonians. The Phoenicians thought of him as a mere priest-king, and he now knew what the Arabs thought of him.[28]

Countless administrative decisions ensnared him. One concerned a slave who deserted his master, a eunuch in the service of the goddess Artemis at her Ephesus shrine. This runaway had fled to another shrine and taken refuge. The eunuch knew that simply removing the slave from the place would be wrong. Instead he wrote Alexander and asked for royal permission to do it. Don't, Alexander replied. Give the slave a hearing, as was customary. Although Alexander sometimes took liberties with suppliants, he prudently did not allow others to. Yet he was to blame. If he had been less powerful, a eunuch in faraway Ephesus never would have written in the first place.[29]

He could strike back, but only with artwork. The painter Apelles painted him with a thunderbolt in his hand, the same as on the Indian commemorative medallions, and Alexander donated the picture to the temple of Artemis at Ephesus. Greek viewers paid this work the compliment of saying it was lifelike, not god-like. They did not worship it.[30]

For the first time, Alexander had to wait for news about his army rather than create the news himself. He still had 10,000 Greeks and Macedonians in and around Babylon, but some of his best officers and men were on their way home with Craterus. Alexander did not know where Craterus was, for that matter, nor when Antipater would reach Babylon with reinforcements.[31]

As a respite, Alexander took short boat trips. He sailed downstream to inspect the ruined canal beside the Euphrates, and visited the Alexandria lately established by Hephaestion in the delta. He resumed looking for royal tombs, an interest that would grow into an obsession. When he got back, he entertained a sculptor's proposal to turn Mount Athos, in northern Greece, into a colossal statue of him. No, he decided, but he listened to proposals for some other extravagant projects.[32]

To keep his companions busy, he sent some on exploratory expeditions to supplement Nearchus's discoveries. One companion sailed into the Persian Gulf and reached Bahrain and the pearl fishery. Another sailed to the Strait of Hormuz, and a third started in Egypt and apparently reached Yemen. These voyages gave Alexander and his surveyors their first good information about the Arabian Peninsula.[33]

As he studied his improved maps, Alexander seized on a way to escape from Babylon: the tidy conquest of Arabia. While leaving the main body of the army in the city with Antipater, he could lead a light force of some thousands. Nearchus could accompany him with a fleet. To raise the troops, he would pursue his plan to enroll Iranians in the phalanx. Newly promoted Macedonians would train the recruits and teach them enough Greek to follow orders. If necessary, he could recruit more non-Macedonian officers like Mazdai's son.[34]

To get ships, Alexander ordered forty-seven Phoenician vessels disassembled and brought eastward, and he had a harbor dredged at Babylon to house them. To improve navigation along the Euphrates, he repaired the long-impassible drainage canal. In flood season, it would fill with water and carry Alexander's scouts toward Arabia. After flood season, the marshes would dry out, and troops could disembark along the canal and march into the interior. A lock would keep the canal deep enough to be navigable.[35]

Alexander did not call a general meeting about Arabia, and so the companions made their objections one by one or in small groups. Commanders disliked serving with Iranians, and engineers busy with Alexander's canal disliked the prospect of leaving the Euphrates valley for the desert. Everyone disliked the proposed time of departure, summer, when the temperature often reached 120 degrees Fahrenheit. They also wondered about the proposed starting point, on the lower Euphrates. What lay beyond? They did not know the extent of the vast wasteland later known as the Arabian Empty Quarter, but they knew that all the caravan routes lay well to the north. Reaching these routes would take weeks of marching in desert winds that dried up the water in the water skins. Withered herbs were the only food. Camels could live on them, but men and horses could not.

How would Alexander manage the empire meanwhile? If the Greek cities, ever restive, heard that Alexander had vanished in the desert with his army, they might seize the chance to rebel.

Assuming the Babylonians were consulted, they added another caution. The last king before Cyrus, Nabonidus, had gone to Arabia and tried to govern Mesopotamia from there. Marduk and the gods of Babylon took offense. They saw to it that Cyrus took away Nabonidus's throne. The gods might well do the same to Alexander.

Alexander remained obdurate. He said Craterus would be on the scene to suppress any Greek uprising. Besides, the invasion would pay. Babylonian traders said that the Arabs were so rich they wore bracelets and necklaces made of gold and precious stones. According to Babylonian records, the Arabs gave one Assyrian king 30,000 camels as tribute, along with 5,000 bags of spices. Arabia would be India on the cheap.[36]

Above all, Alexander said, the Macedonians must make this expedition to defend their reputation. As he reminded them, the visiting sheiks had refused to submit, even when he insisted.

To resist Alexander, the companions needed help from Antipater, who was postponing his arrival in Babylon. The regent sent his son, Cassander, in his stead. Cassander's younger brother, Iollas, introduced him at court. Iollas was the king's cupbearer as well as the lover of Alexander's new favorite, the ship captain Medius. In the peculiar circumstances of that winter, Medius, Iollas, and Cassander replaced Alexander's older and better-known counselors.

Encouraged by his new clique, Alexander fell into a routine of nightly drinking, late mornings, and dice. He had not lived this way before. When campaigning, he breakfasted at dawn, dined in the late afternoon, and drank moderately. He did not play dice except when he was sick or recuperating from wounds, and then he played for trifling stakes. His private life testified to the insignificance of sex. Drunkenness and sex, he said, reminded him of his own mortality, and he needed no reminders besides his wounds. He was not chaste, any more than he was abstemious, but he did not indulge himself, and he had no romance in his makeup. His three marriages were all arranged, and he arranged them himself. When he had a mistress, Campaspe, pose for a painter, and the painter became infatuated with her, he gave her to the painter as a present. In exchange, he got the picture.[37] He had all the appetites of the men in the Macedonian elite, such as his father, and he indulged these appetites, but he had never let appetites get the better of his ambition. He had been more self-controlled than Philip and than many of his generals. He always had to ask himself whether he was a match for Cyrus, the way Caesar later asked whether he was a match for Alexander.

Now he drank with impunity. He had driven away or killed the older companions who could and would have stopped him. Instead he surrounded himself with men too young and too weak to stop him—the clique of Medius, but also young bodyguards such as Ptolemy and commanders such as Nearchus.[38]

Worse, Alexander had forsaken the cult that helped the king and his companions share risks and rewards. He had not led his companions in an act of public thanksgiving since he celebrated the marriages at Susa a year before. He had not given them much largesse since India. So much for shared rewards. Since coming to Babylon, they no longer shared any risks.

While neglecting his duties as a priest, Alexander explored other religious roles. Some of these roles, such as temple-building, sustained his empire, but other roles did not. In Babylon he consulted his horoscope, a new pastime, and dressed like Amon-Re at dinner, with horns on his head. Court gossips whispered that Alexander was impersonating any god he liked, even Artemis. He carried a bow and arrows on his shoulders, like her, and when he played Heracles he added Persian accouterments.[39]

The companions remembered that one of Philip's doctors had dressed like this at some dinner parties. Philip had laughed at him and then ignored him. Now the king was dressing this way. Yet men like Medius made no objection, and they approved when Alexander said he would recognize his father Philip by building him a pyramid at Giza—the biggest pyramid of all.[40]

The Babylonian priests might have helped Alexander concentrate on his duties. So far, they had helped him in some ways and burdened him in others. Now relations between the king and the priests would deteriorate.

———

BY SPRING 323, Alexander had spent several months in Babylon. The equinox approached, and with it the New Year's festival that would reinvigorate the king's authority. The Babylonians maintained the fiction that the king came to the throne at this time, so the festival marked an anniversary. The priests could not force Alexander to attend, only warn him of the consequences of neglecting his duty. The foolish king who preceded Cyrus, Nabonidus, skipped the festival during the nine years he lived in Arabia. That especially explained why he lost the throne to Cyrus. Nabonidus would not have Marduk, so Marduk would not have Nabonidus. Always cooperative with the priests, Alexander agreed to participate.[41]

The festival was very ancient, and it would go on for several centuries more. Descendants of Alexander's generals celebrated it as late as 204 BC.[42]

Esangil, the main site of the ceremonies, was usually off-limits, even for the king. Now the shrine would welcome the king and a select few of his subjects. The main gate, usually closed at night and guarded by day, would be open throughout, and Alexander, after a few days of coaching, would arrive from the palace, many blocks away, and enter the shrine and even the temple. A master of ceremonies, the *sheshgallu*, would perform the rites that preceded the king's arrival, and then guide Alexander through a second coronation, a grand tour of several shrines in and around Babylon, and a sacred marriage. By the end of the festival, Alexander would have a new wife as well as a new lease on the throne of thrones.

On the first day, April 5, the main gate to Esangil opened and "insiders" with the right to enter the shrine, appeared in force to make preparations. Waiting in the palace, Alexander learned his lines from one of the priests. On the next day, the *sheshgallu* rose two hours before dawn and prayed to Marduk on Alexander's behalf. "Display your womb," he asked this male god, a Babylonian phrase meaning "show pity." Then the *sheshgallu* asked, "Establish the exemptions for the sons of Babylon, the protected people." Alexander had learned of these exemptions during his negotiations with Mazdai.

For the rest of the day functionaries came and went while the king remained in the palace. He kept rehearsing for two more days, as temple craftsmen fashioned figurines to place before the patron god of judges, and the *sheshgallu* prayed to Marduk and to Marduk's consort, Zarpanit, asking them to protect the temple of Esangil. At night, from the courtyard of the shrine, the *sheshgallu* gave thanks to the constellation of stars the Greeks later called Pegasus. The Babylonians said that Marduk modeled Esangil on this constellation.[43]

On the fourth day, Alexander's work began. The priests escorted him from his palace to Esangil and ushered him into a chapel for the scribal god Nabû, Marduk's son, where they gave him a scepter. This sign of command in his hand, Alexander sailed ten miles downriver to another temple of Nabû. There Alexander and the priests picked up a statue of Nabû, put it aboard the royal barge, and sailed back to Babylon. This excursion reminded Alexander of his duties in Egypt, but Nabû was not what Egypt would lead one to expect. This god was not imposing or heroic, like Horus; he was a clerk. Still being coached, Alexander took Nabû by one hand. The god held a cuneiform tablet in the other.

Meanwhile, the *sheshgallu* remained in Babylon, reciting the Babylonian creation epic to a statue of Marduk. This long poem resembled the Greek creation epic, Hesiod's *Theogony*. In the Babylonian poem, Marduk rose to power over other gods, as Zeus did in Hesiod. Zeus, though, did little with his power. Marduk did much more, planning canals and dams and creating an inferior breed, mankind, to do the work. Marduk meant most humans to be slaves, but exempted the Babylonians. Marduk had not exempted foreigners, but Alexander was no longer a Macedonian. He had become the pupil of Nabû.[44]

The festival reached its peak at Esangil on the fifth day: the *sheshgallu* rose at two, the gods ate by eight, an exorcist purified the sanctum of Marduk, banging an enormous drum while aides held up torches and sacrificed a sheep, and a second exorcist did the same in chapel of Nabû. The peripatetic *sheshgallu* inspected the gold-spangled blue cloth, called "the Heavens," which hung from the walls of the chapel. Attendants brought Alexander into the courtyard of Esangil, and the "insiders," depilated and dressed in white, led him into the temple.

The *sheshgallu* stepped forward out of the darkness, took away Alexander's scepter, ring, and staff, and deposited them in another room. He returned and slapped Alexander on the face. Then he took him by the ears and led him into the sanctum, where Marduk awaited him. The *sheshgallu* pushed Alexander to his knees and held down his head while the king said his long-prepared lines:

> *I did not sin, lord of all lands.*
> *I did not neglect your godhead.*
> *I did not ravage Babylon.*
> *I did not order its downfall.*
> *I did not strike the cheeks of the clergy.*
> *I honored Babylon.*
> *I did not smash its walls.*

The *sheshgallu* raised the suppliant and called for the regalia, which he returned to Alexander. Then the *sheshgallu* slapped him again. If Alexander shed a tear, he would receive Marduk's blessing. If he did not, the priest ought to slap him a third time, and a fourth, until he cried. He must.[45]

After so many battle wounds, Alexander is unlikely to have cried. As the son of Philip, he would be ashamed to weep, and as the son of Amon, he would not know why he should. He wept when he forgave his men, but now they were on the road to Macedon. He wept when Hephaestion died, but Hephaestion was now a ghost, waiting in limbo for the burial in Egypt Alexander promised to give him.

At dusk that day, the *sheshgallu* and the king prayed together and sacrificed a white bull in the courtyard of Esangil. On the sixth day, priests decapitated the figurines placed before the patron god of judges, slaying the past. On the seventh day, all the gods gathered in Nabû's home, and the priests announced the astral destiny of Babylon for the coming year. The next morning, a procession took the gods out of Esangil. Marduk, Nabû, and many other gods paraded around the city on carts. The *shatammu* and other dignitaries walked behind them, as did colleges of exorcists. Everyone watched for ominous movements by the statues. Then Alexander and the *sheshgallu* ushered the gods aboard a barge to visit a rural shrine reserved for New Year celebrations.[46]

There Alexander got married, Babylonian style. His wife was Marduk's consort Zarpanit. In earlier times, Babylonian kings impersonated Marduk and made love to a priestess who impersonated Zarpanit. In the Babylon of Alexander's time, statues impersonated the divine couple while the king and the priestess drank beer and ate mutton. In Egypt Alexander spoke to gods, and on campaign omens spoke to Alexander, but in Babylonia symbols spoke to each other and Alexander did not know what they said. Officially rejuvenated, Alexander returned to the city.[47]

After his experiences in Egypt and Phoenicia, Alexander could not have found the New Year festival reassuring. It gave him too little to do, and it gave the priests too much. All Near Eastern societies had priests, but not even Egypt had priests who made such ceremonial and scientific claims. Of all Babylon's rulers, Alexander and his Macedonians were least prepared to understand these claims. They came from a society where priests did not go to school and where gods appeared on stage to be apostrophized and upbraided.

In the weeks after the ceremony, the waters in the rivers rose, making sailing easier, and Alexander escaped from Babylon. Now that the companions had got him back from the priests, they gladly accompanied him. Aristobulus needed to map the waterways to build the Euphrates canal, and the boat captains had to learn their routes. Alexander would supervise, but he also wished to resume his hobby of tomb-hunting.[48]

Late that spring he made several short trips to the land of the first Mesopotamian kings and cities. Because the Euphrates branched into a skein of waterways, the royal barge sometimes went astray. Changes in the river's course rendered many places inaccessible. Some tombs were no longer along main waterways. Even if the royal party found a site, they might not recognize it. At some sites, only bricks remained, stamped with words like

Palace of sleep,
Tomb of rest,
Eternal residence
Of Sennacherib, king of Ashur's country.

Looking around, Alexander and his fellow tourists might see no sign of the royal residence, or of the king supposed to be resting there. Wild pigs abounded, so the hunting was good, but there were poor prospects for finding any of the tombs on Alexander's list (if the priests gave him one). Mesopotamia was nothing like Egypt.[49]

The companions seem to have recorded just one incident that took place during these trips. Alexander was piloting the barge when the wind came up and blew away his sun hat and diadem. A sailor jumped into the water and retrieved them, putting the hat and diadem on his head to keep them safe as he swam back to the barge. For this piece of impertinence Alexander whipped him. The companions talked about this incident after they returned to the city. Some regarded the sailor's innocent mistake as a bad omen for Alexander.[50]

Babylonian literature listed many ominous events, but the priests could not find any entry about a sailor's picking a Persian diadem out of a canal and putting it on Alexander's head. In any case, the priests would have discounted the incident because it did not correspond to a celestial sign. (A drowned cow, for example, was an omen only if the moon was dark.) Marduk wrote celestial signs across the face of the heavens by causing stars and planets to move, and Babylon's learned men read the god's writing. No layman—certainly no Macedonian—could read it. The companions were fretting over events beyond their understanding.

Alexander had been in Babylon for some months when the priests announced that the king was in great danger. The companions were never able to learn why. Perhaps the astronomers feared the eclipse due to occur in May. It might cause the king to die within a year. Perhaps they objected to Alexander's tearing down part of the city wall to build Hephaestion's memorial. That would anger Marduk. They could not want more money for repairing Esangil. Alexander had reduced the cost of the repairs by putting his own men to work on the project.[51]

Whatever the reason, the priests told Alexander he must undergo a substitution ritual to protect himself. They would enthrone a mock king and give him enough privileges to lure misfortune away from Alexander. Then, after the signs in the heavens or elsewhere became favorable, the danger would pass. The priests would dispose of the mock king. Alexander would be safe and could resume the throne. The Babylonians and their neighbors had employed this rite for many centuries. Priests in Assyria had performed it for Esarhaddon, conqueror of Egypt, four times.[52]

Alexander should leave everything to the Babylonians. They would pick a proper substitute, such as a simpleton or a prisoner. The substitute would have to volunteer—the rite depended on that—and sign a contract agreeing to attract evil omens. Then the priests would mix into his food a text describing the omens, and he would eat it. They would train him to act as king and see to it that he dined and drank well. He would have a queen to share his bed and his fate. In due course, the priests would kill the pair of them in some place of decent obscurity.

Throughout the rite, Alexander must avoid the mock king and the priests in charge of him. Interfering was out of the question. Alexander could continue to run the army and the empire, but in private. He should avoid the palace and travel incognito.[53]

Alexander agreed. He had sometimes used his half-brother as a substitute for performing sacrifices, so being replaced by a simpleton did not trouble him. He did not grasp that the priests must control the rite. As a chief priest in Macedon and even Egypt, he expected to remain in charge himself. As for the companions, they could not conceive that anyone but a prince or a regent could replace the king. If anyone else tried, that man would count as a traitor. The Babylonians may have explained the rite to them, but they did not understand it well enough to prevent a mishap that occurred soon after the priests had enlisted their human scapegoat and put him to work.[54]

On that day the companions were in the throne room. Alexander was out of the way, getting a massage or visiting an exercise room. Then a man the companions took for an escaped slave or prisoner entered, put on the king's mantle and diadem, and sat on the throne. Babylonian eunuchs accompanied him, and when he sat down they beat their breasts and lamented. The companions asked the man on the throne what he was doing, but he gave no satisfactory answer. The companions sent word to Alexander. Ignoring the priests' instructions, he came to the throne room. Various seers happened to be in the room and warned the king that the incident was ominous. Alexander listened to them and ignored the Babylonians attending the mock king. After the seers called for the imposter to be killed, Alexander ordered that he be executed.[55]

Alexander either did not realize who the mock king was, a remarkable oversight, or let the seers prevail against his better judgment. That would be even more remarkable, for he had always dealt with seers confidently, even arrogantly. Most remarkably, he did not listen to the Babylonians, who made some attempt, however poorly translated, to point out his error. His religious aptitude deserted him.

In response to the execution of the mock king, the Babylonian clergy abandoned the rite and withdrew from Alexander. They would no longer advise or aid him, even if he became sick. This reaction dealt Alexander a third blow in as many years. The companions' refusal to advance farther into India had cost him his mission of conquest. The death of Hephaestion had cost him his intimate. Now came a religious blow that cost him his mandate. Alexander told one companion that he was at a loss to know what he should do for the rest of his life.[56]

Philip or Parmenio might have said that Alexander had too many advisers. Babylonian astronomers told him to obey the stars, Egyptian priests told him to be the son of Amon, and Greek intellectuals told him he was son of Philip. Macedonian comrades expected him to honor the cult of the companions. He was a Greco-Macedonian Egypto-Semite ruling the Persian Empire. Philip and Parmenio, though, were no longer there to advise him, or even drink with him.[57]

ON THE FIFTEENTH of the Babylonian month of Aiaru, Alexander received favorable oracles about Hephaestion. He invited Nearchus to dinner to celebrate the good news. Later that night he let Medius talk him out of bed and take him drinking. The next night, Alexander dined at Medius's along with twenty others. Among them were Iollas and his brother Cassander, Medius's chums, and important leaders such as Nearchus and Eumenes, as well as top generals. Rumor said Alexander drank a toast to each guest, or twenty-one in all. That did not keep him from reciting a passage from Euripides's *Andromeda,* a now-lost play about a damsel whom Alexander's flying ancestor Perseus rescued from a Phoenician monster.[58]

According to the daybook kept by Eumenes, Alexander mostly slept the next day, and went back to Medius's for a second night of drinking. The third day,

Alexander needed to be carried on a couch to make the morning sacrifice, then rested before summoning his councilors. They discussed the Arabian expedition, which was to set sail four days later, one day after the army broke camp. Perhaps they discussed other plans of the king's, such as rebuilding more shrines in Greece and also Macedon. Alexander was still vigorous. After the meeting, he left the palace of Nebuchadnezzar and took a boat to a Persian hunting ground on the other side of the river. There he rested and took his second bath of the day.[59]

On the nineteenth of Aiaru, or early June, he sacrificed, played dice with Medius, and called a meeting for the next day, but lay feverish all night. He was not seriously ill. During the next two days, he sacrificed and met the council twice, but suffered more. The following day he was able to try the palace swimming pool, and also able to sacrifice, but the day after that, when the fleet should have sailed, all he could do was sacrifice. On the twenty-fourth even sacrificing became difficult, and he lost his voice, and on the twenty-fifth he could not worship. His generals, regimental commanders, and captains came to the palace, but he was too sick to meet with them.[60]

By now, rumors of his illness were spreading, and rumors of his death spread in their wake. The next day, soldiers broke into the palace, overwhelming the guard. They demanded to see their king. The companions gave way and soldiers began to file past the bed. As long as he could, Alexander gestured to them. Even when he no longer could gesture, soldiers continued filing past. Thousands came. They wore him out.[61]

Perhaps his doctors did, too. The doctor who had cured him after his illness in Cilicia attended him, and probably used common Greek methods for regulating bodily humors—emetics, diuretics, and bloodletting. Perhaps the doctor thought that Alexander suffered from an excess of black bile. That would cause low spirits. Was it curable? Absolute rulers tended to be bilious and melancholic. The doctor wounded Alexander here, and wounded him there, drawing blood into cupping vessels.[62]

That failed, and perhaps Babylonian doctors came. Where did the fire inside the patient come from? they wondered. From the sky? The heat of the sun was one source, sending fire in its rays. One of the fourteen gods that guarded the gates of the Underworld, Umma, sent fever to the ill from the opposite quarter.

In mild cases, the physician might recommend burning fox grape and milk plant. That would tear out the fever. In severe cases, he regarded the fever as a demon to be thwarted. To ward off the demon, he might sprinkle flour around a patient's bed. He brought substances representing the demon's body, cursed them, and cast them out, one by one. He and his assistants looked around the palace for drains or crevasses by which demons might have entered, and plugged them. Alexander's palace had windows—always tempting for demons. Had the Macedonians closed off the porches and checked the roofs for holes? What about the doors? Had anyone performed a ritual to bring the doors to life, so that priests could pray to the doors and ask them to protect Alexander?[63]

The doctors did not know that he had compromised his immune system. Nor did they know what threats a weakened immune system exposed him to. To know that, they would have had to check the city's water supply, the transmission of bodily fluids, and the circulation of moisture and parasites. At most, they knew that grief, depression, and drink can be hazardous to one's health.[64]

The companions sacrificed and accomplished nothing. Desperate, they turned to the Babylonians. Half a dozen of them, including Peucestas, the satrap of Persia, went to a Babylonian temple, but found it closed. They waited by the temple gate all night. At dawn the gatekeeper admitted the temple bakers, butchers, and porters delivering foodstuffs and supplies. The Macedonians asked to be admitted, but the gatekeeper said they had no right to enter. They went away without speaking to any priests.[65]

Several days passed. The king lay speechless and motionless. A rumor spread that Alexander left his bed and tried to drown himself in the river. His body would disappear, and his men might believe he had been taken to heaven. Roxana supposedly prevented him. She might have said that Alexander could not propitiate Anahita by drowning.[66]

Another false rumor blamed a young soldier named Proteas, who made a sport of drinking. He happened to be the nephew of Clitus. On the night Alexander dined with Medius, he passed a double-size cup to Proteas. Proteas drained it, refilled it, and passed it back. Never one to be outdone, Alexander did the same. Then he collapsed on his couch and never recovered.[67] The older companions agreed that drinking had made Alexander ill, but did not blame Proteas. Dionysus had made Alexander drink too much on the night he killed Clitus. Now the wrathful god had made Alexander drink more. The companions thought Dionysus was still angry with Alexander because of the siege of Thebes, twelve years before.

To judge from the daybook, Eumenes lost track of how long Alexander was sick, but the Babylonians calculated accurately. They counted the days from the middle of the month, when the moon moved in front of the constellation called the Magician. Since then, fifteen days had passed, so the patient died on the afternoon of the twenty-ninth of Aiaru. At age thirty-two, Alexander succumbed to the astronomers' empire over time.[68]

ALEXANDER WAS A good friend to death. In that respect he was a godly man, and a likely posthumous convert to religions that provided for the resurrection of the dead. One of these religions was Judaism. The Hebrews believed Alexander worshipped in Jerusalem, and that he listened to Talmudic sages in Babylon. Some episodes of the *Alexander Romance* take a Christian perspective toward him, as when angels came to warn him after he flew into the air. The common theme of these Christian and Hebrew responses to Alexander was that his own death was a goal toward which he unwittingly traveled. Beyond his own death lay a possible second goal: participating in some eschatological revelation.[69]

According to one episode found in the *Alexander Romance*, he reached his long-sought destination, the end of the world, and learned of the waters of life. In the following excerpt, Parmenio appears unnamed, in the guise of an old soldier. Callisthenes, whom Alexander falsely condemned for treason, appears as an adviser. Three other characters—Alexander's sacrificial assistant Andreas and his concubine and daughter—are apocryphal.[70]

For three days Alexander journeyed through places where the sun did not shine. This was the land of the blessed. Then he decided to leave behind his baggage train and his infantry, along with the old men and the women, and investigate this region with a select force of young men. Callisthenes advised him to go with 40 companions, 100 slaves, and a thousand troops. Alexander gave word that no old man should accompany them, and set out.

One spry old man with two sons who were soldiers said to them,

"Boys, take me with you. You won't find me useless. Some time or other you may need to seek out an old man. Don't be afraid the king will kill you for disobeying orders. Cut my hair and beard."

They did, and took him with them.

The army found itself in a dark country. Because it was hard to traverse, they couldn't advance, and had to throw away their tents. The next day Alexander took his soldiers to reconnoiter, in case they had reached the end of the world. When they headed to the left, they found the country less dark. They passed through empty, rocky terrain for half a day. The sun didn't guide them, and instead they used measuring rods. Frightened by this kind of marching, Alexander turned back. Then he decided to try heading to the right. A smooth plain lay there, but murky and dark. He was at a loss, and the young men advised him not to venture into the murk. If their horses panicked on the long, dark trail, the men would never get back. "Comrades," Alexander said to them, "you all know that in war no good deed can be done without planning and cooperation. We need some old man's advice about how to make our way through the murk. Someone should go back to the baggage train and find a man like that." No one was willing. The road was too long, and the sky too dark.

A leaf bearing an illustration of Alexander beside the waters of life in Firdausi, by Qazvin or Mashhad, 1580.

Sotheby's, London, April 22, 1980, lot 27, ms. fol. 341a.

The old man's sons said to the king, "If you will listen to us with an open mind, we'll talk to you."

King Alexander said, "If you want to, speak. I swear to do you no wrong." The sons talked to him about their father and ran and got him. Alexander embraced him and bade him advise them.

The old man said, "King Alexander, we know this: if the horses do not get us out of here, you will never see the light of day again. Pick out the mares with colts and leave the colts here. We will rely on the mares to get us out."

Among his many horses, Alexander found only one hundred mares with colts. He rounded up them, plus grooms to care for them, and then he and the men went in and shooed the colts away from their mothers. The army took the mares and other horses and left the colts behind. The old man also told Alexander to order the troops to pick up anything they found on the ground and put it in their sacks.

Alexander and 360 of his men ventured on. When they had traveled 15 leagues, they came to a place with a shining fountain, where the water gleamed like lightening. The air was fragrant and very sweet.

Alexander happened to be hungry and wanted some bread to eat, so he summoned Andreas, the sacrificer who killed victims for him, to find him some meat. Andreas got some fish and went to clean it in the fountain. As soon as the fish got wet, it sprang to life and jumped out of his hands. Andreas drank the water and stored some in a silver vessel, but he told no one what had happened, not even the king. . . .

Alexander ordered his men to pick up whatever they could, be it stone, earth, or wood. Some did, but others thought the order senseless. . . . Once they reached a well-lit country they looked at one another in amazement. Their clothes were golden all over, and the stones they had picked up had turned to gold.

The mares soon led them to the camp where they had left the colts. From there the horses took the army out of the land of darkness and back to safety.

Later, Andreas confessed how the fish came to life. Furious, Alexander whipped him. Andreas said, "Why regret the past?" He denied that he drank or kept the water. Alexander had a daughter, Belle, by a camp follower named Ouna, and Andreas seduced her by promising to give her some of the water to drink. Once she drank it, it immortalized her. When he heard of this miracle, Alexander ordered her to come before him, and remove her clothes. She undressed, and he realized she had become a phantasm. He banished her.

This Byzantine story does not say what became of the banished daughter, but folktales say that she went to live in the sea and became a mermaid.[71] Feeling lonely, she has accosted sailors ever since. She asks them the question that is the epigraph to this book: "Does King Alexander live?" If they give the answer, "He lives and reigns," they escape with their lives.

12

Dead Men and a Living King

AFTER ALEXANDER'S DEATH, the body lay in his bedchamber while the council of war tried to decide what to do with it. Alexander left no will and gave no instructions, except, some said, to Craterus, who was on his way to Macedon. So far as the companions knew, Alexander had made only one request, to be buried at the oracular shrine at Siwah. He wished to be the first pharaoh buried at an oasis—the first buried at a frontier. He also wanted to be the first European worshipped alongside Amon. At Siwah both Greek and Egyptian pilgrims might grant him that honor.[1]

Aside from this request, Alexander had supposedly made a few stray remarks that were no more credible than the story that he wished to drown himself in the Euphrates. The most plausible remark was that he expected his companions to compete with one another as if they were contestants at funeral games in his honor.[2]

To comply with his burial request, the council must give the body to the priests of Amon among the entourage and the priests must consign it to embalmers. After that, the council would have to build a hearse and appoint an escort to deliver the body to Siwah, a journey of several months.

The council temporized. Embalming the body was indispensable, for otherwise it would deteriorate and become unfit for funeral ceremonies. Sending the body to Egypt, though, would be unpopular. The funeral of Alexander would take place amid Egyptians with at most a small delegation of Greeks and Macedonians. Hardly any of Alexander's officers and men would receive the graveside blessing they craved. Greek seers told the councilors that Alexander's ghost would protect the vicinity of his tomb, but in Siwah mostly Egyptians would benefit.

The council could guess what Alexander's mother, Olympias, would say: that the army should bring her son's body home to Aegae, the family burial place. If she and the troops did not see the body, they might doubt whether Alexander died of natural causes. Olympias would accuse Cassander, Medius, and others of poisoning Alexander. She had quarreled with Cassander and Cassander's father, Antipater, for years.[3]

Yet Macedon was unattractive, too. If the funeral took place in Aegae, who would perform the ceremony? Alexander's half-brother, Arrhidaeus? He was not king, and officiating at the funeral would make him look like a king. That would suit Olympias, but not Antipater, who was still in Macedon, or Craterus, who would soon arrive there. In Macedon there would be too many possible religious contestants, just as there would be too many absent contestants in Egypt.[4]

The veteran Perdiccas took charge of the deliberations. With Craterus gone, he was the senior military commander. He had commanded an infantry regiment as early as the siege of Thebes in 335, when Ptolemy and Nearchus were striplings and Polyperchon was low-ranking. At Thebes he had attacked without Alexander's permission, showing himself to be impulsive and ambitious. He slaughtered the rebels in Samaria in 331. Lately he had been preparing his new command, the companion cavalry, for the risky march into Arabia. He knew the army well.

He also knew more about embalming than the others. When Hephaestion died, Alexander had ordered Perdiccas to bring the body from Ecbatana to Babylon, and Perdiccas had asked Egyptians in the entourage to embalm it. Perdiccas now ordered these experts to ply their trade on Alexander.[5] A week had passed since Alexander's death.[6]

The embalmers took charge of the king's body and removed the king's diadem and signet ring, both commandeered by Perdiccas. The most elaborate ritual Alexander ever underwent now began.[7]

A lector read prayers, and the Master of the Mysteries, who served the jackal-headed god, Anubis, supervised as a surgeon cut open Alexander's left flank, a place where he had never been wounded, and thrust an arm into his guts up to the elbow. As fluid poured out, the surgeon removed the major organs one by one. The surgeon and his aides were better acquainted with human anatomy than many physicians, but they were working blind, and so they seldom attempted the delicate task of removing the lining of the chest cavity. They never removed the heart. In the next life Alexander, like any other person, would have to present his heart to Anubis, god of the dead as well as of embalmers. The god would weigh the heart, and if it was heavy with guilt, Alexander would be condemned to a second, everlasting death. If the heart was light, the king could proceed into the afterlife. On this journey, his royal status scarcely mattered. Alexander would at last be an ordinary man.[8]

Next, the surgeon and his aides drilled into the nose and removed the brains with a hook. After disposing of this useless stuff, they exercised all their dexterity to pack the mouth with linen or resin and pack resin behind the eyes. How should they pack the empty cranium? The Babylonians supplied two materials, salt and cedar sawdust.

Alexander's lungs, liver, stomach, and intestines posed bigger questions. Should the embalmers replace the viscera in the body, or wrap them in packages and put them on the dead man's thighs, or put the viscera in alabaster jars? All these choices had been fashionable at one time or another; in Alexander's day, all were acceptable.

It would have been idle for the experts to explain them to the companions, or to explain the next steps—laying the corpse in a bed of soda ash, mummifying it, fashioning a coffin and some cartonnage, and then a catafalque and a tomb complete with female figurines serving as concubines to the dead. They were not preparing a military hero for foreign mourners. They were preparing a pharaoh for eternity.

Perdiccas kept council deliberations private. No common soldiers attended, no Persians, no Babylonians, and perhaps no Greeks other than Nearchus and Eumenes. Only one bodyguard, Leonnatus, attended, for the others were protecting the embalmers. To help the councilors concentrate—or to allay Alexander's ghost—Perdiccas put Alexander's throne, diadem, and signet ring in front of them and nailed Alexander's armor to the throne.[9]

The king's Asian regalia and armor were Alexander's personal property, but the empire was not. It belonged to the companions, especially the councilors. The Macedonian throne belonged to the Temenid family, and the council could choose whom to elevate. The new king would become priest of the cult of the companions. The cult of Alexander as son of Zeus-Amon had never taken hold, and the council could leave it in abeyance.

Perdiccas proposed that the council name some senior commander as regent. This companion would take the lead in naming a new king and dealing with the funeral and the empire. Perdiccas wanted the post for himself. Nearchus and others argued that they must first name a successor. Alexander's son by Barsine would do. If the pregnant Roxana bore a son, he might become king. By naming a king first, and not a regent, the council would provide religious continuity. Ptolemy and others wanted to name a successor, too, but not one born to a Central Asian mother. These councilors preferred someone less foreign (Nearchus in particular preferred a son of Barsine's, for he was married to Barsine's daughter).

Another top commander, Meleager, suggested Arrhidaeus, who had accompanied them from the start of the expedition. Arrhidaeus would require a regent, just as a child would, but he could perform some sacrificial duties. Some councilors feared that Arrhidaeus might be hard to control. Incapable of leading troops, he was nevertheless a physically healthy, middle-aged prince perfectly capable of marrying. Philip had wanted to marry him to the daughter of Pixodarus. (That had motivated Alexander to try to marry the daughter himself.) If Arrhidaeus wanted a wife, he would find plenty of candidates, and no one could force him to marry the stupidest and the weakest. He might marry a termagant like Olympias, and she might interfere with the regent, and even with the council.

Egos clashed; precaution won. The council dismissed Nearchus's idea of promoting the son of Barsine, a woman without important relatives, and decided that if Roxana did bear a son, he would become king. If Roxana did not, they would revisit the matter. Meanwhile, there would be no king. Perdiccas and Leonnatus, a general and a bodyguard, would be co-regents. Craterus, Antipater, and Antigonus must accept this fait accompli.[10]

The council also made several other decisions. First, they abandoned Alexander's Arabian invasion and other plans. Second, they left the satrapies mostly as they were. Perdiccas arranged for some of the bodyguards, a set of ambitious men, to get posts in the provinces. He did not want them at court, and so he told them there would be no king worth guarding. Ptolemy got Egypt, and part of Anatolia went to Eumenes, a lifelong bureaucrat who now wanted out of Babylon. Last, the council disposed of Alexander's women. Roxana would live in Babylon and Barsine in Anatolia, where she had been before the war. The council did not have to concern themselves with two others: Darius's daughter, whom Alexander had married at Susa, and Darius's mother, Sisygambis. Roxana killed the daughter as soon as Alexander died, and Sisygambis killed herself for fear of what the companions might do with her.[11]

By now, the Egyptian surgeon was finishing his chef d'oeuvre. After cleansing the innards with palm wine, he poured in myrrh mixed with cassia, and sewed up the wound with linen thread. Alexander had never had so many stitches. Would the council let the troops into the palace to admire them? Not yet, came the answer. The doors remained closed.[12]

Some 10,000 Macedonian troops still guarded Babylon. The cavalry, who served under Perdiccas and thought of themselves as the original companions, accepted his decision. So did the shield bearers, led by Seleucus. By yielding to Perdiccas, they endorsed the arrangements he and the council had made for the empire.

The heavy infantry defied Perdiccas. They marched on the palace, and the frightened councilors locked themselves in the room where the body lay. The infantry pursued them and broke down the doors. Arrhidaeus encouraged the infantry, and so did Meleager, the councilor who nominated Arrhidaeus as king. The troops saw the body of their king and demanded that another Temenid, someone as closely related to Alexander as possible, replace him. Put Arrhidaeus on the throne. Cavalry and heavy infantry, who had fought separately on the battlefield, thought differently about the monarchy.[13]

At one point the two sides camped separately, cavalry outside the city and infantry inside. The disagreement between them might lead to fighting, and the cavalry, facing the infantry's long spears, might not prevail. Very reluctantly, Perdiccas and the council majority agreed to make Arrhidaeus king. They insisted, however, that Arrhidaeus share the throne if Roxana bore a son. If there were two kings, the council could better control Arrhidaeus. Perdiccas himself would become the one and only regent.[14]

Within days, Perdiccas retaliated against his foes. He ordered that the army assemble to be purified, a ritual accomplished by marching the troops between the severed parts of a bitch. Arrhidaeus killed the dog, and Perdiccas killed Meleager after Arrhidaeus denounced him as unpurifiable. That put an end to the political aspirations of the infantry, much as Alexander had put an end to infantry opposition when he killed the ringleaders at Opis. Perdiccas had maintained council unity and his own position.[15]

He delayed the funeral for similar, practical reasons. Yet he also had a religious, even superstitious reason for delaying the funeral. As long as he and his fellow generals kept the body, they kept the power that emanated from it. They remained suspended, and protected, within the prolonged last rites for Alexander.[16]

———◉———

ALL COMPANIONS SWORE to give dead comrades a funeral. Alexander had done this duty again and again—for Nicanor, Erigyius, Coenus, and Hephaestion. Now Alexander's body lay in the palace in Babylon week after week. The embalmers, who had already preserved the body well enough so that it could travel, set themselves a new task. Knowing that Alexander wished to be laid to rest at Siwah, they prepared him for the trip to the oasis.

They asked for divine blessings on their efforts, and then they opened the dead man's eyes, one at a time, followed by the ears, nostrils, and mouth. When Alexander was pharaoh, he opened the mouths of statues in the same way. Both statues and corpses were inert bodies to be revived. For the next five weeks, the embalmers performed a ceremony for each of the four main organs, for each arm and leg, and for the back. Then they cleared away the soda ash in which the body had lain. After seventeen ceremonies in seventy days, they declared themselves ready to mummify Alexander so that he might travel to Egypt. The goddess Isis required that the incarnation of Horus, her son, return to his homeland.

Then Perdiccas pretended to discover what he had known all along—the companions had no hearse in which to transport Alexander. Disingenuously, he invited Arrhidaeus to build one. Arrhidaeus would need extra time, Perdiccas warned him, to accomplish what should be the stupendous task of building a four-wheeled palace worthy of a transcontinental emperor. Perdiccas assigned him a ranking companion as a subordinate, and supplied ample funds.[17]

Nearly two years after Alexander's death, Arrhidaeus finished his task. The Egyptians had contributed a sarcophagus of human shape, as was their custom.

They embossed it with gold leaf, a symbol of divinity, filled it with myrrh, and added a golden lid. Around it Greek craftsmen had built a small temple, adorned with sculptured lions guarding the entrance. A barrel vault studded with jewels rested atop Ionic columns; Apollo's olive wreath topped the roof. At each corner a figure of Nike stood holding a battle trophy—one for the Granicus, one for Issus, one for Arbela, and one for the Jhelum. The animal that was the familiar of Amon, the Nubian ibex, peered out from the cornices, and tinkling bells hung from garlands draped around each curling horn. Friezes ran from one beast to the next. In one, Alexander rode in a chariot followed by Persian as well as Macedonian guards. Others showed parading war elephants, the companion cavalry, and a fleet of ships.[18]

Perdiccas and his supporters had run out of excuses. The body must go somewhere, so he decided to send it where it would do him the most military good. That was Anatolia. Antigonus was warring against Perdiccas's forces there, as were Antipater, Craterus, and Polyperchon. Soon after assigning the task of building the hearse to Arrhidaeus, Perdiccas himself had gone to Anatolia with most of the 10,000 Macedonians stationed in Babylon.

Perdiccas formed a two-step plan. First, he would order his subordinates in Babylon to bring the body and the royal family to him. His enemies would not dare to stop him, let alone fight. The cortege would serve as a talisman. Next, he would take the cortege and the royals to Aegae, where he would serve as master of ceremonies while Arrhidaeus interred the sarcophagus in the family vault. Perdiccas would stage games in Alexander's honor, and inaugurate worship of him as a hero. Since heroes loitered around their tombs, Perdiccas would benefit from Alexander's aura. He could become king in all but name. To improve his chance of success, Perdiccas arranged to marry one of Alexander's sisters.[19]

Sometime in 321, the cortege left Babylon and set off to join Perdiccas in Anatolia. An honor guard led the way, and sixty-four mules pulled the catafalque by collars set with gems. Perdiccas ordered the royal family to travel some ways behind. He did not want them closely associated with the body. He would bring Roxana to Macedon, to live under the gaze of Olympias, and Barsine and her son would retire in Anatolia.

Aboard the catafalque, the embalmers periodically checked the body and the jars intended for the organs. The weather was hot, the pace slow. The mules could not travel more than a dozen miles a day. As the cortege traveled north, through Mesopotamia and Syria, crowds gathered in Babylonian towns, Macedonian outposts, and Arab caravansaries. They admired Nike with her trophy and the other showy Greek features of the catafalque. Few if any saw the lid of the sarcophagus, where Alexander's face appeared like that of a pharaoh.

After a journey of three months, the cortege reached Syria. Perdiccas had achieved a coup de théâtre, and the Egyptian embalmers, still tending to the body, could boast that their pharaoh had weathered a preliminary afterlife of two years. The cortege should arrive in Anatolia in a few more weeks.

Then a messenger from Syria arrived in Anatolia with shocking news. Ptolemy had bribed the companion who assisted Arrhidaeus. The honor guard withdrew, and Ptolemy made away with the hearse. The body of Alexander was now traveling to Egypt. Just as Perdiccas wished to use the body to gain legitimacy throughout the empire, Ptolemy wanted Alexander to help him govern Egypt.[20]

The embalmers accompanied the body back to their native land. They expected Ptolemy to entomb Alexander at Siwah, but Ptolemy disappointed them as well. He put the sarcophagus on display in the Greek quarter of Memphis, before a temple of Amon. This location, next to the Asian quarter, was respectable but not obtrusive. Greeks and Macedonians could sacrifice to Alexander as a hero— Ptolemy certainly would—and Amon would approve.[21]

Perdiccas marched south to reclaim the body, and his army arrived opposite Memphis in the summer of 320. Ptolemy's army awaited them on the other side of the Nile. Perdiccas did not display Alexander's knack for water crossings. He did find a ford, and deployed his elephants upstream to slow the current. Seleucus's shield bearers and some others managed to cross in spite of the chest-high water. Then the weight of the elephants caused the streambed to deepen and the rest of the army could not cross. Isolated, the men who had crossed tried to swim back. Two thousand drowned.[22]

Ptolemy met secretly with Seleucus and other senior officers, offering generous peace terms. He would not attack the invaders, and he would let all Macedonians come to Memphis to pay their last respects to Alexander. Knowing Perdiccas would not accept these terms, Seleucus and some shield bearers put him to death, and then the invaders withdrew from Egypt.[23]

That summer, the leading generals met near Damascus at Trisparadeisos, "the place with three Persian royal gardens," where they redistributed the empire. Antipater became regent and got custody of the royals, plus the elephants used by Perdiccas. When Antipater died a few years later, his son Cassander replaced him. Antigonus became chief commander, and also got elephants. Ptolemy kept the body. Seleucus, the assassin of Perdiccas, got Babylon as his reward. In military terms, they had nothing to fear but each other. The Macedonian army had been the best before Alexander, and it would be the best after him.[24]

Without the body nearby, Alexander's family lost the aura of divinity that had protected them, and they became vulnerable to machinations in the Macedonian court. Arrhidaeus had finally married, and his ambitious wife made an enemy of Olympias, who had the pair of them assassinated. Roxana gave birth to Alexander IV, but he survived only until age thirteen, when Cassander executed him and his mother. Cassander did not forget the inveterate intriguer Olympias. He arranged for the relatives of her victims to put her to death. Of Alexander's wives, only Barsine remained, living privately with her seventeen-year-old son Heracles in Anatolia.[25]

Polyperchon, a Macedonian traditionalist and one of the last of Philip's generation of soldiers, wanted Heracles to succeed to the throne. He brought the young man to Greece and presented him to Macedonian troops as a Temenid fit to be king. Unwilling to share power, Cassander outmaneuvered Heracles. He promised Polyperchon control of southern Greece in exchange for killing the prince and his mother. Polyperchon agreed and killed the pair of them, but he never got southern Greece. The Greeks kept him out of most of the region, and Macedonian rivals kept him out of the rest.[26]

The empire broke up into familiar pieces: Egypt under Ptolemy, Mesopotamia under Seleucus, Anatolia under the sexagenarian Antigonus. The kingdom of Macedon fell to Cassander, and then to a son of Antigonus. The new political map resembled a time before Alexander made his conquests, and even a time before Cyrus the Great. The two conquerors seemed to have accomplished nothing. They were not even properly buried. Cyrus's tomb was empty. Alexander's was in the wrong place.

The companions had deprived Alexander of his army, crowns, women, and children.[27] They even did away with the cult of the companions. They no longer used this term, preferring the saccharine "friends." Yet millions now began to worship Alexander. His afterlife had just begun.[28]

ALEXANDER'S ASCENT BEGAN slowly, before his death. After he marched through Asia Minor, some Greeks cities revised their calendars and made the

Anonymous line drawing of Alexander's catafalque, 1888.
Photograph: Franz Heinz-Deitler, Alamy Stock Photographs.

time of his arrival Year One. Immediately after his death, all the cities named after Alexander began to worship him as a hero. So did the people of Macedon. The original Alexandria, in Egypt, honored him on the anniversary of his death. Worshipping him as a god probably began somewhat later. (The Greek and Persian oracles in Asia Minor had told Greeks to honor Alexander as a god, but did not instruct cities when or where.) Sometime after his death, the island of Thasos erected a temple and sacrificed to him. A league of Greek cities including Miletus and Ephesus probably did, too. Six years after his death, a satrap and his troops honored Alexander as a god (and honored Philip as well—these troops were Macedonian veterans).[29]

For the most part, the leading companions did not dare imitate Alexander by making themselves gods while they were alive, but after their deaths they gained a share of Alexander's symbolic spoils. Their descendants worshipped them alongside Alexander. Rather than gods in their own right, Alexander's generals became companion gods.[30]

In Asia, Seleucus and his successors founded Greek cities that eventually worshipped both Alexander and Seleucus. These cults, one for Alexander and one for the ruler, legitimized rulers, but also benefitted the worshippers. When kings ranked as gods, they were more obliged to help their subjects. Realizing this, Greek cities took the lead in establishing the new cults. Athens worshipped Alexander alongside Antigonus while Antigonus was still alive, and the city worshipped Antigonus's son, too. This cult began when Antigonus briefly controlled Athens.[31]

Ptolemy accomplished more, by making use of Alexander's sarcophagus. In Memphis, it had lain in public view for several decades, one pharaonic memorial among many. Ptolemy moved the sarcophagus to Alexandria and made it the centerpiece of a royal precinct in the city. Ptolemy's grandson removed the gold lid, with its Egyptian image of Alexander, and replaced it with a glass cover. Visitors could now see Alexander's face for the first time. Eventually the royal precinct grew to accommodate the tombs of Ptolemy, his son Ptolemy II, and their successors. Egyptians would call this place Soma (the body), meaning the body of the kings, but especially of Alexander. Elsewhere in the city, statues of Alexander dominated main intersections and shrines—an equestrian statue honoring him as city founder, a cult statue in his temple, and an ensemble showing Alexander being crowned by the Earth herself, attended by Luck and Victory.[32]

Displaying an Egyptian touch, Ptolemy II ordained worship of his own mother as well as of his father and Alexander. To celebrate all three new gods, he established an annual festival, the Ptolemaia. A Greek travel writer who attended in 274 described the extravaganza. A long parade wound through the city and into a stadium before arriving at a royal pavilion where Ptolemy II and his "friends" recreated the court of Alexander. They dined and drank on 300 couches in a circle. Two gold tripods for making small sacrifices stood by each couch. So did silver tables and accouterments weighing, the writer claimed, an entire ton. Wooden columns, carved like palm trees or like staffs used in Dionysiac ritual, rose fifty feet in the air. These alluded to Alexander's imitating Dionysus in India and in the Persian wine country.[33]

Massive floats honoring the founder of the dynasty, the first Ptolemy, entered the stadium first, followed by floats for the Olympian gods. One float honoring Dionysus carried a deified Mount Nysa, that center of the world Alexander had visited. The seated goddess periodically rose to her feet, thanks to hidden machinery, poured a libation, and sat down again. Power for this device came from the sixty slaves pulling the float. Statues of Alexander and the first Ptolemy, adorned with ivy garlands made of gold, rode side by side on another float.

The last float in the parade displayed an enormous statue of Alexander in armor, as though marching at the head of his men. Yet here he stood to the rear of an army of slaves with ropes over their shoulders for pulling floats. The only armed men on the scene served as marshals controlling the vast crowds. The city Alexander founded some fifty years before had become home to several hundred thousand Jews, Greeks, and Egyptians, plus tourists and visitors from throughout the Near East and Greece. Not all honored him as a god, but all admired the spectacle.

The city of Alexandria found several other ways to make Alexander its own. One was mythical. A story spread that the substitute king whom Alexander had put to death in Babylon was an Egyptian, sent to Babylon by an Egyptian god, Serapis. Serapis was the father of Horus, as Amon was, and so Serapis was in charge of Alexander. Serapis wanted Alexander to return to Egypt and be worshipped after death, and got his wish by tricking Alexander into killing the substitute. Alexander lost both his throne and his life, and then Ptolemy stole his body and brought it to Alexandria.[34]

Another way was the *Alexander Romance*, composed in Alexandria sometime after Alexander's death. It soon became popular throughout the ancient world. In every version of the story, Alexander was some sort of Egyptian.

A third way was official. Ptolemy II began to claim that Alexander's father, Philip of Macedon, was his own grandfather. In 272 Ptolemy established a cult for himself as Alexander's descendant, and also for his wife, so that the Greeks and Macedonians in Egypt would worship them as gods. To help pay for the new cults, he taxed every vineyard in Egypt.

Meanwhile, the Egyptian priests continued to worship in the old way. They regarded Alexander as a dead pharaoh, and not an especially prominent one, and they regarded each Ptolemaic pharaoh as a son of Horus, given divine standing and a *ka* to go with it, but not immortality. In 238 Ptolemy III ordered Egyptian priests to expand their pantheon by worshipping Alexander and the Ptolemies.

Now Alexander became a god for the Egyptians. Even at Siwah, he had never asked for so much.[35]

With the new cults came revised rules for rituals and a calendar reform ensuring that the overburdened priests stuck to their schedules. This reform established the 365-day year plus leap years. The last five days of the year belonged to the cults of Alexander, the pharaoh, and his family.[36]

This Greco-Egyptian religious machinery operated for centuries, even after Egypt fell to the Romans. Pompey, Caesar, and Augustus all paid their respects to the shrine of Alexander in the royal precinct. Augustus, the first Roman to rule as pharaoh, preferred Alexander to the other Macedonian rulers of Egypt. After he visited the chapel where Alexander lay, the priests offered to take him to the tombs of the Ptolemies, but he declined. "I have come to see a living king," he said, "not a row of dead men."[37]

Gossips in the emperor's court claimed that Augustus not only saw Alexander but broke off his nose. Although untrue, this story testified to the uncanny power of the body. People doubted whether Alexander was subject to the vicissitudes of mortality.[38]

In AD 215 Emperor Caracalla visited the Soma, and the sight of Alexander's face seemed to mesmerize him. After laying his purple cloak on the sarcophagus in a gesture of grief, he announced that he was a reincarnation of Alexander. He had the same twist of the neck and out-of-kilter eyes. When Alexandrians scoffed, he raised a detachment of pseudo-Macedonian companions to rampage through the streets and butcher them. He also enclosed the Soma with high walls and watchtowers, turning it into a fort. In 264 a rebellious Roman general took refuge there, and the ensuing siege may have damaged Alexander's chapel. More destruction followed, and by the 300s little of the Soma survived.[39]

Then came two cataclysms, Christianity and the tidal wave of 365. If the new religion did not efface what remained, the wave did, and around the year 400 a Christian author mocked the pagan gods by asking, "Where is the tomb of Alexander? Show me. On what day did he die? Tell me." The tomb was gone, and the annual celebrations held on the day of his death had ceased.[40]

Yet Alexander was not quite dead. Centuries later, Muslims venerated him in a chapel that one pilgrim described as being amid the ruins in the middle of the city. A small shrine marked the place where worshippers thought Alexander lay buried. They esteemed Alexander as a prophet described in the eighteenth book of the Koran. They asked him for blessings, brought him votives, and celebrated the anniversary of his death with prayers and a procession, customary honors for a prophet or a saint. In the 1880s an Egyptian government bent on westernizing the city demolished the chapel and the veneration of Alexander along with it.[41]

Alexander's body has never been found.[42]

Line drawing of the shrine of Alexander, by Edward Clarke, 1798.
V. Denon, *Voyage en Égypte* (Paris 1803), pl. 9.

IN THE EIGHTEENTH book (or sura) of the Koran, Alexander appears as the
prophet called "the two-horned man." The shrine at Siwah conceived Amon this
way, and Alexander wore horns to imitate Amon. Coins spread this image of
Alexander throughout the Near East. Many Muslim writers knew about it. One
called a mosque at Alexandria "the mosque of the two-horned man."[43]

A few Muslim authorities identify "the two-horned man," or Dhul Qarnayn,
as Cyrus the Great and not Alexander. Either is plausible. The Koran says that the
Dhul Qarnayn traveled to the limits of the known world in the course of his conquests, and Cyrus seemingly anticipated Alexander in accomplishing this feat.[44]

In the verses quoted below, God addresses Muhammad. God is the upper-case
"We." "He" is Alexander.

> We granted him power in the land and gave him paths leading to all things.
>
> He took one of these paths, and when he reached the limit where the
> sun goes down, he found it setting in a pool of murky water, and he found
> a people. We said, "Dhul Qarnayn, you may either punish them or treat
> them with kindness."
>
> He said, "If a man does wrong, we will punish him. Then he will be
> remanded to his Lord and the Lord will punish him terribly. If a man has
> faith and acts righteously, he will have the best reward, and we will rule
> him gently."

He then followed another path, and when he reached the limit where the sun rises, he found a people to whom We gave no shelter against the sun's rays. . . .

He followed yet another path, and reached a place that lay between two barriers. The people scarcely understood a word, but said to him, "Gog and Magog are despoiling the country. Should we pay you tribute to build a bulwark to protect us?"

He said, "The path my Lord has shown me is better than your tribute. Help me, and I will make a bulwark for you. Bring me sheets of iron." When he had filled the gap between the two barriers, he said, "Blow!" When they had set it aflame, he said, "Bring me molten copper to pour over it." Gog and Magog could not scale it or make a hole in it.

He said, "This is an act of mercy from my Lord. But when my Lord's promise is fulfilled, my Lord will make this bulwark crumble."[45]

The Lord makes a "promise" to summon mankind before Him on the Day of Judgment. On that day, Alexander predicts, the wall he has made will collapse, and Allah will divide mankind anew between heaven and hell. In all of the Koran, only Muhammad, Abraham, and Alexander speak in their own words of this consummation of man's time on earth.[46]

FINIS

Chronology

359 *BC*—Accession of Philip II to the throne of Macedon.

356 *July*—Birth of Alexander III.

338 Battle at Chaeronea.

336 *autumn*—Assassination of Philip II and accession of Alexander III.

335 *spring*—Alexander's campaigns north of Macedon.

335 *October*—Siege of Thebes.

334 *early spring*—Dedication of shrine to Jason at Abdera and sacrifices for crossing the Bosporus and invading the Persian Empire.

334 *late spring*—Visit to Troy and the battle at the Granicus River.

334 *summer*—Occupation of Ephesus and Priene.

334 *autumn*—Campaign in Caria.

333 *spring*—Visit to the shrine of Zeus in Gordium.

333 *summer*—Passage through the Cilician Gates.

333 *autumn*—Occupation of Cilicia and the battle at Issus.

332 *winter and spring*—Siege of Tyre, lasting six months.

332 *late autumn*—Siege of Gaza, lasting two months.

332–331 Occupation of Egypt and accession or coronation ceremonies for Alexander at Heliopolis, Memphis, and perhaps Thebes. Visit to Siwah.

332–331 Religiously motivated revolt in Samaria.

331 *early spring*—Official foundation of Alexandria.

331 *spring*—Suppression of the revolt in Samaria.

331 *summer*—Passage of the Euphrates River.

331 *Sept. 20*—Eclipse of the moon.

331 *Oct. 1*—Battle near Arbela.

331 *autumn*—Occupation of Babylon and coronation of Alexander. Occupation of Susa.

330 *winter*—Occupation of Persepolis and visit to Pasargadae.

330 *summer*—Death of Darius.

330 *fall*—Execution of Philotas and assassination of Parmenio.

330 *winter*—Arrival at the Hindu Kush.

329 *spring*—Passage through the Hindu Kush.

329–327 Campaign in Bactria and Sogdiana.

329 *late spring*—Surrender of Bessus. Foundation of Alexandria *Eschate*.

329–328 Winter quarters in Bactra. Violation of the shrine of Anahita.

328 *autumn*—Defeat and decapitation of Spitamanah.

328–327 Fall and winter quarters in Samarkand and elsewhere. Murder of Clitus.

327 *spring*—Marriage of Alexander and Roxana.

327 *summer*—Conspiracy of the pages and trial of Callisthenes.

326 *early spring*—Departure for India. Visit to Mount Meru at Nysa. Sacrifices for crossing the Indus.

326 *summer*—Campaign in Punjab. Visit to Taxila. Battle at Jhelum River. Dedication of altars at the Beas River.

326 *autumn*—Departure downstream, toward the lower Indus Valley.

326 *winter*—Campaign against the Malavas.

325 *midsummer*—Arrival at Patala. Sacrifices on the shoreline and at sea.

325 *early autumn*—Departure of Nearchus and the fleet, and of Alexander and Craterus with the troops and baggage.

325 *late autumn*—March through the Gedrosian Desert.

325–early 324 Occupation of Carmania and Dionysian celebrations. Flight and supplication of Harpalus.

324 *spring*—Second visit to Pasargadae and arrival in Susa. Marriages of Alexander III and leading companions to Iranians.

324 *late spring*—Mutiny of the army at Opis.

324 *autumn*—Death of Hephaestion at Ecbatana and destruction of temple there.

324 *winter*—Arrival in Babylon.

323 *June 10*—Death of Alexander III in Babylon.

323 *summer*—Birth of Alexander III's posthumous son, Alexander IV. Regency of Perdiccas.

321 Departure of cortege of Alexander III from Babylon and seizure of the cortege by Ptolemy in Syria. Supplication and death of Demosthenes.

321–320 Burial of Alexander III in Memphis.

320 *summer*—Assassination of Perdiccas by Seleucus.

320 *summer*—Redistribution of commands and provinces at Trisparadeisos.

317 Murder of Philip Arrhidaeus by Olympias.

316 *spring*—Execution of Olympias.

310–309 Murder of Roxane and Alexander IV by Cassander.

309 Betrayal and death of Heracles, son of Alexander III and Barsine.

ca. 300 Removal of Alexander III's body to Alexandria.

A Glossary of Gods and Lesser Beings

Achilles The greatest Homeric warrior, important to Alexander III both as a military role model and as a reputed ancestor of Olympias, his mother. Alexander worshipped him at Troy.

Ahura Mazda The chief god of the Persians, sometimes worshipped together with two others, Anahita (q.v.) and Mithra, a sun god. Unlike his Greek counterpart, Zeus, Ahura Mazda, or "Lord of Wisdom," personified good in combat against evil.

Alexander III King of Macedon and acknowledged leader of Thessaly and Greece, positions inherited from his father, Philip II; reputedly the son of Nectanebo according to Egyptian sources, and half Persian according to some Persian sources. In Greek and Egyptian sources his mother was Olympias, but in Persian sources she was a Persian princess.

Alexander IV Co-king of Macedon and of the Macedonian empire in Asia, positions inherited from his father, Alexander III. His mother was Roxana, the Sogdian wife of Alexander III.

Ambhi Ruler of Taxila, the first important Indian city conquered by Alexander III and his army. Ambhi was the first native ruler to become a provincial governor under Alexander.

Amon, or Amon-Re The chief god of Egypt, responsible for making Alexander III pharaoh of Egypt, and worshipped in Greece as Zeus-Amon. As pharaoh, Alexander ranked as Amon's son; however, he had no divine mother. The priests of Amon-Re became important advisers to Alexander.

Anahita, or Sarasvati As Anahita, a goddess of water, fertility, and culture among the Iranians; the same as Sarasvati among the Pakrit-speaking peoples of India. The most important shrine of hers that Alexander III visited was in Bactra, the capital of Bactria.

Antigonus A veteran of the wars of Philip II, given the task of subduing and controlling Asia Minor by Alexander III. After Alexander's death, a leading successor in control of Asia Minor, and sometimes Syria, Mesopotamia, and western Iran.

Antipater A veteran of the wars of Philip II, given the task of controlling Macedon and Greece during the Macedonian invasion of the Persian Empire. After the death of Alexander III, a leading successor in control of Macedon and Greece, which eventually came under the control of his son, Cassander.

Aristander The chief diviner of Philip II and later of Alexander III. He accompanied Alexander into Asia and was the most influential priest in the army before Alexander encountered the priests of Amon-Re.

Aristobulus An engineer, architect, and virtual chief of the technical staff of Alexander III. He was the author of the most important account of Alexander's career from a civilian rather than military viewpoint.

Artabazus, or Ashavazdan A Persian exile who lived in Macedon and then returned to Persia, serving Darius III. He was one of the most prominent Persian leaders to switch sides and enter the service of Alexander III, who took his daughter, Barsine, as a mate.

Athena An Olympian goddess worshipped for her military qualities by the kings of Macedon, notably Alexander III.

Baal Haman The chief god of the Semites of western Syria and also the god of the mountain beside which the battle of Issus was fought, and thus for Alexander the III a local form of Zeus.

Barsine The daughter of Artabazus, who became Alexander III's mate when captured after the battle of Issus. She bore Alexander a son, Heracles.

Bessus, or Artaxshasa A Persian noble who was Darius III's governor of Bactria, a post establishing him as heir to the Persian throne. After Darius's death, he took the royal name Artaxshasa.

Calanus The most prominent of the Indian religious leaders who joined the entourage of Alexander III. Evidently a Brahmin, he committed suicide during the army's return from India.

Cassander The son of Antipater, who joined Alexander III in Babylon in the months before Alexander's death, and who established himself as his father's successor in Macedon in part by killing Olympias and Heracles, Alexander's son by Barsine.

Chares Steward and master of ceremonies for Alexander III, and the author of memoirs of court life.

Clitus Surnamed "the Black," a Macedonian cavalry commander assigned by Alexander III to be the first Macedonian governor of Bactria. Alexander murdered him following a quarrel at a drinking party.

Coenus A veteran of the wars of Philip II, he served first as a leading infantry commander and later as a commander of cavalry and independent detachments. He led the faction of generals who compelled Alexander III to abandon the conquest of India and return to Babylon.

Craterus A veteran of the wars of Philip II, he served as a leading infantry commander and later replaced Parmenio as the virtual second in command of the army. He died shortly after the death of Alexander III, and thus did not become one Alexander's successors.

Cyrus the Great Ruler of Anshan, a small Persian kingdom, who made himself ruler of Iranian Central Asia and then of the entire Near East, save for Egypt. Admired by many Greek writers, he offered a role model to Alexander III.

Darius III, perhaps né Codomannus King of the Persian Empire at the time of the Macedonian invasion, but of dubious ancestry, since he was only a collateral descendant of Cyrus the Great.

Demosthenes The most famous of Greek orators; also an outstanding opponent of both Philip II and Alexander III, and convicted of taking bribes from Alexander's fugitive treasurer, Harpalus.

Diades Alexander III's leading engineer, a Thessalian, who wrote a book on siege warfare describing innovations such as towers on wheels and wall drills.

Dionysus An Olympian god important to Alexander III as the patron god of Thebes, which Alexander sacked, and as a god reportedly worshipped in India, where Alexander hoped to establish himself as ruler under Dionysus's sponsorship.

Eumenes The most important Greek companion of Alexander III, whom he served as secretary and to whom he lent money in India. After Alexander's death, he was briefly one of his successors, only to be defeated by Antigonus.

Harpalus A childhood friend of Alexander III, who became treasurer of the empire, eventually residing in Babylon. He was the first companion known to have deserted Alexander, fleeing to Athens in an unsuccessful attempt to establish himself in Greece.

Hephaestion A childhood friend of Alexander III, becoming his lover and later a top administrator and also commander of the companion cavalry. His death in Ecbatana, less than a year before Alexander's own death, marked the beginning of the king's final, fatal decline.

Heracles, son of Alexander III The son of Alexander by Barsine, he took no part in politics until the Macedonian general Polyperchon persuaded him to try to become king of Macedon, and then betrayed him to Cassander.

Heracles, son of Zeus The greatest of Greek heroes, important to the kings of Macedon both because of his military qualities and because he was reputedly an ancestor of the Macedonian royal family. Heracles was also the most important of the Argonauts, a group of heroes providing a precedent for the companions of Philip II and Alexander III.

Heracles Melkarth The patron god of Tyre, the chief city in Phoenicia, and identified by Greeks with Heracles the son of Zeus, and thus identified by Alexander III as an ancestor. Sacrifices to Heracles Melkarth were an important prerogative of Tyrian kings.

Jason Leader of the Argonauts, the heroes who brought back the Golden Fleece from Colchis, in eastern Asia Minor. Parmenio built a shrine to Jason at Abdera, an act comparable to Alexander III's worship of Achilles at Troy.

Leonnatus The same age as Alexander III, this companion was a bodyguard of Philip II before holding the same post under Alexander. In Central Asia he held independent commands; after Alexander's death, he became a provincial governor in Asia Minor.

Marduk The chief god of the Babylonian pantheon, and thus the patron of Alexander III once he became king of Babylon. Unlike Amon-Re, Marduk did not adopt Alexander III as his son.

Mazdai A leading Persian general in the service of Darius III, he switched sides and surrendered Babylon to Alexander III, who made him governor of Babylonia.

Memnon of Assyria This legendary figure died fighting against Alexander III's ancestor Achilles at Troy, and was regarded by the Greeks as the chief builder of the city of Susa, one of the capitals of the Persian Empire.

Memnon of Rhodes A Greek mercenary in the service of Darius III, Memnon was the first husband of Barsine, and thus the son-in-law of the Persian notable Artabazus, who later became Alexander's leading Persian supporter.

Nearchus A childhood friend of Alexander III who in India served as his leading admiral and commanded an independent force that sailed from the Indus to Mesopotamia.

Nectanebo, or Nakhtnebef The last native pharaoh of Egypt, regarded by some Egyptian sources as the father of Alexander III. The Persians drove him from power twelve years before Alexander invaded Egypt.

Olympias, née Polyxena The mother of Alexander III by Philip II, and thus the most important of Philip's seven wives. The relatives of those she had put to death did the same to her in 316, seven years after Alexander's death.

Onesicritus The helmsman of Alexander III's vessel, noteworthy for his philosophy of Cynicism, ironically combined with gross flattery of Alexander in reporting, for example, that the king made love to the queen of the Amazons.

Parmenio The most important general of Philip II, a distinction that he retained under Alexander III until he was assassinated in Ecbatana shortly after the execution of his son Philotas. Another son of his, Nicanor, commanded the shieldbearers.

Perdiccas A veteran of the wars of Philip II, this general commanded an infantry regiment and afterward succeeded Hephaestion as commander of the companion cavalry. After the death of Alexander III, Perdiccas became regent for Alexander's two successors, Alexander IV and Philip Arrhidaeus.

Philip II Son of King Amyntas III of Macedon, he came to the throne after being appointed regent for an infant king. He had daughters by two of his seven wives and a son, Philip Arrhidaeus, by a third. By Olympias he had a son, Alexander III, and a daughter, Cleopatra.

Philip Arrhidaeus Half brother of Alexander III by one of Philip's Thessalians wives, he became co-king after Alexander's death.

Philotas Son of Parmenio and commander of the companion cavalry until executed by a court-martial in eastern Iran. He was an early and vocal critic of Alexander III's claim to be the son of Zeus-Amon.

Polyperchon A veteran of Philip II, this able soldier became a regimental commander under Alexander and on the return march to Babylon served under his fellow traditionalist, Craterus. After Alexander III's death he replaced Antipater as regent, only to lose power to Cassander.

Porus, or Puru The most powerful of the kings in the Punjab, he was the chief opponent of the Macedonian invasion of India under Alexander III. After being defeated, he became an autonomous subject of Alexander's and also a companion.

Ptolemy, the son of Lagus A childhood friend of Alexander III, he served him first as a bodyguard, then as a commander of independent detachments. After Alexander's death, he became governor of Egypt and later pharaoh.

Roxana The daughter of a Sogdian warlord in Central Asia, she was married to Alexander III as part of his efforts to pacify this region. She bore him a posthumous son, Alexander IV, and like her son died at the hands of Olympias.

Seleucus An infantry commander during invasion of Asia by Alexander III, he replaced Parmenio's son Nicanor as commander of the shieldbearers. After Alexander's death, he at first sided with the regent, Perdiccas, but then betrayed and killed him, receiving the province of Babylonia as a reward.

Sisygambis The mother of Darius III, captured by Alexander III after the battle at Issus. Her daughter Stateira later was married to Alexander, and she committed suicide after his death.

Xenophon A leading Greek mercenary and military writer of the early and mid-fourth century BC, Xenophon was important for Alexander III as the leader of a Greek force that returned home after fighting successfully in the Persian Empire and as a writer extolling Cyrus the Great.

Zeus The chief god of the Greeks and Macedonians, identified with Amon of Egypt and Marduk of Babylon, among others. As Zeus-Amon, he was the divine father of

Alexander III, but as the Greek god Zeus, he was not—a difficulty exploited by Philotas and other critics of Alexander.

Zoroaster, or Zarathustra Born in Central Asia at some unknown date, but before the establishment of the Persian Empire, this Persian religious reformer imparted a dualistic quality to Persian religion, exalting Ahura Mazda over other gods.

Acts of Sacrifice and Related Rituals

This appendix lists acts of sacrifice and related rituals in the Alexander historians and in Strabo. It falls into two parts, 1a for sacrifice and libations and 1b for omens and oracles. The second part effectively overlaps with the first, since all acts of *thusia* included inspection of entrails, and thus provided an omen, and since all oracles given in shrines were preceded by an animal sacrifice.[1] As the diction found in the sources is largely conventional, important terms are mostly paraphrased rather than reported verbatim.

Where more than one source reports an act, Arrian comes first, followed by the Vulgate, which is indented. The burial of Darius, which Alexander facilitated, is included, but no acts in the Persian court are listed, for the Alexander historians very remarkably do not report a single act of sacrifice or libation, or a single oracle or interpretation of an omen, by any *magos* or other Persian priest. The same is mostly true of subject peoples. Also omitted are dedications not expressly said to be accompanied by sacrifices.

These appendices list all reported acts, but not other acts that are unreported yet certain or very likely, such as the funerals after the battle of Gaugamela. Four suppositious acts, no. 38 in Appendix 1a and nos. 1, 3, and 16 in Appendix 1b, are italicized.

Appendix 1a: Occasional Acts of Sacrifice, Including Libations

The following list excludes not only daily, routine sacrifices, as in the *Ephemerides*,[2] and irregular, traditional sacrifices such as the *Hetareida* (Hegesander *FHG* 4 fr. 25), but also regular festivals such as the annual autumn festival to Dionysus (Arr. *An.* 4.8.1, Ephippus *FGrH* 126 F 5). Purification of the army is excluded for lack of any instance in which the historians report that Alexander performed this ritual. Instead this ritual appears at the end of this list, under "Occasional Acts Shortly After Alexander's Death."

Under the heading "God or hero," all funerary offerings are supposed to be directed to "Chthonic gods." Under the heading "Type," *thusia* designates some form of the verb *thuein*; *sphagia* designates *sphazein*; and *sacrificium* designates Latin verbs or nouns from the same root. Under "Request or purpose," terms suggested by the express language of the source are found, e.g., *diabatēria* for river crossings or ocean voyages. At nos. 6, 36, and 40, acts closely associated with one another are grouped, but distinguished according to celebrant, god, or type. Where stated, the species and gender of an animal offering are indicated in a note. Unless asterisked, the *sacrifiant* or *sacrificateur* is Alexander.

Source	Time and place	God or hero	Type	Request or purpose
1. Arr. *An.* 1.4.5	335; Danube	Zeus, Heracles, Danube	*thusia*	*Eucharistēria*
2. DS 17.14.1	335; Thebes	Chthonic gods	unstated	Burial
3. Arr. *An.* 1.11.1	335; Dium	Zeus and Muses	*thusia*	Olympic games[3]
DS 17.16.3	same	same	same	Same
4. Str. 11.14.12*	334; Abdera	Jason	unstated	*diabatēria*; altar dedicated
5. Arr. *An.* 1.11.5	334; Hellespont	Protesilaus	*thusia*[4]	*Diabatēria*
6. Arr. *An.* 1.11.7	334; Hellespont	Zeus, Athena, Heracles	*thusia*	*diabatēria*; altar dedicated
		Poseidon, Nereids	*thusia*[5]	*Diabatēria*
		Zeus, Athena, Heracles	*thusia*	*apobatēria*; altar dedicated
Justin 11.5.4	same	Twelve gods	*sacrificium*	*Apobatēria*
7. Arr. *An.* 1.11.8	334; Troy, altar of Zeus Herkeios	Priam	*thusia*	Appeasement
DS 17.17.9	same	Athena	*thusia*	unstated; armor dedicated

Source	Time and place	God or hero	Type	Request or purpose
Plu. *Alex.* 15.3	same	Athena and heroes	*thusia* and libations	Unstated
Str. 13.21.6–7	same	same	*thusia*	Unstated
8. Arr. *An.* 1.16.5	334; Granicus	Chthonic gods	unstated	burial; armor and statues dedicated at Dium and Athens[6]
DS 17.21.6	same	same	same	Burial
Plu. *Alex.* 16.16	same	unstated	unstated	unstated; armor dedicated at Athens
9. Arr. *An.* 1.18.2	334; Ephesus	Artemis	*thusia*	*epinikia*?; parade
10. Arr. *An.* 2.3.8	333; Gordium	unspecified	*thusia*	*Eucharistēria*
11. Arr. *An.* 2.5.8	333; Soli	Asclepius	*thusia*	*Eucharistēria*
	Curt 3.7.3 same	unstated	*sacrificium*	*Vota*
12. Curt. 3.8.22	333; Issus	*Dis praesidibus loci*	*sacrificium*	pre-battle; altars afterward
13. Arr. *An.* 2.12.1	333; Issus	Chthonic gods	unstated	burial; tomb never built[7]
Curt. 3.12.13	same	same	unstated	Same
14. Plu. *Alex.* 25.1–2	332; Tyre	unstated	*sphagia*	pre-battle
15. Arr. *An.* 2.24.6	332; Tyre	Heracles Melkart	*thusia*	*eucharistēria*; parade, games
DS 17.46.6	same	same	same	Unstated
16. DS 17.46.6	332; Tyre	Chthonic gods	unstated	Burial
17. Arr. *An.*	2.27.4 332; Gaza	unstated	*thusia*[8]	pre-battle

Source	Time and place	God or hero	Type	Request or purpose
Curt. 4.6.10	same	same	*sacrificium*	Same
18. Arr. *An.* 3.1.4	332; Memphis	Apis	*thusia* (sic)	Unstated
		unspecified	*thusia*	Games
19. Curt. 4.8.9	332; Nile	Chthonic gods	unspecified	burial of Hector
20. Arr. *An.* 3.1.5	332; Alexandria	unstated	*thusia*	foundation of city
21. Arr. *An.* 3.5.2	332; Memphis	Zeus Basileios	*thusia*	Unstated
22. Arr. *An.* 3.6.1	331; Tyre	Heracles Melkart	*thusia*	Unstated
Plu. *Alex.* 29.1	same	unspecified	*thusia*	Games
23. Arr. *An.* 3.7.6	331; Tigris	Earth, Sun, Moon	*thusia*	*Apotropaia*
24. Plu. *Alex.* 31.9	331; Gaugamela	Phobos	*thusia*	*Apotropaia*
Curt. 4.13.15.	same	Jupiter and Minerva	*sacrificium*	Same
25. Arr. *An.* 3.16.5	331; Babylon	Marduk	*thusia* (sic)	Unstated
26. Arr. *An.* 3.16.9	331; Susa	unspecified	*thusia*	unstated; games
27. Curt. 5.4.2	330; Persian Gates	unspecified	*sacrificium*[9]	pre-battle
28. DS 17.72.1	330; Persepolis	unspecified	*thusia*	*Epinikia*
29. Justin 12.1.4	330; east of Ecbatana	Chthonic gods	unstated	Burial
30. Arr. *An.* 3.22.1.	330; Persepolis	unstated	unstated	burial of Darius
DS 17.73.3	330; unstated	same	same	Same
Plu. *Alex.* 43.7	330; unstated	same	same	Same

Source	Time and place	God or hero	Type	Request or purpose
Justin 11.15.	330; unstated	same	same	Same
31. Arr. *An.* 3.25.1	330; Zadrakarta	unspecified	*thusia*	unstated; games
32. Curt. 6.6.18	330; Areia	Chthonic gods	unstated	burial of Nicanor
33. Arr. *An.* 4.4.1	329; Tanais	unspecified	*thusia*	unstated; games
34. Arr. *An.* 4.4.3	same[10]	unspecified	*thusia*[11]	*Diabatēria*
Curt. 7.7.8–29	same	same	*sacrificium*	Same
35. Arr. *An.* 4.6.5	328; Polytimetus	Chthonic gods	unstated	Burial
Curt. 7.9.1	same	same	same	Same
36. Plu. *Alex.* 50.5	328; Marakanda	Dioscuri	*thusia*	unstated[12]
	** same	unstated	*thusia*	Interrupted
	*** same	same	*ekthusiasthai*	on behalf of Clitus
37 Curt. 8.2.40	327; unstated	Chthonic gods	unstated	burial of Erigyius
38. *Plu. Alex.* 56	*327? Unstated*	*Chthonic gods*	*unstated*	*burial of Demaratus*[13]
39. Arr. *An.* 4.30.5	326; Rock of Aornus	unstated	*thusia*	*Epinikia*
Curt. 8.11.25	same	Athena and Nike	*sacrificium*	*Epinikia*
40. Arr. *An.* 5.3.2	326; Indus	unspecified	*thusia*[14]	*Diabatēria*
5.3.6	same	unspecified	*thusia*	*Eucharistēria*
DS 17.86.3	same	unspecified	*thusia*	*Eucharistēria*
41. Arr. *An.* 5.8.3	326; Taxila	unspecified	*thusia*	unstated; games
42. Arr. *An.* 5.20.1	326; Hydaspes	Chthonic gods	unstated	Burial

Source	Time and place	God or hero	Type	Request or purpose
43. Arr. *An.* 5.20.1	326; Hydaspes	unspecified	*thusia*	*epinikia*; games
Curt. 9.1.1	same	Sun	*sacrificium*	Same
DS 17.89.3	same	Sun	*thusia*	same; also burial
44. Arr. *An.* 5.25.5	326; Sangala	Chthonic gods	unspecified	Burial
45. Arr. *An.* 5.28.4	326; Hyphasis	unspecified	*thusia*[15]	*diabatēria*; unsuccessful
46. Arr. *An.* 5.29.2	326; Hyphasis	Twelve gods	*thusia*	unstated; altars dedicated
Plu. *Alex.* 62.8	same	unspecified	*thusia*	unstated; altars dedicated
47. Arr. *An.* 6.3.1	326; Hydaspes	Chthonic gods	*thusia*	burial of Coenus
Curt. 9.3.20	same	same	same	Same
48. Arr. *An.* 6.3.1, *Ind.* 18.12	same	Acesines, Hydaspes, Heracles, Amon, and others	*thusia* and libations	*Diabatēria*
49. Plu. *Alex.* 63.13	325; Malli	unspecified	*thusia*	*sōtēria* and *epinikia*
50. Arr. *An.* 6.19.4	325; Indus mouth[16]	unspecified	*thusia*	according to an oracle
DS 17.104.1	same	Oceanus, Tethys, and others	*thusia*	unstated; altars dedicated
Plu. *Alex.* 66.2	same, but an island	unspecified	*thusia*	Unstated
Justin 12.10.4	same	Oceanus	*sacrificium*	Unstated
51. Arr. *An.* 6.19.5, *Ind.* 20.10	325; Gulf of Arabia	Poseidon	*sphagia*[17] and libations	*Diabatēria*

Source	Time and place	God or hero	Type	Request or purpose
52. Arr. *Ind.* 21.3	**** 325; Gulf of Arabia	Zeus Soter	*thusia*	*sōtēria*; games
53. Arr. *An.* 6.28.3, *Ind.* 36.3	325; Carmania	Zeus Soter and others	*thusia*	*Sōtēria*
54. Arr. *Ind.* 36.9	**** 325; Carmanian coast	Zeus Soter	*thusia*	*Sōtēria*
55. Arr. *Ind.* 42.8	324; Susa	unspecified	*thusia*	*Sōtēria*
56. Arr. *An.* 7.11.6	324; Opis	Zeus, Heracles, Dionysus	*thusia*	*Sōtēria*
57. Arr. *An.* 7.14.1	324; Ecbatana	unspecified	*thusia*	*eucharistēria*; games
58. Arr. *An.* 7.14.3–9	324; Ecbatana	Chthonic gods	*thusia*	burial of Hephaestion
59. Arr. *An.* 7.14.6	324; Epidaurus	Asclepius	*ἀνάθεμα*	*apotropaia?*
60. Arr. *An.*7.24.4	323; Babylon	unspecified	*thusia*	*Eucharistēria*

Occasional Acts Shortly After Alexander's Death.

Source	Time and place	God or hero	Type	Request or purpose
61. Arr. fr. 1.4	323; Babylon	unspecified	*καθᾶραι*	Interrupted
Curt. 10.9.11–9	Same	same	lustrare	Interrupted
62. Curt. 10.10.9–20	321–20; Egypt	unstated	*omnis… honos*	Burial

Appendix 1b: Omens and Oracles

The following list includes all expressly reported omens and oracles in the Alexander historians, Strabo providing no examples. Under the heading "Interpreter/source" appears a *mantis* or other expert, or, if none is mentioned, the name of the persons reporting the omen or receiving the oracle. Under "Type" appears the object or incident that brought about the omen, or the word *manteia*, designating an oracle. Under "Interpretation" appears the outcome of the omen or oracle.

Source	Time and place	Interpreter/source	Type	Interpretation
1. Plu. Alex. 14.6	*336–335; Delphi*	*Apollo*	*manteia*	*ambiguous*[18]
2. Arr. *An.* 1.11.3	335; Pieria, statue of Orpheus	Aristander	"sweating"	in favor of expedition
Plu. *Alex.* 14.8	Same	same	same	Same
3. DS 17.19.4	*334; Troy, statue of satrap*	*Aristander*	*fallen*	*death of satrap*[19]
4. Arr. *An.* 1.17.6	334; Sardis	Alexander	thunder	in favor of building shrine
5. Arr. An. 1.18.6–9	334; Miletus	Alexander and Parmenio	bird	against naval battle
6. Arr. *An.* 1.25.6–8	334; Halicarnassus	Aristander	bird	prediction of plot
7. Arr. *An.* 1.26.2	333; near Phaselis	Alexander	change in wind	divine intervention
8. Arr. *An.* 2.3.7–8	333; Gordium	Alexander	thunder	in favor of untying the Gordian knot
9. Arr. *An.* 2.18.1	333; Tyre	Aristander	dream about Heracles	in favor of siege
10. Curt. 4.2.13–14	Same	Aristander	discolored food	in favor of siege
	Same	Tyrians	discolored iron	in favor of defenders
DS 17.41.6	same pair	same	same	same

Source	Time and place	Interpreter/ source	Type	Interpretation
11. DS 17.41.7	Same	Macedonians	whale	in favor of siege
	Same	Tyrians	same	in favor of defenders
12. Arr. *An.* 2.27.4	332; Gaza	Aristander	bird	in favor of siege
Curt. 4.6.12	Same	same	same	same
Plu. *Alex.* 25.3–4	Same	same	same	same
13. Arr. *An.* 3.4.5–6	332/1; Siwah	Priests of Amon	oracle	unstated
Curt. 4.7.25–27	Same	same	same	sundry
DS 17.50.6–51.2	Same	same	same	sundry
Plu. *Alex.* 27.3–4	Same	same	same	sundry and ambiguous
Justin 11.11.7–11	Same	same	same	sundry
14. Arr. *An.* 3.2.1	332/1; Alexandria	Aristander	birds	in favor of foundation
Curt. 4.8.6	Same	unspecified	same	same
Plu. *Alex.* 26.8.	Same	unspecified	same	same
15. Arr. *An.* 3.7.6	331; Tigris	Aristander	eclipse	in favor of battle
Curt. 4.10.1–7	Same	Egyptian priests	same	same
***16.** Plu. Alex. 37.1*	*unspecified; Delphi*	*Apollo*	*manteia*	*in favor of invading Persis*[20]
17. Curt. 4.15.27,	Gaugamela	Aristander	birds	victory
Plu. *Alex.* 33.1.	Same	same	same	same
18. Arr. *An.* 4.15.7	328; Oxus	Aristander	oil flow	eventual victory

Source	Time and place	Interpreter/ source	Type	Interpretation
Curt. 7.10.14	Same	Alexander	water source	divine intervention
Plu. *Alex.* 57.5–9		seers	oil flow	eventual victory
19. Plu. *Alex.* 57.4–5	328; Oxus	Babylonian priests	ἐκαθάρθη [*sic*]	deformed sheep
20. Arr. *An.* 4.13.6	327; Bactra	Syrian prophetess	dream about drinking	protection of the king
Curt. 8.6.16–17		same	same	same
21. Curt. 9.4.27–28	325; Malli	Alexander and seers	entrails	immediate attack
22. Arr. *An.* 7.14.7	324; Ecbatana	Amon-Re	oracle	against worship of Hephaestion
DS 17.115.6	Same	same	same	in favor of worship of Hephaestion
23. Arr. *An.* 7.16.5	324; Babylon	Babylonian λόγιοι	λόγιον	against entry into Babylon
DS 17.112.2	Same	Chaldaeans [*sic*]	τῆς τῶν ἀστέρων μαντείας	same
Plu. *Alex.* 73.1	Same	same	unstated	same
24. Arr. *An.* 7.24.4	323; Babylon	unstated	*manteia*	unstated
Plu. *Alex.* 75.3	same	unstated	χρησμοί	Hephaestion

APPENDIX 2

Acts of Supplication

This appendix provides a list of the acts of supplication, whether in shrines or elsewhere, in the Alexander historians. Where more than one source reports an act, Arrian appears first, followed by the Vulgate, which is indented. As the diction found in the sources is more various than is the case for sacrifice, important terms are often reported verbatim.

Under the column "Suppliant/supplicandus," the latter is the party approached during the act of supplication; in a shrine, this party is nominally a god, but is actually Alexander or some municipal authority. Under "Gesture/word" appears the language in which the source describes how the suppliant approaches the supplicandus and communicates his intent to supplicate. Sometimes the suppliant is not described, but only identified as an *hiketēs* or *supplex*, in which case only this word appears, and any verb is omitted. Under "Response" appears the reaction of the supplicandus to the suppliant, often conveyed either by a gesture or a word.

This appendix lists all reported acts, but it does not include other acts that are unreported yet certain or very likely, such as supplications made by enemy soldiers or civilians during the siege of Gaza. Three suppositious acts, nos. 5, 20, and 30, are italicized.

Source	Date	Suppliant/supplicandus	Gesture/word	Response
1. Arr. *An.*1.8.8	335	Thebans/shrines	πρὸς ἱεροῖς ἱκετεοντας	slain
DS 17.13.6	Same	same	ἐς τὰ ἱερὰ καταπεφευγότας	slain
2. Paus. 6.18.3–4	334	Lampsacenes/Alexander	ἱκετεύειν	request granted

Source	Date	Suppliant/ supplicandus	Gesture/word	Response
3. Arr. *An.* 1.17.12	334 Ephesian Artemis	Syrphax and sons/	ἐκ τοῦ ἱεροῦ ἐξαγαγόντας	slain
4. DS 17.22.4–5	334	Milesians/ Alexander	μέθ' ἱκετηριῶν προσπίπτοντες	φιλανθρώπως προςνvέχθη
5. *Curt. 3.2.17*	333	*Charidemus/ Darius III*	*supplicem*	*rejected*[21]
6. DS 17.35.5	333	Persian noblewomen/ Macedonians	προσπίπτουσαι γόνασι	enslaved
7. DS 17.36.4	333	Satraps' wives/ royal family	προσπιπτούσαις	unstated
8. Curt. 3.12.10	333	Persian women/ Leonnatus	Prouolutae ad pedes	alleuari
9. Curt. 3.12.17	333	Sisygambis/ Alexander	aduoluta… pedibus	alleuans
10. DS 17.41.7–8	332	Youth/Heracles Melkart	καταφυγὼν ἐς τὸ …ἱερὸν	accepted
11. Arr. *An.* 2.24.5	332	Tyrians/ Heracles Melkart	ἐς τὸ ἱερὸν καταφυγοῦσι	spared
12. Curt. 4.4.12–3	332	Tyrians/ temples	supplices	spared
13. Curt. 4.6.15–6	332	Arab/ Alexander	genibus… aduoluitur	assurgere
14. Curt. 5.1.17–19	331	Mazaeus/ Alexander	supplex urbem seque dedens	
15. Curt. 5.3.12–15	331	Persians/ Sisygambis	supplicum precibus	abnuens[22]
16. Curt. 5.10.14	330	Traitors/Darius	preces… suppliciter	forgiven
17. Curt. 6.6.34	330	Rebels/ Alexander	supplicibus semet dedentibus	parceret
18. Curt. 6.7.3–15	330	Dymnus/ Nichomachus	supplex	request granted[23]

Source	Date	Suppliant/ supplicandus	Gesture/word	Response
19. Curt. 6.7.33–5	330	Philotas/ Alexander	complexus	dextram pignus[24]
20. *Curt.* 7.5.33	329	*Didymaeans/ Alexander*	*Supplicum uelamentis*	*slain*[25]
21. Curt. 8.1.48	328	Ptolemy and Perdiccas/ Alexander	genibus aduoluti	request denied
22. Curt. 8.10.34–5	327	Cleophis/ Alexander	genibus regis	ueniam
23. Arr. *An.* 5.1.4–2.4	326	Nysaeans/ Alexander	πεσόντας εἰς γῆν	ἐξανέστησε
24. DS 17.91.4	326	Indians/ Alexander	μέθ' ἱκετηριῶν	ἀπέλυσε
25. DS 17.96.5	325	3,000 Agalasseis/ Alexander	μέθ' ἱκετηριῶν	ἀπέλυσε
26. DS 17.102.7	325	Brahmins/ Alexander	μέθ' ἱκετηριῶν	ἀπέλυσε
27. DS 17.108.3	325	Harmatelians/ Alexander	μέθ' ἱκετηριῶν	ἀπέλυσε
28. DS. 17.108.6–7	324	Harpalus/ Athenians	ἱκέτης	sent on
29. Arr. *An.* 7.11.4–7	324	Troops/ Alexander	ἱκετηρίαν	ἐφίλησε
Plu. *Alex.* 71.6–7	same	same	μετὰ…κλαυθμοῦ παραδιδόντας ἑαυτοὺς	request granted
Justin 12.12.6	same	same	*flentes regem adeunt*	same
30. *Curt.* 10.9.21	323	*Meleager/ unnamed Babylonian temple*	*confugit in templum*	*slain*
31. Plu. *Alex.* 42.1	???	Slave/unnamed shrine	ἱερῷ καθεζομένου	unstated

Formal Meetings of Alexander's Companions

This appendix provides a list of formal meetings of Alexander's companions—in brief, his council meetings—in the Alexander historians and in Aelian. Where more than one source reports a meeting, Arrian comes first, followed by the Vulgate, which is indented. At the end of the list of meetings during Alexander's reign appears a list of meetings shortly afterwards, and a list of Persian meetings. As the diction found in the sources is much more various than in the case of sacrifice, important terms are almost always reported verbatim rather than paraphrased.

Except where indicated, the "issue" is military. "Summons" refers to the words by which the king calls the meeting; if the council meets without his say-so, "none" appears in this column. "Question" refers to the words by which the question is put, or by which information is adduced; if the latter, the question may be deduced from the information; sometimes the question is implied. If the words in this column are underlined, the council puts the question. Otherwise the king puts the question. "Speakers" refers to persons other than the king. "Response" refers to words by which the companions state their opinion, and sometimes to the words by which the king responds to them; except in cases explained below, a verb in the singular refers to the king and a verb in the plural refers to the council. If the companions do not state an opinion, "none" appears in this column. If the king rejects advice, "rejected" appears.

This appendix lists all reported meetings, but not other meetings that are unreported yet certain or very likely, such as meetings to determine the line of march (a generic report of which appears at no. 35).

Source	Date Place/Issue		Summons	Question	Speakers	Response	Results
1. Arr. *An.* 1.1.8	335	Mt. Haemus	βουλὴ γίνεται	implied	unnamed	ἐδόκει[26]	battle orders
2. DS 17.16.2	335/4	Macedon marriage	συμβουλευόντων	προέηκε βουλὴν	Antipater Parmenio	rejected	troops marshaled
3. Plu. *Alex.* 16.2–3	334	at Granicus	implied	εἰπὼν	Parmenio	rejected	battle orders
4. Arr. *An.* 1.25.4	334/3	Pamphylia Lyncestes	συναγαγὼν τοὺς φίλους	προυτίθει ὅτι χρὴ γνῶναι	unnamed	ἐδόκει τοῖς ἑταίρους	arrest
5. Curt. 3.5.11–6.3[27]	333	at Cydnus king's health	admissis…amicis	inquit	unnamed	nulli placebat	cure administered
6. Arr. *An.* 2.6.1	333	Mallus	συναγαγὼν τοὺς ἑταίρους	φράζει αὐτοὺς	unnamed	ἐκέλευον	marching orders
7. Arr. *An.* 2.7.3–9	333	Issus	συγκαλέσας στρατηγούς τε καὶ ἰλάρχας καὶ τῶν ξυμμάχων τοὺς ἡγεμόνας	παρεκάλει	unnamed	ἐκέλευον	battle orders
Curt. 3.7.8–10	same	same	consilio habito	indirect question	Parmenio	ratio…consilii accepta[28]	same

Source	Date	Place/Issue	Summons	Question	Speakers	Response	Results
8. Arr. *An.* 2.16.8–18.1	332	Tyre	συναγαγὼν τοὺς ἑταίρους καὶ τοὺς ἡγεμόνας τῆς στρατιᾶς καὶ ταξιάρχας καὶ ἰλάρχας	ἔλεξεν ὧδε (ταῦτα ἐκράτησε)	unnamed	ἔπειθεν	siege orders
DS 17.45.2		Tyre	τῶν φίλων	none	Amyntas	ἕνα μόνον ὁμογνωμονοῦντα orders	siege
9. Arr. *An.* 2.25.1–3	332	Tyre Darius's offer	ἐν τῷ ξυλλόγῳ τῶν ἑταίρων	ἐπαγγελθέντων	Parmenio	none save to legates	dismissal
10. DS 17.39.2	332	Issus? same	συναγαγὼν τοὺς φίλους	προσήνεγκε τοῖς συνέδρους	unnamed	none	same
Plu. *Alex.* 29.7–8	331	Syria same	ἐκονοῦτο τοὺς ἑταίρους	implied	Parmenio	none	same
11. Curt. 4.10.4–7	331	at Tigris	duces principesque frequentes adesse iubet	uates quid sentiret iubet expromere	priests	none	marching orders
12. Curt. 4.11	331	near Tigris Darius's offer	consilio aduocato	quid placeret ad consilium refert	Parmenio	rejected	dismissal of legates

Source	Date Place/Issue	Summons	Question	Speakers	Response	Results
DS 17.54.3–6	same	εἰς τὸ συν-έδριον παρα-λαβὼν τοὺς φίλους	περὶ αἱρέσεων ἀνακοινωσάμενος	Parmenio	none	same
13. Arr. *An.* 3.9.3–4	331[29] Gaugamela	συγκαλέσας τούς τε ἑταίρους καὶ στρατηγούς τε καὶ ἰλάρχας καὶ τῶν ξυμμάχων καὶ τῶν μισθοφόρων τοὺς ἡγεμόνας	ἐβουλεύετο	Parmenio	νικᾷ Παρμενίων	pitch camp
14. Arr. *An.* 3.9.5–8	331[30] Gaugamela	συγκαλέσας τοὺς αὐτοὺς ἡγεμόνας	παρακαλεῖσθαι	unnamed	ἀντιπαρα-κληθεὶς	pitch camp
15. Curt. 4.13.4–11	331[31] Gaugamela	consilium adhibet	quid optimum factu exquirens	Parmenio Polyperchon	assentiebantur/ rejected	dismissal
Plu. *Alex.* 31.10–14	same[32] same	τῷ βασιλεῖ προσελθόντες	πρὸς ἀλλήλους διαλεχθέντες	unnamed	ἔπειθον/rejected	same
16. Curt. 4.13.17–20	331[33] Gaugamela	duces conuenerant ad imperia accipienda	implied	Parmenio	Parmenio... pronuntiat	troops fed

Source	Date Place/Issue	Summons	Question	Speakers	Response	Results
DS 17;56.2–4	same[34]	none	implied	Parmenio	Παρμενίων πρόσταγμα διέδωκε	same
Plu. *Alex.* 32.1	same[35]	none	implied	Parmenio	παρὰ αὐτῶν παράγγελμα	same
17. Curt. 4.13.37	331[36] Gaugamela	duces	exposito	unnamed	none	monet
18. Curt. 5.4.1	330 Persian Gates	consultare	quid agendum	unnamed	none	marching orders
19. Curt. 5.6.1	330 Persepolis sack	conuocatos duces	unstated	unnamed	none	docet
20. Curt. 5.13.4–5	330 Tabae	ducibus conuocatis	inquit	unnamed	conclamant	marching orders
21. Curt. 6.2.18–21	330 Hecatompylus	praefectos contrahit	implied	unnamed	operam suam offerre	assembly convened
22. Curt. 6.7.17	330 Drangiana unstated	unstated	unstated	unnamed	unstated	ceteris dismissis
23. Curt. 6.8.1–17	330 Drangiana Philotas	aduocato consilio	implied	Craterus	decernunt	trial

Source	Date Place/Issue	Summons	Question	Speakers	Response	Results
24. Curt. 6.11.9–33	330[37] Drangiana Philotas	amicos conuocari	implied	unnamed	in senteniam… transeunt	torture administered
25. Curt. 7.5.9–12	329 Sogdiana king's conduct	circumfusi amici	implied	unnamed	orabant	unstated
26. Curt. 7.7.5–29	329 at Tanais	consilium aduocari iubet	consultanti cum iisdem	Erigyius Aristander	none	marching orders…………[38]
27. Curt. 8.6.28–8.8.20	327 Bactra Hermolaus	consilium adhibuit	implied	Hermolaus	damnatos excruciatos[39]	
28. Plu. Alex. 55.9 327?	Unknown Callisthenes	unstated	ἐν τῷ συνεδρίῳ κριθείη παρόντος Ἀριστοτέλους		imprisoned	
29. Arr. An. 5.25.2–28.1	326 at Hyphasis	συγκαλέσας τοὺς ἡγεμόνας τῶν τάξεων	ἔλεξεν	Coenus	rejection of king	marching orders
30. Arr. An. 5.28.2–3	326[40] at Hyphasis	συγκαλέσας αὖθις	ἔφη	unnamed	same	performance of sacrifices
31. Arr. An. 5.28.5	326[41] at Hyphasis	τοὺς πρεσβυτάτους τε τῶν ἑταίρων καὶ τοὺς ἐπιτηδείους αὐτῷ συναγαγὼν	ἐκραίνει	unnamed	approval	withdrawal

Source	Date	Place/Issue	Summons	Question	Speakers	Response	Results
32. Arr. *An.* 6.2.1	326	at Hydaspes Porus	συναγαγὼν τούς τε ἑταίρους	ἀπέδειξε	unnamed	none	marching orders
33. Curt. 9.6.4–26	326	at Hydraotis king's health	none	Implied	Craterus Ptolemy	rejected royal counterproposal	postponed
34. Curt. 9.7.14	326/5	at Hydraotis surrender of Oxydracae	consilio habito	unstated	unnamed	none	marching orders
35. Ael. *VH* 3.23	324?[42]	unstated	implied	λέγων	unnamed	unstated	marching orders
36. Arr. *An.* 7.25.2	323	Babylon	τοῖς ἡγεμόσι παραγγέλλειν	unstated	unstated	none	
37. Arr. *An.* 7.25.4	323[43]	Babylon	ἀπαντῆσαι τοῖς ἡγεμόσιν	παραγγεῖλαι	unnamed	unstated	none
Plut. *Alex.* 76.3	same[44]	same	ἡγεμόσι παραγγεῖλαι	unstated	unnamed	unstated	none
38. Arr. *An.* 7.25.4	323[45]	Babylon	τοὺς ἡγεμόνας ἐσκαλέσαντα	παραγγεῖλαι	unnamed	unstated	none
39. Arr. *An.* 7.25.5	323[46]	Babylon	ἐσκαλέσαι…τοὺς ἐπικαιροτάτους	παραγγεῖλαι	unnamed	unstated	none

Source	Date	Place/Issue	Summons	Question	Speakers	Response	Results
Plu. *Alex.* 76.5	same[47]	same	τοῖς ἡγεμόσιν διελέχθη	unstated	unnamed	unstated	none
40. Arr. *An.* 7.25.5	323[48]	Babylon	implied	παραγγέλειν	unnamed	unstated	none
41. Curt. 10.5.4–6	323	Babylon	adire iussis amicis	adiectis mandatis	unnamed	quaerentibus	ambiguous
Justin. 12.15.5–9	same	same	none	unstated	unnamed	quaerunt	same

Meetings Shortly After Alexander's Death

Source	Date	Place/Issue	Summons	Question	Speakers	Response	Results
42. Curt. 10.6.1–2	323	Babylon succession	custodes principes amicorum ducesque copiarum aduocauere	implied	unnamed	meeting interrupted	none
DS 18.2.2	same	same	συνεδρεύσαντες	implied	unnamed	διέγνωσαν	envoys sent
43. Curt. 10.10.1–6	323	Babylon	consilium principum uirorum habuit	implied	Perdiccas	iusserunt	commands assigned

Meetings of the Council of Darius and of Other Persian Councils

Source	Date	Place/Issue	Summons	Question	Speakers	Response	Results
44. Arr. *An.* 1.12.9–10	334	Zeleia	βουλευομένους[49]	implied	unnamed	divided	give battle

Source	Date	Place/Issue	Summons	Question	Speakers	Response	Results
45. Curt. 3.2.10–19	333	Babylon	none	implied	Charidemus	divided	councilor slain
DS 17.30.1–5	same	same	συνήγαγε τῶν φίλων Συνέδριον	προέγηκε βουλήν	Charidemus	same	same
46. Curt. 3.8.1–11	same	Issus	none	implied	Greeks, incl. Thimodes	purpuratis displicebat	none
47. Curt. 5.1.4–9	331	Arbela	[amicis] conuocatis	exponit	unnamed	imperium… sequentibus	retreat
48. Curt. 5.8.6–9.13	330	Media	consilio aduocato	oro et obtestor	Artabazus Nabarzanes	divided	disorder

Notes

1. Writers on Alexander commonly make other comparisons—for example, with Napoleon, as at Clausewitz (1976), 580, and with Cortés, as at Bosworth (2000b). The comparison with Caesar first occurred to Caesar himself (Plu. *Caes.* 11.5–6, Suet. *Caes.* 7). Napoleon esteemed Eastern conquests such as Alexander's: "L'Europe... c'est une taupinière. Il n'y a jamais eu de grands empires et de grandes révolutions qu'en Orient," as in Dumas (1840), 41.

2. Lucky Alexander: a tradition going back at least as far as Plu. *Fort. Alex.* Alexander as civilizer: the same down to Tarn (1948). Alexander as sociopath: Worthington (2004), the latest in a long list of writers beginning with Seneca and St. Augustine. Sociopath and even psychopath: Schachermeyr (1973), Badian (1996).

3. For Asian deaths, which came mostly east of the Zagros, see Ch. 3, n. 18; Ch. 4, n. 30; Ch. 5, n. 4; Ch. 6, n. 36; Ch. 8, n. 9; Ch. 9, nn. 24, 63; and Ch. 10, n. 8. Macedonian deaths were far lower; see Ch. 6, n. 4, and Ch. 10, n. 19.

4. Alexander's skipping the ritual at Pasargadae described at Plu. *Arta.* 3.1–2: Arr. *An.* 3.18.10, Curt. 5.6.10. Destruction of the shrine of Anahita at Bactra: Onesikritos *FGrH* 134 F 5, Plu. *Fort. Alex.* 328d.

5. A final sacrifice only four days before his death: Plu. *Alex.* 77.3.

6. Alexander the virtual Anglican: Tarn (1948), 1.114. Similarly, Alexander as "monumentally superstitious" at Cartledge (2004), 209. Scrupulous piety, yet hubris, too: Aubriot (2003).

7. Alexander the deluded god: Wilcken (1932), 109, 114–15, followed by Lane Fox (1973), 497, and Bosworth (1988b), 65, 70, 87, and, with reservations, Cartledge (2004), 209. Dissenting: Wilamowitz-Moellendorff (1931), 265, followed by Kern (1963), 37. The literature on the deification of Alexander could be the subject of a book in itself. To the writers above add the following in English alone: Balsdon (1950), Badian (1981, 1996), Cawkwell (1994), and Chaniotis (2003).

8. Pagan Führer: Schachermeyr (1973). Anticipating this view, but praising Alexander: Berve (1926). Alexander "the indiscriminate opportunist" in matters of religion: Green (1991), 182. Anticipating Green: Badian (1965), 166; following him, Worthington (2004).

9. Alexander's strategy: Lonsdale (2007), esp. ch. 3. Religion in military historians: Pritchett (1979), Jacquemin (2000); also Lonis (1979), 302–15, on victory parades. Also brief: Case (1915), 181–82. Notice of fundamental questions, such as sacrifice and purification: Kern (1915), Schwenn (1920).

10. Alexander's letters, alas, are almost all spurious. When most of them were composed is disputed: Romm (1992), 109–16, preceded by Pearson (1955), 448–49.

11. Errington (1969) assails Ptolemy for his biases. Religion in Ptolemy: Kornemann (1935), 223–27. Criticism of Ptolemy while emphasizing religion: Altheim (1953), 110. Not surviving: the writings of Marsyas of Pella (*FGrH* 135), the brother of Antigonus, another leading soldier.

12. Alexander's contempt for Onesicritos: *FGrH* 134 F 7.

13. Arrian's usage concerning companions: App. 3 #4 vs. 6, 8. Diodorus always uses the Hellenistic term *philoi*: #8, 10, 12, 45. For Plutarch, see #10; *philoi* never being used, although *sunhedrion* is used (28), as it is in DS (12, 45). Outside of these instances, which are all formal gatherings of the companions, Plutarch occasionally uses *philoi* as mere elegant variation: *Alex.* 15.5, 19.5–6.

14. Sundry rites are catalogued in App. 1a, 1b, and 2. For a sample of the many comparanda, see Naiden (2009, 2013).

15. Among the articles and biographies on Alexander contributing to the emphasis on Near Eastern materials: Van der Spek (1998, 2014) and Lenderling (2005). An archeological and art-historical Alexander: Stewart (1993). A recent complaint of continuing underestimation of Near Eastern material: Bowden (2014). Edmunds's standard article on religion (1971) omits Near Eastern aspects of the subject. So does Fredricksmeyer (2003), which is a brief treatment, as is Naiden (2011), which touches on ritualistic aspects of this subject. Alexander as pharaoh: Bosch-Puche (2008).

16. Briant (2010) is a revision of his basic Alexander biography of 1974; see also (2015), insofar as religion affects the relation between Alexander and Darius III. Among recent works, note Hanaway (1982), Abramenko (2000), Blazquez (2000), Asirvatham (2001, 2012), Razmjou (2002), Mari (2002, 2008, 2011), Antela-Bernárdez (2007, 2016), Jamzadeh (1995, 2012), and Bowden (2013). Especially noteworthy is the comparative work of Ross (2016) and Ulanowski (2016a). No one has attempted a study of important rituals performed at a single location since Instinsky (1949). The only book on Macedonian religion remains the compilation of sources in Baege (1911).

17. In many instances, Arrian, Curtius Rufus, and Plutarch's *Alexander* all report some version of an event occurring during the expedition, and sometimes other ancient sources do, too, so any narrative must choose among or combine these versions, as

is my practice in these pages. An introduction to this complex task: Bosworth (1996), ch. 2, "Windows on the Truth," observing that each of these three sources has merits and demerits, a conclusion applicable to religious matters. Where these matters are concerned (but not otherwise), this book seeks to complement Robinson (1932), 13–62, and the commentaries of Bosworth (1980, 1995), Hamilton (1999), Atkinson (1980, 1994), Heckel and Yardley (2009), and Atkinson and Yardley (2010) in tabulating versions of events.

18. Tales drawn chiefly from *HR* and passages in the Talmud, Nizami, and Firdausi, as well as several versions of the *Alexander Romance*. In references at the end of each chapter, a few—and far from all—parallels for these tales are cited. An introduction to this literature: Stoneman (2008).

CHAPTER I
The Mediterranean Comes of Age

1. The flood: Garcia-Castellanos (2009), Hsu (1983). Macedonian flood stories: Decaulion in Thessaly (Apollod. 1.7.2), if not the stories of the Ogygian flood in Attica (Pl. *Lg.* 3.677a, *Crit.* 111–12, *Tim.* 22) and the flood of Dardanus in the northern Aegean (Pl *Lg.* 3.682a). These were local stories; national stories in the Near East included both Israel (Gen. 6–8) and Babylon, whose Noah was Atrahasis (Berossos *FGrH* 680 F 1.6–8, as portrayed on the walls of the Eanna temple as well as in *Atrahasis* (*ANET* 104–6) and SB *Gilgamesh* xi).

2. The Mediterranean as a pond lined by Greeks: Pl. *Phaed.* 109b.

3. The Mesopotamian view: Rochberg (2012). The Egyptian: O'Connor (2012). The Greek: Romm (1992), ch. 1.

4. Zeus's anger at human noise: Cypr. fr. 1. Cf. *Atrahasis* II SBV iv.

5. In a word, a "sacred" but not divine kingship, the full divinization of the king being rare, as in Frankfort (1948), whereas the king's being "infused with the divine," as in I. Winter (2008), was common. The distinction between the divine and human would not perfectly apply to a king of this kind, as at Brisch (2008a), 8–9. Frankfort (1948), 337–38, dismissed the early kings of Greece and Persia, not to mention Macedon, as mere chieftains without the cosmic role of the kings of the Near East.

6. For Pharaonic oracles, see Černý (1935), (1942), and (1962). No comparative work has been done on Egyptian and Greek oracles.

7. For examples of Greek and Hebrew sacrificial mishaps, see Naiden (2005).

8. Ross (2016) compares Greek and Babylonian responses to eclipses.

9. A list of thirty roads, but only at the end of the Classical Period: Hatzopoulos (1997), 12–13, 17–21. Dependent on the king earlier: DS 13.49.1–2.

10. The unmixed wine: Gadaletta (2001), 134. Foresters: Theophr. *HP* 9.31–33. Herdsmen: Arr. *An.* 7.9.2.

11. Royal Zeus: *Olympios*, worshipped by the kings at Aegae as at Baege (1913), 7–12. Rings: Naiden (2013), 94 with fig. 3.

12. Zeus-Amon: Baege (1913), 1–5. Zeus-Amon was also worshipped by Greeks, but given the greater size of Greece, he was perhaps worshipped comparatively less: Paus. 9.6.1 (Thebes in the time of Pindar), 5.15.11 (Olympia, albeit undated), and elsewhere as at Classen (1959).

13. Spear-won land: see Ch. 2, n. 158. Land distribution: cf. Sparta, where the land was given to the Heraclidae, as at Tyrt. Fr. 1, noted by Malkin (1998), 44. Greek precautions: Chaniotis (2004), dealing with late Classical and Hellenistic evidence for the justification of land claims.

14. Heracles at Aegae: Christesen and Murray (2010), 433–34 with refs. The link to Orpheus and Orphism remains controversial, but it cannot be fortuitous that one of the favorable omens given to Alexander concerned Orpheus (App. 1b #2). The "phony man": Polyaen. 4.2.1.

15. Purification of the army: App. 1a #61 with Liv. 40.6.1–7 and Hatzopoulos (1996), 1.319–20.

16. The king and not any temple officials made important contacts with shrines abroad, such as the shrine of Asclepius at Epidaurus. Mari (2007), 36–37, notes that this picture changes after 346, when Macedon joins the Delphic Amphictyony. For both Greek and Macedonian exx. of household sacrifices, see Naiden (2013), ch. 2. A different summary view of the king as chief priest of the Macedonians: Worthington (2014), 15–16; there is, surprisingly, no monograph on this topic.

17. Justin 11.1.8. Choose but not by a vote: Heckel and Yardley (2009) ad loc.

18. The one, doubtful piece of evidence for kings before Philip II being called *basileus*: a now-lost inscription from Oropus, discussed by Ellis (1971) and Lane Fox (2011b), 340. The political consequences of a modest royal style: Errington (1974).

19. The year 360: Hatzopoulos (1982). Priestly magistrates providing names for the dating of decrees, as eponymous archons did in Athens: Hatzopoulos (1996), 1.193–94, 384, and Riethmüller (2005), 174–76, 320–24. The πελειγᾶνες: *SEG* 48.785. Other views giving the people at large an important role: Costanzi (1915), 4–7, and Granier (1931), 13–15, arguing from Homeric comparanda; Hatzopoulos (1996), arguing from Hellenistic epigraphical evidence. Views giving the people only a small role: Errington (1978), although Errington (1990), 198, says that the nobility had to accept a new king; similarly, Borza (1991), 231–52.

20. As in the deaths of Crateuas in 399 (Arist. *Pol.* 1311b); and Pausanias in 394/3 (DS 14.89), for which date see Hammond and Griffith (1979), 170.

21. The Persians' aversion: pace [Dem.] 12.21, which Hammond and Griffith (1979), 103, take to refer to a successful attack by Alexander I on the retreating Xerxes.

22. The Illyrians had begun using shields and spears earlier, around 700 BC, according to Randsborg (2001), but Bardylis apparently raised the funds to arm them, and to reward them (Theopompos *FGrH* 115 F 286).

23. Philip's accession: Hammond and Griffith (1979), 205–8.

24. Justin 7.5.6–10, supported by Satyrus apud Ath. 12.557d–e, implies that Philip became king in 357, but DS 16.2.4 and schol. Aeschin. 3.51 do not mention a regency,

leading Hammond and Griffith (1979), 209, to suggest that Philip became king immediately. Whatever his role, he controlled the court, as shown by his likely killing not only the exiled pretender Argaeus but also a half brother who was the most plausible rival then in Macedon (Justin 7.4.5). A chronology for 360–59: Lane Fox (2011a), 335–37.

25. A warning against facile comparisons: Carlier (2000). Momigliano (1934), 11, observes that the relation between the king and the companions was by far the oldest part of Macedon's unwritten political arrangements. Admission to the royal circle: Marsyas *FGrH* 135 F 11. Once admitted, a companion could use a net, as Leonnatus and Philotas do (Plu. *Alex.* 40.1, Ath. 12.539d, Ael. *VH* 9.3). If kings used nets, no source says so.

26. For battlefield *hetaireia* in Homer, see Esposito (2015), chs. 2–3.

27. No order except when troops are mustered: *Il.* 2.362–63. Very nearly the contrary view: Homeric loose lines in an "open formation" as at Krentz (2007); similarly, Van Wees (2004), 184–99. An altogether contrary view, with a Homeric phalanx: Schwartz (2002).

28. The ceremony, or *teletē*, as performed at Magnesia, another community with official *hetairoi*: Hegesander *FHG* 4 fr. 25. At a minimum, a ceremony had already been established, but Philip greatly enlarged the number of members. Loyalty as a traditional requirement for *hetairoi*: Hes. *Op.* 707–9, Theog. 851–52, Hipponax fr. 15.15–16. Another view: Kienast (1973), 19–20, holding that *hetaireia* came to Macedon from Persia. Most scholars do not discuss any religious aspect of *hetaireia*; e.g., Plaumann (1913); Berve (1926), 1.30–37; Hampl (1958), 66–77; Hammond and Griffith (1979), 2.395–404. Habicht (1958), 12, does not, either, but acknowledges the psychological importance of religiously sanctioned reciprocal ties among *hetairoi*. There is no dispute concerning one religious aspect, the oath, for which see Hammond and Griffith (1979), 65–67, but without mention of *hetaireia*. The oaths sworn to Alexander's successors (as at Plu. *Eum.* 12.2) did not confer the status of *hetairos,* or, for that matter, *philos.*

29. Betrayal would of course be irreparable: Aeschin. 3.91. Seniority was a Homeric concept, too, exemplified by Nestor, who has several Macedonian counterparts: Ruzé (1997), s.v. "Nestor." The ceremony perhaps took place at Aegae, an older shrine than Pella, at which there is no reported religious activity before Archelaus, and older than Dium, with none before the establishment of the cult of Zeus *Olympios.*

30. A dancing companion: Theopompos *FGrH* 115 F 225, which is also the source for the citation.

31. Clubs: Plu. *Lys.* 13.4, Dem. 54.39. Tyrants' clubs: Hdt. 5.71. Arist. *Pol.* 1313b. Oaths even for these scalawags: Plu. *Mul. virt.* 252d. Forbidden in Athens: Hyp. *Eux.* 8, but cf. Th. 8.48.3–4. Counterrevolutionary: Th. 8.54. A quality of all companions, Macedonian and Greek: heavy drinking (Diphil. 20 K-A). An especially censorious attitude: Demosthenes, calling *hetaireia douleia* (Sud. s.v. ἑταιρεία). Eight hundred companions under Philip: Theopompos *FGrH* 115 F 225.

32. Cretans: as at n. 28 above. Enomoties: Lazenby (1985), 69–70. Cf. military *hetairoi* on Methymna perhaps known to Philip: Th. 8.100.3. Thebes, where Philip had lived in exile, had no military companions, only a small sacred band.

33. Philip at Samothrace: Plu. *Alex.* 2.1. Macedonian initiation (or better put, consecration) ceremonies: Mari (2011), 457–58.

34. Sacrifices to found a city: App. 1a #20. Not to mention the obvious duty of giving thanks, as any household head would, or propitiating the gods at frontiers or rivers and straits (*euchatristēria* at 1, 10–11, 15, 57, 60; *diabatēria* at 4–6, 33, 39, 48, 51), or asking for divine help before battle (12, 14, 17, 27). Sacrifices for victory: App. 1a #9, 28, 39, 43, 49. Suppliants: App. 2. Burial as a duty: Curt. 10.5.5, with the reciprocal obligation of the *hetairoi* to bury their leader. A possible parallel: *I. Oropus* 675, as at Henry (2003). Examples from reign of Alexander: App. 1a #2, 8, 13, 16, 29, 34, 37, 42, 43 (DS 17.89.3), 44, 47, 58, 62.

35. An exception proving the rule about named regiments: Arr. *An.* 7.14.7. Cf. Classical Athens, where the infantry was raised tribe by tribe, a task for magistrates, but again not locally. A British parallel: regiments named after commanders in the late seventeenth and eighteenth centuries. Regiment size of 1,500: Milns (1976), 102. Purple cloaks: Plu. *Eum.* 8.12. Eumenes went further than Alexander and Philip and gave purple garments to a greater number of officers. Another view of "the purple": Briant (1994), 283–85. In Greece, generals wore purple, too (Ar. *Pax* 1175), showing that the Macedonians did not need to borrow this dress from Persia.

36. Which is not to say all companions, or even most, had been pages, or bodyguards, as observed by Ma (2011), 530–31, comparing the firmer social organization in the Antigonid court. Another view, which was that Philip invented this institution: Arr. *An.* 4.13.1, accepted by Bosworth (1980) ad loc., Heckel (1992), 239–40. Yet it was apparently older: Curt. 8.8.3. If so, Philip again formalized inherited practices.

37. For a description of modern professional officers, see Teitler (1977), ch. 1.2, with bibliography. An attempt to distinguish between the term "profession," with its modern flavor, and "career" or "calling": Naiden (2007).

38. Anaximenes *FGrH* 74 F 4 attributes the *pezetairoi* to "Alexander," meaning to say Alexander II, 371–368/7 BC, in other words, about ten years before Philip came to the throne. If Alexander II did establish the *pezetairoi*, he did not organize them so as to achieve the results Philip would. A different view of this information: Erskine (1989). Arguably, the term *pezetairoi* at first applied not to the mass of infantry, but only to select troops, as at Theopompus *FGrH* 115 F 348 with Anson (1985), 246–48. The opposite view attributes the practice to Alexander III, as at Lane Fox (2011b), 361. For the promotion of officers, see Curt. 5.2.2–5. Promotions into the heavy infantry: Atkinson (1987). Into the hypaspists: Heckel (2013).

39. Power of the nobles: Borza (1991), 238. For the conduct of council business, all evidence dates from Alexander's reign and the regency of Perdiccas, for which see Appendix 3. In some particulars the two stages of development overlapped, so that Arrian uses *hypaspistēs* to mean armor bearer (*An.* 1.11.8, 4.24.3) as well as light

infantryman. Accompanying this overlap was social ambiguity, so that the "king's own" among both the companion cavalry and the shield bearers were more prestigious—and more reliable—than other units that were functionally identical. The command of the "king's own" was likewise prestigious; thus Heckel (2016), 81, suggests that at Gaugamela Hephaestion commanded this unit among the shield bearers.

40. Satyrus apud Ath. 12.557d–e, listing the wives, but whether he lists them in chronological order is controversial; see Tronson (1984), 118. Surely alive at the time of his death: Olympias, Meda, and Cleopatra. Serial monogamy: Green (1982), 138–40.

41. Bardylis fighting at age ninety: Lucian. *Macrob.* 9. Diplomatic complications between Bardylis and Philip make it possible that Philip married first and attacked afterward, as at Carney (2000), 57–58.

42. The pellets: Anochin and Rolle (1998). The bolt: Str. 7.330. An arrow: Theopompos *FGrH* 115 F 52, Dem. 18.67, followed by DS 16.34.5, Justin 7.6.14, Didym. ad Dem. 12.43.

43. Philip and Thessaly: Theopompos *FGrH* 115 F 162. A wedge: Ael. *Tact.* 18.4, Arr. *Tact.* 16.6. A diamond: Asclepiod. 7.2, Ael. *Tact.* 18.2.

44. Female cult membership: Plu. *Alex.* 2.1. Female literacy: Plu. *Lib. educ.* 14b-c.

45. The first tales told the child: Pl. *HM* 285e–86a, on slave women as tellers of mythical tales, and Cic. *N. D.* 2.5, on their greater willingness to believe in tales of monsters. The chief nurse: Arr. *An.* 4.19.3, Curt. 8.1.2, Justin 12.6.10. The cavalryman: Curt. 8.1.20.

46. Alexander and the *Iliad*: DC 4.39. He did not think the *Odyssey* worth the trouble (Plu. *Alex.* 8.2 with other refs. as at J. Hamilton ad loc.).

47. Little more than titles survive of two political works that likely would have interested Alexander and most companions—*Peri Basileias* and *Huper Apoikōn* (as in DL 5.22). Even the date of composition is unknown: J. Hamilton (1999) ad Plu. *Alex.* 7.5. Geography: Stoneman (2015), 63. Alexander's curiosity, or *pothos*, directed at seeing or sailing across bodies of water: Arr. *An.* 1.3.5, 7.1.1, 5.26.1, 7.16.2, *Ind.* 20.1. Similarly, a *pothos* to cross rivers and mountains: Arr. *An.* 1.3.5, 4.28.4, both noted at Bosworth (1980), 30. A similar desire to examine specimens: Ael. *NA* 16.39. The sources never report a *pothos* to enter a shrine, in spite of Alexander's conduct at Tyre and elsewhere. A different view: Seibert (1972), app. 13.

48. Olympias as a priestess, or at least a procession leader: Plu. *Alex.* 2.6. Alexander's youthful offerings: Theophr. *de piet.* fr. 8 ed. Pötscher (1964).

49. Alexander and the hot coal: Val. Max. 4.3. ext. 1, saying that if Darius had witnessed this scene, he would not have resisted Alexander.

50. One hundred sacrificial couches: App. 1a #3. The significance of sacrifice at this location: Mari (2002), 51–60.

51. From Egypt to Dodona: Hdt. 2.55–56.

52. Several sources other than Plutarch contribute to this composite picture. Cowlick: *Itiner. Alex.* 13, Plu. *Pomp.* 2.1. Height: Curt 5.2.13, DS 17.66.3. Kilter: Plu. *Alex.* 4.2, *Alex. fort.* 335b. Voice: Plu. *Quo. adul.* 53d. Philip's wrestling: Polyaen. 4.2.6.

Alexander's dislike of athletics: Plu. *Alex.* 4.10, *Reg. apophth.* 179d, *Fort. Alex.* 331b. The ball held over a basin: Amm. 6.5.14.

53. Nor could the Athenians fight artillery with artillery: Athenian artillery had scarcely begun, as noted by Marsden (1969), 70–71, in spite of the Athenian accomplishments in siege warfare in the preceding century (Ar. *Av.* 363, Th. 3.51.3). The first Athenian fortification meant to serve as an artillery platform, Aegosthena, dates from 335 at the earliest, according to Keyser (1994), 39. n. 53, or 300, according to Marsden (1969), 134–38. Superior numbers: Justin 9.3.9–10.

54. A few of Philip's men in the hills: Hammond (1973), 541.

55. Macedonian distaste for military oracles: discounting Alexander's supposedly consulting Delphi (Plu. *Alex.* 14.6, DS 17.93.4), a doublet for Heracles's consulting Delphi in the same aggressive fashion (Paus. 10.13.8, Apollod. 2.6.2). Ditch-digging Macedonians: Plb. 5.2.4–5.

56. Polyaen. 4.2.2, 4.2.7. Battle narrative: mostly DS 16.85.5–87, with Plu. *Alex.* 9.1–2 for the sacred band. A different view of the dispositions: Ma (2008), 74. The same view, but with topographical details: Hammond (1973), 541.

57. Athenian courage: Justin 9.3.8–4.1. Theban courage: Plu. *Pel.* 18.7. Athenian amateurishness: Polyaen. 4.2.7.

58. Philip's modesty at Chaeronea: Sotiriadis (1902). Philip at Olympia: Paus. 5.20.9–10. A more expansive interpretation: Green (1991), 81 with refs.

59. Scholarly views of combat trauma, but without reference to religion: Meineck and Konstan (2014), notably Tritle (2014). Macedonians consoling themselves with Euripides: Plu. *Fort. Alex.* 331d.

60. A raised dais: DS 16.92.5, referring to those "around the throne," as noted by Spawforth (2007), 91.

61. The oracle: DS 16.91.2, Paus. 8.7.6, regarded as spurious by Fontenrose (1978), 167, who does not distinguish between the vague prediction being made of Philip's death, one that may not have been part of the original oracle, and the clear endorsement of an attack on Persia, which is consistent with pronouncements in Philip's favor at Aeschin. 3.130, Plu. *Dem.* 19.1, 20.1. A similar view of this development: Walser (1984), 49–53.

62. Squillace (2010) calls the Greek appeals to Philip "propaganda" that did not provide any practical plan for Philip's proposed invasion. As Bosworth (1994), 798, notes, Alexander retraced the route of Xerxes in Thrace, but he could not do the same in Asia. Except for Alexander's letter to Darius (Arr. *An.* 2.14.4), the theme of revenge drops out of the Alexander historians until the army reaches Persepolis. The statue: Arr. *An.* 1.17.10–11.

63. Meda: Bengston (1985), 12, also holding that Olympias was "offizielle Gatin," vs. Carney (2010), 415, observing that there was no such position.

64. DS 16.93.4–8; Plu. *Alex.* 10.6 omitting the details, but not the *hybris*; so also *stuprum* at Justin 9.6.5–6, and Arist. *Pol.* 5.1311b.

65. The assassination: DS 16.92.2–5. The theater: Drougou (2011), 248.
66. Other companions: DS 16.91.2. The rumors and counter-rumors: ibid., Arr. *An.* 2.14.5, and Curt. 4.1.12, where the accusation appears in a dubious context, as observed by Griffith (1968). The "sacrifice": Paus. 8.7.6. The same view of this episode: Carney (1992), 179–80. The view that Olympias and also Alexander did hire Pausanias, or that Philip feared such a stroke: Green (1991), 91. Other views: Lane Fox (1974), 22–25; Heckel (1981), 55–57.
67. Alexander's first political maneuvers: DS 17.2.3, 5.2.
68. Alexander the Lyncestian's hastily acknowledging Alexander as king paved the way for this bargain between the new ruler and the most senior companion (Arr. *An.* 1.25.2). Perhaps Antipater coached the Lyncestian, as suggested by Badian (1963), 248. Antipater did not come to the aid of the Lyncestian's brothers, and Alexander put them to death.
69. Death of Amyntas within some months: Curt. 6.9.17, Justin 12.6.14. More than a year later: Arr. fr. 1.22. Cf. Plu. *Fort Alex.* 327c, saying that Amyntas had support throughout Macedon. Yet Amyntas had no military record. Nor was Attalus a candidate for the throne, *pace* DS 17.2.3.
70. The Aegae palace had a total of sixteen rooms with space for 224, according to Kottaridi (2011b), 176–77.
71. This is tomb II at Vergina, identified as the place of burial of Philip II by Andronikos (1984), who at 115 accordingly says Alexander III and Philip II are depicted in the frieze. Bibliography through 2006: Borza and Palagia (2007), who argue that Tomb II holds the remains of Philip Arrhidaeus and his wife Adea Eurydice, and that the frieze accordingly depicts Alexander III and Arrhidaeus, as at 102–3. Bibliography through 2010: Lane Fox (2011a), agreeing with Andronikos. Bibliography through 2011: Carney (2015), 107, 125–26, agreeing with Borza and Palagia. Both interpretations are speculative, as the two figures in the frieze are not identified by name, and only one figure can be identified by role, i.e., the lion-killer, who must be the entombed king. If Philip II was not buried in tomb II, the question arises where he was buried instead. Possibly tomb I at Vergina: Borza and Palagia (2007); Carney (2015), 107. Contra: Lane Fox (2011a), 3–7. The remaining possibility at Vergina, tomb III, is assigned by most writers to Alexander IV.
    Wherever Philip was buried, there was no time to establish a cult in his name, an honor for which funeral games would be only the first step. The putative *hērōon* found by Andronikos was thus established on some other occasion, if not for some other purpose; see Kottaridi (2011a), 24, and Hammond (1991) connecting it with tomb I, vs. Lane Fox (2011a), 7, connecting it with tomb II.
72. Fig. 25 in Saatsoglou-Paliadeli (2011), with 284, supposing that Alexander has killed the boar.
73. The right eye obscured: Lane Fox (2011a), 17. The meaning of the laurel is unknown. Victory is one possibility, but over whom?

74. Hdt. 7.125, Paus. 6.5.5–6, as at Lane Fox (2011a), 10–11.

75. Adapted from *HR* 4–6. Alexander by birth half Egyptian: Ps.-Call. A 1.1–12, Ar. Ps.-Call. 1.4–8. By birth half Persian: Firdausi, as in Ch. 3 below; al-Tabari 697. A Macedonian: al-Tabari, 700; Nizami, 1.15.36.

CHAPTER 2

A Macedonian Priest-King

1. The first of many rumors of Alexander's death: Arr. *An.* 1.7.3. The early campaigns: Arr. *An.* 1.7, the only account to mention units and the companions commanding them.

2. The insults: DS 17.9.4–6. Letting a subordinate take the initiative: Arr. *An.* 1.8.1–4. Doubting the role of Perdiccas: Bosworth (1980) ad Arr. *An.* 1.8.1, regarding the account in Arrian as distorted by Ptolemy's bias against a rival general. Yet the report of a Theban mock retreat is credible, given Theban military skill, and independent action by regimental commanders like Perdiccas, or by their subordinates, appears on other occasions, such as Halicarnassus (Arr. *An* 1.21.1–4, by Perdiccas's men), Issus (2.11.1, by Coenus and Perdiccas), and Gaugamela (3.14.4, by Simmias). The alternative maneuver, fighting in relays, as at DS 17.12.1, is plausible, for Macedonians used it elsewhere, as shown by Sinclair (1966).

3. Supplication: App. 2 #1. The romantic scene with Timoclea, one falling just short of supplication: Aristoboulos *FGrH* 139 F 2 with Plu. *Mul. virt.* 259d–60d.

4. The exceptions: Arr. *An.* 1.9.9–10, DS 17.14.1, Plu. *Alex.* 11.10. Instinsky (1961), 248, mistakenly supposes that the protection due to suppliants in shrines extended to suppliants removed from shrines and then sold; see Naiden (2009), 120–21. The highest reported total of enslaved persons: see the lists compiled by Ducrey (1999), 74–92, and Volkmann (1961), 14–46.

5. Medical details: Bliquez (2014), 23–50, especially carrying cases (Hp. *Decent.* 9.8.8.–9L), sundry iron instruments (*Morb.* 2.28P), rasps (*VC* 14.2, 14.7, 14.9 ed. Hanson [1999]), forceps (*Medic.* 9P, *Nat. mul.* 8.70.5L), tubes (*Morb.* 2.59–60P, 2.33, 2.36), and drills (*Loc. Hom.* 32B). Speculation about anesthetics: Bliquez (2014), 18. Philip: Pl. *NH* 7.37.37. Few wounded commoners are mentioned by name in the Alexander historians: Arr. *An.* 1.8.3, Perdiccas, at Thebes; Arr. *An.* 3.14.3, Curt 4.16.32, DS 17.61.3, Hephaestion, Coenus, and Menidas, at Gaugamela; Arr. *An.* 6.10.2, Leonnatus and Peucestas at siege of the Malli. An attempt to fill gaps in the evidence: Ruffin (1992).

6. Macedonian casualties at Chaeronea: DS 17.14.1. Greek casualties, and large numbers of people enslaved: DS 17.41.1, Plu. Alex. 11.12.

7. Boeotians prevent the engineer, Crates, from proceeding: Str. 9.2.18–20.

8. The satraps owed the king loyalty enjoined by Mithra, but not any obedience peculiar to slaves: Schmidt (1978), 285, citing a parallel in the *Rigveda* 29. There is no evidence, however, that they were initiated into any cult of Mithra.

9. The consensus of Dandamaev and Lukonin (1989), Briant (2002), and the essays in Frei and Koch (1996): considerable control exercised by satraps over provinces, and by generals over garrison towns. Dandamaev and Lukonin also stress local autonomy, whereas the essays in Frei and Koch stress manipulation of local elites.

10. The doubtful evidence for a recent rebellion in Babylon: Stolper (1994a), 240. If Babylon rebelled, Alexander likely did not know of it, whereas he did know of the Persian difficulties in Egypt.

11. Darius III in Egypt: DS 17.6.1–3, Justin 10.3.4. Babylonian ancestors: Ktesias *FGrH* 688 F 15.47–51.

12. Darius the young soldier: Justin 10.3.4, DS 17.6.1–3. Defending Darius's legitimacy: Briant (2002), 772, citing DS 17.5.5, which concerns descent through the female line. Alexander rejects this claim at Curt. 6.3.12.

13. Impressive Babylonian royal titles also made up for the lack of superlative adjectives in Akkadian (the same as in Hebrew).

14. The alliance between Philip and Persia: Arr. *An.* 2.14.2, doubted by Bosworth (1980) ad loc., but not so strongly as to deny that Philip was surprised and disappointed when Persian interference made it impossible for him to blockade Perinthus in 340 (Arr. *An.* 2.14.5, DS 14.75.2, Paus. 1.29.6).

15. Alexander's opinion of Darius's legitimacy: Arr. *An.* 2.14.4–5, Curt. 6.3.12. A similar formulation: Wilcken (1932), 248. The contrary: Lane Fox (1973), 98, attributing this opinion to "some Greeks," but not Alexander.

16. This view of Alexander's aims reflects the religious rituals performed at the Hellespont and at Troy later in this chapter. Various writers hold that Alexander's aims evolved, and did not at first include conquering the entire empire. Tarn (1948), 1.8, held that at first Alexander was opportunistic, the same as his father had been. Somewhat similarly, Burn (1963), 64, held that his initial aim was to give his large army employment. Bosworth (1993), 18–19, accepts the language in the ancient sources of a war of revenge. For these and other views, Egypt and Babylon are targets of opportunity, not original objectives.

17. Cyrus "the Great": first attested in Agathocles *FGrH* 472 F 6, fl. 2nd cent. BC. Merely Kurash, son of Kurash: *ANET* 316. Elamite cultural mixture: Scheil (1905), 59–61, followed by Amiet (1979). The Achaemenid dynasty, merely collateral descendants from Cyrus, changed the name of Anshan to Paruash, later Persia; see Hansman (1972), 106–9.

18. Hdt. 1.154–56, 61 gives two examples of Cyrus's recruits, Pactyes and Mazares.

19. Cyrus the restorer of neglected cults: *ABC* 104–11, with Jursa (2007). His abundant sacrifices: l. 37, Cyrus Cylinder. His antiquarianism: l. 43, Cyrus Cylinder. His religious policy: Heller (2010), 254–56, expanding on *ANET* 306. Elamite ceremonial dress: *ABC* 7 3.26 with George (1996), 379–81. Or perhaps Cambyses wore this dress—a much more pointed gesture. Another view: Waerzeggers, in which the Cyrus Cylinder expresses Babylonian hopes, which would eventually be

dashed (lecture delivered June 30, 2010, Vrije Universiteit Amsterdam, as reported
by Van der Spek [2014], 250 n. 140).

20. Cyrus receives adulation at Is. 44:28–45:1, where Van der Spek (2014), 251, suggests that the Hebrew prophet was attempting to influence the king.

21. Cambyses thus became *šar mātāti* like his father: Dandamaev (1990). He was king
of Babylon earlier, while crown prince, but only briefly.

22. Cyrus the diviner: X. *Cyr.* 1.6.2. Cyrus's many debts to Assyrian and Babylonian
predecessors were unknown to the Greeks, making it all the easier to idealize him;
see Van der Spek (2014). The superior diet of the ancient hunter: Hughes (2014),
30–31. No doubt the army of Cyrus enjoyed the same advantage over Levantine
opponents.

23. A violent council meeting: App. 3 #45, one of just five councils of Darius reported
in the Alexander historians.

24. Big battle: App. 3 #13–17. Daily route: App. 3 #35. Battles, or courts-martial, or spe-
cial sacrifices: App. 3 #1 (Mount Haemus), 3 (Granicus), 7 (Issus), 8 (Tyre), 13–17
(Gaugamela), 18 (Persian Gates); 4, 23–24, 27, 28 (trials of the Lyncestian, Philotas,
Hermolaus, and Callisthenes); 11, 26 (sacrifice). Line of march: App. 3 #6 (at
Mallus), 20 (at Tabae). Health and safety: 5, 25, 33. Diplomacy 9, 10, 12. Strategy: 8
(Egypt), 29–31 (the line of march to be followed after reaching the Hyphasis, and
thus a question of strategy), 36–41 (Arabian expedition).

25. Seniority as shown by App. 3 under the column "Speakers," #2, 3, 7 (Curt. 3.7.8–10),
9, 10 (Plu. *Alex.* 29.7–8), 12, 13, 15, 16, all Parmenio; 15, Polyperchon; 23, 33,
Craterus; 26, Erigyius; 29, Coenus. Marriage: App. 3 #2.

26. So also Squillace (2004), but without reference to any customary procedures in
the council of war. For customs with the force of law in ancient or tribal societies,
see Pospisil (1971) and Barkun (1968), both omitting military institutions. Skeptical
attitudes toward the council of generals: Bosworth (1980) ad Arr. *An.* 1.25.4; similarly, Atkinson (1980) ad Curt. 3.7.8. Neither writer notices most of the councils
listed in App. 3; nor do Atkinson and Yardley (2009) and J. Hamilton (1999).
A negative but nuanced view: Errington (1978), 114, saying that the council was
only "informal." Earlier expressions of the idea: Meyer (1910), and Adcock (1957)
74, implying that a council was unnecessary since Alexander was "his own chief of
staff and foreign minister." In contrast, Droysen (1833), 127–28, 132–33, 183, 250,
312–13, 425, regarded the council as an institution comparable to a medieval council of barons.

27. Reckoning from the fact that later a hypaspist received a drachma a day, or about
one-half of 1 percent of a talent per month, and from the assumption that, although many soldiers were paid less, cavalry and officers were paid more, so that
one-half of 1 percent is a minimal average. Multiplying by 45,000 yields 225 talents.
The drachma a day: *IG* ii² 329, but see the doubts of Milns (1987), 246–47. Wages
implied by contraction of debts by soldiers: Arr. *An.* 7.10.3. Wages indubitable as of
326: Arr. *An.* 6.9.3, 10.1. Wages since 334: Milns (1987), 246–47.

28. Sixty merchant vessels: DS 17.17.2. Some of these were Greek, perhaps reducing Alexander's burden, but for doubts about financing these ships, see Milns (1987), 246–47, with Arr. *An.* 1.11.6, 1.18.4. Naval costs: Eddy (1968), 142–43, arguing for a slightly lower cost than this conventional estimate.

29. Seven thousand talents: Berve (1926), 1.312. Debts: Arr. *An.* 7.9.6 [−800]; or Onesikritos *FGrH* F 2 [−200]; perhaps plus Plu. *Fort. Alex.* 327e, Aristoboulos *FGrH* 139 F 4 [+70]. Tax relief: DS 17.2.2–3. Plu. *Alex.* 15.2, *Fort. Alex.* 327d, not quite admitting the borrowing discerned by Green (1991), 156.

30. The needed local portent: App. 1b #2. The report of Delphic endorsement at #1 is a doublet as at Ch. 1, n. 55.

31. The common unit sizes, in a summary view with bibliography: Errington (1990), 242–43, leading to a calculation of 2 officers per file of 16, one in front and one in back, or 32 officers in a *lochos* of 256, led by a *lochagos*; 3 commanders called penta-kosiarchs, each leading two *lochoi*; and a taxis commander, or 202 in all, for a notional regiment of some 1,500, or a ratio of 1 to 7. Other accounts of the army: Berve (1926), 1.103–217, Fuller (1958), 39–54, Milns (1968), 194–95, Hammond and Griffith (1979), 405–50, Bosworth (1988a), 273–77. Concentrating on officers: Lazenby (1985), ch. 1, and Wrightson (2010). Cf. the Spartan army of X. *Lac.* 11, with 169 officers (96 enomotarchs, 48 pentakosiarchs, 24 *lochagoi*, and a polemarch), for a force of a notional 600 men in each of six *morai*, or an officer-to-soldier ratio of 1 to 21. (Six hundred: X. *HG* 4.5.15. Five hundred to 900: Plu. *Pel.* 17.3.) Add four file leaders per enomoty, and one man in six was an officer. The ratio falls even further if the Spartans had file-closers like the mostly Peloponnesian mercenaries in Xenophon's *Anabasis*, as argued at Wheeler (2007), 207. A different organization in the preceding century: Van Wees (2004), app. 2, with bibliography on this long-disputed question. The officers' corps of Near-Eastern armies ought to be smaller, if we assume that there was an officer for every ten, hundred, and thousand men, as was the common report for Semitic armies; for Assyria, see Malbrat-Laban (1982), 121–23. Besides biblical examples (2 Sam. 18:1, 1 Chron. 26:26), a Persian garrison of Hebrew soldiers at Elephantine organized by hundreds and thousands: Porten (1968), 29–30. For Persia, the Persepolis ration tablets refer to a *pascadathapatis*, "rear leader of ten," corresponding to the leader of five at X. *Cyr.* 2.1.21, 3.3.10. For Egyptian armies, there is very little evidence for unit sizes.

32. The makeup of the army is more surely known than the precise number, which in the ancient sources varies from 35,000 to 48,500; see Bosworth (1980) ad Arr. *An.* 1.11.3, with refs. The 45,000 total given below includes the forces already assigned to Parmenio in Asia Minor (the admittedly round figure of 10,000 at DS 17.7.10, Polyaen 5.44.4).

33. Infantry half from the highlands: i.e., half *asthetairoi* from Lyncestis, Orestis, and Elimaia, but the first syllable in *asthetairoi* is of uncertain meaning; see Bosworth (1980) ad Arr. *An.* 1.25.4. Another view of the Greeks: Kahrstedt (1936), 122, saying that Alexander kept the Greek force small because he thought it disloyal.

34. Calculations of supplies follow parameters at Sidebotham (2011), Junkelmann (1997), and Roth (1999), used in addition to (or in correction of) Engels (1978).
35. The festival during Daisios: Hatzopoulos (1996), 1.150, 1.411–12, with sources as at Baege (1913), 226–27.
36. Antipater's allotment: DS 17.17.5.
37. Antipater's age: *Sud.* s.v. Ἀντίπατρος and Luc. *Macr.* 2. Delphi in 342: Liban. 23.1.66. Purple and white: Plu. *Reg. apophth.* 180e. The suspicions of Olympias: Arr. *An.* 7.12.5, Plu. *Fort. Alex.* 332f = *Reg. apophth.* 180d, Justin 12.14.3. Antipater's attitude: Arr. *An.* 7.12.6, Plu. *Reg. apophth.* 180d.
38. Parmenio's act of worship: App. 1a #4, an occasion that would naturally occur at the start of the expedition. The only other conceivable date would be the year before, when he went to Anatolia with a small infantry force that would be much harder to compare to the Argonauts.
39. Jason: Hegesander apud. Ath. 13.572d. The only comment linking this precedent to Macedon: Stoll (1884).
40. Dascylium had long been a military headquarters: Bakir (1995), 271–73, (2006), 66.
41. Memnon thus outgeneraled Parmenio by making use of interior lines. A similar view: Badian (1966), 43. A different view, holding that Parmenio's main task was to hold Abydos: Anson (1989), 48.
42. The channel route: Leaf (1912), 400–403. The sacrifices: Arr. *An.* 1.11.5, sacrificing for greater success than the Achaeans had at Troy; DS 17. 17.2, Justin 11.5.10–11, seeking Asia's submission (App. 1a #5–6).
43. A similar view of the Hellespontine sacrifices: Worthington (2014), 131–32, and Cartledge (2004), 165, preceded by Milnes (1968), 56, and Droysen (1833), 24. A less expansive view: Altheim (1953), 62. A fixed but less ambitious aim, to attack the Persian Empire in force: Instinsky (1949), 22–28. An impressionistic but less ambitious aim, to equal Homeric heroes: Lane Fox (1973), 111–12. A caution that Greek hopes of revenge did not encompass the conquest of the entire Persian Empire: Atkinson and Yardley (2009) ad Curt. 10.3.7, analyzing statements by Isocrates.
44. Alexander and Priam: Arr. *An.* 1.11.7–12.1, DS 17.17.6–7 (App. 1a #7). App. 1b #3 is evidently a *post-eventum* prophecy, since Aristander does not in any other instance predict the death of an individual.
45. Troy and Assyria: Pl. *Lg.* 685c, Ktesias *FGrH* 688 F 1.22.
46. Adapted from Ar. Ps.-Call. 1.14.

CHAPTER 3
The S-Curve

1. Lampsacus: App. 2 #2. Janke (1904), 135, identified the inland route, which passed the inland town of Colossae on the way to Hermotum (Arr. *An.* 1.12.6). As Bosworth (1980) observes ad Arr. *An.* 1.12.6, the leader of the delegation of

Lampsacene suppliants, Anaximenes, performed well, being rewarded with a commemorative statue—the only known statue of this kind (*FGrH* ii C. 105).

2. Local shrines: Paus. 10.31.6–7. The eastern Memnon: Hdt. 5.53 (in Susa); Ktesias *FGrH* 688 F 1.22 (at Troy), with Drews (1965), 130.

3. The polis of Zeleia: Arr. *An.* 1.12.8, *Syll.* 279. A tyrant in charge, however, in 334: Berve (1926), no. 551. A tributary of the Granicus may have been bridged at the city of Didymateiche, which may be modern Dimetoka, but the army would still have to cross the Granicus afterward. For Didymateiche, see Hasluck (1909), 125, and Robert (1937), 195. The only other possible bridge over the Granicus would have been at Sidene, an upcountry town garrisoned by the Persians; see *IMT Gran/Pariane,* no. 1097; Jeffery (1961), 372, no. 50. Memnon's plan: Arr. *An.* 1.12.9. As Bosworth (1980) ad loc. observes, destruction of food supplies was a common tactic, one used by Persians at X. *An.* 1.6.2.

4. Daisios and the harvest: *EM.* 252.29.

5. Memnon's council of war: App. 3 #44. Darius's orders: Justin 11.6.8. Spitadatha: DS 17.13.1 as explained by 17.20.2, συγγενεῖς, a word that here refers to a unit. Many passages in the *Yasna* envision war between good and evil, or Ahura Mazda and his enemy, Angra Mainyu: 32.6, 10, 34.8, 44.15, 48.7, and others at Choksy (2012).

6. Persian chain mail: Head (1992), 12–14. The differences between the two sides did not chiefly concern equipment, for the Persians had access to the Macedonians' characteristic weapon, the pike: X. *An.* 4.7, where Chalybian mercenaries in Persian service used long spears. By Alexander's time, the Persians had seen some Greek troops using them: Nep. *Iph.* 1.3. The differences were chiefly tactical and organizational. The Persians fought under standards (*X An.* 1.8.9–10) and were organized in multiples of ten, and not according to tactically convenient multiples, as the Greeks and Macedonians were. A different view, in which the units of ten are not artificial but are functional in combat: Sekunda (1992), 17–18.

7. A nearby derelict village, Cinarköprü, is named after the scrub oak trees. Here, nine miles from the sea, but less than half a mile from the confluence of the Granicus and the Koca Çay, is the only extant bridge on the lower Granicus, seen a century ago by Janke (1904), 139, fig. 20. Recent autopsies by Foss (1977) and Harl (1989), 316–17, find the banks to be less of an obstacle than stated above, provided that the battle took place below the confluence.

8. The council meeting: App. 3 #3. Two-piece Macedonian spears: Andronikos (1970); Markle (1977), 323–26.

9. Alexander controls the calendar: Plu. *Alex.* 16.2.

10. Sacrifices performed in this case, just as they were the night before Issus (App. 1a #12) and Gaugamela (24). Similarly, at the Tanais, where, since battle was not in the offing the night before, Alexander communicated with the gods earlier in the same day (33). Sacrifice at every river: Naiden (2013), 77, 100 n. 100, 101, 336, 342, and 345. Unnecessarily noncommittal about a sacrifice at the Granicus: Stoneman (2015), 72–73.

11. This account: DS 17.18.8–9, except that this source says little about units, the movements of which must be guessed; so also Plu. *Alex.* 16.1–4, Polyaen. 4.3.16. Many writers prefer Arrian's account at *An.* 1.14.6–15.5, e.g., Badian (1977). Beloch (1922), 4.2.296, and Bosworth (1980), 1.114–17 with refs., both prefer Diodorus; Green (1991), 489–512, proposes a compromise. The crisscross reported by Arrian, an unparalleled maneuver, would be difficult to execute in a stream.

12. The countryside at the time of the battle: Rose and Korpe (2005), 325, reporting tombs "undoubtedly associated with estates linked to the satrapal court at Daskyleion." Hunting is implied by the reservation of land for hunting in local regulations (*Syll.* 279.4–5). A late fourth-century sarcophagus with a hunting scene, from modern Çan, on the Granicus about twenty miles upriver from the battlefield: Sevinc (2001), 389, fig. 4.

13. The two plumes: Plu. *Alex.* 16.7, surpassing Cyrus, who wore only one, the same as his entourage (X. *Cyr.* 7.1.2).

14. Three named attackers: Arr. *An.* 1.15.7–8. Only two, but Spitadatha first: DS 17.20.5. Only two, Spitadatha second: Plu. *Alex.* 16.8–10. Among other differences, the sharpest concerns Clitus's weapon: a cleaver (DS, Arr. *An.*) vs. a spear (Plu. *Alex.*).

15. A lack of helmets: as for many Iranian cavalry, to judge from Hdt. 9.22, and later the figures on the Abdulonymus Sarcophagus drawn by F. Winter (1912), pls. 1, 13, 14, and 17, although some Persians had casques (*UCP* 93, from the time of Darius II).

16. Casualties: DS 17.21.6, Plu. *Alex.* 16.15, Arr. *An.* 1.16.2, Justin 11.6.12, with Macedonian totals ranging from 29 (Plutarch) to Arrian (115), and Justin (129).

17. A list of grave goods based on the mass graves at Chaeronea, described by Ma (2008), 73–75, and Sotiriadis (1903), 309. Comparable finds at Derveni: Themelis and Tsouratiglou (1997), 84, 109.

18. Financial largesse: Arr. *An.* 1.16.5, 1.17.1, DS 17.21.6. Perhaps also rent exemptions for those occupying royal lands: Bosworth (1980) ad Arr. *An.* 1.16.5.

19. Troy: Str. 13.1.26–27, as at App. 1a #7. Burials: App. 1a #8. A few statues for infantry also: Plut. *Alex.* 16.7. Twenty-six figures: Arr. *An.* 1.16.4. Thirty-four equestrian figures: Plu. *Alex.* 16.16. One hundred twenty-nine: Justin 11.6.12, Vell. Pat. 1.11.3–4; similarly, Plin. *NH* 34.64 (*turma Alexandri*).

20. The inscription: Arr. *An.* 1.16.7, Plu. *Alex.* 16.17.

21. Although there is no report of a council meeting on naval matters, Alexander discussed them with Parmenio somewhat later, at Miletus (Arr. *An.* 1.18.6–9). Other councilors were surely present, even if the formalities of a meeting were dropped.

22. Supplication at Miletus: App. 2. #4.

23. The Sardis foundation: App. 1b #4. Argives to garrison Sardis—a plum assignment—and others to subdue and occupy other territory in western Anatolia: Arr. *An.* 1.17.8. Unlike Athens, Thebes, and Sparta, three cities of comparable prestige, Argos had never opposed the Macedonians.

24. Supplication at Ephesus: App. 2 #3. The status of a suppliant who was a tyrant: Naiden (2009), 147–53.

25. Celebration at the Artemisium: App. 1a #9. The dispute with the city: Str. 4.1.22, where Alexander makes a generous but undated financial offer to the Ephesians. Goats' horns: Eust. ad *Il.* 8.249.

26. New governments: *OGI* 222, 223, 226, 229, 237. Apelles: Ael. *VH* 2.3, Pl. *NH* 32.95, 35.16.2 with Stewart (1993), 33–34.

27. Taxes: *Priene* 132. Shrine: *Priene* 145.

28. The pause, and then the fire set by Memnon: DS 17.27.4–5. Arr. *An.* 1.23.3 specifies the two remaining strongholds, whereas DS speaks only of a retreat to Cos.

29. Arr. *An.* 1.23.7–8 refers to Ada not only as being satrap, but also as holding sovereign power, or *archein*; so also DS 17.24.2. The adoption appears also at Plu. *Alex.* 22.7. A similar view of the episode: Bosworth (1980) ad Arr. *An.* 1.23.7–8, speaking of Alexander's gaining "legitimacy."

30. The inscription: Plu. *Alex.* 17.4. The nearby tomb of Sarpedon: A. *Supp.* 870. Observing the weaknesses of the military argument for this route: Bosworth (1988), 50, speaking of the "lure of conquest" while referring to earlier scholarship attributing to Alexander a grand strategy for dealing with the Persian navy. The lure of being rid of Parmenio was perhaps a factor also. The port of Telmessus: Arr. *An.* 1.24.4 with Berve (1926), no. 117.

31. The crown at Phaselis: Arr. *An.* 1.24.5. Local honors: Plu. *Alex.* 17.9. The miracle at the Ladder: App. 1b #7. No miracle: Str. 14.3.9. Road-building: Arr. *An.* 1.26.2.

32. This is the rugged region between Side and the vicinity of later Seleuceia Tracheotis, as at Str. 14.3.9. Action at Termessus: Arr. *An.* 1.27.5–28.1.

33. The need to hurry, evidently caused by lack of food: Arr. *An.* 1.28.2. Another route, by the Kestros River, was too rough to use according to Stark (1958), 120, who says that the army retraced its steps for some 8–9 km (5–5.5 mi.).

34. The bloody action at Sagalassus: Arr. *An.* 1.28.7 supp. Roos. A similar episode, but not a doublet: DS 17.28.1–4, where the local people burn their home before fleeing into the mountains.

35. The unfavorable terms: Arr. *An.* 1.29.2; so also Curt. 3.1.6–8, where Alexander begins a difficult siege before the enemy surrenders. Celaenae and vicinity: Thonemann (2011), 54–55. Payment of debts: Curt. 3.1.20.

36. Width of the road: Young (1963), 348–49 with fig. 2. Parmenio's movement: Arr. *An.* 1.29.3.

37. *Alexandrou charax* at Celaenae: Steph. Byz. s.v. χάραξ with Ruge (1941). *Alexandrou pandokeion* (unknown): App. *Mith.* 20 with Ruge, ibid. *Alexandri fontes* (somewhere in Phrygia): Livy 38.15.15, unless the text reads *Alandri fontes*.

38. Memnon's movements: Arr. *An.* 2.1–2, carried on by his successors, 2.4–5; DS 17.29.1–2. Macedonian worries: DS 17.31.3–4.

39. In the Roman period, roads well to the west of Tyana ran from Laranda to places in Cilicia, notably Seleucia Tracheotis, as at Hild and Hellenkemper (1990), 139–40, but there is no evidence these roads were suitable for an army in Alexander's time. Sufferings of the Ten Thousand: X. *An.* 4.1.12–13, 4.5.15.

40. Macedonian Midas: Hdt. 8.138.2 and Euphorion *FGrH* 31 F 35 as at Lightfoot (2009). Alexander's putative ancestor Caraunus expelled Midas (Justin 7.1.7–21), creating a complicated relation between Midas and Alexander: whereas Alexander's ancestor wrested a kingdom from Midas, Alexander would receive a greater kingdom as a gift. Other complications: Roller (1983) and (1984). None of the versions in the Alexander historians, given at Bosworth (1980) ad Arr. *An.* 2.3, mention either the Macedonian migration or any negotiations between Alexander and the temple staff. For these negotiations, Arrian substitutes the formula πόθος λαμβάνει; so also Curt 3.1.16, Justin 11.7.4.

41. Rituals at Gordium: App. 1a #10, 1b #8. A version for the engineers: Aristoboulos *FGrH* 139 F 7a.

42. Memnon's death in the fall of 333, as at Berve (1926), no. 497. Barsine: Berve (1926), no. 206, reckoning she was born around 360 BC.

43. Sabictas (Arr. *An.* 2.4.2) or Abistamenes (Curt. 3.4.1). Cappadocian: Berve (1926), no. 690, although he supposes that the Persian Abistamenes (no. 4) was a subordinate and then a successor.

44. The sea captain: Nearchus, at Berve (1926), no. 544. The brother, Asander, thus Berve (1926), no. 165. Not Parmenio's brother: Bosworth (1980) ad Arr. *An.* 1.17.7.

45. Wells named Midas: Paus. 1.4.5, Tz. *H.* 1.110–12.

46. Anahita at Zela: Str. 11.8.4. The army may have encountered Anahita elsewhere, or heard tell of this goddess, as shown by the sundry evidence in Robert (1948), chs. 2–4.

47. The very long north-south view: Str. 1.2.7.

48. The difference of opinion about a naval omen: App. 1b # 5.

49. Janke (1904), 107, found a space in the Gates that would allow one wagon at a time, as at Xen. *An.* 1.2.21.

50. The rush to the Gates: Curt. 3.4.11–13 (a day attack, Thracians leading) vs. Arr. *An.* 2.4.3–4 (a night attack, Alexander leading); no particulars at DS 17.31.4–6, Plu. *Alex.* 19.2–5, Justin 11.8.1–2. Another view: Bosworth (1980) ad Arr. *An.* 2.4.3, holding that the Cilician Gates could be turned, and that the Persians withdrew in order to establish a better defensive position farther south, even as far away as Syria. Similarly, Curt. 3.4.3–5 says that the Persians withdrew in order to devastate Cilicia and then fall back farther. The only precedent for avoiding the Gates, however, was a campaign of 401 (X. *An.* 1.2.20–21) by a few thousands with no heavy baggage.

51. For a conspectus of the versions of this episode, see Atkinson (1980), 165–69, but with no discussion of the meeting of the council, as is also true at Bosworth (1980) ad Arr. *An.* 2.4.9–10; Atkinson (163) regards the councilors as *amici* "in the style of Hellenistic novels." The council meeting on the subject: App. 3 #5. Alexander's escaping common illnesses: one that may have struck him was typhus, if this was his fatal illness. For speculation as to the cause of his death, see Ch. 11, n. 64. Olympias's gratitude for his recovery: Hyp. 4.19, Paus. 1.23.4. Whatever the illness was, it may

also have killed Frederick Barbarossa, who died after bathing in Cilicia on his way to the Holy Land, as at the *Hist. Frid.* 100–105.

52. The anonymous *Historia Alexandri* supposed that Alexander did not move in an S-curve, and instead went straight to the southern part of the country (*Anonymi Historia Alexandri FGrH* 151 F 2).

53. A new era: Habicht (1970), 23–24.

54. Adapted from Firdausi 17.5–6, 19.1–2. For the motif of Alexander disguising himself as a subordinate or emissary, see Ps.-Call. A 2.13.4–15, 3.18–23; Ar. Ps.-Call. 2.6–7; Nizami 1.38.

CHAPTER 4
The Throne of Tyre

1. A sample of other views of Alexander's aims in the Issus campaign: Droysen (1877), 113; Renault (1975), 95, 99; Milns (1968), 79; Bosworth (1988a), 59.

2. The identification of the stele: Lanfranchi (2003), with refs. Alexander may have supposed the emperor was the Sardanapalus of Arr. *An.* 2.5.4. Chamoux (2006), following Aristoboulos *FGrH* 139 F 9, doubts whether the stele was part of a tomb.

3. Solli: App. 1a #11.

4. Local Syrian coinage: Lemaire (2006), 407, specifying small change. Semitic legends: Lemaire (2000), 128–32. A survey of Alexander's mints: Kremydi (2011), 167.

5. Parmenio thus had nearly half the army. The meeting: App. 3 #6. Some days later, and sauntering: Curt. 3.7, not the quicker, jerky pace that Bosworth (1980) questions ad Arr. *An.* 2.6.1. Discussion of other possible routes south for the two armies: Devine (1986). Another tourist stop: Magarsus (Arr. *An.* 2.5.8). Mount Amanus: Lipiński (1994), 207 n. 24.

6. Nebuchadnezzar's boasting: *WBC* 9.33–56, 10.1–9.

7. Arr. *An.* 2.7.1–2 reports that the patients were killed; Curt 3.8.12–13 reports mutilation.

8. Darius's meeting: App. 3 #45. Curtius reports that another experienced mercenary, Mentor's son Thimodes, later advised withdrawing to Mesopotamia at a council of Darius's held at Issus (App. 3 #46).

9. The victory of the mercenaries came at Cunaxa (X. *An.* 1.8), a tactical and defensive victory for the Ten Thousand, although a defeat for their employer.

10. Information from local observers: Plb. 12.17.2–3.

11. Rapp (1866), 130–31, cites ancient sources for this and other religious possibilities.

12. Royal drinking water: Curt. 3.3.9, with Schachermeyr (1973), 682–85.

13. The location of the Pinarus battlefield, best described at Plb. 12.17.4, is controversial; see Bosworth (1980) ad Arr. *An.* 2.7.1. The essential feature is the riverbanks

that would impede the Macedonian heavy infantry yet not stop the cavalry, a possibility explored by Janke (1906), 2–74.

14. App. 3 #7, one of the few instances of council procedure long noticed by scholars from Beloch (1922), 3.2.263, to Bosworth (1980) and Sisti (2001) ad Arr. *An.* 2.6.1. Arrian and Curtius differ slightly, for Curtius supposes that the meeting took place earlier before the battle, and that Alexander moved south (3.8.13), then back north, glad for the chance to fight where Parmenio had recommended. Other views: Brunt (1976), app. 3.6, and Atkinson (1980) ad Curt. 3.7.8–10.

15. App. 1a #12, where Curtius refers to *dis praesidibus*, evidently including Baal Haman; Bing (1991) suggests the other two. He adduces local coins, which would have made the task of identifying gods easier, but which were not indispensable, for Alexander surely consulted local informants.

16. Divine in its own right: Allen (2015), 230, citing the theophoric name "servant of Ḥamān." If the mountain were El, it would have been compared to Zeus's father, Cronus, and not to Zeus; thus Philo of Byblos *FGrH* 790 F 2. At S. *Andromeda* fr. 126, Cronus is taken to be Baal Haman by Lipiński (1995), 260–61.

17. Another view: Blazquez (2000), calling the rites Persian.

18. The modern name of Issus is long disputed, as at Bosworth (1988a), 109, Hammond (1980), 97–101, and Seibert (1972), 98–101. Speculation rests on the report that the battlefield was only fourteen stades wide and a hundred long, as at Callisthenes *FGrH* 124 F 35.

19. Alexander immediately next to the cavalry, with the *agēma* or elite of the hypaspists: Hammond (1992).

20. The opposing orders of battle: Arr. *An.* 2.8.3–8, preferred to Curt 3.9. The infantry: Cardaces, whether heavily armed (Arr. *An.* 2.8.6) or lightly (Plb. 12.17.7), as these troops were not identified by their armor or weapons, as Greek and Macedonian infantry commonly were. According to Str. 15.3.18, they could be identified by age, and again differed from Greek and Macedonian infantry. Ethnically mixed: Bosworth (1980) ad Arr. *An.* 2.8. Light infantry: Charles (2012), 7, with n. 4 giving bibliography on weaponry and ethnicity. The view that they were hoplites would make Alexander's sweeping thorough or past them more difficult to envisage. A guard of 2,000 means 1,000 infantry and 1,000 cavalry, but 3,000 elite cavalry as well as 1,000 infantry are reported by Curt. 3.9.4 with Charles (2015), 24–26, on the value of this report. These troops plus the Immortals were about as numerous as the Macedonians in the army of Alexander. Another view of this subject: the Immortals no longer existed, as at Fuller (1958), 164 n. 2, and Charles (2011), 114.

21. Tight royal control of troops: Curt. 3.8.9, DS 15.41.5. A similar view: Head (1982), 44. Opposing view: Atkinson (1980) ad Curt. 3.8.9. Darius's gray mare: Plu. *Alex.* 33.8, Ael. *HA* .48. The palisade: Arr. *An.* 2.10.1.

22. Persian archers would be behind the infantry if the latter were heavily armed, in front of them otherwise. In front: Fuller (1958), 160. Arrian does not say (*An.* 2.10.3). A similar view of Alexander's aims during the battle, but without the religious element: Badian (1965), 188, and Wilcken (1932), 149. An aim of fighting

nobly: Rüstow and Köchly (1852), 145; Berve (1926), 1.145–46. Darius as a target of opportunity only: Fuller (1958), 160.

23. The two kings approach each other: Arr. *An.* 2.10.1, Curt. 3.11.7, DS 17.34.5, Plu. *Alex.* 20.7–9. Chares's divergent report that Darius wounded him (*FGrH* 125 F 6) confirms that Alexander had drawn near his quarry.

24. The break in the line: Arr. *An.* 2.10.3–7, a danger noted at Plb. 12.20.6 followed by Hammond (1992), 402. The battle thus in the balance: Bosworth (1988a), 61. Ptolemy the son of Seleucus: Berve (1926), no. 670.

25. One hundred or so officers, reckoned at 1 per file, or 16 per *lochos*, and thus a total of 96 and the commander himself. Casualties: Arr. *An.* 2.10.7. Attributing the high number to "racial animosity": Hammond (1980), 107; so also Milns (1968), 80.

26. Trumpets in emergencies: Ael. *VH* 8.7. The leading regiments near Coenus were those of Perdiccas and either Meleager (Curt. 3.9.7) or Amyntas (Arr. *An.* 2.8.4). The initiative of Coenus and his fellow commanders: Arr. *An.* 2.11.1. Credit given to Alexander for this initiative: Droysen (1833), 63; Fuller (1958), 162; Green (1991), 232. Just as Coenus led the first three regiments, Craterus, at the opposite end of the line, anchored last three regiments—a variation on the standard Greek practice of giving the position of honor, which was on the far right, to the best unit, and the second-most-prestigious position, on the far left, to the next-best. A somewhat different view: Lendon (2005), 125–31.

27. Given Persian methods, Darius did not order the mercenaries to change their place in line after the fighting started, as claimed by Callisthenes *FGrH* 124 F. 35.

28. The attack in swarms: Arr. *An.* 2.11.2, Curt. 3.11.1. There are well-known exceptions to the tendency for horses to shy away from rows of spears or bayonets, such as the charge of the Light Brigade. Whether such an attack occurred at Chaeronea is uncertain: DS 17.86.3, where Alexander breaks the enemy's ranks, is consistent with such an attack, as is Plu. *Alex.* 9.2; Plu. *Pel.* 18.7, where the sacred band resists a frontal attack by Macedonian infantry, perhaps is not; Justin 9.3.9–10 omits cavalry. For the Granicus there is no information.

29. Skeptical of the use of the mare on the battlefield as at Curt. 3.11.1, but not Arr. *An.* 2.11.5 or DS 17.37.1: Atkinson (1980) ad loc.

30. Macedonian deaths of 82 to 450 (Curt. 3.11.27, 3.12.13, Arr. *An.* 2.10.7, 12; Justin 11.9.10, DS 17.36.6) vs. Persians deaths of 110,000 or more according to Diodorus.

31. The funeral and games: App. 1a #13.

32. The sundry Damascus captives: Ath. 13.607f-608a. Cf. the less precise total for ordinary slaves (Curt. 3.13.16).

33. Cicero at the spot: *Ad fam.* 15.4.8–9 with Atkinson (1980) ad Curt. 3.8.22. Unfinished shrine: Theopompos *FGrH* 115 F 253.

34. The misdirected supplication: App. 2 #9, an act that may have led Curtius to suppose that other Persian women supplicated Leonnatus, too (#8). The situation of a slave, or *famula*: Curt. 3.12.24. Another view of the term of address

"mother": Brosius (1996), 22–23, suggesting it was a Persian courtly term Alexander adopted.

35. App. 2 #6. Reports of panicking Persians supplicating each other, as at App. 2 # 7, are dubious. In Iran and Mesopotamia, supplication usually accompanied professions of obeisance, which in this case could be given only to Alexander.

36. Antigone: Berve (1926), no. 86, noting that she came from either Pydna or Pella.

37. Berve (1926), no. 152. The fate of Ilioneus (no. 382), a Persian youth named after Alexander's favorite Greek poem, is unknown.

38. Barsine's son, and a potential heir: Plu. *Alex.* 21.8.

39. Curt. 3.13.14; Justin 11.10.2; Plu. *Alex.* 21.7 and *Eu.* 1.7. Barsine merely a "mätresse": Schachermeyr (1973), 289; and Berve (1926), no. 206, also suggesting that the union between the two did not take place until 331, when the army returned to Syria. Concubines bearing legitimate children were to be found in Athens; we know too little about Macedonian marriage customs to say whether they existed there. Carney (2010), 243, describes her as "no courtesan." Her knowing Alexander as a child: Lane Fox (1974), 177.

40. Rejection of luxury on Alexander's part: Plu. *Alex.* 20.13. Cf. Justin 11.10.1, saying that Alexander admired this degree of luxury.

41. Arr. *An.* 2.14.6–9. Cf. Curt. 4.1.7–14, where Alexander responds to a less generous offer with a similar invitation for Darius to approach as a *supplex,* but mentions the female captives.

42. Coronation by acclamation at Sidon: DS 17.47.6. So also in Judea: 2 Ki. 2.23, 11.14.

43. Thirty-five-foot walls of Arad: Conrad (1992), 318.

44. Negotiations at Arwad: Arr. *An.* 2.13.7–8, Curt. 4.1.5–6.

45. Negotiations at Sidon: Arr. *An.* 2.15.6, Curt. 4.1.15–24.

46. Popular approval of the negotiation: DS 17.42.2, Curt. 4.1.17. (DS 17.47.1–6 mistakenly situates some parts of this story in Tyre.) No comparable political content: Justin 11.10.8–9. Accepting this story in spite of its Clitarchan origin: Lane Fox (1980), 382, and Green (1991), 246, both interpreting it without reference to religious duties. Accepting it in the main: Bosworth (2003), 181–86. Philosophical elements in the story, but again with no effect on the religious aspects of the kingship: Atkinson (1980) ad Curt. 4.1.15–26 with refs.

47. Nebuchadnezzar did do considerable harm to the Tyre's commerce, and perhaps forced a change in government: Ezek. 19.20; J. *AJ* 10.228, *Ap.* 1.156.

48. The shining temple of Melkart: Hdt. 2.44.2.

49. Arr. *An.* 2.18.1–2. The contrary view, that he did not know of the festival: Wilcken (1932), 109. So also Edmunds (1971), 374, assuming that Alexander did not know that Melkart differed in some respects from Heracles.

50. Another view of mutual misunderstandings such as this one: Teixidor (1990), 71–74, arguing for "interpretation in either direction," i.e., Near Eastern reinterpretation of Greek gods being symmetrical with Greek reinterpretation. Macedonian siege engines, however, made the relation asymmetrical in this case. Nor is there

any evidence of Tyrian curiosity about Heracles, as noted by Bonnet (1988), 401. The Tyrians resisted on orders from Darius: Grainger (2010), 2. The religious issue a mere screen for political goals: Droysen (1833), 72–73.

51. App. 3 #8. For problems with the speech reported by Arrian, see Bosworth (1980) ad Arr. *An.* 2.17.8. Events would soon disprove Alexander's claim that siege engines alone could breach the walls of Tyre. Like Alexander, Antigonus in 315 used his navy as well as his siege train to capture the city. Alexander no doubt spoke of his program for future conquests on other occasions as well as here, contra Tarn (1948), 2.286–87.

52. Objections offered by Polyidus, assuming he was still in service: Whitehead (2015), 79–80.

53. The act of sacrilege against the herald: Curt. 4.2.15. Greek immunity for heralds: Rhodes and Larsen (2012). Near Eastern immunity: Parpola (2003), 1047, 1067.

54. Pre-battle omens: App. 1a #9, 11, 14.

55. Modular towers: F. E. Winter (1971), 321.

56. Plu. *Alex.* 24.6–8 gives this characteristically reckless act a romantic cast by making the companion one of Alexander's former tutors, Lysimachus.

57. Chaining the statue: Curt. 4.3.22. The suppliant: App. 2 #10.

58. Scythes and hooks: Curt. 4.3.26.

59. The drawbridge: Arr. *An.* 2.22.7 with Ath. Mech. 10.12, 15.5–6. Its use here: Whitehead and Blyth (2004), 89.

60. Calendar manipulation: Plu. *Alex.* 25.1–2. App. 2 #12. Casualties and more flight: Arr. *An.* 2.24.4–6, DS 17.46.4, Curt. 4.4.17.

61. Flight to Melkart's shrine: App. 2 #11. Offering to Heracles: App. 1a #15. Perhaps Diades thought of the offering as coming from himself and his crews, since he was, as a papyrus fragment says, "the man who took Tyre along with Alexander," as at Tarn (1948), 2.39. Macedonian funerals: App. 1a #16. Funeral games: Arr. *An.* 2.24.4. Captives: Curt. 4.4.17. The donative: DS 17.46.6.

62. The offer: Arr. *An.* 2.25.1 (not mentioning Egypt) differs from Curt. 4.5.1 (western Anatolia only, as also at *Itin. Alex.* 43) and DS 17.39.1 (no specifics). In any event, Darius makes large concessions, whereas in the reported offer of 331 (App. 3 #12) Darius makes the even larger concession of joint control of the empire (DS 17.54.2; according to Curt 4.11.6, Plu. *Alex.* 29.7, and Justin 11.12.10, Darius concedes Egypt and all Asia east of the Euphrates, or effectively the same thing). Parmenio thus has a stronger case at App. 3 #12 than he does at #9–10.

63. App. 3 #9; Plutarch dates a meeting with the same *agendum* to the next year (#10).

64. Alexander's wish to go to Egypt: DS 17.40.2, 45.7, Arr. *An.* 2.17.1–4, 25.4. Scholarly dispute about his aims begins with Droysen (1833), 87, with other bibliography at Bloedow (2004), notably Beloch (1922), 3.1.641. Alexander's interest heightened because he underestimated the distances involved: Yorck von Wartenburg (1897), 31–32.

65. A Macedonian expedition to obtain a sum total of spoils, *ta hola* (DS 18.50.2, 50.5, 54.4), but not an *archē*, as noted at Errington (1976), 158. *Imperium macedonicum* is a Roman concept; "empire of Alexander" is a modern one.

66. Of the two appointed to Cilicia and Syria, Balacros was a veteran, as noted by Berve (1926), no. 200. Little is known about the other, Menon (no. 514). The situation in Thrace: Bosworth (1988a), 166.

67. J. *AJ* 11.302–3. Disputes over the identity and career of this official, named Sanbaallat, begin with Büchler (1898) and continue through Dušek (2012), 128, who rejects a governor of Samaria of that name in the time of Darius III and Alexander.

68. Mount Gerizim: Magen (2008), 152–56, 160. The town: Crowfoot, Kenyon, and Sukenik (1942), 116–17, vs. earlier activity, 94–116.

69. The water tunnel: Sneh, Weinberger, and Shalev (2010), 61. Attributed to Hezekiah, but perhaps newer: Reich and Shukron (2011).

70. The Persian share of the revenue: J. *AJ*. 11.297. Black soil: Crowfoot, Kenyon, and Sukenik (1942), 111–12, for Samaria. Or, to credit the claims of the present Iranian government, a soil of Persian, Achaemenid origin: UNESCO (2010), 394–96.

71. An example of a bicultural coin: Meshorer and Qedar (1999), #42.

72. Enemies: Gen. 19:24. Violators: Lev. 11.1–2, Nu. 16:35. Sexual offenses: Lev. 20:14, 21:9.

73. The survey by Cantarella (2011) shows that Greek legal authorities did not use immolation as a punishment.

74. The tax break for Yehud: J. *AJ* 11.317–18, 326–39. The incineration of Andromachus: Curt. 4.8.9–11. Other views of this episode: Marcus (1966) ad J. *AJ* 6.512–32; Sartre (2001), 79–81. Perhaps Andromachus went so far as to conduct Greek sacrifices in the shrine, as at *ABC* 11, concerning the crown prince Antiochus.

75. The Assyrian siege of Samaria: 2 Ki. 17.5. The escape and the slave registries: Dušek (2007), ch. 4. The Macedonian colony in Samaria: Eus. *Chron.* 19.489 and Jer. *Chron.* 27.504, attributing the colony to Perdiccas, and Syncellus 314.6–13, to Alexander. This reconstruction of events: Cross (1963), 119.

76. Land reallotment after the rebellion: J. *Ap.* 2.42–43. Hebrew mercenaries in the army: J. *Ap.* 1.200–204.

77. *HR* 30–31. Other versions of the visit: J. *AJ* 11.331; and Ps.-Call. Γ 2.24 with a different course of events before the visit. Momigliano (1979) attributes the story to Judean rivalry with the Samaritans. Other scholarly views: Golan (1982).

CHAPTER 5
The Throne of Egypt

1. Mentor of Rhodes: DS 16.49–52.

2. Gaza's hilltop fort was some eighteen to thirty meters (sixty to a hundred feet) above the plain, to judge from the modern situation: Bosworth (1980) ad Arr. *An.* 2.25.4. The rituals at Gaza: App. 1a #17, followed immediately by App. 1b #12; rationalistically, Plu. *Alex.* 25.4 separates the sacrifice and the flight of the bird.

3. The wound: Arr. *An.* 2.27.2, Curt. 4.6.17–20 (with the fainting).

4. The treacherous Arab: App. 2 #13; even more luridly, DH *Comp.* 12.8. Casualties: Curt. 4.6.30. Enslavement: Arr. *An.* 2.27.7. In private life, Alexander's attitude toward supplication was conventional, as at Plu. *Alex.* 42.1–2.

5. Alexander mistakenly put in a chariot: Curt. 4.6.25–29.

6. Plu. *Alex.* 5.7–8, 25.6. The Greek tradition of modest sacrifices: Naiden (2013), 215–17.

7. Amyntas and his men escaped Syria via Tripoli, and thence invaded Egypt (Arr. *An.* 2.13.2, Curt. 4.1.27–33, DS 17.48.2–6). Another 8,000 made their way north, to Caria (Curt. 4.1.39, 17.48.1). Yet others went to Cilicia and eventually fought Antigonus (Curt. 4.1.34–35, DS 17.48.5–6). This division of forces was unlucky for Amyntas but lucky for Alexander. Mazaces, the replacement for the dead satrap (Arr. *An.* 3.1.2), surrendered to Alexander.

8. Clère (1951) describes a statuette placing Nakhtnebef's son in an Iseion at some un-known date, but evidently a generation after his father, and thus in Alexander's time.

9. The two chief temples at Heliopolis: Kákosy (1977), 1111.

10. The return of the statue of Darius to Susa: Razmjou (2002).

11. Gods writing on leaves: Gregory (2013), 33; Lepsius (1849), vol. 3 pl. 169.

12. The text of a stone, perhaps a pedestal, found at Alexander's shrine at Bahariya, as at Bosch-Puche (2008), provides a complete titulary for Alexander, and thus con-firms that Alexander was crowned pharaoh, *pace* Burstein (1991) followed by Stewart (1993), 174, and preceded by Badian (1985), 433. An alternative but very similar text for this stone: Blöbaum (2006), 54–55.

13. "Hymn to Amon-Re," *ANET* 366.

14. Liquid sunlight: Moret (1902), 47–48. Alexander's successor, Philip Arrhidaeus, whose mother was a dancer from Thessaly (Ath. 12.557b), was nourished by, but not born to, the goddess Amaunet at Karnak, as at Hart (2005), s.v. "Amaunet."

15. Pharaonic *ka*: Bell (1985a). Name of Ptolemy IV's *ka*: *Edfou* 1.61.19, 1.433.14.

16. The statues on the occasion of Philip's death: *agalmata* versus an *eidōlon* (DS 16.92.5); see Mari (2008), 235. Other evidence for the worship of Philip during his lifetime is slight. The sacrifices made in Philip's honor at Amphipolis may have lasted only two years, from his accession to the throne in 360 or afterward until his destruction of the city in 357 (Aristid. 1.715d ed. Jebb). No remark on how long these sacrifices took place: Habicht (1970), 11–12. Preserved in spite of the destruction: Mari (2008), 240 with refs. The fourth-century but not precisely dated *temenē* at Philippi, including one for Philip II, as at Ducrey (1988), were estates, not shrines, for they were alienable, as observed by Prestianni Giallombardo (1999), 930–36. Evidence for a tribe named after Philip at Philippopolis (*IG Bulg* 5.512) is of impe-rial date. Two dedications to Philip *Sōtēr* are difficult to date: *SEG* 41.599 and Pouilloux and Dunant (1954), 2.230. The phrase *Zeus Philippios* refers to worship on Philip's part at Eresus, as at Rhodes and Osborne (2003), #83.2.4–5. Other views of this evidence: Habicht loc. cit. and Christesen and Murray (2010), 442–43.

17. Surprisingly, the Alexander historians are silent on the subject of the canal, which for Darius was an important project, as at Tuplin (1991).

18. Boat travel speeds in antiquity: Arnaud (2005), 217.

19. Memphis as at D. Thompson (2012), 8, 15, 24–26, 41.

20. Memphis as at D. Thompson (2012), 18, 20–21, 29, 78.

21. "Pharaoh," i.e., *Pr-ʿȝ*, a phrase used of kings from the Eighteenth Dynasty onward.

22. The only text for a coronation ceremony: Gardiner (1953), 22–23. Coronation here and here alone: Koenen (1977), 29–31, and Manning (2010), 92. Possibly several coronations: Gardiner (1953), 22. Ps.-Call. A 1.33 implies coronation in one place, but divine acclamation in several.

23. The sacrifice to the Apis bull: Plu. *De Is. et Os.* 353a, Ael. *NA* 11.10. The misconduct of Cambyses: Hdt. 3.27–29, an act of sacrilege that did not occur, as noted by Pfeiffer (2014b), 95 with refs.

24. The sacrifice: App. 1a #18. The competition: Plu. *Fort. Alex.* 334e.

25. Alexander's route: Curt. 4.7.5, *a Memphi eodem flumine vectus ad interiora Aegypti penetrat*. (Curt. 4.8.3 rules out travel into Ethiopia.) Amon at Memphis: Guermeur (2005), 9–81. A possible sacrifice to Amon at Thebes by Alexander: Spiegelberg (1906), 222. The objection that the trip would take too long: D. Thompson *per litteras*. On foot or horseback it would, but it would not by boat; see Arnaud (2005), 17. Macedonian Epirus and Dodona: A. Lloyd (1975) ad Hdt. 2.56. Siwah and Dodona: Hdt. 2.32.1, Pi. fr. 58 ed. Maehler (1989); Baege (1911), s.v. "Amon."

26. Luxor inscriptions of Alexander's: Abd el-Razik (1984), 38 with pl. 11. Location: Ullmann (2002), pl. 5. Abd el-Razik (1984), on the outer walls: 10–43. Inner walls: 43–56.

27. The *ka*: Bell (1985a), 251–52, 289.

28. The importance of the Theban priesthood in particular: Veïsse (2004), 240–42. No more likely to rebel than other places, Thebes was more likely to recognize usurpers.

29. As *Diospolis hē megalē*, Thebes was distinguished from other cities of Zeus. The Hebrews called it No-Amôn, from the Egyptian Nw-t-imn, "the city of Amon." "Amon" as Egypt: Jer. 46.25, Na. 3.8–10. Greek *Thebes* was a misnomer, apparently from *Tȝm.t*, the ancient name of Medinet Habu, as shown by Sethe (1929), 53. Karnak: as at Barguet (1962), chs. 1–5 passim, esp. 192–97, on the shrine repaired by Alexander in the Akhmenou. No doubt Alexander saw the colossus of Memnon, as at Klotz (2008), 124; he presumably interpreted it in a Homeric, not Egyptian, sense.

30. Inside the Akhmenou: Barguet (1962), 194–95; Martinez (1989), 112.

31. Chonsu: Murnane (1981), pl. 112 and pl. 1; Traunecker (1987). More for Amon at Luxor: a chapel built to hold a sacred boat, as at Murnane (1985), 2.137–38. For Amon at Medinet-Habu: Hölscher (1939). Memphis: Spiegelberg (1905), 222, no. 1, a hieroglyphic stele indicating royal worship of the Theban triad, plus a demotic inscription that Spiegelberg supposed refers to the hieroglyphic inscription. For Amon at Tukh el-Garamus in the northern Delta: Guermeur (2005), 250. For Thoth at Hermopolis, unless this was the work of Ptolemy I: Roder (1959), 111, 300, and pl. 67 (d).

32. The titles: Bosch-Puche (2008) with a similar interpretation at Bosch-Puche (2013).

33. The Egyptian for "ruler of rulers," *ḥq3w*, is not a translation of "king of kings," as noted by Bosch-Puche (2013), 137; cf. Grenier (1989), 16. Other gods: Chonsu, Mut, Hathor, Neither, and Isis, almost all celestial beings, as at Budde (2003), passim. "Lord of the world," *nb r ḏr*, is likewise only for divinities; in the reign of Nectanebo II, for example, it is for Re-Horakhty, as at Lichtheim (1973), 2.43.

34. Amon and pharaohs: Thutmosis IV (*ANET* 446–48 from *Urk.* 4.1545.4–18); Hatshepsut (*Urk.* 4.342).

35. Amon and ordinary worshippers: Černý (1935), (1942), (1962), (1972). There were no ambiguous answers, save for those reported by Herodotus (2.11.2, 2.133.1, 3.64.4).

36. According to Arr. *An.* 3.3.1, a mere *pothos* motivated Alexander's trip; so also the *ingens cupido* of Curt. 4.7.8.

37. Greco-Egyptian Siwah: Parke (1967), 202–4. Libyan origins: Colin (1998), 1.329–55. The shrine in Alexander's time: Guermeur (2005), 423–28. The satellite shrine, visible in the nineteenth century: Minutoli (1824), 20–23. The failed attack: Hdt. 3.26.1–4.

38. The oracle given to the Macedonians: App. 1b #13, especially DS 17.50.6–51.2, Curt. 4.7.23–25. Cursory accounts: Plu. *Alex.* 27.4–5, Arr. *An.* 3.4.5–6, Justin 11.11.7–11. The one ancient source saying otherwise: Str. 17.1.43, reporting that others accompanied Alexander into the temple.

39. Persian building in Siwah, and elsewhere in Egypt, under the first two Dariuses: A. Lloyd (1983), 294; Briant (1974), 620; Vittmann (2003), 129. No quid pro quo involving Bahariya: Ladynin (2016), arguing for an early Ptolemaic date for the inscription published by Bosch-Puche (2008).

40. A similar bargain, but without Bahariya: Justin 11.11.7–11. Alexander's knowing in advance what the oracle would say, but no bargain: Lane Fox (1973), 212. Undecided as to the bargain: Cartledge (2004), 268–69.

41. Details of the journey: Minutoli (1824), 17–20.

42. The text at the entrance: Guermeur (2005), 425. Soutekhirdisou may have been the founder of the shrine, as at Kuhlmann (1988), 104–5. Alexander was unwittingly imitating or lending himself to a local ruler, not a national or international one. This error or necessity had already occurred at Phaselis, Sidon, and Tyre.

43. The sanctum: Fakhry (1944), 72–73. Scholarly debate as to whether Alexander received an oracle or only a greeting: J. Hamilton (1999) ad Plu. *Alex.* 27.5. The religious purport of the priest's statement: Tarn (1948), 2.354. Religious but also political purport: Kuhlmann (1988), 154–55.

44. A sacrifice to Philip: Aristid. *Or.* 38.14. In other instances, sacrificing to Philip was out of the question, as at Olympia, where Philip erected *eikones* (Paus. 5.20.9). Other views: intimations of worship at Fredricksmeyer (1979), 58; true worship, at Habicht (1970), 3–16, and Fredricksmeyer (1981), but without citing any particular act of worship rendered to him. The same cautious view as here: Prestianni Giallombardo (1975), 37–45. Other *eikones* for generals: C. Hamilton (1979),

67–70. Worship of pharaohs was rare: Menes as at DS 1.74–75; Ramses II and III, as at Nelson (1942), 154–55; Thutmosis III, as at Bell (1985b), 35–36. A similar view of how the two oracles, one royal and one public, interacted: Kuhlmann (1988), 130–37. Doubting the processional oracle: Borchard (1933), 39–42.

45. Bahariya: Fakhry (1972), 1.603; Guermeur (2005), 433–34 with other refs.

46. Bosch-Puche (2008), 37: ΒΑΣΙΛΕΥΣ / ΑΛΕΞΑ<N>ΔΡΟΣ / ΑΜΜΩΝΙ / Τ[Ω]Ι ΠΑΤΡΙ. Cf. Ps.-Call. A. 1.30.5, where Alexander dedicates a shrine to Amon by inscribing Πατρὶ θεῷ Ἄμμωνι Ἀλέξανδρος ἔθηκεν (so also B and Γ 1.30). At Bahariya, it was not necessary to say that Amon was divine.

47. The funeral for Hector: App. 1a #19.

48. The Macedonian-style sacrifice at Memphis: App. 1a #21. Holding that this was a sacrifice to Amon: Bosworth (1980) ad Arr. *An.* 3.5.2. Olympias's gift: Ath. 14.659f-660a, where she adds that the slave is also "skilled in preliminary offerings that [she] happens to make (προθύεται)." Other interpretations: Fredricksmeyer (1966).

49. Philotas's sneers: Aristoboulos *FGrH* 139 F 56.

50. Philotas's opinion: Plu. *Alex.* 48.5–6. Or did the rift between Alexander and Philotas begin earlier, at the time of the Pixodarus affair? Thus Heckel (2016), 52, citing Plu. *Fort. Alex.* 339f. Then religious differences deepened the rift.

51. Winning formula: Justin 12.16.9. Other views of how Alexander's notion of his own divinity developed: Seibert (1972), 192–206; Badian (1981); Bosworth (1988a), 278–90. Droysen (1833), 96–97, thought that Alexander's notion of his status did not develop before Siwah, at the oracle, and that afterward he practiced on the naiveté and ignorance of most of his soldiers.

52. Revenues: St. Jerome, *In Dan.* 3.11, Cicero apud Str. 17.1.13; Le Rider (2001), 229. Egypt vs. elsewhere: Hdt. 3.89–92. Cleomenes was appointed satrap sometime later, as shown by his holding this office at the time of Alexander's death (Arr. fr. 6, Justin 13.4), as well as by [Arist.] *Oec.* 1352a. The disloyal Persian satrap: Hdt. 4.166; so also the first satrap in Lydia (Hdt. 1.155–56).

53. A rebellion under the appropriately named pretender Amyrtaios, or Amenirdis, "Amon has given him," *Ỉmn- ỉr-dỉ.s.*

54. Administration of Egypt: Arr. *An.* 3.5.2–7, Curt. 4.8.4–5. The Persian and the Egyptian: Doloaspis and Petisis, the former having an Iranian name, even if he was of Egyptian origin, as at Arr. *An.* 3.5.2, with Harmatta (1963), 208. The uniqueness of Egypt: Badian (1965), contrasting it with Babylon and Phoenicia. Contrast with Persian administration: Bengston (1937), 7. The Egyptian populace, admittedly, did not always distinguish between a satrap and other administrators, as at H. Smith (1988), 184–86, reporting a demotic ostrakon reading *P3-di-'Ist p3 ih-strpny*, or "Petisis the Satrap."

55. The role of Cleomenes: Curt. 4.8.5.

56. The assignment of offices: Arr. *An.* 3.5.5.

57. Other views of the purpose of Alexandria: Grote (1884), 12.199, a naval base; Cavaignac (1913), 2.432, a new colony, replacing Naucratis, similar to [Arist.] *Oec.*

1352c. A similar view: Ehrenberg (1926), 38, with Alexandria as a counterweight to Memphis. None of these scholars cite religious factors. The date of the city's founding: 25 Tybi, as at Ps.-Call. A 1.32.10, is rendered compatible with App. 1a #20, a ceremony said to occur at an earlier date, by Bosworth (1980) ad Arr. *An.* 3.1.5. Here he suggests Alexander visited the site twice, once at Arrian's earlier date, and once in April. I assume that the foundation ceremony occurred during the second visit, but this point is disputed; see especially Welles (1962).

58. Alexandria's waterworks: *B. Alex.* 5.

59. "[By order of] Peucestas. No entry. Priest's chamber," as at Turner (1974).

60. Egyptian coinage before Alexander: Kraay (1976), 294–95; Dumke (2011), 57–90. Imitation: Buttrey (1982). Demanhur: Newell (1923), 44, 166–67.

61. App. 1b #14, but with characteristic differences among the sources: Arr. *An.* 3.2.1–2, simplifying the omen while implying his source is inferior to Ptolemy and Aristobulus; Curt. 4.8.6, making the use of barley an otherwise unreported *nomos* of the Macedonians; and Plu. *Alex.* 26.8, making the use of barley accidental.

62. Adapted from Ar. Ps.-Call. 1.88–94.

CHAPTER 6
The Throne of Babylon

1. Melkart: App. 1a #22. The Athenian prisoners: Arr. *An.* 1.29.5–6; 3.6.2, Cur. 4.8.12, with the supplicatory term *orabant*. Harpalus: 3.6.7.

2. New diviners in the entourage: the Syrian (Arr. *An.* 4.13.5), and the Greek Pythagoras, a hepatoscopist (Plu. *Alex.* 73.1–4).

3. The discussion of Darius's offer: App. 3 #10.

4. Known Persian losses: at least 112,000 (DS 17.21.6, 36.6). Macedonian losses so far (and up to Gaugamela): 656 to 1,029, i.e., Granicus, 34 to 129 (Plu. *Alex.* 19.8, Justin 11.6.12, Arr. *An.* 1.16.4–5); Halicarnassus, 40 to 50 (Arr. *An.* 1.22.7, DS 17.25.6); Issus, 82 to 450 (Curt. 3.11.27, 3.12.13; Arr. *An.* 2.10.7, 12.1; Justin 11.9.10; DS 17.26.6); Tyre, 400 (Arr. *An.* 2.24.4). Enemies entered his service at Miletus (Arr. *An.* 1.19.6, DS 17.22.4) and elsewhere in Anatolia (Arr. *An.* 2.5.7, Curt. 4.5.18).

5. The arrival at Carcemish: Arr. *An.* 3.7.1–2, Curt. 4.9.11–12. Arrian's "Thapsacus" near Carcemish and not farther south: Engels (1980), 64–65 with refs.

6. Rejection of the Euphrates perhaps also because it became unnavigable in August and thus could not be used to transport supplies on rafts, as at Semple (1919), 160. Lack of forage: X. *An.* 1.4–5. Limits of pharaonic conquests: Manetho *FGrH* 609 F 2–3.

7. Operations of Mazdai: Curt. 4.7.9, 4.7.12, distinct from the similar operation at the Euphrates, as noticed by Lane Fox (1973), 526. The Macedonians crossed somewhere north of the main ford, at Mosul, as noted by Marsden (1964), 20. Nineveh was destroyed by Cyrus according to Amyntas *FGrH* 122 F 2, a report that would interest Alexander.

8. The eclipse: *AD* 1–330 ob. 3 as well as the Alexander historians as at Bosworth (1980) ad Arr. *An.* 3.7.6; the first incident datable to a particular day in both Occidental and Near Eastern sources for the expedition.

9. Previous eclipses during the expedition: NASA (2009), pl. 202.

10. The Egyptian interpretation of the eclipse: App. 1b #15.

11. The council: App. 3 #11. The offerings: App. 1a #23. Another view: Ross (2016), supposing that Alexander understood the cause of the eclipse, rather than interpret it with priestly help.

12. Arr. *An.* 3.8.7. As the battle occurred only eleven days after the eclipse, the Persians had accordingly arrived in Arbela by the date of the eclipse, Sept. 20. The exact location remains disputed but was some fifty to sixty miles north of Arbela, as reckoned at Bosworth (1980) ad loc.

13. Persian panic: *AD* 1–330 obv. 14. As Rollinger and Ruffing (2012), 104, observe, there is no reason to suppose that the mere approach of the Macedonians caused the panic. Ministrations of the Magi: as after the solar eclipse at Hdt. 7.37. Or, if Darius was not reassured, he tried once again to negotiate with Alexander, leading to the meeting reported in Curtius (App. 3 #12), where Parmenio gives much the same advice as at #10.

14. For astronomical progress in Babylon, see Rochberg (1984), especially 134, 136, for the date of the first horoscope in 410.

15. The pre-battle omen: Labat (1965), #71.7.

16. Another view of the cultural differences between Greece and Babylonia: Ulanowski (2016a), 83, comparing *manteis* and *bārûtu*.

17. Dispirited Persian forces: Lenderling (2005), 167–69. The contrary view: Neujahr (2005), arguing that the "Dynastic Prophecy" predicted Darius's victory over Alexander, rather than being composed *ex eventu*.

18. This crucial council meeting before the battle: App. 3 #13.

19. The next meeting: App. 3 #15. Arrian differs from the Vulgate and instead reports a meeting in between #13 and #15. Conceivably, this meeting, which is #14, and meeting #15 both took place, for Alexander summons the meeting at #14 in order to gain the officers' support during the coming battle, and so meeting #15, about tactics, would still be necessary. Alternatively, Arrian has dropped meeting #15 and replaced it with #14.

20. As Atkinson (1980) ad Curt. 4.13.1–10 observes, the rebuke given to Polyperchon in Curtius runs parallel to a rebuke given to Parmenio at Arr. *An.* 3.10.1–2, an informal encounter between Parmenio and Alexander rather than a meeting of the council. Plutarch's report of the meeting (*Alex.* 31.10–14) names no individual speakers. As shown by App. 3, Plutarch never names individual speakers other than Alexander and Parmenio. A Persian version of the moral contrast between a day attack and an attack at night: Nizami 1.25.12–15, where an unnamed adviser tells Alexander to attack Dara by night and Alexander rejects the advice, saying that the sun cannot attack by night.

21. Curt 4.13.15 reports the prayers to Zeus and Athena, and thus to two of the three *dis praesidibus loci* to which Alexander sacrificed before Issus (Curt. 3.8.22). Plu. *Alex.* 31.9 supplies a third god, as immediately below.

22. Adoration of Ishtar by Assurbanipal: the hymn of Assurbanipal at Livingstone (1989), 14–17, rev. ll. 14–17. Cyrus and Ishtar: Borger (1996), 280 and 294, prism B1, ll. 115–17. Alexander and Phobos: App. 1a #24. The cult of Phobos at Sparta and elsewhere: J. Hamilton (1999) ad Plu. *Alex.* 31.9 with refs. Alexander overslept as in the sources at App. 3 #16. The *Astronomical Diary* reports the battle nonetheless began in the morning, as noticed by Van der Spek (1998), 297–98.

23. The informal gathering the morning before the battle: App. 3 #17.

24. The length of the front: Marsden (1964), 74. The size of the army: 40,000 infantry and 7,000 cavalry reported at Arr. *An.* 3.5.1. Devine (1989) estimates nearly the same number.

25. The opposing orders of battle: Arr. *An.* 3.11.3–10, preferred to Curt. 4.12.6–13, although as Bosworth (1980) says ad Arr. *An.* 3.11.3, both may contain errors and omissions. The differences between the two sources are greater than for Issus (as at Ch. 4, n. 20).

26. A somewhat different view of Mithra: Green (1991), 290–91, describing Mithra as a god of "holy war."

27. The numbers for the elite protecting the king are harder to estimate than for Issus, since no author gives a figure for the guard except DS 17.59.2 (1,000 συγγενεῖς).

28. The moves and countermoves: Arr. *An.* 3.13.1–6 with Milns (1968), 122, adding that the Persians also wished to encircle the Macedonians. The omen: App. 1b #17. The focus on Darius: as at Lane Fox (1973), 239, who uses terms compatible with his stress on the Homeric elements (497–98).

29. The Persian cavalry breakthrough: Curt. 4.15.5, as opposed to Arr. *An.* 3.14.5, 3.15.1, which envisions Indians dispatched from the center, presumably by Darius, not from the right by Mazaeus. So also Atkinson (1980) ad Curt. 4.15.5–13 with refs. A different view: Hammond (1980), 147, saying that the phalanx split because of pressure against Parmenio's entire position.

30. The very different version at Curt. 4.15.12 has one important point in common with this version, drawn from Arr. *An.* 3.14.6: a Macedonian subordinate takes charge of the situation. Although reaching the baggage train, the Persians never came close to reaching the women: Fuller (1958), 176. The absurd idea that Sisygambis did not want to be rescued: DS 17.59.7.

31. Poor visibility: Curt 4.15.32, DS 17.61.1. Cf. good visibility at Arr. *An.* 3.13.1. A pre-arranged message: Green (1991), 294. Doubting Parmenio's power to compel Alexander to turn around: Bosworth (1988a), 82–83.

32. The issue of the message: not delivered, DS 17.60.7–8; delivered, Arr. *An.* 3.15.2, Curt. 4.26.3. A second issue: the number of messages, for which see Bosworth (1980) ad Arr. *An.* 3.15.1–7. A third issue: the distance between Parmenio and Alexander. Beloch (1922), 4.2.300, accepts the account at Curt. *Alex.* 4.16.8–10,

which Fuller (1958), 177, calculated as putting Alexander twelve miles from the rest of the army. Both criticize Alexander, as does Lane Fox (1973), 240. Griffith (1947), 82–83, argues that Alexander was pursuing a leading Persian subordinate, Bessus, but not Darius, a switch reducing the distance. Only Marsden (1964), 61, supposes that the gap between Alexander and the main body was planned. The last stand by Darius: *AD* 1–330 obv. 15–18. Cf. Arr. *An.* 3.15.1–3, Curt. 4.15.30–33, and DS 17.60.3, in which Darius has already fled, and Alexander has the luxury of changing front.

33. The wounded leaders: Curt. 4.16.32, DS 17.51.3.

34. A close pursuit would imply panic in Darius's entourage. The Alexander historians report panic (Arr. *An.* 3.15.1 in light of 3.14.3–4; and Curt. 4.16.1, DS 17.60.7, Plu. *Alex.* 33), but *AD* 1–330 obv. 15–18 does not.

35. The Persian council meeting: App. 3 #47.

36. Macedonian casualties are reported to be 100 to 500, more likely the latter (Arr. *An.* 3.15.6, Curt. 4.16.26, DS 17.61.3), vs. the colossal totals reported at Arr. *An.* 3.15.6, Curt. 4.16.26, DS 17.61.

37. The stench of the dead: Curt. 5.10.11. Burial in Arbela: Str. 16.4.1.

38. The tunnels of Sennacherib: Safar and Basmachi (1946). The naphtha experiment: Plu. *Alex.* 35.2–9.

39. "King of Asia" at Plu. *Alex.* 34.1, preceded by Arr. *An.* 2.14.9, is accordingly an anachronism, as it is when used of Bessus at Arr. *An.* 3.25.3, *pace* Fredricksmeyer (2000), 140. A third view, that Macedonians hailed Alexander as "King of Asia" regardless of how Asians would respond: Schachermeyr (1973), 276–85. The Lindos dedication: *Lindos* II 2.105 with *FGrH* 532 F 1 36–38. The pharaoh's statue: Hdt. 2.182.1.

40. Hegelochus: Curt. 6.11.22. Perhaps he had died already, at Arbela. Doubting the story: Badian (1960), 332. Prosopographical complications: Atkinson (1994) ad loc.

41. Antigonus's battles: Curt. 4.1.35. Fall of Halicarnassus, thanks partly to Asander: Arr. *An.* 2.5.7.

42. The battle of mice: Plu. *Ages.* 15.6. The same jealousy on Alexander's part: Curt. 6.1.18–19.

43. Babylon as a city the size of a nation: Arist. *Pol.* 3.1.12; similarly, Ar. *Av.* 552. A population of 250,000: Dandamaev (1996), 364. Only 50,000: Boiy (2004), 229–34.

44. Labor: Jursa (2015), 349, 363, 361. Houses: Jursa and Hackl (2010), 807.

45. The ziggurat was reported to be some 300 feet according to Schmid (1995), 128–30, versus 480 feet. The Elamite ziggurat at Choga Zanbil (as at n. 70 below) had a slightly bigger base, but its height is unknown. The Pharos lighthouse at Alexandria, built in the mid-third century BC, rose some 400–450 feet according to McKenzie (2011), 42. The number of members of the priestly college: fourteen at some point in the fourth century BC, according to Beaulieu (2006), 24. The *Shatammu* and assembly as, in effect, presiding officer and assembly: Van der Spek (1986), 60, and (1987), 61–64, stressing that this body was not a popular assembly. The shrine assembly doubled as a court: Boiy (2004), 218–19.

46. Although the throne had been abolished, the phrase "King of Babylon" continued to be used off and on, a matter of no political significance, as at Stolper (1994b), 214.

47. The effect of the rebellion against Xerxes on archives and management in one city, Borsippa: Waerzeggers (2010), 54. A rebellion against Darius III is doubtful: Stolper (1994), 240.

48. Cyrus diverting the Euphrates: Hdt. 1.191, although the story was untrue, as noted by Beaulieu (1989), 225–26. Darius I needed a year and seven months to capture Babylon (Hdt. 3.150).

49. Evidence for the bargain: *AD* 1–330 rev. 4–7. A different view of the negotiations: Kuhrt (1990), 25–27, stressing Persian and Assyrian precedents. Mazdai's position: *bēl pīḫāti*, the Babylonian preference, as at Stolper (2006), 227–28; or *šakin māti*, even reserving the term "satrap" for lower officials, as at Dandemaev (1988). Simply as "satrap": Arr. *An.* 3.16.4. Cf. "hyparch" at 4.18.3, implying proconsular powers. Mesopotamian coronations with and without a coronation oath: Ben-Barak (1980).

50. The change in accession date: year 8 of Alexander is indicated for *AD* 1–328 left edge of rev. The same honor done to Antigonus Monophthalmos when he was the most powerful man in the region, and was entered on the Uruk king list as king of Babylon for six years, even though Alexander IV was on the throne: *BaM* (1980), 2.88. The juniper garden, besides being a meeting place, contained several temples, including a "House of Deliberation": Boiy (2004), 84 and Van der Spek (2006), 75 n. 4. Suppliants: App. 2 #14, reporting that Mazdai himself supplicated. Arrival in the city: *AD* 1–330 rev. 9.

51. The milestones outside Babylon: Robson (2008), 167 with fig. 6.5. Height of the city walls: Str. 16.1.20. Map of the walls: Wetzel (1944), 48. Alexander's parade: Curt. 5.1.19–23; perhaps BM 36761 rev. 11–14 as at Wiseman (1985), 116–21. Details concerning the approach and the parade route: Koldeway (1914), passim.

52. Twigs thrown for Cyrus: *ABC* 7 rev. 3. Flowers: Curt. 5.1.23. The Babylonians were old hands at welcoming foreigners they had outnegotiated; see Kuhrt (1990), Boiy (2004), 106, Jursa (2007).

53. Inner walls "a frontier as firm as time itself," Al-Rawi (1985), 5–6, quoting Nabopolassar. The water screws: Berossos *FGrH* 141 F 8a. A skeptical view: Bichler and Rollinger (2005). Wherever this remarkable piece of remarkable hydraulic ingenuity was located, Alexander surely saw it and took an interest in it. The citadel gate: George (1992), 365–68.

54. The double New Year: the Akitu festival (*ABC* 283), and the Nisannu festival, attended by Antiochus II (*AD* 2–245 A obv. 12–13) and by Antiochus III (*AD* 2–204 C rev. 14–19). Perhaps not in 245: Van der Speck (1993), 72.

55. The ceremony for Nabopolassar: *ABC* 26.78–96. Some such ceremony performed for Alexander: Pallis (1927), 174–83, followed by Bosworth (1980) ad Arr. *An.* 3.16.5, with refs., to which add Altheim (1953), 66, to the scholars rejecting the ceremony. A possible location: Wiseman (1991), 231. Alexander "was seated on the throne of royalty," as at *ABC* 1 3.12 (Mušezib Marduk); 1 4.33 (Šamaš-šuma-ukin);

2 15 (Nabopolassar); 5 obv. 11 (Nebuchadnezzar), 13 rev. 6 (Seleucus II), 13 rev. 9 (Seleucus III). His installation was immediate; *AD* 1–330 rev. 11, referring to him as *šar kiššati*. Variations on his name: *Aleksandari*, or *Aleksandaru*, as at Boiy (2004), 48. Nabû: George (1996), 375.

56. The inaugural sacrifice: App. 1a #25. The palace: Wiseman (1985), 55–60. Water-cooled: Dalley (2013), 62–63.

57. Hdt. 1.181–82 lists those who may ascend the ziggurat.

58. The Greeks presumably responded to an innovation found in the Babylonian calendar, a seventy-six-year cycle for reconciling the movements of the sun and moon. Callipus of Cyzicus, a pupil of Aristotle, introduced this innovation in Greece, as at G. Lloyd (2001), 176–78. In the Persian Empire, the Babylonian calendar had already spread; see Stern (2011), 99–114. Earlier kings in Mesopotamia, like Greek kings and magistrates, controlled the calendar by manipulating intercalation, by fiat, or both. Intercalation: Parpola (1970), 2.285, 2.504–5. Fiat: Brown, (2000), 195.

59. For an illustration of the relation between the heavens and acts of extispicy, see Gurney and Finkelstein (1957), no. 73.110–17.

60. Tour guides and sights: George (1992), passim. The shrine of Anahita: Berossos *FGrH* 680 F 11. Gardens at Nineveh: Dalley (2013).

61. The Macedonian sacrifice: *AD* 1–330 rev. 13–15.

62. Maintenance of Esangil: Boiy (2004), 110–11. Persian neglect of temples fell short of the now rejected view that they attacked Babylonian temples (Arr. *An.* 7.17.1–4, DS 2.9.9), and that Alexander wished to rebuild Esangil in particular (Str 16.15, DS 17.112.3); see Van der Spek (2006), 24–25. The standard set by Cyrus: *ANET* 315–16. The ziggurat had not been destroyed: Messerschmidt (2015), 241, in the course of a discussion of controversy about this point, 236–41. Financial disputes between the priests and Alexander: Arr. *An.* 7.17. A complication: rerouting of funds through tithes collected by individuals, not the temple, as at *CT* 99.5.15–17.

63. Kings' quarrels with priests: Waerzeggers (2010), 54 n. 282 with refs. The same conflict under the Neo-Babylonians: Dandemaev (1979), 591. Defeating the priests by appointing them: Frame (1991), 79, and Beaulieu (1989), 126. By creating new posts, at least in Assyria: Löhnert (2007).

64. The food fight aboard ship: Chares *FGrH* 125 F 9.

65. Bitumen and other uses of naphtha: Forbes (1964), 1.1–124. *Hacksilber* in the east: Le Rider (2001), 170–71. Babylonian example: C. Thompson (1999). The lack of darics in the east: Lewis (1989), 227–34. Lack of *sigloi* in Mesopotamia before the fourth century BC: Carradice (1987), 89–90. There is no evidence for Susiana in this period, but for the lack of currency in neighboring Persis see Joannès (1994), 142–44.

66. Arr. *An.* 3.16.4 mentions two of the four appointees; Curt. 5.1.43 mentions the other two. Mazdai's remark: Plu. *Alex.* 39.9.

67. Massive donatives in Babylon: Curt. 5.1.45. Olympias on luxury: Plu. *Alex.* 39.7.

68. The alternative to Babylon as capital: Susa (Str. 15.3.9–10). Babylon reportedly the chief capital of Cyrus: X. *Cyr.* 8.6.22. For Alexander's regular provincial revenue, no good figures are available, since those in Herodotus date from more than a century before, but Holt (2016), 181–93, shows that other reported payments to Alexander, minus reported expenditures, netted some 150,000 talents over thirteen years. The only ancient source to estimate Alexander's income, Pompeius Trogus, said that the royal treasures, plus other revenues, amounted to 30,000 talents a year (Justin 13.1.9). Only 8,000 a year: Berve (1926), 1.312. Complications involved in such estimates: Holt (2016), 8–19. Comparatively slight Macedonian revenues engrossed by Antipater: Arr. *An.* 1.16.5, *SEG* XII (1955), 314. Harpalus may at first have followed Alexander to Ecbatana, as at Berve (1926), no. 143, in which case he moved to Babylon in 330.

69. The thirty-four days of relaxation: Curt. 5.1.36, 5.1.39.

70. The ziggurat: Choga Zanbil. Dimensions: Travlos (1960), 71–72; F. König (1965), no, 21, 28a.

71. The chief buildings in Achaemenid Susa: Potts (1999), 323. Horns on temples: 284, 346.

72. The entry into Susa: Arr. *An.* 3.16.6–9, Curt. 5.2.12–15. Possible resistance: Kaboli (2000), interpreting numerous Macedonian spearheads and arrowheads in the vicinity. Vandalizing the statue: Razmjou (2002).

73. Statues of the two tyrannicides restored by Alexander, apparently in 325/4: Arr. *An.* 3.16.7–8, 7.19.2; Pl. *NH* 34.70, although other sources date the restoration of the statues to the time of the Diadochi; hence Bosworth (1980) ad loc. holds that Alexander only promised to restore the pair.

74. Opulence and grandeur: Arist. *De Mundo* 398a, comparing the Persian king to a god; Ath. 5.206d-e; and Esth. 1:6–7, with Perrot (2013), passim.

75. The temple of Inshushinak, which largely survived until the nineteenth century AD: Harper (1992), 122–27. Mesopotamian statues in the temple: Beran (1988); Foster (1993), 304–7.

76. Similar problems for the *interpretatio graeca*, but in an Egyptian setting: Van Lieven (2016).

77. Sacrifice in Susa: App. 1a #26.

78. Susa appointments: Arr. *An.* 3.16.9. Parmenio's house: Plu. *Alex.* 39.10.

79. Sisygambis: Curt. 5.2.18–22, whereas DS 17.67.1 reports no weaving incident. Atkinson (1994) ad. loc. adduces evidence for weaving by Persian women, but not by queens or princesses. The objection to manual labor is akin to her earlier, but more polite, objection to being in the situation of a slave (Curt. 3.12.24).

80. In the winter of 334/3, Antipater helped Coenus and Meleager recruit 3,000 Macedonian infantry and 300 cavalry (Arr. *An.* 1.29.4). In mid-333, Antipater sent another 6,000 Macedonians and 9,000 others (Curt. 3.7.8). By the end of the year, Antipater added 5,000 more infantry and 800 cavalry (unless the source for this

report, Plb. 12.19.2, confused them with the troops sent earlier). The next winter, Antipater added 500 Thracian cavalry and 400 Greek mercenaries (Arr. *An.* 3.5.1). Not all these troops arrived in time for the battle of Issus, but if even only half did, they accounted for a large part of the Macedonian and total force. For total reinforcements, see Seibert (1986), 848. The last installment: DS 17.49.1; Curt. 4.6.30, 7.1.37–40. Alexander had been waiting for these troops for a year (Arr. *An.* 2.27). Consequent depletion of Antipater's and Macedon's manpower: Bosworth (1986), 5–9.

81. Adapted from *Tamid* 31b–32a. Besides references to Gen. 1–2 in the first two questions, the answer to no. 2 refers to Ps. 103.11–12. No. 4: Mishnah *Afot* 4.1. Of the two answers to no. 5, the second, practicing humility, was proposed by Rashi. Cf. the somewhat similar accounts at Plu. *Alex.* 64 and *Epit. Mett.* 78–84, with ten questions but set in India, and the very different account at Ps.-Call. A 3.6, also set in India. Shorter and less informative accounts: Arr. *An.* 7.1.5–2.1, Str. 15.1.61–65.

CHAPTER 7
A Vacant Throne

1. Some 40,000: Curt 5.8.3, listing 37,300 without mentioning royal guards. DS 17.73.2: 30,000, but no cavalry mentioned. Arr. *An.* 3.19.5: a mere 9,000, far too low in the light of Darius's decision to resist rather than flee.

2. The misconception of the Caucasus: Baeton *FGrH* 119 F 2a, with miscalculation of the distance from the Caspian to India (F 26). Prometheus ended up buried in the Hindu Kush, a part of the Caucasus (Arr. *An.* 5.3.3).

3. The intercession: App. 2 #15, attributing Greek gestures to the principals. The preceding campaign: Curt. 5.3.3–9. A version without supplication, except perhaps (δεηθῆναι) by Sisygambis to Alexander: Arr. *An.* 3.17.1–6.

4. The battle at the Gates: Arr. *An.* 3.18.1–10, without religious aspects, vs. Curt. 5.3.17–4.33, with an omen, a council, and an unperformed burial.

5. The omen and council at the Gates: App. 1a #27, App. 3 #18. A similar story, but involving a Lycian guide, inspired the suppositious oracle at App. 1b #16. Combat: Curt. 5.4.20–34, but enemy suicides as at Arr. *An.* 3.18.9.

6. The total haul, including Susa: up to 170,000 silver talents, as at Holt (2016), 188–89, at fifty-eight pounds per talent, or some 7,000 tons of silver, equaling, at $15 an ounce, some $3.5 billion. De Callatuÿ (1989), 272, revisited in (2011), 21, estimated only 2,000 tons of silver and 90 tons of gold for all treasures together, but at a silver-to-gold ratio of 13 to 1, the values of the metal is still well over $1 billion. Persian workers at Persepolis paid in weighed bullion: Joannès (1994), 142–44.

7. The deaths of the priests: Boyce and Grenet (1991), 3.116, quoting *AVN* 1.3.3–11 to this effect. The report in this Pahlavi text that Alexander burned the Avesta is less credible, since there is no evidence for manuscripts in the fourth century; Ciancaglini (1998), 71–72, 76, rejects the possibility that religious writings of the

Magi were burned rather than Avesta manuscripts. The reuse of the casket: Pl. *NH* 6.108.

8. The council meeting: App. 3 #19. No general destruction: Sancisi-Weerdenburg (1993). Similarly, the Macedonians destroyed the outer precincts of Halicarnassus (Arr. *An.* 1.24.6, DS 17.27.6) but did not destroy the monuments there (Pl. *NH* 35.172). Other views: an act of folly at Green (1991), 319, following the reasoning attributed to Parmenio at Arr. *An.* 3.8.11; partly drunken folly at Badian (1985), 485, following DS 17.72.2–4; an attempt to intimidate Darius at Borza (1972), 244, following DS 17.70.1, 71.3, speaking of hatred toward Persepolis; an act of religiously motivated revenge at Antela-Bernárdez (2016), 45–46, following Arr. *An.* 3.18.12, DS 17.72.5–6.

9. Greco-Macedonian sacrifice at the Persian capital: App. 1a #28. Many Persian gods, including some that were originally Elamite: Fort. 1316.101.28.

10. Sights at Pasargadae: Stronach (1978), 44–50; 107–13 with pl. 60; 138–45.

11. The scant attention given to this episode in the Alexander historians: Arr. *An.* 3.18.10, Curt. 5.6.10. Str. 15.3.7 reports the trip but only briefly, the rest of the section dealing with events from the return visit in 324.

12. The coronation ceremony at Pasargadae: Plu. *Arta.* 3.1–2. Anahita's status: A² Sa, Ha, Sd, all mentioning her as well as Ahura Mazda and Mithra. Her temple at nearby Estakr would be important for the Sassanids, as at Bivar and Boyce (1998). The Plutarch passage may derive from Ctesias; see Lenfant (2004), 145, 178–80.

13. The satraps of Persis: Orxines, Berve (1926), no. 591, replacing Phrasaortes (Arr. *An.* 6.29.2). Regarding the cuneiform inscription on the tomb, Onesikritos *FGrH* 134 F 34 was surely wrong to claim that the inscription was written in Persian characters translating Greek words. A similar meaning for the inscription: Aristios *FGrH* 134 F 1. Alternatively, the inscription was not on the tomb but nearby, as at Stronach (1978), 26.

14. Babylonian aspects of the tomb: Arr. *An.* 6.29.4–11, Curt. 10.1.3–33.

15. The visit to the tomb: Aristoboulos *FGrH* 139 F 51. Alexander's instructions to the priests may be deduced from his anger when he returned to Pasargadae in 324, as at Arr. *An.* 6.29.4–11, Curt. 10.1.30–38.

16. The contrary view: Badian (1996), 17, holding that Alexander was effectively crowned by wearing Persian dress. The Persian dress he wore was not, however, strictly royal. The purple *chlamys* was aristocratic and Macedonian, for he shared it with his generals; the *kausia* was Macedonian. Several sources say that he wore a Persian diadem (Ephippos *FGrH* 126 F 5, DS 17.77.5, Curt. 6.6.4), yet Persian princes wore diadems, just as the king did (X. *Cyr.* 8.3.13, Plu. *Frat. amor.* 488d). The remaining item, the *chiton*, was perhaps royal by virtue of the white stripe (X. *Cyr.* 8.3.13, Curt. 6.6.4); on the terms for "white," see Collins (2012), 387. For the upright tiara, see n. 45 below. Another contrary view: Briant (1996), 697, holding out the possibility that Alexander worshipped Persian gods in Anatolia, and thus gained legitimacy among Persians; rejected by Fredricksmeyer (2000), 143–45, also disallowing Alexander's worship of local gods in Anatolia.

17. Arrival of the mercenaries sent by Antipater: Curt. 5.7.12.

18. The Persian council: App. 3 #48. The cavalry: Arr. *An.* 3.19.5, Curt 5.8.3. At Arr. *An.* 3.19.4, however, Darius plans merely to flee, a plan that no council was likely to have reached.

19. Bactrian satrap as heir apparent: Sancisi-Weerdenburg (1980), 129–30, followed by Lenderling (2005), 214. A list of governors, many of whom became king: Rawlinson (1912), 149–50.

20. The winter march through the Zagros: Curt. 5.6.12–20. Better conditions: 5.7.12.

21. The statues at Ecbatana: Paus. 1.16.3, 8.46.3, returned to Greece by one of Alexander's successors, Seleucus, but not by Alexander. The donative: Arr. *An.* 3.19.5.

22. The new policy announced at Ecbatana: Arr. *An.* 3.19.5–8, Plu. *Alex.* 42.5. At Curt 6.3–6.4.1, Alexander dealt with army grievances at an assembly at Tabae, an illustration of this author's greater interest in this kind of meeting.

23. The Thespian inscription: *IG* vii 3206. The number of men dismissed: at a maximum, 7,000 allies (as at DS 17.7.4), plus allied reinforcements totaling 16,000 (as at Ch. 6, n. 80), but surely much smaller, because of the assignment of some men to garrisons and the reenlistment of others. A further 1,500 Thessalians and the total is very roughly 10,000.

24. The council meeting at Ecbatana: App. 3 #20, located by Curtius (6.3–6.4.1) in Tabae. In Curtius, however, Alexander makes no concessions to the generals, any more than he does to the troops.

25. The narrative of the pursuit of Darius: Arr. *An.* 3.20.1–21.1. Curtius reports that the news about Darius came in stages (5.13.3, 5.13.6–7), plus other differences and complications noticed at Bosworth (1980) ad. Arr. *An.* 3.21.1.

26. The narrative through Darius's death: Arr. *An.* 3.21.1–10, but with details taken from Plu. *Alex.* 43.1–5 (the force of 60 and the cloak) and Curt 5.13.7 (the interpreter) and 5.13.23–24 (the wagon).

27. The system was one of *qanats*, by which the underground pipes were developed from natural underground channels. In the era of Darius I, this system came into use at the Kharga oasis, where Darius built a shrine. Perhaps it was imported from Iran, as at Goblot (1963), 503–5. Alexander's use of the system: Plb. 10.28.

28. The burial in the wastelands: App. 1a #29.

29. The treacherous suppliants: App. 2 #16.

30. The burial of Darius: App. 1a #30. Stealing Darius's money: DS 17.74.5. Paying the sutlers: Pl. *NH* 35.110. Paying for luxuries: Plu. *Alex.* 54.2.

31. For the claims of Bessus, see n. 19 above. Lenderling (2005), 214, cites *ABC* 8 chr. 8, obv. 3–4, where the name of Bessus must be supplied, and the possibly lacunose *ABC* 8.112–13. Naveh and Shaked (2012), no. 1a, does not make clear which Artaxerxes is mentioned in the text.

32. Ancient views of the Verkana expedition: to capture fugitives (Arr. *An.* 3.23.1) and to protect adjoining territory (Curt. 6.4.1).

33. The three-way split of the forces: Arr. *An.* 3.23.2, Curt 6.4.2.

34. Measuring the underground river: Curt. 6.4.4–7, Arr. *An.* 3.23.4, neither acknowledging that the usual method for tracing an underground river was to use chaff, as at J. *BJ* 3.511–15.

35. Exaggerating Artabazus's ties to Philip through Pammenes: Lenschau (1949), failing to remark that Artabazus suspected Pammenes of treachery. Mercy for tribesmen: Arr. *An.* 3.24.2–3. No mercy for horse thieves: Plu. *Alex.* 44.2–3, *Fort. Alex.* 341b.

36. Caspian sacrifices: App. 1a #31. Caspian appointments: Autophradates, Berve (1926), no. 189 and Amminapes, no. 55.

37. Funeral of Nicanor: App. 1a #32.

38. The narrative of the rebellion: Arr. *An.* 3.25 (including forty men and the long march), Curt. 5.4.25–32 (only the march).Would-be suppliants denied a chance to beg before they were enslaved: Arr. *An.* 3.25.7, Curt. 6.6.33.

39. The first mountain siege of the expedition: Curt. 6.6.25–32.

40. The supplication: App. 2 #17. The drill: Ath. Mech. 10.11–12. This device would not have impressed defenders manning stone walls, as at Halicarnassus.

41. Brunt (1976), 497–99, explains the choice of route by Macedonian fear of further rebellion in Areia. Engels (1979), 186–91, explains the choice by the need for food and fodder following the unsuccessful pursuit of Shatibrzana. Lane Fox (1973), 282, emphasizes Alexander's distrust of the Persian satrap to the south.

42. Zarin, old Persian *Zranka*, as at Db 1.6, or modern Dāhān-e Gholāmān: Scerrato (1966a), (1966b). According to (1979), 733, the cult site is not Zoroastrian. Books from Harpalus: Plu. *Alex.* 8.3.

43. The *Euergetae* and Cyrus: Arr. *An.* 3.27.4–5, Curt. 7.3.1–3, neither describing the encounter with the Persian conqueror.

44. Some Persian elements in the mixed array that was Alexander's dress: Badian (1985), passim, summarized at 491 n. 2. Literary sources: Ritter (1965), ch. 1. Visual sources: Tuplin (2007a), 77–78. When Alexander began to wear Persian dress is unclear: Hyrcania at DS 17.77.4–7; Parthia at Plu. *Alex.* 45.1–4; Sogdiana implied at Arr. *An.* 4.7.4. Effeminate belt: Curt. 3.3.18, Plu. *Alex.* 51.5. Arrian on the clothes: *An.* 7.29.4. Plutarch (*Alex.* 45.1–4) and Diodorus (17.77.4–7) add that Alexander wished to dress in some fashion that would put foreigners at ease. A Persian companion: Plu. *Alex.* 43.1, Curt. 6.2.10.

45. No upright tiara for Alexander: Plu. *Alex.* 45.2, *Fort. Alex.* 329f. The upright tiara versus other tiaras, which did not designate the Persian king: Hdt. 7.61, X. *An.* 2.5.23, *Cyr.* 8.3.13, Klitarchos *FGrH* 137 F 5, Phylarch. *FGrH* 81 F 22. The upright tiara was not indispensable, for it is missing from extant Persian art, as noted by Tuplin (2007a).

46. The council meeting about Philotas: App. 3 #22. Curt. 6.7–11 allows an institutional role to the companions while reporting rivalries among them, and introduces the issue of Alexander's being the son of Amon (6.9.18, 6.10.23).

47. The council meeting about Alexander the Lyncestian: App. 3 #4. The bird omen: App. 1b #6.

48. The Lyncestian suffered so much in confinement that he could not speak coherently in his own defense (Curt. 7.1.8–9).

49. Philotas's supplication: App. 2 #19, although Philotas cannot have used the florid gestures found only in Curtius. Having the pages supplicate each other at an earlier stage of the conspiracy (#17) is perhaps dramatic license on Curtius's part. A second council meeting about, but this time without, Philotas: App. 3 #23. A violation of Philotas's right to attend: Hatzopoulos (1996), 331. Philotas and Alexander at dinner: Curt. 6.8.16.

50. The assembly of the army, as opposed to a council of officers, meets about Philotas: Arr. *An.* 3.36.2–3.

51. The third and last council meeting about Philotas: Ap. 3 #24.

52. The Greek custom of stoning those hateful to the gods: Cantarella (2011), 74–84. Stoning as a Macedonian custom: Curt. 6.11.38. It was not, however, the only method of capital punishment: Curt. 7.1.9.

53. The narrative as at Curt. 7.2.11–34, giving the only highly detailed account; cf. Arr. *An.* 3.26.3, Plu. *Alex.* 49.13, and other sources as at J. Hamilton (1999) at Plu. *Alex.* loc. cit.

54. For details concerning the fate of generals under Alexander, see Ch. 10, nn. 47–48. Alleged co-conspirators of Philotas acquitted: Arr. *An.* 3.27.1–2; Curt. 7.2.5–7, with a hint of supplication by the accused. Alexander's accusing three brothers of being co-conspirators of Philotas (Curt. 7.10–7.2.10) was inspired or at least excused by the Macedonian custom that the blood kin of those who commit capital crimes should be put to death (Curt. 8.6.28–29). The execution of the Lyncestian: Curt. 7.1.1–9 and DS 17.80.2, a proceeding dominated by council members. Another view, ignoring the council: Badian (2000), 57–60.

55. Other views: a long-laid plan against Parmenio that takes an unexpected form, as in Badian (2000), 63, relying on Plu. *Alex.* 48; a cabal by officers jealous of Philotas, as at Heckel (1977) and Bosworth (1988a), 101–4, relying on Plu. *Alex.* 49. In contrast, Droysen (1833), 145–48, thought that the conspiracy was genuine and that Alexander's orientalism was the reason for it. Droysen is partly right on both counts: the conspiracy was genuine, if insignificant, and "orientalism" of a sort was manifest in Alexander's obsession with his status as son of Amon.

56. Antipater's response to the Philotas affair: Plu. *Apophth. reg.* 183b. Antipater's hostility to Alexander's claim to be the son of Amon, or Zeus-Amon: Berve (1926), 2.50, citing Suid. s.v. Ἀντίπατρος.

57. Dispersal of powers: Arr. *An.* 3.29.7, partly because of the need to operate in smaller units on the Iranian plateau, a need that would only become greater in Bactria and Sogdiana. Parmenio's cavalry left at Ecbatana: Arr. *An.* 3.19.7. More cavalry and javelin men left in India: 6.15.2. Through these reassignments, along with the dismissal of the Thessalians, Alexander dismantled the left wing of the army. Corresponding forces on the right wing mostly remained with him. The Agrianians fought at the Hydaspes (Arr. *An.* 5.12.2), the *prodromoi* at the Tanais (4.4.6).

The Paeonians alone leave the scene earlier (last reported at Gaugamela, 3.13.4). *Prodromoi* absorbed by companion cavalry: Brunt (1976), lxxxv.

58. The only detailed account of Erigyius's expedition: Curt. 7.4.32–38; cf. Arr. *An.* 3.28.3. First use of Asiatics: Curt. 7.3.1.

59. Passes blocked by the Persians: Seibert (1985), 121. Which pass is uncertain: perhaps the Khawak or Kushan Passes, both 14,000 feet, or the Salang Pass, 12,700, or the Sibar Pass, 8,900; see Schachermeyr (1973), 676–81. Porters in the army: Arist. *Rh.* 1.7.32; Ar. fr. 896 K-A, and *Ran.* 8. Rigors of the climb: Arr. *An.* 3.28.9, Curt 7.3.12–18, DS 17.82.

60. Adapted from Firdausi 19.2. Alexander present at Darius's death: Ps.-Call. A 2.20, Al-Tabari 696, Nizami 1.30.110. Only at Nizami 1.29.105–14 is Darius murdered with Alexander's connivance. Cf. Alexander's eliminating Zoroastrianism at Nizami 1.32 and his even more violent attack on Zoroastrian libraries as well as temples at al-Tabari's Persian counterpart, Gardīzī 16.

CHAPTER 8
Sogdian In-laws

1. The rule of "warlords" in the countryside: the useful term of Holt (2005), passim, although Holt refuses to regard Artaxshasa as a warlord (36, 39).

2. Bactrian irrigation: Gardin (1980). Wealth: Hdt. 3.89–97. Poorer than Bactria, paying 360 talents: Syria (350 talents), Susa (300), Parthia (300), Moschi (300), Scythia (250), Matiene (200), Caspian region (200), Gandara (170). In spite of this wealth, few large cities: MacDowall and Tadei (1978), 214–18. The 1,000 cities of Justin 11.41.4 are settlements. Persian signal fires: Herzfeld (1947), 1.224 with refs.

3. The scene at the Amu Darya: Arr. *An.* 3.29.1–5. Six days to cross: Curt. 7.5.18.

4. The bargain with Spitamanah: Arr. *An.* 3.29.6, mentioning an embassy, as opposed to the melodramatic version at Curt. 7.5.19–26.

5. The degradation of Artaxshasa, with further grim details: Arr. *An.* 3.30.1–5, 4.7.3; Curt. 7.5.38, 7.10.10. The use of saplings: Plu. *Alex.* 43.6.

6. Alexander's fibula broken: Arr. *An.* 3.30.11. The less important tibia: Plu. *Alex.* 45.5, Curt. 7.6.2–8.

7. A vacant throne: so also Hammond (1986) and Fredricksmeyer (2000), except they posit that a throne of Asia replaced that of Persia. No political vacancy: Altheim (1953), 68, describing the struggle against the invaders as a pan-Iranian "Volkskrieg." Worthington (2014), 142, notices Alexander's religious limitations, but without reference to ceremonial requirements at Pasargadae or elsewhere.

8. The councilors gathered informally (App. 3 #25). The name "City of Cyrus": Benveniste (1943). Scythian diplomacy: Arr. *An.* 4.1.2.

9. The next injury: Arr. *An.* 4.4.3, but only Curt. 7.6.22–23 reports fainting and loss of speech. The casualties and slave sale: Arr. *An.* 4.3.4. Many in these campaigns were killed, as at Arr. *An.* 4.2.4, Curt. 7.6.16.

10. The engineering achievement at Alexandria *Eschatē*: Curt. 7.6.25. Dwarf apples: Theophrast. *HP* 4.4.2.

11. The companions vs. Alexander: App. 3 #26. More offerings: App. 1a #33 (festal sacrifice) vs. 34 (*apobatēria*). Cf. Curt. 7.7.8–9, 22–29, where the author sides with Alexander's seer against Alexander.

12. Macedonian casualties during the pursuit of the Scythians: Curt. 7.9.16, Arr. *An.* 4.4.6.

13. Versions of the battle: Arr. *An.* 4.5.4–9, following Ptolemy in portraying a breakdown among Macedonian officers; 6.1–2, following Aristobulus in blaming the Macedonians rather than Pharnuces; and Curt. 7.7.31–39, giving credit to Spitamanah for outflanking and surrounding the enemy.

14. Tardy burial: App. 1a # 35. The date of the battle is uncertain. Fall 328: Tarn (1948), 1.73. The following winter: Berve (1926), 207.

15. Macedonian casualties: Arr. *An.* 4.3.7, 4.5.9, Curt. 7.9.21. Blame given to Alexander: Arr. *An.* 4.3.7, 4.5.2–6.2, encasing this response to the defeat in a difference of opinion between Ptolemy and Aristobulus.

16. Economic and military elements in Alexander's formula of mixing ethnic groups: Bosworth (1988a), 247–48. The contrary view of the Central Asian cities, one condemning Alexander's policy as aggressive and counterproductive: Holt (2005), 70, 154–55.

17. Anahita, irrigation and fertility: *Yasht* 5.1–5. Medes: Plb. 10.27.12. Persians: as at Boyce (1984), 61–62; so also Berossos *FGrH* 680 F 11, who knew of the Mesopotamian cult of the goddess. The statue at Bactra: *Yasht* 5.126–31, as interpreted by Müller and Darmesteter (1898), 2.53. Worship of her image "among the Bactrians," hence in a shrine in Bactra: Berossos *FGrH* 680 F 11.

18. Sogdiana: Boyce and Grenet (1991), 191. Yet these customs were not universal or unaffected by other practices: Grenet (1984), 65; Boyce and Grenet (1991), 192–93.

19. The Macedonians report to Alexander, and he bans the burial practices: Onesikritos *FGrH* 134 F 5, Plu. *Fort. Alex.* 328d. The invaders should not have been surprised, since Hdt. 1.140 reports similar customs in connection with the Magi. Accepting the essentials of Onesicritus's report: Boyce and Grenet (1991), 7. Harder to credit: Pahlavi reports that Alexander destroyed manuscripts of the Avesta at Samarkand at this time, as at Ciancaglini (1998), 73.

20. The petroleum omen: App. 1b #18. Olive oil: Arr. *An.* 4.15.7, Plu. *Alex.* 57.5–9. Water: Curt. 7.10.14, with the Persian religious touch noticed by Jamzadeh (2012), 128.

21. Babylonian diviners at work in Central Asia: App. 1b #19.

22. The capture of Peithon: Arr. *An.* 4.16.5–7, followed by the counterattacks of Craterus and Coenus, 4.17.1–6. Mere "pockets of resistance": Bosworth (1988a), 116.

23. The last campaign of Spitamanah: Arr. *An.* 4.17.3–6. His death: 4.17.7. Curtius does not connect any late campaigns (8.2.13–19) to the death (8.3).

24. Alexander's new haughtiness: Plu. *Phoc.* 17. Censorship: Justin 12.5.7–8. Less loot in the way of silver: Holt (2016), 181–93, although he does not divide income by

province. Bactria and Sogdiana contributed far less than large regions either before or after, excepting only Egypt and Babylonia, which provided no slaves since they had surrendered without a fight.

25. Planned or eventual garrisons: Arr. *An.* 4.22.3, DS 18.7.2.

26. The appointment: Curt. 8.1.19, 35. The reluctance of Clitus: Lane Fox (1973), 310–13. A survey of older scholarly literature on this episode: Bosworth (1995) ad Arr. *An.* 4.8, observing "all sources have something to contribute," and J. Hamilton (1999) ad. Plu. *Alex.* 50–52.2.

27. The ominous sacrifice on Clitus's behalf, preceded by his sacrifice and Alexander's: App. 1a #36.

28. Companions jointly supplicate Alexander, a *hapax drōmenon*: App. 2 #21. This version of events: Curt. 8.1.22–52.

29. The second version of Clitus's death: Plu. *Alex.* 50.8–51, derived from Chares as at J. Hamilton (1999) ad loc. It is characteristic of Plutarch that Clitus had proved himself a cultural match for Alexander (as he previously had in another way, by commissioning a portrait by Apelles, as at Pl. *NH* 35.93).

30. The third version: Arr. *An.* 4.8–9, which is also the source for the sacrifices discussed above and below.

31. The boundary stones of Dionysus: Curt. 7.9.15. The intellectuals (and Alexander) knew E. *Ba.* 15–16, referring to Dionysus in Bactria, and even if they did not, because these lines were interpolated later as discussed at Bosworth (1996), 120 n. 106, they recalled the offense given to this god by the mistreatment of suppliants at Thebes (App. 2 #1).

32. No weeping by Alexander at Arr. *An.* 4.9.2, where he is not said to have attempted suicide; tears, groans, and a suicide attempt at Plu. *Alex.* 51.11; stern self-condemnation and a suicide attempt at Curt. 8.2.2–4. These reactions correspond to the kind of killing found in each author—voluntary manslaughter in the first two, since Alexander kills Clitus on the spur of the moment, as noted by Bosworth (1995) ad Arr. *An.* 4.8.9, and murder in Curtius, since Alexander stalks his victim. However, ancient Greek legal categories, or at least those known to us, differ somewhat from those of the contemporary English-speaking world. There was no contrast between "murder" and "manslaughter," but instead a contrast between *phonos ek pronoias* and *phonos akousios*, or intentional homicide and unintentional homicide, with intentional homicide sometimes being construed broadly, so that killing with an intent merely to do harm would be considered "intentional." All three sources would thus render Alexander guilty of the more serious crime, *phonos ek pronoias*. See MacDowell (1978), 115.

33. Aristander's way of blaming Clitus: Plu. *Alex.* 52.1. Companions preferring to blame Dionysus: Arr. *An.* 4.8.1. Badian (1964), 197, regards the suicide attempt as a fake.

34. A negative view of the situation in Bactria and Sogdiana in early 327: Holt (2005), 93. A positive view: Bosworth (1988a), 116–17.

35. The disastrous fire: Curt. 8.4.1–19, Val. Max. 5.1 ext. 1.

36. The largesse of the warlord: Curt. 8.4.19–20.

37. Rewards for scaling the heights above the Rock of Sogdiana, an event presented here using Arrian's chronology, nomenclature, and list of principals (*An.* 4.18.5–19.4), not those of the Vulgate, preferred by Bosworth (1988a), 116 with refs. Rewards for each of the first ten climbers, as in Curt. 7.11.2–21, raise the total to fifty-five talents, still a modest sum in light of the figures in Holt (2016), 181–93.

38. Success of the settlement reached between Alexander and Huxshiartas: Arr. *An.* 4.21.1. If Curtius is right to report that some captives were sent to new colonies (Curt. 7.11.29), Huxshiartas may have guessed at Alexander's colonization plans.

39. According to Arr. *An.* 4.19.5, the marriage took place at or near the Rock of Sogdiana, as here, but according to Curt. 7.11.1, 8.4.23, it took place elsewhere in Sogdiana, the version preferred by J. Hamilton (1999) ad Plu. *Alex.* 48.7 with refs. In Arrian, the marriage is an act of infatuation that the author does not endorse, as noticed by Bosworth (1995) ad loc.; in Curtius, the companions condemn the infatuation (8.4.30); neither author regards it as a political act.

40. Ancient Iranian marriage customs: Karimi Zanjani Asl (1999). Contemporary use of these customs: de la Porte (2004), 12.

41. The Iranian, not Macedonian, custom of bride and groom breaking bread together: F. von Schwarz (1906), 82, correcting Curt. 8.4.27.

42. An Iranian, not Macedonian, marriage ceremony: Lane Fox (1973), 317; Berve (1926), 1.357. Macedonian: Bosworth (1988a), 117 with refs. Mixed: Radet (1931), 254. A marriage to a slave, not an ally's daughter: Curt. 8.4.26–30, reflecting the view of some offended companions.

43. In regard to Alexander's children, *Epit. Mett.* 70 reports that Roxana bore Alexander a son in the summer of 326, only to see the baby die very soon afterward.

44. The most important resistance after the settlement achieved in Sogdiana: Curt. 8.1.6, with 1,000 casualties inflicted by Craterus in Paraetacene in the summer of 327. Other views: Howe (2016), 172, holding that some warlords wished to succeed Artaxshasa; Lane Fox (2007), holding that Alexander did not wish to duplicate Persian titles or methods; Bosworth (1988a), 117, holding that this phase of the campaign was "an act of conquest" as opposed to pacification.

45. Numerous Persians in the entourage: Curt. 6.2.9, reporting "a thousand" leading Iranians switched sides. As early as 328, Alexander made use of Persian guards—one of Clitus's complaints (Plu. *Alex.* 51.1). The leading versions of the *proskynesis* episode (Arr. *An.* 4.10.1–4.12.7, Curt. 8.5.5–8.6.1, Plu. *Alex.* 54–55) all describe pressure exerted by Alexander on the companions, but not an ukase on his part, as noticed by Badian (1981), 48–54. Cyrus the Great as a possible model for this and other changes made by Alexander: Olbrycht (2014), 52–54. Further references: Sisti (2001), 2.400–411.

46. *Proskynesis* by Themistocles: Plu. *Them.* 28.1–29.2. Varying definitions of *proskynesis* to the Great King: Briant (2002), 222–24. The relation between supplication and *proskynesis*: Naiden (2009), 236–39. A survey: Delatte (1951).

47. The response of Leonnatus: Arr. *An.* 4.12.2. The response of Polyperchon, who does not appear in this passage in Arr. *An.*: Curt. 8.5.22–26.1. Later high command for Polyperchon: Curt. 8.11.1 with Heckel (1992), 190–91.

48. Different views of this episode: Bosworth (1988a), 287, holding that Alexander, like other Greeks and Macedonians, did not understand *proskynesis* as the Persians did, and thus believed that he was asking his own men to treat him as a god; Badian (1996) agreeing that Alexander was asking for divine treatment, but insincerely. Bowden (2013) traces interpretations of this kind to authors of the Imperial period as opposed to Alexander's contemporaries. Scholars minimizing any misunderstanding on Alexander's part: Wilcken (1932), 168–70; Lane Fox (1973), 322–23; Spawforth (2007), 104. Further refs.: J. Hamilton (1999) ad Plu. *Alex.* 54.3.

49. One hundred is merely an estimate of the number of pages; Berve (1926), 1.37 n. 3, identified only thirteen individuals as pages, as noted by Heckel (2016), 248. Callisthenes's claim that Greek oracles recognized Alexander as a god: Kallisthenes *FGrH* 124 F 14, the oracular reports being thought genuine by Habicht (1970), 23.

50. Callisthenes and *proskynesis*: Plu. *Alex.* 54.3–6 and the very similar Arr. *An.* 4.3.5. *Proskynesis* by the waves of the Mediterranean: Kallisthenes *FGrH* 151 F 1.2.

51. The hunting incident: Arr. *An.* 4.13.2, Curt. 8.6.7. Hermolaus's father: Berve (1926), no. 736.

52. The omen discerned by the Syrian prophetess: App. 1b #20. The trial of Hermolaus: App. 3 #27.

53. Hermolaus's critique of Alexander the god: Curt. 8.7.13, 8.8.14. The political leanings of Sopolis and the fathers of the other pages are unknown.

54. The manner of punishment chosen for Hermolaus and his co-defendants: Arr. *An.* 4.14.3.

55. The trial of Callisthenes: App. 3 #28.

56. Callisthenes rejects the tyranny and divinity of Alexander: Arr. *An.* 4.11.6–7. Only his tyranny: Plu. *Alex.* 55.2. The banality of the contrast between *nomos* and *bia*: Bosworth (1995) ad Arr. *An.* 4.11.6 with refs.

57. Callisthenes's death due to mistreatment: Chares *FGrH* 125 F 15, Aristoboulos *FGrH* 139 F 33. Otherwise he was hanged (Ptolemy *FGrH* 138 F 17), or died after being tortured (Curt. 8.9.21). Both Callisthenes and Alexander had annotated copies of the *Iliad* (Kallisthenes *FGrH* 124 T 10), but Callisthenes also wrote on Homeric topography (F 6–7).

58. The funeral of Erigyius: App. 1a #37.

59. Three among many views of Alexander and the Iranians: Briant's claim in 1979 that Alexander was the last of the Achaemenids followed by the responses of Lane Fox (2007) and Wiemar (2007).

60. The size of the army taken to India: 120,000 (Curt. 8.5.4); cf. 120,000 at the start of the voyage down the Hydaspes (Arr. *Ind.* 19.5), and 135,000 at the end of the Indian campaign (Plu. *Alex.* 66.2). Forty thousand reinforcements: see Ch. 6, n. 80. Forty-five thousand in Central Asia: Arr. *An.* 4.22.3. Some 10,000 dismissed:

Ch. 7, n. 23. The number may also be calculated by using the sums of money paid these troops; see Bosworth (1980) ad Arr. *An.* 3.19.5.

61. Scylax's voyage: Skylax *FGrH* 709 T 3a as in Kaplan (2009) with refs., especially Schiwek (1962), 8–19, warning against drawing anachronistic distinctions among war, commerce, and exploration.

62. The first Indian in the entourage, Sasigupta or Sissicottus, as at Berve (1926), no. 707. Scylax on kings: Skylax *FGrH* 709 F 5.

63. The performance of Indian troops at Gaugamela: Arr. *An.* 3.8.3–6, 14.5–15.2; Curt. 4.9.2.

64. Semiramis as Alexander and the Greeks thought they knew her: Ktesias *FGrH* 688 F 475, 570. Similar name: Sammuramat, regent of Assyria 811–806, although many other elements of history and also myth entered into the "Semiramis" of the Greeks, as at Pettinato (1988), 305–8.

65. Specimens for Aristotle: cotton and rice (Str. 15.1.18–20), volumes (Pl. *NH* 6.26), elephants (Thphr. *HA* 596a).

66. Specimens or experiences attractive to Alexander because of his *pothos*, manifest in India as follows: Arr. *An.* 5.2.5, to see Nysa; 7.7.2, to keep company with an Indian sage at Taxila; Arr. *Ind.* 20.1, to sail from India to Persia. Tigers called "manticores": Ktesias 688 *FGrH* F 16.15.

67. The plan of campaign: Arr. *An.* 4.22.7, 4.23.1, Curt. 8.10.2–4. As Bosworth observes ad Arr. *An.* 4.22.7, the main force may have often been split in two, one part under Hephaestion, one under Perdiccas.

68. The Nysaeans supplicate: App. 2 #23. Mount Meros: Arr. *An.* 5.1.5–7 with *Ind.* 1.4–6. Skeptical: Str. 15.1.8. Nysa in Ethiopia: Hdt. 2.146. Accepting the essence of the story—the visit to the city and the link to Dionysus—are the numerous scholars listed by Bosworth (1995) ad Arr. *An.* 5.1.1.

69. Midas and India: Hyg. *Fab.* 91.

70. Ionian Greeks in the east: Str. 14.1.5, Curt. 7.5.28–31, Hdt. 6.9 (a threat to send Greeks into exile in Central Asia). Dionysus in the East: E. *Ba.* 13–15 with later sources at Bosworth (1996a), 119–23. Bosworth attributes the myth to Alexander's interpreters, not to his hosts, as also at (1996b), 166–68. Attributing the myth to the hosts: Narain (1965), 157. Attributing the episode to the Alexander historians rather than Alexander or his hosts: Biffi (2005), 149.

71. Shiva and Skanda: Daniélou (1982), 91–98 with refs. Dionysus as Shiva, not Skanda: Karttunen (1989), 212–16. Supposing that these identifications would lay the foundation for a kingdom in India: Antela-Bernárdez (2007).

72. The campaign prior to the Rock of Aornos: Arr. *An.* 4.23–27, Curt. 8.10.5–7, 8.10.19–28. Leaders wounded in the Kabul Valley: Arr. *An.* 4.23.3.

73. The wound suffered by Alexander in the Kabul Valley: either the ankle (Arr. *An.* 4.26.4), the calf (Curt. 8.28), or the leg (Plu. *Alex.* 28.3)—the usual anatomical contrast between the more decorous Arrian and the less decorous Vulgate. Extermination of the population of the first large town: unless, against all odds, the mother and

daughter of the now-dead king survived, as in Curt. 8.10.23–35, and thus the mother was able to supplicate, using the rare and exclusively Greek gesture of sending an infant son of hers toddling over to the supplicandus, Alexander, as at App. 2 #22.

74. Avarna or the Greek Aornos: Bosworth (1995) ad Arr. *An.* 4.28.1 with refs. The identification: Stein (1929), 128–53, and (1937), 1–104, acting on a suggestion from Col. R. Wauhope, RE, who had surveyed the western bank of the upper Indus during the Black Mountain campaigns in 1880s—the first European invasion of the area since Alexander. Doubts: Karttunen (1997), 49.

75. The struggle at Avarna: Arr. *An.* 4.28–30.5, used here, as opposed to Curt. 8.11.2–24. Doubts about Krishna being the model, or at least the only model: Karttunen (1989), 211–12. Alexander was not above combining gods in selfish or idiosyncratic fashion, as happened at Tyre.

76. The sacrifice atop Avarna: App. 1a #39. No supreme god is named, but perhaps Alexander sacrificed to this god, Athena, and Heracles, following the pattern on display at Issus. Curt. 8.11.24 prefers Athena and Nike.

77. The story of the aerial flight is adapted from Ps.-Call. Γ 2.41. Muslim versions are numerous. Among Hebrew versions: *'Abodah Zarah* 3.1, *Numbers Rabbah* 13.14.

CHAPTER 9
Self-Defeat

1. Movement of the Indian plate: Verma (1991), ch. 1.

2. Comparative size of great rivers: Kretch, McNeill, and Merchant (2004), s.v. "Indus River." So also Ar. *Ind.* 4.12, and Pseudo-Krateros *FGrH* 153 F 2, putting both the Indus and the Ganges ahead of the Nile.

3. The history of the Sarasvati River: Kenoyer (1998), 27. Sarasvati's course: Bryant (2001), 168. The change of course occurred before the notice taken at Rig Veda 3.33, where the Sutlej is already joined to the Beas as opposed to the Sarasvati. Another view: Francfort (1985), 260, holding that the desiccation of the Sarasvati occurred well before the second millennium. Early origin of the desert: Trivedi (2009), 45.

4. Mount Everest rising a little each year: Swiss Foundation for Alpine Research (1999), 11–12. Five to six centimeters (2 to 2.3 inches): National Geographic Society (1999). Indian notions of a world mountain: Kirfel (1991), 15–19; de la Vallée Poussin (1971), 3.156. Water quality at this mountain: *L'Abhidharmakośa de Vasubandhu* 3.144. Hindu rings around the mountain: Kirfel (1991), 57–127. Buddhist version: *L'Abhidharmakośa de Vasubandhu* 3.138. Jain version: Schubring (1962), 217–18.

5. A more generous view of Persian knowledge of India: Briant (2002), 754–58. Pre-Persian knowledge, which died away in the second millennium BC during the decline of the Mohenjo-Daro civilization: Karttunen (1989), ch. 2. Doubts about Persian contacts with the Ganges valley: Karttunen (1989), 64.

6. Harahvati from Sarasvati: loss of the initial sibilant. Similarly, *Hindush*, the Persian term for the Indian province in the Achaemenid Empire, as at Kent (1950),

136–38, where the term appears in the Persepolis and Naqsh-e Rustam inscriptions, is derived from the ancient Indian *Sindhu*, meaning the same region as modern Sind. *Hindush*, in turn, yielded the Greek name *Indos* by loss of the initial aspirant. Alexander's intellectuals, however, did not realize that the name *Indos* derived from a word that referred to a single region rather than the entire subcontinent.

7. Elephants flinging themselves over a cliff to escape capture by Alexander and his party: Arr. *An.* 4.30.8. The invaders did not use the native hunting methods known to Megasthenes, *FGrH* 175 F 20.

8. The Indus bridge: Arr. *An.* 5.3.5 with Rollinger (2013), 67–72, on "Schiffsbrücken." The likely spot: Udabhanda, as at Foucher (1942), 51. The modern crossing point near Attock is hilly and especially difficult in flood season: Caroe (1958), 33. Sacrifices at the Indus: App. 1a #40, preceded by #1 (Danube) and 6 (Hellespont).

9. Information available at Taxila: Engels (1980), 328. Misinformation about Ambhi's name: Curt. 8.12.14.

10. Marshall (1951) describes culture and science in the city at 1.45–49, but without remarks about religion. Study of the Vedas at Taxila in the Achaemenid era: Prakash (1976), 140–42.

11. A generation later, Megasthenes described some of the differences between Greek and Indian practices at *FGrH* 715 F 32. Strangulation etc.: *Kātyāyana Srauta Sūtra* 6.5.17.

12. Writing in northwestern India: Nearchos *FGrH* 133 F 23. *Arthśāstra* 1.2, 6 refer to religious works likely to have been among the first compositions reduced to writing.

13. Ascetics mistaken for Cynics: Onesikritos *FGrH* 134 F 17, Plu. *Alex.* 65. No Cynicism: Aristoboulos *FGrH* 139 F 41. Tirthankara: Stevenson (1908), 1.414–15. Locating the encounter with the gymnosophists at Taxila: Aristoboulos loc. cit., Ps-Call. A 3.13.9–10. Just outside the city: Onesikritos loc. cit. Locating it somewhere in the kingdom of Samba (or Sabba): Plu. *Alex.* 64.

14. Vasuveda as Heracles: Curt. 8.14.11.

15. The issue of Alexander's response to Indian religion: Karttunen (1989), 228–29, noting that he surely paid attention to the Brahmins, the most powerful of the three and also the most interested in sacrifice. Stupas at Taxila, perhaps in the Achaemenid period: Dani (1986), 41–42. The earliest securely dated examples of stupas admittedly date from the third century BC, not the late fourth, as at Coningham (2001).

16. Gifts by kings sometimes forbidden: *Law of Manu* 4.84. In Pallad. 3–4, Alexander does make one acceptable gift, oil, which may be used to honor the fire on which it is poured (*Law of Manu* 3.210).

17. Gifts and tribute: 200 talents before reaching the city (Arr. *An.* 5.3.5), or 600 (*Epit. Mett.* 52), and then 80 talents in coin (Curt. 8.12.15), amounting to less than the 1,000 given to Ambhi by Alexander (Plu. *Alex.* 59.5). The promised booty and the complaint of a jealous companion: Curt. 8.13.15–17, concerning Meleager, who, as

observed by Green (1991), 387, never received another promotion from Alexander. The Macedonian, not Indian, sacrifices at Taxila: App. 1a #41. The garrison and other particulars: Arr. *An.* 5.8.3.

18. As shown in App. #3, this is the only major battle without a council to discuss plans rather than hear orders as at Curt. 8.14.15–16, and a meeting is thus supplied to let the Macedonians plan both the division of forces (Arr. *An.* 5.9.2–3) and the *dolus* described by Curt. 8.13.17. Alexander's personal plan: Fuller (1958), 186. The complex orders for the subordinates, which must have been discussed collectively: Hammond (1980), 210.

19. Alexander's stratagems and difficulties: Arr. *An.* 5.10.1–4. The use of skins was no new trick: the Assyrians used inflatable skins, as at Barnett, Bleibtreu, and Turner (1999), no. 273.

20. The number of troops: Arr. *An.* 5.14.1, somewhat lower than suggested by the roster given at 5.12.2, a difference to be explained by lack of boats, as at Bosworth (1995) ad loc. Cutting up the boats: Casson (1971), 160–61. The error about the island in the river: Arr. *An.* 5.13.2. Alexander's pre-battle stratagems became canonical: Front. *Strat.* 1.7.9–9a, Polyaen. 4.39. Modern praise of Alexander's generalship during the battle begins with these stratagems: Fuller (1958), 186–88; Milns (1968), 215; Green (1991), 293.

21. Handling the enemy chariots: Curt. 8.14.4, more elaborate than Arr. *An.* 5.13.3. The comparison of elephants and castles: Curt. 8.14.13.

22. Coenus's maneuver: Arr. *An.* 5.16.3, Curt. 8.14.15–18, in each case one of several orders given by Alexander to subordinates riding with him. As Bosworth (1995) observes ad Arr. *An.* 5.16.3, Coenus is replacing Parmenio as chief commander on the left, but leads cavalry alone.

23. Coenus may have ridden behind the entire Indian force, a route placing greater responsibility on him: Green (1991), 398. In front of the elephants but behind cavalry forces that Porus sent forward to halt Alexander, an alternative giving Coenus less scope: Fuller (1958), 192; Milns (1968), 212; Hammond (1980), 213.

24. Attack and elephant counterattack: Arr. *An.* 5.17.3; Curt 8.14.22 says only that Porus ordered the elephants forward. Alexander's attack also sought to draw out Porus's cavalry, a preliminary step: Fuller (1958), 196–97; Milns (1968), 214. The timing and coordination displayed by the Macedonians: Fuller (1958), 188, asking, "How was it possible to carry out all these operations in [about] 15 hours? The staff work of the Macedonian army must have been superb." That, General, requires numerous, structured meetings. Heavy Macedonian casualties: DS 17.89.3 reporting 980 and the *Mett. Epit.* 61 1,200. The 310 at Arr. *An.* 5.18.3 is much too low. The Indian losses reported at Arr. *An.* 5.24.3, DS 17.89.2 are exaggerated, but numbered some thousands.

25. The approach made to Puru: Arr. *An.* 5.18.6–7, except that Arrian does not acknowledge Puru's charge of treason, found at Curt. 8.14.36. The question of the identity of Meroes is vexatious. Candragupta Maurya was identified as Arrian's

Indian messenger "Meroes" by F. F. Schwarz (1968), 225, although the identification is rejected by Karttunen (1997), 259, as well as by Berve (1926), no. 518, and Bosworth (1995) ad loc. If Schwarz is right, *Meroes* or *Maurya* must be explained as a clan name, and *Sandracottus*, the Hellenization of *Candragupta*, must be a personal name. Arrian calls him an "old friend" of Puru's, whereas Plu. *Alex.* 53.9, preferred to Arrian by J. Hamilton ad loc., says he was only a *merakion*, and thus unsuited for this diplomatic mission.

26. "Porus" in Pakrit: *paurava*, a tribal name of the ancient Punjab, as in Bevan (1935), 349–52.

27. The bargaining between Puru and Alexander: "Treat me like a King" (Arr. *An.* 5.19.2, in an account that minimizes Alexander's concessions, which are confined to restoring Porus's kingdom to him), and "Treat me as this day shows you should" (Curt. 8.14.43, including the concessions of additional territory and status as a companion, or *amicus*, at 8.14.45). Plu. *Alex.* 60.14–16 combines Arrian's reply with territorial concessions. DS 17.89.6 agrees with Arrian's report of one concession. The version given by Curtius is the only one to allude to the Indian army's competent performance during the battle. Other views: Bosworth (1995) ad Arr. *An.* 5.18.4–19.2.

28. A somewhat different view of the problem of conquering a vast, hostile area: Droysen (1833), 210, recognizing that Alexander had to control leaders, not peoples, but supplying a feudal context. The contrary view, regarding the battle as a complete victory, and the surrender terms as unproblematic: Bosworth (1988a), 129.

29. Religious rituals after the battle: App. 1a #42, 43.

30. The only report of numerous Indian coins: Curt. 8.12.15. A description of the famed medallions including not only these decadrachms but also tetradrachms with similar iconography: Holt (2003), 93, observing that some were overstruck on Babylonian staters. Other views: Holt (2003), 96–101.

31. Alexander is perhaps carrying a scepter, not a spear: Holt (2003), 121–22. No such contradiction between divine and human instruments: the lost portrait by Apelles, showing Alexander with a thunderbolt, provided that this portrait showed Alexander on a throne (Plu. *Alex.* 4.2, Pl. *NH* 7.125).

32. Foraging: Arr. *An.* 5.21.4. Twenty cubits of high water on the Chenab at the time of the summer solstice: Nearchos *FGrH* 133 F 18, Aristoboulos *FGrH* 139 F 35. Wrecked boats and a "great many" drowned: Arr. *An.* 5.20.9.

33. The Nile supposedly found in India: Arr. *An.* 6.1.4–5. The lotuses found in India: Nearchos *FGrH* 133 F 20. The Chenab, not the Nile: F 10b. Cutting wood: Curt. 9.1.3–4. Teakwood was commonly used in ancient Indian boats, especially for long voyages such as Alexander contemplated. An example: Sidebotham (2011), 225–26.

34. India's "big monkeys": Str. 15.1.29; so also Ael. *VH* 17.25. Stone-throwing monkeys: Str. 15.1.56. Multicolored: Kleitarchos *FGrH* 137 F 19.

35. Sangala described here as in Diodorus: App. 2 #24. The Macedonian funerals: App. 1a. #44. Almost 100 Macedonian dead: Arr. *An.* 5.24.5. Arr. *An.* 5.22–24 and

Curt. 9.1.1–18 report no supplication but the same result, unconditional surrender. As Bosworth (1995) observes ad Arr. *An.* 5.22.1–24.8, the three versions essentially differ, just as the versions of the Granicus battle do.

36. Differing estimates as to how much Alexander knew about the Ganges: Bosworth (1996a), 186–200; Green (1991), 404–5. The best single piece of evidence: a letter supposedly written to Alexander by Craterus, who tells the king the Ganges is enormous (Str. 15.1.35). Ten years later, the forces of north India would reportedly total either 600,000 infantry, 30,000 cavalry and 9,000 elephants (Pl. *NH* 6.22.4), or 400,000 altogether (Megasthenes *FGrH* 715 F 32). The estimated number of enemy elephants: 4,000 (DS 17.93.2) to 6,000 (Plu. *Alex.* 62.2). Indian advice given to Alexander (but not mentioning Sandracottus): Curt. 9.2.1–18.

37. Disaffection: Arr. *An.* 5.25.2, Curt. 9.2.3, DS 17.93.2–3, with characteristic differences, Arrian reporting complaints about the toils of campaigning, Curtius reporting that Alexander provoked discontent by giving an address to the army, and Diodorus reporting bad weather as well as exhaustion.

38. Council meetings on the morale problem: App. 3 #21. Assembly meetings: Curt. 6.2.21–6.4.1, 9.2.12–9.3.18. Foraging: Arr. *An.* 5.21.4, and also DS 17.94.2–4, where Alexander promises food to camp followers.

39. Seventy days of rain: DS 17.94.3, Str. 15.1.27.

40. The first meeting: App. 3 #29. For this and two later meetings Curtius substitutes a *contio* (9.2.12–9.3.18) and Plutarch a mass supplication (App. 2 #29). Independent commands for Coenus: Arr. *An.* 3.18.6, Curt. 5.4.20 (Persian Gates); Arr. *An.* 4.6.2, 4.17.3 (Sogdiana); Arr. *An.* 4.27.5, Curt. 8.10.22 (Western India); Arr. *An.* 5.21.1, Curt. 8.12.1 (India). The same for Craterus: Arr. *An.* 3.18.6, Curt. 5.4.15 (Persian Gates); Arr. *An.* 3.23.2 & 25.6 (Hyrcania); 4.2.2 (Sogdiana); 4.22.1, 4.23.5 (Western India); 4.28.7 (near the Rock of Aornos); 5.11.3 (Hydaspes battle), 5.20.2 (at same site); and perhaps Curt. 8.10.4 (near Nysa). Similarly, leadership of wings of the army: Arr. *An.* 5.17.1, Curt. 8.14.15 (Coenus); Arr. *An.* 2.8.4, 2.20.6 (Craterus).

41. Opinions of Alexander's speech: Hammond (1999), 248, saying that the speech is substantially accurate, vs. Bosworth (1988b), 124–25, calling it largely invented. Both views underestimate Ptolemy's contribution—his command of social niceties like the role of seniority, and his confidence in geographical detail latter proved to be erroneous, like the location of the mouth of Ganges. A view that the speech is unsatisfactory, but that Alexander meant it to be so, in order to discourage his men: Endres (1924), 12–15, followed by Heckel (2003), 25. Unlike many speeches attributed to Alexander, this one is very similar in Arrian and Curtius Rufus, for both writers emphasize the theme of conquering all Asia (Arr. *An.* 5.25.3–26, Curt. 9.2.12–30).

42. The second council meeting: App. 3 #30.

43. Antipater's literary work: *Suda* s.v. Ἀντίπατρος. Greek famine: *GHI* 196.3, 6, 22.

44. The third council meeting: App. 3 #31. The announcement of bad omens: App. 1a #45.

45. Other views of this episode: Worthington (2004), 95–96, saying that Alexander would lose his throne if he did not keep his men busy fighting; and Badian (2000),

73–74, saying that it was risky for Coenus to speak. Similarly, Keegan (1993), 42, speaks of a "mutiny," whereas Carney (1996), 42, rightly prefers "quarrel." After a mutiny, Alexander might have ordered a purification of the army, as after the disturbances at X. *An.* 5.7.35 and Curt. *Alex.* 10.9.11. A romantic link between king and soldiers broken (and no role for the officers as a group): Wilcken (1932), 150.

46. Alexander's commemorative altars: App. 1a #46.

47. Supposed use of the altars by Indian rulers: Plu. *Alex.* 62.4–7. Washed away, leaving no remains: Stein (1937), ch. 1. Another view: Foucher (1938), 350, holding that Alexander had reached the easternmost Persian possessions, and erected the altars for this reason.

48. When Sandracottus rose to power is uncertain. As soon as Alexander left: Narain (1965), 162, following Buddhist tradition. By 317: Lamotte (1958), 239–41, closer to Jain tradition, which is 312. Philostrat. *VA* 2.43 says that an unnamed Indian ruler erected a brass obelisk saying only, "Alexander stopped here." This inscription implies that the altars had already decayed so much that they were not identifiable.

49. The council meeting before the voyage: App. 3 #32. The funeral of Coenus: App. 1a #47; Arr. *An.* 6.3.1 adds, "as elaborate as circumstances permitted." That of Bucephalas: Plu. *Alex.* 61.

50. Alexander borrowing money: Plu. *Eum.* 2.3–5, saying that he borrowed 300 talents from Eumenes, who had 1,000.

51. The sacrifice to the Indus at the start of the voyage. App. 1a #48. Arr. *Ind.* 18.11 adds rivers in the Punjab, perhaps as remembered by Nearchus; thus Pédech (1984), 177. Fleet of 1,800 vessels: Arr. *Ind.* 19.7.

52. The hazards of the confluence of the Jhelum and Chenab: Arr. *An.* 6.5; Curt 9.4.9–14, DS 17.97.

53. Complaints of troops tired of fighting: Curt. 9.4.19–23.

54. The Malavas are the Malli of Arr. *An.* 6.8.8–6.12, Curt. 9.4.15–9.6, and Plu. *Alex.* 63, and the Mandri of Justin 12.9.3–12. The refusal to cooperate: Arr. *An.* 6.14.2. The chief town was perhaps modern Multan.

55. The Malava campaign and final siege: chiefly as at Arr. *An.* 6.8.4–6.13.5. The acts of sacrifice: App. 1b #21 and App. 1a #49.

56. The wound suffered by Alexander during the siege: Arr. *An.* 6.10.1–2, Curt. 9.5.25–27, DS 17.99, Plu. *Fort. Alex.* 344–45, which are unanimous about the seriousness of the injury. The need to extract the whole arrowhead: Hipp. *Epid.* 5.1.94–95 = 7.1.121. The surrender of the Malavas: Arr. *An.* 6.14.1–3.

57. The council meeting on the issue of Alexander's leadership: App. 3 #33. The king's unacceptable number of wounds: head (Granicus), neck (Sogdiana), shoulder (Gaza), chest (India), thigh (Issus), lower leg (at the Jaxartes), ankle or foot (beside the Kabul R.), the largest number of wounds reported for any ancient person according to Salazar (2000), 184. By comparison, Philip II was wounded on three occasions, described at Gabriel (2010), 10–14. The problem of fighting and being wounded versus commanding: Curt. *Alex.* 3.11.7, 10.5.27; Arr. *Ind.* 13.4; and the

longer passage at Plu. *Pel.* 1–12, implying that this was a commonplace of ancient military history. Modern notice of the problem: Delbrück (1900), 1.259; Griffith (1947), 89; Garlan (1975), 146. Ancient comparanda: Wheeler (1991).

58. Achilles the bad councilor: he attended only one comparable meeting (*Il.* 19.303–37), and then gave Agamemnon instructions, not advice. Alexander's admiration for Agamemnon: Plu. *Fort. Alex.* 331c. This side of Alexander is little noticed: cf. Bosworth (1996b), 4–6, linking Alexander to Achilles alone; and Hampl (1958), 84, and Fox (1973), 497–98, linking Alexander and Achilles to Alexander's advantage.

59. The council meeting after the victory over the Malavas: App. 3 #34. The appointee: Philip the son of Machatas, Berve (1926), no. 780. Although Philip had been appointed as satrap for northeastern India at Taxila (Arr. *An.* 5.8.3), he effectively shared control of this region with Ambhi and Puru. The only other Macedonian appointee since Clitus: Nicanor, Berve (1926), no. 556. A different view of the Malava campaign: Bosworth (1996b), 142, seeing "terrorism" rather than the violent, but less indiscriminate, practice of extorting submission and supplies.

60. The fleet lost at night: Arr. *Ind.* 42.7. The Ambashthas, as at McCrindle (1893), 155 n. 2, were the Abistanoi of Arrian (*An.* 6.15.1), the Sambastae of Diodorus (17.102), and the Sambagrae of Curtius (9.8.4–7), all identified as living in southernmost Punjab. Honoring the Macedonians as gods: Curt. 9.8.14. (The other possibility, heroic honors, was impossible for a living person). A guess as to what these divine honors were: Bosworth (1996b), 128, "a fire sacrifice," meaning a holocaust as at n. 11 above.

61. Mushika appears at Arr. *An.* 6.15.5–7, with the refusal to cooperate; and 6.17.1; at Curt. 9.8.9–11, 16; and at DS 17.102.5 and 102.6–7, with refusal in the form of flight.

62. Mistreatment of Brahmins: Bosworth (1996b), 94–96. Some Brahmins supplicate: App. 2 #26. Supplication at Hamartelia: App. 2 #27. Other Indians begging for mercy: App. 2 #24, 25 (Polyaen. 4.3.30 being unspecified). Near Eastern begging: Naiden (2009), 21–24, 367–70, with many examples from Josephus alone. Indian surrenders after the withdrawal from the Beas, all after fighting, by author: Arr. *An.* 6.15.1 (Ossadians), 6.15.6 (Musicanus), 6.16.2 (Oxicani), 6.16.4 (Sindimana), 6.17.2 (Patala); Curt. 9.8.7–8 (Sambagrae); DS 17.91.7 (Sopeithes), 17.93.1 (Phegeus), 17.96.2 (Sibians), 17.102.3 (Sambastae), 17.102.4 (Sodrae and Massani). In all India, just two reports of conditional or negotiated surrenders: Arr. *An.* 5.20.4 (Glaucae), DS 17.91.2 (some Adrestians). Among major Indian cities, only Taxila capitulated; similarly, only Herat did in Iranian territory. The tribe that identified itself with Dionysus, imitating Nysa, but too late: Str. 15.1.8.

63. Indian casualties and the enslavement of Indians: Arr. *An.* 4.25.4; 5.24.3, DS 17.89.2; DS 17.102.7. The total of as many as 110,000 casualties surpasses the total for all previous battles, ignoring the incredible 300,000 reported for Gaugamela. For enslavement, the Indian total of 110,000 surpasses the total for fighting east of the Zagros, again omitting 300,000 reported for Gaugamela. No figures for the enslavement of the Malavas, of the people of Mushika and Samba, and of other places: Arr. *An.* 4.27.8, Curt. 9.4.6, Arr. *An.*

6.7.3, DS 96.3, Curt. 9.8.13, DS 102.5, Arr. *An.* 6.17.1. By any estimate of the Persian Empire's population, Indian casualties made the Macedonian invasion a costly one compared to Greek, Roman, or modern wars as at Krentz (1985), Brunt (1987) & Rosenstein (2004), or McPherson (2002), 3, 177 n. 56.

64. Calanus's piece of symbolism: Plu. *Alex.* 65.6–66.1, taking the "center" to be the middle portion, presumably Babylon, although a similar story told of Cyrus, Aristid. *Or.* 26.18, is said to mean that the ruler must be constantly on the move—the opposite conclusion.

65. Shifting banks of the Indus: Aristoboulos *FGrH* 139 F 35. Patala: Arr. *An.* 6.17.5–6.

66. Tidal bores: *Peripl. M. Rubr.* 45–46. This report of one: Nearchos *FGrH* 133 F 1. Another view: Engels (1980), 335, holding that the natives withheld this information. Mangrove swamps that disappear: Pl. *NH* 13.25.51.

67. The mishap for Alexander's crew: Kleitarchos *FGrH* 137 F 26.

68. Nearchos and the whale: Nearchos *FGrH* 133 F 1; similarly, Curt. 10.1.12, DS 17.106, Str 15.2.11–13.

69. Amon's oracle for the vicinity of Karachi: App. 1a #50. Plu. *Alex.* 66.1, however, omits the oracle and situates the sacrifice on an island, in what is arguably a distinct act, as at Eggermont (1975), 28–29. Other views of this sacrifice: a commemoration of Siwah's alleged instruction that all nations worship and obey Alexander, as at Altheim (1953), 204; mere *apobatēria* comparable to the sacrifices made after crossing the Indus and Hellespont, as at J. Hamilton (1999) ad Plu. *Alex.* 66.2.

70. The sacrifice to Poseidon: App. 1a #51. Another view: Ehrenberg (1933), 292–93, saying that Indian *gymnosophistai* advised Alexander.

71. Adapted from Ps.-Call. Γ 2.38. Although Firdausi and Nizami lack this story, Muslim versions are numerous. Among Hebrew versions: *Midrash Tehillim*, Ps. 93.5, *HR* 40.

CHAPTER 10
Persian In-laws

1. The comparison to Napoleon: Strasburger (1952), 489.

2. The plan to divide the army in three: Str. 15.2.4. Cf. Arr. *An.* 6.17.3, 6.21.3, a pair of passages implying no general plan, as is also true of Curt. 9.10.3–4.

3. Nearchus volunteers for the difficult voyage: Arr. *Ind.* 20.4.

4. Alexander's competition with Cyrus: Arr. *An.* 6.24.3. The "fish-eaters": Arr. *Ind.* 32–37. Other ancient sources for the "fish-eaters": Eggermont (1975), 64–67, 77–82.

5. Estimates of the size of the army: Ch. 8, n. 60, excluding noncombatants as noticed by Berve (1926), 1.180. The number of Argonauts: AR 1.1–227.

6. An estimate of Alexander's allotment of fighting men: Strasburger (1952), 490. Other estimates: J. Hamilton (1999) ad Plu. *Alex.* 66.5.

7. Human requirements for water: a gallon and a half per man, at Sidebotham (2011), 12; two to four gallons, at Junkelmann (1997), 172–75. Less generous: half a gallon

per man, Engels (1978), 125. Horses needing on average sixteen times as much: Engels, ibid. Seven to 15 times as much: Roth (1999), 62. Mules about ten times: Roth (1999), 66–67.

8. Crossing in a single night: Arr. *An.* 6.21.4. The battle and massive slaughter: DS 17.104–105.

9. The mistake about the prevailing winds: Arr. *An.* 6.21.1–3. Alexander's much noticed route: Strasburger (1952) with refs.

10. Aristobulus's investigations: Aristoboulos *FGrH* 139 F 49a.

11. The flash flood in the desert: Arr. *An.* 6.25.5, Str. 15.2.6.

12. Stealing supplies: Arr. *An.* 6.23.4. Phoenician foraging: Aristoboulos *FGrH* 139 F 49a.

13. The chief study of the journey through Gedrosia, Eggermont (1975), speculates (61–63) that the fourth-century inhabitants were Iranians, in the light of DS 17.105.1–2, since this source reports the exposure of the dead, but also speculates that they were perhaps Dravidians, or were partly or mostly speakers of Pakrit, implying different burial customs.

14. The king refuses proffered water: Arr. *An.* 6.26.1–3. Curt. 7.5.10–12 and Plu. *Alex.* 42.4.6–7 locate the incident elsewhere, and do not report that Alexander poured the water on the ground. Other views, especially those preferring Arrian's version because it may come from Aristobulus: J. Hamilton (1999) ad Plu. *Alex.* 42.7 with refs.

15. Devouring the army's animals: Arr. *An.* 6.25.1.

16. The short trip to the seashore: Arr. *An.* 6.26.5.

17. Personnel changes made in Carmania: Arr. *An.* 6.27.3, naming Stasanor and Phradasmanes, Berve (1926), nos. 719 and 812 respectively.

18. Abulites: Berve (1926), no. 5, and his son Oxyathres, no. 597.

19. Desert losses: some 50,000 according to Strasburger (1952), 489. Three-quarters lost: Plu. *Alex.* 65.5, but without specifying a number. Only a minority of Alexander's force: Tarn (1948), 1.107.

20. Craterus's forces: Arr. *An.* 6.17.3. Also some cashiered mercenaries: DS 17.106.3. Some 200 elephants under his command: Arr. *An.* 6.2.2, 6.5.5, leaving aside unspecified numbers acquired at 6.15.5, 6.16.2. Roxana and Barsine: *Epit Mett.* 70, reporting Roxana's giving birth to a child in India, meaning that she accompanied one of the three forces back to Babylon, the force of Craterus being the prudent choice. Barsine was likely given the same escort, or perhaps did not make the Indian journey in the first place, as implied by Justin 13.1.7. Craterus's little-studied route via the Bolan Pass: Ar. *An.* 6.17.3, Str. 15.2.4–5, 15.2.11, Justin 12.10.1 with Berve (1926), 2.224–25. The Indus ford: McCrindle (1893), 354.

21. Menon: Arr. *An.* 3.28.1. Rebels: Curt. 9.10.19.

22. The satrap Astapes: Curt. 9.10.21, 9.10.29 with Berve (1926), no. 5.

23. The revel and the kiss for the eunuch: Curt. 9.10.24–27; Plu. *Alex.* 67 adding the kiss.

24. Imitating Dionysus: Curt. 9.10.24–27, Karystios *FGrH* 358 F 4.
25. The customary sacrifice and games: App. 1a #53.
26. Nearchus's mission: Arr. *Ind.* 32.10–13. His odometer: Engels (1978), app. 5.
27. The inaugural sacrifice made by Nearchus: App. 1a #52.
28. The Ladies' Place: Arr. *Ind.* 21–22. Ladies' Place as Karachi: Eggermont (1975), 54–57.
29. Nearchus's trade with Leonnatus: Arr. *Ind.* 23.7–8.
30. Six hundred savages outwitted by Nearchos: Arr. *Ind.* 24. These unnamed people were among the "fish-eaters," to judge from the similarity of the name of their town, Homerus, to the names of other towns in this region, as at Eggermont (1975), 64–66.
31. The trick played on the seaside settlement: Arr. *Ind.* 27.6–28. No offering is mentioned, but the location was sacred to the sun god of the natives, whether Mithra or Surya.
32. The story of the nymph: Arr. *Ind.* 31, Str. 15.2.13.
33. The reunion with Alexander: Arr. *Ind.* 33.5–36.7.
34. The seaside sacrifice: App. 1a #54.
35. The islands of Oaracta, or Qeshm, and Ogyris, perhaps Masira: Arr. *Ind.* 37.1–4 and Str. 16.3.35. Topographical complications: Atkinson and Yardley (2009) ad Curt. 10.1.14. Arab offerings: Arr. *Ind.* 41.7–8.
36. The reception given Nearchus: Arr. *Ind.* 42 with App. 1a #55.
37. The marshes of Mesopotamia: Arr. *Ind.* 41.1–6.
38. The archaeological evidence for this scene: Stronach (1978), 30–31. Curt. 10.1.32 mistakenly adds that Alexander put a crown on the coffin.
39. Versions of who was to blame: Plu. *Alex.* 69.3, Str. 15.3.7; least plausibly, Curt. 10.1.31–35. The assignment given to Aristoboulos: *FGrH* 139 F 51b.
40. Alexander unqualified to be king: Badian (1996), 22–24, who sees the desecration of the tomb as an act of Persian resistance. Other views: Cascon Dorado (1990), 257–58, seeing Curtius's account as blaming Alexander for the disorder; and Brosius (2003), 174–75, holding that Alexander's attitude toward Cyrus was ambiguous rather than modest or admiring.
41. Death at Pasargadae: Str. 15.1.68. Burial elsewhere in Persia: Arr. *An.* 7.3.1, DS 17.107.1. Sundry accounts of this episode: J. Hamilton (1999) ad Plu. *Alex.* 69.6, which reports Calanus's last words. Impiety and death by fire for Brahmins: *Law of Manu* 11.74. The use of fire would also be improper for a Jain.
42. The pretender in Media: Arr. *An.* 6.29.3. The defiant Caucasus satrap: Autophradates, as at Berve (1926), no. 189.
43. The dead satrap to the west of the Indus: Nicanor, with Berve (1926), no. 556, which assumes that Nicanor died in 326. To the east: Philip the son of Machatas, with Berve (1926), no. 780.
44. Sins of the generals in Media: Arr. *An.* 6.27.4, Curt. 10.1.3. Similar sins committed by Parmenio, according to Justin 42.3.5, mistakenly reporting that Parmenio sacked shrines of Jason, to whom he sacrificed at Abdera at the start of the

expedition. Aside from the familiar Greek and Hebrew sources on sacrilege (no contemporary Persian sources for the topic surviving), see Freedman (1998), 19, 161, 169 for similar Akkadian ideas about the subject.

45. The companion killed by the Scyths: Zopurion, as at Berve (1926), no. 340.

46. Execution of the troops: Curt. 10.1.6, although the number, 600, is doubted by Atkinson and Yardley (2009) ad loc. A different view of Alexander's policy, seeing the reaction to Macedonian sacrilege as a "reign of terror": Badian (1961), 16–18; so also Schachermeyr (1973), 474; Bosworth (1988a), 148, 240.

47. [In this and the following two notes, B = Berve (1926), v. 2, and H = Heckel (2006).] A total of thirty-nine companions are sure to have attended the formal meetings listed in App. 3. Lost due to illness: Nicanor (B 554 = H s.v. no. 1), Erigyius (B 302 = Heckel s.v.), Coenus (B 439 = H s.v. no. 1). Lost in combat: Amyntas Andromenou (B 57 = H s.v. no. 4), Andromachus Heronos (B 75 = H s.v no. 1, dying either of wounds or by drowning), Hegelochus (B 341 = H s.v.). Punished for sacrilege: Cleander (B 422 = H s.v. no. 1), Sitalces (B 712 = H s.v.). Sent home: Sopolis (B 736 = H s.v.). Four dead at the hands of Alexander and the war council: Clitus, Parmenio, Philotas, and Alexander the Lyncestian, as in Ch. 7.

48. "Less" meaning eighteen companions with military commands but not sure to have attended the formal meetings listed in App. 3. Among these, one dead in combat: Menedemus (B 504 = H s.v.). Put on trial: Heracon (B 354 = H s.v.). Sent home: Epocillus (B 301 = H s.v.), Gorgias (B 233 = H s.v.), Clitus the White (B 428 = H s.v. no. 3). If the fourteen bodyguards identified by Berve (1926) are included, there were three additional deaths due to illness or combat: Arybbas (B 156 = H s.v. no. 2), Ptolemy Seleucou (B 670 = H s.v. no. 3), and another Ptolemy lacking a patronymic (B 672 = H s.v. no. 1). One was executed: Demetrius (B 260 = H s.v. no. 2). Three of the five Persians put to death: Shatibrzana (B 697), Ordanes (B 590), and Zariaspes (B 335). The two who fought at Arbela: Bessus (B 212), Orxines (B 592). One who retired: Artabazus, co-commander with Coenus in 328 (Arr. *An.* 4.16.2–3).

49. The Cypriot: Stasanor of Soli (B 719 = H s.v.). The trustworthy Persian: Phrataphernes, (B 814). The Macedonian: Sybirtios (B 703 = H. s.v.). The murdered Macedonian in charge of two satrapies in India: Philip (B 780 = H s.v. no. 7).

50. The recruitment and integration of Iranians: Arr. *An.* 7.6.2–5, reprised at 7.8.2. Only one mixed cavalry unit: 7.6.4. Mixed infantry: Arr. *An.* 7.23.1–4 (only in Babylon), DS 17.110.2 (at Susa). The timing of the reforms is thus partly uncertain, as is the number of troops raised. A matter of speculation: the Persian attitude toward the reforms. Brosius (2003), 176–77, suggests that this attitude was negative, citing evidence of Macedonians insulting Persians, such as Alexander's promise that the offspring of Macedonians and Persians would be raised in Macedon (Arr. *An.* 7.1.2, DS 17.110.3)

51. New companions included the seven named at Arr. *An.* 7.6.4–5, but surely there were others.

52. The Susa sacrifice: App. 1a #55, although Arrian does not mention local gods. Thirty thousand Iranian recruits: Arr. *An.* 7.6.3, Plu. *Alex.* 71.1. Persian bodyguards: DS 17.74.5. Honors for Nearchus, not Craterus: Arr. *An.* 7.5.4–6.

53. The group wedding, including incomplete lists of brides and grooms: Arr. *An.* 7.4.4–8, speaking of a "Persian manner." A Persian degree of luxury: Chares *FGrH* 125 F 4, Ael. *VH* 8.7. The number of couples: eighty to one hundred, with sources as at J. Hamilton (1999) ad Plu. *Alex.* 70.3.

54. The drinking contest: Chares *FGrH* 125 F 19b. A very similar view of this episode: Bosworth (1988a), 156–57 with refs. Marriages made to secure legitimacy, and not soldiers, for Alexander: Pirart (2002), 148–49.

55. A profit turned from the wedding: Plu. *Alex.* 70.3. Alexander's wealth more or less reflects the size of the coinage he minted; evaluating this coinage is a complex task that begins with estimating the number of dies used to mint these coins and then multiplying by 10,000 to 40,000. De Callatuÿ (1995, 2011) estimated 1,000 to 1,400 dies for the king's staters, his main gold coin; 2,500 to 3,500 for his silver tetradrachms; and 2,700 to 3,300 for drachms. The total is some 8,000 to 10,000 dies. Multiplying the dies by 20,000 silver coins per die, but just 10,000 gold coins per die, yields the equivalent of 90,000 talents of silver coins. Add coins of Philip II, de Callatuÿ reckoned, and the total rises to about 120,000 talents, comparable to the estimates of Holt (2016), 181–93, for Alexander's surplus in extraordinary payments. If we suppose 10,000 coins per silver die, the total is still 60,000 talents. Melted down, 60,000 talents yield 1,240 tons of silver. At the ancient Greek conversion rate of 13 to 1 for silver and gold, the tonnage in gold would be about 90. This estimate allows the comparisons to the nineteenth-century United States. In 1876, the gold contained in the United States currency amounted approximately 22.5 million troy ounces, or about 75 tons of gold. American silver money made little difference; see *United States Monetary Commission* (1879), 2.xiv. Additional literature on estimating the number of coins per die: Carter (1983). Low estimates based on Carter: Sellwood (1963) for 11,500 to 20,000 coins per obverse die; Buttrey (1993) and (1994), for 10,000 to 13,000 per die. High estimates: Crawford (1974), 2.694–697, for 30,000 coins per obverse die; Kinns (1983), 1–22, for 40,000 coins per obverse die.

56. Fear of Alexander's defeat, or even death: Bosworth (1980) ad Arr. *An.* 3.6.4. Other views of Harpalus's defection: because he expected Alexander to remove him, as at Badian (1960), 246, or kill him, at Badian (1961), 23; because he expected Alexander to punish him for misconduct, at Heckel (2006), 129; because Harpalus intended to serve as a spy, at Green (1991), 222; or because he wished to join Alexander I of Epirus, at Jaschinski (1981), 12–15. The greed of Harpalus: Curt. 9.3.21, DS 17.108.9.

57. Plu. *Alex.* 35,5, *Fort. Alex.* 648c–d. He cannot have known that the Babylonians worshipped some statues of early kings and queens.

58. Ath. 13.594f; Paus. 1.37.4. The politician's nephew's building contract: Plu. *Phoc.* 22.2–3.

59. Money and troops: DS 17.108.6. Harpalus comes to supplicate: App. 2 #28 with Hyper. 1.18; see Naiden (2009), 159, 168, 177.

60. Macedonian demands that Athens, the *supplicandus*, surrender the suppliant: DS 17.108.7. A synopsis of the affair: Berve (1926), no. 143, here pp. 78–79, but with no focus on the use and abuse of supplication, as is true of Heckel (2006, 20016), s.v., and sundry other treatments, including Badian (1961).

61. The offer of Gorgos the armorer: Plu. *Alex.* 41.8, Ephippos *FGrH* 26 F 5. Perhaps Gorgos had a selfish motive for his gesture: he was an informal patron for Samos, which resented recent Athenian meddling in Samian affairs, and so he encouraged Alexander to attack Athens in order to please his clients, as suggested by Pédech (1984), 353.

62. The death of Harpalus: Berve (1926), no. 143, p. 79. The death of Demosthenes and the attendant legal complications: Naiden (2009), 202–4.

63. Adapted from Nizami 1.23.10–24.

64. The tale of the mirror and the dragon: Mulla (1893), 12. The global mirror: Steingass (1892), 1108.

CHAPTER 11
The Waters of Life

1. Alexander's new foe, boredom: Curt. 6.2.1–2: *militarium rerum quam quietis otiique patentior.*

2. Hephaestion's expedition: Arr. *An.* 7.7.1, 7.7.6.

3. The last assembly of the army, at Opis: Arr. *An.* 7.8.1–11.1. The lacunose Curt. 10.2.13–14 lacks the participation of the officers, and the offer of commands to Persians, as does DS 17.109.2–3. Plu. *Alex.* 71.2–8 lacks these features and also the arrest and execution of the leaders of the troops. Mockery of Amon appears at Arr. *An.* 7.83, DS 17.108.3, and Justin 12.11.6.

4. The executions after the assembly: Arr. *An.* 7.8.3. Alexander now had Persian guards (Plu. *Alex.* 71.3) and attendants (Justin 12.11.6), but did not give them this sensitive assignment.

5. Here as at the Hyphasis, Arrian and Curtius give somewhat similar accounts of Alexander's speech, even in regard to the army's performance under Philip (Arr. *An.* 7.9–10, Curt. 10.2.15, 30), a theme otherwise found only in Curtius (3.10.3–10, 4.14.1–7). A similar view: Sisti (2001) ad loc., with refs. Skeptical views: Bosworth (1995) ad Arr. *An.* 5.25.3, detecting Roman models; Tarn (1948), 2.287–90, detecting invention; Atkinson and Yardley (2009) ad Curt. 10.2.12–4.3, detecting a familiar contrast between the two authors, one pro-Alexander and one anti.

6. The companions' ethos of share and share alike: Samuel (1988), reflected not only at Arr. *An.* 7.9.9–10.3 but also at 5.26.7–8; for Alexander it was a trope available in times of emergency.

7. How seriously did he mean his offer of commands to Persians (Arr. *An.* 7.11.3)? Very seriously, to judge from Bosworth (1988a), 272–73; even more seriously according to Briant (1974), 110–11. The ancient sources for Alexander's Persian troops, reviewed by Bosworth (1980b), 12–19, do not mention Persian officers, save for the Bactrian Hystaspes, as at Berve (1926), no. 763.

8. The Macedonians are driven to supplicate: App. 2 #29, but with no supplication at Curt 10.2.13–3–3.14 and DS 17.109.2–110.1 as opposed to Arrian, Plutarch, and Justin. Arr. *An.* 6.11.1 and Plu. *Alex.* 71.7–8 report an interval of three days in which Alexander was incommunicado, a doublet for his action at the Hyphasis, and Curt. 10.3 and Justin 12.11.9–12 report a speech made to the Persian troops, one that Atkinson and Yardley (2009) ad loc. observe has more Roman than Persian points of reference.

9. A similar view of this, the largest act of supplication in Macedonian if not Greek history: Errington (1990), 112. Other views: Heckel and Yardley (2009) ad Justin 12.11.4, calling the events at Opis a *secessio*, or "strike"; Droysen (1833), 273, "Kampf zwischen dem Alten und Neuen"; Grote (1884), 2.252, "mutiny," implying no political consequences; Schachermeyr (1973), 224–28, an unsuccessful exercise of the rights of the army assembly. A supplication, however, is better described as a pressure tactic than as an act of resistance or an exercise of a political right; see Naiden (2009), ch. 1.

10. Alexander's latitudinarian if not ecumenical sacrifice: App. 1a #56.

11. The decree or ἐπιστολή, directed at the exiles as well as at the Greek cities, and thus undermining the cities: DS 18.8.4. Orders first published later the same year: Curt. 10.2.2–4. Murderers: Justin 3.5.2. Traitors, i.e., Thebans: Plu. *Fort. Alex.* 221a. Religious language used by Alexander at Opis: Arr. *An.* 7.5.6. Only one city, Tegea, is sure to have complied with the decree before Alexander's death (*GHI* 202). The selection of secondary literature given by Atkinson and Yardley (2009) ad Curt. 10.2.4–7 omits the religious issues; Cawkwell (1994) rightly observes that the decree was not a demand that Greeks worship Alexander.

12. Mercenaries dismissed by Alexander in 325: DS 17.106.3, 17.111.1. Paus. 1.25.5 says 50,000 mercenaries reached Europe.

13. A similar view of how new assignments affected social cohesion within the officer corps: Wilcken (1932), 175.

14. Satraps brought to Babylon: Peucestas for Persis, Philoxenus for Caria, and Menander for Lydia (Arr. *An.* 7.23.1), and apparently Stasanor for Arachosia and Gedrosia and Phrataphernes for Parthia and Hyrcania (6.27.3)

15. Sixty or more invited to meals: Ephippos *FGrH* 126 F 5.

16. En route they saw the bas-relief and inscription of Darius I at Behistun, which would have been known to them as the Bagistanon of Ctesias (*FGrH* 122 F 1b.13.2). None of the Alexander historians say how Alexander and the entourage reacted to this monument, which Ctesias may have led them to attribute to Semiramis. Resisting the idea that the Macedonians regarded this Persian artifact as a

Mesopotamian one: Briant (2002), 124. No comment: Lenfant (2004), F. W. König (1972) ad loc. If the Macedonians noticed the long stairway at the bottom, this feature of the monument surely aroused Alexander's and his engineers' interest. The Persians destroyed the stairway in order to prevent the monument from being defaced, as at Luschey (1968), 92–94. The Macedonians had perhaps seen a copy of the inscription in Babylon. The feast: App. 1a #57. The regular sacrifices to Dionysus: Ephippos *FGrH* 126 F 5.

17. Rage against the Persian "Asclepius": Arr. *An.* 7.14.4. We do not know who the Iranian god was; perhaps Alexander did not. The order to douse the sacred fires: DS 17.114.4. Arguing that Diodorus did not mean "put out," and that the request was proper: Jamzadeh (2012), 135 with n. 104. Amon's raising Hephaestion to the godhead: App. 1b #22 (DS 17.11.6).

18. The burial of Hephaestion: App. 1a #58.

19. Honors for Hephaestion: Arr. *An.* 7.23.7. The immediate heroization of a prominent deceased individual, such as a king or general, was unusual but not unheard of. The first known example: Brasidas at Amphipolis (Th. 5.11.1). A transition from commemoration to worship was more common: see examples at Loraux (1986), 39–40; R. Parker (1996), 135–37; Currie (2005), 112–19. Alexander surely wanted annual funeral games for Hephaestion, one point on a continuum from commemoration to worship: for examples, see Roller (1981), 6–7, and Seaford (1994), 120–21. Whether Hephaestion's cult was to include *enagismata* rather than *thusiai* is unknown, but for *enagismata* to historical persons see *SEG* 13.312.13 (Megara), Plu. *Arist.* 21.3–5 (Plataea). Prohibited in Athens: Plu. *Sol.* 21.6. The term *herōs* for historical persons: Pi. fr. 133.5–6; Ar. *Ra.* 1039 (Lamachus). Unapologetic offerings to Asclepius: App. 1a #59.

20. The refusal to rename Hephaestion's unit: Arr. *An.* 7.14.7.

21. The campaign against the highwaymen: Arr. *An.* 7.15, *Ind.* 40.6–8 and Plu. *Alex.* 72.4, with a characteristic difference between the two authors, Arrian envisioning a military purpose for the campaign, and Plutarch a quasi-religious one by which Alexander turned the Cossaeans into a tardy human sacrifice to the ghost of Hephaestion. Forty days of fighting: DS 17.112.

22. Events in Babylon in Alexander's absence: In 328, an astronomical diary recorded a movement of troops from Susa to the land of the Hannaeans, the archaic term for "northwesterners" that the priests assigned to Macedonians and Greeks (*AD* -328 rev. 26: ˡúGAL ki-ṣir, "chief of the troops."). The same year, the absent Alexander gave some unspecified order (*AD* -328 rev. 23). Alexander pledged tithes: Van der Spek (2006), 270. The work of the exorcist: *RAcc.* 40, 113. The rites for temple repair: Linssen (2004), 100–107. Repair of Esangil would continue for centuries (*CT* 49, 154). Price rises: Van der Spek and Mandemakers (2003). A new crown for Marduk: *AD* -324 B rev. 23.

23. Trouble in Babylon on his arrival: App. 1b #23. The leader, "Belephantes": DS 17.112.2. The reason for this warning may have been a solar eclipse predicted for

May 12, some months in the future, at Labat (1965), 81.1. A solar eclipse neutralized by ritual during the reign of Cyrus the Great: Beaulieu and Britton (1994). The liver-reader: Arr. *An.* 7.19, vindicating Greek divination; Plu. *Alex.* 73.3–5, saying that Alexander regretted entering Babylon, and thus tacitly vindicating the Babylonians. The problem of the correct route: Arr. *An.* 7.16.5–17.1; DS 17.112.4, referring only to another route of entry; Plu. *Alex.* 73 and Justin 12.13.3 giving no particulars, as also at App. *BC* 2.153. It would seem that only Ptolemy was well informed about the warnings given by the priests. Alexander's response: Arr. *An.* 7.17.6, App. *BC* 2.153. Rough ground: Bosworth (1988a), 168. Arrian's claim that the Babylonians wished to keep him out of the city for selfish, pecuniary reasons (7.17.1–4) is erroneous; see Boiy (2004), 201–2; so also Smelik (1978), 93–94.

24. Alexander holds court: Ephippus *FGrH* 126 F 3.
25. Mazdai's half-Babylonian son: Berve (1926), no. 154.
26. Temples in Greece and also Macedon respond to Alexander: DS 18.4.4–5. Honors: Arr. *An.* 7.23.2, saying only that the Greeks gave him a golden crown, an honor Arrian mistakenly thinks is only for gods; no details at DS 17.113.1–2. The contrary view: Meyer (1910), holding that Alexander demanded deification as reported at Ael. *VA* 2.19. The intransigent Arabs: Arr. *An.* 7.19.6. They perhaps knew, even if Alexander did not, that faraway Carthage paid tribute to Esarhaddon (Prism B 5.54–6.1 at *ANET* 291).
27. Hephaestion worshipped only as a hero: Despinis (1997), no. 23; Stewart (1993), 453–55, fig. 72. Alexander insulted by the Spartans: Plu. *QG* 219e. Ael. *VH* 2.19. An Athenian insult: Plu. *X orat.* 842d. A lawsuit against worshipping Alexander in Athens: Hyper. 6.21–22. Similarly, Hyper. 5.2 mentions an *eikōn* of Alexander, but not an *agalma*. Ephippos *FGrH* 126 F 5 speaks of incense being offered and silence being observed, but gives no locations. A similar view: Cawkwell (1994), 297. A contrary view: Habicht (1970), 30–34; Fredricksmeyer (2003), 276. The contempt expressed by Demosthenes: Hyper. 6.31. So also Dinarch. 1.94, saying that Demosthenes allowed Alexander honors in heaven, but not in Athens. Additional sources: Mari (2002), 239–41, linking the Greek response to the contemporary, and likewise unenthusiastic, response to the exiles' decree.
28. The Greek oracle on Alexander's divinity: Kallisthenes *FGrH* 124 F 14, unless this author invented the oracles, in which case it can still be said that he thought the invention plausible, given previous developments in Anatolia. The date of the oracle, which was reportedly announced to Alexander while he was in Memphis in early 331, must have been sometime in 332. The Persian oracle, preserved in Greek, is described at Boyce and Grenet (1991), 13.
29. A routine supplication: App. 2 #30, assuming that owner, Megabyzus, was one of the hereditary priests known by this name, as at Str. 14.1.23. Eunuchs: Munn (2006), 159.
30. A life-like portrait of a deathless Alexander as at Ch. 9, n. 31. This compliment was given to the entire oeuvre of Apelles: Pl. *NH* 35.79. Other images of Alexander

blurring the distinction between mortal and immortal: Atkinson and Yardley (2009) ad Curt 10.5.33.

31. A minimum of 8,000 stationed in Babylon: Bosworth (1988a), 267, following Brunt (1976), 23.

32. Mount Athos and other extravagant projects: Plu. *Alex.* 72.5–8.

33. The pearl fishery: Arr. *An.* 7.20.7. The Greek Androsthenes sailed farther, and wrote the requisite book (Str. 16.4.2, Ath. 3.93b). Red Sea voyages: Str. 16.4.2, Tzet. *Chil.* 7.174. Alexander must have known about the circumnavigation of Arabia from Hdt. 4.44, if not from the Chalouf Stela, as at Redmount (1995), 60–61. Alexander was thus using Greek navigators to make himself as well informed as a Persian predecessor about erstwhile Babylonian possessions. He may not have known about the desert campaigns of Esarhaddon and Assurbanipal (Prism B 6.1–13, 7.82–10.5 at *ANET* 291–92).

34. Curt 10.1.16–19 retrojects Alexander's naval plans to the previous year. The motive, punishing the Arabs, appears at Arr. *An.* 7.19.3–4 and Str. 16.1.11, but Schachermeyr (1973), 131–40, followed by Atkinson and Yardley (2009) ad Curt. 10.1.16–19, accept the notion, reported at Aristoboulos *FGrH* 139 F 59 and Str. 16.1.11, that Alexander wished to make himself a third god among the Arabs, who worshipped only two, Zeus (or Uranus) and Dionysus. Yet Alexander could not have been so uninformed as to suppose that the Arabs were bitheists; Hdt. 3.8.1 and 1.131.3 name a total of three Arab gods.

35. The forty-seven vessels: Arr. *An.* 7.19.3. The Pallacopas canal: 7.21.1–7.

36. Arab tribute to Babylon: *Sargon & Sennacherib*, 123–28.

37. Moderation on campaign: Plu. *Symp.* 1.6. An ambitious man's objections to drink and sex: Plu. *Alex.* 22.3. Some degree of restraint in sexual predation: Plu. *Amat.* 760c, *Fort. Alex.* 333a. The exchange of a woman for a picture: Ael. *VH* 12.3, Lucian. *Im.* 7.

38. Drinking with impunity: Plu. *Q. conviv.* 623f–24a (during the life of Callisthenes), *Alex.* 70.1 (at Susa), Ael. *VH* 3.23 (some month other than the one described in the extant *Ephemerides*). Reports of earlier drinking: Curt. 5.7.1 (Persepolis); 6.2.1 (a general statement concerning 330 onward); 8.1.22 (the night of Clitus's death). These passages lend some force to Tritle's claim (2003) that Alexander drank because of post-traumatic stress disorder, provided that the stress was provoked by conditions in Central Asia.

39. Temple-building: DS 18.4.5, reporting 9,000 talents were to be spent at locations starting with Dodona.

40. Dressing like Amon: Ephippos *FGrH* 126 F 13. Other people dressing like gods, but only at symposia: Ath. 7.289b–c. More vanities of Menecrates, Philip's doctor: Plu. *Ages.* 21.10, *Reg. apophth.* 191a, *Lac. apophth.* 213a. A pyramid for Philip: DS 18.4.5.

41. A third possibility, besides attending or not: a curtailed ceremony, as at *ABC* #7, col. 3.7–8. A fourth, the use of a substitute, is doubted by Kuhrt and

Sherwin-White (1987). Alexander's participation from the perspective of two recent Assyriologists: affirmed by Dalley (1998), 39; no opinion offered by Kuhrt (1990). Alexander's activities in 323 make it certain he had already arrived in the city by early April. Otherwise he would not have had time to sail to the marshes near the Gulf, visit the colony there, return to Babylon (Arr. *An.* 7.21), and then sail into the marshes a second time and return to drill his fleet (7.23.5), all before falling ill at the end of May.

42. The New Year's festival: *RAcc*, 127–48; Linssen (2004), 215–37. Descendants at the festival: Linssen (2004), ch. 6, n. 391.

43. No easy translation for "Pegasus," since the Babylonian for this constellation, *iku*, means "ditch." Other translations were easier: Virgo for the "furrow," Capricorn for the "goat-fish." Knowledge of the entire zodiac perhaps began to reach Greece in Alexander's time: Rochberg (2010), 13.

44. Marduk as in the *Enūma Eliš* (*ANET* 60–72), 6.1–8, 6.129–31. Purpose of the recitation: 7.145–10.

45. Alexander's words, "I did not strike the cheeks of the clergy," are to be taken figuratively, i.e., "did not consume their wealth."

46. The rural visit at the end of the ceremonies: Black (1991), 45–46.

47. Disputes about changes in the celebration of the symbolic royal marriage: Falkenstein (1959), 162–63. Leading interpretations of the festival do not discuss Alexander, e.g., the interpretation that it symbolizes natural cycles, as at Frankfort (1948), 315–28; or the mock-death of the monarch, as at Eliade (1959), 51; or serves as nationalistic religious propaganda, as at J. Smith (1976).

48. An earlier king with Alexander's hobby: Xerxes, but we cannot tell where he looked (Ktesias *FGrH* 688 F 13.25, Ael. *VH* 13.3, Str. 16.1.5). Lenfant (2004), lxxxviii–lxxxix, suggests one such tomb was discovered in the palace of Nebuchadnezzar in Babylon.

49. Royal tombs in the swamps: Str. 16.1.1; an attested example at *ABC* 18 col. 5.6 with Beaulieu (1988), no. 53. Just two locations of royal crypts—Uruk and Choga Zanbil, in Elam—are known, but the latter was destroyed by Ashurbanipal ca. 640, and neither could have been known to Alexander. A pious brick stamp of Sennacherib's: *Sennacherib*, 151 no. 14 followed by no. 13.

50. The story of the sailor: Aristoboulos *FGrH* 139 F 22.

51. Death within a year: see n. 23 above. Tearing down the city wall: DS 17.115.1. Cost of repairs: Str. 16.1.15.

52. The substitute king: Arr. *An.* 7.24.1–3, DS 17.116.2–4, Plu. *Alex.* 73.7–9, first interpreted as reflecting a Babylonian substitution ritual by Kümmel (1967), 184–86, followed by Lane Fox (1973), 549–550, and Bottéro (1987), ch. 9. What the ritual involved: Parpola (1993), 2 nos. 1, 2, (ingestion of texts), 3–4, 12, 25 (on the throne), 89–90, 189 (royal dress), 219, 220 (execution after fifteen or a hundred days), 221 (private life as a "farmer," *ikkaru*), 240, 314, 350 (execution after a

hundred days), 351, 352 (a simpleton, a consort, and their execution, followed by a funeral), 377

53. Perhaps during the ritual the temporarily isolated king conducted business in the *qersu*, some kind of wooden chamber or vehicle, as suggested by Pomerantz-Leisten (1997), 99 with ref.

54. Any Babylonian explanation given to the companions ought to have compared enthroning a substitute king to a Greco-Macedonian apotropaic ritual, but the enthronement was an instance of a subtly different rite, *namburbi,* that Maul (1994) calls "Löserrituale." Only one Greek apotropaic ritual, for a scapegoat, involved putting a substitute to death.

55. Eunuchs around Alexander: Arr. *An.* 7.24.3. *Manteis:* ibid., DS 17.116.4, Plu. *Alex.* 74.1. No details: D. Chr. 4.66–67, Zonar. 1.14. In Arrian and Plutarch, the substitute is removed rather than killed, another way of interrupting the ritual. A similar view: Boiy (2004), 113. A somewhat similar view: Abramenko (2000), 364, holding that the Babylonians conducted the ritual in secret to avoid interference from the companions.

56. Alexander's despair: Plu. *Reg. apophth.* 207d.

57. A similar view of the role of the Babylonian astronomers in Alexander's last days, although differing concerning the mock king: Lenderling (2005), 343–54.

58. Favorable oracles about Hephaestion: App. 1b #24 (Plu. *Alex.* 74.4). In Arrian, a sacrifice for *eucharistēria* takes place on the same occasion (App. 1a #60). Onomarchus knew who attended the dinner at Medius's, but discreetly refused to list them (*FGrH* 127 F 1). Lists appear in later sources, Ps.-Call. A 3.31.8–32.1 and the *Epit. Mett.* 97–98, analyzed at Heckel (1988), ch. 4. A drunken Alexander recalls Andromache: Nikoboule 127 *FGrH* F 2.

59. The records kept by Eumenes (or his assistants) were evidently far more heterogeneous than what survives in the only two sources, Arr. *An.* 7.25–26 and Plu. *Alex.* 76, only one of which reports meetings and sacrifices. Many scholars have found sundry reasons to regard the *Ephemerides* as a pastiche or a fabrication, starting with inconsistent dating. Atkinson and Yardley (2009) ad Arr. *An.* 10.1.5–6 provide a synopsis of this skeptical bibliography. A fabrication that served the interest of officers in Babylon: Brunt (1983), 289. A fabrication that served the interest of Antipater: Bosworth (1988a), 157–64. The Arabian expedition: App. 3 #36. Alexander's repairs to shrines: Mari (2002), 249–63, observing that some of these were major shrines chosen to maintain Alexander's prestige as national priest of the Macedonians.

60. Successive attempts to sacrifice and meet during the final illness: App. 3 #36, 37, 38, 39, 40, in the course of six days; Bosworth (1988a), 165–67, doubts so many meetings occurred.

61. The parade of mourners also appears in Ps.-Call. A 3.32.12–13 with other versions as at Merkelbach (1977), 220–25.

62. Diseases of absolute rulers: Pl. *R.* 9.573c, Arist. *Prob.* 30. Another view: the Greek doctors administered a fatal overdose of the purgative drug hellebore, as reported, along with other explanations, at Romm (2012).

63. Babylonian nostrums: Stol (2007), passim. In some houses, and particularly palaces, bas-relief sculptures at these locations did this apotropaic work, as at Dalley (2013), 139.

64. Contemporary doctors envisioning the scene: Oldach et al. (1998), diagnosing *Salmonella typhi* enteritis, with further remarks on their report by Borza and Reames-Zimmerman (2000), who add weakening of the immune system because of bereavement, 27–28. Encephalitis due to West Nile virus: Cunha (2004). Malaria: Atkinson and Yardley (2009) ad Curt. 10.5.6.

65. The supplication by the worried companions: App. 2 #31. The god is Serapis according to Arr. *An.* 7.26.2–3 and Plu. *Alex.* 76.9. To explain this error, Bosworth (1995) ad. loc. identifies Serapis as Marduk, an impossibility, given that Marduk had only one shrine in Babylon. (For a later view, see Ch. 12, n. 34.) Quack (2013), 229–30, says that the suppliants sought to incubate, but shrines in Babylon were not used for this purpose. *Interpretatio graeca* in this episode: Heller (2010), 413–14.

66. Roxana's intervention: Arr. *An.* 7.27.3. Another view of this episode: Jamzadeh (2012), 148.

67. Proteas's age: Ael. *VH* 2.26. Nephew of Clitus: Curt. 8.2.8. Son of Alexander's nurse: Ath. 4.129a. Drinking bout: Ephippus *FGrH* 126 F 3.

68. The date: *AD* 1–322B obv. 8; also Sachs (1955), no. 209. The hour: Depuydt (1997). The companions' inaccuracy: the duration of the illness is 11 days in Arr. *An.* 7.25–26 and ten in Plu. *Alex.* 76. Similar disagreement about the date of death: 28th Daisios at Plu. *Alex.* 76; 30th at Plu. *Alex.* 75; 29th according to Beloch (1922), 4.2.27. All Macedonian dates derived from Babylonian ones because of the synchronization of Macedonian and Babylonian calendars, as in Samuel (1972), 141. The Greek term *ephemerides*, used of the day-books kept by Eumenes, has a different sense in astronomical literature, where it refers to tables for making predictions about the movements of heavenly bodies.

69. Resurrection according to the Pharisees, but not the Sadducees: Acts 23.8; so also J. *AJ* 8.14–15, *BJ* 2.8.14.

70. Adapted from Ps.-Call. Γ 2.39–40. Considered in its entirety, this story, which features a forest journey followed by a journey to the end of the world, resembles the *Epic of Gilgamesh*, as noted by Meissner (1894). Nizami, however, attributes the story to Zoroastrianism (1.58.36). Cf. other versions of the story, such as Nizami 1.68–70, and Firdausi 20.3, where Alexander is unenlightened rather than deceived as in Ps.-Call. Γ 2.39–40 and also in B 2.39–40. Hebrew versions: *Tamid* 32a–b, *HR* 37.

71. Folktales influenced by the *Alexander Romance*, as argued in Leigh Fermor (1958), 187, and in particular by Ps.-Call. B 2.41. Versions of the folktale: Politis (1904), #551–52.

CHAPTER 12
Dead Men and a Living King

1. The council meets to dispose of Alexander's body: App. 3 #42. No will: *pace* the sources for App. 3 #41, which mention *mandata*. The various purposes served by the posthumous "will" found in *Epit. Mett.* 87–123 and Ps.-Call. A 3.32.8–10, 33.1–25: Bosworth (2000a). The instructions to Craterus: DS 18.4.1. The instruction to be buried at Siwah: Ar. fr. 25, Curt. 10.5.4, DS 18.3.5, Justin. 12.15.7, Paus. 1.6.3.

2. Alexander envisioning competition, as at athletic games: Curt. 10.5.5, although Curtius mistranslated "strongest," an athletic term, as *optimus*; so also Justin 12.15.8, *dignissimus*. Cf. *aristos* (DS 18.1.4) and *kratistos* (Arr. *An.* 7.26.3). Less plausible remarks: Curt. 10.5.6, Justin 12.15.5, both with Roman *topoi* noticed by Atkinson and Yardley (2009) ad Curt. 10.5.2.

3. The charge of poisoning: Arr. *An.* 7.27.1–3, DS 17.118.1–2, Curt. 10.10.14–18, and Plu. *Alex.* 77.1–3, each with characteristic reservations: Arrian rejects this explanation, Diodorus attributes the report of it to his sources, Curtius is scandalized that the report was repressed, and Plutarch is skeptical. Poisoning charges as multilayered propaganda: Bosworth (1971), 115–16, and (2010), considering poison a possible cause of Alexander's death. Poisoning not a possible cause: Heckel (1988), 1–5.

4. The tradition that the body was to be buried in Macedon: Arr. fr. 24.1–2, Str. 17.1.8, Paus. 1.6.3, Ael. *VH* 12.64. Only Curt. 10.10.20 omits this tradition.

5. Perdiccas at Thebes: Arr. *An.* 1.8; DS 17.12.3 denies Perdiccas the initiative. Perdiccas and embalming: DS 17.110.8.

6. A week spent unattended in a coffin: Curt. 10.10.9. Ael. *VH* 12.64 says the corpse lay unattended for thirty days, an impractically long time in the summer heat of Mesopotamia.

7. This is the ring used to communicate with Greeks and Macedonians. Alexander used another to communicate with Persians (Curt. 6.6.6). Perhaps he used a third ring to communicate with Egyptians, as suggested by Rathmann (2005), 21. The story that Alexander gave the ring to Perdiccas, although found in all the Vulgate authors (Curt. 10.5.4, DS 17.117.3, Justin 12.1.5.12), does not appear in *Ta meta Alexandrou*, the *Ephemerides*, or the Metz *Epitome*; it turns a senior officer into a regent. Atkinson and Yardley (2009) ad Curt. 10.5.4 discern yet another Roman *topos*.

8. The embalming of Alexander is not described by the Alexander historians, save for Curt. 10.10.13, so it is reconstructed by using Smith and Dawson (1924), 57–72, and later works by Egyptologists analyzing mummies of the late Persian and Ptolemaic periods—Loynes (2015), 204–5, 225; Dodson (1994), 1–3; and Janot (2000), 187.

9. Perdiccas's stage management: Curt. 10.6.1–4. Curtius regards the following meeting as an assembly of the army (10.6.3–7.15) combined with, or colliding with, a council (App. 3 #42). Schachermeyr (1970), 49–73, makes an archaeological

objection to this assembly, which was that the likely meeting place, the *regia* in the palace of Nebuchadnezzar as at Curt 10.5.7, was far too small for such a meeting. App. 3 provides a procedural argument: no other meeting of the council is ever interrupted. Some of what Curtius reports the troops saying is also unprecedented, especially the regret expressed for never having worshipped Alexander while he was alive (10.5.11).

10. If we assume that the council met by itself, two events reported by Curtius must be rejected: first, that the *volgus* (10.6.4) offered Perdiccas the crown, and second, that Meleager failed to mention Arrhidaeus to his fellow generals (10.6.20–24). The only comparandum, Justin 13.2.5–12, reports neither of these two events. Other views of this passage: Atkinson and Yardley (2009) ad Curt 10.6.5–24, "something of a construct"; Bosworth (2003), 179, dismissing the offer of the crown to Perdiccas; Schachermeyr (1970), 94, arguing that Nearchus did not belong at the meeting.

11. The allotment of satrapies may have occurred later, as at App. 3 #43; the latest treatment is the relevant entries in Heckel (2016). The disposition of, and deaths among, the women: Justin 13.2.7, putting Barsine in Anatolia already; Curt. 10.5.21–25, Plu. *Alex.* 77.6.

12. The use of honey, aloes, and myrrh on this occasion: Ps.-Call. 3.34.4.

13. Protests by the infantry, but after the meeting, not during it: Arr. fr. 1a.1–2, Curt. 10.7.6–15, and especially Justin 13.2.13, reporting that the infantry protested at being ignored.

14. Separate camps followed by a virtual siege: Curt. 10.7.20, DS 18.2.3–4; Curt. 10.8.1–14. Schachermeyr (1970), 99–101, notices the conflict between two kinds or grades of companions.

15. The purification: App. 1a #61, followed at Curt. 10.9.21 by an act of supplication that would be impossible in Babylon, as at Naiden (2009), 24. Curtius says an assembly previously condemned Meleager (Curt. 10.8.5–7), which, if true, would render the supplication ineffectual in typical Greek circumstances.

16. Similarly, Errington (1976), 142, posited delay in disposing of the body, but not for religious reasons; whereas Erskine (2002), 171, citing Arr. fr. 24.1, posited delay so that Perdiccas might "control" ($\kappa\rho\alpha\tau\hat{\eta}\sigma\alpha\iota$) the body.

17. The catafalque project: Arr. fr. 1.25; DS 18.3.5, 18.26.1, 18.28.2.

18. The completed catafalque: DS 18.26–27, in the light of Stewart (1993), 215–21.

19. The proposed marriage: Arr. fr. 1.26. Another view, that Perdiccas wanted to become king *tout court*: Waterfield (2011), 46.

20. No theft: DS 18.28.2, Paus. 1.6.3. Theft strongly implied: Arr. fr. 1.24.1–8, Str. 17.1.8. A trick and not a theft: Ael. *VH* 12.64.

21. The burial of Alexander: App. 1a #62. Memphis: Marmor Parium *FGrH* 239 F B.111 under 322/21 BC; Curt. 10.10.20, DS 18.28.3, Str. 17.1.8, Paus. 1.6.3, Ael. *VH* 12.64, as at Fraser (1972), 2.32 n. 79. The temple of Amon (and Thoth): Chugg (2002), 20, citing Préaux (1939), 298–99. Redford (1992), 228, describes the

temples of Bel and Astarte. Another suggested location: the tomb of Nakhtnebef at Saqarra, as at Schmidt-Colinet (1996).

22. The fiasco crossing the river: DS 18.33–36.1 Perdiccas also built a canal for some unknown purpose; see Heckel (2016), 181 with refs.

23. The withdrawal of Ptolemy's foes: Nep. *Eum.* 5.1. The date of Perdiccas's death, May/June 320: *ABC* 13c. BM 35, 660 v. 4. The alternative view, placing this event a year earlier: Bosworth (1992) with refs.

24. Babylon as a reward for Seleucus: DS 18.39.5–6.

25. Olympias was assassinated only with some difficulty: 200 picked assassins could not bring themselves to dispatch her (DS 19.51). Then relatives of those she had killed did the deed.

26. The later career of Polyperchon: DS 20.20, 20.37.1, 20.100.6, 20.103.5–7; Heckel (1992), 189.

27. Aside from the deaths of Alexander's mates, three sisters were also all eventually killed, one by Perdiccas, one by Antigonus, and one by Cassander's son, as at Carney (1988).

28. The shift from *hetairoi* to *philoi*: Corradi (1929), 318–43. See also Introduction, n. 13.

29. Hero cult for Alexander is deducible from the hero cult for Hephaestion at *SEG* 40.547. Graffiti referring to Alexander as a hero: *SEG* 47.933. Returning soldiers responsible: Voutiras (1990), 130. The same honor given to Philip: *IG* xii.2 526 γ 4–5. Honors for Alexander in Alexandria: J. Val. 3.60. The Asia Minor oracles: Ch. 11, n. 28. Worship of Alexander on Thasos: *SEG* 17.415. Ionia: *OGI* 222. Later cult, but with no time of origin: Lucian. *DMort.* 13.2. Retrojecting all these cults to the period of the calendar reform: Habicht (1970), 17–26. Veterans honoring Alexander in 317: DS 19.22.2–3.

30. One companion, Lysimachus, did become a god in his own right, as at Hatzopoulos (1996), App. Ep. 22, 44, dated between 287 and 281, and thus perhaps not beginning until decades after Alexander's death.

31. The cults of Seleucus, Antigonus, and their successors: Habicht (1970), 17–18, 20–26; 82–87, 88–89, 92–99. The Babylonians, however, never worshipped Alexander as a god, even though they eventually worshipped the Seleucids, as at Van der Spek (1985).

32. The sarcophagus on public view: Erskine (2002), 167–79. Only a few years: Fraser (1972), ch. 1, n. 86, following Curt. 10.10.20. Alterations to the sarcophagus: Suet. *Aug.* 15, Str. 17.1.8, Zen. 3.94. The evolution of the Soma: Stewart (1993), 247.

33. The expansion from Alexander to dead Ptolemies, and later to living ones: Fraser (1972), 1.213–46. The visitor to Alexandria in 274: Ath. 5.198.

34. Serapis in Babylon: Ch. 11, n. 65. Altheim (1953), 111–12, saw the story in ethnic terms: Alexander's attempt to unify Macedonians and Persians having failed, Serapis brings about the symbolic unification of Macedonians and Egyptians. Bosworth (1988b), 169, envisions an Egyptian shrine in Babylon, yet one used by Macedonians—a kind of concatenation, but not unification.

35. Ptolemy's order: *OGIS* 56.1–3.
36. A summary of these developments from 272 to 238: Pfeiffer (2014a), 120–22.
37. The words of Augustus: Suet. *Aug.* 18. Presumably, he spoke after the sarcophagus was brought forth, implying that ordinary visitors may not have been able to see it.
38. The faux pas of Augustus: CD 51.16.5. Faux pas aside, this story is of a piece with Augustus's indifference to Egyptian religion and with his refusal to be crowned pharaoh. In these two respects, he was the opposite of the man he admired.
39. Caracalla in Alexandria: Hrd. 4.8.9. Later misfortunes: Fraser (1972), 2.34–35.
40. Christian polemics against Alexander: Theod. *Graec. Affect. Cur.* 8 (*PG* 83.1030); J. Chrysos. *Hom. xxvi in epist. secundam ad Cor.* (*PG* 61.258).
41. One pilgrim: Leo Afric. 8.263, not specifying the mosque in which the chapel was located. Africanus was a Muslim at the time of his visit, and thus may have had better access than Christian visitors who could not find either a chapel or a mosque, as noted by Matthey (2015), 324–25. Apparently Clarke (1805) first proposed that a sarcophagus found in the "mosque of Saint Athanasius" was Alexander's, although it proved to be Nakhtnebef's. Longer versions of this story of how the shrine disappeared: Schlange-Schöningen (1996), Erskine (2002), and Saunders (2006), 269–80 with refs.
42. The most recent fruitless search for Alexander's body, leading to Vergina: Hall (2014), 113–16.
43. Horned Alexanders: Stewart (1993), app. 4, passim, including examples from other media. The religious range of images of a horned Zeus-Amon or Zeus: Cook (1914), 346–409. The mosque of the two-horned man: Ibn Abdel Hakim, as at Fraser (1972), ch. 1, n. 86.
44. Cyrus as the two-horned man: Baljon (1961), 32, quoting the Indian writer and administrator Maulana Abdul Kalam Azad, an early exponent of this view. A son of Japheth rather than either Alexander or Cyrus: Horovitz (1926), 111–13.
45. A Hebrew source for these verses: 1 Macc. 1.3-4. The barrier would seem to be the Great Wall of Gorgan, which ran from the Caspian eastward to the Kopet Dagh Mountains and thus divided Persia from the steppes of Central Asia. Although it was built in the fifth century AD by the Sassanids, tradition attributed it to Alexander. It was abandoned in the seventh century, perhaps in the years when Muhammad was preaching. See Sauer et al. (2013). In sources older than the Koran, the wall or walls breached by Gog and Magog were just south of the Caucasus (Ezek. 37.1–3), although Gog came from the far north; later, the sons of Magog were Scythians (J. *A.* 1.6.1), which suggests a wall somewhere within the Caucasus. Another Muslim report of Gog and Magog: Firdausi 20.4. See also Van Donzel and Schmidt (2010).
46. Abraham: Koran 2.126. Cf. Isaac and Jacob (38.46–47), to whom knowledge of the Last Judgment is imparted, but whose statements about it are not quoted. Cf. also unnamed, unquoted messengers or warning-givers, as at 36.3, 36.14, and 50.2; and the generality of prophets to whom some knowledge of the Last Judgment is attributed. For Alexander and Christ, see Amitay (2010), 147–51.

APPENDICES

1. Not followed by one, as at Curt. 4.7.28.
2. Plu. *Alex.* 76.
3. An annual sacrifice, but modified on this occasion.
4. Probably *sphagia* as at Casabona (1966), 184; exx. include X. *An.* 4.3.18–19.
5. A bull, but probably *sphagia* as at n. 4 above.
6. Which some vegetal or animal offering would accompany.
7. Theopompos *FGrH* 115 F 253.
8. Probably *sphagia* as at n. 4 above.
9. Probably *sphagia* as at n. 4 above.
10. Later that day.
11. Probably *sphagia* as at n. 4 above.
12. Probably *diabatēria.*
13. Supposititious because reportedly occurring at the seaside. A funeral for Demaretus at some other time and place remains possible.
14. Probably *sphagia* as at n. 4 above.
15. Probably *sphagia* as at n. 4 above.
16. At two locations, with a distinct set of gods for each.
17. A bull.
   * Parmenio
   ** Clitus
   *** Aristander
   **** Nearchus
18. The shrine being closed, Alexander supposedly trespassed, and the Pythia quipped, "You are invincible."
19. See Ch. 2, n. 45.
20. Supposedly dating from sometime in Alexander's youth, and inserted here, according to the date at which it was supposedly brought to Alexander's attention.
21. The suppliant's words and gestures being incompatible with his acting as a *supplex.*
22. She later reverses herself.
23. But the supplicandus is lying, and betrays the suppliant. This is perhaps too tidily wicked, if not altogether supposititious.
24. Possibly betrayed, but the author will not commit himself.
25. A fabrication by Callisthenes, *FGrH* 124 F 4a, as shown by Tarn (1948), 2.274–75; cf. Parke (1985), 64, followed by Bosworth (1988a), 108 with refs. Of the several versions of this event, including Plu. *De ser. num vind.* 557b and DS 17 table of contents *K*, only Curtius includes supplication. The act of supplication implies that the Branchidae were in good standing in the eyes of both Apollo and the supplicandus, Alexander.
26. I.e., τῇ βουλῇ καὶ αὐτῷ.
27. Unclear when this meeting ends; the cure is administered sometime later.

28. I.e., *a rege et a ducibus.*
29. Day before battle.
30. Later the same day.
31. Evening before battle.
32. Evening before battle.
33. Dawn of the day of the battle.
34. Dawn of the day of the battle.
35. Dawn of the day of the battle.
36. Immediately before battle.
37. After the trial, whereas previous meeting occurs before the trial.
38. At Curt. 7.8.6, after some delay.
39. I.e., *a consilio.*
40. Next day.
41. Three days later.
42. Bosworth (1988a), 171.
43. Two days later than no. 36.
44. Perhaps not the same date as in Arrian, but the same subject, and mention of the same councilor, Nearchus. The scene is Alexander's bath.
45. Three days later than no. 36.
46. Four days later than no. 36.
47. Perhaps not the same date, and a different subject, military appointments as opposed to the Arabian expedition discussed according to Arrian.
48. Five days later than no. 36.
49. Commander not identified.

Bibliography

In this bibliography, the names of classics journals are abbreviated as in *L'Année Philologique*, but journals in the field of the *Tanakh* and the New Testament are abbreviated as in the *Handbook of Style of the Society of Biblical Literature*, 8.4.2. Journals in the field of Egyptology are abbreviated as at the *Journal of Egyptian Archaeology* 95 (2009): 4–13, and journals in the field of Assyriology are abbreviated as at *Cuneiform Digital Library Initiative*, http://cdli.ucla.edu/wiki/doku.php/abbreviations_for _assyriology. Except for Demosthenes, rendered as "Dem.," Greek and Roman authors and titles of works and collections are abbreviated as in *A Greek-English Lexicon*, ed. H. Liddell and R. Scott, rev. H. Stuart Jones (Oxford, 1968) and as in the *Oxford Latin Dictionary*, ed. P. G. W. Glare (Oxford, 1982). Titles of books of the *Tanakh* and the New Testament are abbreviated as for the Septuagint in *LSJ*, and titles of Plutarch's essays are abbreviated in Latin. Epigraphical works and collections are mostly abbreviated as at *Searchable Greek inscriptions: A Scholarly Tool in Progress*, by the Packard Humanities Institute (Los Altos, CA, 2006–). Achaemenid royal inscriptions are cited as in P. Lecoq, *Inscriptions de la Perse achéménide* (Paris, 1997).

Where translations are cited, the English text is that of the translator. Otherwise, the English text is that of the author.

Additional abbreviations appear below. These are chiefly abbreviations for ancient sources and for modern reference works, but one secondary work is included, Ernst Badian's *Collected Papers on Alexander the Great*. After these items appears a list of nineteenth- and early twentieth-century travel writers and geographers who are not quoted in this book but contributed to the description of certain places and climates.

ABC   *Ancient Babylonian Chronicles*. Ed. A. H. Grayson (Toronto, 1975).

AD   *Astronomical Diaries and Related Texts from Babylon*. Ed. A. Sachs and H. Hunger (Vienna, 1988–1996).

Al-Tabari   *The History of al-Ṭabarī, Taʾrīkh al-rusul waʾl mulūk*. Ed. E. Yarshater (Albany, NY, 1985–2007).

ANET   *Ancient Near Eastern Texts Relating to the Old Testament.* Ed.
                  J. B. Pritchard (Princeton, 1969).

Ar. Ps.-Call.   *The Romance of Alexander the Great by Pseudo-Callisthenes:
                  Translated from the Armenian Version.* A. M. Wolohojian (New
                  York, 1969).

Arr. fr.   *TA META AAEXANΔPON,* in *Flavii Arriani quae exstant omnia,*
                  v. 2. Ed. A. Roos, rev. G. Wirth (Leipzig, 1967).

BaM   *Baghdader Mitteilungen. Beiheft* (Berlin, 1968–1987).

BCP   Ernst Badian, *Collected Papers on Alexander the Great.* Ed. R. Stoneman
                  (*London,* 2008).

CAH   *Cambridge Ancient History.* Ed. J. Boardman, D. M. Lewis,
                  S. Hornblower, and M. Ostwald. 2nd ed. (Cambridge, 1971–2006).

Cyrus Cylinder   H. Schaudig, *Die Inschriften Nabonids von Babylon und Kyros' des
                  Grossen* (Münster, *2001*).

Edfou   *Die Inschriften des Tempels von Edfu.* Ed. D. Kurth (Wiesbaden, 1998–).

EI   *Encyclopedia Iranica.* Ed. E. Yarshater et al. (New York, 1982–).

Epit. Mett.   *Incerti auctoris Epitoma rerum gestarum Alexandri Magni cum libro
                  de morte testamentoque Alexandri.* Ed. P. Thomas (Leipzig, 1960).

Eus. Chron.   Patrologiae Cursus Completus, Series Graeca, vol. 19. Ed. J.-P. Migne
                  (Paris, 1857–1866).

FGrH   *Fragmente der griechischen Historiker.* Ed. F. Jacoby (Berlin,
                  1923–1958).

Firdausi   *The Shahnama of Firdausi.* Tr. A. and E. Warner (London, 1905–1925).
                  Chapters and sections as at *The Epic of the Kings.* Tr. R. Levy
                  (Chicago, 1967).

Fort.   *Elamite Presepolis Fortification Archive,* ed. M. Stolper and
                  W. Henkelman, as at oi.cicago.edu/research/projects/persepolis
                  -fortification-archive.

Gardīzī   *Zain al-'aḫbār: az rū-i du nusḫa-i ḫaṭṭī-i makšūf-i dunyā dar
                  Kambrig̃ wa Āksfurd-i Inglistān.* Ed. Abd-al-Hai Habībī (Tehran,
                  1968).

GHI   *Greek Historical Inscriptions.* Ed. M. Todd (Oxford, 1948).

Hist. Frid.   *Historia de expeditione Friderici imperatoris.* Ed. J. Debrowsky
                  (Prague, 1827).

HR   *An Old Hebrew Romance of Alexander.* Tr. M. Gaster, *Journal of the
                  Royal Asiatic Society of Great Britain and Ireland* (1887): 485–509.

Jer. Chron.   Patrologiae Cursus Completus, Series Latina, vol. 27. Ed. J.-P. Migne
                  (Paris, 1841–1855).

Justin   *Epitoma historiarum Philippicarum Pompei Trogi; accedunt prologi in
                  Pompeium Trogum.* Ed. O. Seel (Stuttgart, 1985).

K-A   *Poetae comici Graeci.* Ed. R. Kassel and C. Austin (Berlin, 1983–).

Leo Afric.	*Léon, l'Africain*. A. Maalouf (Paris, 1986).
Nizami	*The Sikander Nāma, or Book of Alexander, written A.D. 1200*. Tr. H. W. Clarke (London, 1881).
OCD	*Oxford Classical Dictionary*. Ed. S. Hornblower, A. Spawforth, and E. Eidinow. 4th ed. (Oxford, 2012).
Pallad.	*De gentibus Indiae et Bragmanibus*. Ed. W. Berghoff (Meisenheim-am-Glan, 1967).
PG	*Patrologiae cursus completus, series Graeca*. Ed. J. Migne (Paris, 1857–1866).
Ps.-Call. A	*Historia Alexandri Magni*. Ed. W. Kroll (Berlin, 1926).
Ps.-Call. B	*Der griechische Alexanderroman, Rezension Beta*. Ed. L. Bergson (Stockholm, 1965).
Ps.-Call. Γ	*Der griechische Alexanderroman: Rezension Gamma*. Ed. A. Hain (Meisenheim-am-Glan, 1962–1969).
RAcc	*Rituels Accadiens*. F. Thureau-Dangin (Paris, 1921).
RE	*Real-Encyclopädie der classischen Altertumswissenschaft*. Ed. A. Pauly and G. Wissowa (Stuttgart, 1894–1980).
Roscher	*Ausführliches Lexikon der griechischen und römischen Mythologie*. Ed. W. Roscher (Leipzig, 1884–1927).
Sargon & Sennacherib	*The Neo-Babylonian Correspondence of Sargon and Sennacherib. State Archives of Assyria* 17. Ed. M. Dietrich (Helsinki, 2003).
SB *Gilgamesh*	*The Standard Babylonian Epic of Gilgamesh*. Ed. S. Parpola. *State Archives of Assyria Cuneiform Texts 1* (Helsinki, 1997).
Sennacherib	*The Annals of Sennacherib*. Ed. D. Luckenbill (Chicago, 1924).
Syncellus	*Georgii Syncelli Ecloga Chronographica*. Ed. A. Mosshammer (Leipzig, 1984).
ZDMG	*Zeitschrift des deutschen morganländisches Gesellschaft* (Leipzig, 1843–1988).

TRAVEL WRITERS AND GEOGRAPHERS

Bellew, H. W. 1874. *From the Indus to the Tigris: A Narrative of a Journey Through the Countries of Balochistan, Afghanistan, Khorassan, and Iran, in 1872*. London.

Burckhardt, J. 1830. *Notes on the Bedouins and Wahabis, Collected During His Travels in the East*. London.

Burns, A. 1934. *A Voyage on the Indus*. London.

Byron, R. 1937. *The Road to Oxiana*. London = 1982. Oxford.

Cunningham, A. 1871. *The Ancient Geography of India*. London = 1963. Ramapura.

Fellows, C. 1852. *Travels and Researches in Asia Minor, More Particularly in the Province of Lycia*. London.

Ferrier, J. P. 1857. *Caravan Journeys and Wanderings in Persia, Afghanistan, Turkistan, and Beloochistan, with Historical Notices of the Countries Lying Between Russia and India*. Tr. W. Jesse. London. 2nd ed.

Fisher, W. B. 1950. *The Middle East: A Physical, Social, and Regional Geography*. London.

Hamilton, W. 1842. *Researches in Asia Minor, Pontus, and Armenia*. London.

Layard, H. 1894. *Early Adventures in Persia, Susiana, and Babylonia*. London.

Leake, W. 1824. *Journal of a Tour in Asia Minor*. London = 2010. Cambridge.

Masson, P. 1842. *Narrative of Various Journeys in Balochistan, Afghanistan, and the Panjab*. London = 1974. Oxford.

Ramsay, W. 1890. *Historical Geography of Asia Minor*. London.

Steindorff, G. 1904. *Through the Libyan Desert to the Oasis at Ammon*. Tr. T. Ziolkowski. Bielefeld = 1977. New Haven, CT.

Von Moltke, H. 1841. *Briefe über Zustande und Begebenheiten in der Türkei aus den Jahren 1835 bis 1839*. Berlin = 1979. *Unter dem Halbmond. Erlebnisse in den alten Türkei*. Ed. H. Arndt. Tübingen.

GENERAL BIBLIOGRAPHY

Abd el-Razik, M. 1984. *Die Darstellungen und Texte des Sanktuars Alexanders des Grossen im Tempel von Luxor*. *ArchVer* 16. Mainz-am-Rhein.

Abramenko, A. 2000. "Der Fremde auf dem Thron. Die letzte Verschwörung gegen Alexander d. Gr.," *Klio* 82.2: 361–78.

Adams, W., and E. Borza, eds. 1982. *Philip II, Alexander the Great, and the Macedonian Heritage*. Washington, DC.

Adcock, F. E. 1957. *The Greek and Macedonian Art of War*. Berkeley.

Al-Rawi, F. N. H. 1985. "Nabopolassar's Restoration Work on the Wall Imgur-Enlil at Babylon," *Iraq* 47: 1–13.

Allen, S. 2015. *The Splintered Divine: A Study of Ištar, Baal, and Yahweh. Divine Names and Divine Multiplicity in the Ancient Near East*. Berlin.

Altheim, F. 1953. *Alexander und Asien: Geschichte eines geistigen Erbes*. Tübingen.

Amiet, P. 1979. "Archaeological Discontinuity and Ethnic Duality in Elam," *Antiquity* 53: 195–204.

Amitay, O. 2010. *From Alexander to Jesus*. Hellenistic Culture and Society 52. Berkeley.

Andronikos, M. 1970. "Sarissa," *BCH* 94: 91–107.

———. 1984. *Vergina: The Royal Tombs and the Ancient City*. Athens.

Anochin, V., and R. Rolle. 1998. "Griechische Schleuderbleie bei den Mauern von Olbia," in *Archäologische Studien in Kontaktzonen der antiken Welt*. Ed. R. Rolle and K. Schmidt. Göttingen. Pp. 837–49.

Anson, E. 1985. "The Hypaspists: Macedon's Citizen-Soldiers," *Historia* 34: 46–48.

———. 1989. "The Persian Fleet in 334," *CP* 44: 44–49.

Antela-Bernárdez, B. 2007. "Alejandro Magno o la demostración de la divinidad," *Faventia* 29: 89–103.

———. 2016. "Like Gods Among Men: The Use of Religion and Mythical Issues During Alexander's Campaign," in Ulanowski (2016), pp. 235–56.

Arnaud, P. 2005. *Les routes de la navigation antique. Itinéraires en Méditerranée*. Paris.

Asirvatham, S. 2001. "Olympias' Snake and Callisthenes' Stand: Religion and Politics in Plutarch's *Life of Alexander*," in *Between Magic and Religion: Interdisciplinary Studies in Ancient Mediterranean Religion and Society*. Ed. S. Asirvatham, C. Pache, and J. Watrous. Lanham, MD. Pp. 93–125.

———. 2012. "Alexander the Philosopher in the Greco-Roman, Persian, and Arabic Traditions," in *The Alexander Romance in Persia and the East*. Ed. R. Stoneman. Groningen. Pp. 311–26.

Atkinson, J. 1980–1994. *A Commentary on Q. Curtius Rufus*. Historiae Alexandri Magni: *Books 5–7.2 and Books 3–4*. Amsterdam.

———. 1987. "The Infantry Commissions Awarded by Alexander at the End of 331," in Will and Heinrichs (1987), pp. 413–35.

Atkinson, J., and J. Yardley. 2009. *Curtius Rufus: Histories of Alexander the Great, Book 10*. Oxford.

Aubriot, D. 2003. "Quelques observations sur la religion d'Alexandre (par rapport à la tradition classique) à partir de Plutarque (*La Vie d'Alexandre*) et d'Arrien (*L'Anabase d'Alexandre*)," *Métis* n.s. 1: 225–49.

Badian, E. 1960. "The Death of Parmenio," *TAPA* 91: 324–38 = *BCP*, 36–48.

———. 1961. "Harpalus," *JHS* 81: 16–43 = *BCP*, 58–96.

———. 1963. "The Death of Philip II," *Phoenix* 17: 244–50 = *BCP*, 106–13.

———. 1964. "Alexander the Great and the Loneliness of Power," in *Studies in Greek and Roman History*. Oxford. Pp. 192–205 = *BCP*, 96–106.

———. 1965. "The Administration of the Empire," *G & R* 12:166–82.

———. 1966. "Alexander the Great and the Greeks of Asia," in *Ancient Society and Its Institutions: Studies Presented to Victor Ehrenberg on His 75th Birthday*. Ed. E. Badian. Oxford. Pp. 37–69 = *BCP*, 14–53.

———. 1976, ed. *Alexandre le grand. Image et réalité*. Entretiens sur l'antiquité classique, Fondation Hardt 22. Geneva.

———. 1977. "The Battle at the Granicus: A New Look," in *Ancient Macedonia II. Papers Read at the Second International Symposium Held in Thessaloniki, 19–24 August 1973*. Institute for Balkan Studies 155. Thessalonica. Pp. 271–93 = *BCP*, 224–44.

———. 1981. "The Deification of Alexander the Great," in Dell (1981), pp. 27–71 = *BCP*, 244–82.

———. 1985. "Alexander in Iran," in the *Cambridge History of Iran*. Vol. 2. Ed. I. Gershevitch. Cambridge. Pp. 420–501.

———. 1996. "Alexander the Great Between Two Thrones and Heaven: Variations on an Old Theme," in *Subject and Ruler: The Cult of the Ruling Power in Classical Antiquity: Papers Presented at a Conference Held in the University of Alberta on April 13–15, 1994, to Celebrate the 65th Anniversary of Duncan Fishwick*. Ed. A. Small. Ann Arbor. Pp. 11–26 = *BCP*, 365–86.

———. 2000. "Conspiracies," in Bosworth and Baynham (2000), pp. 50–96 = *BCP*, 420–57.

Baege, W. 1913. *De Macedonum Sacris*. Halle.

Bakir, T. 1995. "Archäologische Beobachtungen über die Residenz in Daskyleion," *Pallas* 43: 269–85.

———. 2006. "Daskyleion," *Byzas* 3: 61–71.

Baljon, J. 1961. *Modern Muslim Koran Interpretation (1889–1960)*. Leiden.

Balsdon, J. P. 1950. "The Divinity of Alexander," *Historia* 1: 363–88.

Barguet, P. 1962. *Le temple d'Amon-Rê à Karnak. Essai d'exégèse*. Recherches d'archéologie, de philologie et d'histoire 21. Cairo.

Barkun, M. 1968. *Law Without Sanctions: Order in Primitive Societies and the World Community*. New Haven, CT.

Barnett, R., E. Bleibtreu, and G. Turner. 1998. *Sculptures from the Southwest Palace of Sennacherib at Nineveh*. London.

Beaulieu, P.-A. 1988. "Swamps as Burial Places for Babylonian Kings," *NABU* no. 53.

———. 1989. *The Reign of Nabonidus, King of Babylon, 556–539 B.C.* New Haven, CT.

———. 2006. "De L'Esagil au museion. La organisation de la recherche scientifique au ivᵉ siècle av. J.-C.," in Briant and Joannès (2006), pp. 17–36.

Beaulieu, P., and J. Britton. 1994. "Rituals for an Eclipse Possibility in the 8th Year of Cyrus," *JCS* 46: 73–86.

Bekker-Nielsen, T., and L. Hannestad, eds. 2001. *War as a Cultural and Social Force: Essays on Warfare in Antiquity*. Copenhagen.

Bell, L. 1985a. "The Luxor Temple and the Cult of the Royal *Ka*," *JNES* 44: 251–94.

———. 1985b. "Aspects of the Cult of the Deified Tutankhamun," in *Mélanges Gamal Eddin Mokhtar*. Ed. P. Posener-Krieger. Vol. 1. Cairo. Pp. 39–59.

Beloch, K. J. 1922–1927. *Griechische Geschichte*. Berlin. 2nd ed.

Ben-Barak, Z. 1980. "The Coronation Ceremony in Ancient Mesopotamia," *OLP* 11: 55–67.

Bengston, H. 1937. *Die Strategie in der Hellenistischen Zeit. Ein Beitrag zum antiken Staatsrecht. MBPF* 36. Munich.

———. 1985. *Philipp und Alexander der Grosse. Begründer der hellenistischen Welt*. Munich.

Benveniste. E. 1943–1945. "La ville de Cyreschata," *Journal Asiatique* 234: 163–66.

Beran, T. 1988. "Leben und Tod der Bilder," in *Ad Bene et Fideliter Seminandum. Festgabe für Karlheinz Deller zum 21 Februar 1987. AOAT* 220. Ed. G. Mauer and U. Magen. Neukirchen-Vluyn. Pp. 55–61.

Berve, H. 1926. *Das Alexanderreich auf prosopographischer Grundlage*. Munich.

Bevan, E. 1935. "Alexander the Great," in the *Cambridge History of India*. Vol. 1. Ed. E. Rapson. Cambridge. Pp. 345–90.

Bichler, R., and R. Rollinger. 2005. "Die Hängenden Gärten zu Ninive—Die Lösung eines Rätsels?" in *Von Sumer bis Homer. Festschrift für Manfred Schretter zum 60. Geburtstag 25 Februar 2004. AAOT* 235. Ed. R. Rollinger. Munich. Pp. 153–218.

Biffi, N. 2005. *L'estremo oriente di Strabone. Libro xv della Geografia*. Bari.

Bing, J. 1991. "Alexander's Sacrifice *dis praesidibus loci* before the Battle of Issus," *JHS* 111: 161–65.

Bivar, A., and M. Boyce. 1998. "Eṣṭak̲r̲," *EI 8*.6.643–46.

Black, J. 1991. "The New Year Ceremonies in Ancient Babylon: Taking Bel by the Hand and a Cultic Picnic," *Religion* 11: 39–59.

Blazquez, J. 2000. "Alejandro Magno, *Homo Religiosus*," in *Alejandro Magno, Hombre y Mito*. Ed. J. Alvar and J. Blazquez. Madrid. Pp. 99–152.

Bliquez, L. 2014. *The Tools of Asclepius: Surgical Instruments in Greek and Roman Times*. Studies in Ancient Medicine 43. Leiden.

Blöbaum, A. 2006. *"Denn ich bin ein König, der die Maat liebt": Herrscherlegitimation im spätzeitlichen Ägypten. Eine vergleichende Untersuchung der Phraseologie in den offiziellen Königsinschriften vom Beginn der 25. Dynastie bis zum Ende der makedonischen Herrschaft*. AegMonast 4. Aachen.

Bloedow, E. F. 2004. "Egypt in Alexander's Scheme of Things," *QUCC* 77: 75–99.

Boiy, T. 2004. *Late Achaemenid and Hellenistic Babylon*. OLA 136. Leuven.

———. 2006. "Aspects chronologiques de la période de transition (350–300)," in Briant and Joannès (2006), pp. 37–100.

Bonnet, C. 1988. *Melqart. Cultes et mythes de l'Héraclès tyrien en méditerranée*. Leuven.

Borchard, L. 1933. *Allerhand Kleinigkeiten: seinen wissenschaftlichen Freunden und Bekannten zu seinem 70. Geburtstage am 5. Oktober 1933 überreicht von Ludwig Borchart*. Leipzig.

Borger, R. 1996. *Beiträge zum Inschriftenwerk Assurbanipals. Die Prismenklassen A, B, C = K, D, E, F, G, H, J und T Sowie Andere Inschriften*. Wiesbaden.

Borza, E. 1972. "Fire From Heaven: Alexander at Persepolis," *CP* 67: 234–45.

———. 1991. *In the Shadow of Olympus: The Emergence of Macedon*. Princeton.

Borza, E., and O. Palagia. 2007. "The Chronology of the Macedonian Royal Tombs at Vergina," *JDAI* 122: 81–127.

Borza, E., and J. Reames-Zimmerman. 2000. "Some New Thoughts on the Death of Alexander the Great," *AncW* 31.1: 22–30.

Bosch-Puche, F. 2008. "L'autel du temple d'Alexandre le Grand à Bahariya retrouvé," *BIFAO* 108: 29–44.

———. 2013. "The Egyptian Royal Titulary of Alexander the Great, I: Horus, Two Ladies, Golden Horus, and Throne Names," *JEA* 99: 131–56.

Bosworth, A. B. 1971. "The Death of Alexander the Great: Rumour and Propaganda," *CQ* n.s. 21: 112–36.

———. 1977. "Alexander and Ammon," in *Greece and the Ancient Mediterranean in History and Prehistory. Studies Presented to Fritz Schachermeyr on the Occasion of His 80th Birthday*. Ed. K. Kinzel. Berlin. Pp. 51–75.

———. 1980–1995. *A Historical Commentary on Arrian's* Anabasis Alexandri. Oxford.

———. 1980b. "Alexander and the Iranians," *JHS* 100: 1–21.

———. 1986. "Alexander the Great and the Decline of Macedon," *JHS* 106: 1–12.

———. 1988a. *Conquest and Empire: The Reign of Alexander the Great*. Cambridge.

———. 1988b. *From Arrian to Alexander: Studies in Historical Interpretation.* Oxford.

———. 1992. "Philip III Arrhidaeus and the Chronology of the Successors," *Chiron* 22: 55–81.

———. 1994. "Alexander the Great, I: The Events in the Reign," *CAH* 6.791–845.

———.1996a. *Alexander and the East: The Tragedy of Triumph.* Oxford.

———. 1996b. "Alexander, Euripides, and Dionysus: The Motivation for an Apotheosis," in *Transitions to Empire: Studies in Greco-Roman History, 360–146, in Honor of E. Badian.* Ed. E. Harris and R. Wallace. Norman, OK. Pp. 140–68.

———. 2000a. "Ptolemy and the Will of Alexander," in Bosworth and Baynham (2000), pp. 207–42.

———. 2000b. "A Tale of Two Empires: Hernán Cortés and Alexander the Great," ibid. Pp. 23–49.

———. 2003. "Plus Ça Change…Ancient Historians and Their Sources," *CA* 22.2: 167–98.

———. 2010. "Alexander's Death: The Poisoning Rumors," in *The Landmark Arrian: The Campaigns of Alexander.* Ed. J. Romm. New York. Pp. 407–10.

Bosworth, A., and E. Baynham, eds. 2000. *Alexander the Great in Fact and Fiction.* Oxford.

Bottéro, J. 1987. *Mésopotamie. L'écriture, la raison, et les dieux.* Paris.

Bowden, H. 2013. "On Kissing and Making Up: Court Protocol and Historiography in Alexander the Great's 'Experiment with *Proskynesis*,'" *BICS* 56: 55–77.

———. 2014. "Review Article: Recent Travels in Alexanderland," *JHS* 134: 136–48.

Boyce, M. 1984. *Zoroastrians: Their Religious Beliefs and Practices.* London.

Boyce, M., and F. Grenet. 1991. *A History of Zoroastrianism.* Vol. 3. Leiden.

Briant, P. 1974. *Alexandre le Grand.* Paris. Paris = 2010. *Alexander the Great and His Empire: A Short Introduction.* Tr. A. Kuhrt. Princeton.

———. 1979. "*Des Achéménides aux rois hellénistiques. Continuités et ruptures,*" *ASNP* 3rd ser. 9: 1375–414.

———. 1994. "Sources Gréco-hellénistiques, institutions perses et institutions macédoniennes. Continuités, changements, et bricolages," in *Continuity and Change: Proceedings of the Last Achaemenid History Workshop, April 6–8, 1990, Ann Arbor, Michigan.* AchHist 8. Ed. H. Sancisi-Weerdenburg and M. Root. Leiden. Pp. 283–310.

———. 2002. *From Cyrus to Alexander: A History of the Persian Empire.* Tr. P. Daniels. Winona Lake, IN.

———. 2015. *Darius in the Shadow of Alexander.* Tr. J. Todd. Cambridge, MA.

Briant, P., and F. Joannès, eds. 2006. *La transition entre l'empire achéménide et les royaumes hellénistiques.* Paris.

Brisch, N., ed. 2008. *Religion and Power: Divine Kingship in the Ancient World and Beyond.* Chicago Oriental Institute Seminars 4. Chicago.

———. 2008a. "Introduction," in Brisch (2008), pp. 1–11.

Brosius, M. 1996. *Women in Ancient Persia, 559 to 331 BC.* Oxford.

———. 2003. "Alexander and the Persians," in Roisman (2003), pp. 169–93.

Brown, D. 2000. *Mesopotamian Planetary Astronomy-Astrology*. Cuneiform Monographs 18. Groningen.

Brunt. P., 1976–1983. *Arrian*. Loeb Classical Library 236. Cambridge, MA.

———. 1987. *Italian Manpower, 225 B.C. to A.D. 14*. Oxford. 2nd ed.

Bryant, E. 2001. *The Quest for the Origins of Vedic Culture: The Indo-Aryan Migration Debate*. Oxford.

Büchler, A. 1898. "La relation de Josèphe concernant Alexandre le Grand," *REJ* 36: 1–26.

Budde, D., et al. 2003. *Lexikon der ägyptischen Götter und Götterbezeichnungen, VIII*. OLA 129. Leuven.

Burkert, W. 1985. *Greek Religion*. Tr. J. Raffan. Cambridge, MA.

Burn, A. R. 1963. *Alexander the Great and the Middle East*. London.

Burstein, S. 1991. "Pharaoh Alexander: A Scholarly Myth," *AncSoc* 22: 139–45.

Buttrey, T. V. 1982. "Pharaonic Imitations of Athenian Tetradrachms," in *Actes du 9e congrès international de numismatique, Septembre 1979*. Louvain-la-Neuve. Pp. 137–40.

———. 1993. "Calculating Ancient Coin Production: Facts and Fantasies," *NC* 153: 335–51.

———. 1994. "Calculating Coin Production II: Why It Cannot Be Done," *NC* 154: 342–52.

Cantarella, E. 2011. *I supplizi capitali in Grecia e a Roma. Origine e funzioni delle pene di morte nell'antichità classica*. Rome. 3rd ed.

Carlier, P. 2000. "Homeric and Macedonian Kingship," in *Alternatives to Athens: Varieties of Political Organization and Community in Ancient Greece*. Ed. R. Brock and S. Hodkinson. Oxford. Pp. 259–68.

Carney, E. 1988. "The Sisters of Alexander the Great: Royal Relicts," *Historia* 37: 385–404.

———. 1992. "The Politics of Polygamy: Olympias, Alexander, and the Murder of Philip," *Historia* 41: 169–89 = Carney (2015), pp. 167–89.

———. 1996. "Macedonians and Mutiny: Discipline and Indiscipline in the Army of Philip and Alexander," *CP* 91: 19–44 = Carney (2015), pp. 27–56.

———. 2000. *Women and Monarchy in Macedonia*. Oklahoma City, OK.

———. 2010. "Macedonian Women," in Roisman and Worthington (2010). Pp. 409–28.

———. 2015. *King and Court in Ancient Macedonia: Rivalry, Treason, and Conspiracy*. Swansea.

Caroe, O. 1958. *The Pathans, 550 BC–AD 1957*. London.

Carradice, I. 1987. "The 'Regal Coinage' in the Persian Empire," in *Coinage and Administration in the Athenian and Persian Empires. The Ninth Oxford Symposium on Coinage and Monetary History*. Ed. I. Carradice. Oxford. Pp. 73–107.

Carter, G. 1983. "A Simplified Method of Calculating the Original Number of Dies from Die Link Statistics," *ANSMN* 28: 195–206.

Cartledge, P. 2004. *Alexander the Great: The Hunt for a New Past*. London.

Casabona, J. 1966. *Recherches sur le vocabulaire des sacrifices en Grèce des origines à la fin de l'époque classique*. *Publication des annales de la faculté des lettres* n.s. 56. Aix-en-Provence

Cascon Dorado, A. 1990. "La labor demisitificadora de Curcio Rufo en su Historia de Alejandro Magno," *Neronia* 4: 254–65.

Case, S. 1915. "Religion and War in the Graeco-Roman World," *AJTh* 19: 179–99.

Casson, L. 1971. *Ships and Seamanship in the Ancient World*. Princeton.

Cavaignac, E. 1913–1920. *Histoire de l'antiquité*. Paris.

Cawkwell, G. 1994. "The Deification of Alexander the Great: A Note," in *Ventures into Greek History: Essays in Honour of N. G. L. Hammond*. Ed. I. Worthington. Oxford. Pp. 293–306.

Černý, J. 1935. "Questions addressées aux oracles," *BIFAO* 35: 41–58.

———. 1942. "Nouvelle série des questions addressées aux oracles," *BIFAO* 41: 13–24.

———. 1962. "Egyptian Oracles," in *A Saite Oracle Papyrus from Thebes in the Brooklyn Museum*. Ed. R. Parker. Providence. Pp. 45–38.

———. 1972. "Troisième série des questions addressées aux oracles," *BIFAO* 72: 49–79.

Chamoux, F. 2006. "Le tombeau de Sardanaple," in Φιλολογία. *Mélanges offerts à Michel Casevitz*. Collection de la maison de l'Orient et de la Méditerranée 35. Ed. P. Brillet-Dubois and E. Parmentier. Paris. Pp. 205–11.

Chaniotis, A. 2003. "The Divinity of Hellenistic Rulers," in *A Companion to the Hellenistic World*. Ed. A. Erskine. Malden, MA. Pp. 431–45.

———. 2004. "Justifying Territorial Claims in Classical and Hellenistic Greece: The Beginnings of International Law," in *The Law and the Courts in Ancient Greece*. Ed. E. Harris and L. Rubenstein. London. Pp. 185–213.

Charles, M. 2011. "Immortals and Apple-Bearers: Towards a Better Understanding of Achaemenid Infantry Units," *CQ* n.s. 61: 114–33.

———. 2012. "The Persian *ΚΑΡΔΑΚΕΣ*," *JHS* 132: 23–40.

———. 2015. "Achaemenid Elite Cavalry from Xerxes to Darius III," *CQ* n.s. 65: 14–34.

Choksy, J. 2012. "Justifiable Force and Holy War in Zoroastrianism," in *Fighting Words: Religion, Violence, and the Interpretation of Sacred Texts*. Ed. J. Renard. Berkeley. Pp. 158–77.

Christesen, P., and S. Murray. 2010. "Macedonian Religion," in Roisman and Worthington (2010), pp. 428–46.

Chugg, A. 2002. "The Sarcophagus of Alexander the Great?" *G & R* 49: 8–26.

Ciancaglini, C. 1998. "Alessandro e l'incendio Persepoli nelle tradizioni greca e iranica," in *La diffusione dell'eredità classica nell'età tardo antica e medievale. Forme e modi di trasmissione. Atti del seminario nazionale (Trieste, 19–20 settembre 1996)*. Ed. A. Valvo. Trieste. Pp. 59–81.

Clarke. E. 1805. *The Tomb of Alexander. A Dissertation on the Sarcophagus from Alexandria and Now in the British Museum*. London.

Classen, C. 1959. "The Libyan God Ammon in Greece Before 331 BC," *Historia* 8: 349–55.

Clausewitz, K. von. 1876. *On War*. Tr. M. Howard and P. Paret. Princeton.

Clère, J. 1951. "Une statuette du fils aîné du roi Nectanebô," *RevEg* 6:135–56.

Colin, F. 1998. "Les fondateurs du sanctuaire d'Amon à Siwa (désert Libyque)," in *Egyptian Religion, the Last 1,000 Years: Studies Dedicated to the Memory of Jan Quaegebur, II.* Ed. W. Clarysse, A. Schoors, and H. Willems. Leuven. Pp. 1.329–55.

Collins, A. 2012. "The Royal Costume and Insignia of Alexander the Great," *AJP* 133: 371–402.

Coningham, R. 2001. "The Archaeology of Buddhism," in *Archaeology and World Religion*. Ed. T. Insoll. London. Pp. 61–95.

Conrad, L. 1992. "The Conquest of Arwād: A Source-critical Study in the Historiography of the Early Medieval Near East," in *The Byzantine and Early Islamic Near East: Papers of the First Workshop on Late Antiquity and Early Islam*. Vol. 1. Ed. L. Conrad and A. Cameron. Princeton. Pp. 317–401.

Cook, A. R. 1914–1940. *Zeus*. Cambridge.

Corradi, G. 1929. *Studi ellenistici*. Turin.

Costanzi, V. 1915. *Studi di storia macedonica sino a Filippo*. Pisa.

Crawford, M. 1974. *Roman Republican Coinage*. Cambridge.

Cross, F. 1963. "The Discovery of the Samaria Papyri," *BA* 16: 110–21.

Crowfoot, J., K. Kenyon, and E. Sukenik. 1942. *The Buildings at Samaria. Samaria-Sebaste: Reports of the Work of the Joint Expedition in 1931–1933, and of the British Expedition in 1935*. London.

Cunha, B. 2004. "Alexander the Great and West Nile Virus Encephalitis," *Emerging Infectious Diseases* 9: 1599–1603.

Currie, B. 2005. *Pindar and the Cult of Heroes*. Oxford.

Dalley, S. 1998. "Persian, Greek, and Parthian Overlords," in *The Legacy of Mesopotamia*. Ed. S. Dalley. Oxford. Pp. 35–55.

———. 2013. *The Mystery of the Hanging Gardens of Babylon: An Elusive World Wonder Traced*. Oxford.

Dandamaev, M. 1979. "State and Temple in Babylonia in the First Millennium B.C.," in *State and Temple Economy in the Ancient Near East, II*. Ed. E. Lipiński. OLA 6. Leuven. Pp. 589–96.

———. 1988. "The Title *aḫ šdrapānu* in Nippur," in *Nippur at the Centennial: Papers Read at RAI 35, Philadelphia, 1988*. Ed. M. de Jong Ellis. Philadelphia. Pp. 29–32.

———. 1990. "Cambyses II," *EI* 4.726–29.

———. 1996. "Land Use in the Sippar Region in the Neo-Babylonian and Achaemenid Periods," in *Urbanization and Land Ownership in the Ancient Near East*. Ed. M. Hudson and B. Levine. Cambridge, MA. Pp. 363–87.

Dandamaev, M., and V. Lukonin. 1989. *The Culture and Social Institutions of Ancient Iran*. Cambridge.

Dani, A. 1986. *The Historic City of Taxila*. Paris.

Daniélou, A. 1982. *Shiva and Dionysus*. Tr. K. F. Hurry. New York.

De Callatuÿ, F. 1989. "Les trésors achéménides et les monnayages d'Alexandre: espèces immobilisées et espèces circulantes?" in *L'or perse et l'histoire grecque, REA* 91: 259–64.

———. 1995. "Calculating Ancient Coin Production: Seeking a Balance," *NC* 155: 298–311.

———. 2011. "Quantifying Monetary Production in Greco-Roman Times: A General Frame," in *Quantifying Monetary Supplies in Greco-Roman Times. Proceedings of the Third Francqui Conference held at the Academia belgica, Rome, 29–30 Sept. 2008*. Ed. F. de Callatuÿ. Bari. Pp. 7–29.

De la Porte, J. 2004. *The Caucasus and Central Asia Program Newsletter of the University of California at Berkeley*, 2004 no. 6: 12–14.

De la Vallée Poussin, L. 1971. *L'Abhidharmakośa de Vasubandhu*, I. Brussels.

Delatte, A. 1951. *Le baiser, l'agenouillement et le prosternement de l'adoration. Proskynesis chez les Grecs*. Academie royale de Belgique. Bulletin de la classe des lettres et des sciences morales et politiques 37. Brussels.

Delbrück, H. 1900. *Geschichte der Kriegskunst im Rahmen der politischen Geschichte*. Berlin = 2000. Berlin.

Dell, H., ed. 1981. *Ancient Macedonian Studies in Honor of Charles F. Edson. Inst. for Balkan Stud*. 158. Thessalonica.

Depuydt, L. 1997. "The Time of Death of Alexander the Great: 11 June 323 BC (-332), ca. 4:00–5:00 PM," *Die Welt des Orients* 28: 117–35.

Despinis, G., T. Tiveriou, and E. Voutiras. 1997. *Catalogue of Sculpture in the Archaeological Museum of Thessaloniki*. Vol. 1. Thessalonica.

Devine, A. 1986. "The Strategies of Alexander the Great and Darius III in the Issus Campaign," *AncW* 12: 25–38.

———. 1989. "The Macedonian Army at Gaugamela: Its Strength and the Length of Its Battle-Line," *AncW* 19: 77–80.

Dodson, A., et al. 1994. *The Canopic Equipment of the Kings of Egypt*. London.

Drews, R. 1965. "Assyria in Classical Universal Histories," *Historia* 14: 129–42.

Drougou, S. 2011. "Vergina—the Ancient City of Aegae," in Lane Fox (2011), pp. 243–56.

Droysen, J. 1833. *Geschichte Alexanders des Grossen*. Berlin = 1966. Dusseldorf.

———. 1877. *Geschichte des Hellenismus*, Vol. 1. 2nd ed. Gotha = 1952. Basel. Ed. E. Bayer.

Ducrey, P. 1988. "Des dieux et des sanctuaires à Philippes de Macédoine," in *Comptes et inventaires dans la cité grecque*. Ed. D. Knoephler and N. Quellet. Neuchâtel-Geneva. Pp. 207–13.

———. 1999. *Le traitement des prisonniers de guerre dans la Grèce antique des origines à la conquête romaine*. Paris. 2nd ed.

Dumas, A. 1840. *Napoléon*. Paris.

Dumke, A. 2011. "Gutes Gold. Überlegungen zum Sinnhorizont der *nbw nfr*-Prägungen des Nektanebos II," in *Geld als Medium in der Antike*. Ed. B. Eckhardt. Berlin. Pp. 57–90.

Dušek, J. 2007. *Les manuscrits araméens du Wadi Daliyeh et la Samarie vers 450–332 av. J.-C.* Culture and History of the Ancient Near East 30. Leiden.

———. 2012. "Archaeology and Texts in the Persian Period: Focus on Sanballat," in *Congress Volume Helsinki 2010*. Ed. M. Nissinen. Leiden. Pp. 117–33.

Eddy, S. 1968. "Athens' Peacetime Navy in the Age of Perikles," *GRBS* 9: 141–56.

Edmunds, L. 1971. "The Religiosity of Alexander," *GRBS* 12: 363–91.

Eggermont, P. H. 1975. *Alexander's Campaigns in Sind and Baluchistan and the Siege of the Brahmin Town of Harmatelia.* OLA 3. Leiden.

Ehrenberg, V. 1926. "Alexander und Ägypten," *Beihefte zum alten Orient* 7: 17–66 = *Polis und Imperium*. Ed. A. Graham and K. Stroheker. 1965. Zurich. Pp. 399–448.

———. 1933. "Die Opfer Alexanders an der Indusmündung," in *Festschrift für M. Winternitz zum siebzigsten Geburtstag.* Ed. O. Stein and W. Gampert. Leipzig. Pp. 287–97.

Eliade, M. 1959. *The Myth of the Eternal Return: Cosmos and History.* Tr. W. Trask. New York.

Ellis, J. R. 1971. "Amyntas Perdikka, Philip II, and Alexander the Great: A Study in Conspiracy," *JHS* 91: 15–24.

Endres, H. 1924. *Geographischer Horizont und Politik bei Alexander dem Grossen in den Jahren 330–323.* Mürzburg.

Engels, D. 1978. *Alexander the Great and the Logistics of the Macedonian Army.* Berkeley.

———. 1980. "Alexander's Intelligence System," *CQ* n.s. 30: 327–40.

Errington, R. M. 1969. "Bias in Ptolemy's History of Alexander," *CQ* n.s. 19: 233–43.

———. 1974. "Macedonian 'Royal Style' and Its Historical Significance," *JHS* 94: 20–37.

———. 1976. "Alexander in the Hellenistic World," in Badian (1976), pp. 137–79.

———. 1978. "The Nature of the Macedonian State Under the Monarchy," *Chiron* 8: 77–133.

———. 1990. *A History of Macedonia.* Berkeley.

Erskine, A. 1989. "The *Pezetairoi* of Philip II and Alexander III," *Historia* 38: 385–94.

———. 2002. "Life After Death: Alexandria and the Body of Alexander," *Greece & Rome* 49: 163–79.

Esposito, J. 2015. "*Hetaireia* in Homer." Ph.D. diss., University of North Carolina at Chapel Hill.

Fakhry, A. 1944. *Siwa Oasis: Its History and Antiquities.* Cairo.

———. 1972. "Bahrija, Oase," in *Lexikon der Ägyptologie*. Vol. 1. Ed. W. Helck, E. Otto, and W. Westendorf. Wiesbaden. Col. 601–4.

Falkenstein, A. 1959. "Akiti-Fest und Akiti-Festhaus," in *Festschrift Johannes Friedrich zum 65. Geburtstag am 27 August 1958 gewidmet.* Ed. R. von Kienle et al. Heidelberg. Pp. 147–82.

Fontenrose, J. 1978. *The Delphic Oracle, Its Responses and Operations with a Catalogue of Responses.* Berkeley.

Forbes, R. 1964–1993. *Studies in Ancient Technology.* Leiden. 2nd ed.

Foss, C. 1977. "The Battle at the Granicus," in *Ancient Macedonia II. Papers Read at the Second International Symposium Held in Thessaloniki, 19–24 August 1973*. Institute for Balkan Studies 155. Thessalonica. Pp. 495–502.

Foster, B. 1993. *Before the Muses*. Bethesda, MD.

Foucher, A. 1938. "Les satrapies orientales de l'empire achéménide," *CRAI* 82: 336–52.

———. 1942. *La vieille route de l'Inde de Bactres à Taxila. Mémoires de la délégation archéologique française en Afghanistan* 1. Paris.

Frame, G. 1991. "Nabonidus, Nabu-Sar-usur, and the Eanna Temple," *ZA* 81: 37–86.

Francfort, H.-P. 1985. *Prospections archéologiques au nord-ouest de l'Inde. Rapport préliminaire, 1983–1984*. Paris.

Frankfort, H. 1948. *Kingship and the Gods: A Study of Ancient Near Eastern Religions as the Integration of Society and Nature*. Chicago.

Franz, D. 2009. "Kriegsfinanzierung Alexanders des Großen," in *1000 & 1 Talente. Visualisierung antiker Kriegskosten. Begleitband zu einer studentischen Ausstellung*. Ed. H. Müller. Gutenberg. Pp. 115–50.

Fraser, P. 1972. *Ptolemaic Alexandria*. Oxford.

Fredricksmeyer, E. 1966. "The Ancestral Rites of Alexander the Great," *CP* 61: 179–82.

———. 1979. "Divine Honors for Philip II," *TAPA* 109: 39–61.

———. 1981. "On the Background of Ruler Cult," in Dell (1981), pp. 145–56.

———. 2000. "Alexander the Great and the Kingship of Asia," in Bosworth and Baynham (2000), pp. 136–66.

———. 2003. "Alexander's Religion and Divinity," in Roisman (2003), pp. 253–79.

Freedman, S. 1998. *If a City Is Set on a Height: The Akkadian Omen Series Šumma ālu ina mēlê šakin*. Philadelphia.

Frei, P., and K. Koch, eds. 1996. *Reichsidee und Reichsorganisation im Perserreich*. OBO 55. Freibourg. 2nd ed.

French, D. 1998. "Pre- and Early-Roman Roads of Asia Minor: The Persian Royal Road," *Iran* 36: 15–43.

Fuller, J. F. C. 1958. *The Generalship of Alexander the Great*. London.

Gabriel, R. 2010. *Philip II, Greater than Alexander*. Washington, DC.

Gadaleta, A. 2001. "Efippo, storico di Alessandro. Testimonianze e frammenti," *AFLB* 44: 97–144.

Gaebel, R. 2004. *Cavalry Operations in the Ancient Greek World*. Oklahoma City, OK.

Garcia-Castellanos, D., et al. 2009. "Catastrophic Flood of the Mediterranean After the Messinian Salinity Crisis," *Nature* 462: 778–82.

Gardin, J.-C. 1980. "L'archéologie du paysage bactrien," *CRAI* 124: 480–501.

Gardiner, A. 1953. "The Coronation of King Ḥaremḥab," *JEA* 39: 13–31.

Garlan, Y. 1975. *War in the Ancient World*. Tr. J. Lloyd. London.

George, A. R. 1992. *Babylonian Topographical Texts*. Leuven.

———. 1996. "Studies in Cultic Topography and Ideology," *BiOr* 53: 363–95.

Goblot, H. 1963. "Dans l'ancien Iran, les techniques de l'eau et la grande histoire," *Annales. Histoire, Sciences Sociales* 18: 499–520.

Golan, D. 1982. "Josephus, Alexander's Visit to Jerusalem, and Modern Historiography," in *Flavius Josephus: Historian of Eretz-Israel in the Hellenistic-Roman Period*. Ed. U. Rappaport. Jerusalem. Pp. 29–55.

Grainger, J. 2010. *The Syrian Wars*. Leiden.

Granier, F. 1931. *Die makedonische Heeresversammlung. Ein Beitrag zum antiken Staatsrecht*. Munich.

Green, P. 1982. "The Royal Tombs at Vergina: A Historical Analysis," in Adams and Borza (1982), pp. 129–51.

———. 1991. *Alexander the Great: An Historical Biography*. Berkeley. 2nd ed.

Gregory, S. 2013. "The Role of the *Iwn-mwt.f* in the New Kingdom Monuments of Thebes," *BMSAES* 20: 25–46.

Grenet, F. 1984. *Les pratiques funéraires dans l'Asie centrale sédentaire de la conquête grecque à l'islamisation*. Ph.D. diss. Université de Paris I.

Grenier, J.-C. 1989. *Les titulatures des empereurs romains dans les documents en langue égyptienne*. Pap. Brux. 22. Brussels.

Grieb, V., K. Nawotka, and A. Wojciechowska, eds. 2014. *Alexander the Great in Egypt: History, Art, Tradition*. Philippika 74. Wiesbaden.

Griffith, G. T. 1947. "Alexander's Generalship at Gaugamela," *JHS* 67: 77–89.

———. 1968. "The Letter of Darius at Arrian 2.14," *PCPS* n.s. 14: 33–48.

Grote, G. 1884. *History of Greece from the Earliest Period to the Close of the Generation Contemporary with Alexander the Great. A New Edition*. London.

Guermer, I. 2005. *Les cultes d'Amon hors de Thèbes. Recherches de géographie religieuse*. Bibliothèque de l'École des Hautes Études, Sciences Religieuses 123. Turnhout.

Gurney, O., and J. Finkelstein. 1957. *The Sultantepe Tablets I*. London.

Habicht, C. 1958. "Die herrschende Gesellschaft in den hellenistischen Monarchien," *VSWG* 45: 1–16.

———. 1970. *Gottmenschentum und griechische Städte*. Zetemata 14. Munich. 2nd ed.

Hall, J. 2014. *Artifact and Artifice: Classical Archaeology and the Ancient Historian*. Chicago.

Hamilton, C. 1979. "On the Perils of Extraordinary Honors: The Cases of Lysander and Conon," *AncW* 2: 67–70.

Hamilton, J. 1999. *Plutarch, Alexander: A Commentary*. Oxford. 2nd ed.

Hammond, N. G. 1973. "The Victory of Macedon at Chaeronea," in *Studies in Greek History*. Ed. N. G. Hammond. Oxford. Pp. 534–57.

———. 1980. *Alexander the Great, King, Commander, and Statesman*. London.

———. 1986. "The Kingdom of Asia and the Persian Throne," *Antichthon* 20: 73–85.

———. 1991. "The Royal Tombs at Vergina: Evolution and Identities," *ABSA* 86: 69–82.

———. 1992. "Alexander's Charge at the Battle of Issus in 333 BC," *Historia* 41: 395–406.

———. 1997. "What Philip May Have Learnt as a Hostage in Thebes," *GRBS* 38: 355–72.

———. 1999. "The Speeches in Arrian's *Indica* and *Anabasis*," *CQ* n.s. 49: 238–53.

Hammond, N. G., and G. T. Griffith. 1979. *A History of Macedonia*, Vol. 2. Oxford.

Hampl, F. 1958. *Alexander der Grosse*. Berlin.

Hanaway, W. 1982. "Anāhitā and Alexander," *JAOS* 102: 285–95.

Hansen, M. 2006. *The Shotgun Method: The Demography of the Ancient Greek City-State Culture*. Columbia, MO.

Hansman, J. 1972. "Elamites, Achaemenians, and Anshan," *Iran* 10: 101–24.

Hanson, M. 1999. *On Head Wounds, Hippocrates. Edition, Translation, and Commentary*. Berlin.

Hanson, V. 1998. *Warfare and Agriculture in Classical Greece*. Berkeley. 2nd ed.

Harl, K. 1989. "Alexander's Cavalry Battle at the Granicus," in *Polis and Polemos: Essays on Politics, War, and History in Honor of Donald Kagan*. Ed. C. Hamilton and P. Krentz. Claremont, CA. Pp. 302–26.

Harmatta, J. 1963. "Das Problem der Kontinuität im frühhellenischen Ägypten," *AAntH* 11: 199–213.

Harper, P., et al. 1992. *The Royal City of Susa: Ancient Near Eastern Treasures in the Louvre*. New York.

Hart, G. 2005. *The Routledge Dictionary of Egyptian Gods and Goddesses*. London. 2nd ed.

Hasluck, F. 1909. *Cyzicus*. Cambridge.

Hatzopoulos, M. 1982. "The Oleveni Inscription and the Dates of Philip II's Reign," in Adams and D Borza (1982), pp. 21–42.

———. 1996. *Macedonian Institutions Under the Kings*. Paris.

———. 1997. "L'état Macédonien antique. Un nouveau visage," *CRAI* 141: 7–25.

———. 2001. *L'organisation de l'armée macédonienne sous les Antigonides. Problèmes anciens et documents nouveaux*. Meletemata 30. Athens.

Head, D. 1992. *The Achaemenid Persian Army*. Stockport.

Heckel, W. 1977. "The Conspiracy of Philotas," *Phoenix* 31: 9–21.

———. 1981. "Philip and Olympias (337/336)," in *Classical Contributions: Studies in Honor of M. F. McGregor*. Ed. G. Shrimpton and D. McCargar. Locust Valley, NY. Pp. 51–57.

———. 1988. *The Last Days and Testament of Alexander the Great: A Prosopographical Study*. Historia Einzelschriften 56. Stuttgart.

———. 2003. "Kings and Companions: Observations on the Nature of Power in the Reign of Alexander," in Roisman (2003), pp. 197–225.

———. 2006. *Who's Who in the Age of Alexander: A Prosopography of Alexander's Empire*. Malden, MA.

———. 2013. "The Three Thousand: Alexander's Infantry Guard," in *The Oxford Handbook of Warfare in the Classical World*. Ed. B. Campbell and L. Tritle. Oxford. Pp. 162–79.

———. 2016. *Alexander's Marshals: A Study of the Makedonian Aristocracy and the Politics of Military Leadership*. Routledge.

Heckel, W., and J. Yardley. 2009. *Justin: Epitome of the Philippic History of Pompeius Trogus, Vol. I, Books 11–12: Alexander the Great*. Oxford.

Heller, A. 2010. *Das Babylonien der Spätzeit in den klassischen und keilschriftlichen Quellen. Oikumene 7.* Berlin.

Henry, W. 2003. "Two Verse Inscriptions (*I. Oropos 675, SEG 49.1976*)," *ZPE* 145: 10–12.

Herzfeld, E. 1947. *Zoroaster and His World.* Princeton.

Hild, F., and H. Hellenkemper. 1990. *Tabula Imperii Byzantini 5: Kilikien und Isaurien. Österreichische Akademie der Wissenschaften, phil.-historiche Klasse. Denkschriften* 215. Vienna.

Hölscher, O. 1939. *The Excavation of Medinet Habu, Volume 2: The Temples of the Eighteenth Dynasty.* Chicago.

Holt, F. 2003. *Alexander the Great and the Mystery of the Elephant Medallions.* Berkeley.

———. 2005. *Into the Land of Bones: Alexander the Great and Afghanistan.* Berkeley.

———. 2016. *The Treasures of Alexander the Great: How One Man's Wealth Shaped the World.* Oxford.

Horovitz, J. 1926. *Koranische Untersuchungen.* Berlin.

How, W., and J. Wells. 1928. *A Commentary on Herodotus.* Oxford.

Howe, T. 2016. "Alexander and 'Afghan Insurgency': A Reassessment," in *Brill's Companion to Insurgency and Terrorism in the Ancient World.* Ed. T. Howe and L. Brice. Leiden. Pp. 151–82.

Hsu, K. 1983. *The Mediterranean Was a Desert: A Voyage of the Glomar Challenger.* Princeton.

Hughes, J. 2014. *Environmental Problems of the Greeks and Romans: Ecology in the Ancient Mediterranean.* Baltimore. 2nd ed.

Instinsky, H. 1949. *Alexander der Grosse am Hellespont.* Godesberg.

———. 1961. "Alexander, Pindar, Euripides," *Historia* 10: 248–55.

Jacquemin, A. 2000. *Guerre et religion dans le monde grec (490–322 av. J.-C.).* Paris.

Jamzadeh, P. 1995. "Darius' Thrones: Temporal and Eternal," *IrAnt* 30: 1–21.

———. 2012. *Alexander Histories and Iranian Reflections: Remnants of Propaganda and Resistance.* Leiden.

Janke, A. 1904. *Auf Alexanders des Grossen Pfaden. Eine Reise durch Kleinasien.* Berlin.

Janot, F. 2000. *Les instruments de l'embaumement de l'Égypte ancienne.* Cairo.

Jaschinski, S. 1981. *Alexander und Griechenland under dem Eindruck der Flucht des Harpalos.* Bonn.

Jeffery, L. 1961. *The Local Scripts of Archaic Greece: A Study of the Origin of the Greek Alphabet and Its Development from the Eighth to Fifth Centuries B.C.* Oxford.

Joannès, F. 1994. "Métaux précieux et moyens de paiement en Babylonie achéménide et hellénistique," *Transeuphratène* 8: 137–44.

Jouanno, C. 2002. *Naissance et metamorphoses du roman d'Alexandre. Domaine grec.* Paris.

Junkelmann, M. 1997. *Panis Militaris. Die Ernährung des römischen Soldaten oder der Grundstoff der Macht.* Mainz-am-Rhein.

Jursa, M. 2007. "The Transition of Babylonia from the Neo-Babylonian Empire to Achaemenid Rule," in *Regime Change in the Ancient Near East and Egypt: From Sargon of Agade to Saddam Hussein*. Ed. H. Crawford. Oxford. Pp. 73–94.

———. 2015. "Labor in Babylonia in the First Millennium," in *Labor in the Ancient World*. Ed. P. Steinkiller and M. Hudson. Dresden. Pp. 345–96.

Jursa, M., and J. Hackl. 2010. *Aspects of the Economic History of Babylonia in the First Millennium BC: Economic Geography, Economic Mentalities, Agriculture, the Use of Money, and the Problem of Economic Growth*. AAOT 377. Münster.

Kaboli, M.-A. 2000. "The Apadana Gateway at Shush," *Iran* 38: 161–62.

Kahrstedt, U. 1936. "Das Athenische Kontingent zum Alexanderzuge," *Hermes* 71: 120–24.

Kákosy, L. 1977. "Heliopolis," *LAe*. Vol. 2. Pp. 1111–3.

Kaplan, P. 2009. "Skylax," in *Brill's New Jacoby*. Ed. I. Worthington. Leiden.

Karimi Zanjani Asl, M. 1999. "Marriage in Ancient Iran," *Tchista*, 1999 no. 4.

Karttunen, K. 1989. *India in Early Greek Literature*. Studia Orientalia 65. Helsinki.

———. 1997. *India and the Hellenistic World*. Studia Orientalia 83. Helsinki.

Keegan, J. 1993. *A History of Warfare*. New York.

Kenoyer, J. 1998. *Ancient Cities of the Indus Valley Civilization*. Oxford.

Kent, R. 1950. *Old Persian: Grammar, Texts, Lexicon*. New Haven, CT.

Kern, O. 1915. *Krieg und Kult bei den Hellenen*. Halle.

———. 1963. *Die Religion der Griechen, III*. Berlin. 2nd ed.

Keyser, P. 1994. "The Use of Artillery by Philip II and Alexander the Great," *AncW* 25: 27–59.

Kienast, D. 1973. *Philipp II von Makedonien und das Reich der Achaimeniden*. Munich.

Kinns, P. 1983. "The Amphictyonic Coinage Reconsidered," *NC* 143: 1–22.

Kirfel, W. 1991. *Die Kosmographie der Inder nach den Quellen dargestellt*. Hildesheim.

Klotz, D. 2008. *Kneph: The Religion of Roman Thebes*. Ph.D. diss. Yale University.

Koenen, L. 1977. *Eine agonistische Inschrift aus Ägypten und frühptolemäische Königsfeste*. Beitr. zur klass. Phil. 56. Meisenheim-am-Glan.

Koldeway, R. 1914. *The Excavations at Babylon*. Tr. A. Johns. London.

König, F. 1965. *Die elamischen Königsinschriften*. AfO Beiheft 16. Graz.

König, F. W. 1972. *Die Persika des Ktesias von Knidos*. AfO Beiheft 18. Graz.

Kornemann, E. 1935. *Die Alexandergeschichte des Königs Ptolemaios I. von Ägypten. Versuch einer Rekonstrucktion*. Leipzig.

Kottaridi, A. 2011a. "The Legend of Macedon," in *Heracles to Alexander: Treasures from the Royal Capital of Macedon, a Hellenic Kingdom in the Age of Democracy*. Oxford. Pp. 1–24.

———. 2011b. "The Royal Banquet, a Capital Institution," in *Heracles to Alexander: Treasures from the Royal Capital of Macedon, a Hellenic Kingdom in the Age of Democracy*. Oxford. Pp. 167–81.

Kraay, C. 1976. *Archaic and Classical Greek Coins*. Berkeley.

Kremydi, S. "Coinage and Finance," in Lane Fox (2011), pp. 159–78.

Krentz, P. 1985. "Casualties in Hoplite Battles," *GRBS* 26: 13–20.

———. 2007. "Warfare and Hoplites," in the *Cambridge Companion to Archaic Greece*. Ed. H. Shapiro. Cambridge. Pp. 61–84.

Kretch, S., J. McNeill, and C. Merchant, eds. 2004. *Encyclopedia of World Environmental History*. Vol. 2. London.

Kromayer, J., and G. Veith. 1928. *Heerwesen und Kreigführung der Griechen und Römer*. Munich.

Kuhlmann, K. 1988. *Das Ammoneion. Archäologie, Geschichte, und Kultpraxis des Orakels von Siwa*. AV 75. Mainz-am-Rhein.

Kuhrt, A. 1990. "Alexander and Babylon," in *The Roots of the European Tradition: Proceedings of the 1987 Groningen Achaemenid History Workshop*. AchHist 5. Ed. H. Sancisi-Weerdenburg and J. Drijvers. Leiden. Pp. 121–30.

Kuhrt, A., and S. Sherwin-White. 1987. "Xerxes' Destruction of Babylonian Temples," in *The Greek Sources: Proceedings of the Groningen 1984 Achaemenid History Workshop*. AchHist 2. Ed. H. Sancisi-Weerdenburg and A. Kuhrt. Leiden. Pp. 69–78.

Kümmel, H. 1967. *Ersatzrituale für den hethitischen König*. Wiesbaden.

Labat, R. 1965. *Un calendrier babylonien des travaux des signes et des mois (séries iqqur îpuš)*. Bibliothèque de l'École des Hautes Études, Sciences Historiques et Politiques 321. Paris.

Ladynin, I. 2016. "Defence and Offence in the Egyptian Royal Titles of Alexander the Great," in Ulanowski (2016), pp. 256–72.

Lamotte, E. 1958. *Histoire du bouddhisme indien des origines à l'ère Śaka*. Louvain.

Lane Fox, R. 1973. *Alexander the Great*. London.

———. 1980. *The Search for Alexander*. New York.

———. 2007. "Alexander the Great: Last of the Achaemenids?" in Tuplin (2007), pp. 267–311.

———, ed. 2011. *Brill's Companion to Ancient Macedon*. Leiden.

———. 2011a. "Introduction: Dating the Royal Tombs at Vergina," in Lane Fox (2011), pp. 1–34.

———. 2011b. "Philip: Accession, Ambitions, and Self-Preservation," in Lane Fox (2011), pp. 335–66.

Lanfranchi, G. 2003. "Il 'monumento di Sardanapalo' e la sua iscrizione," *Studi Trentini di Scienze Storiche*, 82: 79–86.

Lazenby, J. 1985. *The Spartan Army*. Warminster.

Le Rider, G. 2001. *La naissance de la monnaie. Pratiques monétaires de l'Orient ancien*. Paris.

———. 2007. *Alexander the Great: Coinage, Finance, and Policy*. Tr. W. Higgins. Philadelphia.

Leaf, W. 1912. *Troy: A Study in Homeric Geography*. London.

Leigh Fermor, P. 1958. *Mani: Travels in the Southern Peloponnese*. London.

Lemaire, A. 2000. "Remarques sur certaines légendes monétaires Ciliciennes (V^e–IVe s. av. J.-C.)," in *Mécanismes et innovations monétaires dans l'Anatolie Achéménide*.

Numismatique et histoire. Actes de la table ronde internationale d'Istanbul, 22–23 mai 1997. Varia Anatolica 12. Ed. O. Casabonne. Istanbul. Pp. 129–41.

———. 2006. "La transeuphratène en transition (c. 350–300)," in Briant and Joannès (2006), pp. 405–41.

Lenderling, J. 2005. *Alexander de Grote. De ondergang van het Perzische rijk.* Amsterdam. 2nd ed.

Lendon, J. 2005. *Soldiers and Ghosts: A History of Battle in Classical Antiquity.* New Haven, CT.

Lenfant, D. 2004. *Ctésias de Cnide. Edition, traduction, et commentaire historique des témoignages et fragments.* Ph.D. diss. Université de Paris IV.

Lenschau, T. 1949. "Pammenes," *RE,* Vol. 19.1. Col. 298–99.

Lepsius, R. 1849. *Denkmaeler aus Aegypten und Aethiopien.* Berlin = 1972. Geneva.

Lewis, D. 1989. "Persian Gold in Greek International Relations," *REA* 91: 227–34.

Lichtheim, M. 1973–1980. *Ancient Egyptian Literature: A Book of Readings.* Berkeley.

Lightfoot, J. 2009. *Hellenistic Collection.* Loeb Classical Library 508. Cambridge, MA.

Linssen, M. 2004. *The Cults of Uruk and Babylon: The Temple Ritual Texts as Evidence for Hellenistic Cult Practices.* Leiden.

Lipiński, E. 1994. *Studies in Aramaic Inscriptions and Onomastics, II.* OLA 57. Leuven.

———. 1995. *Dieux et déesses de l'univers phénicien et punique.* Leuven.

Livingstone, A. 1989. *Court Poetry and Literary Miscellanea.* SAA 3. Helsinki.

Lloyd, A. 1975–1988. *Herodotus, Book II.* Leiden.

———. 1983. "The Late Period, 664–323 BC," in *Ancient Egypt: A Social History.* Ed. B. Trigger. Cambridge. Pp. 279–348.

Lloyd, G. E. R. 2001. *Magic, Reason, and Experience: Studies in the Origin and Development of Greek Science.* London.

Löhnert, A. 2007. "The Installation of Priests According to Neo-Assyrian Documents," *SAA* 16: 273–86.

Lonis, R. 1979. *Guerre et religion en Grèce à l'époque classique.* Paris.

Lonsdale, D. 2007. *Alexander the Great: Lessons in Strategy.* London.

Loraux, N. 1986. *The Invention of Athens: The Funeral Oration in the Classical City.* Tr. A. Sheridan. Cambridge, MA.

Loynes, R. 2015. *Prepared for Eternity: A Study of Human Embalming Techniques in Ancient Egypt Using Computerised Tomography Scans of Mummies.* Archaeopress Egyptology 9. Oxford.

Luschey, M. 1968. "Studien zu dem Darius-Relief von Bisutun," *AMI n.s.* 1: 63–94.

Ma, J. 2008. "Topographies of Commemoration," *JHS* 128: 72–91.

———. 2011. "Court, King, and Power in Antigonid Macedonia," in Lane Fox (2011), pp. 521–45.

MacDowell, D. 1978. *The Law in Classical Athens.* Ithaca, NY.

MacDowall, D., and M. Taddei. 1978. "The Early Historic Period: Achaemenids and Greeks," in *The Archaeology of Afghanistan from Earliest Times to the Timurid Period.* Ed. F. R. Allchin and N. G. Hammond. London. Pp. 87–233.

Maehler, H. 1989. *Pindari carmina cum fragmentis*. Leipzig = 2001. Munich.

Magen, Y. 2008. *Mount Gerizim Excavations, III: A Temple City*. Jerusalem.

Malbran-Labat, F. 1982. *L'armée et l'organisation militaire de l'Assyrie d'après les lettres des Sargonides trouvées à Ninive*. Paris.

Malkin, I. 1998. "Myth, Religion, and Spartan 'Ideology,'" in *Politische Theorie und Praxis im Altertum*. Ed. W. Schuller. Darmstadt. Pp. 43–49.

Manning, J. 2010. *The Last Pharaohs: Egypt Under the Ptolemies, 305–30 BC*. Princeton.

Marcus, R., et al. 1966–1969 = *Josephus: Jewish Antiquities*. Loeb Classical Library 242, 281, 365, 456, 489, 490. Cambridge, MA. = 1929–1965.

Mari, M. 2002. *Al di là dell'Olimpo. Macedoni e grandi santuari della Grecia dall' età arcaica al primo ellenismo*. Athens.

———. 2007. "Macedonian *Poleis* and *Ethnē* in the Greek Sanctuaries Before the Age of Philip II," in *Ancient Macedonia VII: Macedonia from the Iron Age to the Death of Philip II. Seventh International Symposium, Thessaloniki, October 14–18, 2002*. Thessalonica. Pp. 31–49.

———. 2008. "The Ruler Cult in Macedonia," *Studi ellenistici* 20: 219–68.

———. 2011. "Traditional Cults and Beliefs," in Lane Fox (2011), pp. 453–65.

Markle, M. 1977. "The Macedonian Spear, Sarissa, and Related Armour," *AJA* 31: 323–39.

Marsden, E. 1964. *The Campaign of Gaugamela*. Liverpool.

———. 1969. *Greek and Roman Artillery: Historical Development*. Oxford.

Marshall, J. 1951. *Taxila: An Illustrated Account of the Archaeological Excavations Carried Out at Taxila Under the Orders of the Government of India Between the Years 1913 and 1934*. Cambridge.

Martinez, P. 1989. "A propos de la décoration du sanctuaire d'Alexandre à Karnak. Reflexions sur la politique architecturale et religieuse des premiers souverains Lagides," *BSEG* 13: 107–16.

Matthey, P. "Alexandre et le sarcophage de Nectanébo II. Éléments de propagande Lagide ou mythe savant?" in Grieb, Nawotka, and Wojciechowska (2014), pp. 315–37.

Maul, S. 1994. *Zukunftsbewältigung: eine Untersuchung altorientalischen Denkens anhand der babylonisch-assyrischen Löserituale (Namburbi)*. Mainz-am-Rhein.

McCrindle, J. 1893. *The Invasion of India by Alexander the Great as Described by Arrian, Q. Curtius, Diodoros, Plutarch, and Justin: Being Translations of Such Portions of the Works of These and Other Classical Authors as Describe Alexander's Campaigns in Afghanistan, the Punjâb, Sindh, Gedrosia and Karmania, with an Introduction Containing a Life of Alexander, Copious Notes, Illustrations, Maps and Indices*. Westminster.

McKenzie, J. 2011. *The Architecture of Alexandria and Egypt, c. 300 B.C.–A.D. 700*. New Haven, CT.

McPherson, J. 2002. *Crossroads of Freedom: Antietam*. Oxford.

Meineck, P., and D. Konstan, eds. 2014. *Combat Trauma and the Ancient Greeks*. New York.

Meissner, B. 1894. *Alexander und Gilgamos*. N.p.

Merkelbach, R. 1977. *Die Quellen des griechischen Alexander-Romans*. Munich. 2nd ed.

Meshorer, Y., and S. Qedar. 1999. *Samarian Coinage*. Numismatic Studies and Researches 9. Jerusalem.

Messerschmidt, W. 2015. "Babylon in achaemenidischer und hellensitischer Zeit: Eine Stellungnahme zur aktuellen Forschungsdiskussion," in *Religious Identities in the Levant from Alexander to Muhammed: Continuity and Change*. Ed. M. Blömer, A. Lichtenberger, and R. Raja. Turnhout. Pp. 229–46.

Meyer, E. 1910. "Alexander der Grosse und die absolute Monarchie," in *Kleine Schirften I*. Halle. Pp. 283–332.

Milns, R. 1968. *Alexander the Great*. London.

———. 1976. "The Army of Alexander the Great," in Badian (1976), pp. 87–130.

———. 1987. "Army Pay and the Military Budget of Alexander the Great," in Will and Heinrichs (1987), pp. 233–56.

Minutoli, H. F. von. 1824. *Reise zum Tempel des Jupiter Ammon in der libyschen Wüste und nach Oberägypten in den Jahren 1820 und 1821*. Berlin = 1982. Wiesbaden.

Momigliano, A. 1934. *Filippo il Macedone. Saggio sulla storia greca del IV secolo*. Florence.

———. 1979. "Flavius Josephus and Alexander's Visit to Jerusalem," *Athenaeum* 57: 442–48 = 1987. *Pagine ebraiche*. Turin. Pp. 85–93.

Moret, A. 1902. *Du caractère religieux de la royauté pharaonique*. Paris.

Morgan, C. 2001. "Symbolic and Pragmatic Aspects of Warfare in the Greek World of the 8th to 6th Centuries BC," in Bekker-Nielsen and Hannestad (2001), pp. 20–45.

Mulla, D. F. 1893. *Translation and Explanation of the Fifty Odes of Saadi (51–100) Prescribed for the Previous Examination of 1893; Together with an Account of the Life of Saadi, Proverbs and Figures of Speech Occurring in the Prescribed Odes, the Metres and Feet of the Same, etc.* Bombay.

Müller, F. M., and J. Darmesteter. 1898. *Sacred Books of the East, XXIII*. Oxford = 1993. Delhi.

Munn, M. 2006. *The Mother of the Gods, Athens, and the Tyranny of Asia*. Berkeley.

Murnane, W. 1985. "False Doors and Cult Practices Inside the Luxor Temple," in *Mélanges Gamal Eddin Mokhtar*. Vol. 2. Ed. P. Posener-Krieger. Cairo. Pp. 135–49.

Murnane, W., et al. 1981. *The Temple of Khonsu, Vol. 2: Scenes and Inscriptions in the Court and the First Hypostyle Hall*. OIP 103. Chicago.

Naiden, F. S. 2005. "Examples of Rejected Sacrifice in Greek and Hebrew Religion," *JANERS* 6: 187–223.

———. 2007. "The Invention of the Officer Corps," *Journal of the Historical Society* 1: 35–60.

———. 2009. *Ancient Supplication*. Oxford. Rev. ed.

———. 2011. "Alexander the Great as a Religious Leader," *AncW* 2: 166–79.

———. 2013. *Smoke Signals for the Gods: Greek Animal Sacrifice from the Archaic Through Roman Periods*. Oxford.

Narain, A. 1965. "Alexander and India," *G & R* 12: 155–65.

National Aeronautics and Space Administration. 2009. *Five Millennium Canon of Lunar Eclipses: -1999 to +3000*. Technical Publication 2009–214172. Washington, DC.

National Geographic Society 1999. "Roof of the World," available as of June 21, 2017, at http://www.nationalgeographic.com/features/99/everest/roof_content.html.

Naveh, J., and S. Shaked. 2012. *Aramaic Documents from Ancient Bactria*. London.

Nelson, H. 1942. "The Identity of Amon-Re of United-with-Eternity" *JNES* 1: 127–55.

Neujahr, M. 2005. "When Darius Defeated Alexander: Composition and Redaction in the 'Dynastic Prophecy,'" *JNES* 64: 101–7.

Newell, E. 1923. *Alexander Hoards*. New York.

O'Connor, D. 2012. "From Topography to Cosmos: Ancient Egypt's Multiple Maps," in Talbert (2012), 47–81.

Olbrycht, M. 2014. "An Admirer of Persian Ways: Alexander the Great's Reforms in Parthia-Hyrcania and the Iranian Heritage," in *Excavating an Empire: Achaemenid Persia in Longue Durée*. Ed. T. Daryaee, A. Mousavi, and K. Rezakhani. Costa Mesa, CA. Pp. 37–63.

Oldach, D., R. Richard, E. Borza, and R. Benitez. 1998. "A Mysterious Death," *New England Journal of Medicine* 338.24: 1764–9.

Pallis, S. 1927. *Mandaean Studies*. London.

Parke, H. W. 1967. *The Oracles of Zeus*. Cambridge, MA.

———. 1985. "The Massacre of the Branchidae," *JHS* 105: 59–68.

Parker, R. 1996. *Athenian Religion: A History*. Oxford.

Parpola, S. 1970–1983. *Letters from Assyrian Scholars to the Kings Esarhaddon and Assurbanipal*. AOAT 5. Kevelaer.

———. 1993. *Letters from Assyrian and Babylonian Scholars*. SAA 10. Helsinki.

———. 2003. "International Law in the First Millennium," in *A History of Ancient Near Eastern Law*. Ed. R. Westbrook and G. Beckman. Vol. 2. Leiden. Pp. 1047–67.

Pearson, L. 1955. "The Diary and Letters of Alexander the Great," *Historia* 3: 429–55.

Pédech, P. 1984. *Historiens compagnons d'Alexandre. Callisthène, Onésicrite, Néarque, Ptolémée, Aristobule*. Paris.

Perrot, J., ed. 2013. *The Palace of Darius at Susa: The Great Royal Residence of Achaemenid Persia*. Tr. D. and G. Collon. London.

Pettinato, G. 1988. *Semiramis. Herrin über Assur und Babylon*. Zurich.

Pfeiffer, S. 2014a. *Herrscher- und Dynastiekulte im Ptolemäerreich. Systematik und Einordnung der Kultformen*. Munich.

———. 2014b. "Alexander der Grosse in Ägypten: Überlegungen zur Frage seiner pharaonischer Legitimation," in Grieb, Nawotka, and Wojciechowska (2014), pp. 89–106.

Pirart, É. 2002. "Le mazdéisme politique de Darius Ier," *Indo-Iranian Journal* 45: 121–51.

Plaumann, W. 1913. "Hetairos," *RE*, Vol. 8.2. Col. 1376–77.

Politis, N. 1904. Μελέται περὶ τοῦ βίου καὶ τῆς γλώσσης τοῦ ἑλληνικοῦ λαοῦ. Παραδόσεις. Athens.

Pomerantz-Leisten, B. 1997. "Das 'negative Sündenbekenntnis' des Königs anläßlich des babylonischen Neujahrsfestes und die *kidinnūtu* von Babylon," in *Schuld, Gewissen, Person: Studien zur Geschichte des inneren Menschen. Studien zum*

Verstehen fremder Religionen 9. Ed. J. Assmann and Th. Sundermeier. Gütersloh. Pp. 83–101.

Pomeroy, A. 1991. *The Appropriate Comment: Death Notices in the Ancient Historians.* Studien zur Klassischen Philologie 58. Frankfurt-am-Main.

Porten, B. 1968. *Archives from Elephantine: The Life of an Ancient Jewish Military Colony.* Ph.D. diss. University of California at Berkeley.

Pospisil, L. 1971. *Anthropology of Law: A Comparative Theory.* New York.

Pötscher, W. 1964. *Περὶ εὐσεβείας.* Philosophia antiqua 11. Leiden.

Potts, D. 1999. *The Archaeology of Elam: Formation and Transformation of an Ancient Iranian State.* Cambridge.

Pouilloux, J., and C. Dunant. 1954–1958. *Recherches sur l'histoire et les cultes de Thasos, II.* Paris.

Prakash, B. 1976. *Political and Social Movements in Ancient Punjab (From the Vedic Age up to the Mauryan Period).* Lahore. 2nd ed.

Préaux, C. 1939. *L'économie royale des Lagides.* Brussels.

Prestianni Giallombardo, A. 1975. "*Philippika* I. Sul 'Culto' di Filippo II di Macedonia," *SicGymn* 28: 1–57.

———. 1999. "*Τέμενη Φιλίππου α Φηιλιππι*: ai prodromi del culto del sovrano?" in *Ancient Macedonia VI: Papers Read at the Sixth International Symposium Held at Thessaloniki, October 15–19, 1996.* Thessalonica. Pp. 921–43.

Pritchett, W. K. 1979. *The Greek State at War. Part III.* Berkeley.

Quack, J. 2013. "Sarapis: Ein Gott zwischen griechischer und ägyptischer Religion— Bermerkungen aus der Sicht eines Ägyptologen," in *Aneignung und Abgrenzung. Wechselnde Perspektiven auf die Antithese von 'Ost' und 'West' in der griechischen Antike.* Oikumene 10. Ed. N. Zenzen, T. Hölscher, and K. Trampedach. Heidelberg.

Radet, G. 1931. *Alexandre le grand.* Paris.

Randsborg, K. 2001. "From Bronze to Iron: The Rise of European Infantry," in Bekker-Nielsen and Hannestad (2001), pp. 155–65.

Rapp, A. 1866. "Die Religion und Sitte der Perser und übrigen Iranier nach den griechischen und römischen Quellen, II," *ZDMG* 20: 49–140.

Rathmann, M. 2005. *Perdikkas zwischen 323 und 320: Nachlassverwalter des Alexanderreiches oder Autokrat?* Vienna.

Rawlinson, H. 1912. *Bactria: The History of a Forgotten Empire.* London.

Razmjou, S. 2002. "Assessing the Damage: Notes on the Life and Demise of the Statue of Darius from Susa," *Ars Orientalis* 32: 81–104.

Redford, D. 1992. *Egypt, Canaan and Israel in Ancient Times.* Princeton.

Redmount, C. 1995. "The Wadi Tumilat and the 'Canal of the Pharaohs,'" *JNES* 54: 127–35.

Reich, R., and E. Shukron. 2011. "The Date of the Siloam Tunnel Reconsidered," *Tel Aviv* 38: 147–57.

Renault, M. 1975. *The Nature of Alexander.* New York.

Rhodes, P. J., and J. A. Larsen. 2012. "Heralds," *OCD*, p. 666.

Rhodes, P. J., and R. Osborne. 2003. *Greek Historical Inscriptions, 404–323 BC*. Oxford.

Riethmüller, J. 2005. *Asklepios. Heiligtümer und Kulte*. Heidelberg.

Ritter, H.-W. 1965. *Diadem und Königsherrschaft. Untersuchungen zu Zeremonien und Rechtsgrundlagen des Herrschaftsantritts bei den Persern, bei Alexander dem Grossen und im Hellenismus*. Vestigia, Beiträge zur alten Geschichte 7. Munich.

Robert, L. 1937. *Études Anatoliennes. Recherches sur les inscriptions grecques de l'Asie Mineure*. Paris.

———. 1948. *Hellenica 6*. Limoges.

Robinson, E. 1932. *The Ephemerides of Alexander's Expedition*. Providence.

Robson, E. 2008. *Mathematics in Ancient Iraq: A Social History*. Princeton.

Rochberg, F. 1984. "New Evidence for the History of Astrology," *JNES* 43: 115–40.

———. 2010. *In the Path of the Moon: Babylonian Celestial Divination and Its Legacy*. Leiden.

———. 2012. "The Expression of Terrestrial and Celestial Order in Ancient Mesopotamia," in Talbert (2012), pp. 9–47.

Roder, G. 1959. *Hermopolis 1929–1939: Ausgrabungen der Deutschen Hermopolis-Expedition in Hermopolis, Ober-Ägypten, in Verbindung mit zahlreichen Mitarbeiten*. Hildesheim.

Roisman, J., ed. 2003. *Brill's Companion to Alexander the Great*. Leiden.

Roisman, J., and I. Worthington, eds. 2010. *Brill's Companion to Ancient Macedonia*. Leiden.

Roller, L. 1981. "Funeral Games for Historical Persons," *Stadion* 7: 1–18.

———. 1983. "The Legend of Midas," *CA* 2: 299–316.

———. 1984. "Midas and the Gordian Knot," *CA* 3: 256–71.

Rollinger, R. 2013. *Alexander und die grossen Ströme. Die Flussüberquerungen im Lichte altorientalischer Pioniertechniken (Schwimmschläuche, Keleks, und Pontonbrücken)*. Wiesbaden.

Rollinger, R., and K. Ruffing. 2012. "*Panik im Heer*—Dareios III., die Schlacht von Gaugamela und die Mondfinsternis vom 20. September 331 v. Chr.," *IrAnt* 47: 101–15.

Romm, J. 1992. *The Edges of the Earth in Ancient Thought*. Princeton.

———. 2012. "Who Killed Alexander the Great?" *History Today* 62.4: 30–36.

Rose, C. B., and R. Korpe. 2005. "The Granicus River Valley Survey Project, 2004," *Arastirma Sonuçlari Toplantisi* 23: 323–32.

Rosenstein, N. 2004. *Rome at War: Farms, Families, and Death in the Middle Republic*. Chapel Hill, NC.

Ross, M. 2016. "Eclipses and the Precipitation of Conflict: Deciphering the Signal to Attack," in Ulanowski (2016), pp. 99–120.

Roth, J. 1999. *The Logistics of the Roman Army at War (264 B.C.–A.D. 235)*. Leiden.

Ruffin, J. R. 1992. "The Efficacy of Medicine during the Campaigns of Alexander the Great," *Military Medicine* 157: 467–75.

Ruge, W. 1941. "Phrygia," *RE*, Vol. 20.1. Col. 781–860.

Rüstow, W., and H. Köchly. 1852. *Geschichte des griechischen Kriegswesens von der ältesten Zeit bis auf Pyrrhos*. Uarau.

Ruzé, F. 1997. *Délibération et pouvoir dans la cité grecque de Nestor à Socrate.* Paris.

Saatsoglou-Paliadeli, C. 2011. "The Arts at Vergina-Aegae, the Cradle of the Macedonian Kingdom," in Lane Fox (2011), pp. 271–95.

Sachs, A. 1955. *Late Babylonian Astronomical and Related Texts Copied by T. G. Pinches and J. N. Strassmeier.* Brown University Studies 18. Providence.

Safar, F., and F. Basmachi. 1946–1947. "Sennacherib's Project for Supplying Arbil with Water," *Sumer* 2: 50–2, 3: 23–25.

Salazar, C. 2000. *The Treatment of War Wounds in Greco-Roman Antiquity.* Leiden.

Sallares, J. 2012. "Population, Greek," *OCD.* Pp. 1185–7.

Samuel, A. 1972. *Greek and Roman Chronology: Calendars and Years in Classical Antiquity.* Munich.

———. 1988. "Philip and Alexander as Kings: Macedonian Monarchy and Merovingian Parallels," *American Historical Review* 93: 1270–86.

Sancisi-Weerdenburg, H. 1980. *Yauna en Persai. Grieken en Perzen in een ander perspectief.* Groningen.

———. 1993. "Alexander and Persepolis," in *Alexander the Great: Reality and Myth.* Ed. J. Carlsen et al. Rome. Pp. 177–88.

Sartre, M. 2001. *D'Alexandre à Zenobie. Histoire du Levant antique, IVᵉ siècle av. J.-C.-IIIᵉ siècle après J.-C.* Paris.

Sauer, E., et al. 2013. *Persia's Imperial Power in Late Antiquity: The Great Wall of Gorgan and the Frontier Landscapes of Sasanian Iran.* British Institute of Persian Studies, Archaeological Monograph Series 2. Oxford.

Saunders, N. 2006. *Alexander's Tomb: The Two-Thousand Year Obsession to Find the Lost Conqueror.* New York.

Scerrato, U. 1966a. "Excavations at Dahan-I Ghulaman (Seistan, Iran), First Preliminary Report (1962–63)," *EW* 16: 9–30.

———. 1966b. "L'edificio sacro di *Dahan-e Ghulaman* (Sistan)," in *Atti del Convegno sul tema: La Persia e il mondo greco-romano. Roma, 11–14 aprile, 1965.* Rome. Pp. 457–70.

———. 1979. "Evidence of *religious life at Dahan-e Ghulaman,* Sīstān," in *South Asian Archaeology 1977.* Ed. M. Taddei. Naples. Pp. 709–33.

Schachermeyr, F. 1970. *Alexander in Babylon und die Reichsordnung nach seinem Tode.* SAWW 288. Vienna.

———. 1973. *Alexander der Grosse. Das Problem seiner Persönlichkeit und seines Wirkens.* SAWW 285. Vienna.

Scheil, V. 1905. "Documents archaïques en écriture proto-élamite," in *Mémoires de la délégation en Perse.* Vol. 6. Paris. Pp. 57–128.

Schiwek, H. 1962. "Der Persiche Golf als Schiffahrts- und Seehandlsroute in Achämenidischer Zeit und in der Zeit Alexanders des Grossen," *BJ* 162: 4–97.

Schlange-Schöningen, H. 1996. "Alexandria-Memphis-Siwa: wo liegt Alexander der Grosse begraben?" *Antike Welt* 27: 109–19.

Schmid, H. J. 1995. *Der Tempelturm Etemenanki in Babylon.* Mainz-am-Rhein.

Schmidt, H.-P. 1978. "Indo-Iranian Mitra Studies: The State of the Central Problem," in *Études Mithriaques. Actes du 2ᵉ congrès international, Téhéran, du 1er au 8 Septembre 1975. Acta Iranica* 17. Leiden. Pp. 345–93.

Schmidt-Colinet. A. 1996. "Das Grab Alexanders d. Gr. in Memphis?" in *Problematics of Power: Eastern and Western Representations of Alexander the Great*. Ed. M. Bridges and J. Bürgel. Bern. Pp. 87–91.

Schubring, W. 1962. *The Doctrines of the Jainas, Described After the Old Sources*. Tr. W. Buerlin. Delhi.

Schwartz, A. 2002. "The Early Hoplite Phalanx: Close Order or Disarray?" *C & M* 53: 31–63.

Schwarz, F. F. 1968. "Mauryas und Seleukiden. Probleme ihrer gegenseitigen Beziehungen," *Studien zur Sprachwissenschaft und Kulturkunde. Gedenkschrift für W. Brandenstein*. IBK 14.1. Innsbruck. Pp. 223–30.

Schwarz, F. von. 1904. *Alexanders des Grossen Feldzüge in Turkestan*. Stuttgart.

Schwenn, F. 1920–1922. "Der Krieg in der griechischen Religion," *ARW* 20: 299–322; 21: 58–71.

Seaford, R. 1994. *Reciprocity and Ritual: Homer and Tragedy in the Developing City-State*. Oxford.

Seibert, J. 1972. *Alexander der Grosse*. Erträge der Forschung 10. Darmstadt.

———. 1985. *Die Eroberung des Perserreiches durch Alexander d. Gr. auf kartographischer Grundlage*. Beiheft zum Tübinger Atlas des vorderen Orients 68. Wiesbaden.

———. 1986. "Demographische und wirtschaftliche Probleme Makedoniens in der fruhen Diadochenzeit," in *Studien zur Alten Geschichte Siegfried Lauffer zum 70. Geburstag am 4 August 1981 dargebracht*. Ed. H. Kalcyk, B. Gulatt, and A. Graeber. Rome. Pp. 835–51.

Sekunda, N. 1992. *The Persian Army*. Oxford.

Sellwood, D. 1963. "Some Experiments in Greek Minting Technique," *NC* 123: 217–31.

Semple, E. C. 1919. "The Ancient Piedmont Route of Northern Mesopotamia," *Geographical Review* 8: 153–79.

Sethe, K. 1929. *Amun und die Acht Urgötter von Hermopolis. Eine Untersuchung über Ursprung und Wesen des ägyptischen Götterkönigs*. APAW Philosophisch-historische Klasse 4. Berlin.

Sevinc, N., et al. 2001. "A New Painted Graeco-Persian Sarcophagus from Çan," *Studia Troica* 11: 383–420.

Sidebotham, S. 2011. *Berenike and the Ancient Maritime Spice Route*. Berkeley.

Sinclair, R. 1966 "Diodorus Siculus and Fighting in Relays," *CQ* n.s. 16: 49–55.

Sisti, F. 2001–2004. *Arriano. Anabasi di Alessandro*. Rome.

Slotsky, A. L. 1997. *The Bourse of Babylon: Market Quotations in the Astronomical Diaries of Babylonia*. Bethesda, MD.

Smelik, K. 1978–1979. "The *Omina Mortis* in the Histories of Alexander the Great," *Talanta* 10/11: 91–111.

Smith, G., and W. Dawson. 1924. *Egyptian Mummies*. London = 1991. London.

Smith, H. 1988. "A Memphite Miscellany," in *Pyramid Studies and Other Essays Presented to I. E. S. Edwards*. Ed. J. Baines et al. Occasional Publications, Egyptian Exploration Society 7. London. Pp. 184–92.

Smith, J. Z. 1976. "A Pearl of Great Price and A Cargo of Yams: A Study in Situational Incongruity," *History of Religions* 16: 1–19.

Sneh, A., R. Weinberger, and E. Shalev. 2010. "The Why, How, and When of the Siloam Tunnel Reevaluated," *BASOR* 359: 57–65.

Sotiriadis, G. 1902. "Ἀνασκαφὴ δύο τύμβων παρὰ τὴν Χαιρωνείαν," *Praktika tēs en Athēnais Archaiologikēs Hetaireias*. Pp. 53–59.

———. 1903. "Das Schlachtfeld von Chäronea und der Grabhügel der Makedonen," *Ath. Mitt.* 28: 301–30.

Spawforth, A. 2007. "The Court of Alexander the Great Between Europe and Asia," in *The Court and Court Society in Ancient Monarchies*. Ed. A. Spawforth. Cambridge. Pp. 82–120.

Spiegelberg, W. 1906. "Die demotischen Inschriften der Steinbrüche von Turra und Masara," *ASAE* 6: 218–33.

Squillace, G. 2004. *Vasileis ē tyrannoi: Filippo II e Alessandro Magno tra opposizione e consenso*. Rome.

———. 2010. "Consensus Strategies Under Philip and Alexander: The Revenge Theme," in *Philip II and the Alexander the Great, Father and Son, Lives and Afterlives*. Ed. D. Ogden and E. Carney. Oxford. Pp. 69–80.

Stark, F. 1958. "Alexander's March from Miletus to Phrygia," *JHS* 78: 102–20.

Stein, A. 1929. *On Alexander's Track to the Indus: Personal Narrative of Explorations on the North-west Frontier of India Carried Out Under the Orders of H. M. Indian Government*. London = 2001. London.

———. 1937. *Archaeological Reconnaissances in North-western India and South-eastern Īrān*. London.

Steingass, F. 1892. *A Comprehensive Persian-English Dictionary, Including Arabic Words and Phrases to Be Met with in Persian Literature*. London = 1996. Delhi.

Stern, S. 2011. *Calendars in Antiquity*. Oxford.

Stevenson, W., ed. 1908–1931. *Imperial Gazeteer of India*. Oxford.

Stewart, A. 1993. *Faces of Power: Alexander's Image and Hellenistic Politics*. Berkeley.

Stol, M. 2007. "Fevers in Babylonia," in *Disease in Babylonia*. Ed. I. L. Finkel and M. J. Geller. Leiden. Pp. 1–39.

Stoll, H. 1884. "Hetaireia," in Roscher, Vol. 1.2. Pp. 2653.

Stolper, M. 1994a. "Mesopotamia, 482–330 BCE," *CAH*, Vol. 6. Pp. 234–60.

———. 1994b. "The Estate of Mardonios," *AuOr* 10: 211–21.

———. 2006. "Iranica in Post-Achaemenid Babylonian Texts," in Briant and Joannès (2006), pp. 223–60.

Stoneman, R. 2008. *Alexander the Great: A Life in Legend*. New Haven, CT.

———. 2015. "How Many Miles to Babylon? Maps, Guides, Roads, and Rivers in the Expeditions of Alexander and Xenophon," *G & R* 62.1: 60–74.

Strasburger, H. 1952. "Alexanders Zug durch die Gedrosische Wüste," *Hermes* 80: 457–93.

Stronach, D. 1978. *Pasargadae: A Report on the Excavations Conducted by the British Institute of Persian Studies from 1961 to 1963*. Oxford.

Swiss Foundation for Alpine Research 1999. *Elevation of Mount Everest Newly Defined*. Zurich.

Talbert, R., ed. 2012. *Ancient Perspectives: Maps and Their Place in Mesopotamia, Egypt, Greece, and Rome*. Chicago.

Tarn, W. 1948. *Alexander the Great*. Cambridge.

Teitler, G. 1977. *The Genesis of the Professional Officers' Corps*. Tr. C. N. Ter Heide-Lopy. Beverly Hills, CA.

Teixidor, J. 1990. "Interpretations and Misinterpretations of the East in Hellenistic Times," in *Religion and Religious Practice in the Seleucid Kingdom*. Ed. P. Bilde, T. Engerg-Pedersen, L. Hannestad, and J. Zahle. Aarhus. Pp. 66–79.

Themelis, P., and I. Touratsaglou. 1997. *Οἱ τάφοι του Δερβενίου*. Athens.

Thompson, C. 1999. "A New Look at Barrekub's Treasure: Silver from Zinjirli," *Minerva* 10: 48–50.

Thompson, D. 2012. *Memphis Under the Ptolemies*. Princeton. 2nd ed.

Thonemann, P. 2011. *The Maeander Valley: A Historical Geography from Antiquity Through Byzantium*. Cambridge.

Traunecker, C. 1987. "La chapelle de Khonsou du mur d'enceinte et les travaux d'Alexandre," *Karnak* 8 (1987): 347–54.

Travlos, J. 1960. *Poleodomikē exelixis tōn Athēnōn apo tōn proïstorikōn chronōn mechri tōn archōn tou 190u aiōnos*. Athens.

Tritle, L. 2003. "Alexander and the Killing of Cleitus the Black," in *Crossroads of History: The Age of Alexander*. Ed. W. Heckel and L. Tritle. Claremont, CA. Pp. 127–466.

———. 2014. "Ravished Minds in the Ancient World," in Meineck and Konstan (2014), pp. 87–103.

Trivedi, M. 2009. "On the Surface Things Appear to Be…Perspectives on the Archaeology of the Delhi Ridge," in *Ancient India: New Research*. Ed. U. Singh and N. Lahiri. New Delhi. Pp. 39–71.

Tronson, A. 1984. "Satyrus the Peripatetic and the Marriages of Philip II," *JHS* 104: 116–26.

Tuplin, C. 1991. "Darius' Suez Canal and Persian Imperialism," in *Asia Minor and Egypt: Old Cultures in a New Empire: Proceedings of the Groningen 1988 Achaemenid History Workshop*. AchHist 6. Ed. H. Sancisi-Weerdenburg and A. Kuhrt. Leiden. Pp. 237–83.

———, ed. 2007. *Persian Responses: Political and Cultural Interaction With(in) the Achaemenid Empire*. Swansea.

———. 2007a. "Treacherous Hearts and Upright Tiaras: The Achaemenid King's Headdress," in Tuplin (2007), pp. 67–97.

Turner, E. 1974. "A Commander-in-Chief's Order from Saqqâra," *JEA* 60: 239–42.

Ulanowski, K., ed. 2016. *The Religious Aspects of War in the Ancient Near East, Greece, and Rome.* Leiden.

———. 2016a. "A Comparison of the Role of *Bārû* and *Mantis* in Ancient Warfare," in Ulanowski (2016), pp. 65–99.

Ullmann, M. 2002. *König für die Ewigkeit—Die Häuser der Millionen von Jahren. Eine Untersuchung zu Königskult und Tempeltypologie in Ägypten.* Wiesbaden.

UNESCO (United Nations Educational, Scientific, and Cultural Organization). 2010. *Application by the Islamic Republic of Iran for World Heritage Classification for Persian Gardens at Pasargadae and Elsewhere.*

United States Monetary Commission. 1879. *Documents Accompanying the Report of the United States Monetary Commission Organized Under the Joint Resolution of August 15, 1870.* Washington, DC.

Van der Spek, R. 1985. "The Babylonian Temple During the Macedonian and Parthian Domination," *BiOr* 50: 542–62.

———. 1986. *Grondbezit in het Seleucidische Rijk.* Amsterdam.

———. 1987. "The Babylonian City," in *Hellenism in the East: The interaction of Greek and Non-Greek Civilizations from Syria to Central Asia after Alexander.* Ed. A. Kuhrt and S. Sherwin-White. London. Pp. 57–74.

———. 1993. "New Evidence for Seleucid Land Policy," in *De Agricultura. In memoriam Pieter Willem de Neeve.* Ed. H. Sancisi-Weerdenburg, R. Van der Spek, H. Teitler, and H. Wallinga. Amsterdam. Pp. 61–77.

———. 1998. "Darius III, Alexander the Great, and Babylonian Scholarship," in *A Persian Perspective: Essays in Memory of Heleen Sancisi-Weerdenburg.* AchHist 13. Ed. W. Henkelman and A. Kuhrt. Leiden. Pp. 289–346.

———. 2006. "The Size and Significance of Babylonian Temples Under the Successors," in Briant and Joannès (2006), 261–307.

———. 2014. "Cyrus the Great, Exiles, and Foreign Gods: A Comparison of Assyrian and Persian Policies on Subject Nations," in *Extraction and Control: Studies in Honor of Matthew W. Stolper,* ed. W. Henkelman, M. Kozuh, C. Woods, and C. Jones. Chicago. Pp. 233–63.

Van der Spek, R., and C. A. Mandemakers. 2003. "Sense and Nonsense in the Statistical Approach to Babylonian Prices," *BiOr* 60: 521–37.

Van Donzel, E., and A. Schmidt. 2010. *Gog and Magog in Early Eastern Christian and Islamic Sources: Sallam's Quest for Alexander's Wall.* Leiden.

Van Lieven, A. 2016. "Translating Gods, Interpreting Gods: On the Mechanisms Behind the *Interpretatio Graeca* of Egyptian Gods," in *Greco-Egyptian Interactions: Literature, Translation, and Culture, 500 BCE to 300 CE.* Ed. I. Rutherford. Oxford. Pp. 61–83.

Van Wees, H. 2004. *Greek Warfare: Myths and Realities.* London.

Veïsse, A.-E. 2004. *Les "revoltes Égyptiennes." Recherches sur les troubles intérieurs en Egypte du règne de Ptolémée III Evergète à la conquête romaine.* Studia Hellenistica 41. Leuven.

Verma, R. 1991. *Geodynamics of the Indian Peninsula and the Indian Plate Margin.* Rotterdam.

Vittmann, G. 2003. *Ägypten und die Fremden in ersten vorchristlichen Jahrtausend.* KAW 97. Mainz-am-Rhein.

Volkmann, H. 1961. *Die Massenversklaverungen der Einwohner eroberter Städte in der hellenistisch-römischen Zeit.* Forschungen zur antike Sklaverei 22. Mainz-am-Rhein.

Voutiras, E. 1990. "*Ηφαιστίων ήρως*," *Egnatia* 2: 123–73.

Waerzeggers C. 2010. *The Ezida Temple of Borsippa: Priesthood, Cult, Archives.* Leiden.

Walbank, F. 1957–1979. *A Historical Commentary on Polybius.* Oxford.

Walser, G. 1984. *Hellas und Iran. Studien zu den griechisch-persischen Beziehungen vor Alexander.* Darmstadt.

Waterfield, R. 2011. *Dividing the Spoils: The War for Alexander the Great's Empire.* Oxford.

Welles. C. B. 1962 "The Discovery of Sarapis and the Foundation of Alexandria," *Historia* 11: 271–98.

Wetzel, F. 1944. "Babylon zur Zeit Herodots," *ZA* 48: 45–68.

Wheeler, E. 1991. "The General as Hoplite," in *Hoplites: The Classical Greek Battle Experience.* Ed. V. Hanson. London. Pp. 121–70.

———. 2007. "Land Warfare," in the *Cambridge History of Greek and Roman Warfare I.* Ed. P. Sabin, H. van Wees, and M. Whitby. Cambridge. Pp. 186–223.

Whitehead, D. 2015. "Alexander the Great and the *Mechanici*," in *East and West in the World Empire of Alexander: Essays in Honour of Brian Bosworth.* Ed. P. Wheatley and E. Baynham. Oxford. Pp. 75–91.

Whitehead, D., and P. Blyth. 2004. *Athenaeus Mechanicus, "On Machines." Translated with Introduction and Commentary.* Stuttgart.

Wiemar, H. 2007. "Alexander—der letzte Achaimenide? Eroberungspolitik, lokale Eliten, und altorientalische Traditionen im Jahr 323," *HZ* 284: 281–310.

Wiesehöfer, J. 2009. "The Achaemenid Empire," in *The Dynamics of Ancient Empires: State Power from Assyria to Byzantium.* Ed. I. Morris and W. Scheidel. Oxford. Pp. 66–99.

Wilamowitz-Moellendorff, U. von. 1931–1932. *Der Glaube der Hellenen.* Berlin.

Wilcken, U. 1932. *Alexander the Great.* Tr. G. Richards. London.

Will, W., and J. Heinrichs, eds. 1987. *Zu Alexander dem Grossen. Festschrift G. Wirth zum 60. Geburtstag 9.12.86.* Amsterdam.

Winter, F. 1912. *Der Alexandersarkophag aus Sidon.* Strassburg.

Winter, F. E. 1971. *Greek Fortifications.* Toronto.

Winter, I. 2008. "Touched by the Gods: Visual Evidence for the Divine Status of Rulers in Ancient Near East," in Brisch (2008), pp. 75–101.

Wiseman, D. 1985. *Nebuchadrezzar and Babylon.* Oxford.

———. 1991. "Babylonia, 605–539 BC," in *CAH* 3.2.229–51.

Worthington, I. 2004. *Alexander the Great: Man and God.* Harlow, NY.

———. 2014. *By the Spear: Philip II, Alexander the Great, and the Rise and Fall of the Macedonian Empire.* Oxford.

Wrightson, G. 2010. "The Nature of Command in the Macedonian Sarissa Phalanx," *AHB* 24: 71–92.

Yorck von Wartenburg, M. 1897. *Kurze Übersicht der Feldzüge Alexanders des Grossen*. Berlin.

Young, R. 1963. "Gordion of the Royal Road," *Proceedings of the American Philosophical Society* 107: 348–64.

Index